Child Development and Socialization

Child Development and Socialization

JERE E. BROPHY

Michigan State University

SRA

SCIENCE RESEARCH ASSOCIATES, INC.
Chicago, Palo Alto, Toronto
Henley-on-Thames, Sydney, Paris, Stuttgart

A Subsidiary of IBM

This book is set in 10-point Caledonia, with
display lines in Avant Garde Light. The book was
set by Computer Typesetting Services, Inc., Glendale,
California, and printed and bound by R. R. Donnelley
& Sons Company, Crawfordsville, Indiana.

Acquisitions Editor: Michael A. Zamczyk

Project Editor: Ronald Q. Lewton

Photo Editor: Judith A. Chaffin

Designer: Bert Johnson

Chapter-opening photographs by Jean-Claude Le Jeune,
The Stockmarket, and American Stock Photos.

Library of Congress Cataloging in Publication Data

Brophy, Jere E.
  Child development and socialization.

  Bibliography: p.
  Includes index.
  1. Child development.   2. Socialization.
I. Title. [DNLM: 1. Child development.
2. Adolescence.   3. Adolescent psychology.
4. Socialization WS105 B873c]
HQ769.B682   155.4′1   76-49882
ISBN 0-574-17985-2

Preface

This book is a product of my experiences as a student taking courses in child development and as a classroom instructor teaching child development at the undergraduate and graduate levels. It is my attempt to prevent or counteract the sense of frustration that I experienced personally and have observed all too often in students who discover that child development is not as interesting or valuable a course as they expected it to be. In my own case, I did not really appreciate the value of developmental psychology until several years after I had taken my last course in the subject as a student. It was only in my years as a parent, which gave me firsthand and continuing experience with the subject matter, and as a clinician, when I realized that meaningful diagnosis and treatment often were not possible unless one could discover how a person's problems had begun and developed, that I began to see the tremendous value developmental psychology has, both presently and potentially.

Many reasons contribute to the typical failure of developmental psychology courses to convey the excitement and importance of the topic to students, but I would like to call attention to two particular reasons. The first is the lack of fit between the expectations and interests of students and those of instructors and textbook writers. It has been my experience that most students taking child development courses come in with unusually high (often unrealistic) expectations, believing that the course will be an especially practical one that will help them understand children and themselves better, and eventually help them function better as parents. Meanwhile, textbook writers and many instructors act as if all their students were psychology majors with strong research interests, planning to specialize in the field. Among other things, they tend to assume interests and knowledge that students do not have, even those who have taken general psychology courses. The desire of instructors to teach a graduate level (or at least graduate-oriented) course to undergraduate students taking their first developmental psychology course is understandable but unrealistic. I believe that students can and will be eager to learn about the cutting edges of research in the field and take an interest in methodological as well as substantive aspects of it once they understand its importance, but that they must develop this understanding first.

One can be reasonably certain that this prior understanding of the nature and importance of developmental psychology will not be acquired in general psychology courses, which present little if any truly developmental content. In fact, my own belief is that it probably takes an entire course to develop a real appreciation of the importance of and possibilities involved in the developmental approach to psychology—and that is one of the primary goals of this book. Toward this end, I have placed great stress upon the communication of basic developmental principles, discussing them and providing examples not merely to provide instruction in the principles themselves, but also to show why the principles are important and how they apply to practical situations. This material should eliminate or substantially reduce the commonly observed "why am I studying this?" reaction of students prematurely confronted with the intricacies of developmental psychology before they have acquired an appreciation for the general topic.

A second problem, one that I have become aware of primarily in my role as instructor, is an extremely uneven balance of content in most developmental textbooks. Perhaps the most common problem is relatively sparse coverage of middle childhood. Some textbooks go into tedious detail about prenatal development and development in the early childhood years and also provide detailed coverage of adolescence, but have remarkably little to say about the years in between.

Part of this problem reflects the historical development of the field. The vast majority of all developmental research ever done has been done within the past 15 years or so, and the systematic and widespread application of developmental principles to research on children in the middle years has been a relatively recent phenomenon. In any case, I have tried to provide a more balanced coverage of what I consider to be the more important facts about development from conception through adolescence. This has meant omission of explicit coverage of experimental methodology, some aspects of prenatal development, and highly specialized topics in the early development of perception, language, and cognition, in order to allow for some of the other kinds of coverage discussed below.

In addition to what has been said already, this book is unusual in both approach and organization. The approach is an attempt to integrate past and present cognitive, social, and personality psychology, and to present them from a developmental point of view. The result is a very broad and deep scope that presents unique integrations of theory and data from a wide variety of sources. However, in order to concentrate heavily upon integrative concepts and principles, I have not attempted to present research encyclopedically. Instead, I have presented research selectively, to illustrate particular points or applications of general principles.

In addition to concentrating on materials traditionally considered to be developmental psychology, I have given extensive coverage to child rearing or socialization (to the extent that this differs from developmental psychology). This emphasis is obvious throughout the book, but most obvious in the organization of the book. Except for the introductory part, each part of the book consists of paired chapters. The first chapter in each pair presents theory and research on the topic at hand. The second chapter of each pair goes into detail about the socialization implications of the material covered in the previous chapter. For example, Chapter Three contains information on cognitive development in the sensorimotor period (among other things), and Chapter Four contains detailed information about how cognitive development can be stimulated during those years.

I have followed Piaget's four general developmental stages in organizing the book, but the approach is eclectic rather than Piagetian. Influences from existential and phenomenological psychology, Gestalt and field theory, psychoanalytic theory, and especially behavioristic theory, are noticeable throughout. Most of the material in the socialization chapters flows from a preventive mental health or environmental optimizing point of view. Stress is placed on how the probability for optimal development can be maximized through manipulating the environment, especially the nature of adult-child relationships.

I have concentrated on *normal* development in covering the descriptive literature and in discussing how to optimize development. Disordered development is not ignored. On the contrary, such topics as antisocial behavior and anxiety and defense mechanisms are treated at length and integrated with other material, but they are still presented within the general framework of discussing how to optimize development rather than isolated for treatment under a topic such as "Disordered Development" or "Abnormal Personalities." The same is true for topics like environmental disadvantaged, racial stigma, and biological abnormalities. The reason for this positive and prescriptive treatment of such topics is my belief that far too much emphasis has been placed on what *not* to do, at the expense of discussion of what *to do*. Consequently, I have devoted relatively little space to discussing all the ways development can go wrong, and all the ways that unfortunate socialization experiences can harm children. Similarly, I have made no attempt to catalog all the real or supposed deficiencies in children raised under unfortunate circumstances or plagued with birth defects. Instead, I have concentrated on the biologically normal child, and on how socializing agents can optimize development by providing cognitive stimulation and the kinds of social-personal environments that foster general happiness and mental health.

This process necessarily involves identifying certain outcomes as "good," which requires value judgments. Recognizing this, I have made a systematic effort to spell out my assumptions, biases, and value judgments in explicit detail, and to point out to readers how they might disagree with my conclusions and inferences if they were to begin with different assumptions or goals. Where I can see no clear-cut basis for advocating one kind of outcome over another, I have tried to present information about the linkages between differential adult behavior and child characteristics, leaving it to readers to decide what is best. However, where I believed that the data warranted it, I have not hesitated to make explicit and detailed prescriptions and explain the reasons for them. In general, I have tried to strike a balance between what I see as over-conservatism about making prescriptions in the more traditional child and developmental psychology books, and what I see as unwarranted or unsupportable advocacy by most writers of popular "how-to-do-it" books intended for parents or others working with children.

I believe that the explosion of research in the field in recent years has produced enough solid data to warrant a variety of prescriptive suggestions about child rearing, and I have tried to mine these data and provide these suggestions in the book. I also believe that the field is ready for more integration of different strands of theory and research than has taken place heretofore, and I have tried to provide some of this integration.

Readers already familiar with child and developmental psychology books may be surprised to find some of the connections made in this book, such as those between love-hostility and restrictiveness-permissiveness and parental education, competency, and socio-economic status, or those between behavioral modeling, moral development, cognitive development, vulnerability to stress, and the use of defense mechanisms. These and many other topics typically treated in isolation from one another have been integrated in this book, because I think that, like developing organisms, developing scientific fields become much more than the sums of their parts when they become integrated. I also believe that these integrations help show the value of the developmental approach, and thus I hope they will be especially useful in helping readers develop important new insights and make connections between psychological facts they may be aware of but have never integrated or considered important.

I also hope that the integrative material in the book will help illustrate that most different approaches to psychology are merely different, rather than contradictory or competing. A developmental psychology text is an ideal text to do this kind of integrating, because developmental psychology is not so much a substantive field as it is a point of view that cuts across and is applicable to all the various subfields of psychology. Upon finishing this book, readers should realize that no single approach to psychology has all the answers or even all the questions, that each approach has something unique and important to offer, and that integrative knowledge including information and insights from various approaches is much deeper and more powerful than single-theory approaches which typically are limited to questions that "fit" the assumptions of the theory. I believe that most child development researchers already realize this, but that textbooks still tend to stay within a particular theory or to stress the contrasts between different theories without paying sufficient attention to the commonalities. In summary, I think the field is ready for an inventory and integration of theories and facts from diverse sources, and this book is intended as a step in that direction.

Jere E. Brophy

Acknowledgments

Any attempt to acknowledge everyone who influenced me in significant ways that affected the writing of this book would be bound to fail, because my thinking about child development has been influenced by a large number of teachers, a very large number of students, and numerous colleagues and friends. However, I do wish to single out for special mention a few individuals who contributed directly and importantly to my development of knowledge about the field and/or my completion of this book.

Among my teachers, I would like especially to acknowledge and thank Robert C. Nicolay of Loyola University of Chicago, who not only taught me a great deal about psychology but was directly instrumental in and more responsible than anyone else for my decision to pursue a career in this field. In addition, I wish to acknowledge and thank other instructors at Loyola and at the University of Chicago who taught me much of what I know about psychology in general and child development in particular: Ann Bond, Donald Fiske, Robert Havighurst, William Henry, Robert Hess, Lawrence Kohlberg, Robert LeVine, Salvatore Maddl, Bernice Neugarten, Ronald Walker, and Benjamin Wright.

In addition to what I learned from these and other instructors as a student, my knowledge about child development and my professional career generally have been enriched by numerous warm and valuable associations with colleagues at the University of Chicago, the University of Texas at Austin, and the Southwest Educational Development Laboratory. These colleagues include Carolyn Evertson, Thomas Good, Carson McGuire, Shari Nedler, Robert Peck, Virginia Shipman, and Harris Stern.

I also wish to thank Karl Schmidt, Michael Zamczyk, and others at Science Research Associates, not only for the help and encouragement they have

X

provided me, but for their willingness to take a chance on a book that breaks with tradition and strikes out in new directions. I also am indebted to several reviewers whose comments and criticisms helped improve the book as it moved from first draft to the final manuscript:

Dorothy Sailor, Fullerton College

Theresa Chang, Kansas State University

Francine Deutsch, Pennsylvania State University

Richard Scott, Oregon College of Education

David Goldstein, Temple University

Steven Timmons, St. Mary's College

Lewis Konigsberg, SUNY, Oswego

Judith Creighton, Arizona State University

Broncha Stern, Los Angeles Valley College

I am also grateful to Gwen Newman, Barta Stevenson, and Sidney Weaver, who completed the prodigious task of typing successive drafts of the manuscript with amazing efficiency and good humor.

Finally, I would like to acknowledge and thank my two families. My parents, Eileen and Joseph Brophy, consistently provided me with the kind of socialization experiences stressed as ideal in this book, and consequently deserve much of the credit for what I have been able to achieve. My children, Cheryl and Joseph, have provided me with firsthand knowledge and experience of the various tasks and emotions that being a parent involves, not to mention providing numerous anecdotes and illustrations (occasionally upon request, but usually without intending to do so)! Finally, my wife, Arlene, has shared the experience of parenting with me and contributed immeasurably to my knowledge about child development and socialization in indirect ways; in addition, she also read successive drafts of the manuscript very carefully and made numerous incisive criticisms and suggestions. Thus, I am grateful to her not only for putting up with the familial inconveniences that writing a book brings about, but also for providing direct and valuable assistance in the task itself.

J.E.B.

Contents

XII

CHAPTER FOUR
PREPARING FOR AND CARING FOR INFANTS

PART THREE
THE PREOPERATIONAL
YEARS

CHAPTER FIVE
PHYSICAL AND COGNITIVE DEVELOPMENT IN YOUNG CHILDREN

CHAPTER SIX
FOSTERING PHYSICAL AND COGNITIVE DEVELOPMENT IN YOUNG CHILDREN

CHAPTER SEVEN
PERSONAL AND SOCIAL DEVELOPMENT IN YOUNG CHILDREN

XiV

CHAPTER EIGHT
FOSTERING PERSONAL AND SOCIAL DEVELOPMENT IN YOUNG CHILDREN

PART FOUR
THE CONCRETE
OPERATIONAL YEARS

CHAPTER NINE
PHYSICAL AND COGNITIVE DEVELOPMENT IN MIDDLE CHILDHOOD

XVI

PART ONE

INTRODUCTION

CHAPTER ONE

Overview
of the Text

Between them, the fields of *child development* and *socialization* include most of what is known about how newborn infants gradually develop into unique adults. Knowledge in these two areas is complementary and mutually supportive, rather than contradictory. However, there has been little integration of the two fields. This book's title, *Child Development and Socialization*, reflects not only its content but my orientation (or bias, if you prefer) as an author. Most child development texts concentrate heavily on child development but usually have little to say about socialization or parenting, and most books on socialization and parenting fail to take into account important data from child development research. I have tried to combine and integrate these two major areas of research on human development.

My primary goals in these initial chapters are to review the major influences upon my own thinking and to explain my approach to human development. This is done for three main purposes:

1. To spell out my biases, because they pervade the book and affect the way I treat each topic.

2. To provide an overview of some of the main themes and major ideas that will appear throughout the book.

3. To place major theorists and their ideas in historical perspective, so that you will understand not only *what* they said, but *why* they said it.

DEVELOPMENTAL RESEARCH

"Developmental psychology" is not so much a substantive field as a point of view. Whatever the substantive area (intelligence, personality, and so forth), developmental psychologists are interested in describing and explaining the changes which occur as an *undifferentiated* infant becomes a complex, *differentiated* adult. The term "development" differs from both "change" and "growth." It implies more than either of them (Werner, 1957). "Growth" refers to the increases in size and weight that occur over time. To say that children have grown implies that they have become taller and/or heavier, but not necessarily that they have developed by becoming more *complex* or more mature. The term "development" includes simple growth, but it also implies that children have achieved higher levels of *differentiation* or organization, not merely that they have acquired more of the same thing (growth). The term "change" can refer to any kind of change, good or bad. Again, "development" includes change, but it refers to change from simpler to more complex or highly *differentiated* levels of organization. The term "development" usually is not used to refer to undesirable or regressive change.

The field of child development also has been associated with several other concepts and practices in addition to this definition of development. First, child development traditionally has been mostly non-experimental, relying on *observation* and *description* to discover and describe the changes that occur with development. Also, child development usually is associated with use of the *stage* concept. In contrast to the idea that development is a smooth, gradual process, the stage concept implies that development is a *discontinuous* process. There is a steady state, then a developmental spurt, then another steady state, then another developmental spurt, and so on. During the steady state that occurs after each developmental spurt, children explore the new abilities and potentials that the latest developmental spurt has provided.

During this time, children presumably are uninterested in (as well as not ready for) activities associated with later stages. They also are less interested in activities associated with earlier stages, because they have mastered them to the point of overlearning (they already know all there is to know, or have developed their skills as far as they can be developed at present). With time, children gain more experiences and fulfill more of the potential that each new stage provides, so that they approach readiness to move on to the next stage. When this readiness finally arrives, they show another developmental spurt and move on to the next stage. Then they again settle into a steady state to explore the potential of the new stage.

When developmentalists speak of "stages," this is what they imply. However, they differ among themselves in how much they use the stage concept and in how they conceptualize it. Stage theorists who use the term in a "hard" sense use it as outlined above, implying discontinuity or sharp breaks between one level of development and the next. Sometimes they even use the stage concept to imply causality, suggesting that the reason children can do something new is that they have moved into a new stage, or that the reason they cannot is that they have not yet reached that stage. This explains nothing; it merely describes the situation in different words. Other writers use the term "stage" very loosely. Sometimes they mean it only as an observable descriptor or guidepost in development, not necessarily indicative of any major or fundamental change. Terms like "the negativistic stage" or "the boy-crazy" stage are examples. Used in this sense, the term "stage" does not really imply a developmental steady state. Instead, it implies that the behavior is transitory and will shortly disappear without any special efforts by parents or other adults ("It's *only* a stage.").

Theorists using the "harder" definitions of the stage concept usually use the concepts of *critical periods* and *irreversibility*. These terms have been borrowed from embryology (the study of development from conception to birth), where they describe demonstrable facts. When applied to human psychology, they describe undemonstrated hypotheses concerning postnatal development. A "critical period" is an identifiable period of time which is crucial in the development of the whole individual or of some subsystem. For example, the first six months following conception form a critical period for life itself. If the mother should suffer a miscarriage during these months, the fetus cannot survive. Its internal organs are not developed well enough yet to allow life outside the womb. However, once the critical period has passed and these organs and bodily functions have developed sufficiently, babies usually survive even though they may be born a month or two prematurely.

More limited critical periods have been identified for bodily subsystems. These usually correspond to the point in time when the subsystem in question is developing most rapidly in the womb. If some trauma (such as accident to the mother, toxic, chemical, or infection) should occur which affects the fetus, the brain is likely to be most severely affected if the trauma occurs when the brain is developing most rapidly; the limbs will be affected most severely if the trauma occurs when the limbs are developing rapidly, and so forth. Once the critical period of vulnerability for a given subsystem passes, that subsystem is relatively less susceptible to developmental retardation or distortion.

Critical periods often are called "critical" because the effects that occur during them are irreversible: remediation efforts cannot repair the damage. However, like the "stage" concept, the concepts of critical periods and irreversibility of effects sometimes are used in a looser, more relative manner. This is especially true in postnatal human development, where so-called "critical periods" have been proposed for such things as sex role identification, peer-orientation, trust vs. mistrust of other people, and other personality characteristics. Certain periods have been identified for these and other aspects of development during which the personality characteristic first

6

appears. In a loose sense, stages or developmental landmarks do exist in each of these areas. However, to call them "critical periods" probably is inappropriate and misleading. These and other characteristics of human personality development usually do not appear suddenly and as a result of internal biological programming (maturation). Also, they tend to show malleability (openness to change) rather than irreversibility, although irreversibility still is claimed for a few characteristics. The concepts of discontinuous development, developmental stages, critical periods, and irreversibility of effects traditionally have been associated with the developmental point of view. More recently, these terms either have been dropped or have been used in a "softer" form implying that they are real but not absolute, and that they are not causes in themselves but reflections of the effects of other causes.

Regardless of whether particular theorists use the "stage" concept in the hard sense, use it in the soft sense, or avoid it altogether, most theorists agree with certain generalities about developmental sequences. Discussion of development usually involves attention to three major factors: *sequence* (the order in which behaviors appear); *rate* (the speed with which the individual proceeds through the sequence); and *form* (individual outcomes which contain certain elements common to everyone at this stage of development but which also are organized in particular ways unique to each individual).

Certain sequences in development have been established as *universal*. The reality of such sequences is acknowledged by different theorists, whether or not they use the "stage" concept. Within these universally appearing sequences, individual differences in the rate or speed with which people proceed through the sequence have been established, both within and across cultures. Different theorists recognize this fact, although they disagree in their proposed explanations for it. Some tend to stress maturational factors (some people move through the sequence quicker because they mature faster than other people), while others stress environmental factors (speed of progression through the sequence depends on the quality and quantity of environmental stimulation that the individual experiences).

Similarly, everyone recognizes the reality of individual differences in the form of behavior, but there is much disagreement as to the causes of these differences. Again, the major difference is between the *nativists* (those who stress genetics and maturation) and the *environmentalists* (those who stress the importance of the environment and the contrasting effects of different environments). Even when writers of different persuasion agree that a particular sequence is universal, they can differ in their explanations for individual differences in rate and form. They also may differ in whether or not they choose to use the "stage" concept in describing or explaining the sequence. Developmentalists tend to be nativists, while those interested in socialization tend to be environmentalists.

SOCIALIZATION AND CHILD-REARING RESEARCH

The socialization and child rearing approach stresses the role of external forces in *shaping* the child's development, in contrast to the developmental approach, with its stress on naturalistic observation, description, and cumulation of normative information about stages in development which presumably are universal across children and cultures. Writers interested in socialization and child rearing usually take into account developmental stages and developmental changes which appear to be universal and to be somewhat independent of the environment. However, they are more interested in problems such as how to arrange the environment to promote optimal mental and personal development, how to intervene effectively when development has been distorted or retarded, and how to explain (not just describe) development.

Researchers and writers of this persuasion, which include myself, are not content to just describe development and are not convinced by arguments that certain aspects are caused by maturation and "explained" by stage concepts. We find developmentalist statements that attitudes of trust vs. mistrust of other people or sexual identification develop at a certain age or stage to be relatively uninformative, except as clues to when and where to look for explanations. Stages, if accepted at all, are viewed as phenomena requiring explanation, not as explanatory concepts in their own right. Socialization and child rearing research is designed to find out what kinds of environments are optimal for the child, and what kinds of interventions will succeed in reversing distorted patterns.

Socialization and child-rearing researchers try to answer such questions as "How do children develop attitudes of optimism and trust toward others?" or "How do children learn about sex differences and acquire their own individual ideas about their sex roles?" Investigation of such questions requires research on children's *experiences*, particularly knowledge about the kind of socialization they have received from their parents and other important influences in their lives. Ethical considerations usually prevent socialization experiments with humans, so such questions are approached with correlational methods. The investigator with a socialization approach identifies children with contrasting attitudes of trust vs. mistrust, or with contrasting sex role adjustments, and then tries to identify experiences or socialization factors that are correlated consistently with particular outcomes. When such investigators find that certain parental behavior is correlated with a particular child outcome, they usually conclude that the parental behavior *caused* the child outcome. This does not strictly follow from the data, though, because a correlation only establishes that two things occur together, not that one causes the other. It is known that some parent behaviors develop *in response* to child behaviors, so that child behavior sometimes causes parent behavior, rather than vice-versa. This possibility was known but not assigned much importance until recently, when several investigators showed that the degree of child influence on parents is much higher than was believed previously (Bell, 1971; Lewis and Rosenbloom, 1974).

Obviously, the developmental perspective and the socialization or child-rearing perspective are complementary, even though some writers make them seem contradictory. To understand children fully, one must understand both what is going on within them (most of this information has come from developmental psychologists) and the effects of whatever socialization influences are present (most of this information has come from socialization and

8

child-rearing researchers). Unfortunately, these two areas have not been integrated well. The implications of developmental psychology for child rearing and socialization usually are not spelled out. Furthermore, the existing data based, scientific information about child rearing (as opposed to purely speculative hypothesizing about it) has not yet been conveyed very well to parents, future parents, or others who work with children.

Most child development books contain relatively little information about how adults should behave toward children, and most books designed to tell parents how to raise their children are written by proponents of particular theories or methods. Often, they do not take into account the existing wealth of empirical data in these areas. In this book, I have tried both to review and critique the more important data on child development and socialization, and to draw implications and prescriptions for child rearing based on these data.

BASIC ASSUMPTIONS AND CENTRAL THEMES

In this book, it is my intention to integrate developmental psychology with research and theory in socialization and child rearing, and to take an *eclectic* approach in integrating what I see as the most important work in these areas. I believe that eclecticism (taking the best of what is available from different approaches, rather than trying to stick with one approach) is necessary for a reasonably complete psychology of human development. Writings of psychologists are influenced heavily by their interests and by the ideas prevailing at the times and places in which they work. Most psychologists were socialized within the Judeo-Christian religious and philosophical tradition, and also in the scientific tradition established originally in western Europe. However, there is much variation within these broad traditions. The influence of the times and of the prevailing ideas of the day are most evident in my intention to write an eclectic and integrated treatment.

Psychology presently is in a state of transition. Most of the theories that had great influence upon the early development of the field are dead or dying. Elements which stood the test of time and proved useful have been retained, but elements which proved incorrect or unnecessary have been dropped. With few exceptions, the very idea of developing comprehensive theories to explain "everything" has been discarded in favor of research which delves systematically into relatively limited and closely related questions. This approach has been much more fruitful than earlier ones in yielding a great quantity of good quality information. However, the division of the field into small groups working in separate areas has meant the loss of integration that the old theories provided. As a result, I often have had to rely on my own observations and interpretations in selecting and integrating information to present in the book. This means that sometimes I interpret data or even theory differently from how it is interpreted by its originators, and I have tried to indicate this whenever I have done so. Suggestions are provided for follow-up reading for those of you who are interested in consulting the original materials and comparing the interpretations and conclusions of others with my own.

DEVELOPMENT   The infant will be described as already somewhat developed and individualistic at birth, and as *active* in manipulating the environment. Infants will be considered almost completely open to the influences of socialization, however. Genetic endowment is viewed as limiting the range of variation possible in *physical and intellectual development,* but even here, aspects of the environment, especially the quality and quantity of socialization that children receive, are viewed as the causal factors explaining the kind and degree of development that individuals show relative to their potential. In *personal and social development,* environmental influences are viewed as the causal factors explaining almost everything, with the exception of certain sex differences and temperament or arousal level differences due to genes and present at birth.

Human potential for development in the social and personal areas is quite "plastic" (open to molding by the environment). Cross-cultural comparisons of sex roles, social organizations, valued traits, moral codes, and the like, reveal striking contrasts (Kroeber, 1953). Even within cultures, we see a great range of individual differences in these and other physical and psychological characteristics. Development is *cumulative,* though, so that traits tend to become established more firmly with age. Thus, I see some validity to the concept of *"predisposing factors"* (certain individuals are especially likely to develop particular traits or symptoms, because their previous development has made them more open to some possible changes and less open to others). Sometimes, these predisposing factors are genetic. Even here, though, the genes only create a predisposition. Whether or not the trait or symptom appears depends to some extent on environmental causes. In general, then, the idea that genetic programming or even biological maturation acts as a direct cause of behavior is rejected, although the role of the genes and of maturation in acting as predisposing factors and in setting limits on what is possible (in general or within a given time period) is recognized.

The place of the human race as a part of the animal kingdom also is recognized explicitly, so that data from animal studies will be discussed occasionally. However, I view humans as qualitatively different from lower animals. We have unique brains and nervous systems which make us different in kind, not just degree, from lower animals. I think that humans are demonstrably unique, and that, ultimately, the only way to understand them is to study them directly (except where ethical or practical considerations make this impossible). Discussions of many topics important in the developmental aspects of animal psychology have been omitted or minimized, because I see them as irrelevant to *human development.* Facts which have been demonstrated with animals are not automatically considered generalizable to humans. Implicit in this, of course, is a rejection of the idea of searching for general principles of behavior which apply to all organisms.

In particular, it should be noted that I have virtually omitted discussion of the theories and findings of animal psychology such as *ethology* or *comparative psychology,* as well as most of the content of *behavior genetics.* These fields have produced fascinating data and interesting theories, but I see them as irrelevant and inapplicable to human psychology. For a contrasting view of developmental psychology which stresses these and other biologically oriented approaches, see Nash (1970).

Another exclusion criterion has been the level of generality of theories or data. To concentrate on important general principles, I have omitted a huge volume of studies dealing with minor details or specific applications of the more general principles discussed. Students interested in specializing in the area should read relevant handbooks, reviews, and journal articles dealing with such research. Most such material has been omitted here, because I judged it to be too specialized for an introductory text.

Although the book has a heavy emphasis on social and personal development, there is relatively little material about abnormal development. The emphasis here is on healthy development and the positive socialization behaviors which optimize it, because this information is most relevant to the average reader. A personal bias is involved here, too. I believe that there has been too much attention to the relatively unproductive listing of all the ways that development can be distorted, and all of the traumas and environmental problems associated with distorted development. I think useful knowledge will accumulate quicker if attention is focused on bright, happy, and well-adjusted individuals, and on questions concerned with discovering how they got that way. In short, we need to know what *to do,* not what *not to do.* Readers interested in more detail about distorted development should consult books on abnormal psychology (White, 1956).

PRESCRIPTIONS   Regarding *cause and effect relationships,* I view the search for simple and universal one-to-one relationships between causes and effects in human development as doomed from the start, because it is hopelessly unrealistic. I believe that it is the *norm* in human development for a given cause (or stimulus, if you prefer) to have many possible effects, depending upon the nature of the person that it is affecting. Furthermore, I believe that a given effect (personality trait, defense mechanism, attitude or value, self-concept) can be produced by many different causal sequences. This recognition of *multiple causality* and *multiple effects* does not mean that humans are too complex to be understood. It does mean that most universalistic stage concepts which presumably apply the same way to everyone will be rejected as hopelessly simplistic. This includes, among other things, glib psychoanalytic "explanations" which attempt to reduce complex phenomena to simple formulas, and behavioristic "explanations" which take into account observable stimulation and reinforcement but not the person's subjective perceptions and previous experiences. It is possible to understand how people got to be the way they are, to make accurate predictions about what they are likely to do, and to make valid judgments about how they should be treated. However, to do this rationally, it is necessary to have a complete, well-rounded picture of the person that only an eclectic view can provide.

I do not see humans as *completely* predictable. Whether you want to call it "equilibration" (as Piaget does), free will, hedonism, or whatever, the basis of predictability is that individuals *generally* will do what is best for them, as they see it. This makes it possible to determine what people see as best for them and thus to make generally accurate predictions, if you understand them well enough. Nevertheless, people are *not* under the absolute control of external forces. They can and do change their perceptions of themselves and their surroundings, as well as their judgments about what is or is not in their best interest. Consequently, even predictions or judgments based upon what "should be" adequate evidence occasionally will be wrong, because the person will do something surprising or unexpected. Judgments and predictions based upon adequate information which is assessed and applied correctly usually will be correct, however. This makes it possible to generalize about child development and to draw inferences leading to prescriptive advice about what parents and other adults should do in the best interests of children. Bear in mind that these are *probabilistic statements* that will apply most but not all of the time— they are not "laws" which will apply in all cases without exception.

The problems of generalizing about human development and providing prescriptive advice for child rearing and socialization would be difficult enough because of the unpredictability factor, but they are compounded by the lack of an agreed upon model of the ideal person. My strategy for dealing with these difficulties has been as follows. *In the motor and cognitive areas, I have assumed a linear model* (that is, the more intellectual and motor development, the better). I think it usually is best for people to develop their physical and mental abilities up to their genetic potential, as much as possible. Consequently, I tend to favor anything known or believed to foster such development. Some writers have stated that high intelligence or well-developed physical abilities can cause problems, but, as will be explained in subsequent chapters, this is not always or necessarily true. In general, children are more successful to the extent that they are brighter and healthier or more athletic than their peers (Tyler, 1965).

Making generalizations and prescriptions in the social and personal areas is much more difficult. Here, the data are less clear, and interpretations are more likely to be affected by value judgments and prejudices. *I assume that social and personal traits are related curvilinearly to adjustment or mental health* (that is, people who have either too much or too little of the trait will be considered less well-adjusted or less mentally healthy than people who have the "right" amount). This is seen as a societal reality that must be kept in mind when making judgments about what is in an individual's best interest. In some cases, it is accepted as appropriate in a more basic and general way.

The adjustment model which equates *statistical normality* with *goodness* will sometimes be rejected as unfortunate and inappropriate (although the realistic restrictions that societal norms place upon people will not be ignored). A good example here is sex role learning. The women's liberation movement came about because our traditional definition of the "proper" female role became outmoded (or, if you prefer, was "found out"), and began to be recognized as too restrictive. More recently, we have come to see that the traditional definition of the male sex role also is too restrictive. Consequently, both roles are becoming more flexible, and we are starting to reject the idea that the traditional roles are better than any others simply because they are "normal." Both sex roles have been quite restrictive, sometimes causing both men and women needless unhappiness and inhibition. However, it would be a mistake to suggest to a young person of either sex that he or she unthinkingly adopt a sex role that contrasts sharply with the prevailing ones, particularly in communities where such deviations from normality are not accepted. Such advice might be good in theory but bad in practice, because the negative consequences could cause the person to end up more unhappy than if a somewhat more conventional sex role had been adopted.

This brief example illustrates several aspects of my orientation toward prescriptive advice in the social and personal areas. In general, I favor encouraging people to develop along whatever lines they please, and I am less concerned about what people say or do than about why they say it or do it. It probably is ideal if as much as possible of a person's behavior is done deliberately and with full conscious awareness, because the person sees it as necessary or desirable. The only exceptions to this would be violations of the Golden Rule or other behaviors implying immorality leading to suffering or difficulty for other people. Within this constraint of responsibility toward others, I think "do your own thing" is good advice. I also think that people must learn to "do their thing" with their eyes open and with full understanding and acceptance of whatever consequences may be involved. Even where there is no rational reason why people should not just do as they please, societal opposition and the undesirable consequences that may accompany it must be taken into account in decision making. Such decisions cannot be made solely on the basis of right vs. wrong. Usually, they must be made on the basis of what is in the best interest of the person, taking into account all relevant factors.

The task of integrating developmental and socializational theory and research is difficult and complex, and any attempt to draw implications and provide prescriptive advice about child rearing necessarily involves making value judgments. Because of this, child development texts typically minimize prescriptive advice, tending to stick to the data and let readers decide for themselves what it all means. In this book, I have drawn implications and made prescriptions freely, although I have taken pains to warn you that these are probabilistic statements rather than iron-clad "laws" and that they are affected by my personal biases and values. I have tried to specify these, although the book undoubtedly is affected by additional biases and values which have not been made explicit because I am not consciously aware of them.

Prescriptive advice will not be presented in "cookbook" style (providing you with rules to follow and implying that they will surely succeed if you follow them properly). This is not because I take a dim view of cookbook approaches as such. In fact, I would be pleased to write a cookbook for child rearing which was capable of insuring that all children developed their full intellectual and personal potentials. Unfortunately, this is not possible, because of the complexities already noted. The probabilistic prescriptions given in the book are based on solid research data, and individuals who apply them correctly and consistently can expect to get good results most of the time.

While I acknowledge that child rearing is not now and probably never will be an exact and totally predictable enterprise, adults can learn basic principles of child development and child rearing, and can apply these principles systematically in dealing with children. Parents who do so will give their children a good head start toward maximizing their potentials and leading enjoyable and productive lives. Results are not guaranteed or automatic, partly because of the unpredictability factor, and partly because of factors beyond familial control (such as peer groups, physical or emotional trauma, or unexpected frustrations and problems). Parents who do succeed in raising children to plan and live rational lives are least likely to see their efforts ruined by outside influences, because their children will be capable of making independent and correct decisions concerning their own welfare. While child rearing cannot be an exact science or technology in which specific procedures are applied to obtain completely predictable results, it *can* be an applied science, in which well-established principles are applied to maximize the probability of desirable results.

It should be clear that I do not believe that there is a "key" to successful child rearing which involves a single technique or a small set of techniques. Techniques are important, but *the quality of the parent-child relationship* is far more important than the use of any particular technique. It has much greater influence on the child's development than any single experience, good or bad. A relationship characterized by love, respect, and concern for the child is crucial. It will provide the basis for the security and self-esteem needed for optimal development, and it will minimize any negative effects that might result when an adult responds inappropriately to a single isolated event. In contrast, parents who "go by the book" and use all of the techniques discussed here and elsewhere ultimately will fail if they do not love their children and bring them up in an atmosphere of concern and respect. Parents can go a long way toward raising their children optimally simply by caring about them and showing that they do. However, understanding of child development and child-rearing principles also is important. There are no cookbook short-cuts, but you will do much better in the long run by acting systematically and knowledgeably than by stumbling along, learning through trial and error.

SUMMARY

In this brief introductory chapter, I have stated my goals in writing this book and identified some of my biases as a psychologist. Bear these in mind, because they pervade every aspect of the book. This includes not only the ways that topics have been treated, but even the selection of material to be included in the book in the first place. In some cases, decisions about inclusions and exclusions were deliberate, based upon what I consider to be important and relevant. However, some exclusion was not deliberate. Undoubtedly, many topics were not introduced because I have little interest in or knowledge about them, or because they just did not occur to me. Before continuing with the book, you might want to spend some time thinking about your own biases and preferences, especially those relating to your implicit "model" of the ideal person. To the extent that it differs from the one I outlined in this chapter, you might very well draw very different implications from the same data in comparison to the ones I have drawn.

Historical Overview

We begin our consideration of child development and socialization with a review and critique of some of the major theories in psychology generally and in these fields in particular. The review is organized historically in large part to show how ideas developed over time and how old ideas led to new ones. Another reason for the stress on history is the point made in the last chapter about the ideas of theorists being influenced by the prevailing ideas of the times. Child development and socialization both are relatively young fields of scientific inquiry (as we have come to think of this enterprise, at least), but they have a long and rich conceptual tradition behind them.

PRE-SCIENTIFIC IDEAS ABOUT HUMAN DEVELOPMENT

Even though the study of how humans develop, and the optimization of such development, is now considered important, the systematic, scientific study of human development is a relatively recent undertaking. Virtually all systematic data collection in this field (and in psychology in general) has occurred in the past 100 years. In the specific field of human development, probably over 90% of today's body of knowledge has been discovered within the past 15 years. The fact that so much of the material is new is one reason why there are few books integrating scientific data and theory in useful ways for the average parent, teacher, or other adult working with children. Frequently, the data have been compiled by investigators working separately from one another, and often in isolation from situations requiring the practical application of knowledge (Bronfenbrenner, 1974).

RELIGION   For centuries, virtually the only sources of psychological theories were based in theology. In Western civilizations this meant a belief in the Judeo-Christian tradition. Theologians introduced and debated several key questions relevant to psychology, including issues which still are not resolved today. One major unresolved issue is the matter of free will vs. determinism. This controversy continues today, not only in theology, but also in psychology. Behaviorists and other determinists continue to debate humanists and other psychologists who do not believe that people's behavior is determined by forces outside them, and that behavior can be predicted by knowledge of such forces. Deterministic theologians see people's individual destinies as determined by the will of God, and deterministic psychologists see them as determined by their genes and formative experiences. The basic issue of determinism vs. free will is the same in both fields.

A second fundamental issue raised by theologians concerns basic human nature—are we basically good or evil? This controversy is unresolved in theology as well as in psychology. Theologians usually debate it in connection with their concept of God. Those believing in a benign God usually believe that we are formed in that image and therefore are fundamentally good. Those believing in a God who has rejected us because of original sin tend to believe that we are fundamentally evil and must learn to overcome our evil instincts.

Humanistically oriented psychologists tend to assume that we are basically good by nature and will develop into prosocial and altruistic people unless this "natural" disposition is twisted by an unfortunate upbringing (Rogers, 1961). Many psychologists see humans as basically evil and in need of socialization which will teach them to curb their antisocial tendencies (Hall and Lindzey, 1970). Behaviorists and others usually see us as essentially amoral, responding hedonistically to the rewards and punishments that we encounter. They believe that our "goodness" or "badness" will be determined by the kinds of experiences we have. People who are rewarded for good behavior are likely to become prosocial and altruistic, while those who are rewarded for selfish or even antisocial behavior are likely to become more selfish and antisocial (Bandura, 1969).

Psychologists' positions on this issue often are conditioned by their own experiences. Those who have worked with primarily normal and psychologically healthy individuals, and whose counseling experiences mostly involved helping people maximize and fulfill their potentials (rather than overcome serious antisocial problems), often tend to be humanistic. This seems to be the attitude of psychologists working in college counseling centers. In contrast, psychologists working in prisons, in institutions for those who have been declared "criminally insane," or in other settings where they encounter antisocial individuals regularly, tend to look upon humans as fundamentally evil. We must always keep in mind that psychologists' theories about people, just like anyone's ideas about anything, are influenced heavily by their own personal experiences. Often, we must take into account the experiences that led theorists to develop their theories in order to appreciate and understand them fully.

The good-evil problem is not merely a speculative one, either in theology or in psychology. It continues to appear regularly in decision-making situations. Should a prisoner with a violent past but a good prison record be paroled? Can a 30-year old criminal with a 25-year history of antisocial behavior be rehabilitated? Does punishment serve any useful purpose?

In contrast to the free will-determinism debate, which goes on mostly at a highly abstract level in both psychology and theology, the good-evil controversy has produced much useful data in psychology, especially in the fields of human development and socialization. Much of this information will be reviewed in this book, and implications will be drawn for child rearing.

A further theological issue that has affected psychology is the notion that a person is a unified organism. There has been little debate about this among theologians, who tend to agree that each person has an individual soul that provides individuality and uniqueness. Many psychologists share this assumption, although they usually avoid theological terms like "soul" and instead attribute the unity of the individual to "concept of self" (Lecky, 1945) or "sense of identity" (Erikson, 1968). Other psychologists, especially behaviorists, reject such concepts, because they involve assumptions about people which can be neither observed nor measured directly, and because they believe that such concepts are not necessary to understand or explain human psychology (Skinner, 1953).

This area of disagreement recently has been sharpened by Mischel (1971). He has suggested that the person is not unitary at all, and that behavior deviates drastically from situation to situation. He believes that knowledge of the situation, especially of the reinforcement factors operating within it, is usually more useful for predicting people's behavior than knowledge about their major traits or self-concepts. In any case, theologians have contributed the idea that humans are unitary and consistent, while psychologists have produced theory and data both to support and to challenge these assertions.

Another area that has involved challenge of notions generally accepted by theologians concerns a cluster of ideas about human nature and how it should be conceptualized. Theologians usually approach humans from the perspective of their relationships with God and the universe. They see humans as much more important than animals (because humans possess souls and because they have a destiny to join God after death). But theologians also see humans as relatively unimportant in the general scheme of things— we are creatures of God, unique in creation, but still creatures.

In contrast to this approach, most psychologists look at humans only in relationship to observable and measurable aspects of their immediate environments. Non-observables such as gods and devils are ignored, except when people's beliefs about them affect their behavior. So are questions dealing with the nature of the universe or the destiny of the human race. Instead, psychologists concentrate upon learning about people's genetic characteristics and formative experiences from the immediate environment. Even so, some of the theological issues discussed here continue to affect psychology. For example, the continuing issue of human nature as good vs. evil originated in theological conceptions of people torn between the dictates of their own conscience (God) and sinful temptations (the devil). Psychological theories that postulate human nature as either good or evil do so without introducing theological concepts, but the basic ideas and implications are the same.

Considerations like these help show that theological and psychological approaches to human nature are simply different rather than contradictory, for the most part. Still, they often come into conflict. Many psychologists believe that they must restrict themselves to observable and measurable events if psychology is to be a true science. Other psychologists agree that theological concepts should be avoided, but they are not willing to confine themselves only to what is externally observable. These psychologists, often called existentialists or phenomenologists, believe that we must take into consideration unobservable psychological factors in addition to studying concrete actions in order to understand behavior fully.

One final way that theology and religion have affected psychology is by becoming objects of psychological research and writings. Psychologists are quite polarized on this issue. Some see belief in God and practice of religion as necessary and desirable human behavior. Important questions include determining which religions or religious ideas seem to be the most beneficial to individuals and how individuals can be socialized to become committed to them. In contrast, other psychologists look upon religion as harmless superstition at best, and as a source of anguish or even mental disorder at worst. For these psychologists, relevant questions include the development of ways to eliminate need for or reliance upon religion by eliminating the problems that led to these needs or by finding more "rational" substitutes for religions.

Traditionally, most psychologists tried to avoid discussing religion at all, although there were some noteworthy and valuable exceptions (Allport, 1950; Elkind, 1964). Many believed that a weakening of organized religions would improve general mental health. We have seen such a weakening over the past 20 years, and as yet, no such improvement of general mental health has occurred. Perhaps this will occur once people become adjusted to the new situation. But many are now beginning to believe that religions exist because human nature requires them. In any case, the problems that have come with the weakening of established organized religions, and especially the development of a variety of new religions and religion substitutes, have pumped new life into this old issue. Religion and related topics are drawing increasing interest from contemporary psychologists (Campbell, 1975)

PHILOSOPHY   Like theology, philosophy contributed several fundamental ideas and issues which persist in modern psychology. Some of these are essentially the same ones introduced earlier by theologists, but philosophers changed the emphasis somewhat by posing the questions in different ways.

One major philosophical issue is the mind-body problem. Are the mind and body separate? Are they connected, but only accidentally (the mind just happens to be located in the body)? Are they connected functionally (so that one can influence the other)? If so, can either influence the other, or is the direction of influence only one way? How does it all work? These and related questions have been debated among philosophers for centuries, and they are being studied today by psychologists. We now know that the mind can influence the body and the body can influence the mind, and knowledge is increasing daily about just how the processes work (Schachter, 1964).

Another important philosophical issue is existentialism vs. objectivism. Existentialists argue that "reality" is subjective and exists only in the mind of the perceiver. Objectivists argue that the universe is composed of concrete, real elements which have well-defined and constant properties independent of the perception of individuals. Many of the controversies early in the history of scientific psychology were related to this question. At first, psychologists insisted that "scientific" psychology had to concentrate on observable and measurable external reality, and had to avoid discussion of non-observables such as existential experience. Behavioristic psychologists still believe this, although the extremism of the past is waning. Psychologists remain divided on this issue. Some stress subjective perception and existential experience (May, 1969), and others concern themselves primarily with observable and measurable external reality (Skinner, 1953).

The developmental psychology of Jean Piaget (1970) has added a new dimension to this controversy by suggesting that children go through several qualitatively distinct stages in developing their understanding of the world. In a very real sense, children *construct* reality on the basis of their interactions with the environment and the feedback they get from it. The nature of these constructions of reality *changes* several times in the course of development.

Another philosophical issue related both to previous theological debates and to subsequent psychological activity concerns the concept of self. Philosophers agree with theologians in assuming an underlying constant self which provides unity to the individual, although they disagree about the nature of this "self." Existentialists stress the subjective aspects, while objectivists stress the physical and bodily aspects.

Influential philosophers also elaborated upon earlier theological debates concerning human nature as good vs. evil. Darwin, working from an evolutionary perspective, believed that humans shared with lower animals a tendency to be guided by *hedonism*. In short, we repeat behavior that brings pleasure or reward and do not repeat behavior that is not rewarded or that brings pain or punishment. In essence, this is the same as the "law of effect" or reinforcement principle that psychologists, particularly behaviorists, espouse as a basic principle of human psychology. The stress on hedonism often is linked with the assumption that human nature is fundamentally evil, so that people are willing to gratify their hedonistic desires at the expense of others if they go unpunished. But many believe that hedonism and basic evil are not necessarily linked. Darwin himself did not believe in a fundamentally evil human nature, and modern behaviorists maintain that reinforcement based on hedonistic desires can be used to shape people to become humanistic (Hamblin, Buckholdt, Ferritor, Kozloff, and Blackwell, 1971). Philosophy which *did* stress inherent evil as part of human nature led to the kind of psychological theory that stresses our presumed need to struggle against these innate evil instincts. Early psychoanalytic theory, especially Freudian theory, stressed this idea heavily.

Other philosophers, notably Rousseau, held an almost completely contradictory position to the idea that man is basically evil. They saw humans as biologically programmed to be prosocial and cooperative, and saw antisocial behavior as the result of distortion of basic instincts. This is the philosophical position held today by humanistically oriented psychologists.

The philosophy of John Locke, in contrast to the good vs. evil position, attached little importance to biological programming and inborn instincts. Locke saw the newborn infant as a "blank slate," open to determination by socialization experiences. He believed that children raised by people who expected and taught them to be good would turn out to be good, while others raised by evil people would learn to be evil. This philosophy underlies modern behaviorism and other approaches to psychology which stress that people develop their individuality because of factors operating in their environment and the kinds of experiences that they have after birth, and not because of inborn, genetically programmed tendencies that emerge as they mature.

EARLY SCIENTIFIC PSYCHOLOGY

Early theological and philosophical debates set the stage for more scientific study of ourselves. Systematic data collection did not begin until about 100 years ago. Until then, theologians and philosophers carried on debates at purely abstract and logical levels, failing to collect scientific data that might have shed some light on their questions. There is an old story about a man who interrupted a debate about how many teeth a horse has by suggesting that someone go to a horse and count its teeth, only to find that this suggestion was viewed as philosophically naive and generally inappropriate. Whether or not the story is true, it reflects the orientation of the philosophers of the times. Partly because of religious taboos, and partly because of a philosophical preference for abstract debates over the collection of empirical data, very little systematic information was collected about humans until relatively recently.

Many of the earliest scientific efforts to understand people appear very primitive today. Human genetics and most aspects of human biology were in their infancies at the same time that human psychology was, and social sciences such as sociology and anthropology did not even exist then. A major reason for the emergence and temporary acceptance of ideas that are no longer accepted was that few empirical data were available to refute them. The *homunculus* theory is a good example of a once-popular theory. For a time, this was the most accepted explanation for why each individual developed unique physical features. It was believed that, at conception, each new individual was equipped not only with a soul but also with a homunculus: a tiny, invisible replica of what that individual was going to look like later. Presumably this homunculus provided the model guiding the individual's development. Given the almost total ignorance of human genetics and human embryology of the times, the theory seems not only understandable, but quite logical. It helped "explain" many things that *had* been observed, such as the facts that children tend to resemble both of their parents to some degree, that each individual is unique, and that conception is related to sexual copulation in some way. It also was known that newborns already had their sex and their future features determined, although the latter were not yet obvious, and that early in prenatal development, the embryo had a rather amorphous form not at all resembling the human body. The homunculus theory helped to explain how all of this potential was present at birth but did not assert itself until later. It also helped tie together much observational data, especially for those who were deterministically inclined.

Another once-popular theory is that of *phrenology*. Phrenology assumed that behavior was determined by the shape and make-up of the head, with different head areas being related to different aspects of emotions and behavior. If your head area which controlled the trait of aggressiveness had one set of features, you would be inclined toward aggressiveness and criminality. If that same area had different features, you would be inclined toward friendliness and prosocial behavior. Again, this idea had appeal, because it seemed to explain a number of puzzling facts, even though later knowledge about brain functioning showed it to be false. We know today that certain brain areas *are* associated with certain psychological functions, but there is no evidence for the kind of determinism that phrenology postulated.

Phrenology was just one of many early theories that postulated biological determinism as the explanation for human characteristics. While phrenology "explained" behavior on the basis of the nature of head areas, other theories stressed such things as instincts, genes, and hormones. All such theories have appeal, because they are deceptively simple. They give the illusion of explaining phenomena, although in fact all they do is describe or label them. For example, at first it seems sensible and informative to say that aggressive people are aggressive because they have strong instincts for aggressiveness, and that less aggressive people do not have such strong aggressiveness instincts. However, this is mere description, not explanation. All it really says is that aggressive people are aggressive because they are aggressive, and that non-aggressive people are not aggressive because they are not aggressive. Elements of this kind of theorizing still exist, and people sometimes dabble in them or even take them seriously (palm reading, astrology, food fads, gurus, drugs, religious and/or social cults). Such ideas are appealing because they are simple and because they provide the illusion of determinism and predictability (all

A model of the human head constructed by phrenologists, indicating the areas of the brain believed to control and explain various personality traits. Notice that the list of traits is extensive and in some ways discriminating, separating conjugal love from parental love, for example. Notice also that the list exemplifies the time and place in which phrenology developed, both in the choice of traits included on the list and in the language used to describe them.
(Culver Pictures)

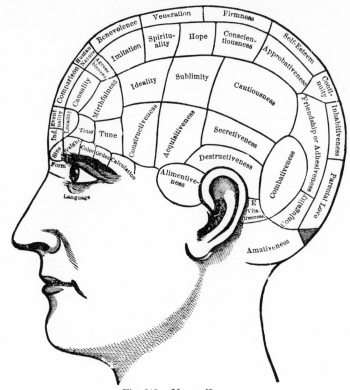

Fig. 245.—MODEL HEAD.

NAMES, NUMBERS AND LOCATION OF THE MENTAL ORGANS.

1. AMATIVENESS.—Connubial love, affection.
A. CONJUGAL LOVE.—Union for life, pairing instinct.
2. PARENTAL LOVE.—Care of offspring, and all young.
3. FRIENDSHIP.—Sociability, union of friends.
4. INHABITIVENESS.—Love of home and country
5. CONTINUITY.—Application, consecutiveness.
E. VITATIVENESS.—Clinging to life, tenacity, endurance.
6. COMBATIVENESS.—Defence, courage, criticism.
7. DESTRUCTIVENESS.— Executiveness, push, propelling power.
8. ALIMENTIVENESS.—Appetite for food, etc.
9. ACQUISITIVENESS.—Frugality, economy, to get.
10. SECRETIVENESS.—Self-control, policy, reticence.
11. CAUTIOUSNESS. — Guardedness, care-taking, safety.
12. APPROBATIVENESS.—Love of applause and display.
13. SELF-ESTEEM.—Self-respect, dignity, authority.
14. FIRMNESS.—Stability, perseverance, steadfastness.
15. CONSCIENTIOUSNESS.—Sense of right, justice.
16. HOPE.—Expectation, anticipation, perfect trust.
17. SPIRITUALITY.—Intuition, prescience, faith.
18. VENERATION.—Worship, adoration, deference.
19. BENEVOLENCE.—Sympathy, kindness, mercy.

20. CONSTRUCTIVENESS.—Ingenuity, invention, tools.
21. IDEALITY.—*Taste*, love of beauty, poetry and art.
B. SUBLIMITY.—Love of the grand, vast, magnificent.
22. IMITATION.—Copying, aptitude for mimicry.
23. MIRTH.—Fun, wit, ridicule, facetiousness.
24. INDIVIDUALITY.—Observation, curiosity to see.
25. FORM.—Memory of *shape*, looks, persons, things.
26. SIZE.—Measurement of quantity by the eye.
27. WEIGHT.—Control of motion, balancing.
28. COLOR.—Discernment, and love of colors, hues, tints.
29. ORDER.—*Method*, system, going by *rule*, arrangement.
30. CALCULATION.—Mental arithmetic, numbers.
31. LOCALITY.—Memory of place, position, travels.
32. EVENTUALITY.—Memory of facts, events, history.
33. TIME.—Telling *when*, time of day, dates, punctuality.
34. TUNE.—Love of music, sense of harmony, singing.
35. LANGUAGE.—*Expression* by words, signs or acts.
36. CAUSALITY.— *Planning*, thinking, philosophy
37. COMPARISON.—Analysis, inferring, illustration.
C. HUMAN NATURE.—Sagacity, perception of motives.
D. SUAVITY.—*Pleasantness*, blandness, politeness.

you have to do to make sure that something will or will not happen is to take the advice of your astrologer or eat the right foods).

Ideas like the homunculus theory and phrenology soon proved incorrect, but they were important steps in the evolution of psychology from armchair theological and philosophical speculation toward the systematic collection of empirical data which we identify with science. They led to systematic observation, record keeping, and experimentation, which ultimately resulted in the science of psychology. Even so, psychology was not firmly established as a discipline in its own right until after 1900. This was also true of most of the other sciences concerned directly with humans. Furthermore, experimental methodology and statistical analysis techniques developed slowly and gradually. The computer and related data processing techniques that make it quick and easy to apply statistics were not developed until quite recently. Because of this, about 75 percent of the scientific studies ever done, and probably more than 90 percent of the studies done in the areas of child development and socialization, have been done in the past 15 years or so. We know much less about ourselves than we do about our environment and the objects in it. This is one major reason why psychology has only just begun to produce significant amounts of applicable information, and why books about child rearing and related topics have been based primarily upon philosophy or unsubstantiated theories rather than systematic data. A large body of data about the relationships between experiences and the formation of personal characteristics now has been accumulated.

Another important reason for the slow accumulation of psychological knowledge was the peculiar history of the development of psychology in general and human development in particular. Until very recently, psychology was dominated by a small number of distinct groups of theorists who worked mostly in isolation from one another. They were interested in different questions and they had conflicting ideas about human nature and about how psychology should proceed.

Knowledge about how psychology developed historically provides the perspective that allows you to learn not only what theorists had to say but why they said it. Such knowledge will enable you to make distinctions between aspects of theory which flow *directly from empirical data* and are supported strongly vs. aspects of theory which are not supported by data and which are part of the theory because of the theorists' philosophical positions or historical circumstances. The ability to make such distinctions is especially important for readers of this book, because of the book's *eclecticism*. Theory and data seen as valuable have been taken from a variety of directions and integrated into a systematic presentation. Unfortunately, there are sometimes disagreements presented among writers with conflicting points of view. While this can present problems of conflict to readers, hopefully the most worthwhile parts of different theories and bodies of data have been integrated into a clear and systematic presentation. Theorists are presented in the context and perspec-

DEVELOPMENT OF SCIENTIFIC PSYCHOLOGY

tive of their places in history and their approaches to psychology. Some of the major groups of writers from whom I have borrowed material will be discussed in the following sections. Some of the strengths and weaknesses of their theories and the reasons why I retain some of their ideas but reject others are also presented.

BEHAVIORISM

The most influential branch of psychology in America, and the one identified most closely with the experimental approach to the study of humans, is *behaviorism*. Although the term itself was not used until much later, its roots go back to the philosophy of Locke and to the early work of the first psychologists working in Germany and the United States. These early psychologists were trying to stake out a territory for the scientific study of humans, in between theology and philosophy on one side, and zoology and other biological sciences on the other.

A major concern of early psychologists was being accepted by the scientific community of the time. Consequently, they took every measure to look, act, and sound like scientists. One result was that early behaviorists tended to restrict their studies to "safe" topics such as memory, sensory psychology, simple learning, and animal behavior. Psychologists felt that by studying simple organisms, general principles of behavior could be established that would apply to humans as well. Another result was excessive concern about the "legitimacy" of certain concepts and methods. Attention was confined to events that could be directly observed, measured, and varied experimentally, and the range of activities was restricted to scientific methods which were acceptable to the scientific community at large.

Although there was concern about building theory almost from the beginning, behaviorists were noted for their *empirical* orientation. They were concerned primarily with producing scientific data about humans and other animals. They insisted on precise specification of everything that was done in the course of carrying out an experiment, and the experiment itself had to be carried out in conformity to a rather narrow set of rules about what was considered appropriate scientific experimentation.

This concern with methodology was useful as far as data collection was concerned. Although the *interpretation* of their meaning sometimes has changed, the *findings* produced in early experiments, even those produced by some of the earliest workers going back to around 1875 (Ebbinghaus, 1885), have stood the test of time remarkably well. As the strengths of their empirical approach and of their scientific precision and detail began to be recognized by the scientific community at large, the attitudes and data collection methods of behaviorists were incorporated into most other approaches to psychology. Even so, these orientations still are identified with modern behaviorism.

The weaknesses of behaviorism lay mostly in the restrictiveness of its concepts and theories. Behaviorists rejected as unscientific and inappropriate for study anything which they regarded as "mentalistic." Unfortunately, this included many aspects of human psychology that are of most interest to the average person (anxieties, attitudes, beliefs, prejudices, and subjective experience in general). Most early behavioristic studies were done with animals, particularly rats, so that behaviorists were able to develop theories adequate to explain their data without any need for "mentalistic" concepts.

Another weakness of behaviorism, particularly for its ability to account for human psychology, was its emphasis on the physical environment and its effects upon the organism. Behaviorists would describe stimuli only in terms of their observable and measurable properties. This works reasonably well, so long as you confine yourself to studying animals. However, humans respond to the stimulation they *perceive,* and different people perceive the same situation differently. Defining the *stimulus situation* for humans requires information about how it is perceived. Careful description of the objective aspects of stimulus situations is not enough, because "objective" stimuli that can be measured and defined may be quite different from subjectively perceived stimuli to which the person is actually responding.

Instincts

Heavy reliance on so-called "instincts" as "explanations" for behavior came into disrepute long ago. Even so, most psychologists retained belief in some instincts, such as self-preservation and "maternal instincts." The latter is called into serious question by the data from monkey studies conducted by the Harlows (1966). Until these studies were conducted and publicized, it was generally believed that animals (and perhaps humans, too) engaged in a complex of behaviors that we call mothering (and perhaps also fathering) for basically instinctive reasons. They apparently did not need to be taught these behaviors. The behaviors appeared to emerge automatically when needed.

The Harlows demonstrated that supposedly instinctive maternal behavior simply did not appear in monkeys who had been removed from their natural mothers and raised in isolation from other monkeys. Isolation from the biological parents and from other monkeys had widespread effects, in fact, touching almost every aspect of monkey life. When returned to the company of other monkeys later, the isolates did not react normally. Instead, they seemed anxious and/or depressed, avoiding other monkeys and not responding in typical fashion to the playful overtures or not so playful aggression directed toward them. In fact, some of the monkeys reared in isolation had to be removed from cages with other monkeys to keep them from being killed or seriously injured.

Presumably instinctual and sexually related mating behaviors were absent in these isolates. They misinterpreted sexual advances by other monkeys and reacted to them as attacks most of the time. Even when they tolerated sexual advances without running away or fighting, they had no idea how to respond. Consequently, they never spontaneously achieved sexual intercourse, despite the best efforts of normal monkeys attempting to seduce or educate them.

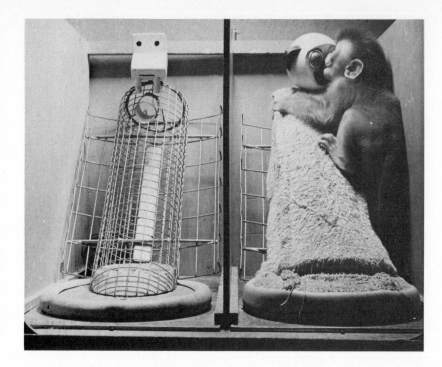

Artificial "mothers" used by Harlow and his colleagues to study the behavior of newborn monkeys removed from their natural mothers. The efficient but cold and impersonal device on the left was used successfully for feeding, but the infant monkeys clearly preferred the warmer, softer, and more "personalized" apparatus on the right whenever they were not hungry and especially when they appeared frightened or in need of comfort. These findings showed that the needs for comfort and security are independent of food needs rather than developed because of associations with feeding, and they suggested that stimulus attributes like warmth and softness might be experienced as soothing and comforting from birth; that is, the predisposition to respond to soft and warm stimuli this way might be a genetically programmed instinct rather than a learned response. (Photo courtesy of Wisconsin Primate Laboratory)

The Harlows wanted to see how some of these "motherless monkeys" would respond as mothers if they gave birth to young themselves, so eventually they arranged for the females to be impregnated with the help of a contrivance dubbed the "rape rack." The motherless mothers found this experience distasteful, and it did little to improve their attitudes toward or their knowledge about sexual behavior, but at least it did insure that they became impregnated and eventually gave birth. This allowed studies of their reactions to their own newborn infants.

These reactions quickly and convincingly demonstrated that interference in the normal course of development of the monkeys had eliminated any "instinctive" maternal behavior. Maternal reactions to newborn young varied from apathy to murderous hostility and aggression. Where no serious aggression was involved, and where repeated attempts to nurse on the part of the newborn infants were continued, some of the "motherless mothers" did learn to interact with their infants reasonably well, but the learning process was slow and painful. Other motherless mothers were so aggressive that their infants had to be removed in order to save the infants' lives. In some cases, removal did not occur soon enough, and the mothers killed and in some cases even ate their own children.

These and other results of the series of monkey studies conducted by the Harlows show convincingly that even genuine instinctive behavior can be strongly affected or even eliminated through environmental intervention. Instinctive behavior is not simply the emergence of genetically programmed activity that is going to occur no matter what; instead, it is the emergence of genetically programmed activities which appear if certain experiences crucial to the "instinct" have occurred previously. In extreme cases like those reported here, important and far reaching behavioral repertoires are entirely eliminated, at least as "instincts" that can be depended upon to appear more or less automatically in the natural course of things. On the other hand, motherless mothers who did succeed in learning to handle their first infant responded much more normally and "instinctively" to subsequent infants, indicating that behavior patterns eliminated through intervention could also be reinstated through intervention.

Finally, before writing off instincts entirely, it is instructive to consider the behavior of the infants of these motherless mothers. The Harlows report that, despite the fact that some of their mothers treated them with unrelenting vicious brutality, the infants "instinctively" kept coming back to nurse, seek warmth, and otherwise react toward their mothers the way that infant monkeys tend to do. These instincts were much stronger than the aversive effects of punishment, so much so that they led to the death or serious injury of many of the infants.

In the case of humans, it seems even more obvious that there is no such thing as maternal or paternal instinct. To the extent that adult humans react favorably and similarly to newborns, it is because of what they have observed and have been taught, not because of genetic programming. This is relevant not only philosophically, but practically, when we turn attention to problems such as child abuse. Child abusers are not individuals who somehow are lacking in appropriate maternal or paternal instincts for biological reasons. Instead, they are individuals who, for a variety of environmental and reversible reasons, have learned to take out their frustrations by abusing their offspring. Just as with the Harlows' motherless mothers, this behavior pattern can be eliminated and replaced by more appropriate parenting. In fact, the process is much easier and more certain in humans than in monkeys, because of human abilities to communicate. However, early diagnosis and intervention are crucial.

A related weakness of behaviorism, also encouraged by the tendency of behaviorists to confine their research to animals (or to restrictive human experiments which confined the subjects' responses to such activities as pushing buttons or memorizing word lists), was a lack of attention to language and the crucial role it plays in shaping peoples' responses. Even in the area of learning, which was behaviorism's strong point, much behavioristic data did not apply to typical human learning situations. Often, behaviorists were studying learning by simple organisms such as rats under conditions involving thrusting them into strange environments and subjecting them to unusual reinforcement contingencies. These experiments were too different from naturalistic situations to allow much transfer of experimental findings to typical human situations. In Bronfenbrenner's terms, they lacked "ecological validity" (Bronfenbrenner, 1974). It is easy to see how this led behaviorists to view humans as passive organisms who could be shaped and controlled by manipulating the stimuli they encountered and the reinforcements they received when they responded to these stimuli. This view also led behaviorists to see learning as requiring the slow accumulation of habits through trial and error, with responses which were reinforced being retained and responses which were not reinforced being dropped. The data produced by behaviorists supported such ideas, but these data were not typical of the everyday lives of humans.

Humans spend most of their time in familiar environments. They learn most things in response to spoken or written language, which provides meaning and definition to both their environment and their own responses. Also, they are not governed *completely* by the law of effect. Some rewarded responses are dropped, and some punished or unrewarded responses persist. Recently, behaviorists have begun to pay more attention to the events that precede responses, although many still stress reinforcement following responses to a degree that I believe to be far out of proportion to its actual importance for human psychology.

Many of the ideas of the early behaviorists, particularly the idea that the best way to understand human nature was to experiment with lower animals, are discounted today. However, they seem no sillier than other early theories, *when viewed in the context of the times.* The early behaviorists' concern about scientific purity was not merely a fad or an ego trip; it was a professional necessity. On the one hand, it provided protection from attacks by theologians and philosophers who believed that humans were not proper subjects for scientific study. On the other hand, scientific rigor provided them with credibility and respect in the scientific community. This was not gained easily; they had to fight for it for a long time.

In many ways, early behaviorists and other psychologists in university settings (as well as psychologically oriented physicians, such as Freud, in medical settings) were in positions similar to modern psychologists who are trying (so far without much success) to establish topics such as ESP and thought control as legitimate subjects of scientific inquiry. Until psychology finally became established as a science, universities of the times looked upon attempts to form psychology departments with the same jaundiced eye that modern universities view attempts to form parapsychology departments. Behaviorists deserve most of the credit for overcoming this resistance and establishing psychology as a science. Furthermore, behaviorists have collected much more empirical data than any other identifiable group of psychologists, and, as noted above, most of these data have stood the test of time.

My stance toward behaviorism probably is evident in what has been said already. Most of the *data* presented in this book were collected by behaviorists or by psychologists influenced strongly by the behaviorist tradition. The primary criteria in judging concepts or assertions are the quality and quantity of data available to support them. Most of the factual information accumulated in experiments by behaviorists are accepted as valid here, although sometimes the data will be interpreted differently. I accept the facts which behaviorists have established through experimentation, although occasionally I will argue that facts established in animal experiments do not apply to humans, or that additional facts also must be taken into account in making generalizations. Although I am sympathetic to behaviorism in many ways, I cannot confine myself to "pure" behaviorism. I believe that subjective experience, language, and the events which precede and elicit responses in the first place are much too important to be ignored or minimized. Behaviorists have recognized this too, of course. Modern behaviorism is much more open to concepts that previously were rejected as "mentalistic." Although the early orientations described above still influence modern behaviorists, they are more a caricature than an accurate description of behaviorism as it exists today. Modern behaviorism, particularly behavior modification and other aspects of applied behavioral analysis, is much less restrictive in its theorizing and much more oriented toward studying human problems of interest to the average person. Behaviorists have introduced the concept of *modeling* and done research on learning which occurs through observation of a model (often without any reinforcement), and they have introduced concepts such as *reinforcement history* to allow them to take into account individual differences that people bring into stimulus situations. The tradition of care in designing and carrying out experiments has continued, so that data produced by modern behaviorists typically are of high quality. Nevertheless, many psychologists still find behavioristic psychology to be too restrictive to be very useful in the areas of cognitive and linguistic development, and in all aspects of development which require attention to the subjective experience of the person (behaviorists still avoid this area, for the most part).

GESTALT PSYCHOLOGY AND FIELD THEORY

Another point of view that became established early in the history of psychology and was important in shaping its development was Gestalt psychology and the related area which came to be called *field theory*. "Gestalt" is a German word corresponding roughly to the word "pattern." Its use reflected the fact that these theorists, in contrast to behaviorists, placed heavy stress on the unity and integration of the person. Where behaviorists were concerned with the objective stimulus, Gestalt theorists were concerned with people's perceptions of situations, or their *subjective experience*. They viewed the person as a patterned, unitary whole (a Gestalt) which therefore had to be conceptualized and studied as such, even though made up of definable parts. The parts were seen as being in dynamic interrelationship with one another, meaning that a change affecting any one part of the system could affect any or all other parts, at least in theory. To the Gestalt theorists, the person was not simply the sum of the parts, but was a unique organization or patterning of those parts. The key to the self lay in the organization of the parts as much as in the parts themselves.

Gestalt psychologists concentrated on events occurring within the person or self. Others with similar ideas who concentrated on relationships between people and their subjective perceptions of the external environment (their *perceptual fields*), were called field theorists. Although there are some differences between Gestalt and field theory, they are relatively minor and technical. For simplicity, therefore, I will use the terms "Gestaltists" and "Gestalt theorists" to refer to both groups (who overlapped anyway).

Gestalt theorists believed that psychologists had to know how people perceived a stimulus situation if they were to make meaningful predictions about how they would act in that situation. To illustrate this point, they produced a variety of experimental data. For example, they used visual illusions to show that different people see and interpret the same stimulus differently. Many of their experiments involved very simple perceptions. They showed that an identical line can be perceived as either longer or shorter than it really is (depending upon the context), that the same patch of gray can be made to appear either lighter or darker (depending upon the brightness of the surrounding area), and that a square of a particular size can be made to look either larger or smaller (depending upon the sizes of nearby squares). In short, they showed that we tend to use context cues in perception. These cues affect not only how we interpret what we see, they actually affect *what* we see in the first place. The same stimulus will look different in different contexts and situations.

Other Gestalt experiments showed that we tend to organize our perceptions. We *instantly* see objects and events, not disorganized bits of information that must be processed and integrated before we can recognize them. Sometimes a stimulus is seen as more complete than it really is, as when a circle with a small segment missing is seen as a complete circle. Conversely, we sometimes see a stimulus as less complete than it really is, as when this same stimulus is seen as the letter "c." Also, we can anticipate and prepare for events (even before they happen), such as when we make a split-second adjustment in batting a ball or driving a car. The tendency to perceive almost any stimulus as meaningful is very compelling, so much so that drawings and nonsense syllables constructed deliberately to be "meaningless" usually are perceived with some degree of meaning.

Just as our *perceptions* are organized, so are our *memories*. This fact forms the basis for *cognitive consistency* (Festinger, 1957), one of the fundamental principles of human psychology that will be stressed throughout this book. Meaningfulness in perception and consistency in cognition (attitudes and beliefs which result from thinking about our perceptions) are not just interesting observations about human psychology. They are basic general principles (at the objective level) and compelling needs or reaction tendencies (at the subjective level) which are important for explaining or predicting behavior.

Although these and other major ideas of the Gestalt psychologists are fundamentally sound and applicable to human psychology, early Gestalt theorists erred in placing too much stress upon inborn mechanisms of perception and not enough on post-natal learning. For a long time, neither they nor the behaviorists with whom they carried on debates had a developmental perspective, so that developmental arguments were carried out on the basis of data collected from *adults*. With the advent of Piaget and the establishment of systematic study of the development of perception and cognition in children, we now know that things once thought to be mostly innate are mostly learned. Cross-age comparisons have shown that children gradually learn most of the meanings that they later apply "automatically" in perception. Cross-cultural comparisons have shown that two people raised in two contrasting environments sometimes learn to attach contrasting meanings to the same stimulus. One obvious example is skin color, which differs in both importance and meaning, depending upon one's race and culture, and depending upon the environment in which a person is raised.

A subtler but in many ways more instructive example is provided by the two illusions shown in the figure below. Cross-cultural comparisons have revealed that people living in modern, industrialized societies are more susceptible to the Muller-Lyer illusion, shown on the left. People living in relatively simple societies, especially if they live in grassy plains unbroken by mountains or man-made structures, are more susceptible to the horizontal-vertical illusion, shown on the right. These differences seem due to learning in different cultures and environments, rather than to genetic differences, although genetic explanations have been proposed (Pollack, 1969).

The most widely accepted explanation probably is that of the investigators who first reported these data (Segall, Campbell, and Herskovits, 1966). They noted that people growing up in industrialized societies live in "carpentered" environments, and that their depth perception development is affected by books, desk tops, table tops, buildings, and other artificial objects and furniture with rectangular sides and tops. Objectively, the nearest edge of such objects appears longer than the farthest edge, but repeated experiences with such objects teaches us that the two edges are equal in length, despite appearances.

These repeated experiences are generalized, so that eventually we learn to "automatically" adjust our perceptions of the relative length of lines according

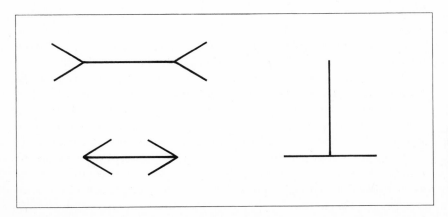

The Muller-Lyer illusion (*left*) and the horizontal-vertical illusion (*right*). Despite appearances, all long lines are exactly the same length. Cultural differences make some people more susceptible to the first illusion, and other people more susceptible to the second.

to our judgments about how far away they are. Since we "know" that a line close to us will look longer than it really is, and that a line farther away will look shorter than it really is, we take this into account when we perceive the lines. Usually, we are correct. In effect, then, we perceive what we "know," and not necessarily what our senses tell us. When there is a conflict between what we "know" and what we see objectively, we tend to *interpret* what we *see* in order to make it conform to what we *know*.

The Muller-Lyer illusion (on the left in the figure) is an exception that proves this rule. Both horizontal lines are exactly one inch long, but the top line looks longer than the bottom line. Apparently, this is because the small lines angling out from the top line make this line appear to be farther away (as if it were the back edge of a table top, for example). The short lines angling up from the bottom line make it appear to be closer (as if it were the near edge of a table top). The "information" provided by these short angling lines is taken into account in judging the length of the longer lines, although they happen to provide misinformation in this case. They make a compelling illusion, because such contours *typically* help us make *correct* judgments when compensating our perceptions of line length to take distance into account. People in primitive cultures, especially cultures that provide little or no contact with objects that have rectangular tops and sides, are less susceptible to this illusion. Apparently, they have not "learned" to compensate in judging line lengths by taking into account apparent differences in distance, at least not to the compelling extent that we have.

The horizontal-vertical illusion (on the right in the figure) shows the opposite cross-cultural difference. Almost everyone sees the vertical line as longer than the horizontal line, to some extent. People who live in flat, grassy plains tend to be more affected by this illusion than people who live in cities or in environments broken up by hills and valleys. One proposed explanation for this is that people who live in flat plains can see all the way to the horizon by looking in a straight line in virtually any direction (Segall, Campbell, and Herskovits, 1966). Such people get much more experience than do city dwellers in learning that the distance from themselves to the horizon is far greater than it appears visually. They get more practice in compensating for the tendency to underestimate such distances.

This tendency to compensate is *adaptive* in *their* environment for the same reason that the tendency to compensate perceptions of line length for distances from the viewer is adaptive in industrialized societies. It usually is correct. People who live in flat plains are especially susceptible to the horizontal-vertical illusion because they "know" that a vertical line is longer than it looks. People in environments with contrasting landscape have fewer such experiences, so that their tendency to compensate when perceiving vertical lines, and thus their susceptibility to this particular illusion, is not as well developed.

These and similar data show that stimuli are perceived in organized and meaningful ways, and that their meanings are determined partially by the contexts in which they are perceived. Our perceptions frequently would be inaccurate if we reacted only to the information provided to our senses, so we learn to compensate for deceptive appearances. Eventually, we "see" reality and reject or compensate for any input that conflicts with what we "know." This applies not only to simple perceptions, but also to cognitions. Much of this is adaptive and correct, as we will see in discussing Piaget. It also makes possible certain incorrect or maladaptive cognitions, such as prejudices, inflexible attitudes and beliefs, delusions, and hallucinations. Sometimes our need for cognitive consistency and our ability to see what we "know" to be correct (regardless of appearances) can become so strong that we maintain incorrect perceptions or cognitions with the help of various *defense mechanisms*. These mechanisms are the same ones we use to compensate for misleading appearances and arrive at correct perceptions and cognitions. However, if the need to maintain a particular perception or cognition (or to avoid it) is strong enough, these same mechanisms can be used to perpetuate incorrect perceptions or cognitions. This will be discussed in detail in the sections on coping and defense mechanisms.

In summary, Gestalt theorists and researchers have stressed that the important aspects of a stimulus are not its objective properties but its subjective meanings to the perceiver, and that these subjective meanings will be influenced both by the context in which stimuli are perceived and by the previous experiences the person has had with similar stimuli. They also have stressed that both perception and cognition tend to be organized and consistent, and that we tend to force such organization even when it does not exist objectively. They also have stressed that the person must be portrayed as a Gestalt: a dynamic, integrated whole consisting of many parts that are interrelated so that a change affecting one part can affect all others (at least theoretically). These ideas from the Gestalt tradition are fundamental assumptions that pervade this book. However, the Gestalt theorists' stress on innate organization of perception and cognition is rejected in favor of the developmental position stressed by Piaget and others.

While it is granted that a change in any part of the system *theoretically* can affect other parts, it should be noted that, in reality, all parts are *not* equal. *Peripheral* parts (such as unimportant beliefs and very minor physical habits which change in the course of learning a skill) are changed easily, but *central* parts (self-concept, strong prejudices or preferences, sex role) are much harder to change, the more so with age. Gestalt ideas apply especially well to situations involving central parts. A change in a central part will tend to force many other changes in the system. In contrast, changes in peripheral parts may have few or no consequences elsewhere in the system. For example, if you think a certain star is 17 billion miles away, and you read that recent work has established that it really is 18 billion miles away, you can change your belief quickly, easily, and without implications elsewhere (unless you are an astronomer). However, if you were told that you were going to live the rest of your life as a member of the opposite sex, starting three days from now, you would be faced with change in almost every facet of your life. Gestalt theory fits well when central parts and subjective experience are vital, while behaviorism fits better in more peripheral and less subjective situations.

PIAGETIAN THEORY   The theory and data of Jean Piaget, who has been studying and writing about child development for over 50 years, are the most comprehensive psychological contributions among those which are explicitly developmental in perspective. They also provide an integrative bridge between the "blank slate" objectivism of the behaviorists and the biological determinism and subjectivism of the Gestaltists. Piaget's many contributions have made him one of history's foremost psychologists.

Piaget never intended to be a psychologist as such. Instead, he was interested in epistomology, a branch of philosophy concerned with the nature of knowledge. Piaget was interested in learning about what human knowledge is and how it is acquired. Rather than remain at the level of philosophical speculation, he made systematic observations of people, particularly children. He focused on how knowledge develops and on the forms it takes as the child grows older and acquires deeper and newer kinds of understanding. This eventually led Piaget to formulate a comprehensive theory of cognitive development, and to invent a variety of experiments which have revealed a great deal of information about what and how children learn. His experiments and writing firmly established developmental psychology and child development as active and important areas of scientific inquiry.

Piaget's theory will be discussed in detail in later chapters. For the present, I will emphasize the role of Piaget in the historical development of scientific psychology, especially in providing an integrative bridge between other points of view. Piaget enjoyed brief popularity in the United States during the 1920s, after some of his early works were translated (he lives in Switzerland and writes in French). He soon came under heavy criticism, primarily because he was not using the "approved" scientific methods of the times. Most of his experiments were self-invented and conducted with homemade materials, and they were not always described to the satisfaction of American behaviorists. Also, he infuriated behaviorists by frequently generalizing from data collected on just a few subjects, instead of conducting experiments involving larger numbers of subjects. Consequently, for the next 30 years or so, Piaget was dismissed as unscientific and was given relatively little attention by American psychologists.

Piaget knew what he wanted to do, and persisted in doing it. He deepened and broadened his studies of child development, publishing an awesome quantity of quality research reports and theoretical writing. More recently, the attitudes of American psychologists towards Piaget have changed, beginning with grudging acceptance of some of his ideas and progressing to the point where now he is not only accepted but generally regarded as one of the greatest psychologists of all time. None of this has affected Piaget much. He continues to pursue his own goals. His work has influenced many others, though, so that a majority of the child development research going on at present is directly related to Piagetian theory, and much other research is influenced by it.

Part of the reason for this acceptance of Piaget is that replication studies by others, including many by scientists explicitly interested in disproving some of

his ideas, generally have shown him to be correct. He has been wrong about certain specifics (for example, in his early work, he gave too much emphasis to age and not enough to individual differences, and he tends to underestimate the importance of language), but his central ideas and the majority of his specific findings have been replicated.

In addition to the sheer quantity and quality of theory and data that he has produced, Piaget's most important contribution to psychology probably has been his demonstration that children go through identifiable and predictable *sequences of qualitatively different stages* as they gradually accumulate knowledge. Stage differences appear both in knowledge (*what* is known) and in the cognitive processes and reasoning strategies available to draw upon in extending and integrating this knowledge (*how* things are known).

Like behaviorists, Piaget stresses that the child acquires knowledge through interacting with the environment and getting feedback from it. Piaget stresses

Jean Piaget interacting with a colleague and two children being observed and interviewed to determine their understanding of the properties of the objects they are manipulating. Using such familiar concrete props, combined with sophisticated questioning, Piaget and other students of child development can assess the degree of cognitive development achieved by the child in various areas of understanding. (Wayne Behling, Photographer) the *informational value* of feedback. Knowledge is confirmed when children receive the expected feedback, while unexpected feedback provides "food for thought" likely to motivate them to experiment and acquire new knowledge. Behaviorists also acknowledge this, but they stress the *reinforcing aspects* of feedback rather than the informational ones (actions that bring desirable consequences are likely to be repeated, and actions that do not are unlikely to be repeated). While there are some differences between the two positions, they both stress that children learn through interaction with the environment.

Unlike the behaviorists, but like the Gestaltists, Piaget stresses the importance of inborn biological factors in determining development. He also stresses heavily the point that the importance of a stimulus is in how it is perceived subjectively rather than in its purely objective qualities. In fact, the Piagetian stages could be described as changes in the ways that children perceive identical stimulus events as they become more knowledgeable about the world. The stimulus events are the same, but children perceive them differently at different stages.

In many ways, the theories of Piaget seem quite compatible with Gestalt theory. However, Piagetian theory differs from Gestalt theory, and provides a bridge between Gestalt and behavioristic theory by stressing that developing children gradually *construct* their knowledge about the world through interacting in it and getting feedback from it. This knowledge is learned rather than biologically programmed to appear automatically. In short, Piaget's view of *adult* perception and cognition is similar to that of Gestalt theory, but he has shown that adults achieve this organization of perception and cognition only after developing through a sequence of stages. The stages involve continual interaction with the environment, and the learning that occurs during the developmental years is governed in large part by the processes described by behaviorists.

Another way that Piaget provides a link between behaviorists and Gestaltists and other cognitive theorists is in the importance he assigns to behavioral interaction with the environment as a determinant of intellectual development. Whereas behaviorists try to confine themselves to observable behavior and to avoid mentalistic concepts, and Gestaltists tend to concentrate on subjective experience rather than behavior, Piaget sees these two major areas of human existence as totally and necessarily intertwined.

Piaget's basic unit of knowledge is called the *schema*. Schemas can be behavioral (skills such as walking, reaching for and picking up something, or driving a car), verbal (knowledge of words and the ability to express one's self in oral or written language), or cognitive (ranging from simple perceptual skills such as matching identical objects or discriminating different ones, through logical reasoning abilities such as the recognition that the number of objects does not change when you move them from one container to another or the ability to draw logical conclusions, to broad beliefs, attitudes, or aspects of knowledge about the world).

Piaget notes that the knowledge of the infant is confined mostly to behavioral schemas. In the first year of life, infants learn a great deal about how to use their bodies and about the properties and uses of familiar objects, but learn relatively little language. Apparently, they do not yet possess the mental structures needed to form cognitive schemas. The quantity and quality of behavioral schemas increases rapidly—infants learn more each day through interactions with the environment.

Most infant behavioral schemas involve their own actions (they know what things they can *do*, what is likely to happen if they perform certain actions). Most of their knowledge about objects in the environment is action-related (their knowledge of objects is concentrated on what you *do* with them, or, more specifically, what *they* can do with them). Early language learning also shows this emphasis. Most of the words and phrases learned earliest concern behavioral schemas (the major exceptions are the names of parents, siblings, and important people or animals). Similarly, cognitive schemas appear to develop, at least initially, through the gradual internalization of behavioral schemas. *Behavior is the foundation for the development of verbal and cognitive abilities.* The child first learns behavioral skills and knowledge about how objects can be used, then learns words for these skills and objects, and then learns to imagine and think about the consequences of actions. These early cognitive activities are the beginnings of the development of intelligence and problem solving abilities.

In putting forth explanations for changes in the nature of intelligence as the child moves through successive stages, Piaget has moved away from his earlier stress on chronological age (which explains nothing) toward a stress on the *sequence* of stages and on the identification of both biological and experiential causes of intellectual development. He stresses that certain stage sequences are universal, that children everywhere progress through the same stages in the same order. Even here, however, the *rate* at which an individual child moves through the stages, and the particular *form* that the organization of knowledge takes within a given stage level, are unique and depend on complex factors. Piaget is eclectic in discussing these causal factors, in contrast to most other theorists, who tend to stress just one or two.

According to Piaget, the rate of progression through the stages (how fast children learn) and the form of knowledge (the specifics of what they learn and the unique connotations that make their understanding of a particular concept slightly different from that of the next child) depend upon both biological and experiential factors. Biological factors include both the genetic endowment, which will set upper and lower limits on children's developmental potentials, and their rates and forms of maturation, which will affect the rates and forms of schema development (at least for those schemas which require a certain minimal level of biological maturation).

Experiential factors include the physical environment, which will cause children to come into contact with certain objects but not others; society and culture, which will cause them to be exposed to certain concepts and attitudes but not others; the information or skills which are directly and deliberately taught by parents, teachers, or other socialization agents (which will differ both across and within cultures); and *equilibration,* Piaget's term for people's unique complexes of interests and intellectual curiosity (which lead them to explore certain aspects of their environments rather than others).

Behaviorists and other determinists dislike the concept of equilibration, partly because it is a poorly defined mentalistic concept. It implies that twins who were identical in genetic endowment and maturational progress and exposed to exactly the same environment and socialization still would develop somewhat differently. Presumably, motivation from unique equilibration needs would cause one child to explore and learn about certain aspects of the shared environment and not others, while the other child would have a different pattern of learning experiences and interests because of different equilibration needs. This idea is understandably distasteful to those who wish to construct a totally deterministic psychology capable of predicting (at least in theory) exactly what children will do in given situations. It is appealing to those (including myself) who believe the development of a totally deterministic psychology is impossible at present and unlikely in the future.

In summary, Piaget has done much more than any other individual to establish the value of developmental psychology and of the stage concept, and he provides a bridge between behaviorists and Gestaltists. His theoretical contributions have been numerous and important, but his most important contributions probably have been his invention of hundreds of different experiments and his accumulation of reams of data about child development. Although many have been attracted by his theories, it has been his experimental data that have gained him acceptance and prestige among psychologists of all persuasions. This has been because most of his findings have been replicated by others, including many who set out to disprove them. In this respect, Piaget probably has the best "batting average" of any major psychologist, particularly when you take into account the great range of topics that he has studied and the large number of findings that he has reported.

Even so, Piagetian psychology is but one approach. It must be integrated with others to form a complete picture. It has certain weaknesses even in its own sphere. One of Piaget's most notable strengths, his steadfast devotion to the study of the nature of human knowledge and how it develops, has resulted in the relative neglect of other areas of study. Because of their cognitive emphasis, Piagetians have little to say about social and personal development. Because of their emphasis on naturalistic observation and the identification of universal stages in cognitive development, they have little to say about individual differences or about how to intervene in order to improve development or provide corrective treatment for children whose development has been distorted. Finally, apparently because their studies have concentrated on intellectually bright and mentally healthy middle- and upper-class children in industrialized countries, they have a tendency to write as if *all* children were happy, bright, and curious young "scientists," busy acquiring knowledge about the world. Consequently, their concepts sometimes are difficult to apply to children with severe problems, low self-esteem or frustration tolerance, inhibitions and fears, apathy or withdrawal, grossly limited intellectual abilities, or other problems that prevent them from being the idealized children described by Piaget.

Piaget and his colleagues are aware of these problems, but they have chosen to concentrate their efforts on intellectual development and leave the study of social and personal topics to others. This probably has been a good choice, because a concentrated and programmatic effort to develop knowledge about a limited area is more likely to succeed than an attempt to answer too many questions at the same time. Nevertheless, Piagetian theory and data, impressive as they are, are applicable only to the cognitive areas for the most part, and even here are applicable primarily only to the developmental aspects of cognition. They cannot stand alone, because too many important areas are left out. They must be integrated with other theory and data.

As with behaviorism, I will accept and draw upon virtually all Piagetian *data* in subsequent chapters, but I will not always *interpret* them the same way Piagetians would. In particular, I think that Piagetians have seriously underestimated the importance of language, especially verbal instruction, for shaping cognitive development, and I see children as much more open to change through planned socialization and educational experiences than do Piagetians. Even though Piagetian theory stresses environmental experience and socialization and education as influences on cognitive development (along with biological influences), Piagetians generally are pessimistic about the importance and usefulness of planned intervention. They believe that the achievement of new concepts and the development of true understanding of principles comes only very slowly and as a result of broad general experience. As a result, they see cognitive development as a slow, gradual process that cannot be speeded up significantly or otherwise improved through planned intervention. Their own studies largely support this position (Piaget and Inhelder, 1969).

However, other, more intervention-oriented workers have produced evidence that planned intervention can have worthwhile effects. Piagetian stages are not as fixed as once believed. They can be advanced with instruction, and, perhaps more importantly, within a particular stage, acquisition of knowledge and skills can be broadened and deepened considerably through systematic efforts to do so (Bruner, 1966). Thus, while the Piagetians are correct in criticizing proponents of early education who believe that the first few years of life are crucial for cognitive development and that planned intervention can eliminate the problems of limited intellectual development associated with disadvantaged environments, it remains true that planned intervention with more realistic goals and proper implementation is both worthwhile and effective.

This will be discussed in more detail in subsequent chapters. For the present, let us turn from Piaget and cognitive development to social and personal development. Both because of its historical importance and because of the quality and quantity of theory it has produced in these areas, this discussion must begin with Sigmund Freud and psychoanalytic theory.

FREUD AND PSYCHOANALYTIC THEORY

Piaget developed a systematic theory of cognitive development that provided a bridge between Gestalt theory and behavioristic theory. Similarly, Freud formulated the first systematic theory of personality and social development, and provided a bridge between earlier theories based upon instincts or other biological concepts and the behavioristic theories of experimental psychologists. Also, like Piaget, Freud did this primarily by combining prolific writing over a long career with persistent work in pursuit of his own goals and interests. Freud personally, and psychoanalysts generally, not only had to contend with rejection by behaviorists but also had to cope with opposition from the established medical authorities of the times. Some knowledge about these problems is essential in understanding psychoanalytic theory, particularly the theory of Freud himself.

Freud was neither a psychologist nor a child development researcher; he was a psychiatrist (although this term was not in use when he began his career). Most of Freud's long career was spent as a practicing and writing psychoanalyst, beginning late in the 19th century and extending until the late 1930s. He began his work in Vienna, but left for England in the late 1930s to escape probable Nazi imprisonment. He died shortly thereafter. Although he had broad interests and was extremely creative in developing theoretical ideas and in being able to look upon old problems from new perspectives, most of what he did was related in one way or another to his clinical practice with disturbed individuals. He collected no systematic data, preferring instead to generalize from individual case histories in developing his theories about the development and treatment of mental disorder. Because of this "unscientific" approach, and because his theories were laden with mentalistic concepts, he and his psychoanalytic movement were rejected by American behaviorists for several decades.

Freud also had to fight for acceptance at home, since his ideas upset his contemporaries by challenging some of the prevailing wisdom of the times. He introduced ideas such as childhood sexuality and the Oedipus complex, which outraged and infuriated most of the community, including his fellow physicians. Freud worked in a hostile atmosphere, and it was many years before his ideas were accepted. Many of them never have been, except by a relatively small number of "orthodox" Freudians. He was never imprisoned or prevented from practicing or writing, however, so that he and his small band of followers, who began to call themselves psychoanalysts, persisted in treating patients and developing their theories despite heated opposition.

Part of the reason that psychoanalysts were able to survive was that most of their ideas (not all) were no more outlandish than the medical theories popular at the time. A typical example concerns hysteria, or conversion reaction, as this disorder is known today. People suffering from conversion reactions lose sensory functions (the ability to see, to hear, or to feel) or motor functions (the ability to move a particular part of the body), even though there is nothing wrong with them neurologically. Freud correctly recognized that conversion reactions were symptoms of a struggle to keep some undesirable impulse or idea repressed (out of conscious awareness). He also recognized that this

Sigmund Freud as a young man. His dress and grooming are typical of his times, as is the stern appearance affected for the photograph. He is not shown with children because he never did systematic research with children, although he did observe and interact with his own six children. (Austrian Information Service, New York)

disorder occurred in men as well as women, although it was more common in women.

Freud's insights were dismissed as ridiculous by the medical establishment of the time. These doctors firmly believed that hysteria occurred only in women and that it was caused by a "wandering uterus" which somehow had become dislodged from its proper place in the woman's body and had moved to another place, where it was interfering with sensory or motor functioning. The doctors of the time literally believed that the reason an hysterical woman could not feel anything in her right hand was that her uterus had lodged itself somewhere between the hand and the spinal cord, cutting off incoming stimulation. Given the times, early psychoanalytic ideas were rather sophisticated in many respects.

Another thing in Freud's favor was that his personal life was above reproach. He lived in the Victorian era, and even though his theorizing contained many elements considered outrageous and immoral, Freud was a model husband and father by the standards of the day. He was devoted to his wife and six children, and led a conventional family life. He did get involved in several professional disputes and unhealthy relationships with some of his colleagues, but most of these problems were known only within the psychoanalytic group, so they did little to harm his reputation. Some of his early colleagues broke with him because they considered him to be too autocratic and conservative. Their attacks probably *helped* his reputation.

Over his long career, Freud periodically introduced new concepts into his theory. He also changed several of his concepts, sometimes more than once. However, he strove to remain consistent and to develop a generalized theory of personality, stressing in particular the ways that disordered personality patterns develop. Although Freud looked upon his theory as a singular entity, certain parts of it have no necessary connection with other parts. For purposes of discussion the theory will be split into five separate pieces because in this book I will accept one part, partially accept two others, and reject the last two. The five parts of Freudian theory are as follows.

1. Freud's theory of anxiety and defense mechanisms (unacceptable impulses or ideas create anxiety, and if this anxiety becomes unbearable, people will use defense mechanisms to help them repress the impulse or idea, because they cannot bear to face it directly).

2. Freud's developmental stages (oral, anal, phallic, Oedipal, latency, and genital) in personality development.

3. Freud's ideas about treatment of psychological disorders (dream analysis, free association, catharsis, unraveling strands of disordered development back to their origins and then attempting to restructure the personality in a healthier form).

4. Freud's concepts of personality structure (id, ego, superego, ego ideal).

5. Freud's ideas about instincts (libido, or life instincts, and Thanatos, or death instincts).

Freud saw these five groups of ideas as necessarily connected with one another, but many psychologists today feel that they are not.

Freud's theory of anxiety and defense mechanisms has been the most widely accepted aspect of his theorizing, and it is accepted in this book more or less as he stated it. The idea that threatening impulses can produce more anxiety than people are equipped to handle, leading them to resort to defense mechanisms to keep the threatening impulse repressed, is accepted as valid. So are most of Freud's definitions of various defense mechanisms, his explanations of how they work to help maintain repression, and his idea that people using defense mechanisms are not aware that they are doing so.

Note that accepting the theory of anxiety and defense means accepting the theory that people can systematically and repeatedly exclude unpleasant thoughts from consciousness *without ever realizing what they are doing.* This may seem intuitively wrong or at least paradoxical, but, as will be argued later, there is considerable neurophysiological and psychological evidence to indicate that this is precisely what happens when people use defense mechanisms (Maddi, 1976; Pribham, 1971). The theory of anxiety and defense does not explain *all* psychological disorders, although it goes a long way toward explaining most of the classical neuroses, many of which were identified originally by Freud himself.

Freud's ideas about developmental stages and his ideas about treatment of psychological disorders are accepted *in part.* Most of the specifics of Freud's ideas about child development have been proved wrong. His general stages and some of his ideas about dynamics have some validity, at least when they are rephrased to eliminate certain unnecessary and undesirable theoretical assumptions. Similarly, many of the methods that Freud stressed as useful for treatment of psychological disorders have proved to be useful. However, they are not as universally applicable as he thought they were, and they are not always the quickest or best treatment even where they do apply. Nevertheless, many of Freud's ideas about therapy persist in treatment approaches popular today.

Finally, Freud's ideas about personality structure and about instincts are rejected. There is no evidence that they exist, and no need for them as theoretical constructs. They are theoretical "excess baggage," although the term "ego" is in common use and will be used occasionally in this book.

Once the initial shock of Freud's ideas had passed, professionals of different persuasions began to see that he had much to offer, even though few agreed with everything he had to say. His structural concepts, and particularly his instinct theories, provided continuity with previous theorizing about personality. Also, his status as a physician gave him a degree of credibility and acceptance among biologically-oriented professionals. Freud clearly saw the course of personality development as determined by environmental causes, particularly early parent-child interactions. This orientation led to a number of hypotheses concerning the relationships between childhood experiences and adult personality. Eventually, behavioristically-oriented psychologists realized this and began research designed to test some of Freud's propositions.

Freud's developmental theory was quite explicit in identifying stages and making predictions about what would happen if development were distorted in a particular way during a particular stage. This led developmentally-oriented psychologists to test many of his stage theories. In fact, up until the last 15 years or so, when non-psychoanalytic theories of social and personality development finally began to appear, psychoanalytic writings were the basis for virtually all hypotheses about social and personality development. Gestalt-ists and Piagetians were confined to perception and cognition, and behaviorists rarely ventured into social and personality development. For many years, psychologists interested in these topics had to look to Freud and his psycho-analytic colleagues for theoretical inspiration. This was the only sizable group that studied these areas in a consistent and programmatic way. Freud was the major influence in shifting the emphasis in personality theory from instinct and trait approaches to developmental approaches and to conceptualization of personality as a product of socialization rather than biological programming. Although Freud did not collect experimental data, his writings introduced a large number of concepts and hypotheses that led to a great deal of research by others.

Freud founded psychoanalysis and easily is its most prestigious and influen-tial proponent, but many other psychoanalytically oriented writers also have been influential. Many of these were early colleagues who broke with Freud and started their own groups. They shared most of Freud's ideas but added or gave greater stress to some of their own (Adler, Jung, Reik, Rank, Reich, and others). More modern writers (the so-called "neo-Freudians"), have integrated psychoanalytic ideas with other, newer ideas and have rejected certain aspects of orthodox psychoanalysis (the instinct theories in particular). Many of these writers are prominent in the areas of psychotherapy and psychodiagnosis. Two of these writers, Anna Freud and Erik Erikson, also are influential in developmental psychology.

Anna Freud, Sigmund's daughter, has had a distinguished career in England directing a psychoanalytic institute for the treatment of disordered children. Her book *The Ego and the Mechanisms of Defense* (Freud, 1946) is a classic in the field that has stood the test of time. It is important reading for anyone interested in anxiety and defense mechanisms. Erik Erikson is best known for his monograph *Identity and the Life Cycle* (Erikson, 1968), in which he reinterpreted and expanded upon the Freudian stages of personality develop-ment. Erikson deemphasizes instinctual components. He places more stress on early experiences and familial relationships as factors affecting personality development. His stage theory will be discussed in detail in subsequent chapters.

While there have been many positive contributions of Freudian psychology, it also has a number of notorious problems and weaknesses. One problem, already mentioned, is that early psychoanalysts did not collect systematic data, preferring to generalize from case studies instead. In contrast to the situation with behaviorism and Piagetian psychology, there are few data from psycho-analysts to accept or reject. Their case studies were not really scientific data.

They were heavily subjective, and usually were selected to illustrate a theoretical point. They tended to be written from a psychoanalytic perspective so strong as to make it difficult to separate facts from their interpretation. Orthodox Freudian *case studies* cannot be accepted unless orthodox Freudian *theory* is also accepted. In this book, many data that bear on psychoanalytic theory will be discussed, but they usually were collected by behavioral scientists other than psychoanalysts. Psychoanalytic theory, however, will be discussed periodically.

Another weakness of psychoanalytic theory is its excess theoretical baggage, particularly the structural concepts (id, ego, superego, ego ideal) and the instinct theories. A related problem is the tendency of psychoanalysts to *"adultomorphize,"* or attribute to young children ideas, impulses, or motives that they perceive in themselves or in other adults. Freud and his colleagues did not realize the seriousness of this problem, partly because differences between the mind of the child and that of the adult (since delineated by Piaget) were mostly unknown at the time, and partly because they spent most of their time working with adults.

In fact, until relatively recently, the major influences on developmental psychology, with the exception of Piaget, came from people who spent little or no time studying children. Behaviorists studied animals, Gestaltists studied the perceptions of adults in unusual perceptual situations, and psychoanalysts studied disordered adults in clinical settings. Each group of theorists generated ideas about child development, but these were extrapolations from work with other populations. They rarely were checked out in scientific studies of normal children. Psychoanalytic theory has proved to be especially vulnerable here, because subsequent studies have refuted virtually every assumption that Freud made about the motives, desires, and general subjective experiences of children (Kreitler and Kreitler, 1966). Freudian developmental stage concepts also have many errors of specifics (penis envy, Oedipus complex, anal theory of birth, castration fear, and so forth), which now are known to be either totally incorrect or applicable to only a small minority of children (Kreitler and Kreitler, 1966).

Finally, Freudian theory appears too pessimistic about human nature and about the reversibility of disordered personalities. Freud saw human nature as fundamentally evil, so he saw the function of socialization as teaching children to overcome their antisocial instincts so that they could get along with others. Freud also felt that an adult neurotic could not be "really" changed without a thorough-going psychoanalysis that lasted several years and involved a total restructuring of the personality. Modern treatment methods have shown that particular "neurotic" symptom patterns can be treated successfully using much briefer treatments that do not involve psychoanalytic exploration of repressed desires, impulses, and memories. While Freud erred on the side of pessimism, modern humanistic theories err on the side of optimism by picturing children as fundamentally altruistic people who will "naturally" grow up to be humanistically inclined unless their development is distorted during socialization.

In contrast to both of these extremes, this book adopts the "blank slate" approach to *personality* development (but *not* to *intellectual* development), for the most part. There is little evidence of instincts or other biological programming in social and personality development, and much evidence that personality is almost entirely a product of the individual's environment and experiences. Personality also undergoes continual development and thus remains open to change at any point in the life cycle. It does not become fixed or stable after adolescence, as many stage theorists imply. These assumptions pervade the book.

THE PSYCHOMETRIC TRADITION

Another major influence on psychology in general and child psychology in particular has been the psychometric tradition. This approach, strong in Britain and the United States, stresses the measurement of psychological characteristics and the development of *norms*. In contrast to the other approaches, which all are heavily theoretical, the psychometric approach is heavily empirical. It is concerned primarily with the collection of data, particularly data describing what is typical and what is abnormal. It is less oriented toward developing theoretical explanations for the data or even toward integrating data from separate investigations. The psychometric tradition has produced IQ tests, standardized achievement tests, personality tests and questionnaires, and age and sex norms for virtually any human characteristic that is of interest and can be measured.

Usually, this has involved application of the assumptions and methods associated with the statistical concept of the *normal curve*. One assumption is that human traits will show the so-called "normal" distribution in the population. Most people will be at or near the mean (average), and there will be equal numbers of people both above and below the mean. As you move farther away from the mean towards either extreme, there will be fewer and fewer people. An example is the average height of adult males in a particular country or area. If this average is an even six feet, and if height is normally distributed among these adult males, there will be more adult males whose height is an even six feet than there will be at any other height measured. The next largest numbers will be at 5 feet 11 inches and 6 feet 1 inch; the next at 5 feet 10 inches and 6 feet 2 inches; etc. Relatively few males will be extremely tall or extremely short.

Using the normal curve and the statistics associated with it, it is possible to compute the percentages of males likely to be found at each given height within the range observed, and also to compile tables of percentiles which will indicate that a given male is taller than a given percent of other males and shorter than the remaining percent. Such *norms* lend meaning to labels like "average," "tall," "fairly tall," and so forth. This kind of normative information can be useful, especially in the early stages of a science, although in the case of human development it is arguable that psychometric information has done at least as much harm as good. The difficulty is not in the information itself, of course; it is in how the information has been publicized and used.

One problem with such information gathering is that some things are given more importance than they deserve simply because they are easy to observe and measure. We have tables giving normative information about infant growth in weight and height, time of appearance of teeth, first mastery of sitting, standing, walking, and the like. Such information is interesting and usually correct, but often it is misunderstood and misused. Parents tend to worry whenever their infant is not above average, forgetting that half of any population necessarily is below average. Also, most of these norms are of no particular importance, because they do *not* correlate with measurements taken later. Except at the very extremes, it makes *no* difference to eventual adult normalcy whether a baby is below average, average, or above average on most of these indices.

Another problem with the psychometric approach is that scores which are merely statistical constructs can be *reified* (treated as if they were real). Probably the best example here is IQ. An IQ is an average of scores on several different tests. It expresses a person's relative standing on that test battery compared to others the same age. There are large numbers of intellectual abilities, so that people with strikingly contrasting patterns of strengths and weaknesses can get the same average score and therefore the same IQ when they take a test battery. The IQ concept tends to mask more than it reveals. Furthermore, it has become so familiar that people sometimes treat it as if it were real; that is, as if it corresponded to something in the brain or the body generally. This is *not* true. An IQ is simply a test score. It is a useful norm, but it does not correspond to anything physical in the person that we might call "intelligence."

A third problem with the psychometric approach is that it tends to assume that attributes are normally distributed in the population. Sometimes this even leads to the use of measurement devices and statistics which give the appearance that something is normally distributed even when it is not. Often, a set of measurements which do not conform to the normal curve are "normalized" statistically, because this makes them more convenient to analyze. Frequently, the fact that the data were normalized are not really normally distributed in the population is forgotten. It is usually assumed implicitly that any trait is normally distributed in the population unless there are clear data to the contrary (such as sex, which is bimodally distributed). However, there are reasons to believe that many traits are not normally distributed (honesty, potential for violence, racial prejudice, attitudes toward authority, and so forth).

Finally, one of the most insidious dangers inherent in the psychometric approach is the tendency for people to equate "average" with "good," or "normal" with "ideal." This is a real problem for human psychology, because we lack a universally agreed upon definition of the ideal person, particularly regarding ideal personal and social traits. As a result, most of us implicitly use an adjustment model, in which a people are considered to have good mental health if they are well adjusted to their society and surroundings but poor mental health if they are not. In effect, being well adjusted means being statistically normal. This leads to problems, because what is normal is not necessarily good (Maslow, 1970).

One set of evidence comes from cross-cultural data, which show that behaviors considered desirable and normal in one culture sometimes are considered undesirable and evil in another. The same behavior which is "good" in one place is "bad" in another. Worse yet, the tendency to link normality with "goodness" implies linking abnormality with "badness" (Murphy, 1976). However, on *some* traits at least, a person who is statistically abnormal attains a superior rather than inferior position in society. For example, aptitude for a particular sport is probably normally distributed in the population, which makes professional athletes statistically abnormal. In this case, being abnormal is socially advantageous, or "good."

In general, normality is equated with the ideal. One must not be either too introverted or too extroverted, too honest or too dishonest, too secretive or too talkative. Norms rather than logical constructs are used to define what is "expected" or "ideal." This tendency to equate normality with goodness will be recognized as a reality throughout the book, although it will be viewed as an unfortunate reality that must be taken into account in studying and raising children rather than as an appropriate or ideal situation.

RECENT DEVELOPMENTS

In the past 15 years or so, there has been an explosion of research about children and on child development. Some of this was fueled by a renewed interest in Piaget, some by interest in socioeconomic status (SES) and concern about the disadvantaged, some by a shift within behavioristic psychology from animal to human experiments and to applied experiments conducted by behavior modifiers, and some by a shift in personality research from interest in studying abnormal adults to interest in prevention of disorder and promotion of positive mental health.

There has been much more experimentation in child psychology, although naturalistic observation remains a popular method. There also has been much more theoretical eclecticism and a focusing of interest on narrower areas. In short, there is less interest in building comprehensive theories and more interest in obtaining reliable information, without worrying much about how one item of information fits with all the rest. The major exceptions to this are Piagetian theory and behaviorism, although there have been changes here, too. Behaviorists, due largely to the influence of Skinner, have retained their stress on experimentation and scientific rigor, but they have moved away from theory building and from experimental paradigms that were producing trivial results toward new kinds of experiments that are producing new and more useful information. Also, experimentation with animal learning has been abandoned almost completely in favor of research on human learning.

In contrast, Piagetians have persisted in the same basic tradition theoretically, although they have begun to conduct carefully controlled and systematic experiments with larger numbers of subjects, replacing the earlier case study method. In some ways, present Piagetian psychology resembles the old behaviorism right before it died: it is starting to get mired in trivia. Piagetians probably will recognize this soon and begin to shift their interests from naturalistic studies of narrower and narrower topics toward applications of Piagetian concepts to intervention with children, although not much of this has happened yet.

In addition to the theories and data presented already, there is a large body of information relevant to developmental psychology and socialization that has been produced by smaller groups of theorists or by individual investigators pursuing particular problems.

SUMMARY   This chapter has presented an historical overview of the development of psychology in general and human development in particular, stressing four major traditions psychology: behaviorism, Gestalt psychology, Piagetian psychology, and psychometrics. In its early development as a science, psychology had to stake out a claim between the well-established fields of theology and philosophy on one side and the newly emerging biological sciences on the other. In the process, many ideas and methods developed that we now can recognize as inappropriate but which were functional and perhaps even necessary given the tenor of the times. Everyone is affected by socialization and surroundings, and these effects show themselves in writings, including "scientific" writings. Often in the case of scientists, the effects show up long before the writing stage. They determine what questions are asked in the first place, and what methods are considered appropriate for trying to answer them. Science once was thought to be truly objective, eliminating human subjectivity and bias through careful specification of experimental procedures and replication of studies by different investigators with different points of view. Science does in fact succeed in producing objective information this way, but now we have come to recognize that it still is a subjective activity (Kuhn, 1962). Different scientists disagree about even the validity of factual information, because one method sometimes will produce one result while another method produces another. More importantly, scientists who agree upon the basic information will then often disagree on the meaning or interpretation of that information.

These disagreements usually end up as subjectively biased arguments among individuals who assign differential meaning and importance to different findings, depending upon whether the findings support or refute their positions. This is hardly the objective, dispassionate search for truth that science sometimes is portrayed as being. This will become quite clear in later chapters when currently "hot" issues are discussed. As we will see, the scientific conclusion about these issues is that they cannot be resolved on the basis of data available at the moment, but this does not stop vast numbers of scientists from arguing their positions, often vehemently. The ultimate point here is that this and other books can provide you with factual information and can try to help you differentiate facts from interpretations of these facts, but they cannot settle all issues or resolve all contradictions for you. To the extent that it is necessary for you to do so, you must do it yourself, hopefully by informing yourself of the available facts and then filling in the missing pieces rationally and remaining open to new information. Child development and socialization are young, interesting, and lively sciences, but they require tolerance of ambiguity and apparent contradiction for the serious student. Those who want "just the facts" will be disappointed.

ANNOTATED BIBLIOGRAPHY, PART ONE

BALDWIN, ALFRED. *Theories of child development*. New York: Wiley, 1967.

This book concentrates on the theoretical aspects of different approaches to child development, comparing and contrasting common sense psychology, field theory, Piaget, psychoanalytic theory, behaviorism, the classical developmental point of view, and sociological theory. Although it is difficult reading at times, it probably is the best single source on the theoretical aspects of developmental psychology.

BORING, EDWIN AND LINDZEY, GARDNER (ED.). *A history of psychology in autobiography*. Worcester, Mass.: Clark University Press, 1930. (The International University Series in Psychology, a continuing series of volumes.)

The authors present a fascinating glimpse of the history of psychology through the autobiographies of several famous psychologists. By reading this and similar sources, you can get a very clear picture of how the particular experiences and the general social environment affecting individuals can creep into the scientific theory building and data collection activities they engage in. It also provides a much more interesting approach to learning about the history of psychology than the more conventional historical account.

FLAVELL, JOHN. *The developmental psychology of Jean Piaget*. Princeton: Van Nostrand, 1963.

Unfortunately, the developmental psychology of Jean Piaget is spread across a very large number of books and monographs, and is extremely difficult to read, partly because of the way that Piaget writes, and partly because the original must be translated from the French. The result is that most readers, even psychologists with good backgrounds, find reading Piaget himself to be frustrating and difficult. Consequently, I recommend Flavell's book as perhaps the most comprehensive treatment of Piagetian theory available from sources other than Piaget himself. A briefer and somewhat easier to follow introduction by Ginsburg and Opper is listed in the annotated bibliography following Part Two.

HALL, CALVIN AND LINDZEY, GARDNER. *Theories of personality*, second edition. New York: Wiley, 1970.

This book surveys and critiques the major theories of personality. It is not a developmental book as such, but it is an excellent source for readers interested in overviews of the theories which have influenced most of psychology, including developmental psychology. The book does not discuss Piaget or cognitive theories, but it does survey theories relevant to social and personality development in detail.

KESSEN, WILLIAM. *The child*. New York: Wiley, 1965.

This is a brief and very readable book on child and developmental psychology that takes an historical perspective. Kessen traces the contrasting ways that children have been conceptualized and treated through the ages in various societies.

KUHN, THOMAS. *The structure of scientific revolutions*. Chicago: University of Chicago Press, 1962.

This surprisingly brief and readable book has been enormously influential. It puts forth and illustrates the thesis that science is not an impersonal, objective accumulation of facts, but instead is a personalized and dynamic enterprise which changes not only in content but even in basic methods over time. Kuhn shows that different theoretical and research paradigms come into and go out of favor over time, so that ideas or approaches considered to be "properly scientific" by scientists working under one paradigm often are later rejected as unscientific when a "scientific revolution" occurs and a different paradigm becomes popular.

MAIER, HENRY. *Three theories of child development: The contributions of Erik H. Erikson, Jean Piaget, and Robert R. Sears, and their applications*, revised edition. New York: Harper and Row, 1969.

This book reviews three major theoretical approaches to development, psychoanalytic theory (as represented by Erikson), cognitive theory (as represented by Piaget), and learning theory (as represented by Sears). Each theory is discussed in detail separately, and then the theories are compared and contrasted and examples are given concerning their practical implications. Considerable attention is given to the implications of these theories for treating children whose development has become distorted. The book is an especially good source for individuals who wish to learn more about theories but do not have much background.

WERNER, HEINZ. *Comparative psychology of mental development*, revised edition. Chicago: Follet, 1948.

Werner was perhaps the foremost of the organismic theorists, combining much of the earlier work of Gestalt psychology and field theory with an explicitly developmental approach. This is an especially good source for promoting understanding of what a truly developmental approach means.

PART TWO

INFANCY

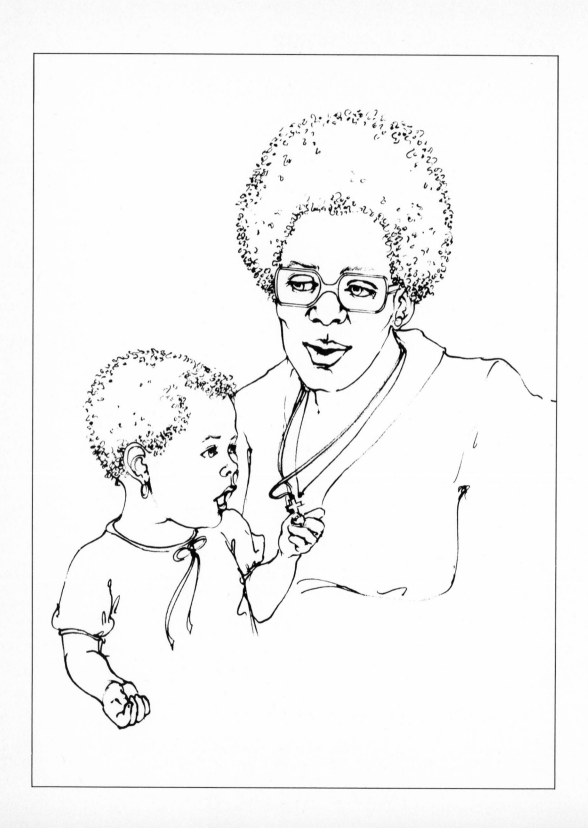

Infant Development

This chapter will present important facts about development during infancy. Here, *infancy* will be equated with Piaget's *sensorimotor period*, which extends from birth until the child shows evidence of memory and imagery used for thinking and problem solving. This is roughly the first 18 to 24 months of age, although there is variation on both sides. Piaget views infancy as *qualitatively* different from the *preoperational* period that follows. His distinction between the two periods is theoretically clear and well supported by research. Thus, I prefer it to distinctions based on more arbitrary guidelines such as age (infancy is the period from birth until age two) or less meaningful developmental markers (infancy is from birth until the child begins to walk).

GENETICS

Normal humans are endowed with 23 pairs of chromosomes, containing matched sets of *genes*, which determine hereditary endowments and limitations. We speak of 23 *pairs* of chromosomes rather than simply a total of 46, because this reflects how the hereditary transmission process works. Half of our genes, one of each matched pair, came from our fathers, and the other half from our mothers. We received half of our genetic endowment from each parent, and genetic influence from each parent operates in every pair of genes. For example, although we may resemble one parent facially much more than the other, this does not mean that all of the genes controlling our facial appearance came from that parent. Half of these genes came from that parent, and half from the other parent. The striking resemblance to one parent rather than the other is due mostly to the fact that we inherited *dominant* genes from the parent whom we resemble, and *recessive* genes from the one that we do not resemble (although there are other causes, too).

Even if all human genes were known and understood (which they are not), and even if the genetic makeup of both parents were completely documented (which is not possible at the moment), we could not predict the genetic makeup of a given son or daughter. This is because it is not possible to predict in advance which particular sperm cell will penetrate which particular egg cell and result in the conception of a unique new individual. Sperm cells are very tiny, and egg cells (ova) are very large. Both are called *germ cells*. The term is related to the same Latin source that produced words like "germination," but germ cells have nothing to do with what we usually call bacterial "germs." Germ cells are formed through a process called *reduction division*, which results in random combinations of genes from each parent. Each parent's gene pattern is fixed, but the reduction division process produces an almost limitless number of combinations of these genes in particular germ cells. The chances of any two germ cells being precisely the same are very slim. The process works like this. Testes in males and ovaries in females produce sex cells. Like all other cells of the body, these contain the usual genes arranged on the 23 pairs of chromosomes. However, during reduction division, the sex cells divide, each forming two germ cells. Each germ cell (sperm or ovum) gets a single member of each pair of genes contained in the original sex cell. During this process, the pairs of chromosomes literally "line up" alongside one another, and, within chromosomes, the corresponding pairs of genes also line up in order. The pairs of genes come together for a while and then separate again, with one member of each pair forming one germ cell, and the paired members forming the other germ cell. Although determining factors may be discovered sometime in the future, at present it appears that the movement of a given gene to one germ cell rather than the other is a random or chance event, and that all potential combinations are possible.

Although it is true that normal humans have half of their genes from their mothers and half from their fathers, it is not necessarily true that they have one-fourth of their genes from their paternal grandfathers and one-fourth from their paternal grandmothers. There are a very large number of genes, and the reduction division process appears to result in random assignment of these genes to germ cells. By chance, we all should receive about one-fourth of our genetic inheritance from each of our four grandparents. However, there will be many exceptions to this general rule. It is true that the most likely result of random placement of genes will be a sperm cell that contains half of the genes which the father inherited from his own father and half which he inherited from his own mother. However, it also is possible that the sperm cells will divide so that one contains 90% of the genes that the father inherited from his father, and the other contains 90% of the genes that he inherited from his mother. This is but one of the many complexities that make it difficult to predict anything prior to conception, except in the (relatively few) cases where well-known genes have quite predictable effects and where the genetic makeup of both parents is known.

A second compounding factor in genetic transmission is that many members of gene pairs are either dominant or recessive with respect to each other. Where this is the case, the combination of a dominant and a recessive gene will *not* result in *phenotypes* (observable characteristics) which are rough mixtures or crosses between the two phenotypes expected on the basis of the *genotypes* (the genetic patterns responsible for producing phenotypes). Instead, the phenotype will be the one associated with the dominant gene. The recessive gene, although it will be carried in the person's cells and *will* be passed on as a genotype in half of his or her germ cells, will not have any observable effects on the phenotype.

For example, certain animals come in either of two skin colors, such as brown or white. In the simplest case, where one gene (such as one for brown fur) is completely dominant and the other is completely recessive, an animal will have brown fur if it has either two dominant brown genes or one dominant brown gene and one recessive white gene. Only animals with two recessive white genes will have white fur. All offspring of unions in which both parents had only dominant brown genes will be brown, and all offspring of unions in which both parents had only recessive white genes will be white. The offspring of parents who each had one dominant and one recessive gene will be mixed in genotype but brown in phenotype. Their brown fur will *not* differ from that of animals with two dominant genes. Random combinations of genes will occur in the offspring of such mixed-gene parents, yielding 25% brown-furred with two dominant brown genes, 50% brown-furred with one dominant brown gene and one recessive white gene, and 25% white-furred with two recessive white genes. Note that these figures are based on random assignment. Although they do apply to large groups, exceptions are typical. It is not uncommon for two parents who each have mixed genes to produce offspring that show only the recessive characteristics (for example, when brown-furred animals produce only white-furred offspring).

The last example shows the futility of trying to make genetic predictions about the offspring of *individual marriages* when one parent carries a dominant gene and a recessive gene and the other parent has either the same combination or two recessive genes. In the former case, 75% of *all* offspring will show the dominant phenotype, and 25% the recessive phenotype. In the latter case, 50% of each phenotype will result. However, these percentages are

58

accurate only for large populations, not for individuals. Each particular combination of genes in a conceived individual is unique, and it is independent of the combinations that appeared in brothers or sisters. Even though it is "expected" that half of the children will show a dominant phenotype and half a recessive one, a family with four children will not necessarily have two dominant types and two recessive types. Many such families will have three of one type and one of the other, and a sizable proportion even will have all four children of one type and none of the other.

There is more to the discussion of genes than just dominance and recessiveness. Many genes show an interactive pattern rather than a dominant vs. recessive one. For example, two dominant genes might produce black fur, a dominant gene and a recessive gene might produce brown fur, and two recessive genes might produce white fur. As knowledge about *human* genetics accumulates, it is being discovered that many more gene pairs than previously believed, perhaps even a majority, operate in this *interactive* fashion rather than as dominants vs. recessives.

Many (probably most) human characteristics are *polygenetic*. That is, they are determined by the interactive influences of two or more genes, not just a single pair. This further multiplies the possibilities for types of offspring, and minimizes the probability of accurate prediction. Unpredictability is not limited to these complex cases, however. Consider the simple case of whether the offspring is to be male or female. The genes that determine sex are on a particular pair of chromosomes (females have two X chromosomes; males have one X chromosome and one Y chromosome). These chromosomes determine other things, too, but they are commonly called the sex chromosomes because sex differences are so pervasive and because the other genes on them tend to interact with sex. Conditions such as hemophilia, color blindness, or certain types of baldness appear mostly in males, because the presence of a single *normal* X chromosome will prevent their expression in the phenotype. Males who receive an unusual X chromosome from their mothers will show the condition, because their only X chromosome is not normal, but females with one of the unusual X chromosomes and one normal one will not. Although such females will not show the condition themselves, they will be carriers capable of passing along the genetic potential for it to their offspring.

The sex chromosomes usually are discussed as wholes rather than with respect to their individual genes, as is typical with other chromosomes. Whether the offspring is to be male or female is determined by whether the ovum is fertilized by a sperm carrying a Y chromosome or an X chromosome. The ovum, since it comes from a female, already has an X chromosome. Females are formed by a combination of two X chromosomes, and males by a combination of an X chromosome and a Y chromosome. Although there are a number of (mostly poorly understood) minor deviations from this norm, the chances of having either a boy or a girl are about 50% in *each* case, regardless of the number and sexes of previous children the parents have had. Each individual conception is unique and independent of all others. Parents with three boys and no girls have precisely the same chance of having a fourth boy as parents with three girls and no boys. The "law of averages" holds for large numbers of individuals, but within a family where only a few children are involved, it is useless as a predictor.

In summary, except for a few specific genetic mechanisms that will be discussed later, predictability of phenotypes in the offspring from knowledge about genotypes in the parents seldom is possible at present. Only a fraction of the human genes have been identified clearly, and the functions of many of these remain unknown. The pervasiveness of polygenetic traits and interaction among genes make it difficult to predict genetic makeup even when the relevant genes of the parents are known. This will not necessarily be the case in the future because knowledge about human genetics is accumulating rapidly. Several applications have already come into use (sperm banks, genetic counseling for parents in danger of producing deformed offspring), and there is every reason to expect that accumulation of such knowledge will make possible the kind of deliberate decision making about offspring that presently is carried out by animal breeders.

As the technology of sperm banks and knowledge about human genetics accumulates, it will become more possible to select sperm that have desirable characteristics for artificial insemination, and to reject those that have undesirable characteristics. As artificial wombs are perfected, it will become possible to do the same thing with ova. In effect, future parents might be able to select the genetic makeup of offspring within the range of possibilities. This would be true whether the offspring come from natural fertilization or from artificial insemination using germ cells from individuals who never had sexual intercourse.

These possibilities introduce obviously basic and very serious ethical considerations. Some considerations already exist and will be discussed in this book. Most involve decisions that do not have to be made at present, but they will have to be made in the future if expected advances in human genetics occur. There is good reason to believe that many of these advances will occur in *your* child-bearing years, if most of them are ahead of you, so you should give some consideration to them. Most of the possibilities are so new that people have not had the time to consider them seriously. Assuming no negative side effects or violations of parental conscience, the idea of insuring that children would inherit the most desirable genes from among the great range of possible combinations available from their parents seems to be a rational and humane one.

The ultimate in genetic determinism, *cloning*, increasingly is a genuine probability, and not just a theoretical possibility. Cloning refers to the artificial production of a new individual with precisely the same genetic makeup as the adult from whom the reproduction cells were obtained. The offspring, or "clones," would have exactly the same genes as the source, or "donor," as with identical twins. In short, cloning involves the genetic duplication of specific individuals. The idea of cloning is not easily accepted, probably because it has connotations of selfishness and egoism (people make exact duplicates of themselves, "uncluttered" by genes from husbands or wives). It threatens time-honored theological, philosophical, and social mores. Proponents can be persuasive in pointing out the advantages to the world of duplicating individuals who have made valuable contributions to society. They dream of a world in which everyone has maximal "good" genes and minimal "bad" ones. Such dreams are based more on wish than reality, however. The personal qualities involved in motivating and enabling people to make great contributions result primarily from experience and environment, not from genes. Present proposals based on cloning or even on genetic selection (eugenics) tend to come from individuals who are relatively ignorant about relationships among genetics, physiology, and developmental psychology. One thing that should become clear to readers of this book is that observed phenotypes result from a long series of developmental changes that occur as the individual interacts with the environment. Simple and direct relationships between genotypes and phenotypes are extremely rare in humans. The genes do exert rather tight control over purely physical and physiological phenotypes, including personal appearance. They also have moderately strong influence on such factors as general abilities (IQ) and susceptibility to certain mental disorders. They have few if any direct effects upon such important human characteristics as attitudes, beliefs, values, morality, personal interests, vocational and avocational interests, or most aspects of what we think of as "personality."

A theory that originated long ago but persists despite clear disproof is the *Lamarckian hypothesis.* Lamarck proposed that acquired traits could be inherited. For example, an individual who became a political leader presumably would pass on this leadership potential and an interest in politics to offspring through the genes. Similarly, a skilled comedian would pass on the ability to make people laugh. We now know that this is completely false: a person's genotype is fixed at conception. Minor mutations sometimes occur, but these tend to be trivial. For all practical purposes, the genes that people can pass to their offspring are fixed at their own conceptions. The genes are unaffected by whatever personal attributes they may develop later. Special education or training which succeeds in raising IQ, producing a dancing or gymnastics champion, or developing a skilled musician will *not* alter the genes in any way and make it easier for the children of these individuals to match these accomplishments. The children may well develop along these lines because of modeling, reinforcement, and other environmental influences, however. Children of political leaders *are* likely to develop political interests and leadership potential, and children of musicians *are* likely to be taught to play musical instruments, but these influences are *environmental.* Remember, *acquired traits do not affect the genes and cannot be passed on to the next generation through genetic transmission.*

EMBRYOLOGY Conception occurs when a sperm penetrates an ovum, forming a zygote, which contains the full 23 pairs of chromosomes and the potential to develop into a human being. With development, the zygote reaches a stage where it is referred to as an *embryo*. With further development, it reaches a stage where it is called a *fetus*. This term continues to be used until birth, when the newborn baby is called a *neonate*. These terms are useful developmental markers for embryologists and others interested in prenatal (before-birth) development.

Debate continues about *when* an unborn offspring should be considered a human being with individual rights, subject to the protection and regulation of society. For a long time, theologians and philosophers set this point at the moment of conception, when the soul presumably entered the body. Some "orthodox" theologians still hold this view. Other views span almost the full range from conception to birth, but the most popular one is that the fetus should be considered a human being around the start of the seventh calendar month of pregnancy, specifically when life-support systems have developed enough to allow survival outside of the womb (usually with benefit of an oxygen tent and other support devices). This is the standard that many courts have used in framing laws about legal abortions, allowing them to be performed as long as the fetus would be unable to live outside of the womb (but preferably as early as possible), but disallowing them once the fetus could survive. This time framework works well enough now, but artificial wombs capable of sustaining prenatal organisms from conception to birth are not far off. Questions that have been "solved" for now (at least for some) will be reopened.

Many stages and developmental markers are observable as the newly conceived zygote develops. In fact, at various stages, it takes on the appearance of embryos associated with lower forms of life. The order in which these stages appear corresponds roughly to the phylogenetic order from simple to more complex organisms. For a while, this led embryologists and psychologists influenced by Darwin and the theory of evolution to cite these stages as evidence of favoring his theory. The phrase "ontogeny recapitulates phylogeny" (the development of the individual organism shows evolutionary remnants of simpler ancestral forms farther down the phylogenetic scale) was popular for a while. This idea was based upon gross general appearances only. It was discredited when finer analyses based on the development of internal structures were performed. While there is much evidence from other sources favoring Darwin's evolutionary theories, the fact that the sequential stages of the human zygote and embryo resemble the embryonic forms of lower species is of no particular significance, evolutionary or otherwise.

Ova usually are fertilized in the fallopian tubes leading from the ovaries, (where they are produced) to the uterus. Normally, a fertilized ovum travels to the uterus and attaches itself to the uterine wall, where it develops. Usually, a single sperm fertilizes a single ovum, producing a single offspring. Identical twins, triplets, and so forth result when a fertilized ovum splits and reproduces itself, forming two or more genetically identical offspring. Fraternal twins occur when two separate ova (one from each ovary or two from the same ovary) are fertilized separately by two different sperm cells. This produces non-identical offspring who share half their genes, just like ordinary siblings born separately. The prenatal environments of multiple offspring are *always* different, whether they are fraternal or identical. This is because different

62

offspring have different placentas and also different locations in the womb.

Typically, the fertilized ovum proceeds through the fallopian tubes and into the uterus, attaches itself to a suitable location in the uterine wall, and begins development of a placenta. The placenta is a sac that completely surrounds and protects it from potentially dangerous substances in the uterus. The placenta also is the tissue through which life-supporting oxygen and nutrients are received from the mother. Once successful attachment to the uterine wall and formation of the placenta are accomplished, development is likely to proceed smoothly (assuming that the mother has an adequate reproductive system and gets good physical care). The womb provides a safe and ideal environment (constant temperature, cushioning against shocks and jolts, etc.)

Most miscarriages occur because development does not proceed in the normal way. One problem occurs when the attachment to the uterine wall is too weak, so that the placenta develops inadequately if at all and development is aborted at the zygote stage. Here, the zygote will be expelled from the uterus, often without the mother even noticing it, and even without her knowing that she had been pregnant.

Another typical problem occurs when the zygote does not travel down far enough into the uterus before attaching itself. Instead, it attaches itself to the wall of the fallopian tube or to the very narrow part of the uterus where the tube enters it. This will cause a miscarriage even if a placenta is formed successfully, because there will not be enough room to accommodate the fetus when it gets larger. The result will be death of the fetus and eventual miscarriage. Both these problems are randomly occurring biological flukes, nothing more, and parents should not be discouraged by a miscarriage of this type. It is unlikely to happen again, since it did not occur for genetic reasons.

DEVELOPMENTAL PRINCIPLES   The principles of development, and the distinction between development and growth, are particularly easy to see in embryonic development. With age, the prenatal offspring not only gets larger (*growth*); it produces new parts that it did not have before. The parts that it does have gradually progress from simple and global subsystems to complex and highly differentiated bodily organs (*development*). Stages, critical periods, and irreversibility of effects also are easily notable in prenatal development. Loosely defined stages can be differentiated on the basis of size and general appearance. More tightly defined stages can be identified on the basis of features that are present or absent, the emergence of new parts beginning to differentiate themselves, and the completion of differentiation of existing

Stages in early prenatal development. Note the cephalo-caudal principle, the proximal-distal principle, the differentiation principle, and the bilateral principle. Some of the gross external features that led to the Lamarckian hypothesis are visible in the early pictures, and all the pictures show the classical fetal position. The closed eyes and the impression of suspension in space accurately reflect what life in the womb is like, except that the body is suspended in supportive and protective fluid within the placental sac. Essential substances are obtained from the external environment through the mother's physiological systems and transmitted through the umbilical cord, not taken in directly from the immediate physical environment. Note: Photos do not show size relationships. (By permission of Dr. Roberts Rugh and Dr. H. Nishimura)

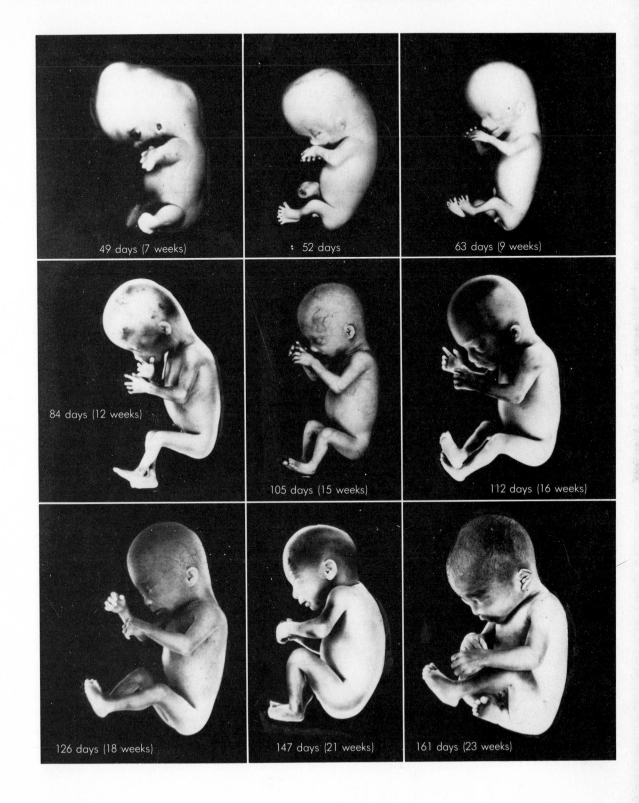

49 days (7 weeks) • 52 days • 63 days (9 weeks) • 84 days (12 weeks) • 105 days (15 weeks) • 112 days (16 weeks) • 126 days (18 weeks) • 147 days (21 weeks) • 161 days (23 weeks)

parts. As with developmental stages generally, the *sequences* are fixed, but the *rates* and *forms* of development vary.

The appearance of particular parts and other stage sequences in prenatal development occur in predictable order. Some sequences are fixed completely, so that part A always appears before part B, which always appears before part C, and so forth. The rate of development varies even in prenatal development, but not nearly as much as in postnatal development. This is mostly because the environment is less variable. We can predict that the baby will be born about nine calendar months after conception.

The form of development varies according to both nature and nurture. Although all humans are more similar to one another than to lower animals, each individual (except identical twins) has a unique genetic makeup. This uniqueness appears even in prenatal development. Independent of genetics, the prenatal environment will affect such factors as the birth weight of the baby and the chemical composition of the blood. All offspring pass through the same sequences of prenatal stages, but they pass through them at different rates and they develop unique forms. This includes identical twins, who have the same nature but do not have identical prenatal environments (nurture).

Development, both prenatal and postnatal, tends to follow the general principles outlined by Arnold Gesell (1954).

1. The *cephalo-caudal* principle: In general, structures in and around the head area develop first, and structures in and around the tail area develop last.

2. The *proximal-distal* principle: In general, the brain and nervous system and the internal organs develop earlier than the extremities and the physiological systems associated with them.

3. The *differentiation* principle: In general, the development of a new organ or subsystem begins with its growth as a relatively undifferentiated mass which nevertheless is identifiable as a separate part of the organism, and then, once this mass has grown, it differentiates into finer and more interrelated subparts.

4. The *bilateral* principle: Humans have bilaterally organized bodies, with many parts appearing in pairs, one on each side. During development, each member of a given pair of parts appears at about the same time and develops at about the same rate as the corresponding member of the pair.

CRITICAL PERIODS AND IRREVERSIBILITY   Many critical periods have been observed in prenatal human development. These are relatively narrow time periods during which something happens that cannot be reversed once the period has passed. As a rule, the presence of a critical period is closely related to the developmental cycle of the body part or function involved. If the problem occurs during the time that a particular organ or function is undergoing a developmental spurt, differentiating itself, and/or establishing itself as an independent organ or function, interference with normal development is most likely to have negative effects. The effects are most likely to be serious and irreversible. Interference occurring early, when the brain and nervous system are undergoing the most rapid development, is likely to produce mental retardation or other brain-related problems. In like manner, major interference occurring later, during the development of the arms, is most likely to produce stunted or distorted arm development. Problems such as these fortunately are rare, but when they do occur they tend to be irreversible. Although much can be done for the unfortunate "thalidomide babies" born without arms and/or legs to help them adjust to their problem and to maximize the quality of their lives, their stunted limb growth is permanent and irreversible.

One of the clearest examples of a critical period in human development is the relationship between rubella (German measles) in the mother and brain damage and other problems in the offspring. Not only is the relationship quite specific (rubella will cause the problem; other varieties of measles will not), it also is confined to a critical period. If the mother contracts German measles during the first three months of pregnancy, there is a strong possibility that the offspring will be damaged. Within these three months, the degree and type of damage is dependent upon when the disease strikes. If this occurs while the brain is most rapidly developing, general brain damage is likely. If it occurs when the eyes are developing, blindness or other visual damage is likely. In any case, some damage is likely if the disease is contracted within the first three months of pregnancy. However, should the mother contract German measles after this critical period, there are no major effects upon the offspring. Critical periods and irreversibility do occur in human development, although they are restricted primarily to prenatal development.

Not all birth defects are necessarily irreversible or uncontrollable, however. One example of this which is easy to see and understand is phenylketonuria (PKU). With this genetically caused disturbance in metabolism, the usual digestive processes do not work properly. Instead of being broken into basic elements which then are either absorbed or expelled, foods containing certain substances (phenylalanines) are broken down only part way, so that the digestive sequence stops at a certain point. The result is a buildup in the blood of substances (phenyl keytones) that are harmless in small amounts but dangerous in large amounts. PKU causes sufficient buildup to result in brain damage. Scientists studying PKU came to understand the processes involved. They were able to develop a simple diagnostic test based on urine analysis, and assemble lists of foods which are especially dangerous for PKU children to eat because their systems do not break them down properly. This led to a treatment involving diet control: these children are kept away from foods containing significant amounts of substances they cannot digest, thus avoiding the buildup of toxic substances and the consequent danger of brain damage.

The PKU example is an instructive one, because the interaction between the genes and the environment is so straightforward and simple. There probably are a very large number of such interactions between genetic endowment and environmental quality that are not yet recognized. Identification is slow because of the complexities involved when a trait is polygenetic in its biological basis and complex in its pattern of development through interaction with the environment. For example, certain severe mental disorders have heavy genetic components (simple schizophrenia, manic-depressive psychosis) that predispose some people toward them, although the causality is *not* purely genetic. Once we find out more about the kinds of environments that foster and inhibit these genetic predispositions, we might be able to design treatments, parallel to the treatment for PKU, which would prevent damage. Treatment might be chemical, psychological, or some combination of the two. In any case, the fact that a particular problem is genetically caused in whole or part does not mean that it cannot be controlled or eliminated; relatively few problems are irreversible.

Just as some genetic predispositions can be prevented through appropriate management of the environment, it is probable that some genetic potentials are never reached because of inadequate or inappropriate environments. This appears to be the case, for example, with regard to the intellectual development of poorly educated children and the physical and physiological development of poorly nourished children. As we learn more about what kinds of environmental supports are needed to insure optimal development, we can reduce the incidence of such failures to reach developmental potential.

THE PLACENTA   The prenatal offspring is protected by the placenta's enclosing sac. Basic life-support processes are maintained via exchanges with the mother through the placenta. The placenta includes a temporary membrane which acts as a buffer and a vehicle of exchange between the systems of the fetus and of the mother. The fetus never is directly connected to the mother's blood system. Instead, interchanges occur by osmosis through the placenta. Oxygen, nutrients, and other required substances travel from the mother's blood stream through the placenta and umbilical cord into the fetal system. Nitrogen, excretory wastes, and other materials that must be removed travel back through the umbilical cord, through the placenta, and out through the mother's own excretory systems.

Although the offspring's development is programmed genetically, its health and general condition is very much dependent upon that of the mother. This is why it is essential that the mother have adequate nutrition and good medical care before and during pregnancy. Severe jolts are not as important a danger as once was believed, because the womb is so well protected. A much greater danger lies in the mother's diet. Maternal malnutrition can cause malnutrition in the fetus, and maternal ingestion of tobacco and certain drugs and chemicals also can affect it. In general, anything that gets into the mother's blood stream can be expected to get into the fetal blood stream, and this can be dangerous if the substance is toxic and the fetus has not yet developed sufficient resistance to it.

Among the more extreme examples of what can happen are mothers who are heroin addicts during pregnancy. They have babies who are heroin addicts at birth. The babies will die within a few days after birth if not gradually phased out of their addiction. The chances are good that similar but less extreme ways that maternal habits can affect a baby's habits and physiological needs also will be discovered. Maternal diet and ingestion of chemicals during pregnancy are extremely important and should be monitored by a doctor.

The last few months of pregnancy involve growth and consolidation of development that has already occurred, rather than new development of more vital parts. Beginning around the seventh calendar month, the fetus is capable of life in the outside world. The growth and development that occurs during the final three months of pregnancy help insure that it will be born healthy and without complications which would require unusual life-support care. Birth occurs about 280 days after the first day of the mother's last menstrual period (Guttmacher, 1973), although deviations of a month or so on each side are frequent and deviations up to two months on each side are not unusual.

Normally, the birth process is triggered automatically as a result of maturation. **BIRTH** It can be induced artificially if the baby is late, or if there is some other reason to do so. For example, if it is known that the mother's pelvic structure is not large enough to accommodate a full term infant, a normal delivery might be possible if the birth process can be induced while the baby is still small enough to emerge successfully. More typically, the baby will be removed through Caesarean section if there is reason to believe that a normal birth process is not possible. This procedure (so called because of a popular belief that it was required for the birth of Julius Caesar) involves cutting into the walls of the mother's abdomen and bringing out the baby through the incision. Technically, Caesarean babies never go through the birth process to be described. If anything, this is probably easier on the baby (but not the mother) than a normal birth (barring complications). However, babies delivered by Caesarean section are a little more likely than average to show problems. This may be because they often are delivered prior to the "natural" time of birth, so that their higher incidence of problems may be due to a higher incidence of prematurity rather than to the operation itself.

In normal births, babies move into position head down, so that they come out head first. Because of the cephalo-caudal developmental sequence, the head is the largest part of the baby, and in most cases, the part that offers the most resistance in passing through the birth canal. As birth approaches, the mother's cervix begins to dilate (the first stage of labor). The result is an opening several times normal size, large enough to allow the baby to come out. These dilations are experienced as labor contractions or "birth pains" by the mother. The time between the first such contraction and the delivery of the baby can be anywhere from a few hours to several days. Occasionally, the process will begin but then stop (the so-called "false labor").

In the first stage of labor, the mother can assist the birth process by relaxing during contractions. In the second stage of labor, the baby moves head-first slowly but surely through the fully dilated cervix, pushed along by muscular contractions in the birth canal. The mother can assist this second stage by deliberately "bearing down," a process similar to what she might use in having a large bowel movement. During birth, there is heavy pressure on the infant, especially upon the head. Apparently, the effects of this are minor, because infant bones are still relatively soft and pliable, and thus are unlikely to be harmed by pressure. Sometimes the head may be distorted into an elongated shape during birth. Medical personnel can remediate this somewhat as soon as the delivery is complete by "molding" the head back into its proper shape. Left to nature, this reshaping will occur anyway over the next few weeks.

Births in which the baby's head is relatively large compared to the size of the birth canal usually take longer and are more difficult, but such difficulties rarely involve danger to the baby. More serious problems occur with breech births, in which the baby does not assume the normal head-first position. Sometimes, such babies can be manipulated into the proper position manually. If not, problems can occur if the baby is forced through the birth canal in an unnatural position and/or if the umbilical cord should get in the way or wrap around the baby's neck. The most serious result of such problems is death. Fortunately, this is rare when birth occurs with adequate medical support. More commonly, such birth traumas reduce the supply of oxygen to the baby's brain. If sufficient and prolonged enough, such oxygen deprivation can cause brain damage. Fortunately, like some of the problems mentioned earlier, these are simply biological flukes that cannot be predicted and are not likely to occur again to the same mother.

Once the baby is born, the umbilical cord is tied and cut. The baby is held upside down to facilitate drainage of fluids from the air passages. The fluids usually are sucked out with a rubber bulb. This usually is sufficient to cause the baby to begin to breathe (and probably cry). Ability to breathe is dependent upon the method of birth selected (see next chapter). Little or no stimulation is likely to be needed if natural childbirth has been used, but it may be required if the mother has been anesthetized.

Following the birth of the baby, the afterbirth, consisting of the rest of the umbilical cord and the placental sac, is expelled (usually a quick and simple process). These temporary biological structures were vital to the life of the baby before birth, but they no longer have a function. If the birth process has been prolonged and pelvic contractions do not expel the afterbirth, it will be removed from the mother's uterus. Once the afterbirth has been removed and the mother's cervix and uterus have returned to their non-pregnant size, the mother is in essentially the same biological condition she was in prior to pregnancy.

If birth is painful for infants, they probably are not capable of experiencing pain the way adults do. Giving birth is hard work for mothers, and is sometimes experienced as painful. The kind and degree of pain experienced is dependent in part upon physical factors such as the size of the baby relative to the size of the birth canal and the physical condition and readiness of the mother. Birth will be easier to the extent that mothers are in good physical conditions and have prepared for it through exercises and practice of relaxation and muscle contraction. Pain experienced by mothers will also depend upon their own pain thresholds, which will differ considerably with individuals.

These and other factors will need to be taken into account in deciding whether to have a natural childbirth, using little or no artificial anesthesia, or whether to use one of a variety of anesthetic methods available. The major advantage of anesthesia is pain reduction during labor, although it may prolong the birth process and thus increase or prolong soreness afterwards. The major advantages of natural childbirth are that the mother can actively assist the birth process through appropriate relaxation and muscle contraction, and she will be fully awake and therefore able to experience the whole process more completely.

THE NEWBORN INFANT

The genes have already done much of their work by the time babies are born. Most of their physical structures already are present, even if they are not well developed. The genes still will affect maturation and growth rates, and they will limit potential variation in many spheres, but from now on, development will be mostly under the control of experience and the environment.

At birth, infants already have developed the vital functions and reflexes they need for survival: breathing, sucking, swallowing, elimination, crying, and various internal functions under the control of the autonomic nervous system. They also have observable but relatively minor reflexes, such as blinking or showing a startle pattern in relation to loud noises or sudden drops. These reflexes form the basis for the development of schemas, which begin immediately.

In addition to reflexes, newborn infants come already equipped with several other genetically programmed traits (they are not *completely* blank slates). First, they are either male or female. This means not only anatomical differences, but also physiological and behavioral ones, right from birth. Studies which have been carefully controlled to eliminate differences in stimulation or reinforcement from adults have shown that boys tend to be oriented relatively more toward manipulation of physical objects, while girls tend to be oriented more toward watching and listening to stimuli in their environment, right from birth (Maccoby and Jacklin, 1974).

Babies also show great individual differences in *temperament*. Some are extremely active "energy burners" with high arousal levels, while others are quiet and passive with low arousal levels. Some are emotionally reactive to stimulation, while others are relatively passive. These differences, in particular the differences in activity level, tend to persist throughout life. Active babies tend to become active children and adults, while quiet and sedentary babies tend to be quiet and sedentary children and adults (Thomas, Chess, and Birch, 1970).

There are also great variations in *sleep patterns*. Many newborns sleep most of the time, remaining awake only around meal times. Some seem to be wide awake around meal times and interested in their environment once their hunger is satisfied. Others seem to be only half awake even while being fed, and they tend to fall asleep again quickly as soon as they are finished. These sleep differences are mostly transitory and meaningless, although parents may attach great importance to them at the time.

These and other recent data on individual differences in infants have forced a re-evaluation of the child-rearing and socialization literature based on correlating the behavior of mothers and fathers with that of their children. Until very recently, such studies almost always have assumed that parental behavior *caused* child behavior, but recent studies are showing that the opposite can occur, and frequently does. This has compounded the already difficult problem of disentangling the strands of causality in parent-child interaction data (Bell, 1971).

The problem is compounded further by the pervasive phenomena of self-fulfilling prophecies (Merton, 1948). In general, people tend to see what they expect to see and to behave in ways that they expect will be successful or appropriate. With regard to parental effects on children, it has been established that most parents treat boy and girl babies differently, independent of any differential behavior that the babies themselves might show (Maccoby and Jacklin, 1974). For example, parents tend to talk to and show things to infant girls, and generally to treat them with great care and tenderness. In contrast, they tend to initiate more physical play and rougher horse play with infant boys (tossing them in the air and catching them, for example). Differences also are seen in the kinds of toys purchased for infants and in the kinds of things that parents try to get infants to do. All of this can cause infants to respond with the kinds of behavior that parents expect.

Infants also can condition the behavior of parents. This is especially likely in the early weeks, when parents are still getting used to infants and trying to decide about their individual qualities. If a child cries a great deal with colic (a purely physiological problem having nothing at all to do with temperament), the parents think that the child is *temperamentally* tense and irritable. This can make the parents tense and irritable. They may begin to treat the child in ways that eventually *will* make the child tense and irritable, although this might not have happened if the parents had behaved differently. Similarly, adults who want to get a warm response from a child, but who try to do so at the wrong time or before the child is developmentally ready, may annoy or frustrate the child and thus provoke a negative response. This may lead the adults to decide that the child does not like them, so that they (consciously or unconsciously) may begin to treat the child with hostility. The end result will be that the child will not like them.

Examples could be multiplied, but the basic point is that parents and others dealing with newborn infants are particularly susceptible to self-fulfilling prophecy effects, because they often jump to conclusions about infants on the basis of just a few experiences. These conclusions may be incorrect, but infants are in no position to understand them, let alone correct them. If they cause the adults to treat the infants in certain ways, the infants eventually will pick up cues and begin to act as adults expect.

PHYSICAL GROWTH

In discussing prenatal development, it was mentioned that spurts are characterized by the *growth* of new subsystems followed by the *differentiation* of parts within these subsystems. Postnatal development mostly involves differentiation of parts within subsystems, since normal babies are born with all of their systems developed fully or primarily. Identifiable and apparently complete systems are present, although they undergo growth and some development involving differentiation and integration of parts and functions.

Some new changes do occur. For example, infants are born with a certain color and amount of head hair (individual differences here are extremely wide). This hair typically falls out and is replaced by hair more like the "more human" kind that the infant will have from then on. The new hair may or may not resemble the earlier hair. Similarly, the eyes change color, gradually developing into the color that will become permanent. This usually happens within a few months, although some children gradually change eye colors over a period of several years. These and other minor external changes are unimportant from the neurophysiological perspective, although they may be important to the children themselves or to people who know them, because they bring on changes in appearance.

The really important postnatal development (other than simple growth) occurs *internally*, particularly in the nervous system. At birth, the brain is a fully developed and functioning organ in a sense, but considerable growth and development will occur for several years. Most important are the development of neural associations and pathways in the brain and the gradual proliferation of myelin sheaths which cover and protect its nerve fibers. This brain differentiation after birth is partly due to maturation, but it also appears to be due partly to stimulation from and interaction with the environment. While brain differentiation does *not* cause behavior directly, it makes possible new behavior that was not possible earlier.

Physical growth and development are controlled mostly by maturation, which in turn is controlled by the genes. Environmental factors, particularly nutrition and health, also are important. Contemporary Americans are measurably taller and heavier than their parents, who in turn were taller and heavier than their parents (on the average), even though the genes obviously did not change. The reason is improved nutrition and general health care. Most children get more and better food today than their ancestors did (particularly calcium, which is vital to bone growth, the primary determinant of height). The same thing can be observed presently in Japan and other countries where nutritional changes have taken place more recently. Thirty years ago, most Japanese fit the stereotype of being small and slender. Today, Japanese children typically grow up to be a few inches taller and several pounds heavier than their parents. These height and weight data are but two examples of the general principle that *the genes set the limits* of development, but *the environment determines the phenotype*, the trait or quality as it appears ultimately (Tanner, 1970).

On the average, girls are already somewhat more mature than boys at birth, and they remain so throughout most of childhood. Growth in infancy is quite rapid compared to later years, but even so, growth rates decelerate gradually with age. The exception to this general rule is adolescence, during which children of both sexes experience both a growth spurt and developmental changes involving the maturation of the sex organs and reproductive systems and the expression of secondary sexual characteristics (breast development in females, bodily hair in males, and so forth). Until adolescence, and except for internal and primarily neural development, physical development is mostly a matter of simple growth. Bodily structures that are already present increase in size, but no new bodily structures develop.

Both within and across different individuals, growth proceeds in fits and starts rather than smoothly and continuously. It is quite common for infants to show little or no growth for a relatively long time, and then to show sudden and quite observable growth spurts. Most of these reflect only maturation. They are unrelated to parental behavior or other aspects of the environment. For example, growth in height or in the length of arms or legs is a function of internal bone growth. The bones are living bodily tissues, just like organs or muscles, and they undergo irregular growth. Certain developmental sequences are observable in this and other growth areas, but they depend upon internal mechanisms, not age. In fact, scientists studying physical growth do not use age as a norm for measurement or prediction, because it is not precise or reliable enough. First, children are of different "ages" when they are born, because age since *birth* and age since *conception* are two different things. Second, individuals have different maturation schedules in different subsystems of their bodies, so that chronological age is not nearly as useful as information about these more specific maturational schedules.

For example, an infant's height at a particular age is not a very useful predictor of ultimate height. However, information about *ossification rates* (the rates at which soft and pliable bone tissue continues to grow versus becoming hardened with calcium deposits to the point where growth no longer is possible) does allow fairly accurate predictions about children's growth rates (Tanner, 1970). Even these predictions involve complexities and subtleties because several different kinds of genetically programmed *growth curves* have been identified for height alone. Some children show a relatively smooth and continuous growth pattern, so that their height at later ages can be predicted reasonably well from information about height at earlier ages. Others show rapid early growth followed by a slowdown, while still others show the opposite pattern of slow growth for a number of years followed by a period of rapid growth. The last group ultimately may be the tallest. Prediction of an individual's adult height requires information about ossification rates and the type of growth curve that the individual is genetically programmed for, as well as information about health and nutrition. Information about ossification rates is too difficult and expensive to obtain for practical purposes, and information about health and nutrition cannot be known in advance. Thus, it is impossible to make very confident predictions about individuals' ultimate heights from their relative heights during their early years. A reasoned guess can be made based upon the heights of parents and other relatives, but this is just a guess, because height is a polygenetically determined trait, and at present there is no way to know which genes have been passed along to the infant. Again, *group predictions* can be relatively accurate, but predictions about *specific individuals* cannot.

What has just been said about height holds for almost any other physical trait. In general, physical growth is largely under the control of maturation—it tends to occur in fits and starts rather than smoothly, and it cannot be predicted reliably on the basis of patterns observed in the first year or two. There is little point in either being happy or worried about physical traits observable in infants, because whether or not infants change, and how fast they change if they do change, is under the control of genetics. Parents should see that their children get proper diets and appropriate exercise, but there is little point in attempting to stimulate general physical growth.

Infant size and body configuration undergo great changes in the first two years. Because of the cephalo-caudal principle, infants are born with large heads and relatively thin bodies, and they remain this way for several months. This changes when they begin to eat solid foods and their lower bodies and extremities begin to develop. These areas develop much more after birth than the head area, so that as infants get older, their heads gradually decrease in their *relative* size, compared to the rest of the body (although the body also continues to grow and develop).

These and other aspects of physical growth and development are relatively unimportant from a biological perspective, because they will occur inevitably due to genetic programming (assuming an appropriate environment). They are important from a psychological perspective. Changes in infants' physical appearances affect the reactions of the parents and others who deal with them, and changes in size and bodily configuration affect the kinds of things they can do physically. Changes in appearance during the first two years are easily observed. Most infants are not attractive at birth because their facial features are not yet well developed and their hair and bodily configurations are very different from those that we view as normal or attractive. Six months later, the infant has filled out somewhat, has become more responsive to adults, and looks much more "human." In another six months to a year, boniness will have disappeared, and facial features will have begun to take on permanent individual characteristics (although considerable changes will continue to occur throughout childhood and into adolescence). This, in combination with increased responsiveness to adults and generally "cute" behavior, usually puts to rest any parental fears about their baby's appearance.

More important than surface appearance changes are gradual changes in size, maturation of subsystems, and body configuration, all of which set limits on the infants' activities. In the early weeks, their ability to hold their heads up and look around depends upon the relative weight of the head and especially upon the maturation of the muscles in the neck, shoulders, and arms. Later, infants' rates of physical growth and development in particular areas will determine how soon they can sit up, crawl, grasp and hold objects, feed themselves, walk, and so forth (Gesell, 1954). These *sensorimotor schemas*, which depend on the maturation of certain physical structures before they can develop, will be discussed in the next sections.

**THEORY AND RESEARCH
OF PIAGET**

Most of the theorizing and much of the data collection about infant development has come from Piagetians, and the Piagetian substages of infant development provide a good overview for organizing the information available about the first two years of life. Piaget sees the *sensorimotor period,* which includes roughly the first 18 to 24 months of age, as qualitatively different from the *preoperational period* that follows. During the sensorimotor period, children lack the visual *imagery* and long-term *memory* capacities needed for the development and retention of cognitive schemas, so that most of their schemas are sensorimotor ones involving physical actions. Piaget posits six substages during this period. These substages are stages in the "soft" sense, describing landmarks in a gradual development from global, undifferentiated responding to the development of differentiated and integrated schemas. For the most part, the infant substages are descriptive rather than explanatory. They are useful because they add rich detail to the general statements about development made above. The six Piagetian substages of the infant or sensorimotor period will be described prior to discussion of development of specific schemas.

Piaget's six substages of infant development

1. *Development of reflex actions into the earliest schemas.* This stage lasts for the first month or so of life, depending upon age and maturational level at birth. The infant is born with a variety of reflexes, but they tend to be purely responsive to external stimulation at first. For example, the sucking reflex will appear if a nipple or similar stimulus is applied to the mouth, and the hands will close around an adult's finger or similar stimulus to the palms, but infants respond only when stimulated in this way. However, they soon begin to "exercise" some of these reflexes in the absence of stimulation or in response to a wider range of stimuli. They will suck virtually anything that happens to touch their mouths, not just nipples. The earliest sensorimotor schemas develop from inborn reflexes.

Newborn infants show no awareness of themselves as individuals, and no distinction between themselves and their environments. They take in information from all of their senses, and they slowly begin to integrate it and develop more complex schemas. For example, the information they gain from watching, listening, and feeling during feeding times is integrated with the information they get from the feeding process itself. The first evidence of *assimilation* occurs when reflexes are repeated apparently for their own sake. The first *accommodation* (formation of new schemas) appears when infants begin to integrate reflex actions with some of their observations, as when they begin to search for the nipple during feeding. Other evidence of early learning is seen in such behavior as the differentiation of crying patterns according to the nature of the distress, and the beginning of responsiveness to parental soothing when distressed.

At this point, maturation is most complete in the head area and the central part of the body (recall the cephalo-caudal and proximal-distal development sequences), so that physical movements during the first month or so are confined to gross bodily movements and to schemas involving the eyes and the mouth. Infants gradually build up funds of sensory information that they will use later in developing other schemas.

2. *Primary circular reactions.* This stage, lasting roughly the next three months, signals the beginning of true schemas and of active exploration and experimentation. Due to maturational factors, physical movement schemas during this stage are confined mostly to manipulation of the infant's own body. Schemas involving manipulation of objects in the external environment begin in the stage of secondary circular reactions, which follows.

Primary circular reactions involve the deliberate repetition and "practice" of bodily schemas such as thumb sucking, watching repetitive hand movements, or bringing things to the mouth to be sucked or tasted. When awake and quiescent, infants will repeat such schemas continually, apparently because they enjoy them for their own sake. No reinforcement or adult attention is required. Infants sometimes also will imitate sounds or visually track moving objects, although they do these things in a passive way that lacks the enthusiasm and determination that appear later. Although they are open to a certain degree of stimulation from others, they are concerned primarily with self-stimulation. They entertain themselves by repeating certain sensorimotor schemas and observing their effects.

These repeated experiences, in addition to demonstrating the active and self-initiated learning activities of infants, also signal the beginnings of concepts such as time, space, and object constancy (knowing that objects have a continuing existence independent of one's self). Probably the most fundamental knowledge that occurs at this time is a rudimentary understanding of *causality*. Repetition of schemas help infants come to understand the relationships between their behavior and its effects. Minor variations in these repetitions facilitate *discrimination learning,* which enables them to make distinctions among different stimuli, different responses, and different combinations of the two.

Finally, the beginnings of *curiosity,* and more generally, the principle of *equilibration,* are evident at this stage. Continued repetition of the same schemas leads to satiation. Gradually, infants begin to prefer visual stimulation and the exercise of schemas which are familiar but not overly familiar. In Piagetian terms, these stimuli induce the greatest amount of disequilibrium and thus motivate infants to observe and explore them.

3. *Secondary circular reactions.* This stage, which lasts from about four to ten months of age, involves continuation and expansion of the activities begun in the stage of primary circular reactions. Infants still show a marked interest in repeating schemas until they reach equilibrium and move on to some new activity, but maturation has enabled them to expand their repertoires from schemas involving their own bodies to schemas involving manipulation of other objects (crawling, pushing and pulling, shaking, manipulating crib mobiles, and so forth). The equilibration principle is even more evident as

infants begin to show clearer preferences for activities high in interest value (especially actions that produce results which can be observed, such as systematically moving a crib mobile).

Infants also begin more active exploration and trial-and-error learning, although not to the degree that will appear later. Their exploratory behavior still is largely "stimulus-bound." They confine their activities mostly to stimuli that happen to come to their attention, showing little of the active searching behavior that will appear later. Also, in reproducing and combining schemas, they still are confined mostly to repetition of familiar activities (practice of existing schemas). There is little evidence of inventing new schemas.

At this stage, infants are much more open and responsive to stimulation from adults. They recognize familiar adults, and for the first time they begin to regularly respond positively to their overtures. Positive responses are particularly likely when adults do things like imitate the infants' sounds or play repetitive physical movement games with them (which allow them to repeat interesting schemas). Much infant development of the object concept also takes place during this stage. They begin to show an understanding that objects continue to exist even when they can't see them.

This is seen in such actions as continuing with an activity related to an object which has disappeared (for example, persisting in the hand movements that they used to manipulate an object that has been dropped), and recognizing an object when only part of it is visible. The object concept still is not as well developed or firmly fixed as it will be later. Activities such as continuing to move the hand in relation to an object which has been dropped, or staring at the place that an object was when it went out of view, indicate some sense that the object exists externally. Infants do not follow through by searching for the object, like they will later.

Similarly, although they can recognize and will go after an object when they can see *part* of it, they will *not* search it out if it is completely hidden from view, even if they watch it being hidden. Even at this stage, infant perception of the constancy of external objects still is quite tenuous. They are capable of responding to an object with apparent great interest one minute, and then acting as if the object had never existed the next. Also, memory and imagery are not yet well developed, so that experiences do not cumulate quickly or systematically like they do later. Parents are likely to be frustrated to discover that their apparent success in teaching the infant to say "mama" or "dada" was misleading. The infant may well be able to utter these sounds, but at first this will just be the exercise of another schema. It will have little or nothing to do with the presence of the parent.

4. *Coordinating secondary schemas.* This brief stage occurs around nine to twelve months of age, when children finally achieve full status as curious manipulators of the environment. They also achieve the concept of the permanence and separate identity of external objects. They gradually move from unplanned and stimulus bound exploration toward goal directed and

purposive activity, in which they set out with a particular intention in mind and follow through with appropriate actions. They now have developed many schemas to the point where they are *mobile*. Mobile schemas no longer are situation bound and attached to a particular stimulus. They can be generalized and used in a variety of different situations. This new mobility of schemas multiplies the infants' learning potential. For example, when faced with a barrier between themselves and a goal (such as something covering or blocking access to a desired object), infants at this stage will strive to eliminate the barrier, instead of simply moving on to something else, as in the past. They still will use only available and well-developed schemas rather than invent new ones on the spot, but as they coordinate schemas for the purpose of goal attainment, they frequently will achieve unique new combinations which constitute new schemas because of their unique organization of subschemas.

Schema mobility also makes it easier for infants to *imitate* the behavior of *models.* In the past, the only behavior they would imitate was their own, perhaps helped along by a model who imitated it back to them (with much the same result that trainers achieve in teaching myna birds to utter speech-like sounds). Now, however, they can begin to imitate what they see models do, including certain actions that are not schemas already mastered. The mobility of schemas allows infants to proceed much more systematically as they learn about the world around them.

One of the most important results of this is that infants finally master the concept that external objects have substance and permanence independent of themselves and their perceptions. They now know that objects continue to exist when they are removed from view or when attention is turned away from them. For the first time, they will initiate purposive searches for missing objects, rather than ignore the fact that they have disappeared. Coordination of visual and motor schemas also allows infants to manipulate and inspect objects systematically and extensively so they can learn about them whenever they want to (rather than only when they happen to come to attention because of factors beyond their control).

Similar changes from stimulus bound and isolated exercise of schemas to combination of schemas into larger and more coordinated and goal directed ones can be seen in the visual and verbal areas, too. In general, the key to changes during this stage is the fact that schemas become mobile. They now can be applied in situations other than those in which they were originally learned, and they can be combined and used together with one another in more complex schemas which allow the child to sustain purposive behavior.

5. *Tertiary circular reactions.* This period, which lasts from about 12 to about 18 months of age, is marked by a general curiosity about the environment and the clear emergence of an interest in novelty for its own sake. This process is aided by the fact that schemas are more and more mobile and easily combined into newer and larger schemas, and by acquisition of the ability to walk, which expands children's horizons in several ways. In contrast to the

previous stage, where they could develop new schemas only by combining old ones, in this stage children experiment with objects and invent new schemas. They are interested in inspecting objects to discover their properties, and in trying out various schemas with different objects to see what schemas apply to what objects. This leads to activities such as throwing or banging toys, and other behavior which parents have to place limits on. In contrast to the previous stage, where schema building was in the context of goal directed behavior, children in the stage of tertiary circular reactions begin to show exploratory behavior and experimentation even in situations where there is no apparent goal. They appear to seek novelty and knowledge for their own sakes. They not only repeat the schemas they discover; they deliberately vary what they do with objects in order to *invent new schemas.*

The concept of object permanence becomes even more clear as children come to know more about objects themselves and become better able to follow movements and changes in the environment. One good example of how children become less stimulus bound with development occurs in relation to object permanence. In the past, they would look for a lost object in the place that they usually found it or where they found it last. Now they begin to look for it where they lost it. If they drop something, they will look for it in the immediate area and show a general grasp of the fact that the object must be in that area because it was there a moment ago.

The main hallmark of this stage is the confluence of mobile schemas, the ability to walk, and the desire to inspect objects and try out and invent schemas which characterize active and exploratory manipulation of the environment. At this stage, toddlers truly are "little scientists." However, as long as they remain at this stage, they still are functioning at a sensorimotor level. This means that they must learn through overt physical manipulation of actual objects in the immediate environment. This limitation is overcome in the following stage.

6. *Transition from sensorimotor functioning to rudimentary thought.* This final stage, which represents the transition between the sensorimotor period and the preoperational period, lasts from about 18 months until about 24 months of age. During this period, development of schemas through active manipulation of the environment under motivation based on the equilibration principle continues, but children acquire vital new abilities that eventually make a qualitative difference in the nature of their cognitive structures and their abilities to conceptualize the world. The most fundamental of these are the ability to represent objects mentally through mental symbols or *images,* and the ability to retain these images in *memory* and deal with them without needing to have the actual objects physically present. This new independence of the immediate physical presence of objects enables infants to store their schemas in memory more efficiently, and to build upon them and assimilate them to one another much more efficiently than they have been able to do in the past.

The presence of these new abilities can be seen in behavior that emerges for the first time during this stage. The most clear-cut is *deferred imitation,* or imitation of a model that the child has observed in the past but which is not present now. Children's ability to do this indicates that they have retained a visual image of the model's behavior that they can use to guide their own imitative efforts. Another example is "pretend play," in which children act out the roles of models with which they are familiar. Again, this indicates the presence in the mind of images concerning the role-related behavior of the models being imitated.

These six substages of the sensorimotor period apply in some degree to all infant functioning. However, they are most evident in the development of sensorimotor schemas, which are the predominant schemas developed during the first 18 to 24 months of life. This is why Piaget calls this the sensorimotor period. Precursors of verbal and cognitive schemas that will develop later are evident, but activity during this time is concentrated on behavioral, sensorimotor schemas.

In addition to his stages, Piaget's key constructs are *assimilation, accommodation, schemas,* and *equilibration.* These can be illustrated clearly by considering the development of infants' grasping schemas.

GENERAL PIAGETIAN CONCEPTS

The grasping schema refers to the infants' ability to visually fixate an object (such as a rattle), reach for it accurately, and then grasp it by closing a fist around the tubular part. The "grasping schema" really involves the coordination of several more basic schemas. Given the necessary maturation and access to a rattle of appropriate size, the infant gradually will learn to grasp it efficiently. Since rattles are made to be grasped and shaken, exposure to the rattle is especially likely to elicit the grasping schema. If the infants were presented with superficially similar tubular stimuli, such as a toothpick or a telephone pole, these stimuli would *not* be likely to elicit the grasping schema. Despite the similarity in shape, they are so different from the stimuli that typically elicit the grasping schema that they would not be even *partially assimilable* to it. Other schemas might apply, but not the grasping schema. For example, if infants noticed the toothpick or if it were held up in front of them, they might attempt to pick it up or take it. This would be especially likely if someone held it up in front of them where they were sure to see it.

Physically, even a well-developed grasping schema is not appropriate for holding something as small as a toothpick. Children who had developed holding schemas involving clasping small objects between the thumb and one or more fingers could use this schema rather than the grasping schema described above. Otherwise, they might attempt to use the grasping schema only to find that their hands kept slipping off the toothpick or that the toothpick kept falling out. Depending upon what other stimuli were available and upon their general state of equilibrium at the time, they might or might not persist in attempting to learn to hold the toothpick. If they did, they would gradually develop a new schema involving holding the toothpick between the thumb and one or more fingers. This situation would have involved considerable *accommodation* and new learning. If the infants did not persist in trying to hold on to the toothpick, they might content themselves with watching it, try to bite it or get it into their mouths, or lose interest and begin to attend to other stimuli. The toothpick is an example of a stimulus that is partially assimilable to available schemas and that may or may not lead to accommodation and the development of new schemas, depending upon a complex of factors.

A telephone pole, in contrast, is not even partially assimilable to a grasping schema or to related schemas involving picking up or holding small objects. Contact with this particular stimulus would *not* lead to accommodation and development of such schemas. In fact, a telephone pole is so foreign to the experience of most young infants, and so different from the stimuli that they have manipulated in developing their presently available schemas, that it would be unlikely to be noticed, unless there were little else to attend to in the environment. If infants did attend to the telephone pole, they might feel it, lean on it, or taste it, but they would not attempt to grasp it.

This example helps illustrate the relationships among different kinds of stimuli and the ways that they can cause changes in schemas. Some force accommodation, because they are novel but partially assimilable. Others are easily assimilated into existing schemas, because they require very little accommodation. The same general principles and interrelationships apply at all ages, and they include reactions in the social and personal area as well as the kinds of cognitive schemas that Piaget has stressed. For example, the various coping and defense mechanisms used in adapting to stressful situations can be looked upon as schemas, and the various stimulus situations that induce them can be discussed from the perspective of the likelihood that they will induce either assimilation or accommodation. Such translation allows discussion of social and personal content in Piagetian terminology.

The Piagetian terms *schema, accommodation,* and *assimilation* will be used frequently throughout the book, often in contexts in which they are not used frequently. Another Piagetian concept that should be kept in mind is *equilibration.* This is Piaget's primary motivational construct. It corresponds roughly to the successive arousal and satisfaction of curiosity. The curiosity involved has a distinct adaptational connotation. Infants are most concerned and curious about themselves and their immediate environments, particularly those aspects having to do with survival, pleasure and pain, and other physical or psychological needs. Equilibration is Piaget's answer to questions about why people choose to deal with one particular stimulus rather than others that are available, and why they eventually switch from this stimulus to one of the others that they could have selected in the first place. The answers to such questions, according to Piaget, lie in the relative degrees of *disequilibrium* that various stimuli produce in the individual.

Theoretically, individuals are at equilibrium with a given stimulus when they know everything they want to know about it (for the moment, at least), and when the stimulus itself is not doing anything to attract attention or cause problems which require a response. Conversely, a stimulus will produce disequilibrium when it attracts attention, either in a positive way because it is interesting or puzzling and stimulates curiosity, or in a negative way because it is frustrating or painful and requires some kind of adaptational accommodation. In theory then, if individuals were at equilibrium with all stimuli in their environments except one, they would devote full attention to the one stimulus, manipulating it or otherwise responding to it in ways that would lead to accommodation and the development of new or broader schemas. This is believed to occur in practice, except that individuals never are in equilibrium with all stimuli except one. Therefore, behavior is determined by the *relative degrees of disequilibrium* they experience in relation to different stimuli. Usually they will turn attention first to the stimulus which engenders the greatest degree of disequilibrium, accommodating to it by developing and exercising relevant schemas. To the extent that this succeeds, disequilibrium with regard to that particular stimulus will be reduced (that is, once the person knows what it is and what to do with it, interest in it subsides). Eventually, full equilibrium with this stimulus will be reached, or the degree of disequilibrium will be reduced to the point that another stimulus will have considerably greater disequilibrium. Then the new stimulus will attract attention, and activities will be transferred to it.

Another cause for a switch in attention might be the introduction of a new stimulus that is much more fascinating or threatening (that is, more removed from a state of equilibrium) than any of the stimuli present previously. Individuals are active and dynamic. Their behavior is determined not only by the nature of external stimuli, but also by internal interests and equilibrium levels. It is for this reason that Piaget prefers to use the term *equilibration*. It connotes the fact that individuals are in active and dynamic interaction with the environment. This is in contrast to the earlier behavioristic term *homeostasis*, which implied that individuals were passive responders controlled by external stimulus events.

The *equilibration principle* implies that, if infants' basic needs are met and nothing is bothering them, their attention will be drawn to novel or interesting stimuli. The most powerful stimuli will be those that induce the greatest disequilibrium. In turn, these will be the ones that are *partially assimilable* into available schemas but *novel* or complex enough to stimulate accommodation. Such stimuli will take precedence over those that are either so familiar that they can be assimilated easily or so foreign that they are irrelevant to existing schemas.

DEVELOPMENT OF SENSORIMOTOR SCHEMAS

At birth, infant behavior is limited primarily to reflex activities controlled by the autonomic nervous system. These activities are initiated and controlled "automatically" by subcortical brain functions. They are controlled by the lower and earlier developing parts of the brain, rather than by the higher and later developing cortex (which is associated with higher mental functioning). Except for certain specific reflexes, most newborn infant functioning is global and undifferentiated. Visual, auditory, and tactile stimuli have to be relatively

Apparatus for studying conditioning and learning in very young infants. This is used to study the process of conditioning infants to turn their heads to specific stimulation, under the control of reinforcement. A tone is sounded to serve as an alerting signal, and the stimulus might be a touch to the cheek. Without reinforcement, the touch to the cheek elicits a turn of the head in that direction only about 25% of the time. With consistent reinforcement, such as an opportunity to suck on a bottle, the rate of head-turning gradually rises to about 80%. Thus, even newborns can be conditioned, at least with respect to certain stimuli and with the use of certain reinforcers. (Photo courtesy of Lewis P. Lipsitt)

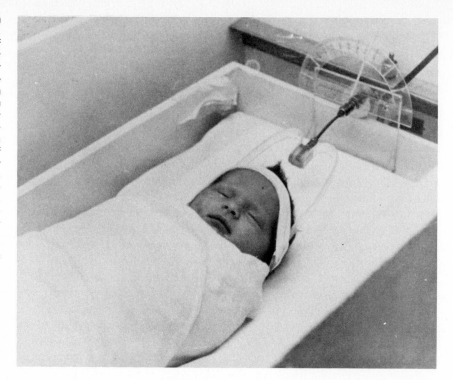

intense for infants even to notice them, and they must be grossly different for them to respond differentially. The *sensory* discrimination abilities they will develop later are mostly absent at birth.

Similarly, *motor* activity is restricted primarily to mass activity involving most of the body. When excited or in distress, infants may cry, flail their arms and legs, and make other bodily movements. These mass activities are primitive reactions to stimuli, not specific responses. Infants have not yet learned about specific responses and their own abilities to make them. They react instinctively and diffusely. These diffuse reactions gradually are shaped into differentiated responses as infants discover that different behavior on their part leads to different consequences.

Infant learning during the early months is much like the learning of lower animals, only *not* as rapid or efficient (at least as far as observable overt behavior is concerned). Most early infant learning involves slow, gradual trial-and-error learning, which produces the kinds of learning curves typically seen in animals (Baldwin, 1967; Bijou and Baer, 1967). The sudden and insightful kinds of learning that appear later are not yet evident. Consequently, learning is described as well (or better) by behavioristic terms as by Piagetian terms.

Piagetians see infants as active and exploratory, while behaviorists see them more as passively controlled by external stimuli, and these two types of theorists tend to use different terms. Nevertheless, they agree on most aspects of observable learning in infancy. Where different results are produced, this usually is because the investigators used different methods of investigation, not because they used the same methods and disagreed about the processes of learning. Methodology is important in all aspects of psychology, but especially so in studying infants, because they cannot tell us their subjective experiences. These must be inferred from observing their behavior.

Researchers usually try to establish that infants behave differently toward different stimuli or in different situations, implying that they can attend to and differentiate between these stimuli or situations. For example, early visual perception has been studied by presenting infants with stimuli varying in shape, color, familiarity, or other relevant visual aspects, and seeing if they notice or show interest in them. Such experiments have revealed interest in certain kinds of stimuli in the first few days or weeks after birth. "Strong" stimuli that are made salient by including bright colors, clear contrast with a white background, placement at the proper distance so the infants can most easily focus on them, and moved around enough to attract their attention (but not so much that they cannot follow them) are more likely to arouse attention and interest than stimuli lacking such characteristics (Kessen, Haith, and Salapatek, 1970).

Similar findings have been reported for other sensory modalities. The general principle seems to be that, in the early weeks, infants are relatively passive (even Piaget acknowledges this). They are open to being affected by certain kinds of stimulation, but not yet active in systematically or deliberately exploring their surroundings.

Infant Attention

Several aspects of the development of the earliest cognitive structures in infants are illustrated in a study by Bronson (1972). He studied infant reactions to unfamiliar people and novel objects, and found interesting differences between reactions to objects vs. people and between positive vs. negative reactions. First, illustrating the importance of active stimulation of infants over mere presence of something in the environment, infant reactions to people were more extreme and emotionally involving than their reactions to objects. Throughout the first nine months of life, infants' primary interest in objects was exploratory. They would manipulate objects according to the sequence and manner described by Piaget, but they did not show much emotional reaction to them, except for occasional wary reactions to novel objects, which began to appear at about nine months of age.

In contrast to the bland reaction to objects in the environment, wariness of strange persons appeared as early as the fourth month of life, and wary reactions became more frequent with age. Three- and four-month-olds typically smiled immediately and repeatedly when approached by a stranger. This fits with earlier data from several studies indicating that infants, at two or three months of age, will smile upon recognition of a human face, but these smiles are "impersonal." They are mere sensorimotor schemas triggered by the stimulus configuration aspects of the human face, and not by memories of interpersonal relationships or interactions. At these early ages, smiling reactions to the parents are no more frequent and intense than smiling reactions to total strangers.

Reactions differentiate over the next few months (the rate depends upon the infant). Familiar faces increasingly begin to provoke smiling responses, but strangers begin to provoke signs of fear or distress. The infants who show distress the earliest tend to be the same infants who have shown distress reactions of other kinds ever since birth.

At six and one half months, reactions depended upon the situation. When infants were held by their mothers, they typically smiled when a stranger approached. However, when they were away from their mothers, they often cried when a stranger approached, especially if the stranger picked them up. Again, infants who had been temperamental all along showed stronger reactions than infants who had been less temperamental. Similar reactions were seen at nine months.

By nine months, individual differences were becoming clearer. These appeared to be related to the quality of care in the home and the nature of previous infant experiences with strangers. Infants who were generally secure and had generally positive experiences were more likely to react positively to strangers than infants who were less secure or who had experienced traumatic encounters with strangers in the past.

This and other studies generally support the idea that infant responses to stimuli (human or non-human) will depend upon the match between stimulus characteristics and existing infant schemas. In general, human stimuli are more likely to be noticed and to evoke responses than are non-human stimuli, and stimuli that are made salient through motion, brightness, sharp contours, and the like, are more likely to be noticed and to evoke responses than stimuli that are less salient. Stimuli of intermediate novelty, those familiar enough to be recognized but not so overly familiar that they become part of the background, usually will elicit the most interest. Depending upon situational factors, including some of the ones indicated in Bronson's study, these stimuli that capture infant attention may produce positive, negative, or relatively neutral emotional responses.

The earliest schemas develop in response to observation of familiar and salient events. For example, research has shown that infants will attend to brightly colored stimuli that are situated at the right distance from their eyes, especially if they are moving. This is why crib mobiles are effective in gaining infant attention. They provide more than entertainment. As infants become familiar with the shapes or objects in the mobile, they will begin to differentiate them from the mass of visual stimulation available and to deliberately focus upon them and follow them if they move.

Visual tracking of this kind is one of the first schemas. Simple as it may seem, it requires development and coordination of the ability to distinguish a stimulus figure from background stimulation and to coordinate eye muscles in order to follow the movements of the stimulus. At first, only the eyes will move. Later, infants will move their whole heads. Still later, when they discover and learn how to use their arms and hands, they will develop repetitive schemas involving deliberately moving the stimuli on a crib mobile and observing the results.

Learning during the sensorimotor period is confined primarily to *sensorimotor schemas*. True *cognitive schemas* do not develop until they acquire the ability to form and remember *images*. This is why infant learning resembles animal learning more than it resembles later human learning. Essentially, infants are not yet using those aspects of the human brain that make it unique and qualitatively different from animal brains. The kinds of sensorimotor schemas that infants develop during this period also are developed by subhuman organisms. In fact, up to a point, monkeys are ahead of human infants in their rate of acquisition of schemas. Human infants acquire schemas more slowly because relatively little of their behavior is instinctive (biologically programmed). Consequently, they must learn almost everything, usually by a slow, trial-and-error process. This apparent disadvantage ultimately is an advantage, however. As schemas become more mobile, infants develop strategies for learning to learn and reach the stage where learning becomes cumulative and somewhat self-generated and regulated. Animals never reach this stage. As long as human learning is sub-cortically controlled, advanced subhuman organisms such as chimpanzees learn faster. However, as cortical control enters the picture, human infants begin to be able to do things that chimpanzees cannot learn to do at *any* age and with *any* amount of training.

This distinction should be kept in mind in considering the results of infant tests which purport to yield baby intelligence quotients (IQ's) or developmental quotients (DQ's). Several normative tests have been developed for use with infants which involve sampling the range and degree of developments of the schemas they possess and computing an average which is expressed as an IQ or a DQ. These terms are unfortunate since they seem to imply that the tests measure the same thing that is measured later on IQ tests which predict school performance. This simply is untrue. Infant performance on the so-called "baby tests," although it tends to be reliable over short periods of time, is uncorrelated with later performance. There is no relationship, positive or negative, between performance on these baby tests and performance on later IQ tests. An "advanced" infant will not necessarily be advanced on later IQ tests, and a "slow" infant will not necessarily be a slow learner later in life (Bayley, 1968).

There are few or no important social class or race differences on these baby tests. For a time, this was taken to mean that all normal individuals start out with equivalent genetic intellectual potential, and that IQ therefore is determined by the environment. This might be good if it were true, but it is not. Baby tests, although they measure certain sensorimotor schemas reliably, do not measure the cortically controlled cognitive abilities that are measured by the kinds of IQ tests given later. The reason is either that these cortical abilities are not yet evident in the infant's behavior, or that they are not being measured by the kinds of items included on traditional baby tests. Performance on baby tests, even standardized ones yielding standardized scores, is of no more importance than isolated incidents such as when the babies say their "first words" or when they begin to walk. These sensorimotor schemas are influenced heavily by neural maturation rates (Kessen, Haith, and Salapatek, 1970). They can be damaged by prolonged exposure to extremely debilitating environments, but they cannot be significantly improved by enriched environments (Gesell, 1954). In many ways, they are like the appearance of the infant's first tooth. They may be noticed and talked about by the parents, and they may be taken mistakenly as indicators of the future, but in fact they are of no special importance and are of little use as predictors.

The futility of trying to speed up sensorimotor schemas through environmental enrichment was shown in a series of *twin studies* conducted by Arnold Gesell and his colleagues (Gesell and Thompson, 1929). They used identical twins, thus controlling completely for genetics and partly for environment (remember that even identical twins have different prenatal environments as well as different postnatal environments). They charted the developmental norms for a number of schemas (behaviors if you prefer), and then conducted experiments to see if special training could speed up schema acquisition. Each experiment involved the same basic design. One twin would be given specialized instruction or practice in a schema (such as walking or stair climbing), while the other twin would be given no special treatment at all. Careful records were kept to see when the schemas first appeared in each twin and how quickly they developed. The results were as similar as the experimental designs. With almost complete regularity, these experiments revealed that training was of little or no practical use. The twin given special training usually showed no progress toward acquisition of the schema until at or near the time it would have developed anyway, and the untrained twin usually developed the schema spontaneously at the same time or very shortly after the trained twin (and very quickly developed it to the same level of proficiency). At most, training speeded up acquisition a little, but not enough to make it worth the effort.

In general, special training will neither speed up sensorimotor schema acquisition nor result in the development of a higher level of proficiency than would have occurred without the training. Instead, sensorimotor schemas develop once the necessary maturation has taken place, and they appear to develop spontaneously (assuming a normal environment) without any special efforts by parents or other socializers. Children begin to walk when their leg muscles and general bodily coordination have matured sufficiently to allow them to walk, and they perfect walking schemas essentially on their own. Assistance from adults (such as "walking" children around) will not speed up the process significantly or help them learn to walk with better efficiency or coordination.

Certain cross-cultural data even indicate that mild deprivation of normal development opportunities does not significantly inhibit sensorimotor schema development. For example, in certain cultures, infants are kept tightly bound or carried about in backpacks that do not allow them much freedom of movement for the first year or more of life. These infants not only receive no special attempt to help them learn to walk; they are prevented from making the kind of leg and body movements that other infants make, and that appear to help build readiness for walking. Yet such infants walk at about the same time as other infants, again underscoring the central role of maturation for the development of such sensorimotor schemas (Dennis, 1941).

Apparently only prolonged and extreme deprivation significantly inhibits the development of sensorimotor schemas. Studies of infants in primitive and understaffed hospitals, who were left most of the day lying in their cribs with minimal human interaction or stimulation, showed serious deterioration over time. Such infants typically showed a pattern of increasing distress, followed by what appeared to be resignation and withdrawal into apathy (Bowlby, 1969). Infants reared this way for the first year or two of life, especially if they were later transferred to an institution that provided minimal care and stimulation, tended to be generally inhibited and apathetic in their behavior and deficient in their intellectual functioning. Short of this, however, environmental deficiencies can be overcome.

A classic study by Skeels (1966) followed up to adulthood two groups of infants who had spent the first year of life under deplorable conditions. He found that infants who had remained in institutions with minimal care and stimulation remained dependent upon others (either in institutions or in the homes of relatives) all their lives, and that a third of them died before age 30. In contrast, infants who had spent the first year of their lives in the same institution, but who then were given a year of stimulation and enrichment in another institution and then were placed in adoptive homes, grew up to be normal in every respect. Most were employed and happily married; all of their children were of normal intelligence and free of psychological disorder; and all were alive at age 30. This study provides dramatic evidence that even severe deprivation can be overcome with environmental improvement.

In summary, the sensorimotor schemas developing in the first year or two of life are controlled heavily by maturation. This will occur as long as the infant goes on living, regardless of the environment. Environmental deprivation or cultural practices may inhibit the acquisition of certain schemas even after the necessary maturation has occurred, but the schemas can be acquired rapidly if the barriers are removed. There is no need to fear that physical restraints placed upon an infant will stunt growth or retard development.

Two cautionary notes about the above material must be inserted before moving on. First, it has been stated that learning during the sensorimotor period is largely under sub-cortical control and is similar to that of subhuman organisms. This does *not* imply that the infant is subhuman. Although baby test scores or even most observations of infant behavior do not reveal it, certain infant activity is unique to humans and probably is building readiness for the later emergence of cognitive schemas.

Activities such as infant sound discrimination and sound production learning help prepare the infant for functional language usage. Linguists distinguish between *receptive* language (words that the child understands) and *expressive* language (words that the child actually uses). With regard to learning in general, there are many things that children learn through observation that do not lead immediately to the development of sensorimotor schemas (except for schemas such as visual tracking). For example, children know a considerable amount about walking before they ever have the opportunity to even try to walk. Similarly, they know about the use of eating utensils, but maturational and parental restrictions delay their attempts to feed themselves. Much of the groundwork for the development of later schemas occurs earlier through schemas that the child picks up through observation, particularly observation of models.

A second cautionary note is that, although it is futile to try to speed up or improve *sensorimotor* schemas through environmental enrichment, it is worthwhile to try to stimulate the acquisition of *verbal* and *cognitive* schemas. As we shall see later, these schemas are much more open to stimulation by parents and other socializing agents. The number and quality of such schemas that individuals develop in these areas are much more dependent upon environmental stimulation.

There is little point in discussing a great variety of sensorimotor schemas. This is partly because the list is virtually endless. It appears that the child has a separate schema for each separate behavior that we can identify. Schema development in various areas all follow the principles and sequences outlined by Piaget. It is useful to trace through some of the developmental landmarks in a particular schema, such as learning to eat with a spoon. During the early months, when babies spend much time lying in the crib and sleeping, and much waking time visually inspecting salient stimuli or stimuli connected with feeding, they usually are unaware of even the existence of spoons. They become aware of spoons as objects later, when they get a chance to observe other family members eating, are given spoons to play with, and/or start to eat solid foods and to be fed with a spoon.

At first, schema development will be restricted to the perceptual sphere. Children gradually learn to recognize a spoon and develop some understanding of how spoons are used. If given a spoon to play with, they will put it in their mouths, among other things. This may partially reflect some observational learning being put into practice, but if they are only a few months old, it more than likely occurs simply because infants will put *anything* into their mouths, if it is small enough. At this point, they probably have not perceived spoons as tools for eating. Spoons are not particularly salient stimuli, so that infants are unlikely to pay them much attention even if they have opportunities to sit up and watch the parents eat.

Recognition of the spoon as a tool for eating comes, if it has not already, when children begin to be fed by a spoon. Now, the spoon becomes quite salient. It has a necessary and immediate association with feeding (and feeding is already well-established as a desirable and important event), and it regularly is moved about within the visual focusing area in a way that is very likely to cause it to be noticed. At this point, infants will begin to associate the spoon with feeding. If given an empty spoon, they may show surprise if they put it in their mouths and do not taste any food. Behavior of this sort represents a repetitive schema that includes such elements as understanding that the spoon is associated with food and that putting it into the mouth should result in the taste of food. At this stage, there also would be some development and coordination of sensorimotor schemas having to do with grasping, picking up, manipulating, and placing the spoon into the mouth.

A true schema involving use of the spoon as a tool would not develop until the period of tertiary circular reactions. Even here, as any parent will attest, a long period of trial and error is necessary. Even if children have well-developed schemas for grasping spoons and putting them into their mouths during play, this is much different from using a spoon in a way that will allow them to get food from a dish into their mouths without spilling it. First, infants must accommodate to the use of the spoon when in a sitting and eating position, because most of their schemas for grasping and manipulating things were developed while they were lying on their backs. Second, they must develop and perfect new schemas needed for scooping up food from the dish and for moving it from the dish to the mouth without spilling it along the way. Some previously learned schemas will be useful here, but considerable new learning will be required.

Children will have general ideas about what they want to do and how to do it, from having watched the parents or others eat with spoons. However, watching someone else perform a motor skill and performing it one's self are two entirely different things. A great many skills can be learned only through direct practice. Before infants develop a smooth schema for dipping the spoon into the bowl and coming up with a spoonful of food, they will have to learn from mistakes such as reaching too far or not far enough, placing the spoon into the bowl sideways or upside down, or holding it too high or too low on the handle. These require improved coordination between visual location schemas, schemas concerning the spatial orientation of objects with reference to one another and to the body, directionality, and general psychomotor coordination.

At the same time, they will have to perfect the schemas involved in moving food from the dish to the mouth, by learning from mistakes such as sitting too close or too far from the bowl, trying to move the spoon too quickly, or turning it sideways or upside down in midair. They also will have to perfect the schemas for getting the spoon smoothly into the mouth and getting the food off of the spoon, learning from mistakes such as missing the mouth and splattering the food, moving the spoon too far or not far enough into the mouth, and attempting to eat before taking the spoon out of the mouth. Each of these sub-schemas will have to be perfected, and they all will have to be mutually assimilated and coordinated into a complex schema that allows the child to smoothly and surely dip a spoon into a bowl, pick up some food, and eat it without difficulty.

Given the importance of eating and the modeling going on all around them, children are very likely to be highly motivated to learn this particular schema (although they enjoy eating with their fingers). This is not the case with all sensorimotor schemas. This brings up a final comment about the relationship between environmental stimulation and the development of sensorimotor schemas: common, universal schemas will develop naturally as soon as the necessary maturation takes place, but unusual schemas (such as eating with a spoon would be, in another culture) will not develop unless the child has the necessary experiences. Some schemas will not appear at all unless children are exposed to them or systematically taught them, unless they should accidentally come upon the idea themselves or encounter it in modeling by someone else.

Individuals in certain societies catch fish by standing in a stream and snatching them out of the water as they swim by. They are taught this skill as children, and they perfect it to the point that most of them can snatch a swimming fish out of the water with the same casual accuracy that we use in eating ice cream with a spoon. Presumably, we have the same genetic capabilities for this skill, but few of us ever developed it because we were not taught and never practiced the skill. This is but one example of an important point: the list of sensorimotor schemas that individuals *could* learn is virtually endless, but the ones they actually *do* learn are mostly ones they see *modeled* in the environment. Although Piaget is right in stating that the child "constructs" reality in moving through the stages of intellectual development, few schemas are truly created. Most involve imitation of the behavior of models the child has observed.

This means that if you possess a specialized or unusual skill that you want children to learn, you probably will have to teach them, or at least let them watch you while you practice it. They are unlikely to learn through trial and error. Skills such as whittling, hand sawing, or whistling with two fingers in your mouth, must be modeled or taught. Even here, genetic endowment will set limits on how far an individual can go. Parents who are champion gymnasts and gifted coaches are likely to succeed in developing their children's gymnastic skills to the point where they are at or near the genetic limits. These limits cannot be exceeded, however, so that the children may end up being just average gymnasts despite the benefit of coaching. Remember, only half of a given parent's genes are transmitted to a given child (and you do not know which half), and that acquired characteristics cannot be inherited (the years of instruction and practice involved in creating champion gymnasts have no effect whatsoever on the genes).

EARLY LANGUAGE DEVELOPMENT

In this book, language development will be treated along with sensorimotor and intellectual development, and not with social and personal development. Language will be viewed as a skill like cognitive and motor skills, although it obviously has uses and ramifications for social and personal development. There has been a continuing controversy about the importance of language and how it relates to other human traits, particularly thought. Some of this will be taken up here, but most of it is discussed in Chapter Five.

Infant language development parallels infant sensorimotor development, so that much of what was said in the preceding section applies as well to language development. The first vocal sounds the infant makes are crying during periods of distress and cooing during periods of contentment. Neither of these truly involve language; they reflect behavior controlled by genetic programming rather than attempts to communicate with the outside world or even to practice repetitive schemas. These beginnings become differentiated as the infant discovers that different sounds bring different results. Early distress crying, which is part of a mass activity also involving thrashing around and general bodily movements, gradually becomes differentiated into simple crying without much bodily movement. Early undifferentiated crying becomes differentiated, so that parents can tell *why* children are crying. They cry one way when they are hungry, another when they are in pain, and so forth.

Babbling often is mistaken for speech by parents anxious to hear the child's "first word," but it is not speech. In fact, at first it is not even a repetitive schema, although it becomes one later. The earliest babbling involves vowel sounds, followed by some of the easier-to-form consonants. Certain of the harder-to-pronounce consonants do not appear until much later. Eventually, babbling does involve repetitive schemas, and children can be heard "practicing" making certain sounds. At the same time, they are exposed to language by persons in their environment, so that certain sounds become salient and familiar to them. Eventually this causes the children to learn to make the sounds which are included in the language spoken in the home. Sounds they are capable of making and that are included in other languages (but not used in this one) tend to drop out.

Children who have developed repetitive schemas will imitate their own sounds persistently. Such imitation can be induced or reinforced by parents who imitate children's sounds for them in much the same way that one can induce a myna bird to imitate you by imitating it. As children move into the stage of tertiary circular reactions, they will begin to imitate the sounds made by adult models, not just their own sounds. They then begin to pick up words and learn the language.

The earliest words children learn include the names of important people, foods, and important objects in the environment, and words that stand for actions that they desire ("eat," for "I want to eat," "out," for "I want to go out," and so forth). The first sentences are brief ones containing words for the main ideas they want to communicate (such as "Mommy, go out," "Billy eat"). Articles, qualifying adjectives, conjunctions, and other aspects of language that are not needed for the communication of babies' needs are not learned until later.

Initially, babies confuse the names for things with the things that they stand for. Often they go through a stage wherein they think that every object has a unique name ("Daddy" refers to one single individual only). Later, this tendency to be over-specific is balanced by the opposite tendency to over-generalize ("Daddy" refers to all males who are roughly the same age as the child's father). In general, then, language learning presents massive discrimination and generalization problems. Children must learn that certain people and places have unique names, but that other words apply to a large number of specific objects (chair, table, mother, and so on). The easiest way for them to learn all of this is to ask questions, and this is how they will learn if adults respond favorably.

Children initially show the capability for making any sound that appears in any human language, but this initial interest in any and all sounds changes as they become more familiar with the sounds stressed in the language they hear. There is no genetic predisposition for children to speak a particular language just because their parents speak it; they learn a particular language because they *hear* it. Frequently heard sounds are imitated (and usually reinforced by parents when they hear such imitations). Sounds that have no meaning in the language receive little attention and reinforcement, so eventually they are dropped. Children retain the capacity to make these sounds, but they do not actually make them under normal circumstances.

For a time, language acquisition was looked upon as just another case of cumulative trial-and-error learning which followed laws of contiguity, reinforcement, and other behavioristic principles. Chomsky (1972) and others have shown that some aspects of language learning do not follow, and cannot be explained by, behavioristic concepts. In particular, infants learn not only specific words and phrases, but also the implicit grammatical rules required by a language. Furthermore, they learn most language without *any* specific instruction or reinforcement. Finally, and most important to the argument, their acquisition of the basic underlying grammatical rules of a language enables them to *construct* sentences which they never have said before and may never even have heard before. In English most sentences begin with a subject, followed by a verb, followed by an indirect object, if there is one, followed by an object. Most adjectives precede the nouns they modify. Children learn these rules implicitly, in the sense that they use them "automatically" in speaking, even though they could not verbalize them if they tried. They do go through stages involving certain kinds of errors, but the errors they make do not violate the grammatical rules of the language. For example, a child may say "Bobby like candy." This is immature speech, in that the child uses his own name instead of "I," and he uses "like" instead of "likes." Such immaturities will drop out as the child gets older. Note, however, that the child's sentence structure follows the typical English language sentence structure. Young children often say things like the example above, but they rarely if ever say things like "Bobby candy like," or "Like Bobby candy." No one ever has systematically *taught* them the proper grammatical order of words in a sentence, and often the particular sentence they say is one they have never said or heard before. Yet they follow the grammatical rules of the language.

Observations of this sort caused Chomsky to postulate that humans have an innate language acquisition device (LAD) which enables us not only to learn particular words and sentences that we hear, but also to master the underlying grammatical rules of the language spoken in the environment. Children need only to be *exposed* to language; they require no specific instruction or reinforcement. This view of early language acquisition, which was controver-

Early Language Development

A great many studies on early language development agree in finding that the first words and sentences of infants and toddlers concern people and objects that are salient and important in their immediate environment. Like other learning at this stage, language learning tends to be fragmented and situation specific (Braine, 1976). Truly systematic linguistic development does not occur until around the time the child becomes operational, as Vygotsky (1962) noted long ago.

A study of infant language development in English, Samoan, Finnish, Hebrew, and Swedish (Braine, 1976) showed that, within each culture and language, children's earliest words were for people and important things in their environment (foods, pets, bed, other furniture) and verbs and directional pronouns important for communicating needs and interests (in, out, up, down, go, eat, more, all gone, and so on). Most spontaneous verbalizations by infants and toddlers communicate emotions or desires.

Another study of interpersonal speech usage by preschool children (Schachter, Kirshner, Klips, Friedricks, and Sanders, 1974.) indicated that most speech prior to age three consisted of mimicking, seeking to get needs met, and generally speaking egocentrically the way that Piaget has described. After age three, speech became less egocentric and more social, indicating greater awareness of the presence and perspective of the listener. Around this time, and increasingly thereafter, expressive language is modulated to take into account the listener, and measures of such speech modulation become more and more closely related to measures of IQ and SES. This is to be expected, of course, given that the content of IQ tests becomes increasingly verbal as children get older, but it is most notable starting around age four. These findings concerning the differential development of language and communication skills in the early years are consistent with the arguments relating measures of the quality of the cognitive environment to measures of cognitive development in children presented in this book, but inconsistent with some of the claims of linguists and psycholinguists.

---

sial when first introduced, now is accepted by virtually all psychologists except for a few die-hard behaviorists (that is, the aspects of the theory presented here are generally accepted; certain additional elaborations remain controversial). All of this means that children will learn the language they hear spoken around them. If they are brought up in New England by parents who have a New England twang, they will, too; if they are brought up in the South by people who have a southern drawl, they will, too. If they are brought up by one parent who speaks to them exclusively in English and another who speaks to them exclusively in Spanish, they will learn both languages, speaking to the first parent in English and to the second parent in Spanish.

Early language is used almost exclusively for social purposes, particularly for the expression of needs and desires. It is *not* used for thinking and problem solving. The words and expressions children learn are related closely to their needs and interests, and in general, language for them is more a vehicle for emotional expression and communication of needs than a method for engaging in mutual conversation. For the most part, words are important only in relation to the things that they stand for. During the sensorimotor period, children have neither the ability nor the interest to engage in conversational talk for its own sake. These children tend to infer the *meaning* of an event or an interaction primarily from what they *see* rather than from what they *hear*. When an adult is talking, children usually pay closer attention to the adult's tone of voice, facial expression, and other affective cues than to the verbal content of the message. Even when they know all the words and could understand the message, they literally may not hear it because they are attending to other things. Children do not begin to systematically listen carefully to the content of verbal messages until they are five or six years old.

Although Chomsky appears to be correct in asserting that children will pick up the *structural aspects of language* simply through exposure to language models, investigations of the *functional use of language* suggest that, in contrast to the situation with sensorimotor schemas, verbal schemas are very dependent upon input from the environment. At the sheer quantitative level (size of vocabulary), it seems intuitively obvious that the number of words children learn will be related to the number of times they hear them. This simple idea has been validated in several studies indicating that parental vocabulary and child vocabulary are highly correlated. Modeling also is involved in the functional use of language, particularly its use for thinking and problem solving. Studies focusing on this aspect of language usage have found that children whose parents regularly model the use of language for thinking and problem solving tend to use language for these purposes in their own communications more successfully than children from homes where the parents do not provide such modeling often.

The implication, then, is that parents can and should take steps to maximize language development in their children. With babies at the babbling stage who are beginning to develop repetitive schemas, they can speed up this process by imitating the children and stimulating them to engage in repetitive schemas that they might not have practiced otherwise. Later, they can play repetitive games and songs which not only will provide mutual pleasure, but also will give the children practice in using language. Studies suggest that parents can help speed up language acquisition by using two related processes: *expanding* upon the child's language and *simplifying* their own language. Both of these can and should be done habitually and spontaneously; there is no need to conduct systematic "drilling" to promote language development (Cazden, 1972). The first way involves simply expanding abbreviated communications into full sentences. For example, if the baby should point to the door and say "Out?" the adult could respond by asking "Would you like to go out?" In this way the adult provides a model of the full sentence for the child, *in the context in which that sentence would be used*. A second method of responding to abbreviated child utterances goes beyond simple expansion by providing some additional relevant information ("You want to go out? All right, I'll open the door for you."). This provides not only language modeling, but also additional relevant information likely to stimulate cognitive development.

Recent studies suggest that parents can make their speech more understandable to very young children if they simplify it somewhat, using shorter sentences, greater emphasis of key words, and more non-verbal assistance through facial expressions, pointing, and other gestures. In the above situation, "You want to go out?" is better than "Are you trying to tell me that you want to play outside now?" Young children should be able to follow the content of the first message, but the second one is a little too long and complex. The need to simplify speech in this manner will vary with the child's age and verbal abilities. It is more necessary the younger and less verbal the child is. As children become capable of understanding longer and more complex verbalizations, they will benefit more from hearing these kinds of verbalizations than from hearing the simpler ones that were more beneficial in the past. It should be noted that the simplified speech recommended is not the same as "baby talk." Simplified speech involves keeping the message short and supplementing the verbal content with non-verbal cues. It does *not* involve the gushy tones or changes in wording that are associated with baby talk ("Baby go play-play now?"). Baby talk not only will *not* help children, it probably will retard their verbal development and perhaps also frustrate them. Children need and usually want correct language modeled for them if they are to learn optimally. Children who use baby talk do so because they have not yet learned to express themselves more maturely, not because they prefer to talk that way. Their receptive language is more advanced, so, when the adult says "play" the child hears the word the same way that adults hear it. If the child attempts to imitate and says "pway," this does not mean that "pway" is preferred. It means only that the word "play" has not been mastered yet. If the adults should start to switch to "pway," the child may become confused or, if old enough to realize what is happening, may become angry or embarrassed.

Another set of information showing the importance of language models for language acquisition comes from studies of twins. Unless kept apart, twins spend a lot of time talking to each other, and in the process they verbalize each other's immature speech. As a result, even though they get the opportunity to practice talking to each other as well as to their parents and older siblings, twins usually are somewhat slower in language development (in terms of group averages). They lag behind singletons on measures of vocabulary and other aspects of language. The problem is not that there is something wrong with them, or that they cannot learn like other children. Instead, they have learned a large number of words and verbal habits that are inappropriate and interfere with the acquisition of more mature language. The language they develop during interactions with each other is useful when they are together, but everyone else will find it meaningless or immature.

In summary, children will automatically pick up the structural aspects (grammatical rules) of the language which is spoken in the home. They even are capable of picking up two or more languages at the same time, especially if they are spoken systematically by different people. In contrast to this automatic acquisition of the structural aspects of language, acquisition of the functional aspects of language (size of vocabulary and ability to use language for thinking, problem solving, and communication generally) is largely dependent upon the quantity and quality of verbal modeling that the children are exposed to. Children from homes where such modeling is rich and frequent will be superior in these functional aspects of language to children from homes where it is not.

SOCIAL AND PERSONAL DEVELOPMENT IN INFANCY

In turning attention to social and personal development, it will be necessary to discuss behavioristic and psychoanalytic theories. The Piagetian ideas discussed so far apply to general stages of development in these areas, but they do not help much in understanding how individual differences develop or why a given infant develops particular traits and not others. Although social and personal traits developed in infancy go through the same stages of development that Piaget has noted for schemas in general, development in these areas does not show anywhere near the universality that it shows in the physical, sensorimotor, and linguistic areas. In social and personal development, questions concerning why certain traits develop and others do not tend to be of more interest and importance than questions about the sequences that can be observed in the development of those traits that are developed. Consequently, behaviorism and psychoanalytic theory are more useful than Piagetian theory.

SOCIAL LEARNING THEORY

Social learning theory refers to that aspect of behavioristic theory which is most applicable to *human* learning, especially learning in the social and personal area. Like behavioristic theory in general, social learning theory tends to minimize attention to subjective perception and other internal events and to stress the effects that external stimuli have in shaping behavior. Certain stimuli are important because they capture attention or cue behavior, and others are important because they are reinforcements that have motivating functions.

The basic unit of learning (corresponding to Piaget's schema) is the association between a stimulus situation, a response, and a resulting reinforcement. The basic conditions for learning are *contiguity* and *repetition*. Contiguity refers to the fact that the stimulus, the response, and the reinforcement must occur in rapid succession (and in that order) if the infant is to become aware of their relationship. Repetition refers to the frequency and consistency with which a given sequence of stimulus, response, and reinforcement occurs. In general, learning is more likely under the contiguity principle if infants are aware of a particular stimulus, aware of their own response to that stimulus, and able to get immediate feedback or reinforcement about the effects of their response to that stimulus. If feedback or reinforcement does not follow immediately or almost immediately after the response, infants may not be able to make the association between what they have done and its effects. Instead,

Apparatus for infant discrimination learning. The infant is seated comfortably and in position to observe and react to the three lights, each of which is extremely sensitive to any touching movement by the infant and wired so that such movements will be recorded. This apparatus can be used to study such problems as which of the given combinations of colors will elicit most attention and response consistently to a light that is reinforced consistently, or whether the infant can learn oddity problems; that is, learn that the light that is different from the other two is "correct," independent of the particular two light colors used. (Photo courtesy of Lewis P. Lipsitt)

they may think that the reinforcement occurred randomly or occurred because of something else that has happened since the response was made. The consistency principle is related to the principle of familiarity discussed earlier. Sequences that infants observe over and over again are much more likely to be learned than sequences which happen rarely or just once.

At the infant level, the social learning view of development is very similar to that of Piaget. At first, infants are almost completely passive and under the control of external stimuli. Attention and responsiveness are affected by stimulus saliency factors such as brightness, novelty, and movement. As maturation and learning occur, infants become more active, beginning to initiate exploratory learning and to imitate models. They also begin to combine two or more smaller schemas into more complex larger ones. These and other general developmental phenomena are agreed upon by both Piagetians and social learning theorists—the differences in theories are in emphasis rather than substance.

Social learning theorists do not accept the concept of equilibration or any similar concept that implies environmentally independent, purely internally initiated behavior. Instead, they see all infant behavior, even that which appears on the surface to be highly exploratory and self-generated, to be under the control of external factors. Essentially, the external factors are the combination of the infant's past experience ("reinforcement history") and the immediate stimulus situation. Social learning theorists make similar comments to those made by Piagetians concerning what stimuli would be of most interest to the infant, but they couch their explanations in terms of the characteristics of the stimuli themselves and the relation of the stimuli to the infant's past experience with them. The explanations do not include mentalistic, internal concepts like equilibration, a desire for novelty, or a desire to explore. This view is quite suitable, perhaps even ideal, for early infancy when the infant *is* passive and under the control of external stimuli. It becomes less appropriate as the infant becomes more and more active.

Behaviorists also discuss the process of mutual assimilation of schemas into larger and more complex ones, except that behaviorists refer to this process as the chaining of responses into larger and larger chains. Again, the general idea is the same, the difference is in emphasis. Such labels fit young infants who combine only those schemas they already possess. Older infants who begin to invent new schemas are not labeled so easily.

The really important contributions of social learning theory to our understanding of child development occur in the area of *imitation*, where this theory provides a method of understanding why one infant develops in one direction and another infant develops in another direction. This is one of behaviorism's strong points, and one of the weakest points of Piagetian theory. Social learning theorists stress that infants can and do learn through imitation. Some of this is direct and immediate behavioral imitation, as when a child reproduces a sound or a sensorimotor schema that a model has just demonstrated. The social learning concept of imitation also includes learning through observation even when it does not show up immediately (or necessarily at all) in overt behavior. Behaviorists make the distinction between *learning* and *performance*. Learning is the *acquisition* of the response (schema) which occurs when infants observe models perform something that the infants are capable of performing themselves. Performance refers to the overt *acting out* of this learning, which already is present. This distinction is an important one, because it allows social learning theory to explain many kinds of learning which do not result in overt behavioral performance, or which produce such performance only after considerable delay. Earlier behavioristic theory could not handle these kinds of learning convincingly (Bandura, 1969).

All social learning theorists stress reinforcement, but the way that this concept has been treated has changed over time. Early behaviorists distinguished between primary reinforcement (relief from hunger, thirst, pain, or other bodily needs) and secondary reinforcement (contact with parents or other stimulus events that were associated with primary reinforcement). In early theory, infants were initially controlled by primary reinforcements but gradually shifted interests to secondary reinforcements as they came to learn that primary reinforcements would be taken care of and that parents and other important people and things in the environment were associated with pleasures derived from primary reinforcement.

Modern social learning theorists, like most behaviorists, have been influenced by Skinner (1953), who defines a reinforcer as anything that will increase the probability of some behavior. This is a circular definition which often causes theoretical problems, but it provides flexibility to the theory. It also avoids some of the problems that came up when behaviorists tried to extend to humans the primary vs. secondary reinforcement distinction that had worked well with animals. In the case of humans, except for strong bodily needs, the so-called "secondary" reinforcers usually were more powerful and apparently important to infants than the so-called "primary" reinforcers (in contrast to most animal findings).

Early behaviorists also contented themselves almost exclusively with what now is called *classical conditioning*. In this kind of learning, infants refine existing schemas by distinguishing more clearly the appropriate vs. inappropriate aspects of the stimulus situation (*stimulus discrimination*), discovering new stimulus situations in which a given response applies (*response generalization*), refining responses to particular stimulus situations in order to make them more specific and efficient (*response discrimination*), and/or discovering similarities between new and familiar stimuli (*stimulus generalization*). These processes, which are commonplace among animals, also account for much of human learning, particularly in infancy. Many of the processes were discovered originally by the Russian psychologist Pavlov (1927). His most famous experiment was one which showed that dogs who salivated at the sight or smell of food could be taught to salivate in response to a sound, if the sound regularly preceded presentation of the food. The dog's "natural" response to a "natural" (unconditioned) stimulus was transferred to an "unnatural" conditioned stimulus. Essentially the same procedures and processes were involved in the famous experiment by Watson (Watson and Raynor, 1920) demonstrating that infant emotional reactions were under the control of external stimuli rather than internal maturation. In this experiment, Watson conditioned an infant boy named Albert to approach and respond positively to a white rat when the appearance of the rat was associated with pleasurable consequences. The boy was then conditioned to respond with avoidance and fear to the same rat when its appearance was associated with undesirable consequences.

Classical conditioning probably is the basis for many of the positive and negative emotional reactions learned in infancy. If the appearance of a new or previously neutral stimulus is followed by some pleasurable experience, lifelong enjoyment or a positive response to this kind of stimulus might begin. Similarly, if a new or previously neutral stimulus is followed by some painful or disagreeable consequence, the result may be a "traumatic" experience, causing the infant to fear or avoid such stimuli in the future, perhaps permanently.

Many modern social learning theorists, while not ignoring classical conditioning, are interested in instrumental or *operant conditioning*. This approach is based upon the work of Skinner (1953), who demonstrated that behavior is much more open to shaping by environmental influences than was previously realized. Not only can existing schemas be altered, as in the case of classical conditioning, but entirely new schemas can be developed through *behavioral shaping* involving successive approximations moving from existing behavior to the desired end point.

As long as the desired end point is within the range of possibilities presently open to the organism, it is possible (at least theoretically) to reach this end point through operant conditioning procedures, regardless of where the organism is now. This is accomplished by stimulating change in the direction of the desired end point (not all the way, but to some degree), and then reinforcing this new response. More stimulation to produce behavior still closer to the desired end point follows, along with more reinforcement. Through repeated successive approximations, behavior gradually is changed from its initial state to the desired end point. The key processes are *stimulation* (which elicits changes in existing responses) and *reinforcement* for such changes (which helps establish them as stable responses likely to be repeated).

Obviously, the approach and terminology of operant conditioning are more appropriate than those of classical conditioning when infant schemas become mobile, and when infants begin to invent new schemas rather than just repeat and combine old ones. Again, the differences between social learning theorists and Piagetians are more in terminology and emphasis than in substance. Social learning theory becomes especially valuable at this point, because its advocates have amassed data and theory about why infants attend to certain stimuli and not others and why they develop certain responses and not others (when all were equally possible initially). These aspects of the theory are most useful for social and personal development, where questions about what is developed and how and why it is developed tend to be more important than searches for universal stages or sequences in development.

An especially important contribution of Skinner's, which has many implications for social learning theory, has been his demonstration that the effects of reinforcement vary depending upon frequency and consistency. Reinforcements are not cumulative, as was thought previously. Responses which have been easily learned and retained because they have been reinforced 100% of the time usually are dropped rather quickly if they stop being reinforced. In contrast, responses which are reinforced only sporadically take longer to develop, but usually are much more difficult to extinguish when reinforcement stops (Ferster and Skinner, 1957).

These findings, which appear to apply about as well to humans as to animals, have many ramifications for parental consistency vs. inconsistency in socializing children. For example, an attention getting mechanism or other behavior in which infants try to manipulate adults is likely to persist much longer if the adults often punish but sometimes reward the behavior than if the adults consistently ignore the behavior. When adults behave inconsistently, infants tend to persist despite punishment, because they are confident that their behavior eventually will be rewarded. Infants who are ignored consistently will be more likely to change their behavior, because they soon will come to the conclusion that the particular behavior no longer will be reinforced.

The distinction between learning and performance is important when considering the effects of punishment. Once learning has occurred, it presumably is *permanent.* Theoretically, it could show up in performance at any time. Performance tends to be regulated by its consequences, so that unreinforced or punished behaviors usually are not acted out, even though infants are capable of performing them. A large number of experiments have shown that punishment affects only performance, not learning. Although infants can be inhibited from performing undesirable behavior through punishment, punishment will *not* eradicate the learning itself. The potential for performing this behavior remains. Punishment will not influence the desire to perform the behavior either. Punishment only inhibits the behavioral expression of impulses, *it does not change them.* Change can be induced only through teaching alternative responses and inducing infants to prefer these over the undesirable responses. The potential for an undesirable response will remain, but the impulse to act it out in behavior will be reduced or eliminated because it will have been replaced by impulses to act out other behaviors in the same stimulus situations. This is why distraction of attention to something interesting usually is more effective than admonishment or threat of punishment for dealing with infants' fears and anger. These data have many more implications for the use of punishment as a socialization technique. These will be discussed in detail later.

PSYCHOANALYTIC THEORY   Freud and the early psychoanalysts created a theory of personality development which included several well-delineated stages. The theory included specific hypotheses about what would happen to infants or children whose development during a certain stage was distorted in certain ways. These ideas have been vastly influential in generating hypotheses that researchers set out to test and in affecting the advice given to parents in books on child rearing. In literal form, the psychoanalytic stages are purely and simply *wrong.* The basic problem is that they attribute to infants and young children perceptions, cognitions, and motivations which clearly are beyond their existing cognitive capabilities. This is an example of the fallacy of *adultomorphism*—attributing the subjective experiences of adults to infants and young children not yet capable of such sophistication. Those who formulated the psychoanalytic stage theories did so at a time when little was known about the mind of the infant. The work of Piaget and others in this area was either not yet done or little known. Despite modern research findings which are contrary to Freud's psychoanalytic stages, these stages still are taken quite literally by some "orthodox" psychoanalysts.

The psychoanalytic stages are in the developmental tradition, implying qualitative changes from one stage to the next, critical periods, and a tendency toward irreversibility of effects (unless the personality is "restructured" through psychoanalysis). Key concepts are *libido,* a loosely defined term used by different writers to mean sexual energy or life instincts, and *maturation,* which produces changes in the bodily parts and functions with which the infant is primarily concerned at a given time. Freud termed the first stage the *oral stage,* because infants interact with the world primarily through their mouths during the first year of life. He termed the next stage the *anal stage,* because he felt that children were primarily concerned about toilet training and aspects of their bodies related to toilet training for the next year or two. Each of these ideas contains some truth. Unfortunately, though, Freud based his stages on bodily parts and functions and on internal maturation rather than on *universal human experiences,* which provide a much more defensible basis for his stage theory of personal and social development.

Psychoanalysts see newborn infants as hedonistic creatures completely under the control of instincts which guide them to seek pleasure and avoid pain. At first, infants are totally under the control of libido, or the pleasure-seeking instinct. Although the pleasure involved sometimes is referred to as "sexual" pleasure, psychoanalysts do not mean that infants have sexual urges and pleasures like those experienced by adolescents and adults. Instead, they mean general bodily pleasure, a sense of relief from discomfort or of pleasurable sensations resulting from bodily manipulations such as rocking or cuddling (as opposed to specific manipulations of the sex organs). Because these general bodily pleasures are especially associated with cuddling during feeding, infants soon associate the two and become especially preoccupied with pleasure needs and of satisfaction of these needs through feeding.

For psychoanalysts, the key to successful resolution of this and other stages is parental consistency in meeting the child's needs and parental ability to provide the optimal kind and frequency of responses to these needs. Deviation from the optimum by providing the child with either too much or too little, or inconsistency in meeting needs optimally, presumably will cause immediate difficulties leading to unsuccessful resolution of the stage. Long-range difficulties could result as well. When a stage is not properly resolved, future development will be distorted or limited.

In the oral stage, infants' primary needs are proper feeding and appropriate behavior accompanying feeding. If this is provided, the infant should be generally happy and secure, and will trust and like other people (because they can be depended upon to meet needs). Failure to meet needs properly will result in various problems, depending upon the particular failure. Inadequate feeding, unnecessarily prolonged delays in feeding, and/or inconsistency in feeding presumably will cause the child to become insecure and mistrustful of others. One presumed result will be a tendency toward hoarding. If infants cannot be sure that their needs will be met in the future, they may "stock up" by getting as much as they can now. During infancy, this would show up in such behavior as unusual distress while waiting to be fed and tendencies to gulp liquids and foods and to overeat beyond the point of physical satiation. Later, this same tendency would generalize to include hoarding of all material goods, not just foods. As an adult such a person might become what is known as an *oral incorporative personality,* a person who smokes, overeats, overdrinks, and shows other evidence of high "oral needs." Such people also show underlying fears that they must act quickly to get what they want *now,* because it might not be available later. This might be observed in such behaviors as regularly trying to be first in line, special sensitivity to possible shortages leading to hoarding, and difficulties in sharing or cooperating with others because of fear that they will not get their share.

In contrast, if infants' feeding needs are met reasonably well, but they are treated with hostility, indifference, or some other form of rejection during feeding, they might retaliate by becoming *oral aggressive personalities*. In infancy, this shows up in such behaviors as spitting, rejecting food, or biting (initially the nipple, then other things). If continued, this pattern could result in adult forms of oral aggression such as general negativism and hostility, sarcasm, a hostile sense of humor, and frequent use of profanity and insults.

These examples, taken from orthodox Freudian psychoanalytic theory, show how Freud combined nature and nurture in developing a personality theory (Baldwin, 1967). The combination of instinctual energy and internal maturation produces a given stage, but the outcome of that stage is dependent upon the behavior of socializing agents, particularly the parents. Inadequate resolution of a stage would lead to neurotic behavior which persists throughout life, but the particular pattern of neurotic behavior depends upon the nature of the infant's experience during this stage.

Erik Erikson (1963) has modernized the Freudian stages somewhat by reducing the emphasis on instincts and bodily functions (although these aspects of the theory are retained and used to some degree) and stressing instead the social aspects of each stage. He notes that the crucial aspect of the oral stage is the infant's total *dependency* upon others for seeing that needs are met. As a result, the basic developmental crisis that must be resolved during this stage is the issue of *trust vs. mistrust* of other people. If the infants' needs are met reasonably well and consistently, they will come to trust others and look favorably upon them. They will tend to be sociable, outgoing, and generally happy. In contrast, if needs are not met adequately or consistently, they may come to mistrust others and develop paranoia and/or hostility towards people in general. This will lead not only to hoarding tendencies, as in the classical oral incorporative personality, but also to a more general and fundamental paranoia marked by a "you have to get them before they get you" mentality.

Freud termed the next stage the *anal stage*, because the primary concern of both infants and parents gradually shifts from feeding to toilet training during the second year of life. Again, Freud's theories about the anal stage combined his ideas about infant concerns about mastering toilet training with his theories about the results of different kinds of parental behavior. If toilet training were accomplished smoothly and without conflict, the stage would be resolved successfully and the infant would not acquire neurotic traits. Difficulty in mastering toilet training, especially if accompanied by parental hostility and rejection, bribing and over-attentiveness, or inconsistency, would result in neurotic outcomes. For example, Freud believed that punitive toilet training marked by unreasonable parental insistence that children "produce" when called upon to do so (and punishment or rejection if they did not) would result in an *anal retentive personality*. Freud's thinking here was that the only way infants could retaliate against such mistreatment effectively would be to frustrate the parents by withholding their feces (an infant's only product). During the anal stage, infants would deliberately inhibit defecation when placed on the toilet, stubbornly refusing to "let go" until the parents punished sufficiently, gave up, or offered some kind of bribe or reward. This would set the pattern for a more general behavioral trait of refusing to give up anything unless either pressured or rewarded. Eventually, this pattern would lead to such adult traits as stubbornness, stinginess, and a tendency to drive hard bargains.

If parent-child interaction during the anal stage focused more on the idea that bodily elimination is dirty and disgusting than on the issue of obedience to parental demands, the infant might become an *anal expulsive personality*. Such infants would come to see bodily wastes, and later dirt in general, as unusually important, perhaps to the point that they became preoccupied with wastes and dirt. If the infants were more cowed than sullen or hostile in response to parental behavior during the anal period, they might come to view wastes and dirt as disgusting and horrible. Ultimately, they might develop such traits as obsessive cleanliness, neatness, and orderliness, and abhorrence for anything messy or dirty. Conversely, infants who were resentful of the parents and who tried to get back at them might learn to do so by deliberately wetting or soiling their clothing and surroundings, much to the frustration and disgust of the parents. This would form the basis for a more permanent anal expulsive personality, in which hostility is expressed by provoking disgust through such behaviors as frequent and pointless obscenities, telling dirty jokes and raunchy stories, and personal uncleanliness and vulgarity. In short, this type of person "dumps on" others as a way of expressing hostility.

As with the oral stage, Erikson generally accepts these ideas but deemphasizes them in favor of stress on the idea that the key to the anal stage is the fact that parents for the first time begin to place limits and demands on children (not just in toilet training, but elsewhere as well). Consequently, children must come to terms with the fact that they cannot always have their own way, and sometimes they will have to do what they are told by others. Erikson has termed this the crisis of *autonomy vs. shame and doubt*. He believes that proper resolution of the stage will cause children to accept the fact that limits will be placed on their freedom and behavior, but they will still be able to retain a sense of autonomy (ability to decide certain things on their own) and competence and self-confidence (awareness of capabilities as well as limitations). Children who experience continual failure and conflict with parents during this stage may lack these positive qualities. Because of continued failures, they may develop a general sense of shame and poor self-concepts rather than high self-esteem and confidence. Sustained attention to failures rather than successes may leave them hesitant and doubtful rather than confident about their capabilities, even their capabilities for controlling their own bodies.

Although Erikson's theory is a considerable improvement over the Freudian original, it still assigns far too much importance to feeding during the stage of trust vs. mistrust (Freud's oral stage) and to toilet training during the stage of autonomy vs. shame and doubt (Freud's anal stage). While it is true that these activities are centrally important at each stage, they have been assigned far more importance than they deserve. This is true both within psychoanalytic theory, and, because of its influence, within society at large. One result has been that feeding and toilet training probably are the two major aspects of infancy that parents are concerned about, even though several other aspects are at least as important. We tend to *see* them as important because of the conditioning effect that exposure to psychoanalytic theory has had on our society in general, *not* because they have inherent primary importance to infants.

One of the best bases for universal stages in social and personal development (to the extent that the stage concept is valid at all) lies in *universal human experiences,* not instincts, maturation, or bodily parts. As Erikson has noted, the truly important aspect of infancy is that children are in a state of total dependency upon their parents and others to meet their needs. They can signal their needs through crying and other active behavior, but they cannot take direct action to get food or reduce discomfort. Freud was aware of this, and he used the term "oral" as a metaphor for the entire range of infant needs. Since most of Freud's writings were explicitly on oral behavior, they sometimes are taken to mean that nothing of any importance occurs outside of the oral realm during the first year of life. Had Freud been disposed somewhat differently, he just as easily could have called the first stage the "need for cuddling" stage or the "need for reducing discomfort" stage. If he had, books for parents probably would treat these as important problems, and give relatively little attention to feeding.

Similarly, although toilet training is one universal example of how parents begin to place limits on and state expectations for children's behavior, it is not the only or even necessarily the most important one. Again, Erikson is closer to the truth in noting that the key to this stage is not toilet training, but the universal human experience of having to come to terms with the fact that you cannot continue to do anything you want without expectations or limitations. Instead, you must accommodate to the demands of your family and of society at large. If Freud had stressed this aspect of the stage rather than the more narrow aspect of toilet training, today we might discuss this part of the life cycle much like we presently discuss adolescence (conflict between the will of the child and the demands of the parents and society). Or, if he had focused attention on parental limit setting on child exploration in the home, today we might be much more concerned about this than we are about toilet training.

The notion of stages in social and personal development has the most basis for validity in that certain experiences are universal to all human infants. These experiences produce what Erikson calls "crises" that the infant must resolve. It is reasonable, although not logically necessary, to state that failure to resolve these crises adequately during a given time period will lead to undesirable traits that remain stable thereafter and are very difficult to change. There even is some loose evidence for this. Adults who fit the Freudian personality clusters can be identified, and their childhood histories (as reported by themselves or their parents) have a good probability of revealing difficulties of the sort that Freud postulated. In a sense there is some evidence favoring psychoanalytic stage theories (Hall and Lindzey, 1970). However, two cautions should be kept in mind here. First, the evidence is weak, coming as it does from self report data and being comprised of statistically significant but relatively weak relationships. Second, and more important, psychoanalytic stage theories (and, for that matter, any stage theory of personal and social development) tend to focus on parent-child interaction during the stage, ignoring interaction that occurs before and/or after the stage. This is inappropriate, because interactions in other stages also are important for the development of the personality traits under consideration. For example, it may well be that parents who are excessively concerned about "filth" will make this concern abundantly clear to the child during the anal stage, and the child may grow up to be at least as concerned about "filth" as the parents. However, parental concern about "filth" does not assert itself only during the anal stage. It appears both before and after the anal stage, and it can be one of the main aspects of the child's socialization. It is an oversimplification to state that adults' concern about cleanliness came about because of poor toilet training or other aspects of their parents' behavior during the infants' anal stages. Adults who are overconcerned about cleanliness probably had parents who were also overconcerned about cleanliness, and showed this concern *throughout their childhoods.*

There usually is at least some evidence favoring Freudian ideas about childhood experiences and adult personality traits, but the relationships are neither as universal nor as specific as Freud or his followers would have us believe. The development of particular traits almost always reflects modeling by parents and significant others, as well as general social learning in response to general socialization forces that exert themselves throughout development. Specific interchanges with parents that occurred during a relatively brief stage are unlikely to have broad ranging effects. If minor events are consistent with broader patterns of behavior, they are just a small part of these patterns, rather than critical parts which have major and disproportional influences upon later development. For this reason, I reject the "hard" forms of psychoanalytic stage theories (Erikson's as well as Freud's) in favor of developmental explanations based on social learning theory. However, certain psychoanalytic ideas about the relationships between formative experiences and later personality traits are accepted with certain reservations.

DEVELOPMENTAL TASKS Robert Havighurst (1953) has proposed a quasi-stage theory of development that relies on the concept of *developmental tasks.* In contrast to psychoanalytic stages, which occur mostly due to internal maturation and preoccupation with bodily parts and functions, developmental tasks are behavioral, cognitive, and social-personal skills that individuals must master because these skills are expected of everyone in society. Havighurst has identified a large number of such tasks as they exist in American society, and has grouped them roughly by age and to some degree by sex. They include such tasks as learning to walk, learning to get along with peers, and coping with school demands.

His conceptual scheme is useful for some purposes, particularly for parents and teachers interested in the problems of normal children who may experience difficulties in self-esteem or peer relationships because their behavior is statistically abnormal or because they cannot do something that most of their friends can do or because they cannot do that which is expected of them. Like psychoanalytic stages, developmental tasks must be taken in the broader context of the child's total development and socialization. Like some of the proposed Freudian stages, developmental tasks are not universal to all children or even to all children in our society. Their relative importance to individuals depends upon the treatment the skills receive from significant others in the environment. Although the development tasks idea has some validity and will be used from time to time in discussing specific topics, it does not explain why individuals develop in particular directions.

INFANT SOCIAL AND PERSONAL DEVELOPMENT: GENERAL PRINCIPLES   In general, social and personal development in infancy follows the same developmental sequences as physical, sensorimotor, and language development. There is movement from the global and undifferentiated to the specific and differentiated, from the passive to the active, from external control to more internal control, and from repetitive and reactive behavior to exploratory and inventive behavior. Although the same general principles apply, development in the social and personal area is much more individualistic. It involves few (some say no) sequences of development which are universal to all children in the world or even within particular cultures.

Recall that individuals already are well developed and are observably unique at birth. They are both sexually differentiated and consistent in their general level of arousal and temperament. Boys are treated differently from girls from birth, independent of their behavior. As the sexes begin to differentiate, this reinforces the tendencies of others to treat them differently. In the early months, these differences show up in the color of clothing and bedroom decor, the behavior of the children themselves (boys tending to be more physically active and manipulative, and girls tending to be more observant and inclined to watch and listen), and in differential behavior by the parents (different toys given to boys vs. girls; boys treated more roughly and physically and girls treated more gently and verbally).

These differences between boy and girl children and between how parents treat boy and girl children cumulate and reinforce one another, gradually increasing differences in sex role differentiation. Differences do not peak until around seven or eight years of age, but they increase throughout childhood until that time. Children during the sensorimotor stage show clear-cut sex role differentiation in toy and game interests, activity preferences, objects selected for exploration and methods used to explore, and so forth. The specifics of sex role development are controlled largely by external forces, but boys and girls are different genetically, physically, and physiologically. These differences will exert themselves to some degree regardless of parental behavior or other external events (Maccoby and Jacklin, 1974).

The same is true of differences in arousal level and temperament. Babies who are "energy burners," who are fussy and irritable, and/or who are physically active from birth will tend to retain these general tendencies relative to babies who are passive and unreactive. These inborn differences are largely predisposing factors. The causal events that determine the infants' later personality traits lie in their socialization and general experiences. Unreactive infants who are raised by introverted parents and/or who "turn off" the parents because of their unresponsiveness may develop into passive and introverted individuals. In contrast, the same infants would be likely to become sociable and person-oriented if raised by parents who modeled and reinforced this behavior pattern. They would not be as physically active and initiatory as more extreme extroverts born with higher arousal levels and different general temperaments, but neither would they be passive and introverted.

Similarly, infants who were both active and irritable might continually "cause problems" because of this activity. They might respond poorly to parental attempts to control behavior through socialization (frustrating and angering the parents by being irritable), so that the ultimate result might be hostile and antisocial personalities. In contrast, the same infants could turn out to be prosocial activist leaders if their parents encouraged exploratory activities, built positive self-concepts, and were unbothered by early irritability. Even though certain behavior patterns are present at birth, ultimate personality traits are shaped by socialization and experiences.

While certain predisposing factors are genetically programmed, there is no evidence for genetically caused social and personal traits in human development. This does occur in lower organisms such as insects, where certain social behaviors appear automatically when genetically programmed instincts mature. No one is *born* happy or sad, good or bad, generous or selfish, fun-loving or inhibited. These and other social and personal traits develop in response to experience. Genetic claims to the contrary are made occasionally, but further investigation inevitably proves them incorrect.

A recent example was the brief furor over the XYY chromosomal condition, a genetic abnormality in which males have an extra Y chromosome in addition to the normal XY chromosome pair. It was discovered that the incidence of this abnormality among prisoners, particularly prisoners incarcerated for violent crimes, was roughly double that in the population at large. This led to the belief that a genetic predisposition to violence had been discovered, and to debates about what should be done to protect society from such individuals. After more data were gathered, it became established that this abnormality is associated with greater than average height and arousal levels in males (Jarvik, Klodin, and Matsuyama, 1973). These traits at most could be predisposing factors rather than causes of criminal misbehavior. A greater than average arousal level can just as well be used for positive, prosocial activities as for antisocial activities. Furthermore, closer inspection of the prison studies revealed that the proportions of such individuals, both in prison and in the general population, are minuscule, being about 2 per 1000 among male prisoners and about 1 per 1000 among non-imprisoned males. Even the already tiny figure for the imprisoned males probably was inflated by the sample selection procedures which concentrated attention on criminals with a history of violent antisocial crimes to the exclusion of criminals convicted of more solitary and passive crimes. If all male criminals were examined (including those white collar criminals who never have been convicted or who receive fines rather than jail sentences), there might be no difference between males who show "criminal tendencies" and males who do not. At best, this chromosomal condition might be a predisposing factor for a life style marked by physical activity. This would mean that individuals who committed crimes would be likely to commit active rather than passive crimes, but they would not be any more likely than anyone else to commit a crime in the first place.

The weakness of genetic influences *in the social and personal area* can be seen in a number of other ways, too. First, consider individuals from the same family. Despite common genes, the differences among individuals in a family are usually more striking than the similarities, unless the different individuals have been raised in very similar milieus. Identical twins are especially instructive. Most parents of identical twins make a conscious decision either to treat the twins as identical by giving them similar names, matching wardrobes, identical gifts and experiences, and so forth, or else to deliberately treat them differently and try to see that each establishes an independent identity. In the latter approach, parents play down the fact that infants are twins and take steps to see that each gets a chance to develop in different milieus with different friends and different experiences. As expected, twins raised as "twins" tend to be very much alike, while twins raised as individuals tend to be quite different. Curiously, few investigations of twins have taken this parental variable into account.

Observation of individuals or ethnic groups who change cultures also shows the lack of genetic influence on social and personal behavior. Although Americans are far from homogeneous, it is clear that the majority of ethnic groups who migrated to this country from some other country have dropped most or all of their "old country" behavior and adopted American behavior. Sometimes this takes two or three generations, although often it is observed in a single individual over a remarkably short period of time. It is always the environment, not the genes, that is responsible for the change.

GENERAL SOCIAL RESPONSIVENESS   For the first four months or so of life, infants are not truly socially responsive, although certain schemas can be activated through deliberate behavior by adults. Infants begin to show differential attention toward and interest in adults familiar to them, but at this level, the interest is not truly social. The adults are not yet recognized as qualitatively different from other kinds of familiar stimuli. With increased age, infants become much more "human" in their responses to the environment in general and in their interest in parents and significant others in particular.

They gradually become more and more interested in the people around them and in interacting with them, and they become more responsive to stimulation and social games. They enjoy being cuddled, tickled, or otherwise stimulated physically, and they begin to enjoy "peek-a-boo" games and other forms of cognitive stimulation. They also enjoy games involving imitation of sounds. Around age six months or so, they recognize and respond positively to their parents' faces, although they still are unlikely to show much interest or surprise if they should disappear from view because they are hiding or have left the room.

Infants also gradually become more adept at communicating their needs, although their learning here is a matter of simple conditioning rather than conscious or deliberate attempts to communicate with the parents. For example, parents will note that infant crying becomes differentiated rapidly. One kind of crying indicates one need, while another kind indicates another need. This ability to communicate becomes vastly expanded as infants begin to talk regularly and to use expressive gestures. Many of their earliest words and phrases are used to communicate needs or desires to the parents. The infants' needs and desires are almost always granted during the first 12 to 18 months of life. Most parents indulge infants during this time, and do not expect them to exert self control or to be able to respond to socialization demands. For the most part, much of infancy is spent seeking and receiving gratification for needs and desires. If this is provided consistently, the infant is likely to develop trust, outgoingness, happiness, and a generally positive orientation toward people and the world. If needs and desires are continually frustrated or treated with notable inconsistency, then mistrust, insecurity, and a general orientation of fearfulness and inhibition may develop.

INFANT ATTACHMENT   Recently, much theoretical and research interest has concentrated on infant attachment. This is the observed tendency (and hypothesized need) for infants to become very closely attached to a single attachment object for a few months, typically the mother (Ainsworth, 1969). Attachment usually peaks at 24 to 30 months, although infants develop toward it gradually.

In the first few months of life, infants appear oblivious to human beings although they will show distress if biological needs are not met. Over the next year or so, they show definite interest in humans, particularly parents and significant others. Infants smile when parents come into view for example. With further development, infants begin to differentiate among humans they encounter, responding favorably to familiar figures, and especially to familiar figures who are associated with pleasant experiences. As infants develop and become more aware of their own vulnerability, they begin to show a fear of strangers and strange situations. When attachment reaches its peak, they not only fear strangers, but also show a positive need for the physical presence of the attachment figure when in strange situations. If attached to the mother, for example, they will tend to leave a room and follow her when she moves from one room to the next. If they are playing on one side of the room when the mother is in a different part of the room, and a stranger enters, the infant probably will begin to cry and show signs of general distress. These signs will disappear quickly as soon as the mother approaches. These and other observations indicate that during this period children are closely attached to the mother, not merely in the sense of loving her and wanting to be with her, but also in the sense of psychologically requiring her physical presence in order to feel secure. As they gradually grow out of the attachment phase, such behavior disappears. They become less and less in need of their mothers' presence in strange situations.

At present, a controversy is continuing concerning the question of whether these observations imply that human infants are genetically programmed to *need* this attachment experience, or whether it is something that appears in most infants but is not particularly necessary. The evidence now favors the latter interpretation. The attachment cycle as described above is typical but not universal, and so far no one has demonstrated any consistent differences between infants who experienced the attachment cycle and those who did not. As yet there is no evidence that failure to experience the attachment cycle has undesirable consequences.

The attachment data have been used by some to argue that institutional care for infants and toddlers (or any other child care arrangements which do not allow for experiencing the attachment cycle) are "bad" for children and should be avoided. To date, this appears to be yet another example of the tendency to believe that what is statistically abnormal is bad. It may be true that most infants are raised in circumstances that allow or even foster the development of the attachment cycle, but this in itself does not demonstrate that the attachment cycle is either good or necessary. Barring data to the contrary, there is no reason to believe that children who do not experience the cycle are worse off than their peers in any way. In fact, there even are some arguments that they may be better off. This does *not* mean that institutional care for infants and toddlers is necessarily good, either. The quality of care in these institutions varies dramatically. Some appear to be beneficial, while others appear to be detrimental.

INFANT EMOTIONAL DEVELOPMENT   Infant emotional development is much like other aspects of infant development—it progresses from mass reactions of quiescence or distress to more differentiated and specific reactions to specific stimuli. The early mass reactions are not really emotions as much as they are generalized instinctive responses.

The first identifiable emotions are a generalized distress response and a generalized "delight" response. Both of these gradually differentiate later, with the negative emotions generally differentiating before the positive ones. This pattern of development reflects both the immediacy of the infants' needs and their capacities to comprehend and respond positively to enjoyable stimulation. Negative distress reactions gradually differentiate into such emotions as disgust, anger, fear, and jealousy. Generally positive "delight" reactions gradually differentiate into such emotions as elation, affection, and joy. The development of positive emotions can be both speeded up and reinforced through systematic provision of pleasant experiences (such as cuddling) and stimulating experiences (such as games).

In addition to differentiating the *quality* of emotions, children gradually learn to differentiate their *causes*. Very young infants experiencing painful distress because they are hungry will make undifferentiated mass distress responses. However, eighteen-month-olds who are hungry and not being fed by parents who could be feeding them will experience not only painful distress because of hunger pangs, but anger at the parents for not feeding them when they need to be fed. Similarly, very young infants in quiescent and happy states might show undifferentiated "delight" reactions, but toddlers playing enjoyable games with adults will express happiness and joy specifically in response to the adults as well as to some of the events that occur during the games.

INFANT MORAL DEVELOPMENT   If infant emotional development is primitive, infant moral development is virtually non-existent. Infants are hedonistic and egocentric. It would *not* be correct to say that they are immoral, though, because this implies that they are aware of the rights of others and of their responsibilities toward them. Clearly, this is not the case. Instead, infants are *amoral.* They are not yet cognitively differentiated enough to have the faintest understanding of mutual rights and responsibilities, the concept of truthfulness and honesty, or other fundamental aspects of morality. Their behavior can be socialized through conditioning and controlled through arranging the environment, but these are external manipulations. Infants do not show self-control reflecting internal self-guidance.

Most parents and others recognize this during the first year or so of life, but often they do not realize it (or they forget it) when dealing with infants in the second year of life. In particular, parents often take it personally when infants fail to show interest in them or say that they do not like them. Such infants are merely behaving according to their level of development, perhaps imitating things they have heard without having the slightest idea of their impact upon the adult. Similarly, partly because of Freud, parents often interpret toilet training or other behavior involving compliance or non-compliance as evidence of general obedience or stubbornness.

All of this is inappropriate. Until infants develop some perspective and the ability to take the role of others, their behavior is neither moral nor immoral (in the sense of conscious and deliberate compliance or non-compliance with moral expectations they know and can understand). To use Kohlberg's term, infants are *premoral:* they are not yet cognitively developed to the point where words like "moral" and "immoral" can be used meaningfully (Kohlberg, 1969).

In many ways, sensorimotor infants are much like animals with respect to morality. They respond to contingencies of reinforcement and other aspects of behavioral conditioning, but they are not able to understand moral reasoning. This does not mean that they should not be exposed to moral reasoning. Even though they may not be able to express it or use it at the moment, they *should* be exposed to such reasoning. The earlier and more often they hear it, the sooner they will learn it receptively and, in all probability, begin to express it in behavior.

SUMMARY

Human genotypes are fixed at conception, but they interact with the environment from that point on to determine phenotypes. Genotypes will set limits on developmental possibilities, but within these limits, the environment will shape development and determine the ultimate phenotypes.

Development includes both growth, in the sense of expanded mass, and differentiation toward higher levels of organization. Prenatal and early postnatal development follow the cephalo-caudal, proximal-distal, differentiation, and bilateral principles. Critical periods involving irreversibility of effects have been identified in prenatal human development, but there is no convincing evidence for critical periods of this kind in postnatal development. Although the genes are primary determinants of physical development and strong determinants of intellectual development, they have little or no influence upon the development of social and personal characteristics.

The quality of the prenatal environment depends upon the mother's personal habits and health and upon the location and quality of the placement of the placenta in the uterus. Birth occurs approximately nine months after conception, although there is considerable variability. Because conception and birth are normal human biological processes, and because female bodies are constructed to accommodate these processes, they normally progress without difficulty. Occasionally, however, tragedies will occur. Fortunately, most of these are random accidents unlikely to happen again to the same woman.

Cognitive development in the first two years or so of life is described in great detail by Piaget and his colleagues. They refer to this first stage as the sensorimotor period, and have identified six substages in this period. The chapter described these substages and gave examples of how schemas develop successively through them. Piagetians see infants as constantly in interaction with the environment, building schemas through assimilation and accommodation, guided by internal equilibration. Both internal maturation and external environmental stimulation and feedback are important in cognitive development. The sensorimotor period comes to an end when the toddler develops imagery and memory that allow cumulation of experience and rudimentary thought processes.

Early language development proceeds through conditioning processes. Exposure to repeated sounds and sound patterns causes infants to imitate and practice familiar ones and to stop practicing unfamiliar ones. Gradually, this practice enables them to become familiar with the specific sounds and the tones and inflections used in the environment. Language can be learned through specific instruction (which might or might not include reinforcement), but most language is acquired simply through exposure, without any deliberate instruction and without any reinforcement. In addition to learning individual sounds and words, children learn the underlying structure of language, so that they form sentences according to

113

the implicit grammatical rules in effect, even though they do not understand these rules yet.

Social and personal development in infancy is described more richly by psychoanalytic and social learning concepts than Piagetian concepts, because Piagetians concentrate almost exclusively on cognitive development. Social learning theorists describe the shaping of behavior through stimulation, modeling, and reinforcement. Psychoanalytic theorists have postulated stages that involve the interaction of genetic programming with socialization by parents to determine ultimate outcomes. The first year or so of life is known as the oral stage or the stage of trust vs. mistrust, and the second year or so is known as the anal stage or the stage of autonomy vs. shame and doubt. Presumably, lifelong personal traits can begin during these stages, depending upon the nature and consistency of infant care.

Although Piagetians have concentrated on cognitive development, early social and personal development show the same general kinds of progressions that can be seen in the cognitive area. A complete understanding of infant development requires attention to and integration of several different lines of theory and research. The same is true for development in later stages.

CHAPTER FOUR

Preparing for and Caring for Infants

Genetics, embryology, the birth process, and the development of infants during the sensorimotor period were discussed in the last chapter. In the present chapter, some suggestions will be offered to individuals who have decided that they want to have children, and some important considerations will be raised. This chapter assumes that the couple already has decided to have children; the issues involved in making this decision will be discussed in the final chapter.

GENETICS

Once the decision to have a child is made, it is simplest and usually best to let nature take its course, unless the couple already knows that sterility might be a problem for them and that special medical supervision is needed. For most couples, however, pregnancy will occur within a year or so if they simply enjoy sexual relations naturally and do not practice birth control.

Conception is less likely to occur if

117

the couple is experiencing sexual difficulties or if they share sexual intercourse infrequently. Conception usually occurs about two weeks before the next (expected) menstrual period. The exact time of conception is difficult to establish without extraordinary procedures because many women have irregular ovulation patterns. Many differ from the "typical" norm, and a given woman may show variation from her own norm on occasion. Couples desiring to have children can increase their chances by having intercourse during the period of the month when conception is most likely. This only increases the odds of pregnancy occurring; it does not insure it. It is not at all unusual for couples to enjoy normal and mutually pleasing sexual relationships for many months without conceiving a child, even though no physical or physiological barriers to conception exist. Couples should not become discouraged or overreact if conception does not occur quickly.

If conception does not occur within a year or two despite regular intercourse, couples can and should be examined to see if there are any biological barriers to parenthood. Both partners should be examined, as a biological problem which prevents conception is at least as likely to occur in a male partner as in a female. There is no reason for couples to hesitate or feel anxious about seeking medical help in this situation. Such problems are frequent, and many gynecologists specialize in diagnosing and treating them. Unless they are experiencing infrequent and/or incomplete intercourse because of difficulties in sexual adjustment, problems in conceiving children have nothing to do with people's capacities for receiving and giving sexual pleasure or with sexual adjustment generally. In males, the most common problem is that the testes produce an unusually low volume of sperm cells. As a group, males with this problem are no more or less "masculine" than other males in any other respect. The reduced sperm volume in their semen may reduce or eliminate the possibility of impregnation (sperm cells are only a very tiny portion of the semen, so that the sexual experiences of such males are the same as those of other males).

Females may have parallel problems caused by abnormally low output of egg cells from the ovaries, although sometimes problems are caused by purely physical difficulties (unusual placement of the uterus, blockage in or unusually small fallopian tubes). The problem usually can be diagnosed and often can then be treated. Where treatment is impossible, the couple must resign themselves to the situation and look to adoption if they wish to raise children.

Genetic counseling will be needed for couples whose genetic endowments raise the possibility (or even the certainty) of genetic defects in their offspring. If it is known that a genetic defect is carried in the family of one or both partners, the couple should be examined at a clinic that provides genetic counseling services. Here they can be informed of the possibilities, probabilities, and certainties (if any) for genetically based defects in their offspring. In the *rare* instances where a genetic defect is *certain* to occur, the choice of whether or not to risk pregnancy becomes a moral decision that couples must make jointly.

Notice that the term "couple" has been used consistently in this discussion of parental decision making about having children, instead of terms like "woman" or "mother." Exposure to controversies about abortion and related topics has conditioned most of us to think in terms of "a woman's rights over her own body," and consequently, to think of women as having the primary, if not the only, rights to decision making about conception and abortion. This may be true for unmarried women, deserted wives, and other pregnant women who are in situations where the biological fathers have no legitimate claims to decision-making rights, but it is *not* true for married couples planning to share the work of parenthood.

For these couples, decision making about conceiving and caring for children is both a right and a responsibility, and it applies to both parents, not just to the mothers. Furthermore, it must be shared in a total sense: there must be full agreement by both parties. Anything less, such as grudging compliance by one partner in order to put an end to arguments, is irresponsible behavior that is virtually guaranteed to backfire in the future by straining the marriage and depriving the child of full parental commitment. Parents faced with a possible genetic problem cannot evade this reponsibility or take it lightly without risking tragic consequences, and this includes fathers as well as mothers. It does not include anyone else, however. The advice of relatives and others should be given serious consideration but, ultimately, decisions must be made jointly by the prospective parents.

Besides making decisions jointly, parents must make them *in advance*. This is most obvious where genetic problems are certain. Here, parents must search their consciences and determine whether they wish to conceive a child with the genetic problem involved, and whether they are emotionally and otherwise prepared to cope with whatever special parenting problems will be presented by such a child. Ideally, this should be settled prior to marriage itself, so that both parties enter the marriage agreed on planning to have children despite the problem or planning to remain childless or planning to adopt. Calling off a wedding is embarrassing, but is nothing compared to the problems involved when the lives of many people are scarred because parents failed to face up to their decision-making responsibilities when genetic problems were predictable.

In the more typical case, where a genetic defect has some (usually estimable) probability, the options increase, but so do the decisions that must be made. A genetic defect in the fetus can often be detected early enough to make abortion possible, so that the couple must consider carefully and decide jointly, *in advance*, what they would do if this choice were facing them. If they cannot accept either a defective child or an abortion, they should prevent pregnancy. No couple should allow pregnancy to occur when a genetic defect is known to be possible until and unless they agree on what they will do if the problem appears.

A number of genetic problems are preventable or treatable, and thus should not deter couples from seeking to have children. In such cases it is often critically important that the problem be anticipated and diagnosed as early as possible. One such problem is an incompatibility between the Rh components of the blood of the mother and the fetus, resulting in the birth of "blue babies." This term originated because such babies' red blood cells were diminished by antibodies built up in a small percentage of mothers whose blood types were incompatible with the blood of the fetus, producing anemia in the babies. The problem would get more serious with each pregnancy, as more antibodies built up in the mothers' systems.

Although it sounds serious, medical advances have eliminated Rh incompatibility as a threat to successful pregnancies (assuming proper medical care). For a time, the problem was handled successfully in most cases by giving the newborn infants blood transfusions shortly after birth. It was important that the medical team attending the mother anticipate the problem and be prepared to deal with it quickly. More recently, an antidote has been developed which will prevent the problem completely in most women. Sensitization to Rh-positive blood components in Rh-negative women can be prevented with a drug called Rhogam. This elimination of maternal sensitivity also eliminates the buildup of antibodies in the mother's blood system that will attack the blood system of an incompatible infant, thus preventing the Rh incompatibility problem altogether. The diagnostic and treatment procedures involved here are simple, but it is essential that information about the blood types of prospective parents be known and that the antidote be administered to the mother within a few days after delivery (Guttmacher, 1973).

Another genetic defect with preventable effects, if diagnosed early enough, is phenylketonuria, or PKU. Although all babies born with two recessive genes will carry the PKU genotype, this genotype can be prevented from affecting the phenotype adversely through early diagnosis and diet control. An inexpensive, quick, and simple test has been developed which can identify such infants with certainty. A few states already have made it mandatory. If it is not mandatory in your state, it is strongly recommended that you take advantage of it. Even though the chances of having a PKU child are slim, the small cost of the test is worth the investment, in view of the serious and irreversible damage that can result if the problem goes undiagnosed for very long.

Even where there is no known danger of genetic defects, genetic counseling often is useful in putting to rest groundless fears or suspicions based on oversimplified or inadequate knowledge of genetics. Offspring receive half of their genes from each parent, so they usually resemble one or both to some degree. However, most phenotypes are polygenetic. Also, recessive traits that have not appeared in either family for many generations may reappear in an offspring with two recessive genes.

These and other factors mean that couples who are dark-haired and dark-eyed, and whose relatives also are dark-haired and dark-eyed, can have a blond, blue-eyed child, and vice versa. Similarly, large and healthy parents can have small or sickly offspring, and vice versa. Examples could be multiplied, but the point is that no one should jump to conclusions when offspring do not resemble their parents. Lack of physical resemblance to the father does not mean that the offspring was sired by someone else.

If it should be important enough, for legal or other reasons, to determine whether or not a certain male is the father of a particular offspring, there are relevant genetic tests. These tests can only rule *out* a man as the father with certainty; they cannot establish with certainty that any specific man *is* the father. At best, they only can establish (perhaps with an accompanying probability statement) that a certain individual *could* have been the father. This may change, but at the moment there is no way to establish scientifically that a specific male is the father of a specific offspring.

EMBRYOLOGY

The womb provides an ideal physical environment for the fetus since it is a biological structure designed specifically for this purpose. Unless some abnormality has been discovered, there is nothing special that the mother should do to stimulate or insure optimal prenatal development. Special diets and special exercises can prevent malnutrition or excess weight gain and can prepare muscles for labor, but other measures probably will not have measurable positive effects.

It is vitally important for the mother to receive early and continuing medical supervision once pregnancy is discovered. The most important biological preparation for childbirth is regular medical counsel coupled with scrupulous care in following medical advice. Ordinarily, this will involve some instructions concerning the mother's diet and some suggested exercises. In some cases, special drugs might be prescribed. Diet instructions often are confined to urging the mother to eat a balanced diet and watch her weight, because overweight mothers generally have more difficult deliveries. Weight can be a problem even for a woman who was not overweight before pregnancy, because some women are especially prone to excess weight gain during pregnancy.

There might be restrictions or limitation of certain dangerous dietary or behavioral habits. The most serious dangers involve toxic chemicals that could injure the fetus if ingested through the mother's bloodstream. Mothers may be taken off some medications and asked to cut down or eliminate smoking and the use of alcohol or other drugs taken for personal pleasure. Any addictive drug, such as heroin, will have an addictive effect on the fetus, and it might have more serious effects also. Pregnant women should also avoid or minimize contact with X-rays or other exposure to radioactivity.

Exercises are not intended to stimulate the development of the fetus, but they will get the mother into the best possible physical shape for delivery. Exercises will involve breathing and moving and stretching muscles in the upper leg and uterine area. Having these muscles in good physical shape and having practiced the movements involved in the relaxing and "bearing down" process that facilitates birth is one important way that mothers can speed up and simplify the birth process.

APPROACHES TO CHILDBIRTH

A variety of approaches to childbirth are available and in common use, and some of them involve more intensive and specific exercises than the kinds just discussed. Options can be divided into two major types: natural childbirth and childbirth accomplished using some kind of artificial anesthetic. For a time, the development of reliable anesthetic methods led to their very widespread use, at least in deliveries conducted in hospitals. Doctors and parents often favored one form of anesthesia over others, but they usually accepted the idea that some kind of anesthesia should be used.

Recently, natural childbirth, accomplished without the use of artificial anesthetics, has come back into vogue. In part this has been due to publicity about some of the dangers inherent in using chemical anesthetics. These dangers have been grossly exaggerated, but they do exist. At minimum, they tend to prolong the birth process by immobilizing the mother and preventing her from actively assisting through relaxation and muscle contraction. Longer deliveries increase the chances of difficulties, so that this is a factor to be considered. More serious dangers occur when anesthetics have not been administered properly, especially if general anesthetics should be used in overly strong doses. General anesthetics render the mother completely unconscious. If the dosage is strong enough and/or the delivery is long enough, the anesthesia can enter and build up in the baby, perhaps causing serious damage. Medical personnel are quite aware of this so that "fail safe" methods of checking the dosage of anesthesia and monitoring its entrance into the mother are standard operating procedures in delivery rooms. Even so, errors leading to unfortunate accidents occasionally occur. These are rare, but they do happen. Consequently, prospective parents should question doctors and generally inform themselves about the pros and cons of various anesthetic methods if they decide that some form of anesthesia will be used.

In addition to concern about possible dangers or side effects of anesthesia, enthusiasm for natural childbirth has developed because it has been propounded vigorously by advocates who promote it with active zeal. Much of the initial impetus came from the writings of Grantly Dick-Read (1959). This British physician argued that childbirth was intended to be and should be a natural process conducted with active preparation and participation by the parents and without unnecessary reliance on doctors and especially dependence upon anesthetics. He also argued that the pain of childbirth had been exaggerated vastly, and that it could and should be a very positive "peak experience" rather than a painful ordeal, if it were approached with the proper attitudes and preparation. These ideas found favor with many doctors and parents, and for a time this method of natural childbirth was something of a fad.

More recently, it has been replaced for the most part by the Lamaze method. This method was developed by physicians in France, although many of its principles go back to the early studies of learning conducted by the Russian psychologist Pavlov. This method combines physical preparation through exercises and simulations with the development of the attitude that pregnancy and birth are basic human experiences in which both parents should participate. An important feature of this method, and one that makes it popular with many couples who desire to share the experience, is that the father participates in active and continuing ways. The couple attends classes together, where they are given information about pregnancy and birth and taught exercises to help prepare them for it. The father then works with the mother as her "coach" or "trainer," helping her to learn and practice the exercises by providing instructions and manual assistance. This continues up to and including labor, and, depending upon the willingness of the medical personnel and hospital involved, it may continue through the birth process itself. The father may be present in the delivery room and allowed to participate actively by "coaching" the mother and providing direction in breathing, relaxing, and muscle contracting (Vellay, 1960). There are references dealing with the topic listed at the end of this chapter. Presently, a number of approaches to natural childbirth and to anesthetics are available to prospective parents. The choice of approach to childbirth is theirs if they inform themselves about alternatives and exercise this choice actively.

Biological preparation for birth must be supplemented with psychological preparation. First, the parents will need to inform themselves, if they have not already, about the options available to them in various hospitals in their area. Once the relevant information is collected, the parents need to discuss thoroughly and to agree upon such matters as the method of delivery (particularly whether or not anesthesia is to be used and, if so, what kind) and whether or not the father will be present and/or will participate during the delivery.

PREPARING FOR THE BIRTH ITSELF

Once such decisions are made, and especially if the parents have strong preferences for particular procedures, they should make sure that their doctor and hospital will allow these procedures. If not, the parents will have to change either their plans or their hospitals and/or doctors. One should not hesitate to question doctors and/or hospitals about these matters; many of them involve personal preferences, because no particular choice is clearly superior to the others on a purely medical basis. Under these circumstances, the right and responsibility for making choices resides in the parents.

At this stage, prospective parents should inform themselves through reading and/or enrolling in parental preparation courses (usually sponsored by hospitals) about the specifics of preparation for birth, according to the method they have chosen. It is important for them to get solid knowledge from competent sources. Although the problem no longer is as extreme as it once was, pregnancy and birth have been taboo topics to some degree. As a result, many future parents are woefully ignorant, or, worse yet, possess incorrect information picked up from relatives or friends. In particular, future mothers should be wary of the harmful tales they may hear from well-meaning friends and relatives. Frequently, a discussion that begins as an attempt to reassure the future mother that pregnancy is enjoyable and that the birth process is nothing to fear gradually evolves into a series of gory, frightening "blood and guts" stories. Fortunately, most of these are false or exaggerated, and even those which are true usually recount unfortunate incidents which were flukes or which occurred prior to the introduction of modern medical techniques that have removed most of the dangers and difficulties involved in birth. A future mother who did not know any better could easily be terrified by such stories. Both for their own peace of mind and for the inherent value that the information will have in helping them prepare for birth, future parents should educate themselves by obtaining information from reliable sources.

Other matters requiring discussion and preparation include selection of names for the child and preparation for quick mobilization in informing the doctor and getting the mother to the hospital when the time comes. The selection of names would seem to be of obvious importance; yet, an amazing number of newborn children remain unnamed for days or even weeks, because the parents did not agree on a name or agreed on a name only for the opposite sex. To avoid such embarrassment, and to be fair to the child, parents should give careful thought to naming. Names should be prepared for a child of *either* sex (unless the sex of the unborn child has been determined prior to birth). Parents should give every effort to choosing appropriate names. They should avoid stuffy or funny-sounding names. Many studies of names agree in finding that children with such names usually suffer some degree of humiliation or even rejection from others (McDavid and Harari, 1966). Most children with this problem learn to cope with it, but it assumes such importance in some children that it leads eventually to personality disturbances. It is not good common sense to give a child a name that is likely to cause trouble.

Giving an unusual name often is an ego trip on the part of the parents or other relatives. A desire to see one's own name or that of a relative carried forward in a new generation is understandable, as is the desire to demonstrate inventiveness or creativity in thinking up a unique name. Satisfaction of such desires is not justifiable if it comes at the child's expense. Parents must also be cautious when contemplating naming a son after his father. This practice can be harmful, especially if the child has to cope with being called "Junior," "little Jimmy," or some other nickname or substitute name that may be disliked. Again, most children cope with the problem, but parents should think carefully before naming a child after themselves.

Preparation for the birth itself should include collection of relevant information and development of a specific plan (with contingency plans if the husband should be unavailable when the wife begins labor). If the birth is to be in a hospital, plans should be made in conjunction with the doctor and the hospital. The parents must be clear about what to do when the time comes. Should they go straight to the hospital? Should they call the doctor first and ask what to do? Will the doctor inform the hospital, or are they expected to do this themselves? And so forth. Phone numbers for the doctor (office and home) and for the hospital, as well as phone numbers of the back-up doctor to be called if the regular doctor is unavailable, should be kept near the home phone and also carried by the mother at all times. The route to the hospital should be determined and a practice run should be driven to make sure that the parents know exactly how to get to there most quickly and know where to go and what to do when they get there. The birth process usually takes many hours from the first labor contractions until the delivery, especially with the first child, so that a frantic rush to the hospital is unlikely. Nevertheless, parents should be prepared for it, just in case.

In many ways, preparing to assume the role of parent is more complex than the specific preparation involved in getting ready for the birth itself. For most parents, the birth of their first child is easily the most important single event in the early adult years, even more so than falling in love or getting married. True, love and marriage, even with the loosening of earlier legal and social sanctions against divorce and common law marriage, involve commitments that many individuals find difficult to make. However, these commitments are minor compared to the commitment of having a child. This commitment involves commitment to a whole life style.

A life style based on seeking personal self-actualization, either individually or with a mate, particularly through social and recreational activities, no longer is possible to the same degree once a couple has a child. Infants and children present immediate and continuing demands for time, attention, and care. These demands cannot be delayed, ignored, or subordinated to parental desires for personal gratification. A commitment to a child is much more total and permanent than a commitment to a mate. It is relatively easy to break a marital commitment through divorce, but usually any children resulting from the marriage will remain as the continuing responsibility of the parents. The decision to have children is a crucial one that should be made with full knowledge and commitment.

This commitment and some of the considerations involved in it will be discussed in more detail in the final chapter. For now, let us concentrate on some of the things that must be done once the commitment has been made. Many things must be done long before the child is born. These include physical preparation of the home for the arrival of its new occupant, and psychological preparation by both parents to help insure smooth transitions into their new roles.

Physical preparation involves much decision making and the acquisition of new furniture and equipment. First, where will the child sleep? In the first month or two after birth perhaps in the parents' bedroom. After that, though, the child should have separate sleeping quarters (when possible). This may mean moving to large living quarters or converting a room presently used for some other purpose into a bedroom for the baby. At minimum, a baby bed, storage for clothes, and a place to be used for changing the baby and for storing diapers and other items will be needed. Other preparation will depend on individual preferences and family finances. For example, if the baby is to be bottle fed, all of the equipment required for this will have to be purchased and ready for use when the baby is brought home. Most of this will be unnecessary with breast feeding, but even here, some supplementary bottle feeding usually is needed for times when the mother is not available or does not have enough milk at the moment. Baby clothes, diapers, powders, ointment, and an assortment of other supplies and equipment also will be needed. If costs are a

PREPARING FOR PARENTHOOD

problem, a budget review might be in order. This will require getting information specific enough to allow good estimates of probable costs.

Checklists of (mostly optional) items that parents might wish to purchase or rent can be found in most books for prospective parents. These will provide good general guidelines, although they will have to be adjusted for geographic and other local factors as well as for budget constraints. Insurance policies should be checked to see what is and is not covered. Benefits for pregnancy vary widely, and parents can expect to have to pay something (perhaps a lot) before taking the baby home from the hospital.

Just as the mother (or both parents working together) practice for the birth process itself, both parents should practice using the equipment that they will need to use when the baby arrives. The list will vary, but it may include cloth and/or paper diapers, safety pins, bottles and nipples, sterilizers, and special equipment used for such things as changing or washing the baby. While these are all relatively easy pieces of equipment to use, most of them do require at least some practice to eliminate the inefficiency and general fumbling that occurs whenever we try to use something completely unfamiliar. Needless to say, any such practice should be accomplished before the baby arrives, so that parents can be efficient and feel confident in knowing what they are doing when the infant comes home.

The final preparation will be that parents will have to be ready to adjust from a life style in which they are relatively free to do what they want in their spare time to a life style geared to meet the *immediate* needs of the baby. Most household jobs or other things that adults have to do can be done at convenient or preferred times. Particular jobs seldom *must* be done *right now*. However, many of the babies' needs will be immediate ones that will have to be met on the spot. Prospective parents can ease this adjustment by discussing it in advance and agreeing upon how demands will be met, who will have basic responsibility for what, and when each job will be done.

THE NEWBORN INFANT

First-time parents who are unfamiliar with newborn infants and whose expectations have been affected by pictures shown in baby food ads are in for shock and disappointment. Newborn infants who possess the well-formed features and fleshy bodies shown in advertisements are exceptions. Most newborns are thin and bony and have facial features that are relatively formless and unattractive. Fortunately, this is temporary. As infants develop, their bodies flesh out and their facial features gradually become better defined. In most cases, adults and even toddlers are not recognizable from pictures taken when they were only a day or two old. Parents should not worry about unsightly physical features in newborn infants, unless they exist because of birth defects or injuries. Unsightly features that exist because of normal biological immaturity will disappear with age.

Parents should try to remain aware of their own reactions. They should avoid becoming conditioned or developing rigid expectations on the basis of early experiences with their infant which may lead them to draw false conclusions. Newborn infants brought home from the hospital have existed outside of the womb for only a few days in most cases, and have developed only very few and very primitive schemas. The infants will encounter many experiences for the first time, and many of these will produce crying or other signs of distress. This is perfectly normal, so parents should not become upset or conclude that they are incompetent parents or that the infant does not like them.

At this stage, infants' cognitive schemas are so primitive (so far as is known) that they have no concept at all of their parents or other aspects of their surroundings. It will be several months before they do. Their reactions are primarily to bodily sensations resulting from internal stimuli, or from such external stimuli as temperature, physical motion, or noise. Reactions are not personal reactions to parents or other caretakers. This does not mean that parents cannot profitably stimulate and interact with infants; quite the contrary. It does mean that parents must guard against the tendency to "adultomorphize" by attributing non-existent motivations and personal reactions to infants. Newborn infants will benefit from stimulation of all their sensory capacities, although stimulation that is too intense (especially sudden loud noises or sudden drops) can startle them and produce crying. It is important for parents and other relatives to understand that such reactions by the baby reflect little or nothing about temperament or personality, and absolutely nothing about reactions to other people (which do not yet exist).

The optimal stimuli for newborn infants are intense and salient enough to attract their attention but not so intense as to produce a startle reaction. Certain constant stimuli that infants can learn to recognize are useful, especially stimuli that move somewhat and/or are well suited to manipulation (Kessen, Haith, and Salapatek, 1970). These include crib mobiles that can be watched when infants lie awake on their backs, small rattles and teething rings, and other small and colorful toys made for very young infants. Auditory stimulation can be provided through talking and singing, especially through repetitive games and songs that allow them to hear sound patterns repeated over and over again. Using the infant's name and repeating certain phrases frequently probably are helpful, too. Tactile stimulation also is important, especially cuddling and stimulating through hugging and rocking (but not shaking or startling).

Infants' biological limits and rhythms must be respected. Stimulation should be confined to times when they are alert and favorably disposed toward it. They should not be awakened from sleep unnecessarily, shaken right after they have been fed, or otherwise disturbed in ways likely to have undesirable biological consequences. Parents usually learn not to do such things, and to leave infants undisturbed when sleeping. However, others may have to be dissuaded from continuing their well-meant attempts to play with infants at the wrong times or in the wrong way. In general, infants' biological rhythms will provide cues as to what kinds of activities are appropriate for them at the moment. If they seem tired, put them to bed. Do not try to play with them, because this probably will lead only to crying and distress. If they seem hungry, feed them, regardless of how long it has been since their last feeding. Do not fear "spoiling" infants. Contrary to former belief, this is not a real danger, and it may be impossible. Infant cognitive development is so primitive that concepts like "spoiling" simply do not apply yet. Their development most likely will proceed smoothly if their needs are met quickly and consistently. Deliberate delay or refusal to respond to infant needs can do no good and may well do harm by causing physical distress or psychological anxiety.

PHYSICAL GROWTH

New babies grow slowly during the first few months, but they begin to grow more rapidly in both height and weight once they start eating solid foods. Unless there is a severe problem in feeding, there is little reason to be concerned about physical growth. In general, babies' preferences and habits should guide parents in deciding when, what, how much, and how often they eat. There is no cause for concern if infants do not finish all of the formula or food "prescribed" for them simply because they seem to be satisfied. Similarly, there is nothing to gain, and there may be some undesirable effects, if parents attempt to force infants to eat when they are full. In the short run, this can cause physical and psychological distress, and in the long run, it may establish an eventual lifelong pattern of overeating and obesity.

For many years, it was thought that infants automatically would balance their diets if given free choice of foods. This was based on a widely publicized experiment (Davis, 1939) in which infants were presented with a wide array of foods at each meal and allowed to eat whatever they wanted and as much or as little as they wanted. The results of this study were that although certain individual meals were nutritionists' nightmares, the infants did balance their diets over periods of a week or so. Eventually it was noticed that most of the foods offered in the study were nutritious in the first place, and that the menu did not include such things as soft drinks, candy, or ice cream. These "empty calorie" foods, heavy in carbohydrates but lacking in protein and other important nutrients, are very attractive to infants and young children. Given this, it seems reasonable to expect that infants and young children would *not* necessarily eat a balanced diet if the choices available to them included these especially tasty and attractive but not very nutritious foods. Infant and child diets do need monitoring by parents for both quantity and quality of food intake. Although infants and children should get to enjoy these treats, just like adults, portions and frequency of servings should be moderate. Children's visions of "snacks" also should include more nutritious foods like cereals, nuts, fruit juice, raisins, or raw fruits and vegetables.

Parents should be prepared to adjust to their baby's individual patterns in physical growth. Occasionally a baby will go through a growth spurt or will not grow at the rate parents expect. These and other aspects of physical growth rates in infancy are unimportant except in so far as the parents make them important. The main thing is that the child be kept happy and healthy. Although physical growth does not *cause* the development of sensorimotor schemas, such schemas often require a certain degree of physical growth before

Early Cognitive Stimulation

Clarke-Stewart (1973) investigated the development of first born children between nine and 18 months of age, studying the relationships among measures of child behavior and between measures of child behavior and measures of mother behavior. She found that, in general, different measures of child competence were intercorrelated significantly, and that these measures showed consistent relationships with maternal behavior. Measures of development in cognition, language, and social skills were related strongly enough to be taken together as a combination measure of competence.

Competence scores were related to the quantity and quality of stimulation that these children got from their mothers. Verbal stimulation from mothers was especially strongly related to *verbal* development in children, *cognitive* development and measures of the complexity of play with objects were correlated with the amounts of time that mothers spent playing with materials with their children, and measures of good *social* development were related to high maternal scores on traits such as affection, stimulation, and responsiveness. Interestingly, measures of the quality of the physical environment were not related to competence, but measures of mother behavior were. These data, although correlational, suggest strongly that opportunity to observe even rich environments is of minimal importance to infants compared to active stimulation and appropriate responsiveness by adults (in this case, mothers).

Qualitative differences were observed even between groups of mothers who spent similar amounts of time with their children. Mothers who were verbally stimulating and who allowed the children opportunities to do things and then responded to these things with attention, approval, and additional stimulation tended to have more competent children than mothers who stressed control and physical care of the children over stimulation of them and playing with them. Sex differences also were observed. All of the children gradually became more interested in and competent in manipulating the physical environment over the age span studied. However, boys became notably more oriented toward manipulation of objects and girls more toward social interactions and verbal interactions with the mothers. These differences were caused at least in part by differences in the children which affected the mothers, and not vice-versa. The author concluded that, in general, maternal influences on the children were primary in cognitive development, but that child influences on the mothers were relatively strong in social development. This is a lengthy and somewhat technical monograph, but it is well worth reading because it brings together in a single study many of the measures and findings discussed in this part of the book.

they can appear. Parents interested in stimulating the development of sensorimotor schemas in their baby must take into account physical growth if they are to optimally match environmental stimulation to the infant's present needs, interests, and abilities.

**STIMULATING SENSORI-
MOTOR SCHEMAS**

During the early months, the infant's schemas are little more than elaborated reflexes. Apparent verbalizations usually are just babbling, and apparent personal reactions such as smiling or crying are more likely to be responses to internal causes than to external causes. Although the infant will benefit from stimulation, parents must be intellectually and emotionally prepared for the fact that most responses in the first six months of life will be impersonal. Infants have not developed enough to perceive and respond to the parents as people yet. Nevertheless, stimulation is important in these early months, particularly stimulation that is *patterned* and helps the child develop the abilities to discriminate figure from ground. Visual stimulation can be provided through crib mobiles, holding up colorful objects in front of children and moving them around (at a distance of about 12 inches from their eyes), and allowing them to sit up and watch what is going on around them at times when they are awake and alert. Allowing them to watch while food is prepared is especially helpful. These often-repeated activities make for easy pattern recognition learning, and infants also learn that these food preparation activities mean that their hunger is about to be relieved. In this way, they not only get cognitive benefit from such experience, they also will be more likely to calm down and become secure in the knowledge that food is on the way.

Auditory stimulation in the early months can be provided by exposing infants to music or other pleasant and rhythmic auditory stimulation, by repeating names and frequently used phrases, and by sing-song and other rhythmic verbal activities. Tactile stimulation can be provided through cribs which rock in response to the infants' movements when they are awake, through cuddling, hugging, and other soothing activities, and through manipulating infants' arms or legs or holding them up or moving them around in the air. The latter activities, of course, should not involve extreme or sudden movements which might produce a startle or distress reaction.

During the second six months of life, infants still are largely sedentary, but they are able to respond much more accurately and to a wider variety of activities than in the past. "Peek-a-boo" games and other activities that involve capturing their visual attention and curiosity are especially good for visual stimulation. Auditory stimulation can be provided by imitating their speech and trying to get them to repeat sounds deliberately, and by introducing new songs, games, and frequently used phrases. Motor development can be facilitated by providing teething rings, rattles, and other manipulative toys. Stimulation in all areas can be provided simultaneously through such activities as helping infants learn to feed themselves with a bottle or use a spoon. Infants also will be able to do such things as roll a ball back and forth or play with blocks, if they are seated on the floor.

In all of these activities during the first year, and for the next several years as well, it is important to keep in mind that schemas appear *unevenly*. A given infant might have well-developed schemas in one area but poorly developed ones in another. It is frequent, perhaps even typical, for new schemas to appear and then disappear for awhile before they reappear consistently and become well established. These temporary regressions and imbalances in development are of little importance unless parents or others in the environment make them important by over-reacting to them. Within limits, it is best if parents and others stimulate infants and try to maximize their development of schemas, but they must have realistic expectations and not react negatively if the infants do not respond as they had hoped.

Development of schemas proceeds rapidly during the second year of life, especially after infants learn to stand and walk around. In addition to

Infants everywhere respond with curiosity and an urge to explore objects that induce what Piaget calls "disequilibrium," as this African mother and her friend illustrate. In this particular social situation, the watch served not only as a stimulus for cognitive development to the infant, but also as a method of keeping the infant happily preoccupied and thus allowing the adults to converse without too much distraction. (UNICEF photo by Alastair Matheson) elaborations of the visual and auditory stimulation that were important earlier, they now become especially interested in the development of sensorimotor schemas. They both learn and practice these through *playing* with blocks, sand, manipulative toys and equipment, playground equipment, and other toys that involve physical manipulation and body movement.

Infants should not be allowed to do things which are dangerous or which involve destruction, but otherwise they should be given as much freedom as possible and as many toys and activities as they seem to want. They should be both allowed and encouraged to explore and manipulate the environment. They should not be restrained or kept passive any more than necessary when they are alert and apparently interested in activities. When they do have to be kept in a playpen, provide manipulative items for them to explore and play with, and place the playpen where there are people and activities to watch.

LANGUAGE DEVELOPMENT

Early language development is fostered primarily by imitating the sounds that infants make, until they eventually learn to respond by repeating them. Gradually, infants progress from these isolated word repetitions toward infinitely more complex language usage. Much of the groundwork for this is laid by exposing them to much language, and by directing much language to them. Even though they cannot respond expressively yet, these kinds of experiences foster the development of receptive language. They help build schemas for perceiving the sound system of the language spoken in the home and for some of the specific words used.

When speaking to infants, *it is important to get eye contact*, maintain their attention, and speak distinctly. Again, infants still are learning figure-ground discriminations. Adults have learned to notice subtle language cues and to hear minor sound differences important for conveying meaning. However, infants still are learning which sounds are meaningful and which are not, as well as what the meanings of these sounds are. Activities which make sounds salient, and repetition of activities so that they become recognized as patterns which are repeated regularly, are helpful to the infant in forming schemas. Once infants begin to repeat words, you can respond by repeating them back with gusto, expressing delight, and otherwise providing positive reinforcement. The earliest words will tend to be the name of the infant, the names of parents and siblings, and the names of objects in the environment which have special importance or significance (bottle, nipple, spoon, milk, and the names of favorite toys, for example).

As a general rule, systematic attempts to teach language should involve modeling and repetition of words, but not attempts to correct the mispronunciations. An important point that adults should bear in mind is that most mispronunciations made by infants and young children do *not* result from failure to hear the word correctly. Infants hear words correctly, but they have not yet mastered the motor schemas needed for pronouncing them correctly. Attempts to correct infants' expressive language almost always are pointless. Switching from pronouncing the word correctly to imitating how infants say it (such as, talking in baby talk) not only will *not* help infants, it will confuse them.

Expressive language is much like any other motor activity: infants know *what* they want to say, but they have to learn *how* to say it correctly through practice. For infants learning language, attainment of the ability to say a word correctly every time is very much analogous to attainment of the ability to roll a ball accurately every time. It is something that is learned gradually and solidified with practice, not something that is learned in one trial. Adults often do not understand this, because adults *are* capable of learning correct pronunciation in one trial. However, infants are not, and should not be expected to do so.

In addition to fostering language development by talking to infants frequently and by exposing them to patterned sounds and to language, verbal games and songs are especially useful. They also are enjoyable activities that parents can share with infants. Stimulation of language development will occur more or less automatically through such interactions, so that special activities or techniques are not required. It is more important that the parent and infant enjoy the activities and participate in them often.

SOCIALIZATION

Socialization in the first 12 to 18 months is primarily a matter of controlling the environment and modeling behavior. Until infants develop a sufficient fund of schemas, they will not be able to understand, let alone follow, verbal instructions or explanations.

In the early months, it is important for parents to recognize and adjust to infants' individual needs in such areas as sleep patterns, amounts and types of activities desired, eating habits, and the like. Parents should be sensitive to crying or other behavior that may signal particular needs or desires. Most infants learn to respond one way when hungry, a different way when in distress, and so forth. Such sensitivities can minimize stress and develop feelings of security and general happiness in the infant.

Before infants are able to respond much to verbal instruction, they can learn many things through observation and through physical guidance (in which parents take their hands and guide them through the motions of some activity). Physical guidance often will make the difference between whether an infant can learn to do something or not at a given time. Just as infants may be unable to pronounce a word correctly even though they hear it correctly, it is common for them to be unable to perform an action correctly even though they know what they want to do and have observed someone else do it. Observation of a model does not automatically transfer to the development of motor ability to perform the action the way the model does. Physical guidance can help children develop the ability to perform activities themselves more quickly. Here again, though, it is important that the right kind of guidance be given under the right conditions. Guidance should be help to infants who appear to want it, not physical forcing that they do not want.

FREUD'S ORAL STAGE   Freud dubbed the first year of life the "oral stage," and attached great significance to infant feeding. This produced much unfortunate concern about matters that really were not worth worrying about, or at least would not have been worth worrying about had not Freud made an issue of them. Perhaps foremost among these has been the controversy over breast vs. bottle feeding. Despite occasional claims (not evidence) to the contrary, there is no significant advantage in social-personal development to the infant in either form of feeding. Breast milk has some advantages, usually minor, from the standpoint of nutrition and health. The matter becomes significant only to the extent that the parents *think* it is significant.

In this age of commercially prepared baby foods and formulas, bottle feeding is convenient, safe, and efficient. It is more expensive than breast feeding, however, and it does not allow the mother the intimate nursing experiences that many women desire. In most cases, the decision to feed by breast or by bottle should be made on the basis of the mother's personal preference. Parents opting for breast feeding should be prepared for the fact that maternal milk supply sometimes is insufficient or irregular, so that the baby may need an occasional bottle or may have to be taken off the breast. This has no implications whatsoever about the mother's sexuality or femininity, so there is no reason for a woman to be ashamed or upset, although she may well be disappointed.

Another possibility, even more frequent, is that a mother will expect breast feeding to be a happy, blissful experience only to find that it is uncomfortable or even painful. Often this is merely temporary, and the discomfort is minimized through treatment or eliminated after a few days as the mother's nipples become adjusted to the infant's suction. It often happens that the mother finds the feeding experience too uncomfortable. If this persists, it is better to switch to bottle feeding than to have a hungry baby *and* upset parents. Experiences like these could be disappointing, but they do not indicate that anything is "wrong" with the mother and usually are of no great importance, but any mother contemplating breast feeding should educate herself about them (Guttmacher, 1973).

Regarding the "oral stage" and related theory, accumulated evidence and historical perspective suggest that the whole thing should be classified as a "non-problem." It is not worth worrying about, and probably never would have been worried about, had not Freud made an issue of it. The important things about infant feeding are that the infant's needs be met consistently and efficiently, that feeding be an enjoyable experience for both the infant and the parents, and that feeding be accompanied by hugging, cuddling, and other expressions of warmth and love. For example, infants will not get much stimulation from feeding from bottles mechanically placed to allow (and require) them to feed themselves, but being bottle fed while simultaneously being held and cuddled by a parent probably is equivalent to breast feeding. These factors, and not minor issues such as breast vs. bottle feeding or demand vs. scheduled feeding, form the basis for a sense of security and well-being.

FREUD'S ANAL STAGE   Another "non-problem" that receives much more attention and concern than it deserves is toilet training. Again, this is because of the central importance placed upon toilet training in Freud's theorizing about the anal stage. Freud noted that the period from around 18 to around 24 months of age is when parents begin to place socialization demands on their children, and that the child's future personality is shaped in part by the number and kinds of demands the parents make, the skills with which they present and enforce them, and the child's subjective reactions to them. In particular, Freud focused attention on the demands placed upon the child during toilet training, postulating that inappropriate parental behavior could result in anal retentive or anal expulsive personalities. Although certain of Freud's ideas have merit when rephrased to eliminate theoretical "excess baggage," the emphasis upon toilet training was unnecessary and unfortunate.

Toilet training is only one of many situations in which socialization demands begin to be placed upon the developing infant. Demands here are no more important than demands related to such activities as naps and bedtimes, learning to eat independently and with minimal accidents, and restrictions on where to play and what to play with. Toilet training is important, but it is not the predominant event that psychoanalytic theories suggest. The really important universal human experience at this stage of development is the experience of encountering socialization demands for the first time and learning to adjust to them. As long as children are considered infants incapable of controlling or assuming responsibility for their own behavior, adults do not expect them to exert such control. However, as they learn to walk and talk, and as they become more responsive to verbal instruction, parents begin to place demands upon them and expect them to live up to these demands. One important set of demands concerns toilet training, but there are many others. Children's development will be influenced by the demands made upon them and by how they respond to these demands. Their attitudes toward authority figures and toward having demands and restrictions placed upon them may well be affected by their reactions during this stage. Just as the "oral" stage might better be called the "dependency" stage or the "development of trust" stage, the "anal" stage might better be called the "adjustment to socialization demands" stage.

Erik Erikson (1963) has referred to this as the stage of autonomy vs. shame and doubt. He notes that parents who avoid unreasonable demands, and who present their demands in ways that do not overwhelm or deflate children, are likely to produce children who can adjust to limits and socialization demands without losing their sense of autonomy. Children will know that they must keep certain rules and live up to certain expectations, but they also will develop the general idea that they are in control of their behavior and environment and able to make autonomous decisions and follow through on them. In contrast, parents who make restrictive demands, especially if they punish or berate children for failing to meet them, may induce a sense of shame. The children may come to doubt their abilities to make decisions and control their bodies and environments generally.

While many other factors enter into the picture, it does appear true that, other things being equal, parents who make reasonable and essentially supportive socialization demands are likely to foster autonomy and self-confidence in their children. Also, parents who reject or belittle their children for failure to meet their demands are likely to produce inhibition, insecurity, uncertainty, low self-esteem, and related traits that Erikson has grouped under "shame and doubt."

SOCIALIZATION AS STIMULATION AND EDUCATION Early psychoanalytic theory and early behavioristic theory shared the unfortunate tendency to view children as possessing impulses that had to be curbed through parental intervention. This negativistic point of view meant that many came to see socialization as equivalent to limit setting and punishment. We now know that socialization is most successful when conducted through positive methods such as modeling and providing prescriptive instruction. It is least successful when conducted through negative methods such as threats and punishments (Hoffman, 1970).

This is true even in the sensorimotor stage, when the children are much less responsive to verbal instructions than they will be later. Although it will be necessary to forbid them to do certain things, and perhaps even to slap their wrists and firmly say "No!" if they should repeat dangerous behaviors such as poking around electrical outlets or reaching for pots on the stove, socialization should be conducted through positive methods whenever possible. The child should be shown and told what to do, and, where appropriate, physically guided through the motions. It is important that positive expectations be communicated consistently and from the start. Consistency and seriousness of purpose build credibility. If parents avoid idle threats or other evidence that they do not mean what they say, their children will come to understand that there is a direct and consistent relationship between what parents say and what they do. This will minimize the "testing" behavior seen in children who want to find out whether or not the parent really intends to enforce a demand or limit that has just been verbalized.

Other important aspects of building credibility and establishing positive expectations are keeping demands *reasonable and appropriate,* and presenting them to the child in a way that communicates the expectation that they will be *understood and followed.* To do this, parents must pay careful attention to what they say to children. If they continually change their minds or otherwise act inconsistently, eventually they will teach the children that their statements do not mean much. If parental demands are reasonable and are presented in ways that implicitly suggest that the child will understand and follow them, the child will be most likely to do so. In contrast, if parents make demands that are unreasonable and must be changed, or if they communicate the idea that they are not sure that the child will obey (such as by threatening punishment if the child does not comply), the child may come to doubt the parent's seriousness of purpose and may begin to test many or even most demands.

One important implication here is that parents must discuss and agree upon what they will and will not allow their child to do, so that they will be clear and consistent in responding to the child's behavior. Negative demands and limits involving forbidding certain activities should be made firmly but matter-of-factly. There should be no threatening voice tones or gestures, and no mention of punishment if the child does not comply. Socialization demands should be accompanied by verbal explanations. When the baby is very young, these will have to be quite simple explanations ("No, no—hot!"). Even these are useful, because they help give babies assurance that prohibitions are meant for their own good and are not arbitrarily imposed. Explanations of the rationales behind socialization demands become increasingly important as children get older and understand more language. They help foster understanding of cause-effect relationships, help them understand the linkages between their own behavior and its effects, help them understand that there are reasons why the parents make demands and impose limitations, and help them understand that these reasons are for their own good and not just parental whims or desires to dominate. In short, explanation can make the difference between socialization demands perceived as reasonable and helpful vs. punitive, and consequently they can make children more likely to internalize the socialization and use it to guide their own behavior (vs. obeying parents only when they are present and ready to enforce their demands).

Successful socialization during the early years involves application of positive methods in conjunction with proper timing of demands relative to the child's emerging capabilities. Because of its complexity and general interest, toilet training will be used as an example. First, biology must be respected here. Attempts to toilet train children before their control mechanisms mature are utterly futile. They cannot possibly succeed, and the ordeal very probably will upset the child and damage the parent-child relationship. Toilet training should not even be attempted until the child shows evidence of being able to exercise voluntary control over bladder and bowel movements. This usually begins around 24 months of age, although there is much variance on both sides. Toilet training often is more arduous and complex than it need be, because adults approach it with misconceptions about children. They often "adult-omorphize," treating the children as if they had the same degree of control over their bodies that adults do. They do not. As with other psychomotor schemas, attainment of voluntary control over the bladder or the bowels is a slow, cumulative process requiring integration of several simpler schemas and frequent regressions along the way before permanent control becomes established. Nevertheless, one of the most common mistakes that parents make is to assume that children are "toilet trained" if they go a few days without soiling themselves. This is unfortunate, because once parents draw this conclusion, they are tempted to blame children personally and respond with anger if they should regress and soil themselves again (which they are very likely to do).

If adults do not over-react to such regressions, they will be relatively minor events in the child's life, just like any other minor setback on the road to mastery of some motor skill. However, if the parents over-react by frightening or rejecting the child, the whole area of bowel or bladder elimination may become a source of anxiety. If this happens, further regressions are even more likely, because anxiety will interfere with the child's already tenuous ability to control these functions. To avoid this, parents should accomplish toilet training with a combination of proper environmental manipulation, modeling, instructions, and attempts to share pleasant interactions with the child so that learning occurs naturally and with minimal anxiety. A small potty chair is preferable. A device that fits on an adult toilet is too difficult for the child to manage, and usually requires parental help in getting into it. This also is the time to switch from diapers to training pants. Use of the toilet is learned most easily if it is modeled for the child regularly. The child can watch and interact with the adult when a parent is using the toilet. This should be done in a nonchalant manner, much the same way as when the adult allows the child to watch tooth brushing or dressing. In this way, the child will come to see using the toilet as an everyday routine, and not as a mysterious or threatening "big deal."

Children probably are ready for toilet training when they can begin to indicate *in advance* that they need to use the toilet. Parents can tell them that, now that they are getting bigger, they can use a potty similar to the toilet the parents use. This should be presented to children as a new and interesting experience to look forward to, rather than as a task being forced upon them. Children then should be instructed to come and use the potty whenever they think they need to. Parents can help by inviting them to use it at times when they are most likely to use the toilet (based upon observation of their typical behavior). If they are content to sit on the potty and amuse themselves with books or toys, it may be best to leave them there until they indicate that they have finished or do not need to use the toilet. If they seem to want companionship, parents can remain with them and read a story or just talk. If they do empty their bladders or have bowel movements, they should be praised (but not too effusively) and wiped clean (children will not be able to do this themselves very well until they are four or five years old). If they remain on the potty for some time without voiding or eliminating and indicate that they do not need to (either spontaneously or in response to a quesion from the parent), they should be allowed to get off without argument or criticism. ("Okay, I guess you don't need to go now. Let me know if you think you need to go later.")

In addition to the inevitable regressions that occur in the process of achieving firm control, parents also should be prepared for the fact that most children will achieve firm control in one area earlier than in the other (usually the bowels before the bladder). These two areas and functions are entirely separate, so that control of one means little or nothing with regard to control of the other. Furthermore, both are very complex.

Bladder control involves feeling and recognizing sensory signals that children need to urinate, being able to withhold urination until they can get to the potty and get undressed, and then being able to urinate into the potty. Difficulty can be encountered at the initial stage if children have trouble recognizing biological signals telling them that they need to use the toilet.

Even when they have no difficulty here, the development of firm control over urination still is complex. They must learn simultaneously to inhibit urination until the proper time and then to produce it. This is no simple task for a toddler.

Similarly, learning bowel control means learning to recognize biological signals that a bowel movement is necessary, learning to inhibit the bowel movement until they get to the toilet, and then learning to have a bowel movement with maximal efficiency. Again, this is complex and difficult learning. It can proceed with relative ease, similar to the learning of other complex motor skills, provided that parents handle it appropriately. However, if they make children anxious by over-reacting, or if they try to force them to learn before they are mature enough, they are asking for trouble.

These comments about toilet training apply to the socialization of almost any sensorimotor schemas. The keys to success are careful observation, paying attention to children's behavior and verbalizations so as to know when to introduce a new demand or challenge, the ability to combine control of the environment with the presentation of demands in positive ways likely to make them desire to acquire the new skills, taking steps to make the experience as enjoyable as possible, and providing help in the form of modeling, instructions, or demonstrations, so that they can learn the new behaviors as quickly and easily as possible. Negative approaches stressing criticism and punishment for failure should be avoided, especially harsh over-reactions to failure which will induce anxiety and compound difficulties in helping the child master skills in the future. Children will learn almost anything *unevenly but steadily* if taught properly, but they probably will show fixation, regression, and anxiety if parents try to force them to do something before they are biologically able or if parents present demands in negative and threatening ways. This is true not only for toilet training, but also for such diverse tasks as rolling a ball, using a spoon, talking, climbing, operating toys, and similar skills typically mastered in the sensorimotor period.

SUMMARY

Once prospective parents have decided that they wish to have children, much information gathering, mutual planning, and specific practice will be required. This includes genetic counseling where necessary, medical supervision during pregnancy, selection and appropriate follow through concerning method of childbirth, selection of names, and making physical and psychological preparations for assuming the parent role. In the early months after birth, parenting focuses mostly on meeting infants' biological needs, because the maturation necessary for truly psychological interaction with parents has not occurred yet. As it does occur, parents will have increasing opportunities to stimulate infants by providing a variety of sensory experiences, especially repeated patterns that the infants can come to recognize and discriminate. As the infant makes the transition out of the sensorimotor stage and becomes a toddler capable of interacting socially and exploring the environment, parents will have to begin setting limits and socializing generally in addition to providing stimulation. Such socialization is most successful when it is positive and prescriptive, using modeling and explanations as much as possible and minimizing threats and punishments.

ANNOTATED BIBLIOGRAPHY, PART TWO

CHURCH, JOSEPH. *Understanding your child from birth to three: A guide to your child's psychological development.* New York: Random House, 1973.

This book, written by a prominent developmental psychologist specializing in infant development, concentrates on the psychological development during the first three years of life. It nicely complements the book by Dr. Spock by providing psychological information to go along with the medical and physiological information provided by Spock. Dr. Church takes an eclectic view. The book is organized and written topically and information and suggestions are based upon the general fund of knowledge available, not upon narrower ideas stemming from a limited theory.

DICK-READ, GRANTLY. *Childbirth without fear: The principles and practice of natural childbirth,* second revised edition. New York: Harper and Row, 1959.

This book, written by the individual most personally responsible for the revival of interest in natural childbirth, provides a wealth of information on the subject for interested prospective parents. It is written from a definitely pro-natural childbirth position, but it does contain a wealth of useful information on natural childbirth generally and on the "Dick-Read" method in particular.

DODSON, FITZHUGH. *How to parent.* New York: Signet, 1970.

This paperback is packed full of good advice about child rearing, especially about dealing with children in the first few years of life. Dodson is eclectic, but he also is prescriptive enough to provide specific guidelines concerning a great variety of problems. His orientation is toward preventive mental health and provision of optimal environments, and away from stress on ages and stages or on dealing with specific problems in isolation from the more important task of building a solid relationship. This is illustrated by his refusal to provide an index for the book, in order to frustrate those who might be tempted to look up "what to do" when faced with a specific problem instead of reading the book in its entirety. An especially valuable feature of this book is the inclusion of several appendices giving information about children's books, toys, and games, annotated with comments about appropriateness and possible uses.

GESELL, ARNOLD, *et al. The first five years of life: A guide to the study of the pre-school child.* New York: Harper, 1940.

Although supplanted by many newer publications from the Gesell Institute, this classic work presents many of the findings from the Gesellian approach to the study of child development. The book includes numerous timetables giving expected dates for the acquisition of particular schemas, and in general it is organized by chronological age, characterizing children at various ages and stages. It is fascinating reading and can be informative, but readers are cautioned that Gesell and his colleagues gave much more emphasis to the "stage" concept than it appears to deserve, and overly specific age and stage norms pervade the book. One must read it with determination to avoid the temptation to worry about infants and young children who are "below average" or "behind."

GINSBURG, HARVEY, AND OPPER, SYLVIA. *Piaget's theory of intellectual development: An introduction.* Englewood Cliffs, New Jersey: Prentice-Hall, 1969.

This is an unusually readable and clear account of Piagetian theory, probably the best place to start for someone who is completely unfamiliar with it. It is listed at the end of this part of the book because it contains an unusually complete treatment of the Piagetian infant stages, along with numerous instructive examples.

GUTTMACHER, ALLAN. *Pregnancy, birth, and family planning: A guide for expectant parents in the 1970s.* New York: Viking, 1973.

This is an unusually complete and well-written guide for individuals who are or thinking about becoming prospective parents. It contains detailed information about the biology of reproduction, the course of pregnancy, and the birth process, discussing various possibilities and options objectively and informatively. It also contains important information on the relative advantages and disadvantages of various family planning options and other considerations involved in choosing whether or not to have children in the first place. Those who read and are persuaded by some of the books listed above written from a definite bias should read this and other more objectively written books before making final decisions.

LEHANE, STEPHEN. *Help your baby learn: 100 Piaget-based activities for the first two years of life.* Englewood Cliffs, New Jersey: Spectrum Books, 1976.

The title describes the content of the book, which is written particularly for parents who want to stimulate their infant's development systematically. Infant development from the Piagetian perspective is discussed, and the author draws upon Piagetian psychology to make specific suggestions about how parents can stimulate their infants through specific activities, mostly activities that go on every day anyway.

LALECHE LEAGUE INTERNATIONAL. *The womanly art of breast feeding.* Franklin Park, Illinois: LaLeche League International, 1963.

This book, published by an organization of individuals who favor breast feeding, contains a wealth of information about the pros and cons of breast feeding and the specifics involved. It probably is the most complete source of information about breast feeding, although readers should be aware of its clear pro-breast feeding bias.

OLDS, SALLY WENDKOS, AND EIGER, MARVIN. *The complete book of breast feeding.* New York: Workman Publishing Company, 1972.

This book is a collaboration between a mother who breast fed her own three children and a pediatrician who advocates breast feeding and natural childbirth generally. It is similar to *The womanly art of breast feeding* in being a complete and informative manual on the subject, written from a clear pro-breast feeding bias.

SPOCK, BENJAMIN. *Baby and child care.* New York: Pocket Books, 1976.

This volume, which comes out in new and often somewhat revised editions each year, has earned a well-deserved place as "the" manual for baby and child care in the home. Despite the vehemence of critics of "the Spock generation," the book actually contains relatively little information or suggestions of a psychological nature. However, it does contain a wealth of important and useful information about general health and preventive medical care. It is especially important for helping parents to recognize possible symptoms and to differentiate between problems that might be serious and problems that are minor and not worth worrying about. It is a valuable manual, likely to be used repeatedly by parents, especially new parents.

VELLAY, PIERRE, *et al. Childbirth without pain.* New York: Dutton, 1960.

This book provides information on the Lamaze method of natural childbirth. It contains both lectures on the technical specifics of the method and testimonials of experiences by mothers who have used it. Along with the Dick-Read method, the Lamaze method of natural childbirth is perhaps the best-known and most widely used. Prospective parents interested in natural childbirth should investigate these two methods. If they select one of them, they also should attempt to find a doctor and hospital familiar with and favorable toward the method selected.

WHITE, BURTON, AND WATTS, JEAN. *Experience and environment.* Englewood Cliffs, New Jersey: Prentice-Hall, 1973.

This volume reports one of the most important recent studies of infant development and socialization, often referred to as "the Harvard Infant Project." Attempts were made to identify components of infant competence, and to relate these to differential socialization behavior by parents that might help explain why some infants become more competent than others. For the serious student of child development, this book is rich in theoretical, methodological, and substantive content.

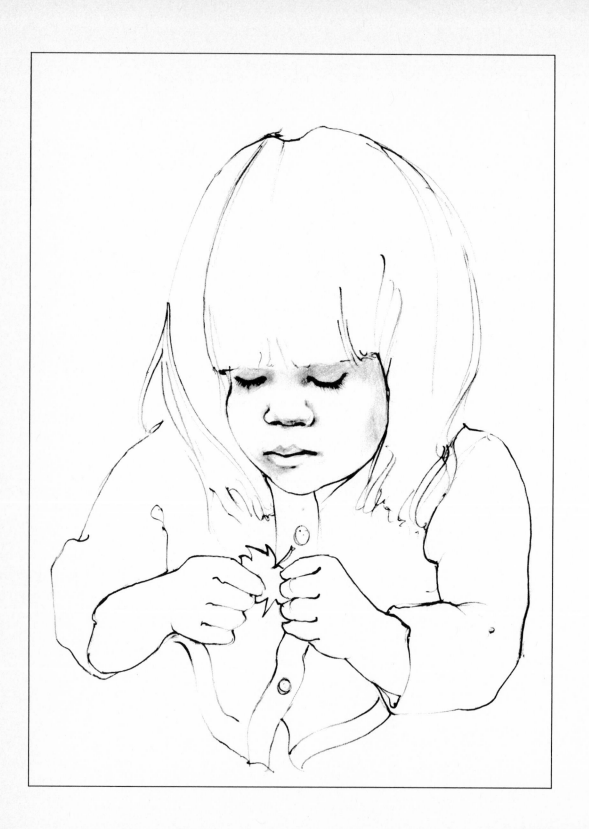

PART THREE

THE PREOPERATIONAL YEARS

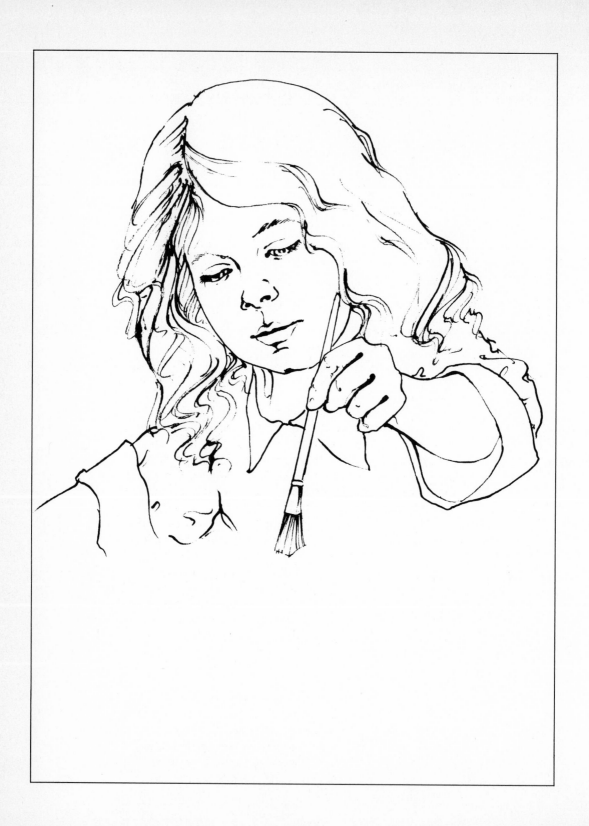

Physical and Cognitive Development in Young Children

For purposes of discussion, development will be divided into the major stages proposed by Piaget. Early childhood is equated with the preoperational period. This extends from the end of the sensorimotor period, when children learn to use memory and imagery to accumulate knowledge and to think, until they become operational. The latter event, which will be discussed at length at the end of this chapter, occurs sometime between the ages of about 5 and 7 or 8, depending on the child's native brightness and the quality of the environment. This corresponds roughly to the period most societies define as between infancy and school age (if formal schooling exists).

PIAGET'S PREOPERATIONAL STAGE

Until the work of Piaget and others who followed in his footsteps, early childhood usually was not considered very important for cognitive development. It was seen primarily as a time of maturation and mastery of basic physical skills, with most cognitive development coming later, especially after children entered school. Piaget and others have shown that children make great strides in *cognitive* development during this time, constructing knowledge of the environment and the people and things in it (but in a piecemeal fashion). Every day brings new adventures, experiences, and discoveries which enable children to gradually solidify and expand their spotty and tentative knowledge base. Most of what children learn during these years is commonplace from the adult's perspective, but we now know that this knowledge is not acquired through simple maturation of other "automatic" mechanisms. Instead, children slowly and unevenly *construct* their knowledge. Each new item of information is a discovery and a revelation *for them* (Piaget, 1954).

Preoperational children's minds work in predictable and logical ways, but the premises which underlie their reasoning often are wrong. Also, the reasoning processes themselves are different in many ways from those used by adults. Piaget and others discovered that systematic differences between child and adult knowledge and reasoning exist in the first place, that universal sequences of development can be identified, and that play and other childish activities formerly thought to be of little importance actually are fundamental to general intellectual development. Eventually, this led to a surge of interest in preoperational children. There was an over-reaction for a time. This included the suggestion that the first six years or so of life were crucially important, perhaps even constituting a critical period for intellectual development (Bloom, 1964). This over-emphasis of the importance of the early years is disappearing, but it is generally agreed that children's activities in these years affect and reflect their cognitive development. They are not "mere play" or "childishness," as was once thought.

A few still claim that the problems of the disadvantaged can be eliminated or that all children can be stimulated to attain high levels of cognitive development if given optimal environments in the early years (White, 1975). Most theorists do not go this far, but they do recognize that the quality of the environment affects children's development, including their cognitive development. Opinions differ about how much can be accomplished by providing optimal environments to all children, and definitive data on the matter are not yet available. Nevertheless, it is obvious that many children are being raised in ways that do not optimally stimulate their cognitive development or their development generally, and that significant improvements in their environments can make significant improvements in their development.

GENERAL CHARACTERISTICS OF PREOPERATIONAL CHILDREN

The preoperational child's knowledge base is spotty, tentative, and poorly organized. In contrast to older children, who have achieved concrete operations and have organized their schemas into clusters which fit together into consistent systems with interrelated and mutually supporting parts, preoperational children have loose and shifting collections of schemas, which at first are interrelated only tenuously, if at all. Even the schemas they do possess are only partially correct. In many cases, they will have to unlearn or partially modify a schema that seemed right when it was acquired but which turned out to be wrong, at least in some respects. Most of this correcting will have to be done through unsystematic trial and error. Preoperational children do not yet grasp basic underlying organizing principles, so that they cannot yet identify and correct errors in their systems easily and efficiently (Piaget and Inhelder, 1969).

Most adults do not remember what life was like during these years, so at first they have a difficult time putting themselves in the places of preoperational children and seeing the world from the children's viewpoints. One way to do this is to observe children systematically, noting their interest and behavior patterns and questioning them about their beliefs. Similar knowledge can be gleaned indirectly by reading the examples of childish thinking that have been published by Piaget and other researchers. It should be noted as a caution that most of these examples come from bright and articulate children who are unusually skilled at describing their perceptions and cognitions. Such examples often show great imagination and inventiveness, drawing analogies between situations or generating explanations for observed events. They help to highlight the thought processes and general logical rules used by preoperational children, but they usually are most typical of bright and articulate children. Less gifted children use the same kinds of logical processes, but with less efficiency and creativity.

Another way to grasp the problems facing preoperational children is to generalize from personal experiences that you *can* remember. The best examples are experiences that you encountered in the process of beginning to learn some complex and difficult body of knowledge, such as one of the sciences or foreign language. If you entered such a course with little or no previous background, it is likely that the first few weeks (at least) were spent mastering an assortment of facts that did not seem to fit together. It is likely that your correct learning was interspersed with a certain amount of incorrect learning, mistakes that were picked up and then discarded later when they were discovered. In the early stages, responses to questions or assignment exercises were more likely to be guesses than to be the end products of chains of systematic reasoning which occurred because you understood the problem, knew what principles applied to it, and were able to apply those principles systematically and correctly to reason through to the correct conclusion. You *were* able to do these later, if you stayed with the subject long enough to learn it as a systematic whole. Knowledge at this level enables you to move back and forth between general principles and specific facts, to solve problems efficiently and appropriately, to make accurate predictions, to reason through problems logically and correctly rather than resort to guessing, and to notice and correct errors more easily. These differences between early and late stages in adult learning are analogous in many ways to the differences between preoperational children and children who have achieved concrete operations.

Preoperational children must rely on fairly primitive learning processes, such as noting the relationships between stimuli, responses, and consequences,

The Subjectivity of Emotions

We often think of emotions as specific physiological conditions that reflect or are caused by psychological experiences. Research indicates that the psychological and experiential aspects of emotions are much more differentiated than the physiological ones. In fact, physiological states which are apparently identical can be experienced subjectively as very different emotions. This was shown in a famous series of studies conducted by Schachter (1964). These experiments led to the conclusion that emotions combine a state of general physiological arousal with a cognitive assessment of the situational factors that presumably are responsible for such arousal. The cognitive assessment leads to the labeling of the physiological arousal, and ultimately to the subjective experience of emotion.

Schachter demonstrated this in some ingenious studies demonstrating that physiological arousal experienced in ambiguous situations could be experienced very differently, depending upon people's expectations, and that these expectations could be influenced by exposure to models. The experiments involved administration of physiologically arousing pills or placebo pills having no physiological effect, combined with different modeling conditions. The models were confederates of the experimenter, but the subjects who were exposed to them thought that they were fellow subjects in the same condition who had experienced the same treatments that they had. The models simulated experiencing strong but very different emotions, such as intense anger vs. euphoria marked by behavior such as "uncontrollable" giggling and laughing.

Subjects who received a placebo pill that did not affect their physiological arousal still experienced some emotions in reaction to observing the models, presumably because they developed the expectation that the "medication" would have a similar effect upon them. A second group of subjects who had received the physiologically arousing medication but had also received some realistic information about the probable effects of the medication showed similar reactions to the models as did the placebo group. They were somewhat affected, but not very strongly. However, a third group of subjects who had received the physiologically arousing medication but had not been given any instructions about what to expect showed very strong responses to the models, apparently experiencing and later reporting experiencing emotional states similar to those they observed in the models. In situations where subjects were physiologically aroused but unclear about the nature of their arousal state, exposure to models which led them to develop hypotheses or expectations about the reasons for and the nature of this arousal state led them to experience quite different emotions, even though the physiological arousal was the same prior to exposure to the models.

This experiment and variations have demonstrated that strong emotions do involve physiological arousal, but, at the same time, the subjective experiences of these emotions depend upon the perception of the situation and the expectations or beliefs about what is likely to happen or what is "supposed to" happen. We tend to feel happy in situations where we are supposed to feel happy, to feel sad in situations where we are supposed to feel sad, and so on. A more recent application of this line of research concerns people's reactions to physiologically arousing or depressing chemicals, including alcohol and marijuana, along with numerous medications. There is good reason to believe that, independent of any direct effects that these substances may have upon the body, the subjective experiences of people who ingest them are affected strongly by their expectations. Among other things, this implies that people who expect to get drunk if they consume a given amount of liquor or to get high if they ingest a given amount of marijuana probably will do so, and people who do not expect to do so probably will not, at least in part because of their expectations.

Which piece has more clay? The girl seems to think that the piece rolled into a "hotdog" shape does. If this piece began as a sphere the same size as the other piece, the girl has not yet mastered conservation of mass. (Photo by Dianne Smith)

and exploring through trial and error, because they do not yet have a firm, systematic knowledge base from which to operate (and into which to assimilate new experiences). They are fooled easily by misleading appearances, prone to overgeneralize from just one or a small number of experiences, likely to draw logical but false analogies, and likely to reason correctly and even creatively but be mistaken because the original premises were wrong. These and other errors associated with preoperational thought processes occur because these children do not have stable systems of factual knowledge and dependable logical principles that will allow them to recognize and avoid such mistakes. Nor are they disturbed by the mistakes they discover. Their days are filled with new discoveries, many of which contradict or qualify what they thought they knew. As a result, discrepancies between expectations and observations do not produce a sense of disturbance and a strong curiosity to find out what really is going on, as they do in older children and adults whose daily experiences generally reconfirm rather than challenge what they know.

Typical child reactions to Piaget's problem of conservation of mass are good examples here. This problem often is presented with two balls of clay which are put on scales to show the child that they are equal in weight (and presumably therefore in amount of clay). If one of the balls then is stretched and rolled into a hot dog shape and the child is asked whether one now contains more clay than the other, children who possess concrete operations will state unhesitantly that neither has more clay than the other. They know that amounts remain the same unless you add or subtract, and that changes in shape do not change the amount. In contrast, preoperational children are likely to be confused by this manipulation, and to state that one of the two pieces contains more clay than the other.

The reactions of preoperational vs. operational children also will differ if they are given feedback about the correctness of their responses. If preoperational children are told that they are wrong, that the two pieces of clay still contain the same amount, they will accept this but will not react strongly. Furthermore, they are just as likely to accept the idea that one piece weighs more than the other, because they do not know enough about weight, density, and related factors to be able to make reasoned judgments about this problem. Nor are they motivated enough to care much one way or the other about the correct answer.

Children clearly in the concrete operational stage react very differently. If the experimenter should "cheat" by pinching off some of the clay from one of the pieces without letting them see it, and should then inform them that they are wrong, and that the one piece weighs less than the other, these children will *not* just accept disinterestedly the news that they have been wrong. They may become agitated and express confusion and concern, or they may smugly inform the experimenter that they know that some kind of trick is being played on them, even though they might not know exactly how it was done.

Children who have achieved concrete operations have *structures* sufficiently *stable* that experiences of this sort will not make them change their ideas. They are *certain* that they are correct, and that the answer to the mystery lies in some sort of trickery or illusion rather than in the correctness of their ideas about what will and will not change the weights of clay pieces. The ideas of preoperational children have not yet crystallized into such stable systems, so that experiences like this easily can cause them to change their ideas about factors that can influence the weight of clay. In fact, they are likely to take the experimenter's word for whatever they are told, without even asking to have clay re-weighed so that they can check for themselves.

This brief example illustrates a major characteristic of the mental structure of preoperational children: they lack stable structures to relate and anchor their schemas, so that schemas are relatively unstable and unrelated to one another. As a result, they believe many things that make sense from *their* perspectives, although they seem silly from the viewpoint of an adult. They maintain contradictory beliefs without noticing the contradictions. They change their minds quickly, and with little or no concern, about matters that an adult would find more puzzling. In general, they take experiences at face value, as they see them, seldom questioning the validity or meaning. The more unstable their schemas, and the fewer connections that have been made among them, the more they will show this behavior. As schemas become more stable and interconnected with logical principles, they begin to act more and more like children who have reached the stage of concrete operations. This happens unevenly, however. Children who act in logical ways (from an adult viewpoint) in one area still will show largely preoperational logic in another area.

Throughout the preoperational years, children show continuous physical growth and developmental changes in bodily configuration. Physical growth patterns are determined largely by the genes, although extreme malnutrition can stunt growth and excessive or unbalanced diets can cause children to weigh more or less than they should for their heights and developmental stages. **PHYSICAL GROWTH**

Height and weight at a given age in early childhood are not very reliable indicators of height and weight in adulthood. Although growth is programmed and controlled genetically, it is not orderly and systematic. Instead, it proceeds in cycles, with children showing relatively brief growth spurts followed by longer periods of *relative* inactivity. During the latter periods, obvious features such as height or the sizes of hands and feet do not change much if at all, but other bodily changes do take place. Growth spurts are caused primarily by spurts in the growth of *bones*. These spurts in bone growth produce temporary stages in which the body is relatively elongated compared to what it was before. Growth in muscle and fat tissues follows this bone growth, so that the body configuration eventually fills out again, and the child's appearance returns to what we expect as "normal" for a child of a given height (Tanner, 1970).

Assuming appropriate nutrition, maturational changes in size and bodily configuration are merely temporary and are of no great importance except as conversation pieces for parents and relatives. For example, many babies get noticeably fat in the few months immediately before they begin to walk, but they quickly lose this "baby fat" when they learn to walk and begin to get much more exercise. Older children show similar, but less extreme, vacillations between thinness and chubbiness, depending upon the time since their most recent spurt in bone growth. Children may keep the same clothes and shoe sizes for many months, but then suddenly move up several sizes during a growth spurt.

Long term growth is determined by the ossification rates of the bones. A given child may show a growth pattern which follows any of several different *growth curves*, which is why two children who appear identical at one age may show different growth patterns later, and why relative size in the early years is not a very reliable predictor of relative size later. The relative sizes of the parents and the kinds of growth curves that they experienced as children are somewhat better predictors, although growth curves are not inherited in any simple direct manner (Tanner, 1970). It is common for a child to be one of the largest children in the peer group throughout childhood, and yet be relatively small as an adult. This happens because bone ossification occurs more rapidly in such children than in their peers, causing them to grow relatively less during adolescent growth spurts and to stop growing sooner. Conversely, other children who are relatively small throughout most of childhood can end up relatively tall because ossification of their bones proceeds more slowly. They grow considerably during adolescence, and they continue to grow for several years thereafter because ossification is not completed until many years later.

In summary, physical growth is determined almost entirely by genetically programmed maturational factors. Other than providing adequate nutrition and exercise, there is nothing that parents can or should do to promote growth. There are a number of things that they should *not* do: make assumptions about young children's ultimate sizes and statures on the basis of their present sizes; worry about children being "too big" or "too small"; complain when children outgrow clothes or shoes (in ways that make the children feel that they somehow are at fault); or make children feel deviant or abnormal by calling attention to their unusual sizes or physical features. Physical appearance will become extremely important later, when adolescent concerns about sexual attractiveness develop. However, in early and middle childhood, children tend to accept their own physical features and those of other children without attaching any great importance to them, unless they are led to believe that these things are important by what they pick up from adults or others in their environment. This is not to say that they are uninterested; quite the contrary. Young children enjoy looking at themselves in mirrors and making comparisons between themselves and others, and physical size and appearance are important aspects of self-concept at any age. However, children ordinarily do not *worry* about their bodies or appearance unless the seeds of such worry are planted by someone else.

New physical growth opens new vistas for schema development in children. As they get taller and their arms get longer, they can reach, and therefore inspect or manipulate, many new objects. This potential is multiplied as they learn to climb. Preoperational children enjoy activities involving large muscle play (climbing, jumping, running, riding), play which involves manipulating their whole bodies through space (swinging, flips, and other gymnastic movements), and other activities involving the body as a whole (crawling under or into things, squeezing into tight spaces, assuming unusual physical positions). In addition to the inherent enjoyment such activities provide, they allow children to test the limits of their bodies' capabilities and to develop schemas related to body control.

In these and other activities, preoperational children are "on the go" much of the time, usually being involved in some physically active, energy burning activity. They often require a lot of food to provide this energy, but the nature of their digestive tracts and their daily activity patterns are not well-matched to the typical adult pattern of three meals with little or nothing in between. Instead, they may need to eat more often, although they probably will not and should not eat very large amounts at one time. Young children may need to have two or three snacks (juice or milk with nuts, crackers, dry cereal, fruits, or vegetables) between meals, and they should not be expected to eat large portions or even to be especially hungry at adult mealtimes, especially at the evening meal. Unless there is some reason to doubt their sincerity, it is best to take children at their words when they say they are hungry, and to provide them with some kind of snack or meal. This often will mean providing a snack to children who "shouldn't be hungry because they just ate lunch an hour ago." An hour ago is a long time in the life of a young child. Given the small capacity of their digestive tracts and the rapid energy consumption that may be involved in their play patterns, it not only is possible but probable that some children might be hungry and/or thirsty only an hour after eating lunch. If you doubt this, you should observe the activities of such a child or, better yet, try to duplicate them. Any adult who can keep up with the child for even an hour is in very good physical condition.

Although the development of cognitive and verbal schemas becomes increasingly important as children develop through the preoperational years, most of their activities still center upon the development of sensorimotor schemas. They still learn primarily by doing, and most such learning is the development of skills based on sensorimotor schemas. Even the verbal and cognitive schemas which do develop tend to follow and be related to sensorimotor schemas developed earlier. This has led Piaget, Bruner, and others to state that *what children learn is what they do*, and that *cognitive development involves the internalization of sensorimotor schemas*.

The general model is that the child first learns a sensorimotor schema as a physical, behavioral response to a particular stimulus. With repetitive practice, the schema becomes better established and more finely differentiated, and it gradually broadens to include more and more stimuli. Ultimately, it becomes a basic part of the child's sensorimotor or behavioral repertoire. Once it is well established as a *sensorimotor schema*, it can be internalized as a *cognitive schema*. Children gradually learn to use imagery to picture themselves

SENSORIMOTOR SCHEMAS

behaving in situations in which they use the schema. As they practice such imaginative activity, they call upon the schema but do not physically act it out. This helps the schema become internalized as a generalized action possibility. Eventually, it can be imagined and evoked in situations involving stimuli which never have elicited it before. For example, through a variety of repeated experiences with nuts and bolts (real ones or toys), bottles and bottle caps, toothpaste tubes, and other stimuli that involve the basic principle and the physical motions connected with the schema of screwing and unscrewing, children develop a generalized schema which assimilates these different stimuli and the relevant physical motions. The presence of such a generalized schema then can be observed in new behavior. Children who have forgotten precisely how to screw a particular screw into a particular nut might immediately try to do so when they encounter the screw and nut, indicating that they are aware that the two can be fastened together through screwing motions. Later, their behavior will show that the generalized schema has been internalized to the point where it is applicable to a broad range of potential stimuli. They may go through a period where they try to unscrew anything that can be unscrewed (ballpoint pens, screws, nuts and bolts), or even looks like it can be unscrewed (pencil erasers, nails, wheels on wheel toys). Evidence that the schema has become truly internalized and cognitive as well as sensorimotor is especially obvious with the latter kinds of stimuli. Children are likely to show frustration or puzzlement if they are unable to unscrew something that looks like it can be unscrewed. In such situation, they even may ask questions or make comments which clearly show that they have the concept of screwing and unscrewing ("Why doesn't it come off?").

Within the purely sensorimotor domain, children go through several stages and sequences, many of which are universal or near-universal. The more universal sensorimotor schemas are developed through normal play, with no special action or environmental arrangement required if children have normal health, freedom, space, and toys for play. Schema development will tend to follow the principles mentioned by Gesell (1954), especially the central-distal principle. In general, children master sensorimotor schemas involving large muscles before they master ones involving small muscles, and they master gross-motor coordination in a particular area before they master fine-motor coordination in the same area. They will be able to roll a ball much earlier than they will be able to catch or throw it; they will learn to catch and throw a ball with two hands much earlier than they will learn to catch or throw with one hand; and they will be able to handle large balls that they can clasp with their hands and arms (without needing to use their fingers) much earlier than they will be able to handle small balls that require fine-motor coordination of the fingers.

Other developmental principles already discussed also apply to developmental changes in sensorimotor schemas across the preoperational years. Schemas at first are isolated and tentative, but they become more firmly established and mutually assimilated to one another with repetitive practice. At first, children have only sporadic success at using shape sorter toys which require them to drop blocks of a particular shape into holes of corresponding shape (triangular, circular, square). They will tend to fumble around with the blocks, using their whole hands but not their fingers separately. Their success in dropping blocks through holes more often will depend on pure luck than systematic skill. With practice, they learn to inspect the shapes of blocks and to search for the right holes, and they become more adept at getting blocks into the holes efficiently. At this point, their schemas for using shape sorters are well developed. They know how to process the shapes of blocks, search out the appropriate holes, and get the blocks lined up with the holes properly. Their skill in using shape sorters will continue to improve as their fine finger dexterity improves and becomes assimilated with other schemas used with the particular toy. Children will achieve some success in dropping blocks into holes using both hands, but they will be much more efficient at the task later when they learn to hold blocks in the fingers of one hand. This developmentally more advanced method of getting blocks into holes not only allows them to manipulate blocks for purposes of getting them lined up with holes more effectively; it also allows them to see the holes better because they are not covering their views with their other hand. This is but one example of how separate sensorimotor schemas become assimilated and coordinated into larger and more differentiated schemas.

As individual schemas are being assimilated into broader ones, they also are becoming more firmly established and better articulated and differentiated. They become more *stable* in one sense, and more *labile* in another sense.

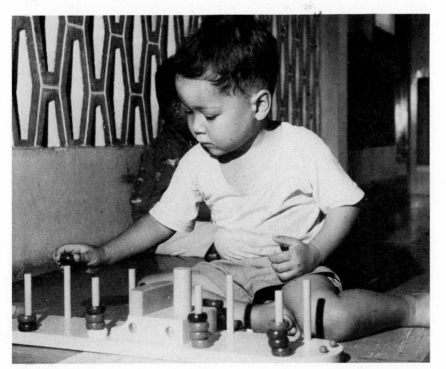

"Educational toys." This boy is carefully putting plastic rings around wooden pegs at a day-care center in Thailand. The toy fosters color discrimination (the rings are of different colors and can be grouped accordingly), shape discrimination (note the different shapes of the different parts of the toy, especially the difference between the large cylinder in the center and the small cylinders that the rings fit around), and fine sensorimotor skills (such as those involved in grasping small rings and fitting them around pegs). This particular toy has many other potential uses for cognitive and sensorimotor simulation as well, although it does not have the self-corrective features common to some educational toys. That is, although the rings will not fit around the larger peg in the center, the toy is not set up so that certain rings only will fit on certain pegs, or so that square or triangular holes correspond with square or triangular pegs, and so on. (UNICEF photo by Prathana Konsupto)

Stability increases in the sense that the schema becomes more dependable and efficient with practice, more predictable in its occurrence and degree of success, and more individualized and routinized in the way it is expressed. In short, well-established schemas start to work "automatically" in certain situations. They come to have certain stable and individualistic qualities that reflect the child's personal way of expressing the schema. In this sense, schemas become increasingly stable with development. At the same time, they become more labile in another sense. Originally, most schemas were highly situation bound. They are drawn out of the child by specific stimuli that appear in specific situations. With development, the schema becomes more and more internalized and generalizable, along the lines described above. When it reaches the point where it is internalized and generalized, the child can apply it to new stimuli to which it has not been applied before. Well-established schemas are labile in the sense that they can be transferred or applied to increasingly greater numbers and varieties of stimuli as they become established more firmly.

Although the principles involved in schema development are the same for all schemas, some schemas are much more important than others. Once they are acquired, they can be applied to a great range of situations, so that they add important dimensions to children's developing abilities to explore the environment and acquire new knowledge and skills. Many of these are universal schemas that appear in all children everywhere, regardless of culture (walking, climbing, grasping, opening, inspecting, imitating, eating without help). Such universal schemas are *learned* (they do not just appear automatically after some kind of maturational event, as in imprinting), and they show the same general developmental progressions as other schemas. They appear to be a part of the basic human behavioral repertoire, in the sense that they develop in all children regardless of environment.

Other schemas are much more specific and dependent upon specific environmental experiences or stimulation. These become increasingly important as the young child masters the more universal schemas and begins to become more and more subject to the principle of *canalization* (Murphy, 1958). Canalization is basically the "twig is bent" principle, the idea that once children's interests or abilities start down a given path, they are likely to continue down that path. With age, children's mental structures (quantity and quality of schemas) become more and more canalized. Children are born with the potential to learn anything that is possible for a human to learn (to some degree, at least), but they actually do learn only a subset of these things, depending upon the environmental stimuli they encounter and the interests they develop. Interests are partly dependent on the culture and general environment into which the child is born, and partly on the specific experiences and modeling the child encounters. According to Piaget's notion of equilibration (or some concept like it), they also are dependent on the child's own individual (and apparently unpredictable) development of specific interests and curiosity about particular things. It is clear that predictions about the development of universal schemas can be made with confidence about all children, but predictions about the development of non-universal schemas can be made with much less confidence. Depending on your basic philosophical orientation, this is either because we do not yet have the knowledge needed in order to make such predictions, or because we never will have such knowledge because people are not totally determined by their environments.

The importance *to the child* of developing some of the more important and universal schemas has been discussed by several developmental writers, most notably Havighurst (1953) with his concept of "developmental tasks." Early in the preoperational years, children are so egocentric and non-reflective that concepts like self-esteem do not really apply to them. They are much more like Piaget's "little scientist," exploring their surroundings and developing sensorimotor schemas. They continually encounter frustration, in the sense that they are unable to accomplish what they are trying to do, or are able to accomplish it only with great difficulty. However, they are not at all frustrated in the adult sense of the term, because they have not yet developed the expectancy that they should be able to do these things without difficulty or the idea that there is something wrong with them if they cannot.

The canalization principle applies even in these early years, in that children who make a few tentative attempts to do something and achieve no success at all are likely to move on to something else, whereas children who achieve partial success are likely to keep at it and try to accomplish higher goals. Even though frustration does not yet have much personal meaning, children are subject to the general law of effect: behavior that succeeds and is rewarded is likely to be repeated, while behavior which brings no results or which brings negative consequences is unlikely to be repeated.

Most schema development occurs in the everyday activities that adults call "play." As many have pointed out, *play is the child's work*. At these early ages, play is largely physical, and much of it involves manipulation of toys and materials. While in one sense children merely are playing when they build block towers, pull pull toys, use playground equipment, ride tricycles, and the like, at the same time they are building schemas. Furthermore, the largely sensorimotor schemas that developed at this time are the foundations for later cognitive schemas.

The foundation for the development of the "self" concept is laid in these early years, also. Part of this occurs through inspection of the body and observation of the self in mirrors, to form a body concept. Another part occurs in interactions with parents and significant others in the environment. Children hear definitions of themselves and hear themselves described as having various qualities. Perhaps the most significant factor in the first few years of life is the development of sensorimotor schemas, particularly the mastery of developmental tasks. Unless they have been inhibited or traumatized somehow, children normally will be curious about and interested in their surroundings, so they develop sensorimotor schemas "automatically."

Even from the beginning, but increasingly with age, certain schemas have inherent or acquired value over and above the satisfaction of curiosity. Many of them are important because they allow children to do things that the children

This youngster obviously has made good progress in sensorimotor schema development, at least with respect to climbing and manipulating the body through space. There is no hint of fear, only concentration on the task at hand. Activities such as this help foster gross motor development, and also help build schemas about the body and its limitations and relationships with respect to the physical world. (Dick Swartz, U.S. Office of Child Development)

want to do (learning to walk probably is the most important of these). Others are made important to children through formal or informal socialization. Children see that older children and adults can do certain things that they cannot do, and they develop desires to do these same things themselves. This may be reinforced if parents or significant others praise the children for progress toward development of abilities, expressing delight or satisfaction and noting that the child is becoming a "big boy" or "big girl."

These children are enjoying the opportunity to climb and manipulate their bodies through space. The play here is more associative than parallel: the children remain primarily concerned with their own climbing, but they socialize a little and enjoy imitating and talking to their friends. Later on, the social aspects of play on this apparatus may become more important to them than the physical aspects. (Photo by Myron Papiz)

These motivational factors can be helpful, especially if they are confined to positive encouragement and rewards. They provide additional incentive to master problems and develop schemas in addition to the incentive provided by simple curiosity. Children who have strong desires to master schemas because they want to prove something to themselves and/or to others will tend to persist longer and work harder than those who are practicing the schema out of idle curiosity. Many writers, notably Robert White (1959), have assigned special developmental importance to this factor, noting that young children develop needs or *desires for mastery* as part of their motivational systems if they repeatedly encounter such experiences. If attempts to satisfy mastery needs are gratified with success repeatedly, children will develop a sense of competence. They will have a growing awareness of their abilities and a generalized expectancy that they can and will learn to do what they set out to learn to do. Such early development of mastery motivation and a positive sense of self-confidence are thought to be important precursors to later development of confidence, high self-esteem, high frustration tolerance, and a generalized "can do" attitude. All of these are considered to be desirable aspects of self-concept.

Mastery motivation theory seems reasonable and essentially correct for many children, but it assumes success experiences and appropriate reactions by important others in the child's life. The development of mastery motivation and a sense of competence also has a negative side: if for some reason children encounter undue frustration and difficulty in trying to meet their goals, or if parents or significant others react to them in ways that make them think their achievements are insignificant or inadequate, they are unlikely to develop healthy self-concepts. Instead, they are much more likely to become inhibited, easily frustrated, anxious, dependent, and lacking in confidence and self-esteem. The development of schemas (particularly the more important ones labeled as developmental tasks by Havighurst) is important not only in laying the foundation for the development of higher level schemas in the sensorimotor area, but also for schemas in other areas, including self-esteem and other aspects of self-concept.

Very little occurs automatically or universally just because children encounter certain developmental tasks and acquire certain schemas. The implications of these events for the development of self-concept depend upon how they are interpreted to the children and, ultimately, on how the children interpret the events to themselves. Regardless of their absolute levels of ability, children are likely to develop self-esteem and generally positive self-concepts if they come to believe that they are capable and competent. They are likely to develop low self-esteem if they come to believe that they are inadequate and incompetent. In the early years, children lack the generalized norms and expectancies to make independent judgments of their own competency, so that they are especially dependent upon and prone to believe what they hear about themselves from others (Coopersmith and Feldman, 1974).

Before leaving the topic of the development of sensorimotor schemas, we will discuss a controversial theory that has been an issue in developmental psychology and socialization in recent years. Most observers of child development have come to agree with Piaget that the largely physical and sensorimotor activities of the young child are important, not only in their own right, but as functional way-stations in the development of later cognitive schemas. Some theorists have carried this point to a much more specific and somewhat different set of conclusions than those discussed so far. The best known and most controversial of these has been Delacato (1963).

Delacato's theory of the development of the brain and nervous system assumes, among other things, that normal brain and neural development will occur only if certain schemas appear in a specific order and are developed to at least a minimum degree of efficiency. An implication of this is that, if a schema should be skipped, or if it should not be developed to at least the minimally necessary level, difficulties will appear later because the brain's development will be distorted from its normal course. Perhaps the most widely publicized application of this idea has been the notion that certain difficulties in reading and other school skills can result from distorted development of the brain and nervous system, which in turn can result from inadequate development of particular schemas.

In particular, Delacato has claimed that children with reading difficulties have them because they did not spend enough time creeping along the floor and crawling on their hands and knees in infancy, moving too quickly from pushing and pulling themselves around on the floor to being able to stand and walk. According to Delacato, creeping and crawling help *organize* the brain and nervous system, and a certain amount and level of development of creeping and crawling is necessary to organize brain development so that it proceeds properly. This has led to remediation programs in which children having difficulties with reading (and in some cases, all of the children in a school) spend some time each day creeping and crawling, on the theory that this will stimulate brain organization or development that is or might be missing.

Several things should be said about this theory. First, it is perfectly legitimate as a *theory*. In fact, it is better than most, because it is more elaborated and specific, as well as more testable. On the other hand, critics (Robbins, 1966; Glass and Robbins, 1967) have concluded that the theory does not make neurological sense (there is much evidence against it) and that it is not backed by any empirical data (there is no evidence for it). Second, remediation programs based upon this theory have succeeded, or at least have claimed success, in remediating children's learning problems. However, the critics who have reviewed the evidence systematically have concluded that studies containing systematic data do *not* support the theory, and that studies making claims for its effectiveness do not provide convincing data to back up their claims. In short, there is no evidence of any kind favoring the theory, and there is considerable theoretical and empirical evidence against it.

What about the children who were enrolled in remediation programs based on this theory and showed improvement? No one knows for sure, but my interpretation is that good results were observed in some cases for the same reason that good results are observed in a percentage of cases involving almost any treatment: *expectation effects*. The programs are run by people who are enthusiastic about and strongly committed to the theory and treatment approach, and their enthusiasm rubs off on the parents and the children involved. Expectations are changed from "the child is inadequate and cannot learn," to "the child's problem is being solved."

A certain percentage of the families acquire and maintain these expectations

164

by virtue of becoming involved in such a treatment program. In cases where the child's difficulties in school have resulted from low self-esteem and frustration tolerance due to a history of repeated failure (rather than to any genuine biological problem), improved expectations can lead to improved motivation, frustration tolerance, and persistence. The result of all this will be real progress, which then can become self-motivating and eventually can help the child overcome deficiencies. As with most treatments that have no evidence to support claims that they work systematically or that they work for a particular reason, this treatment produces positive results in a percentage of cases because of expectancy effects. However, so will acupuncture, hypnosis, and a host of other treatments which are capable of inducing the same kind of expectancy effects. Success in a certain percentage of cases is due, not to anything inherent in the treatment, but to a change in the attitudes of the people involved. These expectancy effects are real and perhaps permanent, even though they do not occur for the reasons specified in the theory.

COGNITIVE DEVELOPMENT

As noted earlier, the development of memory and imagery make it possible for preoperational children to develop cognitive schemas which correspond to their preexisting behavioral or sensorimotor schemas. They literally internalize sensorimotor schemas to form cognitive schemas. This happens gradually and unevenly. Some children develop faster and ultimately farther than others, because of a combination of native abilities and differences in environmental stimulation. The same child develops unevenly in different areas because of specific environmental effects and because of differential interests that develop gradually under the influence of principles such as equilibration and canalization.

Early in the preoperational period, learning is heavily associationistic, like the learning of lower animals. Young children learn to associate specific, concrete stimuli with one another largely on the basis of *similarity in gross, concrete characteristics*. They also associate stimuli with responses in very specific ways. The result is that, although they learn a great variety of things, their learning is "stimulus bound" and situation bound. Connections between events which are related *logically* but not *perceptually* are not learned until later, and most behavioral schemas are learned with little or no symbolic understanding at first. Later, as cognitive schemas develop and as specific schemas of all kinds become assimilated into larger and more differentiated ones, children begin to develop logic more similar to that used by adults.

As an example of these processes, consider a specific little girl's development of counting abilities. When this little girl was about three years old, if she were asked to count, she would say "One, two, three, four, five, six, seven, eight, nine, ten, eleven, twelve, fifteen, fourteen, thirteen." This was a stable schema for a time, in that she counted out precisely these numbers in precisely the same sequence anytime she was asked to "count." Later, she corrected the order of the last three numbers. Even so, for a while there was no relationship whatsoever between what she said when asked to count and the number of objects present (if she were asked to count objects). If someone gave her only three or four objects and asked her to count them, she would count out the whole 15-number sequence. If she were asked to tell how many objects there were (instead of to "count" them), she was confused by the question and unable to respond.

At this stage, then, her understanding of "counting" was "say your number words," or something like that. Later, after she had acquired the concept of one-to-one correspondence (you sound out one number for each object, but stop giving numbers when you run out of objects), her understanding of "counting" became more similar to an adult's understanding. She now knew that counting did not simply mean emitting a list of number words, but instead it meant telling how many objects were in a group. Once she had mastered these concepts, she *understood* counting. At this point, her ability to count was limited mostly by her vocabulary of number words. For example, she might count correctly up to 19 and realize perfectly well that another number word was required for the twentieth object, but be unable to continue counting correctly because she did not know the word "twenty."

Her counting ability in specific situations also was affected by certain aspects of the objects to be counted. Early in her progress in learning to count, she could not count more than a few objects correctly unless they were laid out in a straight line and she could move her finger from one to the next (or, alternatively, if she could move them one at a time from one pile to another pile). At this point, her counting schema still had heavy psychomotor components. She had to rely on (use as a "crutch") pointing or physically handling the objects as a way to help her keep her place. If the objects were in a circle, she could not remember where she started. If they were in a formless jumble, she would be confused completely unless allowed to move them.

At still later stages, she could handle these more difficult problems without actually touching the objects, but she would point at them and use other physical movements to help her keep track of which objects she had counted and which she had not. Only several years later did she reach the point where she could count a group of objects in a formless jumble without moving her hands, the objects, or her lips. Even here, there is a limit on how many objects can be counted. Most adults cannot count more than ten or twelve objects in a formless jumble accurately. Beyond this, they have to begin lining up the objects, moving them around, or using other sensorimotor schemas used by young children.

This sequence of steps that the little girl went through in learning to count silently, relying only on visual and cognitive schemas without having to use sensorimotor ones, is typical. Different individuals go through the sequence at different rates, but most if not all go through the same sequence. Schemas that begin as purely sensorimotor schemas activated by very specific stimuli and occurring in only a narrow range of conditions gradually become more and more internalized. They end up as primarily cognitive stimuli that can be activated in many and varied situations and can be used to process many and varied stimuli. Even so, many cognitive stimuli still require sensorimotor activity under certain conditions, such as the counting example discussed above.

In general, adults frequently are able to understand a problem but unable to cope with it at the purely cognitive level. Instead, they are forced to take some kind of action (use sensorimotor schemas) in order to work the problem out. We can do relatively simple arithmetic problems in our head, but if the problems begin to get too long or complex, we need to get a pencil and paper and write out the numbers. We can give simple directions verbally, but if the directions are complex, we need to draw a map. We can apply basic logic successfully in solving simple problems in our head (If Ed is taller than George and George is taller than Jim, who is the tallest?), but if the problem becomes too involved or lengthy, we have to begin writing things down in order to keep track (if one car leaves Chicago at 2 P.M. Central Time headed for New York at 55 m.p.h., and another car leaves New York at 3 P.M. Eastern Time headed for Chicago at 42 m.p.h., how far will each car have traveled and what time will it be when they pass each other?).

These are but a few examples of what Piaget means when he says that all cognition originally begins in sensorimotor schemas, and that thought is essentially internalized action. He means this quite literally, and in my judgment he is largely and perhaps completely correct. He certainly appears to be correct concerning cognitive development in the preoperational stage.

PIAGET'S DISCOVERIES   Much of what we know about cognitive development in this period comes from the work of Piaget and those who have been influenced heavily by him and his work. Perhaps the most widely known and publicized aspects of cognitive development in the preoperational period concern *conservation* learning. It was mentioned above that the very young child's learning is situation specific and "stimulus bound." They tend to notice and make associations among mostly the more obvious and external aspects of stimuli. With age, they gradually learn to distinguish between those aspects of stimuli which are non-essential and variable (even though they may be quite striking), such as color, size, and shape, and those aspects of stimuli which are essential and *invariant*.

The foundation for all of this is the acquisition of the concept of object constancy, or the knowledge that objects exist independently and maintain their existence even when the child cannot see them. Later, children learn that certain properties of objects are invariant unless something is done to change them: length, number, weight, density, volume, and certain features common to things which all belong to the same larger category (regardless of external appearances). For example, dogs come in many different varieties, but all have four legs, fur, bilateral bodies, and other features common to all dogs (as well as certain ones unique to dogs alone). The development of *conservation* refers to the development of the concept that these essential and invariant properties remain invariant despite non-essential changes in surface appearances.

Attainment of conservation is a special case of learning to distinguish figure from ground and to avoid context effects (in which background factors change the way a stimulus object is perceived). Young children may change their judgments of the length of an object depending on whether it is next to a shorter or a longer object. Or, they may think that a set of seven objects which are spread out contains more objects than a set of ten objects which are bunched close together. Or, they may think that there is more liquid in a test tube than there is in a pitcher, simply because the liquid level in the test tube is higher than the level in the pitcher. As children overcome these sources of confusion, they learn to *conserve the essential or invariant properties of objects from one situation to the next.* Hence the term "conservation."

The conservation studies conducted by Piaget and his colleagues have become so popular in recent years that there has been a tendency to assign the acquisition of conservation and related abilities a much greater degree of importance than they appear to possess. It *does* appear true that *all* children in *all* cultures learn these invariant properties of objects, and also that they learn them in the sequence that Piaget has outlined. In a sense, they are somewhat more fundamental and important than specific cultural knowledge, especially if one wants to develop a general theory of how young children come to understand the world (as Piaget does). Other than in these respects, the acquisition of conservation of invariant properties probably is no more important than the acquisition of many other bits and pieces of knowledge.

It certainly is *not* true, as some had hoped and suggested, that acquisition of a conservation ability produces a notable "quantum jump" in general knowledge or cognitive development (Rohwer, Ammon, and Cramer, 1974). In the first place, conservation is acquired piecemeal. Some aspects of objects are conserved before others, and even within a given area, children show uneven development. Children who can conserve liquid volume in one situation may not do so in another situation, when faced with different stimuli. In addition, the rate at which conservation abilities are acquired shows only moderate correlations with measures of general intelligence, measures of school achievement, and other measures of general cognitive development (Wachs, 1975). There is no evidence that conservation ability is special or crucially important relative to other cognitive abilities. It appears that conservation has been overstressed for the same reasons that a number of other psychological concepts have: there are well-established and easy to use measurement techniques available to study it; it is identified closely with a person and a theory; and there is a rich research literature connected with it.

A number of aspects of cognitive development show sequential stages but do not fit the concept of conservation easily. For example, most children initially refer only to their mothers as "Mom," then generalize the term to include all women roughly similar in age to their mothers, and then develop a generalized concept of what a "mother" is. Usually, this concept undergoes several changes as children eliminate their confusions. Most children go through a period of confusing the term "mother" with the term "wife." A "mother" is a young or middle-aged female adult who runs the household and who lives with a "father" (regardless of whether or not there are any children in the family). This traditional finding may change in response to social changes in adult sex roles, but it still holds for most children.

Preoperational children usually cannot distinguish "father" from "husband" or "mother" from "wife." These and other familial relationships (grandparent, cousin, and so forth) are learned only gradually, and children may be eight or nine years old or older before they get them all straight. Acquisition of these and other universal conceptual schemas may be just as important as the acquisition of conservation abilities.

Another large set of cognitive acquisitions that appear to be important includes schemas involved in thinking and problem solving. Earlier it was mentioned that certain sensorimotor schemas such as walking, opening, and inspecting probably are especially important because they multiply children's possibilities for assimilating schemas to one another and for extending their fund of schemas more rapidly. The same thing no doubt goes on at the more purely cognitive level, although it is harder to see and has not been studied as systematically as conservation abilities. It would seem that abilities such as systematically noting similarities and differences, counting, systematically scanning the environment visually and/or listening carefully to verbal input, and the like, also are very important aspects of cognitive development.

PREOPERATIONAL LOGIC   One of Piaget's major contributions was to show that the thinking of preoperational children is quite logical, given their knowledge base and fund of schemas, but that it is different from adult logic because of certain *qualitative differences* in these knowledge bases and schemas. In general, children reason logically from their own experience and from their immediate observations, but they frequently reach false conclusions because their experience or the immediate situation is misleading.

Certain false assumptions and conclusions are common in children because they are quite reasonable inferences from observations and experiences which are salient to them. One of these is *animism*, the idea that everything is alive and/or that everything is caused by someone acting deliberately. Some children, when very young, believe that everything is alive in the sense that it has feelings and reactions similar to the child's own. Other children never develop the idea that everything is alive, but do develop the idea that anything that moves is alive (such as cars, blowing leaves, clouds). Later on, these children (along with other children who never had the previous ideas) may develop the idea that anything that moves is *being* moved by somebody who is doing it on purpose. Many children develop the idea that the sun and the moon, certain vehicles, and other inanimate objects that move (or even appear to move) are alive, have someone inside of them who is moving them, or are being moved in some mysterious way by someone. These animistic ideas gradually disappear as children learn to identify the essential and invariant properties of living things, and as they learn some of the ways that inanimate objects can move without human intervention.

An even more general and universal characteristic of preoperational logic is *egocentrism*. Early in life, infants cannot distinguish between themselves and the outer world. Even after they learn this clearly, their thinking is egocentric in the sense that they tend to assume that everyone else sees things the way they see them, knows what they know, and so forth. In addition to simple vocabulary problems, some of the difficulties in communication that young children experience are caused by such egocentrism. They do not realize that the listener does not always understand exactly what the child means when the child approaches and asks something like "Go now?"

Egocentrism is manifested in a great variety of ways. Children may think that the sun or their shadows are following them. They will be unable to assume the perspective of another person so that, if they are looking at a photograph, they may think that someone else who is facing toward them and looking at the back of the photograph can see the front of the photograph, just like they can (Flavell, Botkin, Fry, Wright, and Jarvis, 1968). As they learn to be able to predict when certain events will occur (nightfall, the beginning of a favorite television show, dinner time), they may come to believe that they *cause* these events to happen by *willing them*.

When children return to a setting that they have visited before, they may expect to have *precisely* the same experiences they had the last time. They may be surprised (either pleasantly or unpleasantly) to find that the movie they go to today is not the same as the one they went to a week ago, that this week's ice cream cone does not taste the same as last week's ice cream cone, or that certain unusual-looking dogs still are "doggies," even though they do not look like any of the dogs with which they are familiar.

Another aspect of egocentrism is that children speak untruths which are "lies" from the viewpoint of the adult but which are consistent with children's own egocentric views of the world. Given that their funds of schemas are spotty, tenuous, egocentric, and riddled with misconceptions, it is understandable that they have difficulty differentiating the true from the false, the reliable from the unreliable, the invariant from the variable. Early in the preoperational period, contradictions are the norm rather than the exception in children's lives. Their schemas are so tenuous that they are changed easily by new experiences. It is common for children to change their conceptions about something in a matter of seconds, or to maintain two or more totally contradictory ideas without realizing their connection, let alone their contradiction. At this stage. children have no real conception of the meanings of terms like truth and lying, so they may tell the most outrageous of "lies," such as claiming that they were not touching the cookies even though they presently are eating one and have a hand in the sack grabbing for another.

Later, when schemas have become more assimilated to one another, children develop structures that remain relatively stable and are not so easily changed by new experiences. They become much more aware of discrepancies between what they thought was true and what their present experiences tell them. If anything, they may become overly concerned with precise and total consistency at this point. In contrast to their previous lack of concern for truth, they may become truthful to a fault ("out of the mouths of babes . . .").

When "caught red-handed" doing something they know they are not supposed to do, they still may attempt to lie, but lies now will be consistent both with their cognitive structures and with their desires to please adults.

They will not attempt to deny that they have the cookies if they are caught eating them, but they may claim that they were given permission or that they forgot that they were not supposed to eat them. If they merely are caught touching the cookies without actually having eaten any, they may deny that they had any intention of eating them and claim that they were just looking at them (or give some other story that acknowledges the fact that they have the cookies, but at the same time denies the intention of disobeying the rule).

EXPERIMENTAL CHILD PSYCHOLOGY   Complementing the work of the Piagetians, experimental child psychologists influenced by the behavioristic tradition have accumulated a sizable body of information about cognition in early childhood. Initially, this was accomplished by using methods developed originally for animal research, although more recently, experimental child psychology has developed into a field of its own. Psychologists in this tradition approach the study of children very differently from Piagetians. They tend to see children as more passive and manipulable through control of the environment, but the information they collect is complementary rather than contradictory to that collected by Piagetian developmentalists.

Probably the most important general finding of experimental child psychologists has been the demonstration that *learning in the preoperational years is primarily associationistic*. In short, preoperational children are subject to almost exactly the same kinds of learning laws that apply to animals (Martin, 1975). Most of the kinds of cognitive activities that are uniquely human appear only after children become operational (this will be discussed at the end of the chapter).

A typical example occurs with *transposition problems*. Through conditioning, humans and animals can be taught that a circle of two-inch diameter is "right," while a circle of one-inch diameter is "wrong." Learners presented with this choice and reinforced for selecting the "right" alternative every time learn very quickly to select that alternative every time. Once this is learned, the transposition situation is introduced by exposing the learners to a circle of two-inch diameter (the same one that was "right" before) and a circle of four-inch diameter. Animals and preoperational children still will pick the circle of two-inch diameter in this situation, because it is *identical* to the one that was "right" before (Stevenson, 1972). In contrast, adults and children who have reached the concrete operational stage will pick the circle of four-inch diameter, because they perceive the problem as "choosing the larger one." Preoperational children respond to this problem like animals do, because *relational concepts* like smaller and larger are not yet developed in them. If they are rewarded for choosing a specific stimulus, they are likely to fixate on the precise nature of that stimulus, and to pay little or no attention to its relationships relative to other stimuli in the broader perceptual field.

In older children and adults, the properties of the perceptual field in general, and more specifically the larger vs. smaller relationships of the two key stimuli, become more salient than the precise physical attributes of the "correct" stimulus. When they are rewarded for choosing the "correct" circle in the first problem, they perceive this as being rewarded for choosing the larger circle, not for choosing a circle of a particular size. Consequently, in the transposition problem, they choose the larger circle, even though the smaller circle is exactly the same as the one previously "correct." Animals and preoperational children do the opposite.

When asked to sort or group objects and/or to explain how objects are similar or different, preoperational children make decisions on the basis of *salient physical attributes* of objects. Older children and adults are more likely to use *conceptual and logical relationships*. A young child might group pictures of apples and fire trucks together because they are red, and pictures of bananas and taxicabs together because they are yellow. An adult would be more likely to group the fruits together and the vehicles together (Sigel, 1971). Preoperational children are differentially sensitive to different physical attributes (size, shape, color, brightness, and so forth) at different ages (Suchman and Trabasso, 1966), but there is little sensitivity to conceptual or logical similarities and differences in objects until children become operational.

Similar differences between young children vs. older children and adults are seen in the number and kinds of devices used to aid memory in memory tasks. Consider the following list of words: red, cow, chair, green, horse, table, yellow, dog, couch. If adults are instructed to listen to this list of words read repeatedly until they memorize all the words, they are likely to take advantage of the fact that the words group into three clusters (colors, furniture, and animals), and to use this information in helping them to remember. As a result, they probably will be able to remember all of the words after only two or three trials. In contrast, preoperational children will not recognize these clusterings, or at least will not use them to aid memory. Instead, they will try to memorize the words in order, tending to learn words early on the list first, then words late on the list, and finally words in the middle. They usually will take many more trials to learn the list than adults will (Flavell, Beach, and Chinsky, 1966; Kagan and Kogan, 1970).

These and other experiments indicate that the young children have not yet developed their information processing and "learning to learn" skills enough to be able to use them in problem solving situations. Consequently, there are numerous problems that adults can solve that children cannot solve, because they do not yet have the needed strategies. Also, where a given problem can be attacked with any of several strategies which differ in efficiency, adults are likely to use the most efficient strategy and thus solve the problem quickly, while young children are likely to use developmentally more primitive and less efficient strategies and thus take longer to solve the problem, if they solve it at all (Flavell, Beach, and Chinsky, 1966).

The associationistic nature of young children's learning also makes them especially susceptible to "superstitious" learning. This results when a combination of events occurring in close contiguity are perceived as cause and effect, even though they may be unrelated to each other. This is the basis for much of what Piaget calls egocentric thinking. Children may observe that the clock tends to chime six times right before dinner is served. If this happens regularly enough, they may come to believe that dinner cannot be served until the clock chimes six times, or even that the chiming of the clock *causes* dinner to be ready. If they think about the matter more consistently and begin to anticipate and wish for the chiming of the clock, they may even get the idea that *they* cause the clock to chime (and dinner to be served) by willing it.

"Superstitious" learning is especially likely if children *do something imme-diately prior to a very salient event.* If they happen to look at the telephone right before it rings, they may think that they made it ring. If they happen to look up at the sky immediately prior to a thunderbolt, they may think that the thunderbolt occurred because they looked up at the sky. Most such learning is extinguished quickly and corrected through repeated experiences, although incorrect associations formed originally through such "superstitious" learning can persist indefinitely if *disconfirming experiences* are not encountered. The fear of a certain stimulus (such as dogs) can persist indefinitely because a traumatic childhood experience causes the child to avoid that stimulus in the future.

One of the most important laws of learning, originally documented at length by Skinner (Ferster and Skinner, 1957), is that responses are established more firmly and are more difficult to extinguish when reinforced *intermittently* than when reinforced 100% of the time. Associations which show the expected relationship most of the time but not quite all of the time are especially difficult to extinguish, and have the greatest potential for confusing the child. This is one reason why conservation of weight and volume are relatively more difficult and thus acquired later than conservation of quantity or length. Children are led astray by perceptual cues that not only are salient to them but also are usually (but not always) reliable.

Difficulties with weight and volume conservation often stem from confusion of weight and volume with size. This is understandable, because, in general, large objects tend to be heavier than small objects, and containers filled close to the top tend to have more liquid in them than containers filled only partially. There are many exceptions to these generalities, and children have to learn most of them one by one, through trial and error. Sometimes weight can be extremely confusing and difficult, particularly when weight differences are caused by differences in density. Consider the problem confronting children feeling the weights of two metal bars that are painted the same color and appear to be made out of the same kind of metal, but one is several times heavier than the other. Understanding or explaining this will be extremely difficult, especially when the children find out that the most typical reason for such a difference (one of the bars is solid and the other is hollow) is not correct. In fact, for a short time, when children have acquired basic conservation concepts but still do not understand the concept of density, they may reject the idea that both bars are solid (if that is the only explanation they can think of). On the other hand, if they figure out or are told that the two bars are made out of different kinds of metal, even though they look alike, they then can accept and understand the weight difference easily.

THE COGNITIVE ENVIRONMENT   Up to this point, cognitive development has been discussed as if all children went through the same stages in the same ways. Although many sequences are universal in cognitive development, the rates at which children proceed through these sequences and the ultimate forms of their cognitive structures show great individual variability dependent upon genetic endowment and differences in favorability of the environment. By now it is well known, despite American ideas concerning the melting pot, equal opportunity, and the like, that there are socio-economic status (SES), racial, urban-rural, ethnic, and other group differences in measured intelligence and achievement. This means that, on the average, some groups develop their cognitive abilities more fully than others. Some groups acquire more and better schemas, and they assimilate them to one another more completely. Such differences are difficult if not impossible to deny. For a short time, many educators and psychologists interested in group differences attributed them to differences in familiarity with the content of the tests, familiarity with tests and test situations, rapport with the examiner, and the like, implying that the differences were artifacts caused by weaknesses in the tests and in the ways that they were given rather than by real differences between groups. This led to attempts to develop "culture fair" tests that contained only items that dealt with content that children from all racial, ethnic, and SES backgrounds were familiar with, thus avoiding putting anyone at an advantage or disadvantage. Furthermore, in many studies, steps were taken to insure that good rapport with the examiner was established, and that the examiner was of the same racial, ethnic, and/or SES background as the child taking the tests. All of these efforts did not make the group differences go away. Often the group that scored lower on the standardized IQ or achievement tests did somewhat better on the "culture fair" tests, but the group that scored better on the standardized tests also did better on the "culture fair" tests, sometimes so much so that the relative difference between groups increased rather than decreased (Jensen, 1969). In short, attempts failed to eliminate differences in measured intelligence and achievement by changing the tests or the ways they were administered, and almost everyone now agrees that measured group differences reflect real differences in the cognitive abilities of the groups involved. The questions of interest now concern the causes of these differences and the possibilities for improving the cognitive development of groups who typically perform relatively poorly.

A series of arguments related to these questions was set off by a long article by Jensen (1969). In it, he reviewed evidence on and drew interpretations concerning a number of issues related to the nature-nurture controversy concerning intellectual development (see Chapter Nine). After reviewing considerable evidence, Jensen concluded that most (about 80%) of the variance in intelligence test scores is accounted for by genetic causes, and that most of the remaining 20% or so, which is accounted for by environmental causes, is caused by prenatal differences in maternal nutrition, favorableness vs. unfavorableness of the placenta and the womb, and the like. If Jensen is correct, a major implication here is that "intelligence" is essentially fixed by the genes and the prenatal environment. It follows from this that SES, racial, ethnic, and other group differences are due to differences in genes, and that the family, the school, and other aspects of the environment will not make any significant difference in children's cognitive development. Another implication is that governmental or other programs designed to improve the cognitive development of disadvantaged groups are doomed to failure from the start, because they are trying to change genetically programmed factors that are not open to environmental intervention.

Numerous studies have indicated that group differences in intellectual development do not appear until after around age two (Jensen, 1969). This is because, prior to that time, children are tested on baby tests. These tests do not test cognitive schemas, apparently because they do not yet exist in sufficient quantity or level of development to be tested accurately. Consequently, baby tests concentrate on sensorimotor schemas. Sensorimotor schemas appear to develop universally more or less regardless of the environment, so that group differences do not appear. As IQ tests begin to include more and more items that draw upon cognitive schemas, group differences appear and increase over time.

When the tests are normative, such as IQ tests or standardized achievement tests that produce scores which place people relative to others their age, *group differences increase with age*. This has been called the "cumulative disadvantage" effect, indicating that disadvantaged children fall further behind their more advantaged peers as each year goes by. The reason for this can be seen in the accompanying figure which shows two hypothetical curves indicating the growth of cognitive schemas. The curves for both children rise with age and eventually level off. However, the more advantaged child makes more rapid gains and continues to gain for a longer time before leveling off. As a result of

The differences in rates and ultimate levels of cognitive development between highly competent (A) and less competent (B) individuals. Note that the differences in rate of development cause the differences in levels of development attained at any given time to increase with age, until the curve for the more competent person finally levels off.

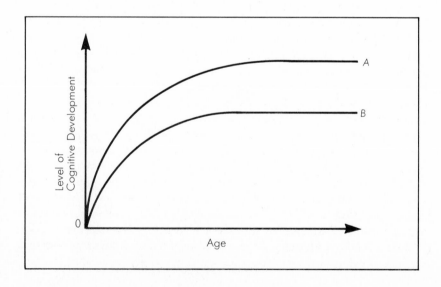

these differences in rates of cognitive development, the *relative difference* as well as the *absolute difference* between the two children increase each year. The relative degree of disadvantage to the disadvantaged child cumulates over time.

Despite the arguments of Jensen and others, I believe that these differences in rates of cognitive development are influenced significantly by differences in the quality of cognitive stimulation in the child's environment, or the nature of the "cognitive environment," if you will. There are huge differences in the cognitive environments of children raised by parents who are concerned with their children's cognitive development and have some knowledge about how to maximize it vs. children raised in homes where the parents are unaware that they can influence children's cognitive development and lack information which would tend to make the parents help foster cognitive development. These differences in cognitive environments are correlated with educational level, race, ethnicity, income, occupation of the family breadwinner, and numerous other indicants of SES or family status in the society, all of which tend to be mutually related to one another (Hess, 1970).

Of these group designations, educational differences appear to be the most important by far. Studies have shown that, once the influence of educational differences is controlled statistically, the influences of other group difference variables such as race, ethnicity, or income either disappear altogether or are reduced to miniscule amounts (Hess, 1970). Parental education is probably the best predictor and in many ways the direct cause of the quality of the child's cognitive environment. It should be kept in mind that educational level is correlated with the other aspects of familial status mentioned previously. Highly educated people, compared to less educated people, are more likely to be white than black, to be anglo-Americans than members of a disadvantaged white minority or ethnic group, to have higher incomes, to have more expensive and better homes, to live in better neighborhoods, to send their children to better schools staffed by better teachers, to work at higher status and better paying jobs, and to have more power and influence in the community. Education does not automatically bring high family status, mental health, or parenting skills, but it probably is the most important single determinant of these things. For simplicity of communication, I will discuss differences between "more educated" and "less educated" parents, although readers should bear in mind that these are group generalizations that do not necessarily apply to particular individuals. Many highly educated persons are terrible parents, and many ill-educated individuals are very good parents. Many psychologists believe that group differences in cognitive development clearly are correlated with, and are partly caused by, differences in the cognitive environments in which children develop. Further, differences in cognitive environments are due primarily to differences in the educational levels of the parents.

One important difference in cognitive environments is the sheer *quantity of interaction with adults*. In general, individuals and groups who show good cognitive development also show evidence of high frequencies of parent-child

The world outside the home. Encounters such as these provide an almost infinite range of possibilities for cognitive stimulation. Through them, youngsters can learn about such matters as the make-up of their families and the tangible symbols associated with their families (names, addresses, residence), individual and racial differences, occupations, responsibilities (this child will personally "deliver" the mail to a parent), and many more. At this stage, the child is probably most interested in the functions of mail carriers and the uniforms they wear. Later, interest will develop about more specific aspects of this particular mail carrier: Why does he wear sunglasses? What is that metal thing in the middle of his cap? What is that chain hanging down from his belt? Why is his skin so dark? Where does the mail come from? How does he know where to take it? (Photo by Herb Comess)

interaction in the home, compared to individuals and groups showing less cognitive development (Deutsch, 1965). Differences here include both the number of interactions and the nature of these interactions. In more highly educated homes, parents and children interact frequently, parents often initiate interactions, and a large portion of these interactions are social or educational in nature. In less educated homes, parents and children interact much less frequently, the majority of the interactions that do occur tend to concern disciplinary or housekeeping matters rather than purely social or deliberately educational ones, and parents tend not to initiate interactions with the child except for disciplinary or managerial purposes. Children of less educated parents may interact with them only a few times a day, and most of these interactions may involve managerial or disciplinary matters. Children of highly educated parents may interact with them dozens of times each day, and many of these interactions are purely social or involve educational stimulation by the parent. These interactions with adults are important. Frequent interactions with adults tend to foster optimal cognitive development. Over time, the cumulative differences increase, and it is likely that they have a cumulative impact on cognitive development. Prior to entrance to elementary school, for example, children of educated parents may have had many thousand more interactions with their parents than children of less educated parents, and differences are especially pronounced in the numbers of social and educational interactions that are especially likely to foster cognitive development. These differences occur mostly spontaneously, but nevertheless they are predictable from parental education and other indicators of cognitive environment. Several studies have investigated the differences in the cognitive environments of preschool children more thoroughly, and they show remarkable agreement and consistency in their findings. One of the largest of these was a study I was involved in, and examples will be given from this research (Hess, Shipman, Brophy, and Bear, 1968). These examples typify the findings of many other investigators.

The study involved 163 families divided into four groups containing 40 or more families each. All of the families were black, and they were selected because they fit into one of four categories of social status and family constellation. The study was restricted to black families to avoid confounding race with social status, a problem that has appeared in several studies which compared advantaged white families to disadvantaged black families (Sroufe, 1970). In this study, the parents in the Group A families all had at least four years of college, the mothers were not working at the time, and the fathers were employed in professional or managerial jobs. The parents in Group B all attended the twelfth grade, but did not have any further formal education. Again, the mothers were not working at the time, and the fathers were employed in white collar or skilled blue collar jobs. The parents in Group C had no more than a tenth-grade education (many had considerably less). The mothers were not working, and the fathers worked at unskilled or semiskilled jobs. Finally, Group D was composed of mothers with no more than a tenth-grade education (again, many had considerably less) and their children. There were no fathers present in the Group D homes, and the families were supported through welfare. At the time they were studied, the child of interest in each family was within three months of his or her fourth birthday. Half of the children in each group were boys, and half were girls.

This study produced a large volume of findings, but only a few of the more important and relevant ones will be discussed here. First, there were large social status differences on measures of *locus of control*, the mother's perception of her ability to control environmental events through her own efforts (as opposed to perceiving herself as powerless in the face of overwhelming forces beyond her control). The more highly educated mothers (who also tended to be the mothers who provided the best cognitive environments for their children) felt that they were wholly or partly in control of their lives, and that they were capable of reaching goals or making desired changes through their own efforts. In contrast, the less educated mothers felt that most of what happened to them was due to chance, luck, the actions of political bodies or social institutions, or other forces larger than themselves which they could not control or even predict. These differences in feelings of control vs. powerlessness extended to their expectations for their children and their definitions of their own roles as parents. Few differences were observed when the mothers were asked about their hopes concerning their children. Mothers in each group gave very similar answers concerning the kinds of education, personalities, and general quality of life that they hoped to see their children achieve. *There were no notable group differences in values or goals; there were huge differences in the degrees*

*to which the mothers felt capable of taking actions to insure that these goals
were realized or at least made probable.*

The more educated mothers felt that they could help insure that their
children turned out the way that they wanted them to by providing the
children with appropriate social and educational experiences. The less educated mothers did not perceive determining their children's future as part of
their roles. Instead, they tended to see their children's existing qualities as traits
that the children were born with or that they somehow developed independently of anything that the mothers did. They also tended to see their
children's futures as unpredictable, to be determined by events outside their
control. Less educated mothers usually were *not* aware that they could affect
their children's development significantly by providing certain experiences or
interacting with them in certain ways. Consequently, they usually did not do
so. If they did, it was because they enjoyed it or because the children initiated
the interaction, not because the mothers initiated it because they knew it was
good for the children. There was a broad, fundamental difference in the degree
to which mothers were even aware of their role in creating cognitive
environments which affect children's cognitive development.

There also were large differences even when questions were restricted to
matters that all of the mothers dealt with all of the time. This information was
determined by asking mothers about such matters as what they would tell their
children to prepare them for their first day at school, what they would do if the
child accidentally broke something, what they would do if the child did
something that was clearly wrong (such as beat up a younger child without any
particular reason), or what they would do if the child were having problems at
school because the teacher was incompetent.

Answers to the questions about preparing the child for school were scored as
"imperative" or "instructive." Imperative statements were those in which the
mothers simply gave the children orders of some kind, without explaining very
much, providing any new information, or giving a rationale for the orders
(warnings to be careful crossing the street, to mind the teacher, to raise their
hands anytime they wanted something, to remember their coats, and so forth).
In contrast, instructive statements gave the children some orientation information about school, telling them what they could expect when they got there,
why they were going, what the role of the teacher was, or how they should act
and why. Instructive responses included suggesting taking children to the
school in order to point out the route to them and generally give them
information about going to school and coming home; explaining the role of the
teacher and noting that the teacher would take care of their needs and that
they should let the teacher know if they had problems; giving the children
some expectations concerning school by mentioning that they would learn
various things there, that they would meet new friends, or that some of the
children they knew from the neighborhood would be going with them. About
half of the statements of the mothers in Group A (college educated) were coded
as instructive, and about half as imperative. In contrast, only small percentages
of the statements of mothers in the other three groups were coded as

instructive. The less educated mothers tended to "prepare" their children for school by giving them lists of orders with relatively little explanation or information. College-educated mothers tended to be aware of the need to give children information and expectations about school in addition to telling them how to behave.

Mothers' responses to the "what would you do if . . ." questions were coded as status-normative, personal-subjective, or cognitive-rational. Coding was based upon what the mother stated as her rationale for her response to her child in the hypothetical situation. Responses coded as status-normative either included no rationale at all or had only a pseudo-rationale. The latter "justified" the response by appealing to social norms (whether or not they made any sense) or to children's present status relative to other children or to people in general (again, whether or not this made any sense). Examples included such statements as "Big boys don't do that," "Good girls don't do that," "You are not old enough to do that," "You are too old to do that," and the like. Personal-subjective rationales were based on "Golden Rule" morality. They appealed to the children's own feelings or their empathy for others ("How would you feel if someone did that to you?" "How do you think Jimmy felt after you did that to him?"). Cognitive-rational rationales pointed out the relationships between children's behavior and its consequences, noting that inappropriate behavior led to undesirable consequences ("If you go around beating up people, they will think you are a bully and won't like you," "You have to be more careful; if you get careless and break things, we won't have them any more, or we will have to pay to buy new ones, and that will cost money that we won't be able to use for other things.").

About half of the rationales of the mothers of Group A were coded as status-normative, while the others were coded in one of the other two categories. Most of the remainder were personal-subjective. Cognitive-rational responses were rare and limited almost exclusively to the Group A mothers. Mothers in the other three groups had high percentages of status-normative rationales. Furthermore, when the mothers in Group A did give status-normative rationales, they tended to be verbal ones for the most part ("Good boys don't do that."). The responses coded as status-normative given by mothers in the other three groups were less likely to contain this degree of verbal explanation. In fact, fully one-half of these responses were statements that the mother would punish the child physically. In responding to questions about how they would handle typical disciplinary situations, the more educated mothers mentioned punitive methods much less often and mentioned provision of information in addition to behavioral rules much more often than the less educated mothers.

Striking group differences also were seen on interaction tasks in which the mothers were required to teach their children to do something (sort toys and blocks and explain the rationales for the sortings, and cooperate with them in drawing figures with an Etch-A-Sketch toy). Again, there were large differences in both the *quantity* and the *quality* of information given to the child on these tasks. The more educated mothers were much more likely to provide advance orientation to the children before the tasks began, giving them some expectations of what was to come and of what role they would play (this is similar to the orientation provided in the responses coded as "instructive" on the questions concerning preparing children for their first day at school). Once into the tasks, these mothers tended to make *each* separate response (sorting a block on the block task or making a line on the Etch-A-Sketch task) a *meaningful* one. They made sure that the children understood what they were supposed to do *before* they tried to do it, and they gave specific *instructions* about exactly how to respond (Brophy, 1970). On the block task, these mothers typically would ask their children to get a block and then either would describe it or see if the children could describe it themselves. Then, they would review the attributes of the group that the block was to be placed in, before allowing them to place the block. In contrast, the typical behavior of the less educated mothers was to simply tell the children to get a block and "put it where it goes." There usually was little attempt to discuss the attributes of the block before the children tried to place it. Instead, the mother would wait until the child made a response and then would give feedback.

These differences in the specificity of pre-response instructions also were seen on the Etch-A-Sketch task, even though specific pre-response instructions were *essential* on this task. The children used a knob to make vertical lines, and if a figure were to be copied correctly, it was essential that they turn their knob in the correct direction in order to make the line go either up or down, as the occasion demanded. If they turned the knob the wrong way, they would produce a short line or "tail" hanging off the edge of the figure that could not be erased or eliminated. Under these conditions, the Group A mothers told the child which way to turn the knob almost all of the time, but the mothers in the other groups told the child which way to turn the knob only about half of the time. Unsurprisingly, the children in the latter groups made many more mistakes.

Differences even occurred in post-response feedback, although they were relatively less extreme here than in the earlier stages of pre-task orientation and pre-response instructions. Even so, however, the Group A mothers generally were superior to the mothers in the other groups in providing specific and instructive feedback to their children after they made mistakes. If the child had placed a small block into a group with some large blocks, these mothers were likely to say something like "No, you had a small block and you put it with some big ones. You need to put it with some small ones." In contrast, mothers in the other groups were more likely to note that the child was wrong but to fail to provide instructive information, saying something like "No, that's not right. Put it where it goes."

In summary, the teaching styles and general interacting styles of the less educated mothers could be characterized as *reactive*, in the sense that their responses to the child primarily were just that: responses to the child. Apparently, most of the interactions that such mothers (and presumably also fathers) share with their children are initiated by something that the child says or does, or by some need which arises and calls for action (such as asking one of the children to call the rest of the family because it is time for dinner).

In contrast, the interaction styles of the more educated mothers (and presumably fathers) were considerably *proactive,* meaning that, in addition to interacting in reactive fashion when circumstances more or less forced them to react, they *initiated* numerous interactions with the children. These interactions were not in direct response to something that the child said or did or to some kind of obvious need. Apparently, these mothers initiate either because they want to for some reason or because they just do so spontaneously (but not in reaction to some direct stimulus). These include social interactions, asking children what they are doing, playing games with them, and teaching them things.

Examples from this and other studies could be multiplied, but the basic points and inferences are clear. On the average, better educated parents interact with their young children much more frequently, and they interact in ways much more likely to stimulate cognitive development, compared to less educated parents. These interactions provide children growing up in the homes of educated parents with a rich *context of meaning.* Objects and events are labeled, cause and effect relationships are explained, future activities are discussed in advance, and discipline is accompanied by instructions containing considerable information. All of these things in combination probably make a great difference in helping young children to acquire verbal schemas and to assimilate their verbal, cognitive, and behavioral schemas to one another. A greater percentage of their experiences are meaningful to them, and a correspondingly lesser percentage are seemingly random, confusing, or contradictory. The parents answer questions and provide information needed to interpret experiences meaningfully.

Children who do *not* get much of this kind of cognitive stimulation at home will be forced to figure out many more things on their own. The most probable result will be a reduced quantity and quality of development of schemas in all areas, but most especially verbal and cognitive schemas. Also, because a greater proportion of these children's experiences will be (or at least will appear to be) random and confusing, the children are likely to persist longer and in a greater variety of situations with more primitive, trial-and-error approaches to problem solving. Their development of more reflective and cognitively based problem solving strategies is likely to be delayed. They not only get a lesser quantity and quality of input from the environment, they are less likely to successfully develop "learning to learn" strategies that will allow them to acquire information on their own. These differences, cumulated over several years, can make a great difference in cognitive development.

Just how much difference remains a topic of controversy. Jensen and other nativists claim that little can be done to affect cognitive development significantly, and environmentalists contend that cognitive development is largely a product of a child's environment. As usual, the truth probably is somewhere in between. My own interpretation of presently available data is that the genes exert strong influences at the extremes of the population, while the environment exerts correspondingly greater influence on people more near to the average. Environmental manipulations, unless they are of the most extreme sort, are unlikely to make much difference in children who are biologically handicapped (such as Mongoloid or hydrocephalic) or who are destined to become all-around geniuses.

Optimal environments will produce optimal cognitive development in the first type of child, but such optimal cognitive development might be limited to simple self-care skills and recreational and work skills. These children may never learn even simple reading or arithmetic, for example. Similarly, unless subjected to extremely deprived environments for prolonged periods of time, children with extremely high genetic potential for intellectual development and accomplishments probably will actualize much of this potential despite obstacles. In any case, it seems clear that, if children already are being raised in good homes and attend good schools, any improvements that could be made in the environment would be unlikely to have a major impact.

The story is very different for more average children, especially for the typical "disadvantaged" child whose IQ is 95 or so at age four but sinks gradually to 75 or 80 by adulthood. In his famous article, Jensen claimed that early education had failed as a device for eliminating or remediating this IQ drop or the cumulative disadvantage, but the data available at that time consisted mostly of evaluations of early Project Headstart programs that were far from ideal by any criterion and had little or no structured cognitive curricula. More recent data have shown that several different projects have succeeded in producing and maintaining over a period of several years significant differences between treatment and control groups. These successful projects tend to have generally good facilities and staff, a favorably low child-to-teacher ratio, a curriculum which is structured to some degree and which contains specific learning objectives that are systematically taught to the children, and a strong parent-involvement component which at the very least enlists the good will and cooperation of the parents and more ideally enlists them as aides in the school and gives them information about how to interact with their child in the home (Miller and Dyer, 1975). Very recent intervention efforts based on the idea of teaching the parents how to raise their children (in other words, working with the parents rather than with the children, or working with both) have produced very encouraging results, although it is still a little too early to pronounce them a success (Robinson, 1975; Weikart, 1969).

In any case, it now can be stated with reasonable assurance that a good intervention program used with children whose IQ average is about 95 when they are four years old will produce children who end up with IQs averaging about 100. These same children's IQs would have dropped to 75 to 80 without such intervention. These numbers are statistically significant, but their practical importance is even more significant. A person whose IQ is about 100 very probably will graduate from high school and become a fully employed, self-sufficient "member in good standing" of our society. In contrast, people whose IQs are 75 or 80 probably are marginally literate at best, unemployed or underemployed for lack of skills, and stigmatized and dependent because they are forced to subsist on some form of welfare. Needless to say, these differences are important by any criterion.

Preoperational children use language primarily for expressing thoughts and desires. At this point, language is for socializing and communicating needs and interests, but not for thinking or problem solving. Only later, when verbal schemas become sufficiently assimilated to other schemas, can children use language for thinking and problem solving.

The development of language in young children has been studied by three main groups of investigators, each asking different questions and using different methods. The first group is primarily developmental in orientation, concerned with identifying sequences in language development and relating them to chronological age or to *developmental* events in the child's life. The second group, including most who call themselves linguists or psycholinguists, focus on the development of language structure, studying children's gradual mastery of the *structural* aspects of their native tongues. The third group, which includes myself, is mainly interested in the development of the ability to use language to communicate and to think and solve problems. The latter observers are most interested in the *functional* aspects of language, or children's abilities to use it to cope with adjustment situations. For the most part, the findings of these three groups are complementary to one another, because they have asked different questions and gathered different information. There is a certain amount of conflict, or at least apparent conflict, between those stressing language structure and those stressing language function.

Studies of the developmental aspects of language have produced much information about norms for language development and about the sequences with which different words and language abilities are acquired. Typically, the earliest language consists of labels for common objects and names of important persons, along with verbs for common actions. Common adverbs and adjectives are picked up next, along with additional nouns and verbs. In general, children's vocabularies begin with words for objects and actions that they are most familiar with and most interested in (Braine, 1976; Brown, Cazden, and Bellugi, 1969).

The first sentences usually contain only a single verb and noun, telegraphically communicating some important need ("Go play." "Eat now?"). Children now are past the point where they must rely solely on sounds of distress and on pointing and gestures to communicate their needs, but their vocabularies and general language abilities still are quite limited. Language abilities improve gradually as vocabulary expands and becomes more precise, and as they become more familiar with the structural aspects of their language, they can form increasingly more complex sentences (Dale, 1976).

New words are added to the vocabulary quite easily. In fact, it is common for even very young children to acquire a word in one trial. Most words are acquired informally simply by hearing them used by parents or others in the environment, although most children acquire some words by directly asking the names of objects. Coming to understand the specific meanings of words is considerably more difficult than simply acquiring them. Children overcome errors caused by over-generalization (any four-legged animal may be called "doggie" for a time), over-specificity ("oven" is a generic word that applies to ovens in homes everywhere, but some children think for a time that it applies only to the ovens in their own homes), confusion of polar words that have opposite meanings (large-small, ask-tell) and confusion of words that have overlapping meanings (bigger-taller-older, mother-wife-woman, behind-next to-under-over, above-on top of). These and similar sources of confusion may cause children to use certain words incorrectly for many years, although the confusion eventually is cleared up through experience.

Even if they are not confused about word meanings, children must overcome other difficulties. For example, they may know exactly what they want to communicate, but be unable to do so, for any of several reasons. Perhaps the most common reason is simple lack of relevant vocabulary. If children want a parent to get a particular toy or game which is stored on a high shelf where they cannot get it themselves, they may be unable to remember the name or to describe what they want specifically enough so that the parent can understand. This may result in frustration, or at least in a delay which results because the parent has to point to everything on the shelf and wait until the children signal what they want. Interactions like these can be vexing to both parents and children if the children are interested in something that cannot be communicated through pointing or gestures. They may want to know if tomorrow is "cartoon day," but they may confuse "tomorrow" with "yesterday" (a common occurrence). They may not know specific words for cartoon shows, so that they will have to substitute words that identify them as shows specially for them but do not provide much information to the parents. The result might be something like "Can I see *my* shows yesterday?" A perceptive parent may disentangle all of this, ultimately figuring out what the child is asking and answering the question, but often the parent and/or the child becomes frustrated and drops the matter before such understanding is reached.

Even when children do know the words they want to use, they may have difficulty using them. Generally receptive vocabulary (knowing words and understanding their meaning) precedes expressive vocabulary (being able to use the words in speech). Children may be able to recognize the word they are searching for if they hear it, but be unable to remember it themselves. This is analogous to the situation where they know what they want from the shelf but cannot name it. In this case, they will have to wait for the parent to guess correctly, so that they can nod positively. Later, children possess enough expressive vocabulary to make themselves understood.

A more advanced form of difficulty with expressive language occurs with certain syllables and words that are especially difficult for young children to pronounce correctly. Some of these are specific to individual children, while others are common, perhaps universal. Most children say "aminal" before they learn to say "animal." Many such errors are caused because children reason by analogy from their general fund of language (sheeps, throwed, runned), and because certain unusual words do not contain the sound patterns and combinations that are typical for the language (spaghetti-piskety; specific-bacific). Other words are difficult simply because they require unusual or difficult mouth manipulations in order to be pronounced correctly (statistics). These are the same words that adults have trouble with. Similar problems develop with the kinds of word combinations that are used in tongue twisters. During the preoperational years, children gradually overcome such problems and increase their abilities to make themselves understood. Developmentalists have identified stages in the development of early language and common difficulties that young children encounter in learning language.

Information of a different sort has come from those who have focused on language structure. These linguists and psycholinguists have focused much more attention on language than was given to it previously. In the process, they have developed much information relevant to child psychology, especially documentation of language learning which does not fit the "laws of learning" that behaviorists previously believed to be universally applicable to all learning.

Perhaps the best known structuralist is Chomsky (1972), who has contributed several important theoretical papers and empirical demonstrations. Chomsky argues that the human brain and nervous system is designed so that, among other things, the capacity for language learning is programmed genetically. Language learning will occur in any child simply through exposure to the language spoken by people in the environment, without any deliberate instruction or reinforcement. Chomsky refers to this pre-wired language learning capability as a "language acquisition device," or LAD. His ideas were not accepted by psychologists at first, because they implied that learning could occur without systematic stimulation and reinforcement. However, the data overwhelmingly support his conclusion that children acquire language (first receptively, then expressively) "automatically." Except for the relatively few words that children ask about or that someone deliberately teaches them, most of their vocabularies are learned simply by being exposed to language spoken by others in the environment. Furthermore, children not only acquire vocabulary, they also acquire implicit understanding of the structural aspects of their native languages. They learn how to put words together in proper combinations to form meaningful sentences without getting any particular instruction or correction. In short, they learn *language structure as a generalized paradigm* independent of particular words or sentences. This can be seen in the fact that they are capable of saying sentences they never have said or even heard before. Children may have heard all of the words in the sentence many times before, and used the words in different sentences, but they never have formed this particular combination of words together into this particular sentence before.

Children's ability to do this indicates that language learning goes far beyond the kinds of learning typical of conditioning and imitation. It even goes far beyond the kinds of new behavior that learning theorists describe with terms like "transfer" or "generalization," although a few behaviorists still claim that such concepts are sufficient for explaining language acquisition. Most observers, including most behaviorists, now acknowledge that many of the well-documented aspects of learning language structure cannot be explained by traditional learning theory concepts and probably do require a concept something like Chomsky's LAD.

One example, already noted, is that children are capable of generating well-formed sentences (that is, sentences that conform to the grammatical rules of their native tongue) even though they never have spoken or even heard these sentences before. Related evidence comes from analyses of the language errors that children make. These errors almost always fall within the "rules" of the language. For example, children might say "Tow me the ball" or "Throw me the baw" or some other variation of "Throw me the ball" which involves minor mispronunciation but which is phrased in a linguistic structure that fits the rules of the English language. They never would say things that seriously violated these linguistic rules, such as "Me ball the throw" or "The throw ball me."

Preoperational children have no explicit, formal knowledge about language structure. They will not acquire this until many years later, when they learn to diagram sentences in language arts courses at school. Furthermore, they usually have no knowledge of linguistic terms such as "noun," "verb," and so forth. Nevertheless, analyses of their language proves beyond a doubt that they have acquired language structure implicitly. The sentences children say are well formed, conforming to the grammatical rules of the language they speak, even though they may be imperfect in other respects. This is true regardless of the language spoken by the child, an additional point of evidence suggesting that Chomsky is correct in postulating a genetic mechanism common to all humans as the basis for this ability.

Further evidence of young children's mastery of language structure is seen in their ability to make language transformations necessary to communicate effectively. For example, if a young child should be told "Ask Mom if she is ready to go," he will be able to carry out this task effectively by making the necessary linguistic transformations. When he gets to his mother, he will not rotely imitate by saying "Ask Mom if she is ready to go." Nor will he address his mother with a grossly inappropriate transformation ("She ready to go?"). Instead, he will address her with well-formed sentences appropriate to the situation, such as "Are you ready?" or "Dad wants to know if you are ready to go." Behavior such as this, which is common in young children, also defies the traditional "laws of learning," because the children are transforming language instead of repeating or imitating it.

Chomsky and others now have convinced almost everyone of the validity of their basic contentions that children learn both specific vocabulary words and, more importantly, the basic structure of their language, without any systematic instruction or reinforcement (necessarily). Other aspects of Chomsky's theorizing, particularly some of his ideas about the nature of language structure, remain controversial, even among linguists.

An additional statement commonly made by structuralists is *not* well accepted. In fact, it is coming under increasing attack of late. It is a major bone of contention between structuralists and those who approach language from the aspect of function or communication ability. Reasoning from their basic findings that children learn their native language simply by being exposed to it, and from their observations (accepted here) that children eventually master the full structure of their language so that they can use any of the kinds of sentences that exist within this language, many structuralists conclude that all languages are essentially equivalent. Their basic idea is that, once children have mastered all of the structures of their language, they are capable of using their language to think about any kind of concept or problem. Different languages are simply different; there is no basis for claiming that one person's language or language ability is superior to another's. All this is perfectly logical and acceptable at the theoretical level. It follows logically that if all languages are equally useful for thinking and problem solving, and if children have mastered the full structure of their language, then any differences between languages or between individuals who speak the same language are trivial differences. Such differences would not imply that one language or individual is superior to another. This is where functionalistic studies of language come in. While the above may make good theoretical and logical sense, it does *not* hold up in practice. Studies of communication ability and other aspects of language functioning show quite clearly that some people can communicate much more effectively than others. The acquisition of a full language structure is not sufficient (although it may be necessary) to insure that people can use their language effectively to think and solve problems or to communicate efficiently (Neimark and Santa, 1975).

One line of evidence here comes from studies like the one described previously concerning social class differences in child rearing. Recall that the mothers in the study showed great differences in their ability to communicate relatively simple content to their four-year-old children. These differences did not occur because certain mothers did not have the appropriate vocabulary or language skills needed to do the job. The linguistic demands, in terms of the number and difficulty levels of vocabulary words and the kinds of sentences that were needed, were relatively simple. Nevertheless, many mothers failed to communicate even the barest essential information to their children, even though they possessed this information themselves and were capable of expressing it. Although possession of the appropriate language is a prerequisite for adequate communication, it is not sufficient by itself. It does not automatically insure that appropriate communication will appear when needed.

Another line of research which has focused on the functional use of language has been conducted by Basil Bernstein (1962) and his colleagues in Great Britain. Bernstein distinguishes between *restricted code* language and *elaborated code* language. Restricted code language is used primarily for social purposes and in face-to-face situations. It is restricted to relatively simple and often technically incorrect verbalizations, but it does the job in communicating the speaker's intentions. This is because much of the meaning being communicated is *implied* through expressions, gestures, situational cues, immediately preceding events, or prior interactions between the individuals involved. These considerations make the message perfectly understandable and appropriate in the context in which it is spoken, even though it might be puzzling or ambiguous to someone who read it printed on paper. During a conversation between two co-workers, one may say to the other, "You ready?" Depending upon the context, this may be a short form for "Are you ready to start working?" "Are you ready to stop working and go for lunch?" or any of a large number of other possibilities. Because *the individuals share the same context,* the listener understands exactly what the speaker means and will respond appropriately. There is little or no ambiguity because the preceding conversation and the general context shared by the two individuals lends much meaning to these two words that is not there when they are printed on paper out of context. Conversely, if the same words were printed on paper and people were asked to explain what the speaker was asking, they would not be able to do so with any degree of confidence. There are too many possibilities and ambiguities.

In contrast to restricted code language, where the meaning is communicated through many factors other than the words themselves, elaborated code language is stated in more lengthy (usually), formally correct, unambiguous, and *specific* terms. It is the kind of language which is used (or should be used) in scientific writing, in "how to do it" instruction books, and in textbooks. Communications phrased exclusively in elaborated code language are phrased so that *the entire meaning is communicated through the words alone,* without any dependence upon additional cues from any other source. Elaborated code language requires not only well-formed sentences with appropriate structures, but also very specific and precise statements of what is being communicated. The need for such precision in scientific communication is the reason for the development of so much scientific jargon and so much concern about precise definition of terms. Although it may be frustrating to outsiders, the use of detail and jargon usually is necessary to insure accurate and unambiguous communication among scientists.

Besides being useful in their own right, Bernstein's concepts of restricted and elaborated codes have received much attention because they seem to provide some explanation for certain differences in language development and usage between people of different social classes. Bernstein himself attributes these social class differences to differences in the communication requirements of occupational, social, and other roles played by individuals at various social class levels. People of all social classes can and do use restricted code language in certain situations and with certain people, because these situations appear in the lives of everyone (discussions about familiar, everyday things with family members, relatives, and friends in informal settings). The roles, particularly occupational roles, played by higher social class members require them to use elaborated code language much more often than do the roles played by lower social class members. Bernstein believes that the differences in these roles and in their respective requirements for language usage are the basic reasons for the social class differences in language usage: people of all social classes use restricted code language, but elaborated code language is used primarily by members of higher social classes.

Other writers concerned about social class differences in language usage accept what Bernstein has to say but believe that he does not go far enough, noting that Bernstein's statements take into account only present role demands and do not address questions like why members of different social classes are there in the first place or whether people who do not use elaborated code language often cannot learn to do so if they try. Briefly, many would argue that both social class standing and language usage are results of more fundamental causal variables such as educational level, which in turn are results of still more fundamental causal variables such as native intelligence and the quality of the cognitive environment. These writers would cite linguistic studies suggesting that some people not only do not but *cannot* use elaborated code language with any consistency or effectiveness, and that some individuals never get past Piaget's stage of concrete operations. Such individuals are unable to conceptualize abstract or symbolic materials consistently or effectively. These points will be taken up in more detail in Chapter Seven.

Many psychologists, the author among them, believe the structuralists to be correct in stating that children will master the full structure of their native language simply by being exposed to it, but I would add that the data from functionalists' research seem to indicate that mastery of the basic structure of a language is not by itself sufficient to insure that the individual can use the language to communicate or solve problems effectively. What is undeniably a reasonable theoretical possibility appears to be untrue as an empirical fact. People can and do differ considerably in their capacities to use language. Slipping into Piagetian terms, this difference can be described as a difference in the comparative development of different kinds of schemas. The mothers who were unable to communicate the block sorting and Etch-A-Sketch tasks to their four-year-old children in our study possessed the appropriate psychomotor and cognitive schemas to do the tasks themselves, but they did not possess the necessary verbal schemas (and probably also to some degree the necessary cognitive schemas needed to judge their children's understanding of the task and need for information). As a result, they were not able to successfully communicate what they knew, even though they knew it quite thoroughly.

This is not at all unusual. We all know many things at the level of psychomotor and/or cognitive schemas that we are unable to communicate effectively to others because we lack the appropriate verbal schemas to do so. In some cases, this is because the appropriate verbal schemas simply do not exist. This is the problem one is confronted with when one makes a genuinely new and creative discovery and must grope for words to describe it or else coin a new term and attempt to define it specifically enough to communicate its meaning to someone else. More typically, communication problems occur because people learn how to do things or to conceptualize things without at the same time learning how to communicate this learning to others. Mechanics who fix your car or technicians who fix your television set may or may not be able to explain to you in fully comprehensible language exactly what they did, why they did it, or how they did it. Similarly, someone who owns a car and could get you to where you wanted to go in 15 or 20 minutes might be unable to give you coherent directions about how to get there if you were asking "only" for directions instead of for a ride. It probably is easier in many if not most situations to *show* someone how to do something than to try to *explain* it. Thus, I flatly disagree with those who state that the language of different individuals is merely different and that possession of a full language structure somehow automatically enables the individual to be able to conceptualize or communicate anything and to deal with difficult symbolic or abstract material effectively. Research has shown that people differ greatly in their cognitive and linguistic abilities, and that the language abilities of some people are so poorly developed that they have difficulty communicating even the most simple ideas.

THOUGHT AND LANGUAGE

There is much interest in the relationship between thought and language, and much disagreement about the nature of this relationship. Piaget places great emphasis on thought (cognitive schemas), looking upon language (verbal schemas) as merely a vehicle for expression of thought. He does concede that language development involves acquisition of an especially important set of schemas, much like the development of the ability to walk, in that it multiplies the individual's possibilities for cognitive development. However, he does not give language the special status that he gives the acquisition of imagery and memory, which allow the transition from the sensorimotor to the preoperational stage, or the acquisition of the ability to think without concrete imagery, which marks the transition into the stage of formal operations. In contrast, certain linguists and psycholinguists sometimes talk as if thought were secondary to language.

For a brief time, the so-called "Whorfian Hypothesis" was popular. It was named after Benjamin Whorf (1956) whose writings inspired it, although the hypothesis as expressed in popular form was a gross oversimplification of what Whorf actually said, and somewhat of an embarrassment to him. In its briefest and most oversimplified form, the hypothesis stated that language caused thought, rather than vice-versa. Although this seems (and is) untenable, the idea had some popularity, partly because of its novelty and partly because certain data seemed to support it. The data were mostly anthropological findings that different societies had very different vocabularies to describe their surroundings.

Probably the most common example was that the Eskimos had a large number of words for different kinds of snow, whereas Americans had only a single word for it. If Americans want to distinguish among different kinds of snow, they have to use adjectives (heavy, light, packed, good for skiing, deep, and so forth). The fact that Eskimos had different words for these and other aspects of snow, combined with the fact that Eskimos obviously had given much more thought to snow, suggested that perhaps the quantity and quality of concepts developed about some object was a function of the number of words available in the language. Such words would indicate, and thus foster the development of perceptual discrimination of, differences in various types of the object or various conditions of the object in different situations. It is recognized that the presence of specific terms in a language *does* make it easier

Thought and Language

Recent work has accumulated impressive evidence supporting the idea that the thinking and communication aspects of language are much more important than the purely social aspects, and supporting Vygotsky's (1962) ideas about the functional importance of egocentric speech in helping children make connections between previously separate cognitive and verbal schemas. A recent review concluded that linguistic competence is necessary but not sufficient for adequate communication, and that communicating requires many cognitive skills in addition to purely linguistic ones (Glucksberg, Krauss, and Higgins, 1975). Children who communicate successfully must be able to separate relevant stimuli from irrelevant background, determine which attributes of stimuli are important, formulate a tentative message, evaluate this message to see if it sounds appropriate and is likely to be understood *from the viewpoint of a listener,* change or elaborate the message if needed, encode and transmit the message, and process feedback from the listener.

Stress is placed upon the important role of levels of development of communication skills of listeners, because these can facilitate or inhibit communication independent of the skills of the speaker. In short, it is much easier to communicate with an intelligent listener who understands all of the words spoken, picks up verbal and non-verbal cues to subtle meanings, and provides feedback which enables the speaker to know whether or not the message has been understood as intended. The communication skills of individuals acting in the roles of speaker and acting in the roles of listener tend to be closely related, and relatively independent of intelligence and social class, except among the lowest fourth or so of the population, where notably reduced communication skills are evident (Glucksberg, Krauss, and Higgins, 1975).

One example is a study by Spivack and Shure (1975), relating social class and child-rearing measures to the development of interpersonal communication skills and problem solving abilities. The authors concluded that the important SES differences were not so much in possession of language but in the ability to use it to communicate. These differences were observable not only in primarily cognitive communication situations, but also in anxiety provoking situations that led to the use of defense mechanisms. Individuals who were more sophisticated in their ability to communicate tended to use more sophisticated defense mechanisms. Furthermore, children tended to resemble their parents, both on the initial question of whether they reacted to threat by attempting to solve the problem vs. attempting to defend against it, as well as on the secondary question of what kind of defense mechanisms were used if defense was undertaken. Parental behavior seen as especially important for producing optimal development included extracting children's own thoughts from them through questioning, getting them to generate relevant solutions to problems, being willing and able to act as a catalyst, model, and guide in helping them solve problems, and supporting them when they showed skills or made decisions. Behavior seen as destructive included ignoring attempts to get help or reinforcement, criticizing or attacking children for their efforts, and solving problems for children or solving them in ways that did not encourage decision making or thought by the children.

These and numerous other recent findings suggest that the cognitions underlying expressed language are more fundamental and important than the language itself. In fact, a recent reviewer (Ortony, 1975) goes so far as to dismiss linguistics completely, arguing that its basic assumptions do not fit what we know about human psychology and that its methods and data are completely artificial. I would not go this far, because I believe that linguists have demonstrated convincingly that language is learned spontaneously without deliberate instruction or reinforcement (necessarily). Beyond this, however, I believe that it is correct to state that cognitive development is much more fundamental and important than linguistic development.

---

to note particular similarities and differences in objects. Specific terms even might foster thinking and acquisition of knowledge about the object that would not have occurred otherwise. However, in the main, the evidence is heavily against this idea. First, Piaget and others have shown rather clearly that thought ordinarily precedes language, and that much thought occurs without any corresponding language at all (for example, perceptual, motor, and/or cognitive schemas can be acquired without corresponding verbal schemas). The statement that language causes thought is simply incorrect if stated as a generalization.

Functional analyses of some of the data supporting the Whorfian Hypothesis suggest more plausible explanations. As an alternative to simply stating that Eskimos think more about snow because their language contains more words about snow, it makes more sense to conclude that Eskimos *both think more* about snow *and have more words* about snow in their language because adaptation to their environment requires careful attention to the qualities of snow. A rich vocabulary concerning snow *results* from adaptation-related discriminations; it does not *cause* them. In contrast, snow is relatively unimportant to the adaptation and general life styles of most Americans, so that there is much less need for careful attention to it, thought about it, or special words to describe special kinds of snow. Where snow *is* important, as in the case of skiers, thinking and development of vocabulary concerning different kinds of snow has progressed beyond that typical of the average American who rarely sees snow or who does not ski. I would go along with Piaget as far as saying that both thought and language probably are effects of the need to adapt to the environment and/or satisfy equilibration motivation, rather than claim that either causes the other in any ultimate sense. However, I believe that Piaget has underestimated the importance of language and its centrality to thinking.

I think the most lucid and generally valid statement of the relationship between thought and language is that of Vygotsky (1962). Basically, Vygotsky holds that thought and language are essentially separate and relatively unrelated for the first five or six years of life (in Piagetian terms, cognitive schemas and verbal schemas develop separately without becoming mutually assimilated to one another). Thought is used primarily for adaptational and equilibration purposes, while language is used primarily for social purposes and communicating needs and emotions. Young children's thought is nonverbal, and their language, although present, is not yet used for purposes of thinking and problem solving. Later, when cognitive and verbal schemas become mutually assimilated, children become able to use language for thinking and problem solving. This change is very important in making their thought processes more effective and in speeding up the general assimilation of schemas that is involved in moving from the preoperational to the concrete operational stage.

Much evidence supporting these ideas was accumulated by Vygotsky himself, and more has been accumulated since by others (Kohlberg, Yeager, and Hjertholm, 1968). Most of it concerns the nature of the preoperational child's egocentric speech. First, the egocentric speech of young children increases for a while, then peaks, and then decreases and largely disappears. Second, there are certain constant differences in the quality of egocentric speech, depending upon whether it is early, middle, or late in the development curve. Early egocentric speech is typical of the speech shown in children involved in parallel play (children playing in close proximity and *apparently* in communication, but actually preoccupied with their own concerns). Their speech mostly expresses whatever is on their minds. It is essentially social, serving little or no problem solving function. As the children get older, their egocentric speech becomes less typical of social speech and more typical of *inner speech*, the kind of speech we use when we talk to ourselves, especially when thinking or problem solving. Egocentric speech changes from purely social to clearly problem solving in focus. For example, during sand play, children early in the egocentric speech curve might make random statements about their sand castles and about other things going on in their lives. There would be no particular relationship between anything said and anything done in the process of building sand castles ("I've got a new shovel . . . I got it for my birthday."). Late in the egocentric speech curve, the children involved in sand play would be talking and mumbling to themselves, giving themselves directions about what to do next in the process of building the sand castle the way they wanted to build it (". . . more water . . . bigger window . . .").

Observations like these led Vygotsky and others to reject Piaget's notion that egocentric speech is nothing more than another example of children's *general* egocentrism during the preoperational stage. Instead, Vygotsky saw egocentric speech as a *functional stage*, marking the transition from thought and speech as separate and unrelated systems to the assimilation and coordination of cognitive and verbal schemas. Children talk to themselves during this stage to give themselves directions for the same reason that they use their fingers in counting: they need this sensorimotor activity as a reinforcement or "crutch," because their cognitive schemas are not yet developed well enough to allow them to think silently without such props. As their schemas do develop, they have less and less need to spell out everything they are thinking, so they begin to mutter and to use short, telegraphic phrases similar to adult inner speech. These take the place of the full sentences (typical of social speech) that they used to use. As schemas develop further and become more assimilated, they no longer need to do even this, because they now are able to *think in words*, to "talk to themselves" in inner speech as a way of thinking. At this point, thought and language no longer are separate systems. Now they can be used in tandem, and this acquisition of the ability to use language for thinking and problem solving greatly increases the quality and efficiency of the child's thinking and problem solving. A developmental observation that adds to the force of this argument is that brighter children tend to go through this egocentric speech cycle earlier than duller children, and also to move into the stage of concrete operations sooner (Kohlberg, Yeager, and Hjertholm, 1968).

Clearly, egocentric speech is *not* mere childish rambling. Just as children's play is their method of perfecting their sensorimotor and cognitive schemas, their "egocentric" speech is their method of perfecting their verbal schemas. As this progresses, the need to verbalize out loud decreases, as does the need to verbalize in complete sentences. This reflects assimilation of verbal schemas into larger schemas that can be activated with only one word instead of a string of words, as well as assimilation of verbal schemas with cognitive and sensorimotor schemas. Once the process is completed, children have much more powerful and well-integrated sets of tools for thinking and problem solving, and they are well on their way toward moving into the period of concrete operations.

BECOMING OPERATIONAL

When children move out of the preoperational stage and into the stage of concrete operational thinking, they begin to acquire and use logical reasoning abilities just like those used by adults. This was recognized long before systematic child psychology existed by theologians and philosophers who spoke of children attaining "the age of reason." Once this stage is attained, children no longer show much of the egocentrism and other common aspects of the thinking of preoperational children. Their experiences, formal education, and language development are not the same as those of adults, but children at the stage of concrete operations reason logically in the same ways that adults do. The only difference is that they require the presence of concrete physical props, or at least the mental imagery of past experiences with such props, as the basis for reasoning. They will not be able to deal with purely abstract matters that require reasoning without concrete objects or the use of imagery until and unless they enter the stage of formal operations.

So many different things happen and are involved in the process of becoming operational that this stage transition cannot be attributed to the attainment of just one or two key schemas, as is the case with other stage transitions. However, a number of important changes can be identified. Perhaps the most important one is that children's mental structures (that is, their existing sensorimotor, cognitive, and verbal schemas which are developed and assimilated to one another in varying degrees) become firmly established, internally consistent, and well integrated. Most or all of the problems of identifying the necessary and invariant properties of the environment and separating them from the accidental and varying properties have been worked through, so that reasoning is now not only *logical* given children's assumptions but also much more often *correct* (because their assumptions are correct). Furthermore, as this *structure gains stability and reliability*, it is less and less easily swayed by a single experience which conflicts with previous ones. Instead of changing schemas quickly and without much questioning in response to an unexpected new input, children may question the unexpected input to find out if there is an explanation that makes it comprehensible in its own right and yet at the same time consistent with their previous experiences. In short, mental structures now are stable and reliable enough to enable children to begin to trust their own judgment about what "must be," even if some new experience seems to challenge these expectations. Children still accommodate, of course, but they no longer accommodate "automatically" if a new experience conflicts with what they expect. Instead, they will investigate the matter systematically to try to eliminate inconsistencies and incongruities.

Part of this process, and another important part of becoming operational, is the assimilation of schemas into the larger cognitive units that Piaget calls *logical operations.* Among other things these include understanding of fundamental logical relationships and mathematical operations. Children not only acquire these cognitive abilities, they acquire them to the point that they are *reversible*. They can reason both backward and forward in a chain of logic to make decisions about what answer is correct or about what should happen in a given situation. The combination of stability in mental structures in general and the ability to use logical operations (including reasoning with reversibility where appropriate) makes them likely to reason correctly. They no longer are so susceptible to the kinds of errors that they used to make in the preoperational stage. In the past, an adult who pinched off a piece of clay in a conservation experiment could fool children by making them think that one of the two balls of clay weighed more than the other after their shapes were changed. Children in the concrete operational stage no longer are fooled by this trick. They will not decide that they were wrong in their conclusions. Instead, they will decide that a trick is being played on them, or that there is something unusual or strange about the clay. In any case, they will not give up their fundamental understanding of the fact that mass does not change if nothing is added or taken away.

The ability to reason backward and forward through such logical sequences means, among other things, that henceforth their cognitive structures will be relatively stable and permanent, less susceptible to change from the influence of a single event. It also means that, for the first time, children will be highly susceptible to the principle of *cognitive consistency*, so that when they do encounter discrepancy between their expectations and their observations, they will tend to take actions to investigate and remove these discrepancies.

A host of other changes in children's general cognitive structures appear about the same time that children become operational in the Piagetian sense.

When they encounter problems that they used to be able to solve only through developmentally primitive mechanisms, they now solve them more quickly and easily using developmentally more advanced mechanisms. They no longer show much production deficiency either. In contrast to the past, when they possessed knowledge receptively but were unable to use it expressively when it would have been helpful, they now can use it when it is helpful and thus can solve more problems more quickly and correctly. The assimilation of sensorimotor and cognitive schemas with verbal schemas described by Vygotsky takes place around this time, too, so that children now can use verbal processes to assist in or even to carry out cognitive reasoning processes. At first they may have to do this literally out loud, talking to themselves, but gradually they will learn to do it silently, using inner speech.

Children also acquire a number of "learning to learn" schemas at this time, and develop a general interest in learning for its own sake. A large proportion of their questions will be "why" questions, reflecting their attempts to resolve apparent inconsistencies and fill gaps that remain in their cognitive structures. The "cute" questions of earlier years tend to disappear, because children no longer make gross errors due to gross misconceptions or false assumptions. They now begin to ask very difficult questions, including some that have no answer because even adults do not know how to answer them.

This process coincides with the beginnings of formal schooling (approximately), and once children learn to read, they can vastly expand their input through reading about things that are not in their immediate environments. The result is a large addition to their funds of sheer factual knowledge, and the new input also triggers a number of questions about matters that they were not concerned about or even aware of previously (geography, history, politics, and so forth). All children will tend to master the universals identified by Piaget in the process of moving into the stage of concrete operational thinking. What schemas they acquire in addition to these fundamental universals will depend upon their environments (both their physical environments and their cultures). Within this, their gradually individualizing interests will take shape in response to unique experiences, discovery of special talents and abilities, or the internal factors that Piaget describes as equilibration.

Direct experience, especially experience that involves physical manipulation of the environment, still is a primary factor in learning, even after children enter the stage of concrete operations. However, they now can reason correctly in response to problems presented to them verbally, provided that the problems deal with familiar content that lends itself to the use of imagery. Once basic logical operations are mastered, children's reasoning follows the same logic as that of adults, although children differ from one another in degree of development of these abilities and number and variety of stimuli to which they can apply them successfully.

Piaget sees these differences as more quantitative than qualitative. Bright and dull children use essentially the same kinds of cognitive operations. The difference is that brighter children can use them more quickly and more efficiently, can use them more consistently when they are appropriate (in other words, they less often show production deficiency), and can use them in relation to a wider range of stimuli and a somewhat higher level of difficulty of stimuli (presumably because of more stimulating experiences and richer cognitive environments).

SUMMARY

The preoperational stage begins when children develop the ability to use mental imagery and retain it in their memories. This allows them to accumulate knowledge in a way that was not possible before, and to reason logically without being totally dependent upon the presence of concrete objects to manipulate and observe. The logic and general mental structures of preoperational children are qualitatively different from those of older children and adults. Schema development is spotty and uneven, so that there are many gaps in the cognitive structure and it contains contradictory elements that may not be cleared up for some years. Perhaps the most salient trait of preoperational children is their egocentrism. Their perceptions and thinking focus solely on their own subjective experience. They cannot put themselves in the place of others, tending instead to believe that others see things the same way that they do. Preoperational children also are "bound" by specific stimuli and situations. Well-established perceptual and sensorimotor schemas dominate newly developing cognitive schemas for several years, until children gradually learn to differentiate the stable and invariant aspects of the environment from the unstable and variable ones.

Eventually, as more and more schemas become assimilated to one another, preoperational children become aware of and eliminate the gaps and contradictions in their cognitive structures. One result is the achievement of stable and internally consistent structures. This brings with it the development of more adult-like logic, featuring reversibility, or the ability to think backward and forward through chains of cause and effect reasoning. Another result is the development of the need for cognitive consistency, so that surprising events which might have been accepted with little notice or concern in the past become causes for concern and curiosity. This provides motivation for learning through exploration as well as the possibility for maintaining distorted perceptions through defense mechanisms. Toward the end of this period, when children finally become operational in their thinking, their logical reasoning is similar to that of adults. However, lacking formal operations, they are dependent upon the physical presence of concrete stimuli or at least mental images of such stimuli to support their thinking. They cannot yet handle purely abstract material. The sequences through which children progress are universal, but the rates at which they progress and the ultimate forms that development takes are dependent in part upon the quality of the environment, particularly the quality of the cognitive environment provided through stimulation from parents, teachers, and other adults.

Fostering Physical and Cognitive Development in Young Children

Probably the most important thing for adults working with preoperational children to bear in mind is that, although these children think logically and have a great interest in and aptitude for learning, they have not yet acquired the knowledge base and logical operations that the adult has acquired. Consequently, they think differently and often do things or ask questions that can be confusing or frustrating to the adult.

THE CHALLENGE OF SOCIALIZING PREOPERATIONAL CHILDREN

Fostering optimal development during early childhood is a complex and difficult task. First, it is *time*-consuming. It means spending many hours with children, reading to them, playing games with them, answering their questions, inspecting and making comments upon their latest discovery or accomplishment, and the like. Second, it involves continuous responsibility and *availability*. In contrast to contact with other adults, which usually can be scheduled at mutually convenient times, children need attention or information *now*. This includes times when a tactful adult would not dream of imposing. Young children are *not* tactful. They cannot and will not be for several years, because being tactful requires sophisticated knowledge about people and situational factors that make some behavior appropriate, other behavior inappropriate, and still other behavior appropriate in some situations but not in others. Young children have learned little or nothing of this yet, so that they will become upset and mystified, but not enlightened, by a rebuff such as "Can't you see I'm busy?"

Finally, trying to carry on a productive relationship with young children is often an unusual or unnatural burden to the adult. Adults who are willing and theoretically able to have a productive relationship often have difficulty because of the limited ability of young children to "hold up their end of the conversation." Unless they interact regularly with young children or with handicapped individuals (blind, deaf, and so forth), adults usually are unaware of the limitations of their own communication abilities. Because most adult communication is between individuals who share a common language and a rich network of mutual understandings about people and the environment, it is relatively easy for adults to make themselves understood to other adults in an everyday conversation. Listeners usually know the meanings of all of the words that speakers use, so that they are easily able to comprehend what speakers *mean* just by hearing what they *say*. If the listeners are not sure, they can clarify by asking a question or two. Adults who expect to be able to carry on this kind of conversation with young children are in for a jolt. They will find that children frequently do not understand them, or that the children get different meanings from what the adults said than the meaning intended. Such communication failures will often remain unknown for a time, because children will not do anything to indicate that they do not understand. They may even nod or give some other indication that they *do* understand. On those occasions when children do make clear that they do not understand and try to clarify by questioning, both they and adults may be frustrated by the children's inability to find the right words with which to express themselves or to make the adults understand what they want to know. Experiences like these can be frustrating, and some adults end up responding by avoiding children if possible, rationalizing that "talking to children is a waste of time." While these reactions to frustration are quite understandable, they also are quite unfortunate. Interchanges with adults probably are the most important environmental events determining cognitive development in children.

Adults can interact with children enjoyably and productively, but this requires some experience and the use of a different style of communication than that used with other adults. Instead of an equality arrangement, in which all participants "hold up their ends of the conversation," most of the responsibility for "holding up" conversations between adults and children falls with the adults. They must go out of their way to adjust their cognitive and linguistic levels to take into account children's ability to understand. They also must be on the alert for communication failures and be ready to try to diagnose and remedy them (if possible) by taking unusual steps to make themselves understood or by careful questioning to clarify what the children know. Adults must do all of this for the simple reason that children cannot. Consequently, if a conversation between an adult and a child is to continue for any length of time without communication failures, it will be up to the adult to see that it does. These and related points will be discussed in detail throughout the chapter. For the moment, however, we will turn to the area of physical growth in early childhood and its implications for socialization.

Because physical growth is so determined by genetics, there is little that adults need to do specifically other than provide adequate nutrition, exercise, clothing, and sleep. Beyond this, adults probably are best advised to respond to physical changes in children by enjoying them and by sharing in the children's delight at attaining new milestones. Adults are unlikely to go wrong if they *accept children for what they are,* and if they *fight the temptation to apply age norms and worry if children are "below average."*

RESPONDING TO YOUNG CHILDREN'S PHYSICAL GROWTH

Accepting children for what they are is vital, even more so with regard to physical features than with regard to personality or behavior. This is because physical features are determined genetically and cannot be changed significantly. Adults who are disappointed or feel cheated because children did not turn out the way they wanted them to turn out physically are reacting to something which cannot be changed and which the children did not cause. There is nothing to be gained and much to be lost if the reaction results in the rejection of the children or in low child self-esteem because children are made to believe that something is wrong with them. Physically, children are what they are. Psychologically, they are products of their genes *and* their environments, and there is much that adults can do to optimize development here.

No warning against inappropriate concern about age norms could be phrased too strongly. Failure to understand what age norms do *not* mean, along with a tendency to apply them inappropriately, is by far the most common mistake that adults make in dealing with young children, *especially* well-educated adults, who "should" know better. This is one reason why age norms have been minimized in this book, despite their interest value and popularity in other books. Age norms can do more harm than good, and this will continue to be the case until we discover a way to present norms to people that will enable the information to be used appropriately and overcome what appears to be a strong psychological tendency to apply the norms inappropriately.

Perhaps a good place to start would be to note that, by definition, half of any population is "below average." We all want our own children and our relatives' children to be above average on *everything,* and we do not seem to understand that this is wildly irrational. Some parents want to be able to point to a long list of positive qualities in their children in order to take credit for them. Even where such feelings are less selfish, they still are inappropriate. Almost all children have strikingly uneven patterns of scores and relationships to age norms, being considerably above average in some qualities, average in others, and considerably below average in still others. This is not merely a fact of life that must be accepted because it is true; it is true because of the very nature of the norms themselves. As soon as you measure children on *any* trait and provide a set of *norms,* you automatically have classified half as "above average" and half as "below average." The children are the same whether or not the norms exist, but they may not stay the same if parents or others important in the environment become concerned about them being "below average" and communicate these concerns. The tragedy is compounded by the fact that age norms are virtually useless for predicting eventual adult status on the basis of relative status in the early years. Except for unusual conditions caused by biological disorders, it is of absolutely no importance when children get all of their teeth, are large or small, learn to walk or ride a tricycle, and so forth, relatively early or late, compared either to general age norms or to the children of relatives or neighbors. It simply does not make any difference.

PHYSICAL NEEDS   Young children need adequate exercise, both to promote physical growth and to promote the development of sensorimotor schemas. Ordinarily, they will get this exercise spontaneously in the process of engaging in the kinds of large muscle play described in Chapter Five. As far as is known, there is no special kind of play or exercise which is specially important or essential to optimal development. There is no point in trying to get children to play with certain toys or to engage in certain kinds of activities because they are "good for them." Activities such as running, jumping, climbing, riding, playing hide and seek, using playground equipment, and many others probably all are equally useful for getting physical exercise.

For the sake of variety, it probably is good for children if the family can provide opportunities to use different kinds of play equipment, such as a sandbox, swings, slides, monkey bars, tricycles, and the like. If these cannot be purchased, they can be used at public parks, but adults will have to make time to take the children to the park. Children can and will find plenty to do in an "empty" lot, and they will convert such materials as crates and boxes, old tires and inner tubes, sticks and pieces of wood, and other materials that adults do not look upon as toys into play materials if they are available. Children who do not have access to manufactured equipment will manufacture their own, to some extent. Nevertheless, manufactured large muscle play equipment which is purchased or used at parks probably is physically good for children. In any case, they will enjoy it.

NUTRITION   Providing for children's nutritional needs involves some familiarity with the basic food groups and the principles involved in balancing diets, as well as adaptation to the children's unique eating habits, as described in Chapter Five. The importance of providing balanced and nutritious diets can be seen in changes which have appeared in countries where diets have improved significantly. A generation or more ago in the United States and Western European countries, and more recently in Japan and other countries, improvements in diet have led to significant improvements in physical health and growth patterns. Children grew to be two or more inches taller and correspondingly heavier than their parents or grandparents. Some of the credit for this goes to preventive medicine, but mostly it is due to improved diets.

Those concerned with purchasing and preparing food for families in general and young children in particular should acquaint themselves with the basic nutritional principles important for dietary planning. This is an area in which misinformation is common. Some of it is obvious nonsense (such as carrots are especially good for the eyes, spinach is a necessary and especially valuable vegetable). Usually, though, the problems of misinformation are more subtle. Most people grasp the basic ideas that a balanced diet is important to general health and that imbalances can lead to susceptibility to diseases, stunted growth, or obesity, among other things. However, there is a tendency to think of balanced diets on a meal by meal basis, instead of using somewhat larger time units, such as days or weeks. Although it is important for young children (or anyone, for that matter) to get appropriate amounts of each of the basic food groups on a regular and continuing basis, this can and should be done without resorting to overly restrictive or unnecessary diet rules. For example, there is no single necessary food. Many foods, such as milk, are especially nutritious and thus important to the basic diets of most people. However, some individuals (relatively more blacks than whites) are physically allergic to milk, and others simply do not like the taste. These people can get the same benefits they would have gotten from milk by consuming other dairy products and other foods that are more acceptable to them and at the same time provide the same nutritional benefits that milk provides. It would be inappropriate to require all children to drink a certain amount of milk per day or per meal, and it would be inappropriate to require some children to drink any milk at all. All of this is equally applicable to any other *particular* food. Nutritional balance is achieved in any of a great number of ways. There are no simple rules and no rigid quotas of certain "necessary" foods. As long as the children's diets meet general nutritional standards, it makes little difference what specific foods they eat or when they eat them.

Young children often need to eat more frequently than adults because they burn more energy but have smaller digestive tracts. Snacks between meals or even five or six small meals per day are ideal for some children. Many nutritionists believe that this pattern would be ideal for everyone. Our familiar three-meals-a-day pattern is an historical accident of social evolution in Western cultures. There is nothing inherently appropriate or biologically ideal about it. However, once we have become thoroughly socialized to it, it becomes a strong psychological force, causing us to automatically get hungry at "mealtimes." Adults should bear in mind that this does not apply to young children. There is no reason why they "should" be hungry at times when adults have learned to be hungry. Learning to be hungry at culturally established mealtimes requires socialization (distortion, if you will) of naturally occurring biological rhythms. It is not difficult to learn, but it usually develops only gradually over several years. If children say they are hungry, they probably *are* hungry, regardless of the time of day or the time since they last ate. If children say that they are not hungry at mealtime, they probably are not, so that forcing them to eat is comparable to insisting that a satiated adult have a third helping. Children will have to be socialized gradually to the eating patterns of the family, through such methods as reminding them about mealtimes and providing briefer and less filling snacks when they request a snack shortly before a meal. Gradually, they will learn to adjust their eating cycles to those of the other members of the household. This will take time, however, and it will not necessarily succeed fully with all children. The eating habits of some households may be so out of phase with the hunger cycles of certain children that the children never adjust to them completely.

Adults also should bear in mind that children's tastes will not necessarily match their own, and that tastes will change over time. One cannot assume that children will like a particular food just because their parents like it, and it is futile to attempt to convince children that it "tastes good" when their taste buds tell them otherwise. Children may go through phases of wanting to eat a certain food regularly for some time, and then lose taste for it to the point that they do not want to eat it at all. Such children will find the argument that they should eat something "because you always liked it before" to be incomprehensible, and they will be right. Adults also should remember that *they* determine what the family eats, based upon *their* own likes and dislikes. Unless forced to eat non-preferred foods due to economic hardships, adults tend to purchase and eat foods that they like and avoid foods that they do not like. This should be taken into account when children protest that they do not like something.

Children's vitamins can be useful, although ordinarily they are not necessary if the child is getting an adequate diet. Parents should follow the advice of their doctor here, studiously ignoring television ads, sales pitches based on scare tactics, and claims by relatives or acquaintances that certain vitamins are extremely important because they will promote growth or because they are "natural."

In addition to their own spontaneous taste reactions, children will be guided by the behavior of their parents and others in the family in their reactions to foods. If others' behavior communicates the expectation that the food will taste good, children will expect it to taste good, and vice-versa. Children will pay much more attention to the eating behavior they *see* than to the verbalizations directed at them, and for good reason. Parents who do not eat a particular food themselves should not even attempt to get their children to eat it if they say that they do not like it either. Conversely, parents are wasting their time if they try to tell children that they "won't like" a food that the parents obviously relish. The children will not believe this until they taste the food themselves and form their own opinions. Furthermore, having observed the parents, they will taste it with the expectation that it will taste good. Combining these two mistakes, parents can get themselves into a double bind by insisting that children eat a food that they dislike in order to get to eat a food (usually dessert) that they like.

This is a special application of what behavior modifiers call the "Premack principle," a restatement of the basic law of reinforcement that is useful in behavior modification applications (Premack, 1965). The principle states that a low frequency behavior (in this case eating a disliked food) can be increased if it is made contingent upon the opportunity to indulge in a high frequency behavior (in this case, eating desired foods). The principle clearly works in the short run, both in general and in the case of getting children to eat foods that they do not like by withholding dessert until they do. At least in the case of food preferences, it typically results in the children being somewhat resentful of the whole situation, developing a deeper loathing for the disliked food, and coming to over-value dessert to the point where it becomes their primary interest and concern about every meal. This problem will disappear or at least minimize in time, as the child comes to appreciate a variety of foods.

In summary, it is important that children have balanced diets that meet basic nutritional principles. There are no single crucial foods and no single balanced diet. Diets can be balanced in an infinite variety of ways. It is pointless at best for adults to criticize children's eating habits for the wrong reasons. Mealtimes should be for the enjoyment of the food and for pleasant conversation. They should not be battlegrounds featuring continuous arguing and coercion about food.

Socialization concerning nutrition is best accomplished through a combination of good nutritional planning and the modeling of good eating habits by adults. Accommodation to children's needs for smaller but more frequent meals can be done through nutritious snacks of grain products, cheese, fruits and nuts, juice and milk, and fresh vegetables (but not TV-promoted junk foods that provide lots of calories and sugar but little else). Between-meal snacks can be reduced and gradually phased out as children become accustomed to eating just at "mealtimes."

CLOTHING   If the family has the resources, they can simply purchase whatever clothing children need when they need it. If the budget is a problem, parents will need to keep in mind the sporadic growth spurts of children in planning the clothing budget. Young children grow at such a rapid rate, but grow so unevenly, that clothing purchases for later use are chancy at best. It is not wise to "stock up" by purchasing a large number of items at children's present sizes, since they may not be at that size much longer. This is especially true for more expensive items such as "dress up" outfits that young children rarely wear anyway. Underclothes, socks, and everyday play clothes will be used regularly, and these will need to be on hand in quantity. Ordinarily, it is best if they are somewhat loose-fitting, partly because they will last longer as the child grows into them, and partly because tight clothing is restrictive and uncomfortable. Of course, this should not be carried to the point that children are wearing clothes several sizes too large for them.

Shoes are a particular problem, both because they are relatively expensive and because a good fit is especially important. It probably is in this area that it is most vital for parents to resign themselves to the realities of children's growth rates. Unfortunately, it is the norm, not the exception, for children to

206

go through shoes quickly (active children can wear out even a good pair of shoes in three months or less). It is also frustratingly common for children to be fitted carefully for a pair of shoes and then end up wearing them only a few weeks because they enter a growth spurt and the shoes become too small. It is *not* a good idea for parents to buy large sizes and wait for children to grow into them, because foot growth can be impaired by ill-fitting shoes. About all parents can do here is resign themselves to the situation and make the best of it, taking care not to do or say things that might make children feel guilty about having outgrown shoes before they "got the wear out of them."

PHYSICAL GROWTH AND THE SELF-CONCEPT   Children are keenly interested in their physical size and appearance, and they will ask many questions and make many comments about it. Adults should respond to these with accurate information but with care to see that they foster self-acceptance and the development of positive self-concepts. Sheer experience and information can be gotten through looking in the mirror, measuring with a yardstick or tape measure (and perhaps marking off height on the wall every six months or on every birthday), getting on the scale and weighing, comparing hand and foot sizes, and so forth. Children find these activities interesting and enjoyable for their own sake, and in addition they help build their fund of information about themselves and other people.

Young children usually are full of questions about what they are going to be like in the future. Will a boy be as tall as Daddy? Could he get even taller than Daddy? When will he be that tall? Why doesn't Daddy keep getting taller? Why is Daddy taller (or shorter) than Mr. Schmidt next door? When he is as tall as Daddy, will Daddy be as small as he is? These are just a few of the questions typically asked by children concerning physical growth and their own size relative to parents or others in their environments.

Parents should answer such questions factually and matter of factly. This is especially important when children ask questions about whether they are "below average." The children may not understand the implications of such questions because they have no idea of norms or averages; they just will want the information. Consequently, parents should provide it in a normal and natural way, without giving any indication that they do not want to answer the question, that the topic is unpleasant, or that the whole thing is a "big deal." Children generally will accept themselves for what they are spontaneously, unless they are taught that there is something wrong with them. It is not necessary to tell children flatly that they are inadequate because they are ugly, too short, and so forth. The same effect can be accomplished inadvertently by well-meaning adults who try to "protect" the children by giving them reassurance "Yes, you are short, but don't worry about it. People who make fun of short people are ignorant. You don't have to feel bad just because you are short." Such "reassurance" might be appropriate in certain circumstances, such as if the child had expressed concern about being short. Where no such concern was present, a reply like this to a simple question about height could *create* concern. Such an over-reaction by an adult would tell the child that being short was a "big deal," perhaps something to be worried about or ashamed of.

In summary, information given to children should be as accurate as possible, so that their self-concepts will be as accurate as possible. Meanwhile, the problem of self-esteem will take care of itself if they are accepted implicitly for what they are. Self-esteem problems may come up, however, if the adults create them, either directly by criticizing or rejecting children, or indirectly through well-meant but inappropriate attempts to "protect" them from knowledge about their "inadequacies." Unless children have some clear-cut handicap (such as blindness), and unless they show some concern over being "below average" on some measure or ability, it probably is best not even to mention the subject.

Achievement of many psychomotor schemas, particularly the universal ones, occurs automatically as a result of normal, everyday activities. Adults can be helpful here by providing attention, encouragement, and praise as children acquire and "show off" new abilities. Such positive responses will help speed up and solidify the development of mastery motivation and a sense of competence. Comments which call children's attention to progress they have made over time are especially useful ("Look! Jeanie put the puzzle together all by herself!"). In contrast, comments that praise children but do so by calling attention to their performance relative to that of other children should be avoided, because these may lead to jealousy and related problems. Compari-

**FOSTERING
PSYCHOMOTOR
DEVELOPMENT**

Mastery and achievement. This boy is past the stage of mere exploration with the blocks. Industry and determination show on his face as he concentrates on testing his limits. Assuming sufficient success, the goals he sets for himself will continue to become more and more complex as he masters the easier ones. (Photo by Myron Papiz)

sons with others tend to socialize children toward competitiveness against others, rather than toward striving for mastery for its own sake. Much of the foundation for so-called "intrinsic" motivation (which actually is learned, of course) is laid in the reactions by parents and significant others to children's early accomplishments. If these early reactions cause children to develop the generalized schema that problem solving and goal striving situations are enjoyable in their own right (partly, but not only, because they lead to success experiences in the end), the children are likely to develop the qualities that we call "intrinsic" motivation.

In addition to providing the freedom, opportunity, encouragement, and praise for the development of psychomotor schemas, there are many more specific actions adults can take, especially for stimulating the development of non-universal schemas that are important in a particular culture or important because the adults and/or the children are interested in them. For most children, motivation to learn something new is present more or less continually. The problem facing the adult is one of matching new learning tasks to children's present readiness, providing appropriate materials, and, in some cases, providing modeling and instructions.

AN EXAMPLE   Readiness can be judged by observing children's present activities. Consider puzzles, for example. Puzzles are useful manipulative stimuli for developing a variety of sensorimotor schemas, and they are available in numerous varieties and difficulty levels. To introduce children to puzzles, begin with very simple ones. Those constructed for two-year-olds usually are made of wood, contain only four to eight pieces, and are designed so that each piece is a complete object (person, animal, and so forth). To introduce the puzzle, show it to the child (describing it as a new and enjoyable toy), and demonstrate how to use it. The demonstration should involve slow and deliberate movements that the child can easily follow visually, coupled with careful instructions. Stress any key terms that will help link verbal labels with pieces of the puzzle, and describe the physical operations conducted in the process of putting it together.

Adults might begin by showing the child the puzzle while it is still intact, describing the picture shown on it. Then they could explain that a puzzle is a picture that you take apart and put back together again, and proceed to demonstrate how to do so. The demonstration (and accompanying explanations) should feature such essentials as making sure that all of the pieces are right side up, indicating that you have to look back and forth between the puzzle outline and the pieces to figure out where a given piece goes, modeling how to pick up pieces and drop them into place, and demonstrating how to rotate a piece in order to get it lined up properly. Because you are dealing with a two-year-old and not an adult, the task is much more difficult than it seems. The puzzle should depict something familiar if the child is to know which side is "right side up." If it does not, the child will have great difficulty mastering even this step. Children may have considerable difficulty even if the picture *is* familiar.

One problem may be simply the seating arrangement. Children seated across a table or on the floor across from the puzzle will benefit little if at all from adult attempts to talk about lining up the pieces so that they are right side up. This is because they will be looking at the whole operation upside down, and will not be able to mentally put themselves in the place of the adult and "see" the situation the way the adult sees it. In contrast, most adults would be able to do this. Children must be seated next to the adult, so that *both have the same perspective* in looking at the puzzle during the demonstration.

There are many ways that the actual construction of the puzzle can go wrong. Many adults make the mistake of putting in a single piece and then inviting children to repeat or to attempt to put in another piece themselves. This is premature, confusing, and probably somewhat uninteresting to the children. Instead, adults should put together and take apart the puzzle several times, so that the children get clear concepts of how you "make the picture" by putting all the puzzle pieces in place together. Children's motivation for working on the puzzle is likely to be much stronger once they have this idea.

Even if children want to work the puzzle and have a general idea of what to do, there probably will be numerous problems when they do it. Lacking the perceptual development and fine finger dexterity of adults, they are likely to reach for a piece and try to put it into place using both hands (effectively blocking out their vision). When they release the piece, they are likely to put it almost anywhere in the puzzle, perhaps even turning it over so that it no longer is right side up.

These and numerous other possible difficulties will have to be worked out through repetition, demonstration, and verbal instructions, often given while guiding the child's hands on initial trials. These should help children make connections between different sensorimotor schemas ("You have to line it up just right over the hole, so it will drop in") and between sensorimotor schemas and cognitive schemas ("Now, where does the tail go?" "Put the wheel in the place where the truck has a wheel"). Eventually, it should be relatively clear whether or not the child presently is "ready" for the puzzle. When children *are* ready, they will maintain interest and will learn at least enough to enable them to work on their own. In turn, this will enable them to learn more through trial and error. If they are not ready, they soon will lose interest in the adult's attempts to get them to try to put pieces in the puzzle frame. They may begin to fuss or physically move away because they have become interested in something else. If things like this happen, put away the puzzle and try again a month or two later.

On the other hand, if children are ready for the puzzle and begin to work at it, they gradually will increase their skills in using it through trial and error, eventually reaching the point where they can put it together quickly and efficiently. At this point, they are ready for a more difficult puzzle involving more and smaller pieces, or more difficult pieces which are parts of objects in the puzzle rather than complete wholes. The adult will not have to go to such lengths in presenting new puzzles, because the child now has acquired several general schemas about the nature of puzzles and what one does with them.

Nevertheless, it will be helpful to build interest by pointing out that this is a newer and more difficult puzzle (for "bigger kids"). Adults probably should let children try the puzzle on their own at this point, although they should observe carefully to make sure that the puzzle is not too difficult and should provide encouragement and praise as the child begins to show success.

This extended example concerning puzzles is representative of what adults need to do generally in providing manipulative stimuli, modeling, and instructions in order to foster their development of sensorimotor schemas in preoperational children. The general principles are: present children with materials they seem ready for; provide complete demonstrations with rich accompanying verbalizations; gradually phase in child responses, providing physical guidance or other help when necessary; phase out physical help but continue to provide verbal guidance and encouragement as the children begin to catch on; gradually let them take over by themselves and praise them as they show consistent success and generally "get the idea." If they make no progress at all and seem uninterested in the new object, put it away for a while and try again a month or two later. In general, match experiences and opportunities to children's present states, letting them proceed at their own paces. Particularly in the sensorimotor area, attempting to speed up development by trying to get children to do something before they are ready is almost certain not to work (Gesell, 1954). Further, such experiences are likely to be frustrating to both adults and children.

LARGE MUSCLE DEVELOPMENT Adults can do much to encourage the development of sensorimotor schemas by providing children with a variety of manipulative stimuli and with special equipment that will enable them to do things that they could not do otherwise. Young children cannot do much with marbles or small balls, but they can handle large, light balls such as soccer balls or rubber utility balls, and most children enjoy playing with them. Two- or three-year-olds who are too young for tricycles will enjoy wheel toys that they can sit on and push. Later, they will enjoy small tricycles designed for use by three- and four-year-old children. At this point, they are capable of operating pedaled vehicles, but have not yet developed the fine motor skills and coordination required to successfully operate large tricycles or bicycles.

Climbing toys such as playground sets and monkey bars are invaluable, because of their multiple uses. Children not only climb and manipulate their bodies through space on them, but they can use them for imaginative play, for crawling under and through, and for many other favorite activities. Large plastic toys with holes in the center large enough for children to crawl through or climb inside also have this multiple purpose capability. Most parks have such equipment, and it can be purchased for home use where budgets allow. The same thing can be achieved with cartons and boxes, too (although refrigerators or anything else that has a lock and involves the danger of children locking themselves in must be avoided).

SELF-CARE SKILLS Adults can do a lot to help children help themselves by providing the right kinds of materials and equipment. Most children are more than willing to assume personal responsibility for eating, dressing, getting out and replacing toys, and other daily self-care responsibilities, if adults encourage them, make it possible for them to do so independently, and do not nag them.

Concerning meals, for example, once children are past the stage where they must be lifted into high chairs and either fed completely or heavily assisted in eating, they can and will manage most of the tasks involved in eating on their own if given certain help. A booster chair or even an ordinary chair equipped with some kind of safe and effective booster adapted from materials from around the home will enable children to graduate from high chairs. This will eliminate dependence upon the parents to lift them into high chairs and get the high chairs properly assembled, and it will make them feel less like babies and more like "big people" who sit in regular chairs.

By providing unbreakable dishes and utensils, and by seeing that the utensils are both large enough and dull enough so that children do not hurt themselves eating with them, adults can both encourage and make it easier for children to feed themselves. They still will need to have cutting done for them, but they will be able to handle most foods with spoons and forks if they have the right kinds of utensils and if they are seated in front of their plates.

Concerning care of personal possessions, children can be helped through such methods as providing stools or short step ladders for them to use to get up to the sink to wash their hands and brush their teeth (although adults probably will have to assist until the children are about four years old, and may have to monitor them for several years more). Children can manage going to the bathroom if they have potty chairs that they can sit on and clothing that they can get off by themselves. They can hang up their outdoor clothes if hooks in closets are placed low enough for them to reach. They can take out and put

Mother and son frolic at the pool. Obviously, this is an opportunity for both of them to enjoy themselves and each other in a common activity that involves lots of physical contact. In addition, through modeling and explicit instruction, the mother familiarizes the boy to water play and, later, to swimming. (NFB Photothèque/Photo by Ben Law)

away many of their toys if they are stored in containers that they can handle and are placed on shelves or other storage space low enough for them to reach. Storage of balls and other items difficult to keep on shelves is helped by providing a toy box.

FROM SENSORIMOTOR TO COGNITIVE SCHEMAS   Sensorimotor schemas that are important in their own right but also are important because they underlie later cognitive schemas can be facilitated through providing children with toys and other equipment appropriate to their ages and levels of development. For example, two-year-olds can (and are very much likely to) play with pounding benches that allow them to use hammers or mallets to pound plastic or wooden pegs through holes. They will repeat this activity over and over again, sometimes for hours. Children whose motor development of the hands has progressed a little bit beyond this will enjoy peg boards involving tapping pegs into small holes with a hammer that has a smaller head. Still older and more developed children will enjoy working with child tool kits or even with regular tools, pounding real nails into boards. At first, children will simply pound away, but as they get older and more skilled, they will become interested in and capable of creating primitive but credible versions of ships, airplanes, and other objects of interest to them.

Three-year-olds and even some two-year-olds will enjoy playing with toys involving large plastic screwdrivers and large plastic screws. At first, about the most that they can do is screw and unscrew, although later they will be able to use screws and bolts (both plastic) more functionally to fasten things together and perhaps to make things. Just as with hammering, as their skills develop they will be capable of more difficult tasks involving smaller screwdrivers and screws. Gradually, they can make the transition between plastic, child-oriented toys to the use of real screws and screwdrivers. This can be done not only with manufactured toys such as erector sets, but also with ordinary screwdrivers and screws used in various construction projects.

The precursors of later writing skills can be stimulated by providing young children with chalk boards and chalk and/or sets of thick crayons that they can use with coloring books or blank paper. They will need writing instruments like chalk or thick crayons at this stage, because they will not yet be able to handle thin crayons, pens, or pencils. They will tend to grasp writing instruments with their whole fists, and "write" by making global motions with their whole arms, rather than just their fingers. The ability to manipulate a thinner writing instrument by holding it between the thumb and only two fingers, and the ability to make fine writing movements using just the hand and forearm, do not appear until much later. Two-year-olds are capable of scrawling on chalk boards or paper with chalk or large crayons, but they will only break thin crayons or pencils, because they do not yet know how to hold them properly or treat them with appropriate delicacy.

As abilities develop, children acquire more differentiated motor skills. They can hold and manipulate writing instruments with greater efficiency, and they graduate from mere scrawling to more deliberate copying (copying letters and numbers, copying their names, tracing). Still later, they will be able to work dot-to-dot puzzles (after they also have learned their numbers) and pencil mazes (after they have learned the spatial concepts involved in following a path from start to finish). Once they have learned how to form certain letters efficiently through repetitive copying, they will be able to print their names and other words of their own choosing if adults help by telling what letters to make.

Examples could be multiplied, but the basic principles remain largely the same. In each case, children move from gross motor movements which are fairly primitive in intent and actuality, and which involve manipulation of large-scale objects, toward more purposive and cognitive tasks, which involve manipulation of smaller-scale objects and the use of fine motor skills. Adults can stimulate such development by presenting new toys in ways that create or enhance the child's enthusiasm for them, by demonstrating how to use the equipment and providing the child with help if necessary, and by maintaining an encouraging posture and praising noteworthy accomplishments. It is important that adults let children *"do it themselves,"* as much as possible. Enjoyment that leads to persistent practice is primary, much more important than "doing it right." Efficiency will come with practice, but children can be "turned off" if pushed too hard or too fast or if relegated to a passive role by adults who take over activities themselves because they lack the patience to let children make mistakes and learn. In coloring, for example, children will not stay within lines or use the "right" colors at first. So what is wrong with green faces?

Always keep in mind that development is gradual and cumulative throughout the early years, but it also is uneven and punctuated with regressions. Regressions can be frustrating, but the only sensible response for adults is to remain encouraging and to help if necessary by repeating rules or demonstrations. Given the newness and uncertainty of so many schemas, it is not at all uncommon for children to be unable to do today what they could do efficiently yesterday. Although such regressions occasionally will be deliberate (see next chapter), usually they will occur spontaneously, because the schema involved was not established nearly as well as the adult thought it was. The wise adult is resigned to and prepared for such regressions, looking upon dealing with them as "part of the job" of child rearing.

FOSTERING COGNITIVE DEVELOPMENT

Most of what has just been said about fostering sensorimotor development also holds for fostering cognitive development, although in the cognitive area there are many more specific things that adults can do to stimulate specific development or even to teach particular cognitive schemas. Once again, though, the general quality of the adult-child relationship is much more important than any isolated, specific actions that adults may take. A child who already is well along the way toward development of high self-esteem and a desire for competence and mastery in the sensorimotor area probably will develop these same kinds of positive motivational systems in the cognitive area. Adult encouragement and availability, positive expectations and positive responses, and modeling of desired behavior remain vital. Key steps in stimulating children to become interested in new areas, such as presenting them with new challenges and providing instructions if they show interest and aptitude, also remain vital.

LEARNING THROUGH PLAY   Many cognitive schemas are acquired through play. Adults can assist this process by providing children with a variety of stimulating toys. Many of these will be so-called "educational toys," although many toys that carry this label are not particularly helpful, and most any toy has educational value of some sort. Nevertheless, most educational toys do appear to "work," in the sense that they do foster the development of sensorimotor schemas and, eventually, related cognitive schemas. For the young child, such toys will develop the sensorimotor schemas involved in fine sensory discrimination and motor coordination (shape sorters, puzzles, peg boards, self-correcting toys requiring the child to match or compare objects correctly). As would be expected on the basis of work by Piaget and others, toys that allow or require the child to make some kind of *discrimination* and *manipulation* and then get *feedback* are especially valuable.

Young children can be introduced to letters and numbers through play long before they are able to read or count or even understand what these symbols are. Sets of numbers and/or letters come in a variety of types of materials, and they can be used for matching or manipulation exercises. So do building blocks with letters or numbers. One useful and flexible letter and number toy consists of a metal tray painted to resemble a chalk board and a set of letters and numbers containing magnets. The magnets allow them to stick to their painted outlines on the tray or to stay in place when children put them on the lower

If it wasn't clear already, this boy now realizes that his plastic wheel toy has many things in common with complicated mechanized vehicles used by adults. At the moment, he is preoccupied with observing a particular part of the machinery, but it is likely that he will observe many different parts and note similarities and differences between his vehicle and the motor bike before he becomes bored with this fascinating stimulus. (Frank Siteman/Stock, Boston)

part of the tray if they are trying to spell something. The letters are big enough for children to see clearly and to manipulate (about two inches high, an inch or more wide and ¼ inch thick), but yet small enough so that all 26 letters and all 10 numerals can fit easily on the tray.

Children typically begin by playing with letters and numbers for their own sake—poking them, inspecting them, feeling the force of the magnet as it pulls them toward the tray, stacking them, rotating them in various spatial positions, learning to fish the magnet out of its compartment and put it back, finding out what else the letters will stick to besides the tray that they come with, noting that the letters and numbers will stick to one another as well as to the tray. These and a host of other insights are just as important to the young child as learning to use the toy "the way you are supposed to use it." Later, they will be ready for and interested in some of the activities useful for building familiarity with numbers and letters. These include learning the names of the letters and numbers, learning to recite them in order, learning to match each letter or number to its proper outline on the tray, learning the sounds of the letters, and, ultimately, learning to use the letters to "spell" words. The words should be names of familiar people and short words that the child is familiar with and interested in. As they are spelled out, the adult should touch each letter and pronounce its name, finishing by giving the whole word ("There, D, O, G, DOG!").

The Functional Value of Play

Developmental psychologists have long considered play to be "the child's work." By this they mean that play not only provides recreation and enjoyment for children, it is the primary method by which children explore and learn about their environments. Piagetians in particular long have stressed the importance of play, especially exploratory play motivated by curiosity, as an important mechanism fostering cognitive development.

More recently, investigations have accumulated additional evidence favoring this point of view. The work of Kohlberg, Yeager, and Hjertholm (1968) on egocentric speech during play has been described in the text. Moore, Evertson, and Brophy (1974) observed the free play of children attending kindergartens, and found that, contrary to the assertions of some psychoanalysts, solitary play was positively related to maturity and generally healthy development. Only a very small percentage of the solitary play observed could be classified as indicative of inhibition, immaturity, or other undesirable characteristics. Furthermore, about half of the solitary play that was observed was goal-directed constructive play that appeared to have functional value for fostering cognitive development.

Smilansky (1968) found that both interpersonal play with other children and imaginative solitary play in which children acted out dramas involving interactions with real or imaginary characters appear to have functional value. This kind of play seemed to both reflect and to a degree mediate cognitive development generally and linguistic skills in particular.

These findings were extended by Rubin, Maioni, and Hornung (1976), who observed the free play of middle and lower class preschool children. In general, the middle class children were more advanced than the lower class children in nature and variety of play. They showed more associative-constructive play and more cooperative-dramatic play than lower class children, who showed more solitary play involving mere repetition of motions and more parallel play. More of the play of the middle class children was interpersonal or at least verbal in nature, and more of the solitary play they engaged in involved constructive or exploratory activities rather than simple repetition of sensorimotor schemas.

Taken together, findings such as these illustrate how play can be either a solitary phenomenon reflecting internal equilibration needs or an interpersonal and social activity, and how it can be both an external indication and a functional cause of level of cognitive and linguistic development.

Depending upon the children's levels of comprehension and interest, such activities can progress to more complex ones, such as having them name words that they would like to see spelled out or having them imitate by getting the letters and spelling the words themselves after they watch an adult do it. Similar games can be played with the numerals, using important numbers such as the home address or telephone number and the ages of various members of the family.

A detailed listing of useful educational toys, grouped according to appropriate ages, is given by Dodson (1970). Any of these toys should be helpful in stimulating the cognitive development of young children, especially if adults take an active role in the play process.

In addition to providing toys and play materials that children can manipulate, a second major method of stimulating cognitive development through play is through the use of games. Many very simple table games in which pieces are moved along the game board according to the dictates of a die or spinner have been designed specifically for use with young children. Children find most of these enjoyable, and such games help stimulate cognitive development. Such games inherently involve number recognition, colors, counting, observation of who is ahead and by how much, using concepts such as following a particular path and moving the piece a particular number of spaces, and reacting with appropriate happiness or displeasure when good or bad things happen. These and all of the other aspects involved in playing such games can be made into learning experiences for children if adults remain appropriately aware of their potential and capitalize upon it through effective modeling and instructions. In the case of very young children, this will mean almost a continuing "play-by-play" announcement of events as they occur, because, until and unless they learn the game, children literally will not know what is happening, even though they are sitting there watching. The game will have meaning to them to the extent that the adult is successful in *making it meaningful.*

Once children grasp fundamental numerical and spatial concepts, they are capable of playing numerous table games and card games with adults, sometimes with a little help, and sometimes with no help at all. Very simple games like "Old Maid" can be played with three-year-olds, and games like "Concentration" and "Crazy Eights" can be played with four- and five-year-olds. Often, the biggest stumbling block in these games is not the children's concepts of the game and how to play it, but their ability to hold the cards in their hands and manipulate them without dropping them. Sometimes it is easier to allow them to keep their cards behind some kind of screen, but leave them on the table or floor rather than try to hold them. In addition to being enjoyable experiences shared with adults, games help children learn numerical and spatial concepts, and, where strategy is involved, help them develop the ability to think ahead and to make reasoned strategic decisions.

EDUCATIONAL EXPERIENCES   In addition to toys and games, adults can stimulate cognitive development by exposing children to educational experiences in and out of the home. As always, the most valuable ones are those which involve direct, concrete experience, especially ones which involve the opportunity for the child to make some kind of behavioral response.

One type of educational experience is a trip to a zoo, museum, or other public place of interest. Such visits will be very special for young children, and their educational value will be enhanced because they involve direct, immediate experience rather than the more vicarious kinds of experiences they can get through books or television. The cognitive meaning and value of such experiences can be maximized if children are prepared for them *ahead* of time by being told what they will see and do, if the adults provide continuing commentary and explanation about what is going on *during* the experience itself, and if they stimulate memory through questioning the children and reminiscing about it *later.* Such experiences, especially family vacations or one-time-only trips to see or do something special, often remain as high points of children's early lives, providing many important and happy memories for them. They also help broaden and correct their funds of schemas. For example, most children are confused about the sizes of some animals, because of the differing pictures that they see in books or on television. A trip to the zoo, where they get to see the genuine articles, will change this. An opportunity to visit a place that is geographically different from anything that children are accustomed to will broaden their vistas and provide unforgettable experiences such as playing on a beach and swimming in an ocean or very large lake; leaving the city to visit the country, or vice-versa; being up on high mountains and scenic overlooks; hiking or camping in the woods; going up to the top of tall buildings and looking out over cities; riding trains, airplanes, buses, or subways; or visiting an amusement park that has roller coasters and other "thrill" rides. These and similar experiences produce not only pleasure but a wealth of eye-opening experiences and a desire for more information.

Things which are less unusual or costly but which involve personal, firsthand experience also are important (firsthand physical contacts with animals; opportunities to try things that they see parents and other adults doing; tasting new foods; performing household chores themselves or helping adults perform them). Usually children already have the cognitive schemas involved in these activities from having observed adults perform them, but, like learning to eat with a spoon, some firsthand experience and practice is needed before they can successfully accomplish behaviorally what they know they want to do conceptually.

MODELING AND IMITATION   Most children spontaneously imitate adults, especially their parents, and wise adults will capitalize upon this by allowing children to learn things through imitation. Adults can facilitate this by remaining aware of their status as models, maximizing the effectiveness of this modeling by allowing or even inviting children to observe, letting them sit where they can see everything clearly, using slow and perhaps exaggerated movements so that they can more easily see what is going on, and providing a "thinking out loud" type of running commentary on what they are doing in order to make it more meaningful to the children. This kind of modeling can and should be done with virtually any household chore, routine or special. Where possible, children should be allowed to help. With some kinds of chores, such as drying dishes or repairing machinery, it will not be feasible to let them

With the help of a homemade prop (the hat) and some imagination in directions, this activity (*below*) can not only teach something about baking cookies, but can foster identification with adults and adult roles, the sense of personal accomplishment and satisfaction, and many other aspects of development that are cognitive or social-personal, not just sensorimotor. (Dick Swartz, U.S. Office of Child Development)

do the task themselves. They might be allowed to manipulate some of the materials with careful supervision. Children can watch and hear what is happening in any case. With other chores, such as straightening up a room or raking leaves from the lawn, children can participate actively according to their interests and abilities. As they get older, certain chores, particularly responsibility for taking care of their own toys and belongings, can be assigned to them on a regular basis.

PRESCHOOL EXPERIENCES   Cognitive stimulation can be provided through preschool experiences in addition to (but hopefully not instead of) those in the home. A good preschool will be equipped with the kinds of toys and manipulative equipment that usefully stimulate child development in all areas, and will have teachers skilled at working with children and developing their unique potentials. On the whole, enrollment in a good preschool generally is a beneficial experience for a young child. It is neither the threat to proper development nor the panacea for all ills that certain extremists, either opponents or enthusiasts, have claimed.

Until fairly recently, many children were placed in preschools like Project Headstart, to try to improve the child's cognitive development, or they were placed in preschools because the mother worked and needed some form of care for her children during the day. Lately, attendance at preschool has become almost universal across all social classes. This is true even in families where the mother does not work and does not have other young children at home. Children from such families often are sent to preschools for reasons having to do with either their own development (opportunity to meet and play with other children their own age and to get stimulation and experiences broader than what they could get at home), or their mother's well-being (to get the child out of the house for part of the day).

A good preschool should be defined not by its physical plant or tuition rates, but by *the competence and orientation of the staff*. Is the school a pleasant place to visit? Are the staff friendly and at ease with parents, and favorable toward parent visitation? Are the children playing in harmony and happiness and/or participating actively in planned activities? Do the staff seem to enjoy the children, and to enjoy their jobs generally? Is there a general absence of negative signs such as fighting, crying, passive withdrawal, destruction of property, and disruptive outbursts? Is the child-to-teacher ratio small enough so that the teachers can adequately care for all of the children in their rooms without undue difficulty? Are the premises free of safety hazards or other signs of thoughtlessness or neglect? If the answer to all of these questions is "yes," the school is a good one, regardless of its tuition, the paper credentials (or lack of same) of its staff, or its philosophical orientation (Montessori, cognitively oriented, oriented toward the promotion of social and personal growth, oriented toward simple provision of high quality day care featuring play activities). If the answer to one or more of these questions is "no," and especially if the answer to several of the questions is "no," the school probably is not a good place for a young child to be, regardless of its paper credentials.

In selecting a preschool for their child, parents should personally visit

This boy (*on the opposite page*) is beginning to make the transition from purely childish play to more adult-like activities. Here, he uses adult tools and materials to work on a "real" sawing task which is part of a larger and equally realistic construction task. He is not ready to handle all of this from beginning to end on his own, but he can do a great many parts of the task if adults provide the proper guidance, safety precautions, preparation of materials, and general instructions. The finished product is likely to engender tremendous satisfaction and the proud claim, "I did it myself!" (Dick Swartz, U.S. Office of Child Development) possible schools and get firsthand answers to such questions. Parents should never rely upon indirect information, especially when the information deals with a school rather than a specific teacher. Often a neighbor will provide high praise for a particular preschool, but actually it is only one teacher, and not the school as a whole, that is being praised. Unless they are certain that their child will be assigned to the same teacher who taught their neighbor's child, parents are asking for trouble by enrolling their own child in a school solely on the basis of such a recommendation.

Preschools are of no great importance to the *cognitive* development of children who come from homes where the parents continually do a good job of fostering their child's cognitive development themselves. Children from such homes will *not* show notably improved IQ's or other evidence of improved cognitive development due to attendance at preschool. Attendance at preschool may be an enjoyable and beneficial experience because of its social nature and the opportunity it provides for meeting new friends and for learning to function as part of a group. It also broadens the child's world and provides variety and companionship.

Even the best parents and children probably are better off if they are separated from one another for several hours each day than if they are together constantly. By getting away from one another regularly, they will minimize the degree to which they "get on each other's nerves." They automatically will have more to talk about during the time that they do spend together. Formerly, when most children had many siblings and when the nuclear family was surrounded by the extended family, this was much less of a problem. Now, when families are small and living apart from their relatives, it is easy for children and their parents to see too much of each other for their own good. Preschools are one mechanism that society is developing to deal with this problem.

Parents should take a careful look at claims that preschool experiences will have significant impacts upon their children's cognitive development, and they also should ignore claims that particular preschools or other preschool experiences are "necessary" for normal or optimal cognitive development. Such claims are not uncommon of late, given the stress that has been laid on the early years as the basis for the development of general intellectual functioning (Bloom, 1964). As noted previously, it does seem to be true that children coming from homes where they are not getting very much cognitive stimulation will be helped to some degree by a preschool that has a good curriculum, competent teachers, a favorable child-to-teacher ratio, and a good parent involvement program. Even here, however, effects will be relatively modest, not phenomenal.

Just as a few extremists have argued that preschool attendance is vital or mandatory for good cognitive development, other extremists have argued that preschool is a threat to the child's normal development, is undermining the fiber of family life, or even is a Communist plot. This also is nonsense. Because the issues involved are more social-emotional than cognitive, they will be taken up in the following two chapters.

Structuralists have demonstrated that children acquire full language systems merely by being exposed to their native tongues, so it follows that there is nothing in particular that parents need or should do to foster language development. In one sense, this is true. The receptive and expressive oral language that children acquire will accurately reflect the language spoken in their homes and neighborhoods. Where such language is homogeneous, they will learn to talk just like everyone else around them. Where children are raised in bilingual or bi-dialectical environments, they either will learn each of the languages or dialects to which they are exposed, or, more probably, will acquire a mongrelized hybrid, in which elements of each are mixed into a unique blend. By itself, this is not very important, because the only thing that counts is the child's ability to communicate with other people. It is important to the extent that society at large makes it important, even for a young child. It becomes more important later, when the child enters school and begins to learn written language and to hear distinctions made between what is "approved" language and what is not approved language.

During the preschool years, it is much more important to stimulate children to use language regularly for communicating (and thus to speed up their desires and abilities to use it for thinking and problem solving), without being much concerned about language form or grammatical correctness. The vast majority of problems that young children show in pronunciation and grammar are *developmental*—they are characteristic of a certain age or stage of development. They appear spontaneously and then later disappear without any deliberate or systematic intervention by parents or anyone else. Since such developmental phenomena will disappear of their own accord anyway, they should be sources of enjoyment, and not of concern, to adults.

Incorrect language can be corrected through modeling the appropriate language, and eventually the child will catch on. It is not usually worth the effort to call special attention to problems or to "drill" children in the correct ways of speaking. They will correct problems themselves after sufficient exposure to modeling of the correct language anyway. The only exceptions here would include problems which interfere with communication; that is, problems that make it difficult to understand what children are trying to say. In these situations, it would be of some importance to make it clear to the children that their speech is ambiguous and that the listener does not understand them or is not certain what they are saying. Any correcting of children's language should be done casually and matter of factly. Stutterers and other children with speech enunciation problems usually show backgrounds of having the speech imperfections called to their attention consistently and dramatically by parents and others in their environment, to the point that they become overly conscious and anxious about them. This does *not* mean that adults should avoid correcting children's speech for fear of making them stutterers. It does mean that adults should avoid communicating the idea that a minor speech problem is a "big deal," perhaps something important enough that they should become concerned about it ("If you don't stop talking like that, everyone will laugh at you.").

FOSTERING LANGUAGE DEVELOPMENT

221

Adult concern is better focused on the quantity and variety of children's speech, rather than upon its form. Adults who are most successful in fostering language development will be those who teach children to value and use language, both for social communication and for thinking and problem solving. Social communication should become a valued end in itself. Where there is a good parent-child relationship, the parents and children will share many conversations each day and will enjoy talking to one another and sharing one another's company for its own sake. Adults can stimulate this by speaking to children frequently themselves and by showing their receptiveness to questions or communications about everyday activities. *Sustained conversations* are especially important. Here, instead of responding to children's comments by praising or by making some minimal acceptance comment, adults can sustain the conversation by asking questions or making "leading" statements that stimulate children to say something else. In this way, skilled adults can get children to talk for several minutes about what they did during the day, if they wish to do so. They also can get children to use language to describe their drawings and constructions, give their versions of stories they have heard or television programs they have watched, explain why they do or do not like something or someone, and so forth.

As children get older, it becomes especially important to model and help them learn to use language for thinking and problem solving. Perhaps most important here is *receptiveness to children's questions*. By now it should be clear that, given children's special and unique views of the world, no question they might ask is "stupid" or "silly." No matter what the question might sound like from an adult perspective, if children ask it, they probably really want an answer. Furthermore, what is "obvious" to the adult "obviously" is not to children, or they would not be asking the questions. Any questions children might ask should be accepted as appropriate and honest questions that demand answers.

Sometimes children will have difficulty expressing what they really want to ask because of language deficiencies, so that the question may come out ambiguous or nonsensical. Where this happens, adults might have to clarify by asking a few questions designed to identify exactly what it is the child wants to know. This is especially advisable when the child asks a "cosmic mind blower" that most if not all adults could not answer ("Where does electricity come from?"). Given that children know next to nothing about electricity, except that you need it to turn on the lamp, when they ask a question like this one, they probably are really asking something like "How do you get electricity into the lamp?" They do not want an extended explanation of what electricity is, let alone where it may come from. So, the answer is "From the plug in the wall." Adults should bear this in mind, because preschool children regularly ask such questions as why the dog in the picture book is bigger than the giraffe, why the day turns into night and then turns into the day again, where the sun goes when it goes, what makes the noise in thunder, what happens when you die, why Jimmy does not have a father, and so forth. When faced with cosmic mind blowers like these, it is best to question the children a bit to find out what they really want to know rather than taking the question at face value and ending up giving information the children do not want and cannot understand.

Most specific activities involving language are rather obvious. Children should be read to *from infancy.* As they get older and begin to identify their interests, they should be allowed to choose books from the library. They also will greatly enjoy such activities as going through department store catalogs and discussing the various items, particularly toys, pictured there. They will enjoy and benefit from songs and games that help build verbal skills and reading readiness skills. If adults have the time and interest, they can teach children to read at age five or so. Materials designed for teaching children the sound-letter relationships basic to reading are widely available. This is not of crucial importance, because they will learn reading at school later anyway, but it does tend to help them learn easier at school. How much serious reading instruction should be given will depend on children's interests and abilities. It is better not to push it too far, because children usually have difficulty learning when younger, and forced reading instruction before they are ready may make them feel inadequate and/or "turn them off" on reading.

Much verbalization about numbers occurs during games, although counting can be brought into almost any kind of activity. One way that counting can be taught and learned easily is in connection with the counting of small candies. Children almost always divide small candies into color groups before beginning to eat them, and they usually make comments about the relative amounts of each color received. This makes it easy to reinforce color and number concepts at these times by counting with the children or by having them do it themselves to discover how many of each color they have. Counting also can be done with nuts or raisins, and with non-food items such as coins or marbles (an advantage here is that the things being counted do not tend to disappear in the process, as food items do).

Other implications for fostering language development follow rather directly from research on social class differences. Adults should talk to and with children, not at them; initiate interactions with them rather than wait for them to do so; provide positive and informative responses, as opposed to minimal or discouraging responses, to their initiatives; try to be clear, specific, well-organized, and understandable when explaining something; question children to get more information when unsure about what they have said or mean; provide advance orientation before an important event so that children know what to expect and will look forward to it, and provide comments that help them remember salient points by discussing the event afterward; and in general adopt a proactive rather than a reactive stance toward children by initiating and anticipating rather than just by responding (Hess, Shipman, Brophy, and Bear, 1968; Clarke-Stewart, 1973).

BUILDING MOTIVATION

It is important to build in children internal senses of locus of control and general "can do" attitudes. The most important "don'ts" here are "don't continually remind children of their deficiencies and failures," and "don't make comparisons between children." Much more important than the "don'ts," of course, are the things that adults can *do* to help development in this area. Because of the difficulty in research in this area, and because there is not much research available, no one really is sure. Some good bets do include the following.

1. Accept children for what they are. Characteristics like sex, appearance, size, agility, and the like are set by the genes. They represent both limitations and potentials. They are not going to change, and nothing is to be gained by complaining about them or communicating disappointment.

2. Call children's attention to cause and effect relationships, especially those in which effects are caused by their own behavior. Because of egocentricism, animism, and other aspects of preoperational logic, children will be confused about what they are and are not capable of and what they did and did not personally cause. You can minimize this confusion by giving them rich and detailed feedback.

3. Pay attention to, and call children's attention to, the development of their abilities. In particular, verbalize and express satisfaction with their progress in developing skills in particular areas ("Now you can count all the way up to 17!").

4. When children need help from you with something they cannot handle themselves, model and explain as you solve the problem with them. Let them see that it was solved with actions comprehensible to them, not through mysterious ways known only to you. Let them know that eventually they will be able to do it themselves.

5. If the problem is one they *can* solve themselves with instructions and/or help, let them do as much of it as they can and want to.

6. Let the children guide you regarding readiness. Stimulate them to try things and challenge them to push ahead, but do not insist on continuing when they clearly are resisting.

7. Build frustration tolerance and persistence by modeling and reinforcing the ideas that patience and determination pay off, that problems can be overcome, and that skills will improve with practice.

8. Acknowledge your mistakes, but then go on to show how they can be overcome through corrective action.

Learning to tie shoes, for example, is a complex task for young children, usually learned piecemeal over a period of years. Adults often are tempted to tie shoes for children, because it is quicker and easier. However, children will need opportunities to practice if they are to learn to do it themselves. At first, they will progress better if given a commercially manufactured enlarged shoe which has long, thick laces for them to practice with. Instructions with feedback (and patience in undoing knots) are needed here. When they can succeed with enlarged laces, switch them to ordinary shoes, but do not expect them to be able to tie their own shoes *while they are wearing them*. Because of the physical obstacles and the differences in perspective and ease of movement, tying shoes while wearing them is much more difficult than tying them when they can be manipulated freely. The task will be mastered in steps, and there may be long time lags between steps. At first, children may be able only to *untie,* and even then they may cause knots frequently until they learn to separate the loose ends from the loops. Then, they can make the first part of a bow knot by crossing the laces, but cannot go further. Later, when they master the complex art of forming loops and following through to form knots, they may require several tries before getting knots that "hold," and the knots are likely to be too loose. It may be several years before the ability to tie tight and otherwise satisfactory knots, every time, without effort, develops. In the meantime, children will need continual encouragement, help, recognition of what they *can* do, praise for progress, and reassurance that eventually they will be able to do the job as well as adults can.

SUMMARY

Adults can do much to foster children's development during the preoperational years, but the adults must be able to accommodate to the special needs of these children that result from their egocentrism and other aspects of preoperational logic that make it difficult to communicate clearly. Adults often have to observe carefully and perhaps ask questions in order to understand what children mean by what they say and/or why they say it, and they must phrase their own communications to the children in language that the children can understand.

Much of children's learning still is learning by doing at these ages, so that development is fostered by providing children with opportunities to observe interesting events and have interesting experiences. Even more important, development is stimulated through continuous interactions with children in which the adults discuss and explain everyday events in ways that make them understandable and meaningful to children. Often this happens quite literally. Preoperational children can watch or even participate in an activity without really understanding what is happening, unless adults provide a context of meaning through demonstrations and explanations.

Development proceeds from the global to the differentiated, and progress in different areas proceeds unevenly according to such principles as canalization and equilibration. Given this, adults will be most helpful to developing children if they observe and question them carefully in order to determine readiness and interests, and then follow through by arranging for experiences that are matched to these child attributes in ways most likely to be both motivating and instructive. Different children at the same age will benefit most from different experiences, and the same child will need different experiences at different ages.

Development can be stimulated both through provision of opportunities for children to learn on their own in play, and in interactions in which the adult deliberately teaches children something. These can include stimulating and unusual vacations or trips, but more typically they involve demonstrations and discussions about everyday things. Preschool experiences are useful supplements (but not substitutes) for stimulation in and around the home.

Personal and Social Development in Young Children

Personal and social development in the preoperational years closely parallels the expanding cognitive development discussed in Chapter Five. Individual characteristics become more truly personal than they were in the sensorimotor period. Cognitive schemas begin to appear and proliferate rapidly, and children change from relatively passive organisms that respond in predictable and often animal-like fashion (and respond mostly to external stimuli) into much more active, initiatory, and reflective organisms who increasingly behave in distinctly human ways. Perhaps the most important of the cognitive schemas that appear and begin to develop during these years is the self-concept schema.

PERSONAL DEVELOPMENT

Different psychologists variously refer to "personality," "the self," or "the self-concept." *Personality* usually refers to any and all social-personal traits that are characteristic of people, whether or not people are conscious of them. *Self-concept* usually refers to the combination, presumably integrated, of perceptions and beliefs about oneself, whether or not accurate. *Self* is a murky and controversial term referring to a hypothesized inner consciousness that is the "real person" beneath the facade visible to others. "Self-concept" will be used frequently in this book; "personality" will be used rarely, and "self" will not be used at all.

Psychologists view the self-concept as either a very rich cognitive schema that includes many separate but well-integrated sub-schemas, or as a term used somewhat inappropriately for that portion of one's cognitive schemas that apply to oneself, regardless of their accuracy or degree of integration. Psychologists with the latter view are at least as impressed with the inconsistencies in personality and with the situational and contextual influences upon it as they are with its consistency and stability (Mischel, 1971). Furthermore, when self-theorists refer to the "self" concept, they usually are discussing only self-definitions as they apply to relatively narrow areas, and not to the total of all cognitive schemas that apply to the self (Allport, 1955). "Self" concept is much like IQ, a sort of weighted average of a large number of components, useful as a concept for some purposes, but not existing as a unitary entity. Like IQ, it often masks more information than it reveals. It is especially important not to think of the self-concept as a unitary entity when discussing preoperational children. Their schemas concerning themselves are just as tentative and subject to sudden and drastic change as are all of their other preoperational schemas. The points discussed in Chapter Five concerning the fragmentary and tentative nature of children's knowledge until they become operational and achieve stable cognitive structures includes knowledge about the self.

The principle of *cognitive consistency*, which becomes so important later, does not yet apply. Preoperational children have not yet achieved cognitive structures stable enough to "demand" consistency. Instead, change and inconsistency are both characteristic of these children and expected by them (at least in the sense that they are accustomed to them and not surprised or upset by them). Consequently, preoperational children do not need to use coping or defense mechanisms (Chapter Nine) to resolve conflicts or inconsistencies within themselves. Because of their limited cognitive development, they are unlikely to note such inconsistencies in the first place. Even if they do, children usually do not respond to inconsistencies with strong negative emotions yet, because the inconsistencies do not yet have the threatening moral implications that they will have later.

This is why preoperational children are capable of "lying" when there is no possibility that they will be believed, capable of forgetting a disagreement or even a physical fight with a playmate shortly after it is over, and capable of being utterly uninterested in a game or activity that they were excited about a few days earlier. In short, preoperational children's personal and social development show the same kinds of egocentrism and tenuousness that are observed in their cognitive development.

SELF-AWARENESS   Early in the preoperational period, self-awareness is relatively primitive and centered around physical appearance, the child's

Stage Development Is Slow and Uneven

It has been noted periodically that development through sequences of broad stages is a long, slow process which involves numerous short-term plateaus and even reversals. This was illustrated in a study by Kuhn (1976), in which children aged five through eight were interviewed three times across a calendar year and scored for their development level according to the stages outlined by Kohlberg.

If development were steady and continuous, repeated testing would show much evidence of advance and little or no evidence of regression. This was not the case when data from the initial interviews were compared to data from interviews six months later, nor when data from the second interview were compared to data taken a year after the initial interviews (six months after the second set). Between the first and second interviews, 25 children showed an increase in stage level, 15 remained the same, and 10 declined. Between the second and third interview, 19 children increased, 17 did not change, and 14 declined. Although both sets of data showed more increases than declines, this difference was not significant in either set and the proportion of children showing declines was much higher than would be expected if stage development were continuous and irreversible.

Comparisons of the third interview with the first interview, which allowed assessment of development over a full year, provided more support for the general validity of Kohlberg's stages. This time, the data favoring increases over declines were statistically significant: 32 children showed an increase, 13 did not change, and only 5 declined. Note, though, that even here, there were five children out of 50 who had lower scores on their interview data from the third interview taken an entire year after the first interview was taken. Such findings are typical, not only for moral development but for conservation and other aspects of more purely cognitive development and for attempts to place children in Piagetian stages. Instability is especially frequent with preoperational children (that is part of what being preoperational involves), but it is common at later stages, too.

name, important possessions, and personal qualities seen as important (usually sensorimotor schemas which children have been striving to master and which cause them to urge anyone who will listen to "Look at me! Look at what I can do!"). As children get older, more and more interpersonal and social qualities become recognized and integrated into other self-concept schemas, but appearance, possessions, and physical abilities remain as especially important aspects of self-concept throughout the early years. This is partly because children spend much of their time in physical play and in developing sensorimotor schemas, so that their attention normally is focused on this area (especially on those developmental tasks which parents or significant others have defined as developmental markers, so that mastering them becomes a

230

special source of pride and satisfaction). In addition to this positive orientation toward physical things, young children's egocentrism and related characteristics leave them undisposed toward and ill-equipped for development of more sophisticated schemas concerning self-definition based on inferences from interpersonal relationships. These begin to appear later, when the necessary preexisting knowledge and abilities have been developed.

Children get direct feedback about their physical skills from successes and failures in performing physical tasks. This feedback is available for integration into the self-concept to the extent that children are aware of their abilities (or lack of them) in various areas. Information concerning personal qualities also is acquired primarily through feedback, but here the feedback comes from other people. Sometimes this is analogous to the situation regarding feedback concerning physical abilities, in that children will do things that consistently provoke particular responses in others, leading children to grasp the concept that particular behavior on their part is good or bad.

Peer Group Status, Self-Concept, and Behavior

Well established self-concepts based upon long standing status in a social group are not easily changed, and they can cause individuals to experience frustration and discomfort if the individuals are suddenly thrust into unaccustomed roles, even roles more attractive than the ones they usually portray. This was shown nicely in a study by Klinger and McNelly (1976). The subjects in their study were boy scouts who had been members of preexisting scout troups in which most of the members had established fairly stable roles (such as leader or follower). For the experiment, the boys were asked to compete in teams of four against teams from other scout troups in various games that were popular with the boys. The instructions for the games, and the method of awarding prizes connected with the games, caused the role of captain of the team to be one of unusual importance, power, and responsibility.

If the boys had been allowed to select captains spontaneously, they probably would have selected the scout in each group of four who had the highest leadership status in the scout troup represented. However, captains were assigned arbitrarily by the experimenters, so that some captains were the same boys who probably would have been elected captains anyway, but other captains were boys who typically occupied low or follower status in their scout troup and would have been unlikely to have been elected as captains. The boys participating in the games were observed and interviewed in an attempt to see how they were affected by their participation, and especially how the experience of acting in a leadership role affected the boys who typically had low status in the group.

As expected, boys who typically had *high* status in the group and were appointed to be captains functioned effectively in that role and enjoyed the whole experience. Also as expected by the experimenters, but perhaps not by people who assume that an opportunity to play "top dog" would be valued by those who rarely experienced it, boys who typically had *low* status in the group were not very effective in trying to function as team captains and did not enjoy the experience. Some even became noticeably withdrawn or anxious, clearly experiencing the task as unpleasant rather than enjoyable.

These findings do not negate what has been said elsewhere in the book about the importance of positive experiences for building positive self-concepts and self-esteem, but they do help illustrate how self-concepts become very powerful and resistant to change through short-term or artificial intervention. Boys who develop into leaders gradually and on the basis of a combination of their own leadership potential and recognition by the group probably would change their self-concepts, but boys who experience a brief treatment like this and have their leadership defined arbitrarily by someone outside the group rather than by spontaneous evolution within the group are unlikely to have lasting positive effects. As the present experiment showed, they may not have even temporary positive effects.

Other feedback is less directly tied to their own specific preceding behavior. It comes in the form of verbalizations to them about themselves, or communication of expectations concerning what they are or should be. Many expectations are verbalized directly in the process of socialization, as when adults tell children that they will be expected to tell the truth or share their belongings with playmates without squabbling. Other expectations relative to self-definitions are communicated indirectly, through such mechanisms as age and sex norms propounded through the media, toys and play suggestions made by parents, comments made about the child to some third person which the child overhears, and various anticipatory behaviors that parents or others engage in in order to facilitate or prevent something that they expect the child to do.

In the early preoperational years, these indirect forms of socialization are communicated primarily through gestural and expressive reactions to the child. Because of their concrete orientations and their poorly developed language systems, young children are especially observant of and reactive to *non-verbal* aspects of communication. More or less independently of what adults may say, young children will observe reactions of approval or disapproval and take these into account in developing schemas concerning their own behavior which provoked the reactions. Later, as verbal abilities develop, they become more and more sensitive to and able to understand verbal communications, including verbalizations not meant for them.

The matter never has been investigated systematically, but based on my own observations, I believe that most children probably pick up more information about how others see them from listening to what is said *about* them than they do from verbalizations directed *toward* them. It is common for parents, older siblings, and others who know young children to talk about them right in front of them as if they were not there, often on the assumption that children do not understand what is being said. Young children are very sensitive to non-verbal communication, and their receptive understanding of language precedes their ability to use it expressively. Consequently, they usually understand much more than adults think they do. Children can learn that they are *expected* to lie, to resist going to bed at bedtime, to dislike certain foods, or to be selfish in their interactions with playmates, simply by listening to adults discuss their behavior or what should be done about them ("That child has a mean streak!").

Children develop concepts about themselves through these various feedback mechanisms. Usually these concepts are accepted without question, unless something comes up to contradict them (just as most other immediate experiences are accepted without question by preoperational children). If the various schemas that children pick up are mutually assimilable and integratable, they are likely to develop generalized expectancies or schemas that justify the use of the term "self-concept." Usually there are so many contradictions and gaps that the "self-concept" is far from unitary or stable.

Preoperational children, particularly before they develop stable cognitive structures that are resistant to change in response to single experiences, are especially susceptible to the principle of the self-fulfilling prophecy. At its simplest, the principle states that children will become what they are expected to become (given the expectations that they perceive). This appears to be generally true, particularly when expectations are consistent with one another and communicated to children regularly. Where expectations are communicated consistently and strongly, as in the case of sex roles, children tend to acquire them easily and strongly and to begin to fulfill them with a minimum of direct and deliberate socialization by parents or anyone else (sex role learning will be discussed in more detail later in the chapter). Expectations communicated less strongly and frequently are less likely to become fulfilled, although the groundwork is laid if children acquire the expectations at all. All other things being equal, children who are expected to be honest and prosocial are more likely to become so than children expected to be dishonest and antisocial.

The power of expectations communicated by socializing agents to influence social and personal development resides in the fact that little if any development in these areas is genetically programmed. With the exceptions of certain sex differences and certain aspects of temperament, children are very open to the influences of significant others in their environment. If they were systematically socialized from birth toward a certain set of behaviors and values, they very probably would acquire these behaviors and values. However, it is typical for children to be exposed to conflicting expectations from parents, siblings, peers, the media, and other sources. This is why socialization outcomes are not so easily predictable, and is one reason why individuals raised in the same families sometimes have very different personalities. It is important for parents and other socializing agents to *expect* children to become the kinds of individuals that they want them to become, and to *treat* them accordingly.

Poor personal or social development in the early years is *not* irreversible, and the undesirable effects of unfortunate or traumatic experiences *can* be overcome. As with cognitive development, however, getting off to a good start makes continued success more likely as well as easier to achieve. Conversely, the development of undesirable characteristics necessitates some unlearning. This must occur prior to and in addition to the development needed to arrive at a certain desirable end point. Adults important in the life of young children can help get them off to good starts by providing facilitative environments, communicating the expectations that they are and will continue to be likeable and competent people, and treating them in ways that will make it very likely that they will in fact *become* likeable and competent people (Stone and Church, 1973).

ACHIEVEMENT MOTIVATION   Although young children do not develop anything like the richly differentiated personalities that they will achieve ultimately, certain important personal traits that become central parts of personality begin to develop in the preoperational years. As might be expected, most of these are traits acquired through feedback from physical activities and play activities frequently engaged in by preschool children.

One set of traits is the complex which includes mastery motivation, achievement motivation, frustration tolerance, level of aspiration, and general self-concept of competence (White, 1959). In general, success breeds success expectations, and failure breeds failure expectations. However, young children's experiences of success and failure can be determined more by the expectations and reactions of others than by their own objective levels of achievement.

Initially, very young children show evidence of curiosity and exploratory interests. They often will persist indefinitely in trying to reach goals. As they become more socially oriented and learn to interact with others in the environment and to solicit their reactions, these reactions will begin to affect their attitudes toward themselves and toward success and failure in meeting goals. If reactions are generally positive, this is likely to motivate them to begin to take more personalized satisfaction when they achieve goals, because they have been taught, or at least have learned, that this *should* make them feel proud. They also are likely to form habits such as bragging about accomplishments or bringing others to see projects in order to solicit (hopefully) favorable reactions from them. In general, they will approach challenges confidently, concentrating upon succeeding at tasks and not worrying about failure. Conversely, if children are criticized or ridiculed for their efforts, they are likely to avoid such activities and develop feelings of failure and unworthiness. To the extent that they develop achievement motivation, it is likely to be an unpleasant type in which fear of failure is prominent, often interfering with performance and thus producing failure through self-fulfilling prophecy effects.

Consider children building block towers. If adults show approval and positive interest, this activity can be social and involve personal satisfactions as well as the exercise of sensorimotor schemas. Adult reactions of "awe" and "amazement" at accomplishments ("Wow! Look at the size of that tower!") will build pride and personal satisfaction. Adult reactions to failure which minimize the "failure" connotations ("Oh, you almost got another one on, but it fell down! Try it again, and see if it will stay on this time!") will build frustration tolerance and persistence. In general, then, positive adult reactions make the experience enjoyable regardless of objective success in block stacking. Contrast this with the probable results of comments like "See, you can't do it—I told you!" (from an older sibling) or "If you can't play with those more quietly, maybe you ought to do something else" (from an adult). Depending on such onlooker reactions, two children whose block stacking had been very similar would come away with very different subjective experiences and attitudes toward block stacking, toward the onlookers, and toward themselves.

As success and failure experiences increasingly involve implications of personal worthiness or unworthiness, these feelings and self-perceptions will begin to affect performance. Children whose mastery motivation has been fostered optimally will develop greater tolerance for frustration and tendencies to persist longer in attempting to overcome obstacles to the attainment of goals. They also will tend to develop stronger achievement motivation, becoming both more desirous of achieving goals and more determined to persist until they succeed in doing so. Their levels of aspiration will be high but realistic, being continually shifted upward to newer levels as lower goals are mastered (McClelland, 1958). In contrast, children whose efforts have been shamed or ridiculed are likely to develop feelings of insecurity, inadequacy, and fear of failure. Although it probably is true that most if not all children initially show curiosity and exploratory behavior, and a degree of mastery motivation and persistence in the face of frustration as well, these qualities are enhanced or suppressed by socialization pressures. As children become older and increasingly sensitive to the evaluational reactions of others, these pressures become stronger.

The development of optimal levels of these characteristics probably is facilitated if significant others model them, stress the satisfactions involved in setting and achieving goals, and provide appropriate attention to accomplishments and praise and encouragement of efforts. Praise of accomplishments should not be over-emphasized lest children develop the idea (rightly or wrongly) that they are valued and appreciated only for what they can *do* and not for what they *are*.

Strong achievement motivation will show itself in such traits as a desire for mastery for its own sake, an ability to tolerate frustration and persist in the face of failure, and a tendency to set high but appropriate levels of aspiration in setting goals. The phrase "high but appropriate" was deliberately used instead of merely "high," because some children with low achievement motivation will state extremely high and difficult-to-reach goals if asked what they think they can do or what they are trying to do (McClelland, 1958). Failure to reach a ridiculously high goal actually is not failure at all. It is defensive avoidance (not failing by not trying in the first place). The appropriateness of goal setting must be judged in relation to children's specific capabilities. Confident children with high achievement motivation will tend to set their goals at difficulty levels beyond what they can achieve presently but reasonably within reach. Theoretically, they will set their goal at a level that they have a 50% chance of reaching. Children who fear failure and do not have confidence in their ability to perform the task may preclude failure altogether by setting very low goals that they know they can reach, or, if they fear the stigma that might be attached to this behavior, they may set unrealistically high goals that they are very unlikely to reach. The appropriateness of a stated goal or level of aspiration cannot be judged on an absolute basis, or even with reference to norms based on age or size. Instead, it must be judged on the basis of the individual child's ability to reach the goal.

6.

INDEPENDENCE   Another major theme in self-development in the early years is the gradual transition from dependency toward increasing degrees of independence and autonomy. As noted in Chapter Three, the need to come to grips with the fact that one is dependent upon adults for basic needs, and the need to accommodate to socialization demands to limit and channel one's behavior in culturally prescribed directions, are two universal human experiences that all children must go through. Much of the discussion in Chapters Three and Four concerning child and adult behavior in relation to the child's striving for independence and autonomy applies also to the preoperational years. Because of their immaturity and inexperience, young children need socialization and limit setting by adults. Ideally, this will come in the form of positive guidance rather than punitive repression.

Child "experts" have waxed and waned over the issue of freedom vs. control in raising children. At various times, some have prescribed careful and complete scheduling of the child's activities, with particular attention to avoiding "spoiling" the child (Watson, 1928). Others have recommended the polar opposite, suggesting that all children automatically are born with a tendency to develop into prosocial and mentally healthy individuals, and that attempts to interfere with their presumed "natural" development through unnecessary socialization pressures will only warp or frustrate them (Rogers, 1961). With hindsight, we now can see that both of these extreme positions are incorrect, and that debates over freedom vs. control tend to cloud the real issues rather than settle them. Children need *both freedom and control*, not one or the other. The really important questions concern what kinds of control are needed and when and how they should be implemented.

Recent research has produced a convergence of agreement on many of these issues. Perhaps the most comprehensive and representative is that of Baumrind (1971). Frustrated with earlier work that classified parents as either authoritarian or democratic in their child-rearing practices (usually by lumping together into one or both categories parents who were different from one another in several crucial ways), Baumrind divided parents into three categories: authoritarian, authoritative, and *laissez-faire*. This typology, which followed up on earlier work showing that the *ways* that parents socialized their children and placed limits upon them were more important than the number and kinds of such limits, proved to be much more valid and useful in the search for relationships between parental socialization behavior and child outcomes.

Authoritarian parents make little or no attempt to provide rationales or explanations for the demands they make upon their children. Instead, they "boss the children around" with an attitude of "you'll do it because I said so," and with the implication that the children will be punished if they do not comply. *Authoritative* parents have a different approach. Although they may place as many or more socialization demands and limits on their children as authoritarian parents do, they regularly explain the rationales for these demands and limits to the children. They help children to perceive their demands as needed, or at least as motivated by a concern for the children's own good rather than by a determination to tell them what to do and force them to do it if necessary. Finally, the *laissez-faire* parents differ from both of the other two groups in that they place few demands upon their children at all. Instead, they tend to ignore them and let them do as they please, as long as they do not become destructive or annoying.

Baumrind, as well as numerous others, has found that the children of authoritative parents tend to show the most advanced levels of autonomy and independence for their ages, and also to show greater confidence and generally healthier self-concepts. The difficulty with authoritarian parents is easy to see and requires little explanation. Children who are continually being told what to do but rarely given clear explanations that would allow them to develop generalized schemas to control their own behavior, and rarely encouraged to assume independence, are very likely to become immature and dependent. They also are likely to become unhappy and angry, although they may be too cowed to express hostile emotions directly. They are likely to disobey parental dictates if they are sure that they can get away with it, because they lack internalized self-control.

The situation with regard to *laissez-faire* families is more complex. Nevertheless, the data make sense when several factors are taken into account. First, parents with a *laissez-faire* approach toward child-rearing often are parents who do not really like their children and/or do not take their child-rearing responsibilities seriously. This pattern often is a form of rejection. Where this is the case and the children realize it at some level, they may devalue themselves, developing feelings of insecurity and low self-esteem. At the same time, in an effort to please the parents and perhaps win their approval, they may do everything they can think of to try to please them, thus becoming extremely dependent. On the other hand, if they have stronger self-concepts and are able to respond to parental rejection with resentment and anger, they may become acting out "problem children." This is not what is ordinarily thought of as dependency, but neither is it mature independence and autonomy.

In addition to the interpersonal dynamics that may be involved in *laissez-faire* families, a *laissez-faire* approach to child rearing appears to be maladaptive for other reasons. One problem is that, contrary to the assumptions of certain advocates, children are *not* born with innate predispositions toward prosocial behavior or self-control. They need to *learn* appropriate behavior, ideally through such mechanisms as modeling, explanations, demonstrations, and the other parental behaviors associated with authoritative child rearing. Like other schemas in the preoperational period, those related to personal and social development are in continuous flux. They do not become assimilated into a stable structure until the child is six or seven years old. One is not necessarily doing young children favors by allowing them "freedom" or granting them "autonomy" in situations where they do not have the slightest idea about what to do, or where they lack the prior knowledge or experience needed to make rational and appropriate decisions. The result can be a great deal of unnecessary and sometimes painful trial-and-error learning, as well as development of traits such as insecurity, anxiety, and fear of failure. In short, even when it is done by parents who mean well, forcing children to handle situations on their own without any help or guidance when they are not prepared to do so is much like throwing them into a swimming pool and ordering them to swim. The experience is likely to be traumatic, and even if the child succeeds, there may be some emotional costs involved.

The young child's needs for socialization and guidance are not always obvious. Throughout the early years, "Let me do it myself" and "Why can't I?" are among the more common verbalizations directed at adults. The "trick" for the adults involved is to allow, and where possible encourage, children's strivings for independence, while at the same time keeping their behavior within appropriate limits and protecting them from potentially traumatic experiences. The criterion for appropriateness has to be the children's ability (or lack of it) to handle the situation on their own, and not the firmness of their demands.

Young children may go through periods of negativism where they try to refuse to do anything they are asked to do or to contradict anything that an adult may tell them. They also frequently ask or even demand to do something when they are not sure whether or not they really can do it, or when they do not even want to do it. It is important that adults recognize such behavior for what it is: *reality testing*.

Children learn mostly by doing, and in order to develop independence and autonomy, sooner or later they must begin doing for themselves things that previously were done for them. Often, they will be inaccurate in judging what they can and cannot do, so that many of their demands will be inappropriate. Where this clearly is the case, the adult should firmly refuse the demands, while explaining the reasons for the refusal.

Whether or not children's judgments about their abilities are correct, they will not always move toward independence in socially approved ways during the preoperational years. They often lack the cognitive and verbal schemas needed to present reasoned arguments or to ask permission to be allowed to do something new in ways that adults perceive as properly respectful and "mature." Instead, they are much more likely to simply go ahead and try something (often with unfortunate results), or to make insistent demands and perhaps throw temper tantrums if they are not indulged. Such behavior admittedly is exasperating, but adults should bear in mind that, for a time at least, it is the only method children have for taking the initiative in seeking to expand their autonomy. Adults who are confronted with such behavior should let children know that it is inappropriate and tell them what to do instead, although they should not expect immediate results.

DEPENDENCY   Although most people see dependence and independence as opposite ends of the same dimension, child development researchers have found it convenient (perhaps even necessary) to discuss them separately. This is partly because young children cannot be scaled validly on a single such dimension; they may be relatively independent in some areas and yet extremely dependent in other areas. Furthermore, vacillation between apparent determination to achieve autonomy and independence and regression to over-dependency and over-concern about security is quite common. Usually, this happens when children "bite off more than they can chew." That is, some of their adventures on the road to autonomy and independence do not work out very well, because they try things before they are ready for them and fail miserably. Children who have decided that they should be drinking their milk by themselves may strenuously resist any attempt to hold the glass for them or help them in other ways. If they should spill the milk during a confrontation over the issue or immediately after they have been given permission to handle the glass on their own, they may not only abandon all attempts at independence in drinking milk, but may even want to go back to a baby bottle or special cup.

Such incidents are just more examples of a general phenomenon mentioned frequently in regard to preoperational children: their schemas are tenuous and not yet assimilated into stable structures, so that they often are affected deeply by single experiences, particularly traumatic ones. When achievement strivings lead to unfortunate outcomes, children may temporarily regress to a dependent state. This is perfectly normal and usually rather unimportant, assuming that adults do not over-react in negative ways and the children are provided with steady diets of reassurance and positive expectations. Eventually, they will overcome their fears and become willing to try again.

Child development researchers also have found it important to distinguish between *instrumental* and *expressive* dependency (Maccoby and Masters, 1970). Instrumental dependency refers to children's necessary dependence upon adults to do certain things for them or to help them do things because of their physical limitations and psychological immaturity. Children who ask adults to get things for them from high shelves are showing instrumental dependency.

Expressive dependency refers to the need for emotional reassurance and security. This may involve only the adult's presence, as in the attachment cycle discussed in Chapter Three, but, in more extreme cases, it may include a need for soothing, reassurance, hugging, or rocking. A certain degree of expressive dependency is normal, particularly during the attachment cycle and following traumatic experiences. Throughout the early years, children who have been injured, who have been humiliated or rejected by their peers, or who have suffered some other unsettling experience often will be upset and will need to be soothed and reassured. Expressive dependency of this sort is perfectly normal for young children of both sexes. Too much expressive dependency usually is considered undesirable, especially if it is part of a more general pattern of inhibition, fearfulness, unwillingness to take risks, and general immaturity and dependency upon adults. Sometimes this is created by adults who reward or even demand such dependency, although it also can occur in children who experience unusually frequent and intense trauma. Children of the latter type probably should be given whatever they seem to require for their own security needs. They should be brought along slowly, since a series of frightening and painful experiences understandably will reduce their ability to tolerate frustration and increase their general fear.

Instrumental dependency is observed more frequently in average children and usually is considered a normal (and perhaps necessary) stage in the progression from dependency to autonomy and independence. In this respect, it is like many other childhood behaviors that appear and then disappear, because the dependency is needed during the time a child is beginning to develop a schema but becomes less necessary as the schema becomes better developed. In a very real sense, instrumental dependency is not dependency at all, but is an early stage in the development of independence.

The distinction between expressive and instrumental dependency helped clear up some confusing child development data which had accumulated over the years. Most studies found older children to be more independent and less dependent than younger children, but there were some puzzling exceptions. Occasionally, older children would be scored as more dependent than younger children in a particular study. We now know that the dependency being measured in these studies was largely or totally instrumental dependency, and the older children showed more of it because they were developing new schemas which required them to seek assistance from adults. The younger children did not yet show this kind of dependency because they were not yet starting to develop the other schemas. Studies of children of the same age who differed in mental development or general maturity showed the same kinds of differences. Frequently, highly developed children will show more of certain kinds of instrumental dependency than less well developed children, because they are developing newer, more advanced schemas (Maccoby and Masters, 1970).

Adults should bear all of this in mind when children "pester" them with questions and requests for help. Telling the children to do it themselves usually is not the answer, because the children ordinarily *would* do it themselves if they could. The very fact that they come to the adult to seek help indicates that they probably really need help. They probably also are looking forward to the day when they *can* do it themselves. In general, requests for help in zipping a zipper, taking apart two or more plastic bricks that are stuck together tightly, tying or untying knots, fixing a toy that is stuck or broken, and the like, are examples of normal and healthy instrumental dependency rather than babyishness or over-dependency. Such requests usually are made only after children have tried to do it themselves. Adults will be most helpful to children when they respond favorably to these requests, allow children to watch, and provide some explanation concerning what they are doing as the adult solves the problem for them. This will speed up the children's acquisition of the ability to handle the problem on their own.

TOWARD A REALISTIC SELF-CONCEPT   As young children learn about expectations held by their families, their peers, and society at large which apply to them, children usually will strive to fulfill the expectations (Kohlberg, 1966). Once children discover that they are considered "babies," they usually become very strongly motivated to drop characteristics and behavior associated with babies and to acquire characteristics and behavior associated with "big boys" or "big girls." Children will often develop sets of ideals to strive for which are far beyond their reach because they are trying to reach perfection in so many different areas that they are bound to fail in some areas. Children often want to be able to do things that they will not be able to do very well for some time, because of developmental immaturity.

Sex Differences in Reactions to Feedback from Peers vs. Adults

In general, success experiences and positive feedback build confidence and motivation in children of both sexes, and failure experiences and negative feedback are likely to engender the belief that the child cannot do the task. Several studies have indicated that there are culturally learned sex differences in the relative importance and meaning attached to feedback from different sources. One common statement, for example, is that girls are more oriented toward people and thus more concerned about personal reactions to their behavior, while boys are less concerned about the reactions of others and more concerned about the immediate feedback that they get from exploratory and manipulative experiences. This has led to the idea that boys learn to try to achieve for its own sake for self-gratification, whereas girls learn to try to achieve in order to please others important in their lives. This appears to be true to some extent, although like most things connected with sex role, it probably is undergoing change at the moment.

More recently, attention has been drawn to sex differences in reaction to feedback from peers vs. adults. A good example is a study by Dweck and Bush (1976). In this study, fourth and fifth grade children were asked to work on school-like tasks and then were given feedback about their relative success or failure on the tasks. The feedback was given by an adult male, an adult female, a same sex child of about the same age, or an opposite sex child of about the same age. In general, girls showed little improvement in performance in response to failure feedback from adult sources, but failure feedback from perceived peers led to immediate and sustained improvement. The opposite pattern occurred for boys: notable improvement occurred in response to failure feedback from adults, but failure feedback from peers made little difference.

Furthermore, it appeared that these behavioral differences were due to differences in the meanings that the children attached to the feedback messages they received. Girls receiving failure feedback from adults tended to attribute their failures to lack of ability. If an adult told them that they had not done well, they assumed that they lacked ability on the task and would never do very well on it. In contrast, they did not make this assumption when given failure feedback from peers, and the peer feedback seemed to provide positive motivation for them to improve. The boys showed the opposite pattern, responding to failure feedback from adults with redoubled efforts to improve, but responding to failure feedback from peers as indication that they lacked ability on the task and were unlikely to improve significantly in the future.

Among other things, this suggests that adults have a much better chance than peers to improve the performance of girls through feedback, but that the opposite is true with boys. Another implication is that the suggestion made earlier that girls generally achieve to please others but boys generally achieve to please themselves was too broad. Apparently, boys' achievement motivation is affected strongly by peer reactions, just as girls' achievement motivation is affected strongly by adult reactions. These data provide many interesting possibilities for improving motivation and performance in children, but they also illustrate how easily unfortunate outcomes can result when girls receive negative feedback from adults or boys receive it from their peers.

Preoperational children usually show strong needs for conformity and social desirability in their characteristics. They find out what they are "supposed" to be doing and try to do it, and then seek praise or reassurance for having done so. They usually are very adult-oriented at this point, being very concerned about being accepted and well thought of by parents and significant others. Peer group relationships are developing at this point, too, but peers usually also are adult-oriented themselves. Peer influences usually reinforce adult influences, rather than conflict with them, as is typical with older children.

One of the developmental tasks that preoperational children must accomplish over these years is to move from a naive striving for perfection in every area to an awareness and acceptance of their limitations and a generally realistic self-concept. This will be relatively easy for children whose parents have made it clear to them from the beginning that they accept them for what they are rather than only for their successes. Less secure children may have some difficulties in emotionally working through and accepting the fact that in reality they are something less than the ideal that they would like to be. Giving up the belief that one is better or more ideal than one really is is unpleasant for anyone, and it is especially difficult for young children whose coping mechanisms for dealing with this conflict are limited (Erikson, 1963). Both as an attempt to avoid facing up to reality by denying imperfections, and (farther along) as an attempt to test reality, children may make numerous false statements about themselves. Many of these may appear to be outrageous bragging, outright lying, or pitifully obvious attempts to tell adults what they think they want to hear rather than what the truth really is. Children may claim that they are capable of or already have done things that they obviously cannot do, that they always win and never lose in competitive games with peers, that they would not be afraid of anything under any circumstances, and so forth. Children sometimes even may back up these verbal assertions through behavior such as cheating in order to win or refusing to continue a game unless allowed to win.

Such behavior does not proceed from "perversity" in children. Instead, it results from rigid but unrealistic self-expectations and/or fears of rejection if they fail to do what they believe others expect them to do. The main problem facing adults here is to move children gradually toward less rigid and more realistic expectations and self-definitions, but without causing them undue anxiety or loss of self-esteem. Just as children previously had to learn to accept limits and socialization demands while still retaining a sense of individual autonomy, now they must learn to accept their limitations and imperfections while at the same time developing a positive self-concept. This is a difficult and time-consuming process, but usually it is accomplished successfully if children are raised in atmospheres of warmth and acceptance and if they get feedback about their limitations and deficiencies in ways that allow them to accept them without feeling shattered or rejected.

FEARS AND ANXIETY   Even after passing through the attachment cycle described in Chapter Three, preoperational children usually are still susceptible to fears and anxieties. Some of these result from traumatic experiences, while others are related to changes in children's lives and in the kinds of experiences that occur as they move into higher levels of development. One very common fear produced by trauma occurs as a result of physical injury, especially in two- and three-year-olds. An unexpected sting or insect bite, a jammed or smashed finger, a broken bone, or an injury that produces blood flow as well as pain can temporarily terrorize a child who experiences it for the first time. This is especially likely in children with newly developed senses of body awareness and vulnerability to injury. For them, a sudden injury may produce fears of death or fears that the pain and bleeding might never stop. Adults can help here both by providing information and, more importantly, by providing reassurance and comfort. Reassurance is provided partly verbally and partly through non-verbal behavior that *shows* the child that the adult knows that the problem is not serious. Comfort is provided by holding or rocking the child and providing reassurance that everything will be all right. Verbal reassurance should be encouraging but realistic and informative. For example, children who break bones and are in casts can be given information about why the cast has been put on, how long they will wear it, and what is happening inside their bodies during healing. They also can be reassured that they will be "good as new" when healed, and can resume their favorite physical activities again.

Other fears and anxieties result from aspects of developmental progress. As children learn more about physical objects, especially their own possessions, they also learn that they are supposed to take good care of them, so that they stay in good condition and do not break. Children who are highly concerned about this might become extremely anxious if a toy should break, even if the problem was entirely accidental. Similarly, children who feel confident and comfortable playing with certain familiar peers may become anxious if a new child, especially an older and bigger one, should appear (and most especially if this child should tease or threaten them). Children who seem utterly unconcerned about physical safety and the whereabouts of their parents when they are in familiar surroundings may become notably anxious if they are taken to unfamiliar places. If they are taken to an amusement park, shopping center, or other place full of people and fraught with the danger of getting lost, they may cling tightly to the adult, refusing to let go even if the adult is standing still. Even much less threatening situations, such as visits to the homes of friends who are unfamiliar to the children, may produce uncharacteristic anxiety and inhibition, and sometimes even refusal to play with children of similar age who live in the house or nearby.

Another particularly common example of childish fear is fear of the dark. Very young children usually do not fear the dark at all, because they have not yet learned that the dark is associated with danger. However, three- to six-year-old children may become very fearful of the dark, so much so that they may plead for night lights and have difficulty sleeping if they are left in darkness.

These, and numerous other examples that could have been cited, all are special cases of the general point that preoperational children have not yet developed stable cognitive structures. They are vulnerable to being overly

A classical example of parallel play. The children are physically close together and involved in similar activities, but they pursue these activities egocentrically, *showing* no interest in or even awareness of each other (although they *are* quite aware of each other). (Photo by Myron Papiz)

impressed by and to over-reacting to a novel stimulus that counters expectations or presents problems they never have dealt with before. They will learn to take these situations in stride, provided that adults give them the necessary information, reassurance, and comfort, although they will not necessarily overcome such fears immediately.

Fear of the dark, for example, sometimes will persist for months, first increasing and then decreasing. Probably the most important single adult characteristic useful for minimizing the trauma of such fears is to respond matter-of-factly and thus *show* children (not merely tell them) that the situation is normal and that there is nothing to fear. Children usually will accept such reassurance when it is given with a confident smile and a clear explanation. In contrast, if the adult also responds with fear or obvious concern, this will reinforce the child's own fearful reaction.

SOCIAL DEVELOPMENT Social development in the preoperational years parallels cognitive and self development in many ways. Most of this occurs during play, in which the child's interests evolve slowly and gradually from a primary concern with exploration and mastery of physical objects to a primary concern with peers and peer relationships. Early in this stage, the children are concerned primarily with whatever activities they are engaged in at the moment. The presence or absence of peers is relatively unimportant to them. Later, they become strongly motivated to seek out and play with peers, and objects are of interest primarily as props for social play rather than as vehicles for individual exploration or mastery.

This is seen in the frequently discussed progression from parallel to associative to cooperative play (Parten, 1932). Social activities of two-year-olds involving peers usually are restricted to *parallel play*. If placed near each other and given similar toys to play with, two children this age usually will begin to play in similar fashion. However, they will play mostly as if they were alone, showing little or no interest in the other child and rarely if ever making attempts to interact. Furthermore, if interaction attempts should be made, they are likely to be ignored.

As children's peer orientation and social (especially verbal) skills develop, they move into what has been called *associative play*. They still play separately and individually, but they show much more awareness of each other's presence and much more social speech, even though their speech is heavily egocentric. Frequently, they will blurt out something that is on their minds, but they will say it as if speaking to no one in particular, rather than turning directly toward and addressing the playmate. Most such statements do *not* elicit replies from the playmate. Instead, playmates confine their verbalizations to similar egocentric messages reflecting what is on *their* minds. The result can be a "dialogue" which really amounts to nothing more than the two children taking turns talking but not really listening to or responding to each other. The presence of the other child is important, however, because the same child typically will not say much if anything out loud if playing alone (Vygotsky,

1962). The presence of a playmate induces much "social" speech, but it does not yet cause children to pay attention to what playmates say and respond to it. The result is "dialogue" such as the following:

John: "I got a new truck for my birthday."
Michael: "My brother's name is Bobby."
John: "It's a fire engine."
Michael: "He's eight years old."
John: "It has a hose and a ladder and two firemen."
Michael: "He's in the second grade."

Such "dialogues" carried on during associative play can go on indefinitely without either child responding to or even showing that he or she has heard what the other is saying. Yet, neither child seems to notice this or be concerned about it. In contrast, both the nature of play and the nature of verbal interchanges become more adult-like as children move into the stage of *cooperative play*. Here, they work together on tasks rather than merely sit near each other and work separately, and they carry on conversations in which each listens to the other and responds appropriately. The result is a genuine dialogue, in contrast to the kind of egocentric speech illustrated above.

Development of strong interests in peers and in playing with them appears to occur spontaneously once children master the sensorimotor schemas involved in basic developmental tasks. Through contacts with playmates and neighbors, contacts with older siblings or relatives, and input from television, books, and other sources, children gradually come to understand that children of their age typically play with similar children, and that certain toys and games are meant especially for them and are fun to use.

As they learn more and more about people, *age differences* become increasingly important to them. They become especially interested in opportunities to meet and play with children similar in age to themselves. Part of this undoubtedly is due to the acquisition of the social expectation that this is what they "should" be doing, although the phenomenon appears to be virtually universal, and children appear to develop strong desires for peer contact with little or no prodding from adults. Some children may need help in overcoming bashfulness or other inhibitions, but the *desire* for peer contact usually is there (Hartup, 1970). Children tend to segregate themselves by age if they have a large number and variety of potential playmates available. They tend to prefer children the same as themselves first, then older children, and then younger children. They also show a slight preference for same sexed peers as playmates, a preference that becomes much stronger with age (this will be discussed later in the chapter).

The preference for children most similar to themselves is part of a more general tendency for children to be interested in and to show a preference for contact with anything that they discover is considered particularly relevant or appropriate to them. Children of similar ages also are likely to be at similar developmental levels (other things being equal), so that they are most likely to share common interests and thus play well together.

The typical preference for older playmates over younger playmates apparently occurs because older playmates tend to be more interesting and to be able to teach younger ones new things. This is important to most young children, who are continually interested in getting inside information from and about "big kids." Often children differing two or three years in age will be able to play well together, especially if the younger one is relatively mature. Where there is a clear age difference between children, sooner or later it is probable that the older children will tell the younger ones to "get lost," or, alternatively, will boss around the younger ones so continually that the younger ones eventually will decide to go home. These sporadic frustrations by older playmates usually are relatively unimportant and quickly forgotten, although if they happen with regularity, they can hurt a child's self-esteem and development of peer relationship skills.

AGE AND SEX ROLES   6.

Social psychologists and sociologists have noted that cultures tend to be organized hierarchically, and that a remarkable portion of individuals' behavior can be predicted and explained on the basis of the status that they hold in the society and the social roles which are associated with this status. Occasionally, a particular status and some of the role behaviors associated with it are prescribed explicitly, as in the case of the protocol surrounding royalty or heads of state. Most of the time an individual's status is implied covertly rather than expressed overtly, and the same is true for the role behaviors associated with this status.

Among preoperational children, the two most important status variables are age and sex, although variables such as race and social class begin to show effects and become increasingly important as children become more aware of them. Most children are not very aware of these latter variables during the preoperational stage, however, but they are very acutely aware of age and sex differences, usually to the point that they become preoccupied with them for a time. This is because age and sex are so important to self-concept. Children usually want to find out everything they can about them, because of their implications for what the children should or might think about themselves.

AGE ROLES   Throughout early childhood, and continuing through most of middle childhood, age is an extremely important variable in the eyes of almost all children. It is a hot topic of discussion among children who are discussing themselves and comparing themselves to others, and it is one of the major variables used in establishing a childhood "pecking order." Other things being equal, an older child usually is afforded greater status than a younger child. This shows up in all kinds of social interactions and on criteria ranging from who gets the biggest piece of cake to who decides what game is going to be played at the moment.

Older children love to remind younger children about the differences in their ages, and they usually do not hesitate to use age as the reason for why they should get their way ("I'm the boss because I'm five and you're only four").

Younger children usually accept this, although they frequently retort by reminding older playmates of their place in the pecking order ("Oh, yeah? Well, you're not the boss of your big sister!"). Because of the importance of age to self-concept and peer status, young children, in contrast to adults, are always looking forward to getting older (children aged three years, six months are not three-year-olds, they are three-and-a-half-year-olds).

The heavy stress on age differences at this stage appears to result from a combination of developmental and socialization reasons. The main developmental reason is that age really *is* a much more meaningful variable for very young children than it is for older children or adults. The difference between a thirty-five-year-old and a thirty-six-year-old adult is trivial, but the difference between a three-year-old and a four-year-old child is very great in magnitude and importance. An extra year at these very young ages means that older children have had many more experiences and possess many more schemas than younger children, so that in most areas they will be more knowledgeable. Their leadership status results in large part simply because they are objectively *more capable* of exerting leadership, not merely because they are *older*.

Age decreases in its importance to individual children and to children in general as they get older, although it remains important throughout childhood. Part of the reason for this is that children who are a year or more older than playmates will be ahead of the playmates in school and thus will continue to have an advantage over them in knowledge and experience. As a result, older children generally are the leaders of peer groups involving children of differing ages.

These age role differences that would exist in any case for developmental reasons are reinforced in most instances by socialization influences from adults. Almost all parents at some time or another rationalize their refusal to allow children to do something on the grounds that they are "too young," and many parents do this regularly. The importance of age as such usually is reinforced in a variety of contexts: children can get a tricycle for their fourth birthdays; they will be allowed to cross the street by themselves "when they are five"; they are going to "four-year-old school" now, but next year, when they are five, they will go to kindergarten. Age not only brings status in the peer group; it often is tied to the ability to obtain desired toys, privileges, or experiences from adults.

SEX ROLES   Like age, sex is an important component of the self-concept and a variable that carries with it numerous role expectations. Again, too, these role expectations vary across cultures and across geographical regions and social classes within cultures. In any case, it makes a great difference, both to the child and to significant others, whether the child is male or female. Sex roles refer to learned behavior associated with being of the male or female gender. They have nothing to do with sexual activity. This should be kept in mind, because, as will be explained later, sex role learning and sexual adjustment are virtually unrelated to each other.

The development of an active interest in finding out about and acquiring the toys, clothes, traits, friends, and other characteristics associated with one's age

248

in one's culture appears to occur spontaneously with little or no deliberate adult socialization or reinforcement (Kohlberg, 1966). One aspect of this orientation toward age mates and the peer group is the development of sex role learning. As noted previously, boys and girls differ somewhat at birth, physiologically and behaviorally as well as anatomically, and they begin to be treated differently at birth in ways likely to socialize the boys toward masculine traits and the girls toward feminine traits (as defined by a given culture).

A clear differentiation of the two sexes and a concern with one's own sex and with fulfilling the expectations of the sex role associated with it does not appear in most children until they are about three years old. Prior to this time, sex differences are noticeable, but they appear to result primarily from the differential toys and games that children are given to play with and the differential treatment they receive from adults. Children themselves do not seem much concerned about (and up to a point, not even aware of) sex differences among themselves. Part of the reason for this is that the children are so egocentric that they are relatively uninterested in *any* personal characteristics of age mates, including their sex. For the first couple of years, infants and toddlers are only vaguely aware of sex differences at best. For the next year or two, sex differences become objects of curiosity, but they do not assume any great importance in the child's scheme of things. Consequently, play groups of children up until around age three or four show relatively little conscious segregation along sex lines. Children this young usually are not especially interested in or concerned about the sex of their age mates.

Once concern about sex differences does begin to develop, sex differences become increasingly important to the child thereafter. As children learn more about and become more interested in sex differences, they also develop sex role expectations that affect their behavior. This gradually leads to a preference for playmates of the same sex and for activities associated with that sex, and also to a parallel distaste for and avoidance of members of the opposite sex and activities associated with the opposite sex. This developmental trend increases until it reaches a peak at about age eight, after which it gradually diminishes. Sex differences and sex roles continue to be important thereafter, but not in the same way that they were during early childhood (Kohlberg, 1966). The latter point is an important one to keep in mind, because most discussions of sex role learning have failed to distinguish sufficiently between *childhood* sex roles and *adult* sex roles. The distinction is extremely important for developing accurate explanations about how sex roles are learned.

Psychoanalytic theory posits that sex role learning results from identification with the parent of the same sex, which in turn is one outcome of resolution of the Oedipus complex. Social learning theorists of course reject explanations of this sort, but typically they do state that sex role learning is based primarily upon imitation or modeling of the same-sexed parent. Sex role learning is seen as a response to socialization pressures both from parents and from the environment in general, rather than from the sexual psychodynamics that Freud postulated. It usually is acknowledged that same-sexed models in addition to the parent are involved. Nevertheless, social learning theorists using concepts like imitation and modeling, and psychoanalytic theorists using the concept of identification, have in common the idea that the primary mechanism for sex role learning is observation and modeling of the parent of the same sex. This appears to be true, to an extent at least, with regard to *adult* sex roles. When acting in their roles as spouse or parent, most adults show both general traits and specific behaviors that apparently were learned as children when they watched their fathers or mothers behave in similar situations. They do not simply duplicate what their parents of the same sex did, of course; many other factors are involved. For one thing, children imitate *both* parents, not just the parent of the same sex. Everyone has certain traits that they picked up from modeling their parent of the opposite sex, whether consciously or unconsciously (Maccoby and Jacklin, 1974).

Adult sex roles are picked up from models of all kinds. These include adults other than parents who were important to the child when younger, contemporary models among respected friends and acquaintances, and vicarious models read about in books or magazines or observed in movies or on television. Some adolescents and adults consciously model themselves after someone other than their same-sexed parent, because they dislike or at least lack respect for that parent and wish to avoid being the same way themselves. For most people, however, modeling some of the behavior observed in the same-sexed parent is an important, and often the most important, source of adult sex role behaviors. Consequently, it is at least partially correct to say that adult sex role behavior results from identification with or imitation or modeling of the parent of the same sex.

This statement does *not* hold up, however, in regard to *childhood sex roles*. Young boys do *not* learn many of the behaviors considered appropriate for their age and sex by observing their fathers, and young girls do *not* learn many of the behaviors appropriate to their age and sex by observing their mothers. Instead, these things are learned by observing and being explicitly socialized by other children, particularly older siblings, friends of the same sex, and media personalities.

KOHLBERG'S THEORY   Most of the material to follow concerning childhood sex role learning is based primarily upon the work of Kohlberg (1966). These ideas stand in contrast to psychoanalytic theory and also to some degree to social learning theory. Kohlberg's theory is based in large part upon Piagetian cognitive developmental research. His theory of sex role learning minimizes the role of socialization (particularly reinforcement), describing instead a process that results from a combination of children's increasing cognitive development and their internal direction based upon the principle of equilibration. Kohlberg does not see sex role learning as genetically programmed or explained by biological maturation, but he does see it as occurring spontaneously in the usual situation, independent of socialization by adults. Kohlberg minimizes the role of identification with the parent of the same sex, the mechanism that other theories stress in their explanations of sex role learning. In my view, Kohlberg's theory is much superior to both of the other two, especially to psychoanalytic theory, but it does need some modification to take into account social learning concepts (Mischel, 1966).

Kohlberg notes that sex typing is universal. All cultures prescribe differential behavior for the two sexes. Most males in a given culture acquire the socially prescribed male characteristics, and most females acquire the socially prescribed female characteristics, to some degree. Sex role behavior obviously is learned, however, because cultures differ dramatically in the kinds of behavior associated with males as opposed to females. Virtually all the traits that are associated with males in our culture, for example, are associated with females in one or more other cultures (D'Andrade, 1966). Furthermore, within cultures, a few individuals with unusual child-rearing backgrounds acquire the characteristics associated with the opposite sex instead of those associated with their own. Sex role learning is culturally and not biologically determined.

Kohlberg points out that the *desire* to acquire the characteristics associated with one's own sex appears to be acquired spontaneously in the typical case. It usually appears shortly after children have discovered, asked numerous questions about, and developed an interest in the differences between the two sexes and the implications of these differences for their own present and future behavior. Although some modeling and, to a lesser degree, reinforcement, probably are involved, the primary motivating mechanism for systematic and deliberate sex role learning seems to be the development of the insight "I am a boy, and therefore I should act like a boy and do the things that boys do," or "I am a girl, and therefore I should act like a girl and do the things that girls do." There is much formal and informal evidence to support this idea. Before children become acutely aware of sex differences, they appear to be uninterested in them and relatively unaffected by them. Afterward, children begin to show clear preferences for same-sexed playmates and for toys, games, clothes, occupations, and other things characteristic of their own sex. They also begin to show an aversion for things associated with the opposite sex, including many activities that they happily participated in previously, rejecting them now on the grounds that "they're for boys," or "they're for girls." All of this usually goes on with little or no deliberate instruction or reinforcement from adults and sometimes in spite of it.

Kohlberg's argument is based primarily upon the close association of sex role learning with cognitive development. The timing of the cycle of sex role learning is closely related to the timing of certain aspects of cognitive development. Children who are cognitively more mature than their age mates begin to show sex role learning earlier, proceed to a peak of concern about sex differences and preference for their own sex earlier, and then gradually become less concerned with sex differences, again earlier, than age mates who are not as well developed cognitively (whether measured in terms of mental age or in terms of Piagetian criteria). In short, sex role learning involves learning about and mastering a set of concepts concerning sex differences and role differences associated with them, and this learning appears closely related to children's general brightness more than to their chronological ages

(Kohlberg and Zigler, 1967). Data like these help bolster Kohlberg's contention that sex role learning is largely a cognitive activity.

Finally Kohlberg argues that other theories of childhood sex role learning have greatly overstressed the roles of the parents relative to the roles of peers and other socialization sources such as the media, and that they have greatly overstressed the role or reinforcement. Most children probably receive direct instruction and reinforcement in a few areas, but it seems clear that most sex role learning occurs without any direct instruction or reinforcement from parents or anyone else. Children clearly are exposed to modeling influences, and thus are likely to develop general social expectations that they should act in certain ways and should avoid certain behaviors. Even where no direct reinforcement has been applied, it is probable that children will come to expect reward or punishment for fulfilling or not fulfilling sex role expectations.

Even so, the fact that most children obviously become motivated in a positive sense toward learning about and acquiring the characteristics associated with their sex role at a stage where they are not yet likely to be very sensitive to covertly implied social reinforcement, combined with the fact that the children seem to positively value and desire the acquisition of behavior and characteristics associated with their sex role, suggest that Kohlberg is primarily correct in asserting that the desire for sex role learning is based primarily upon the development of certain key cognitions and not upon deliberate socialization and reinforcement. His stress on the role of peers and on the media seems especially useful for explaining the acquisition of *childhood* sex role behaviors. The idea that sex role learning involves identifying with and/or modeling the parent of the same sex is useful in explaining how children acquire certain *adult* sex role behaviors that appear later, but it does not explain why they acquire the sex role behaviors typically associated with members of the same sex and age in the culture in which they are growing up. Typically, boys do *not* learn how to play with guns, and girls do *not* learn how to play with doll houses, from watching their fathers or mothers, although parents give them these toys and state or imply that they will enjoy playing with them. Mostly, children learn these things from other children, from observing child models on television and in books, and from such activities as paging through toy catalogues and visiting toy stores.

The primary vehicle for sex role socialization in childhood appears to be peer group socialization. Children pass along information and even instructions about toys and games to one another, more or less independently of adults. These days, adults have more of a say in determining what toys children will play with, because most toys now are advertised on television and in catalogues, but most games that children learn are learned from other children, who in turn learned them from other children. Studies of children's games have suggested that, for the most part, games are passed along from children to children, with adults rarely getting into the act (Herron and Sutton-Smith, 1971).

Much the same appears to be true for childhood sex role learning. Children pick up concepts about what is appropriate for children of their sex primarily

252

from observing and talking to one another and from television, books, shopping trips, and catalogues. Relatively little of this is acquired from adults, and much of it is acquired in spite of adults. Many parents find this out to their dismay when they discover that their children have long and quite specific lists of toys and games that they want purchased for birthday presents, or that they will refuse to wear certain clothes or use certain toys because "they're for boys" or "they're for girls."

Sex role learning proceeds continually and becomes increasingly important in the child's scheme of things throughout the preoperational period. Boys and girls who were close friends and who enjoyed playing with each other by the hour when they were three or four "wouldn't dream of being seen together" when they are six or seven. Neighborhood or nursery school playgroups which used to be organized according to geography or common interests begin to be organized along sex lines, with boys playing almost exclusively with boys and girls almost exclusively with girls. A certain amount of preference for one's own sex and hostility (mostly verbal rather than real) toward the opposite sex develops and increases until it peaks around age eight or nine. This leads to much teasing, name-calling, and occasional shouting and arguing, even among children who once were close friends. Fortunately, the problem takes care of itself and gradually disappears.

Antipathy for the opposite sex can peak at around age eight, although it may be notable in most children through age 11 or 12 (or beyond, in some cases). Spurred by the women's liberation movement and other forces concerned about increasing the flexibility of both sex roles, several experiments have been conducted involving systematic socialization attempts by adults designed to interest children in activities typically associated with the opposite sex, and, in general, to reduce the concern and stress placed on sex differences. To date, these experiments have succeeded in changing children's behavior only as long as deliberate and consistent socialization pressures were applied by the adults involved. As soon as the treatment was abandoned and the children were allowed to do whatever they wanted to do, they reverted to segregation by sex and to clear preferences for activities associated with their own sex (Serbin and O'Leary, 1975).

This does not mean that our sex roles are "natural" or unchangeable; cross cultural data reveal that this is not the case. It does mean that a change in the behavior of only a small portion of the socializing influences affecting children will not make much of a difference. Clear-cut and lasting differences in sex role learning are unlikely to be observed until and unless our society as a whole supports them. An implication for parents here is that they probably will be fighting a losing battle if they should try to prevent children of this age from acquiring aspects of sex role learning which are virtually universal in the neighborhood in which they live and in the culture in general.

SOCIAL LEARNING THEORY   The social learning and psychoanalytic theories of sex role acquisition are worth discussing here, because certain aspects of these theories which have proved to be largely or totally incorrect are especially easy to identify and discuss in relation to childhood sex role learning. Let us begin with social learning theory. Social learning theorists assume that sex role learning, like any other learning, is acquired through stimulation and reinforcement (Mischel, 1966). However, Kohlberg has pointed out that relatively little sex role learning is stimulated directly and deliberately by socializing agents or reinforced after it occurs. Some deliberate socialization does go on in most families: some little boys are told that they should or should not do certain things *because* they are boys, and some little girls are taught that they should or should not do certain things *because* they are girls. Some boys are criticized for certain behavior on the grounds that it is girlish or sissyish, and some girls are criticized for certain behavior on the grounds that it is tomboyish or unladylike. It would be incorrect to say that socialization and reinforcement do not play *any* role at all in sex role learning.

More importantly than reinforcement, *modeling* plays a major role in sex role learning. However, the bulk of this modeling does *not* involve watching and imitating the same-sexed parent. Instead, it involves watching and imitating other children and same-sexed models seen on television, in books, or in other media. While the classical social learning theory explanation of sex role learning as the result of modeling and imitation of the same-sexed parent is rejected (at least with regard to the acquisition of childhood sex roles), social learning principles such as stimulation, reinforcement, modeling, and imitation are acknowledged as important aspects of childhood sex role learning.

PSYCHOANALYTIC THEORY   In contrast, the psychoanalytic theory of sex role learning, and in fact the psychoanalytic stage of theory of development, is rejected almost entirely by most psychologists. It has been previously stated that the psychoanalytic oral and anal stages do contain a certain degree of validity if defined in terms of universal human experiences rather than in terms of metaphors based on bodily functions. However, the psychoanalytic phallic and Oedipal stages cannot be accepted even if reinterpreted, because there are no universal human experiences to support these psychoanalytic ideas as genuine stages. However, psychoanalysis will be discussed because it still remains widely known and to some degree widely accepted, despite overwhelmingly negative evidence.

The phallic stage was the name Freud gave to the stage at which children become concerned about their own bodies and the more general issue of sex differences. The very name he gave to the stage indicates one of the most fundamental difficulties with psychoanalytic theory; it has a definite and pervasive *masculine bias*. Its concepts and explanatory theories usually are at least understandable with regard to males (although usually not correct), but they break down completely and are seen as rather obviously wrong with regard to females. Because of this, the phallic and Oedipal stages will be discussed only as they regard males.

Freud referred to the period at which a boy becomes concerned about his own body and about those of others, especially girls, as the *phallic stage*. He did this because he believed that young children were particularly taken with the

254

fact that boys possess a penis and girls do not. This presumably led young boys to develop a sense of pride and a degree of exhibitionism, seen most directly in attempts to "show off" the penis. The basic idea was extended to include all kinds of "showing off," including some of the things discussed previously under striving for independence and social desirability. In any case, there is no basis or need for such a theory to explain any of the things that it purports to explain. Nor is there any basis for postulating that ordinary children go through a stage of obsessive concern over having or not having a penis.

The phallic stage was thought to be followed by the *Oedipal stage*, so named because certain elements in it were present in the ancient Greek tragedy, *Oedipus Rex*. Although it ultimately proved to be completely wrong, Freud's theory building effort here was quite ingenious. With one stroke, he developed a theory to explain simultaneously the increase and later decrease in relative concern about the body and sexual bodily differences, sex role learning, and the development of conscience. The presumed dynamics underlying all of this were as follows.

The boy (typically four to six years old) develops a sexual lust for his mother and a desire to marry her. He gradually becomes aware that this is not possible because his mother already is married to his father, a powerful authority figure whom he cannot hope to displace. As the boy thinks these matters over, he gradually becomes less concerned with lust for the mother and more concerned about what the father might do to him if he should find out what he is thinking. Ultimately, he decides that the father will become infuriated if he should find out what is on the boy's mind. No doubt he will punish him severely, probably, under the circumstances, by cutting off his penis. Since all of this is too bloody and horrible to contemplate for long, the boy puts it out of his mind permanently by using defense mechanisms, particularly repression (see Chapter Nine) and identification with the aggressor. He forgets that he ever had any lustful interest in his mother (or in females in general, for that matter), and he identifies with his father. In this way, he unconsciously hopes to curry favor from the father and also to share in his mysterious power (perhaps if he begins to act like the father, *he* will grow up to be big and powerful, too). As a result of all this, the boy emerges from the Oedipus conflict situation and enters the *latency stage*. Sexual thoughts remain repressed and latent, so that he presumably does not have another thought about sex until adolescence. Meanwhile, his identification with his father causes him to undertake sex role learning systematically and deliberately, and his need to please his father causes him to introject his father's moral values (internalize them as if they were his own all along), thus initiating the development of conscience.

Needless to say, this theory does not describe the typical situation. It is not totally impossible, however. It *is* conceivable that a few isolated young boys have managed to provoke jealousy in their fathers by showing affection and sexual interest in their mothers, and that some of these boys had fathers both jealous and stupid enough to angrily threaten to punish them by cutting off their penises if they did not change their behavior. In situations like these, which probably do exist, but are extremely rare, dynamics like Freud described would not only be possible but perhaps probable. Fortunately, however, these situations are not typical.

How could Freud go so far wrong? The basic reasons seem to lie in his extremely puritanical upbringing and surroundings, which caused him to be obsessed with sex, and in the fact that he built his child development theory by working backward from the dreams and reminiscences of adult neurotic patients, instead of by observing children. Given who Freud was and the methods that he used, it is not too difficult to understand how he arrived at his theory. However, child development researchers have discovered that children simply do not believe the things that Freud thought that they believed, except in unusual cases (Kreitler and Kreitler, 1966). Among the things that Freud thought were universal, but which research has shown to be non-existent or extremely rare, are the following.

1. Childhood sexuality in the sense of deliberate manipulation of the body, sexual organs or otherwise, for the purpose of obtaining bodily pleasure, definitely exists. Freud deserves credit for calling our attention to this. However, children do *not* lust after their parents (or anyone else, for that matter) in the adult sense of the word.

2. It is fairly common for a young boy to state that he is going to marry his mother when he grows up, and for a young girl to state that she is going to marry her father when she grows up. Again, these childish statements do not have anything like the meanings they would have if stated from an adult point of view. They are made by children who have only the faintest idea of what "marry" means. Usually, they only mean living together in the same house with the other person. Most children who make such statements do not understand adult sexual relationships or even the spouse roles involved in marriage.

3. Both boys and girls typically accept bodily sex differences with the same nonchalance that they accept other information they acquire every day. They do *not* think of boys as having a penis and girls as having nothing; they know that girls have a vagina (or whatever it is called in their home). This difference usually is accepted casually and is not given any more importance than sex differences in toys or clothing.

4. Cases of young boys who fear being punished by having their penises cut off, and cases of children of either sex who thought that girls once had a penis but had it removed, are extremely rare.

5. Childhood sex roles, as explained above, are not acquired through identification with the same-sexed parents. If this were the case, a young son would be reading newspapers and magazines, "working" at his father's desk, fixing things around the house, and working in the yard, like his father does, instead of playing with his toys, which the father usually does not do. He may well be picking up certain aspects of sex role behavior from observing the father that will appear when he is an adult,

but his *present* sex role learning is acquired primarily from interacting with other children and observing children on television, in books, and so forth.

6. Freud believed that most children had an anal theory of birth; that is, that they thought that children were born through the anus. Only about one child in a thousand ever has this idea. Most young children either know nothing at all or have a vague but generally correct idea (the baby grows in Mommy's tummy and then comes out at the hospital).

7. Finally, considering Freud's obsession with sex, his latency stage is particularly ironic. It is true that concerns about the body and about sex differences in bodily construction recede after they peak sometime between ages four and six, and that school-aged children prior to adolescence are concerned primarily with school, peer relationships, and the development of athletic skills and other talents. However, it also is true that sexuality persists and usually increases throughout childhood. Most "latency stage" children masturbate sporadically, play "house" or "doctor," show evidence of sexual arousal when daydreaming or dreaming, and otherwise show signs that they still are sexually active and not in a latency stage in which their sex interest somehow has gone underground until reawakened at adolescence.

Other difficulties in Freud's theory also could be mentioned. Most modern psychologists feel that the theory is totally and hopelessly erroneous, but orthodox psychoanalysts hold on to it tenaciously, despite evidence which proves the theory invalid. This no doubt would scandalize Freud himself, who did not hesitate to change his theories when the facts demanded it. It is unfortunate that some of his more zealous and faithful followers do not have the same vision and respect for the facts that Freud had.

To summarize this section on sex role learning, I believe that Kohlberg's theory fits the facts much better than social learning theory and particularly psychoanalytic theory. However, many of the concepts of social learning theory do appear to apply to sex role learning. A complete explanation seems to require a combination and integration of these two major theories. In contrast, psychoanalytic theory, while fascinating, appears to be completely wrong, and should be eliminated from serious consideration of childhood sex role learning in the future.

It seems important to distinguish between sex role learning in childhood and the learning about adult sex roles that occurs during childhood. Sex role learning in childhood quite obviously involves little or no identification with or imitation of the same-sexed parent, since that parent is performing sex typed behaviors appropriate to an adult rather than to a child. It should be obvious by now that a boy does not learn "how to be a boy" by watching and imitating his father, and a girl does not learn "how to be a girl" by watching and imitating her mother. Instead, this learning of childhood sex roles occurs by watching and imitating peers and child models.

It seems clear that adults often do show behavior that they apparently picked up by modeling their own parents, even though the observation of the parents occurred many years ago when they were children, and the adult behavior occurs many years later. Men whose fathers were authoritarian are likely to be authoritarian husbands and fathers themselves, and women whose mothers were warm and loving are likely to treat their own children similarly. Ordinary social learning concepts cannot explain such events adequately, although concepts like "modeling" can. The above discussion concerning the learning of sex roles in childhood should *not* be taken to mean that children never model their parents. They do model their parents, but not for the purpose of acquiring *childhood* sex role behavior. There appears to be little need or justification for the use of the term "identification" in the way it usually is used by psychoanalysts. The simpler term "modeling" as used by social learning theorists appears to be just as adequate for explaining the phenomenon, but it is preferable because it does not contain the undesirable theoretical "excess baggage" that is tied to the concept of "identification."

ERIKSON'S STAGE THEORY   Erikson (1963) broadened and somewhat reinterpreted the Freudian version of stages in personality development. In the late preoperational stage, he places less stress upon sex per se, as Freud did, and more on the child's need to successfully resolve the conflict of *initiative vs. guilt.* Much of his thinking is tied to ideas about child-rearing practices which relate to this particular conflict and also to the previous conflict of autonomy vs. shame and doubt.

Children who have resolved the conflict of autonomy vs. shame and doubt reasonably well, thus developing a healthy self-concept which includes a sense of autonomy within certain limits, are well on their way to also developing self-confidence that will enable them to take the initiative comfortably in achievement situations or social interactions. They are psychologically free to explore without fear of the unknown, and to experience failure without over-reacting by becoming terror stricken or guilt ridden.

In contrast, parents whose child-rearing beliefs and behavior have produced a strong sense of shame and doubt in a toddler are likely to continue such beliefs and practices, so as to produce a strong sense of guilt in the child at the late preoperational stage (these child-rearing practices are discussed in Chapters Six and Eight). Psychoanalysts stress parental over-reaction to children's normal explorations of their own bodies, and their curiosity about the bodies of playmates or other family members. Theoretically, strong negative parental reactions to such bodily explorations form the basis for more generalized guilt feelings, especially in children who already have a sense of shame concerned with bodily elimination functions and who later are taught that it is wrong to explore or manipulate the body, particularly the sex organs.

All of this appears to be generally true, except that it is only a subset of the more general principle that children who are encouraged or at least allowed to explore their environment generally (not just their bodies) tend to become eager and carefree about initiating such exploration, while children who are overprotected from and/or punished for such exploration of the environment (not just their bodies) tend to become inhibited. If socialization is sufficiently harsh and consistent, they may well develop strong guilt feelings and generalized inhibition and become very dependent and unable to take new initiatives without experiencing anxiety.

As an example, consider a young boy who develops the habit of playing with his penis, sometimes privately but sometimes in the most public and embarrassing situations. Here, parents should not over-react or tell the boy that he is bad or that his behavior is terrible, but they probably will want him to change his behavior in order to avoid embarrassment (and also in order to teach him something about social norms and expectations). In the immediate situation, rather than discuss or call attention to the masturbation, it may be best to get the boy interested in some other activity by making specific suggestions and even perhaps getting him started in the other activity. Later, in private, the boy can be told to be careful about irritating his penis so as not to make it sore. Also, the boy should be told that he should not masturbate publicly because some people do not like it and might get upset by it. At this point the parent might suggest that the boy stop, or if unconcerned about masturbation but only about social reactions to it, might tell the boy that in the future he will be allowed to do it only when alone in his room. In general, in discussing sex with children it is best to use correct terms (penis, vagina, and so forth), and to provide as much information as the children seem to need or want.

The stage of initiative vs. guilt also is tied closely to the emergence of conscience, a topic which will be discussed at the end of this chapter. Basically, the idea is that children who resolve the conflict successfully will learn to control their behavior and respect social conventions and moral responsibilities without losing their psychological freedom to assume initiatives and the responsibilities that come with them. Conversely, children who fail to resolve this conflict successfully will tend to emerge with overly strong and inflexible consciences which inhibit them from taking initiatives in ambiguous situations where they are not sure that they are safe from disapproval.

FAMILY CONSTELLATION FACTORS

In addition to general age and sex roles, some children are affected by family constellation factors such as the number of children in their family, the spacing of these children, and their place in the birth order (Sutton-Smith and Rosenberg, 1970).

The number of children in the family is associated more strongly with cognitive development than with social and personal development. In general, children from large families have lower IQs and less impressive records of achievement in and out of school than children from smaller families. This is partly related to parental education and social class. Higher status, better educated families generally have fewer children than lower status, less educated families. Even where family social class and education are equivalent, however, children from larger families will have less access to material advantages and to parental time and energy than children from smaller families, all other things being equal. This will mean a less favorable cognitive environment, unless the difference is made up by older siblings or other parent substitutes.

There also are some relationships between family size and social and personal development, although these relationships are not nearly as strong or well understood as those concerning cognition. In general, children from large families are relatively advanced in peer relationships for their ages, presumably because their opportunities to interact with siblings (brothers and sisters) enable them to learn social skills earlier than children who get less opportunity to interact with other children. Children from large families typically learn to share and get along with other children earlier and more easily than children from small families, particularly only children or children who do not have a sibling similar in age to themselves. Again, the difference appears to be simply a matter of experience. Since learning to share and cooperate with others is one of the major developmental tasks of social learning during the preoperational years, children necessarily will gain experience in these areas as they interact

Birth Order

Zajonc (1976) has advanced an interesting theory relating IQ and standardized achievement test performance to family configuration variables. He begins with a review of well-known studies indicating a negative relationship between test scores and family size. Children from smaller families tend to score higher than children from larger families. He then reviews a variety of cross-cultural data on birth order and the spacing of siblings in families. Although some data suggest a drop in test performance with increase in birth order, others do not, and the more fundamental relationship seems to be sibling spacing. It appears that children spaced farther apart tend to score higher than children spaced close together, when family size is held constant. This trend is most obvious and exaggerated in the case of twins, who consistently scored lower than non-twins.

Turning to another line of evidence, Zajonc shows that children from one-parent homes score lower on the average than children from two-parent homes. Effects are most severe when parental loss occurred early and when it was due to death rather than separation or divorce.

Finally, Zajonc shows that only children score more similarly to lastborn children than to firstborn children, although most child development literature lumps only children with firstborn children. This historical tendency to combine "oldest and onlies" is arbitrary, because there is just as much justification for looking upon only children as last children as there is for looking upon them as first children. It is just that few investigators have done so.

Data brought together by Zajonc provide a strong argument for the value of doing so because he has developed a compelling hypothesis to explain why firstborns with younger siblings tend to score higher on IQ and achievement tests than only children do. His hypothesis is that such firstborns get the opportunity as children to function as teachers in their interactions with their younger siblings, and it is a widely accepted truism that there is no better way to learn a subject thoroughly than to teach it. This explanation has great appeal because of its simplicity, and also because it does go a long way to explain the surprising (to some) superiority of oldest children to only children, along with certain national, regional, ethnic, racial, and sex differences in patterns of test scores. Furthermore, it has rather obvious implications for how we might go about providing remedial experience to children who have not had the opportunity to serve as teachers or tutors to younger children and thus get the cognitive benefits presumably associated with this experience. The latter has not been tested out yet systematically, although experiments with tutoring in the schools frequently show that the older children tutoring younger ones gain as much or more in tested abilities and achievement than the younger children who presumably are getting all the benefit from tutoring. Obviously, there are exciting possibilities here.

---

with other children. Because children in large families typically interact with other children (their siblings) more often, they tend to develop their social skills more quickly. Large families do not always or necessarily mean quicker or better social development, however. In families where strife and conflict among siblings is more or less continuous, these undesirable experiences may generalize to relationships with other peers and may result in poorer rather than better peer adjustment. However, this happens in only a minority of cases.

BIRTH ORDER Oldest children tend to differ from children with older siblings on several cognitive and personality measures (Heatherington and Parke, 1975). In the cognitive area, they show higher achievement and, in particular, higher verbal abilities. This seems to be because they have more favorable cognitive environments in their early years, getting most of their input from adults. In contrast, children who get much input from siblings (particularly identical twins who spend much time with each other) develop their verbal skills at a slower rate. Peer contact is important for the development of social skills, but adults generally provide a greater quantity and a much higher quality of cognitive stimulation than do peers (including siblings).

Oldest children also tend to be more responsible, dependable, and conforming than children with older siblings, although these differences are much weaker and less clear-cut than achievement differences. Apparently, this is because they are more intensely and thoroughly socialized. Their parents have more time and energy to devote to their socialization, and they can focus socialization upon them alone, in contrast to parents who must divide their time and attention among two or more siblings. Oldest children, not only as children but also as adults, tend to be more socially conventional and more like their parents than do other children (Sutton-Smith and Rosenberg, 1970).

On the whole, they probably are better adjusted (to the extent that effects are strong enough to make any difference), because the differences mentioned

Successful prosocial behavior. An older sister reads to her younger sister, sharing her time and resources and helping the younger girl by doing something for her that she could not do for herself. The activity seems quite successful, judging from the absence of any signs of distress in either girl, the suggestion of satisfaction and enjoyment on the face of the older girl, and the clear interest shown by the younger girl. Incidentally, the clutching of the stuffed animal by the younger girl is very common in young children and fits with the suggestions of the work of the Harlows described in Chapter Four, although some children show little or no interest in clutching stuffed animals or other "security blankets." (NFB Phototheque/Photo by Terry Pearce)

Unsuccessful prosocial behavior. This boy appears to be satisfied in this "sharing and helping" situation, but his good intentions are frustrated by his own egocentrism, because his younger sister is not enjoying it. She seems uncomfortable, perhaps even frightened or upset. Identification and its symbols are evident in this picture, also. Chances are good that this is the boy's favorite toy, and that he requested the purchase of the shirt he is wearing. (Photo by Myron Papiz)

262

are primarily to their advantage. These differences are minor at best, however, and it can be argued reasonably that conventionality can be carried too far. Perhaps oldest children become competent and well adjusted but not as independent or creative as they might have become if they had not been so thoroughly socialized to be like their parents.

SIBLING RIVALRY   Jealousy, bickering, teasing, and general rivalry among siblings is common. Its importance has been greatly exaggerated because of the influence of psychoanalytic writings, although it does become a serious problem for some children in some families. Typically, rivalry is greatest when the children are of the same sex and are a year or two apart in age. Cross-sex children usually do not develop much rivalry other than some teasing, and children spaced three or more years apart usually do not develop much rivalry either, regardless of sex (Koch, 1960).

Part of the reason for greater rivalry among siblings close in age is that they have similar friends and interests, and thus are competing for leadership or privileges. Furthermore, they will be close enough in size so that fights are likely to be common. Fights are unlikely when the size difference is so great that the younger one is in no position to challenge the older one through direct confrontations.

Sometimes sibling rivalry, particularly jealousy, goes back to the birth of the younger sibling. This aspect, in particular, has been over-stressed by psychoanalytic writers, but it does occur in some families. The older sibling, particularly if he or she is the first child, becomes accustomed to being the center of attention in the household, the "apple of the eyes" of both parents and numerous relatives. All this changes with the arrival of the new sibling, and sometimes the older one can get lost in the shuffle as everyone becomes interested in and concerned about "the baby." In some children who have not been adequately prepared for the arrival of a new brother or sister, the event, and more particularly the switch in attention from themselves to the new baby, produces feelings of resentment and rejection, as well as jealousy toward the new baby, who may be perceived as the cause of it all.

This is unnecessary and avoidable if the child is properly prepared. The main essentials here are that the parents build and maintain a positive image of being a "big brother" or "big sister" to the baby. They can allow older siblings the opportunity to do certain things for and with the baby, praise them for doing so, and continue to show (*show*, not just tell) them that they still are interested in them as individuals, independently of their activities connected with the baby. In this way, the arrival of a new baby becomes a positive event that older siblings can look forward to and enjoy along with the parents, and not something to fear or resent.

SOCIAL RELATIONSHIPS WITH PEERS   Orientation toward age peers develops slowly, but gradually it becomes extremely strong. Compared to older children, young children still at the level of parallel play are not very interested in peers, being more interested in the physical world and in mastering sensorimotor schemas. By the time they reach the stage of cooperative play, they not only are capable of playing cooperatively with other children, they usually desire to do so very strongly and continually. From around age three on, most children want to play with peers at every opportunity.

In the early stages, before the social skills of sharing, cooperation, and the like are well developed, children will be somewhat dependent upon adults for suggestions and directions. However, by age five or six, children usually are capable of playing together by themselves for long periods of time, even a whole day, with little intervention by adults (other than to request or even have to demand that they come in and eat or to stop them from dangerous or destructive play).

Contact with peers is important starting around age three, although contact with parents remains important. The child also will need and usually want time alone occasionally. If peers are not available in the neighborhood, it can be helpful to send children to nursery school or playschool, where they will get opportunities to meet and interact with other children their age. Adults who create expectations and give instructions about how to act with peers can go a long way toward preparing children to be able to play cooperatively with others and to learn to solve disputes without turning to adults for aid. Ultimately, though, children will have to put these ideas into practice through direct experiences with age mates.

The rate of social development, and the specific traits children develop, are somewhat dependent upon the nature of their peer group. Children who are the oldest in a peer group are likely to show leadership qualities, simply because they are the oldest and know more than the others. Conversely, younger children probably will be followers if they are in a peer group led by an older child, but they probably will learn more than they would if their playmates were younger. A three- or four-year-old child usually is eager to play with any peer of about the same age, regardless of sex and regardless of the play activities involved. As children get older, they become more interested in playing with same-sexed peers and more choosy about peers and play activities. Certain peers may be preferred as playmates because they are of the same sex, because they are older, because they have games or toys that the child likes to use, or simply because they are more fun to play with.

Interestingly, the degree to which the children get along well together is almost unrelated to their interests in playing with each other. Most preoperational children are aggressive and uncooperative to some degree, not so much in direct and deliberate ways, but simply because they are egocentric and not yet able, let alone willing, to take into account the rights and feelings of playmates in monitoring their own behavior. It is common for young children to casually take away a toy from another child, ignore demands to share a toy, and show similar evidence of what adults would call tactless or selfish behavior. It is not tactless or selfish in the same sense that it would be if done by an adult, because it is done in an egocentric way, without awareness of its effects on the other child. Nevertheless, these children need to learn that they must accommodate to the needs and desires of others to some degree if they are going to get along with them.

Preoperational children. Many of the characteristics of preoperational children are observable in this picture. The children show both assimilation (they seem comfortable and self-assured in a familiar situation) and accommodation (they both clearly are curious and exploratory, thus expanding existing schemas or developing new ones), all under the control of internal equilibration (the infant on the left selects a particular physical stimulus for manipulation, but the "manipulable stimulus" selected by the infant on the right is the infant on the left!). Both infants, but especially the one on the right, illustrate egocentrism, being clearly preoccupied with their own concerns. (Photo by Myron Papiz)

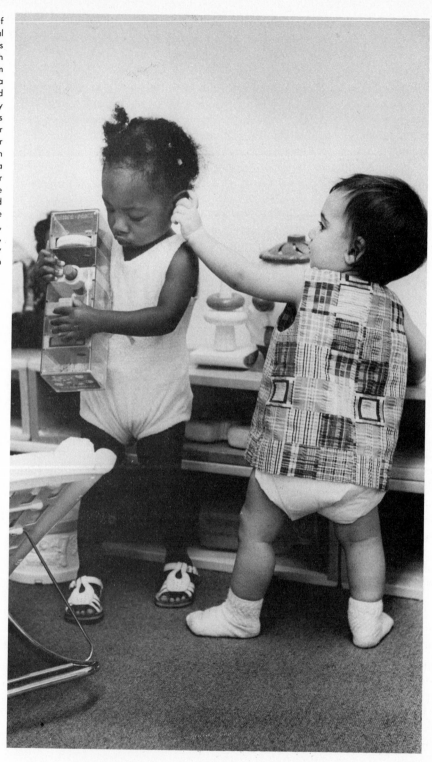

Coupled with these egocentrically aggressive actions is egocentrically tactless speech. Children have been described as "cruel" in verbally attacking one another and pointing out deficiencies in direct and seemingly spiteful ways. Here again, this behavior occurs because they have not yet developed the cognitive structures required for what we call social tact, and does not occur because children are cruel or vicious. Often, in fact, older children teach or help younger ones through "tactless" comments. For example, a younger child could be chided by an older child for not knowing how to color, because the younger child was paying little heed to the lines in a coloring book. These remarks usually would neither upset nor anger the younger child. Instead, they would lead to a tutoring session in which the older child would help the younger child learn to "color better."

Children know nothing of the explanation for "tactless" or "aggressive" behaviors, but they do know that the behaviors themselves are of little or no importance. This is why most fights and arguments are settled very quickly and soon forgotten, so that two children who were striking one another a few minutes before soon are happily playing together. Adults who work with children and observe them playing together should not become upset unnecessarily over such childish disputes. Adult intervention often is needed to solve the problem, but such intervention usually can be confined to a simple suggestion ("Why don't you take turns?"), or a brief explanation as to why a child should or should not do something. Ordinarily, this will be enough both to satisfy the children involved and to cause them to change their behavior. There should be no need to monitor the children carefully to make sure that they do what they are told or to see that the dispute does not evolve into a feud or fight. There usually is no need to dwell on the incident unnecessarily. The children need a short explanation or suggestion, but not an extended lecture that goes on so long that they forget what started it all in the first place. Prosocial development results from a large number of brief experiences such as these, and not from a few "crucial" ones. Disputes that seem serious from the adult's point of view usually are relatively minor from the child's, even if yelling or crying is involved, and they usually are literally forgotten shortly after they have been settled.

Occasionally, the same problem will persist in a variety of situations and will require somewhat stronger action, as when a child persistently refuses to share or always demands to be first. Where ignoring or repeated explanations have not changed the behavior, it usually is simplest to explain to these children that if they do not change their behavior, their friends will have to go home (or if the child's playmate visiting in the home is causing the problem, that the playmate will have to go home). This shows the children that the adult means business, and it also constitutes a powerful threat. For children of this age, being cut off from peers is an extremely powerful punishment. This should not be done often. It should be reserved for situations where unacceptable behavior has persisted despite continued attempts to change it. If adults move in too quickly or too often to settle disputes themselves, children will not learn how to work them out on their own.

266

As the preoperational period proceeds, children gradually move from being egocentrically selfish and aggressive to becoming strongly prosocial and cooperative. This is because their peer orientation remains strong or gets even stronger, but their egocentrism diminishes as their general cognitive development and their more specific social skills grow. The same children who tried to hoard toys or treats when they were three years old will seek to get extra treats from adults in order to give them to playmates when they are five or six. Most children also change from selfishness, competitiveness, and unwillingness to take turns and cooperate to a strong concern about fairness, seeing that everyone gets a turn or an equal opportunity, and the like.

These and related developments in the social area occur partly in response to socialization pressures from parents and peers, and partly as a result of cognitive development that enables children to overcome egocentrism and begin to see situations from the viewpoints of others and to have empathic understanding of others' needs and feelings. By the end of the preoperational period, many social and personal traits have become somewhat stable and obvious. A child who is introverted vs. extroverted, a leader vs. a follower, prosocial vs. antisocial, or afraid of competition vs. normally competitive vs. o erly competitive, is likely to remain this way, at least relatively, until adolescence.

This does not mean that the preoperational period is critical for the development of these skills, or that they cannot change thereafter. They can and frequently do change. However, *the same socialization forces* and general environments that cause children to develop certain traits by the time they are six or seven usually *persist* throughout childhood, so that the forces already at work in shaping development tend to continue and reinforce existing tendencies to develop in the directions they already are headed. As they achieve stable cognitive structures at the end of the preoperational period, their behavior becomes more stable and internally consistent. As a result, social traits, like other aspects of personality, begin to become *generalized schemas* that persist over time and across situations, rather than immediate responses to new experiences, as was the case earlier. For the first time, it is appropriate to talk about the child's *personality* as such, and to discuss personal traits as characteristic of particular children. Those which clearly are characteristic at this point are likely to remain stable, unless the factors that produce them change (Kagan and Moss, 1962).

MORAL DEVELOPMENT

The child becomes a truly moral person for the first time late in the preoperational stage. As noted previously, the behavior of children in the sensorimotor stage and early aspects of the preoperational stage is almost completely under the control of external stimulation and reinforcement. If morality is defined in such a way as to take into account conscious intentions and conscious awareness of the implications of behavior, young children must be described as "amoral" or "premoral" until they overcome egocentrism and begin to become operational in the sense described at the end of Chapter Five.

Until this time, they respond to socialization pressures in much the same way that an animal responds to consistent training pressures: they repeat behavior that brings acceptance and rewards and usually avoid behavior that brings rejection and punishment. Depending upon the nature and quality of the socialization pressures to which they have been exposed, young children will differ in the degree to which their behavior is "moral" by adult standards, even though they have not yet developed *internalized value systems* which bring behavior under *self-control* rather than *external control*.

In a very real sense, the concept of morality and related concepts like mutual respect for rights and privileges or consideration of the effects of behavior on the self and others are utterly meaningless to young children. They simply do not understand them. As children begin to develop the cognitive structures to enable them to understand such concepts, they begin to take them into account increasingly in controlling their behavior. This general idea is agreed upon by theorists of very different persuasions, although their particular explanations for it differ. Theologians and philosophers recognized that the young child was premoral with their use of concepts like "the age of reason." Freudians postulate that the development of conscience (part of the superego) is one outcome of the resolution of the Oedipus complex, so that it does not exist until this time. Behavioristically oriented child psychologists talk about how the child's behavior is controlled initially by physical or material rewards or punishments, then by a desire to please parents and others who are in positions to control access to rewards and punishments, and eventually by the development of internal self-control mechanisms. The role of reinforcement is considered important all along. It is recognized that more and more behavior comes under the control of internal mechanisms as the child gets older, but the ultimate motive for self-control presumably is to maximize social approval and rewards and minimize disapproval and punishment.

The roles of reward and punishment and of general social learning principles should not be minimized as important aspects of moral development. However, the evidence indicates rather strongly that the primary reasons for the transition from external to internal control of behavior and from premorality to a genuinely moral level of functioning lie in the series of related cognitive changes that occur as the child becomes operational at the end of the preoperational period. Piaget has discussed these in terms of overcoming egocentrism and developing the cognitive abilities to put one's self in the place of another, to understand the importance of rules and of seeing that everyone gets fair treatment, and to understand concepts like fairness and reciprocity which underlie "Golden Rule morality" (treating others as one would like to be treated oneself).

KOHLBERG'S MORAL JUDGMENT STAGES   Combining ideas from Piaget and other students of cognitive development with ideas from social learning theorists, Kohlberg (1969) has developed a stage theory of moral development that appears to have both validity and usefulness, despite recent criticisms (Rest, 1974). He identified three primary stages (preconventional morality, conventional morality, and postconventional morality), with two sub-stages within each. The term "stage" is used very loosely here, because children almost always show a mixture of moral judgments typical of several stages, even though their judgments usually cluster primarily at one of the stages. Many individuals, perhaps a majority, never reach the higher stages.

Children at the stage of *preconventional morality* already have been described: they are not really moral at all; their behavior is controlled by external stimulation and reinforcement. Early in this stage, their primary concerns are obtaining direct material rewards and fear of punishment. They will control their behavior in response to socialization demands, but this control will be based solely on desires to obtain rewards and especially to avoid punishments, and not on any general concepts of right and wrong.

Later in this initial stage, children become less concerned with material and physical rewards and punishments and begin to move toward true morality. Much behavior now is under the control of what social learning theorists sometimes call "secondary reinforcement" or "social reinforcement." Schemas have become more generalized and integrated, and one generalized schema is the desire to please parents and other authority figures. An ulterior motive still is obtaining rewards and avoiding punishments, but a more conscious and immediate concern is pleasing significant others.

Another major schema that develops at this time and reinforces the same general kind of morality is the understanding of concepts such as reciprocity and sharing. Children begin to see that, if they show these qualities, they will pay off. They develop primitive versions of the Golden Rule, in which they do certain things because they want to have the same things done for them or because they want to get rewarded. This is not yet a true Golden Rule morality, because motives still are egocentric and somewhat selfish, but children are learning to take into account the probable reactions of others to their own behavior.

The stage of *conventional morality* begins around the time children become operational, and it persists throughout childhood. In many individuals, it persists *throughout life* as the predominant level of moral judgment. At this level, behavior is self-controlled, and motives are social approval (at the conscious level) and desires for acceptance and reward (at the unconscious level). For the first time, children develop the understanding that certain behaviors should be performed because they are "right," and others should be avoided because they are "wrong."

Early in the stage, the content of this morality is determined primarily by parents and other important socializing agents in the immediate environment. Kohlberg sometimes has referred to this as "good boy" and "good girl" morality, because children at this stage develop concepts of the traits that a "good boy" or a "good girl" should have, and usually attempt to acquire these traits. Conscience develops at this point, in that children for the first time are able and likely to take satisfaction in doing things that they associate with being "good," and to feel shame or guilt at doing things that they feel are "bad," even when no one else knows about them. They also become interested in morality for its own sake for the first time, so that they are likely to ask a lot of questions about right and wrong and to show this concern in their social relationships. For example, they may become upset and angry when someone violates the rules of a game or acts in a way that they have been taught is wrong.

Later in this stage, typically not until middle childhood or later, children generalize from immediate experiences and develop an authority maintaining or "law and order" morality. At this point, they think of moral guidelines and social rules as very important in their own right, and as important for the good of people in general or of society, not as important simply because their parents have said that they are important. In addition to a concern with moral codes such as the Ten Commandments, they become concerned with school and game rules, laws, and social expectations. Morality usually is equated with legality, and vice-versa.

Concepts such as the distinction between the intention and the act, or the ability to take into account situational factors that would increase or decrease the justification for a particular action in a particular situation, have not developed and will not develop until adolescence (if and when the child develops formal operations). This level of *postconventional morality* involves the development of generalized moral concepts and their assimilation into an integrated, internally consistent generalized schema which is used as the basis for *all* moral judgments. Lacking such an abstract system, young children respond to the more concrete aspects of specific situations. Young children may believe that it is more seriously wrong to break ten dishes accidentally than to break one deliberately. In general, they think that certain things are wrong at all times and under any circumstances. They also tend to see rules and laws as necessary and unchangeable, rather than as social conventions that were invented and could be changed. These notions of morality affect their perceptions of people. People who break the law are thought of as "bad" in a general way, and it is very difficult for children to understand or even conceive of the idea that political leaders or authority figures could be "crooks" or "bad people."

Gradually, children develop some sense of the distinction between an act itself, the intentions that led to it, and the consequences that resulted from it. Most children, for example, learn the difference between an "accident" and something done deliberately, and often they will attempt to justify the fact that they broke something on the grounds that it was "an accident." This now occurs because the child has discovered that property destruction caused deliberately or carelessly is considered wrong, but destruction considered to have been accidental is not considered wrong and will not lead to blame or punishment (although it may lead to a lecture on the need to be more careful).

There is some evidence that children are more sophisticated in their moral judgments than Kohlberg's work implies. His original moral judgment scales were developed on the basis of responses to questions about moral dilemmas which were posed to children in the 1950s. At that time, our society was more conservative and orderly than it is now, and the moral pronouncements made by parents and religious educators were more likely to be accepted without question by young children. The turmoil of the 1960s and the 1970s made it very clear that there were fundamental disagreements among adults about morality. Especially after Watergate and related incidents that involved immorality by some of the most prestigious politicians in the country, including the President himself, children now are much less likely to naively accept oversimplified moral generalities than were the children of 20 years ago. This increase in moral sophistication may or may not be a good thing in the long run. It will be beneficial if it leads to an increase in recognition of the need for moral behavior, but there also is the danger that it could lead instead to a deep sense of mistrust and cynicism regarding other people. This would reduce the likelihood that people would become more altruistic and pro-socially moral in their behavior.

These considerations lead to a related set of ideas that are extremely important and worth discussing at this time. Students of moral development have made distinctions among *moral judgment* (the child's ability to reason and draw conclusions about the morality of situations, usually measured by posing moral dilemmas and recording the child's responses, as Kohlberg and others have done), *moral affect* (feelings of satisfaction after having done a good deed, and, more typically, feelings of guilt and shame after having done something that one considers wrong), and *moral behavior* (how one treats other people and generally conducts one's life).

Intuitively, most people suspect that these three aspects of morality would intercorrelate strongly, so that people with high levels of moral judgment also would be likely to be moral in their behavior and likely to experience guilt if they should transgress against their moral codes. In fact, many people take this for granted, and automatically assume that someone who scores high on a scale of moral judgment, such as Kohlberg's, is a more moral person than someone who scores low. This definitely is not the case. The intercorrelations among measures of moral judgment, moral affect, and moral behavior are too low to have much practical significance. Moral *judgment* is much more an aspect of *cognitive* development than of morality (in the sense of practicing the Golden Rule in one's interactions with others). Children's scores on moral judgment scales are very closely related to their mental ages and their scores on Piagetian measures of cognitive development, but unrelated to both moral affect and moral behavior. This is because morality is a content area that one can learn about in varying degrees, like mathematics. Unfortunately, learning about morality and being able to make increasingly sophisticated statements about moral dilemma situations in one's interview responses do not insure that one will be moral in one's behavior.

This can be seen in children, but it is even more obvious in adults. People who are marginally literate and who have difficulty verbalizing *anything* are unlikely to score very highly on moral judgment scales, because verbal abilities are so central to these scales, yet they might be models of morality in their behavior. Conversely, we have no shortage of examples of well-educated individuals who are capable of discussing the nuances of moral dilemmas in great length and depth, and consequently of achieving very high scores on moral judgment scales, who nevertheless are grossly immoral in their behavior.

Moral affect does not correlate strongly with moral behavior either, which is why many psychologists counsel against child-rearing strategies that are likely to produce an overly strong and rigid conscience (see Chapter Eight). Unfortunately, compulsive alcoholics, gamblers, wife beaters, and others who indulge in behavior that they know is wrong and then experience deep guilt and shame, only to repeat the cycle again and again, are commonplace. The guilt and shame are very real, occasionally leading to suicide or to punishment-seeking attempts. Nevertheless, they do *not* cause people to change their behavior. Conversely, many individuals who are models of morality by anyone's standards rarely if ever experience guilt. Their prosocial moral behavior is motivated by factors to be described below, and not by fear or the desire to escape punishment or rejection.

In summary, then, moral judgment is largely a cognitive rather than a moral trait. It tells more about people's intellectual abilities and educational levels than it does about their morality. Moral affect, particularly conscience pangs, result from certain unfortunate child-rearing practices that produce a rigid conscience that leads to guilt feelings whenever people transgress against their moral codes, but these guilt feelings do not prevent them from repeating their transgressions. So, *moral behavior* is not controlled or caused to any significant degree by either moral judgment or moral affect. Instead, it results from a combination of modeling influences and child-rearing practices that make people proactive and rational in controlling their behavior.

MORAL BEHAVIOR   Models are by far the most important influences on the behavioral aspects of moral development. Numerous research studies, both naturalistic and experimental, have shown overwhelmingly that children tend to imitate what they see. By and large, it is unnecessary for an adult to tell a child to "do as I do," because the child is likely to do it anyway. Conversely, it is utterly futile for an adult to attempt to tell a child "do as I say, not as I do," because it is not going to work. If there is any conflict between what children hear adults say and what they see adults do, they will end up imitating what the adult *does*, at least when the adult is not around to force them to do otherwise (Bryan, 1975).

This does not mean that children are automatically destined to have the same kind of morality as their parents, because peers, the media, and other socialization forces also influence morality (Kohlberg, 1969). However, unless children eventually become explicitly aware of a particular parental trait and deliberately reject it, they are likely to show it in their own behavior because of modeling influences. Generous parents are likely to have generous children; parents who do not hesitate to tell "little white lies" in order to escape undesirable situations or to rationalize their behavior are likely to have children with equally bad credibility; and parents who have particular vices are likely to have children with these same vices, no matter how much time they spend preaching to the children about how they should not develop these vices themselves.

The correlations between parental behavior and child behavior are especially likely to be strong when modeling influences are supported by expectation effects. The classical, and perhaps most ironic, example of this is physical aggression. There is a very strong positive relationship between parental physical aggression and use of physical punishment (such as spanking and slapping) and the development of these same traits in children (Feshbach, 1970). In most cases, the parents are punishing the children in an attempt to socialize them, and often the punishment is in response to physical aggression by the children themselves. This method of "child rearing" backfires, because by punishing the child with physical aggression, parents are *modeling* physical aggression themselves and also are communicating to the child the *expectation* that one responds to frustrating situations by becoming physically aggressive. Such parents also are likely to be building up funds of hostility and resentment in children, which probably will make them want to "take it out" on others. A vicious circle of child aggression followed by physical punitiveness which increases the likelihood of additional child aggression is established, so that the child grows up to be a hostile, aggressive person. This is especially likely if aggression against peers is *reinforced* (the child usually gets away with it and is able to use physical aggression as a means to control or dominate peers).

Similar effects can be seen in other areas too, even where little or no physical aggression is involved. One sad example combined both modeling and communication of expectations. This case involved a mother who had married because she had become pregnant by her boy friend. This mother was so obsessed with determination to see that what happened to her did not happen to her two daughters, that she waged a systematic and continued campaign to prevent it. She preached the importance of sexual chastity in general and before marriage in particular, lectured the girls about how boys would try to take advantage of them, delayed their dating and other contacts with boys as long as she could, placed heavy restrictions on it when she did allow it, and in general spent an inordinate amount of time and energy drumming into the girls the idea that sex was not going to ruin their lives the way it had ruined hers. Unfortunately, however, all of this overkill, coupled with the facts that the mother had not practiced what she preached and that she preached in such a way as to give the impression that she was trying to stave off the inevitable, resulted in the girls' acquiring the strong impression that sex must really be something fantastic. Why else would their mother place so much emphasis on it and go to such lengths to try to prevent them from finding out anything about it or indulging in it? To make a long story short, both girls became pregnant out of wedlock at age 14.

Additional discussion of the dangers of inappropriate child-rearing behaviors, along with extended discussion of what I believe to be much more effective child-rearing behaviors, will be presented in the following chapter.

NORMAL BEHAVIOR VS. "IMMORALITY"   A few typical child behaviors that appear in the preoperational stage are discussed in the present section because adults often view them as immoral or "bad," although in fact they are perfectly normal developmental phenomena. These include aspects of reality testing that sometimes appear to be lies or obscenities from the viewpoint of adults, masturbation and sex play, and certain behaviors involved in the development of a sense of humor.

As mentioned previously, it is common for young children to "lie" in the sense of telling an untruth, even one that is obviously untrue. Adults need to learn to suppress their frustration and anger in these situations and understand that the child is reality testing, not lying in the same sense that an adult would be in a similar situation. In the process of making the transition from a premoral mode of thinking to conventional morality based on respect for authority and fear of punishment, most children go through a period of believing that they must please parents and other authority figures at all costs. From their point of view, telling parents what they want to hear in order to stay in their good graces is far more important than admitting a transgression that may lead to rejection or punishment. For a time, some children will deny transgressions that they are accused of, especially if they can tell from the adult's manner and tone of voice that the adult is angry and likely to punish them if they admit that they did it.

Another related type of "lie" involves bragging about non-existent accomplishments. Once children learn that they will get approval and perhaps even tangible rewards for positive accomplishments, they may begin to tell tall tales about all of the wondrous deeds that they accomplished in competitive games with friends or in activities at school or at parties. Children can go through a brief period in which they claim, virtually every day, to have won every race or other physical activity conducted in the gym, to have won every game played at a birthday party, and to have won every game or competitive activity engaged in with friends in after school play. An adult can easily reinforce these claims in the early stages, because there would be no reason to doubt the claims and thus respond to tales of victory and success with praise and admiration. Later, as adults realize that success stories were inflated, one should begin making minimal responses and/or observing that "It's really hard for me to believe that you won *every* game."

Provided that the adult does not over-react, these tendencies to deny or exaggerate the truth usually are brief and relatively unimportant. They are one of the ways that the child tests reality, gets feedback, and gradually reorganizes schemas. If adults react to denials of responsibility by pointing out to children that they know the truth and by reminding them about how they expect them to behave, but without exploding in anger about their "lies," and if they respond to exaggerations of the truth by good-naturedly expressing doubts, the children soon will learn that these adults are going to respond to *actions* but not to claims which are not true. Even so, the children may have to learn and come to accept this in stages and over some time. Several repetitions of the same basic situation may be necessary for some children, perhaps dozens of repetitions. This seems irrational and irritating to adults, but it is not for a child. Also, when change does occur, it may occur in stages rather than all at once. For example, a child may at first admit only that certain other children had "tied" him in some races or contests. Later, he would admit losses but also make it clear that he won most of the time. Only after several months would the child reach the point where he would report his performance accurately.

"Morality" Varies with Situations

Studies of moral behavior in children have been puzzling but consistent in indicating that children show great differences across situations rather than a general and consistent level of morality. This conclusion was publicized originally after a study by Hartshorne and May (1930). They studied children's test taking behavior under conditions where the children could cheat and think that this cheating would go undetected. The investigators expected to find consistency in individual differences and relationships between cheating behavior and other measures. However, the frequency of cheating was inconsistent; correlations across different tests usually were not even significant. This means that children who cheated on one test were no more likely to cheat on the next test than children who did not cheat on the first test. Also, measures such as attendance or non-attendance at Sunday School and length of such attendance among those children who did go to Sunday School did not relate to cheating behavior. Many other studies done since on a variety of immoral behaviors have produced similar results.

More recently, research on prosocial behavior has begun to show that there is no general trait of "morality" in the positive sense, either. O'Bryant (1975) studied fifth graders in situations where they had opportunities to *share* (by donating tokens into a collection can presumably for poor children) and to *help* (by assisting kindergarten children in a simple task rather than watch passively while the younger children struggled with it). These two aspects of prosocial behavior were unrelated. Children who shared were no more likely than average to help, and vice-versa. Another recent study (Yarrow, Waxler, Barrett, Darby, King, Pickett, and Smith, 1976) did find some consistent relationships between sharing and comforting across situations, but these prosocial behaviors were not significantly related to helping. Furthermore, depending upon situational variables, these *prosocial* variables sometimes were related positively, sometimes negatively, and sometimes not at all to aggression, an *antisocial* behavior.

Such findings underscore the point that morality in general and even more specific attributes such as aggressiveness, honesty, or helpfulness are not stable traits, at least when measured behaviorally. They interact with a variety of situational variables, so that the same child who appears moral in one situation may appear immoral in another, and vice-versa.

At this point, the child would also understand that adults were more interested in his performance compared to his own past performances or to his capacities, rather than in his performance relative to that of other children.

In addition to "lies," a child may test reality by using words or making statements that adults consider to be obscene, tactless, cruel, or otherwise socially inappropriate. Here again, the child's behavior does not mean the same thing that similar behavior would mean if done by an adult. Children often do not understand the meanings of the words or sentences they use. Even when they do, they do not understand the implications or nuances of what they are saying. They do these things as a way to find out.

Typically, they have seen or heard someone else say or do these things, and they wonder what they mean. So they try to find out by saying or doing them in front of an adult and watching the adult's reaction. This often happens with obscene words. Usually around age four or so, children learn the concept of "dirty words." That is, they learn that there are certain words that adults do not approve for use by children, even though they may use them themselves. Usually the children have no idea at all what these words mean, but they know that they are important, because they produce strong reactions from adults. If children hear a new word and suspect that it may be a "dirty word," but do not know for sure, they may try to find out simply and directly by using the word deliberately in front of adults. In any case, the use of such words, or the making of statements about people that adults would consider to be obscene or tactless, usually is done innocently by children who merely are trying to find out what it all means.

When jolted with an obscenity from the mouth of a young child, adults should try to keep their composure (and a measure of good humor as well) if possible. Ask questions to find out where the word was picked up and what the child thinks it means. Once the necessary facts are collected, correct by explaining what the word means and by noting that it should not be used because some people are upset by it and might get upset with the child if they should hear the child use it.

Occasionally, young children will become so taken with a newly discovered "dirty word" that they will begin to repeat it over and over again, sometimes shouting it out in sing-song rhythmic fashion. Such situations call for calm but very firm limit setting. The children should be told, singly or in combination, that what they are doing is not funny and will not be allowed. This is most likely to be effective if the children get the idea that what they are doing is seen as silly or babyish rather than threatening. In any case, the adult will need to be prepared to back up the prohibition by threatening or following through with some kind of punishment for children who do not accept the prohibition (such as by sending them to the room or sending them home). It is well to remember that, even in situations like this, the child behavior involved is simply reality testing and limit testing. It is not serious and does not indicate anything morbid, evil, or abnormal in the negative sense of the word.

Another major form of perfectly natural and normal developmental behavior that produces needless worry and over-reaction in some adults is masturbation and sex play. Although Freud was wrong about almost all of the specifics he postulated about childhood sexual ideas, he was correct in asserting that sexuality exists in children. Children can and do manipulate parts of their bodies, including their sexual organs, for the experience of sensual pleasure that results. This occurs normally as part of their general exploration of their bodies. Some children develop indirect forms of masturbation by rocking themselves in certain ways or rubbing themselves to produce pleasurable feelings, and some even learn to masturbate directly by stimulating the sex organs. The latter children may even learn to produce a childhood analogue of an adult orgasm.

For the most part, the degree of masturbation and the particular form that it takes is accidental, dependent upon what children happen to discover in their exploratory activities (and perhaps on things taught to them by other children). In any case, masturbation, including masturbation to the point of sexual release, is perfectly normal. Children who masturbate regularly may need socialization to the effect that this is something that one should not do in public. This socialization should be similar in tone and manner to what children are told concerning why they should not spit, cough without covering their mouths, or sneeze at the dinner table. In short, they should be told that these things are annoying and occasionally upsetting to other people, but *not* that they are terrible or wrong.

The one time that masturbation as such might be of some concern is when it appears to be a form of *substitution for social play*. Masturbation conducted during normal quiet periods, apparently simply because the child enjoys it, is normal. However, children who spend most of their time in their rooms masturbating may be experiencing some adjustment problems. The difficulty is not masturbation itself; it is the fact that the children are not indulging in activities normal for children their age. It is a sign that something might be wrong with their social adjustments, perhaps causing them to withdraw from social interactions with peers. The masturbation probably results from spending so much time alone and having nothing else to do, rather than from any abnormal or morbid preoccupation with sex. Children who show this pattern of behavior need help in re-establishing good social relationships, not attempts to stop them from masturbating. If whatever is wrong in the child's social adjustment is corrected, the masturbation problem will take care of itself.

In addition to masturbating, children typically indulge in same-sex and cross-sex "sex play." The latter is something of a misnomer, because typically the children are exploring one another's bodies for the simple purpose of satisfying their curiosity and learning something. They are not engaged in true sexual activity (bodily manipulation for the sake of bodily pleasure). Here again, as with obscenities and masturbation, it is important for adults to provide whatever socialization information is necessary to inform the children about what kinds of behavior are appropriate or inappropriate and in what situations, but at the same time to avoid over-reacting in a way that might cause the children to become fascinated with the behavior or cause them to develop unnecessary or crippling guilt feelings about their own bodies, about nakedness, or about physical intimacy with other children of either sex.

Another area in which young children sometimes vex or irritate adults is in activities related to the development of a sense of humor. Here again, the problem is that children do not understand the concepts involved, so that they may behave in ways that adults see as inappropriate or may test reality by doing things to see what kind of reaction they will get. They may laugh when people fall and hurt themselves, cry when being teased in friendly ways, tell jokes that they think are very funny but which leave adults cold, or fail to see the humor in jokes told to them by adults. All of this is perfectly normal and understandable when you take into account the child's cognitive development and general fund of experiences.

Problems sometimes arise, however, when adults have inappropriate expectations and thus respond in undesirable ways, rejecting or punishing children for no good reason or making them feel anxious or guilty because they did something which was perfectly normal and understandable. Basically, the child's early understanding of humor is heavily weighted in the direction of physical humor (witness Saturday morning cartoons). They are not yet able to understand verbal humor, because they take word meanings literally and cannot yet "play with words" humorously the way an older child or adult can.

There are numerous other things that children do quite normally that sometimes unfortunately are given moralistic interpretations by adults, leading to much unnecessary and unfortunate haggling and unhappiness. Briefly, the following are all developmental phenomena which may require some socialization, but which do *not* involve abnormality or evil intent on the part of the child.

1. Lacking in appreciation for the "benefits" of cleanliness and personal hygiene.
2. Eating habits and preferences that do not correspond well with meal cycles or nutritional standards.
3. "Telling it like it is," even when it is embarrassing, incriminating, or vulgar.
4. Wanting to wear the same clothes every day, to change clothes without need, or to wear no clothes at all.
5. Showing no evidence of a need or desire for sleep at times that adults declare to be nap times or bed times.
6. Painting or drawing on walls, unscrewing screws from furniture, and the like.
7. Spilling food, dropping wet or sticky things on the floor, strewing clothes and possessions all over the house, or getting into the same argument several times a day with the same person, typically a sibling.
8. Showing reckless lack of concern for personal safety in some situations and persistent inappropriate fear and inhibition in other situations.

BECOMING OPERATIONAL

In connection with, and partly because of, the cognitive changes that occur around the time a child becomes operational, several changes in personal and social development appear also. Basically, children switch from being animal-like, with their behavior controlled by external stimuli and reinforcements, to the development of internal self-control and verbal self-regulation. As they develop stable cognitive structures, they also become subject to the principle of cognitive consistency, so that for the first time a measure of stability can be seen in self-concept and personal traits. Also, they begin to develop a conscience and make the transition from premoral to conventional morality.

Although children still have much to learn, they are much more like adults now than they were a few years earlier. Their interests and physical activities move away from the parents and home and out to the community and peer group, although parents and the home remain the most important influences in shaping cognitive and personal development. The personal traits shown at this point are stable and likely to remain so if the general environment remains the same, so that serious adjustment problems that persist past this point are likely to worsen unless corrected through intervention. Conversely, children who get to this point very well adjusted are likely to remain so throughout the rest of childhood and probably the rest of their lives, assuming that the factors that have affected them so far continue to operate in the same fashion.

SUMMARY Personal and social development in the preoperational years shows many of the same developmental trends as, and in many ways is affected by, cognitive development during these years. At first, preoperational children do not possess very many stable or general traits. Their behavior is stimulus and situation bound, and mostly under the control of external stimulation and reinforcement. As they develop a unified and more differentiated cognitive structure, they also begin to develop a unified and stable set of personal and social characteristics.

Much social and personal development in these years is marked by movement from self-preoccupation and egocentrism to peer and adult orientation. Children gradually become more and more interested in other people, both as objects of curiosity and, later, as sources of information and feedback. Feedback about the perceptions and effects of their own behavior is perhaps most crucial, because it lays the foundation for self-concepts.

As children come to understand similarities and differences among people and comprehend expectations concerning themselves, they identify with models perceived as similar to themselves and tend to prefer the company of these individuals and to imitate them in their behavior. This leads to the age and sex typing characteristic of early childhood, and eventually to a strong interest in playing with peers rather than spending time with or around the parents.

During the preoperational period, children develop from amorality or premorality to a childish form of morality based upon being perceived as a "good boy" or a "good girl" by parents and other authority figures. Their moral judgment abilities tend to be closely associated with their general intellectual abilities, but their moral behavior as judged by interpersonal relationships and interactions is determined mostly by the kind of socialization they receive and especially the modeling of socialization agents themselves. In general, children tend to do what they are expected to do and/or what they see important models in their environment doing, more or less independently of what they are told to do.

Egocentricism and other aspects of preoperational cognitive structures cause young children to say and do things which seem immoral or at least tactless from an adult perspective, but which are nothing more than innocent reality testing by children. Adults need to be able to recognize reality testing for what it is if they are to avoid inappropriate over-reactions that are likely to occur if such reality testing is treated as if the behavior had the same meaning it would have if adults did it. Suggestions about how adults can plan for and cope with these developmental changes will be given in the following chapter.

CHAPTER
EIGHT

Fostering Personal and Social Development in Young Children

In this chapter, two schematic models of parental behavior will be introduced. These two models are useful, not only for conceptualizing parental behavior as such, but also for discussing the effects of general parent characteristics and specific behaviors upon children. Many of the basic points made in discussing these two models will underlie what is said about optimal socialization of children, not only in the present chapter but in those to follow.

PERSONAL DEVELOPMENT

The first of these models is the circumplex model described by Schaefer (1959). This model was developed from a series of factor analyses of studies of parent behavior. The factor analyses were designed to see how measures from different studies related to one another, in an attempt to discover primary or major dimensions of parent behavior. The results are shown schematically in the figure. At first,

Schaefer worked with data restricted to mothers, but later work showed that the model fits fathers as well.

Although a very large number of parental characteristics and traits have been studied, including all those mentioned in the figure below, the factor analytic work of Schaefer (since replicated by other investigators) has shown that discussion of much parental behavior can be simplified by reference to two basic dimensions that seem to be primary and fundamental: love-hostility and control-autonomy (also called restrictiveness-permissiveness).

Earl Schaefer's hypothetical circumplex model for maternal behavior. (Reprinted from *Journal of Abnormal and Social Psychology,* 1959, 226–235. Copyright 1959 by the American Psychological Association. Reprinted by permission.)

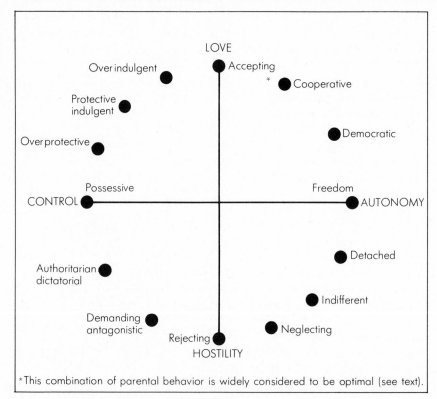

*This combination of parental behavior is widely considered to be optimal (see text).

The love-hostility dimension refers to the degree to which the parents love and value their children. Parents who value their children highly and feel a deep sense of love and affection toward them would be scored highly on this dimension. Parents who did not have much feeling one way or the other, or who had conflicted feelings, would be scored at the middle of the dimension. Parents who rejected and disliked their children and treated them with hostility would be scored low on the dimension.

The term "restrictiveness-permissiveness" is used in preference to the term "control-autonomy," because later work by Schaefer and others has shown that *firm* control (similar to Baumrind's authoritarian methods) has different effects than *lax* control (similar to Baumrind's authoritative methods). This has led to the development of more complex models by Schaefer and others. The circumplex model shown in the figure is used here for the sake of simplicity, although the term "restrictiveness-permissiveness" is substituted for the term "control-autonomy," and the defining information presented below is implied whenever it is used.

The restrictiveness-permissiveness dimension refers to the degree to which the parents closely restrict and control their children's behavior vs. permitting them wide latitude and autonomy in deciding for themselves what they are going to do and how they are going to do it. Parents scored high on this dimension control most aspects of their children's lives, placing numerous and tight restrictions upon their behavior. The children are allowed very little freedom to make decisions or take actions on their own. In contrast, parents scored low on this scale allow their children to make decisions and take action with little or no interference or expectation that they must follow certain rules or live up to certain ideals. In extreme cases, such parents might allow children to do virtually anything they want to do, as long as it does not involve injury or serious destruction of property.

Having briefly stated what these two dimensions *do* imply, it is worth noting what they *do not* imply. The love-hostility dimension does not necessarily imply overt physical affection from parents scored high in love, nor does it necessarily imply physical punitiveness by parents scored high in hostility. Many parents are not particularly expressive or overtly affectionate, but they still manage to convey commitment, respect, and love for their children. Similarly, many parents who rarely or even never physically strike their children nevertheless manage to convey that the children are disliked or rejected. The love-hostility dimension refers primarily to covert valuing and loving, and not necessarily to more overt behaviors such as physical affection or aggressiveness.

The restrictiveness-permissiveness dimension refers to the *degree* to which the parents exercise control over children's everyday decision making and behavior, and not necessarily to the *methods* they use in exercising this control. Many parents are scored very high on restrictiveness because they control their children very tightly, although they rarely if ever use threats, physical punishment, or other authoritarian and punitive methods. Similarly, parents scored as extremely permissive are not necessarily more child-oriented or less authoritarian than other parents. Sometimes, parental behavior scored as "permissiveness" really is not "permissiveness" at all, if the term is taken to mean a deliberately selected and systematically implemented *policy*. Instead, "permissiveness" often means disinterest, apathy, or an implicit attitude of "you stay out of my way, and I'll stay out of your's."

These considerations help explain a finding from the factor analytic studies that many people find puzzling: the love-hostility dimension and the restrictiveness-permissiveness dimension are not correlated with each other (Becker, 1964; Schaefer, 1959). Permissive parents are not necessarily more likely to be warm or loving than restrictive parents, and restrictive parents are no more likely to be hostile or rejecting than permissive parents. This important point should be kept in mind, along with the statements about parental characteristics that the love-hostility and permissiveness-restrictiveness dimensions do and do not include. Whenever the term "restrictiveness" is used in the remainder of the book, it will be used in the sense described above, *not* necessarily implying any hostility or punitiveness. Where the latter parental behaviors *are* meant to be included, this will be made clear. Otherwise, "restrictiveness" should be understood as defined above. The same holds for the terms "love," "hostility," and "permissiveness."

GENERAL PARENTAL CHARACTERISTICS AND CHILD OUTCOMES   A simplified schematic diagram showing the relationships typically found between the parental dimensions of love-hostility and restrictiveness-permissiveness is shown in the figure. These relationships are primarily correlational, so that they do not in themselves constitute *evidence* that the parental characteristics *cause* the child characteristics. In fact, we now know that some of the causality goes in the other direction, with certain types of children tending to elicit certain kinds of parental behavior (Bell, 1971). Nevertheless, these relationships have appeared in a great variety of studies yielding mutually supportive results, and some of them are backed by experimental data which do allow causal interpretations. There is good reason to believe that the correlations between parent and child characteristics shown in the figure below result primarily from parental effects on children.

Relationships among parent behaviors and child outcomes (see text).

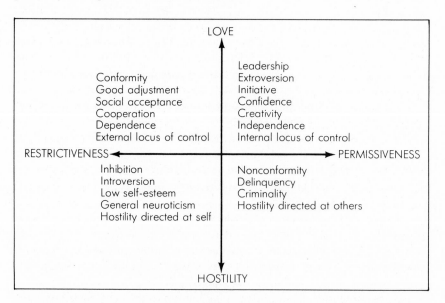

Another important caution concerning the figure is that it takes into account only *parental* characteristics which can affect children. We know that children also are affected by peers, the media, and numerous other influences in addition to parents. In most cases, parents are the strongest single source of influence, but there are numerous exceptions to this. Even in cases which fit the general rule, other influences will play some part in determining ultimate child outcomes. Statements about the probable effects of particular parent characteristics on children must be taken for what they are: statements of *probability*, not statements of *fact* based upon clear or simple cause and effect information.

The figure assumes that the parents are similar in their child-rearing characteristics. Where this is not the case, influences from one of the parents would lead children in certain directions, while influences from the other parent would lead them in other directions. The ultimate result would depend on the relative strengths of these influences, which in turn would depend upon the relative salience and power of the two parents, the degree to which the children looked up to and identified with the two parents, and numerous other factors. To avoid extreme complexities, *the following discussion will assume that the parents are generally similar* in their philosophies and practices concerning child rearing, and thus are exerting generally similar influences upon their children.

Finally, it should be kept in mind that the child characteristics listed in the figure are *stereotypes* which would result from rather *extreme* examples of the parental behaviors involved. Since *most parents are not extreme* on either of these dimensions, their influences on their children will be less extreme, although they will tend to be in the directions indicated in the figure.

Bearing these cautions in mind, let us examine the figure and discuss the relationships between parent and child characteristics that have been discovered repeatedly in child development and socialization research. Briefly, the love-hostility dimension seems most closely associated with the child's self-esteem and orientation toward others. The basic rationale here is very similar to the one for the stage of trust vs. mistrust in infancy. Parents who value and love their children are likely to develop in them a high degree of self-esteem and an attitude of trust and sociability toward others. In contrast, parents who dislike and reject their children are likely to produce children with low self-esteem who dislike and mistrust others as well as themselves.

The permissiveness-restrictiveness dimension appears to be most closely related to child traits such as initiative, autonomy, independence, and conformity. Parents who are extremely restrictive tend to produce children who are highly conforming and well socialized, perhaps too much so. In contrast, parents who are extremely permissive tend to produce children who are non-conforming and independent, although not necessarily in productive ways.

By considering these two major dimensions simultaneously and observing how they interact with each other, it is possible to be much more specific about probable child outcomes. Parents who combine love with permissiveness tend to produce children who combine high self-esteem and sociability with independence and nonconformity. Such children often are social leaders and/or highly creative types.

Parents who combine love with restrictiveness tend to produce highly conforming and very well-adjusted children (in the sense that they meet the demands of the parents with little or no difficulty or resistance). However, because of the high restrictiveness, such children sometimes are overly dependent upon the parents, non-creative and non-initiatory, and overly conforming.

Parents who combine permissiveness with hostility tend to produce antisocial, hostile, aggressive, and paranoid children. In this case, "permissiveness" usually is apathy or a form of rejection rather than a commitment to permissiveness as a child-rearing policy. In effect, then, such children grow up in homes where they are rejected and largely left to their own devices as long as they do not get in the parents' way. They tend to respond to parental hostility and rejection by developing hostility and rejection of their own. This usually includes low self-esteem, although it may be covered by antisocial and aggressive behavior toward others.

Finally, parents who combine hostility with a high degree of restrictiveness tend to produce children who have very low self-esteem, inhibitions, guilt, feelings of inadequacy, and general neurotic tendencies. Such parents tend to "break the spirit" of children by in effect convincing them that they are not very worthwhile. The child continually gets the message "You're no good, you never were any good, and you never will be any good," and comes to *believe it*.

The question of what kind of parental behavior is optimal cannot be answered unequivocally, because it involves *value judgments*. The most frequent answer given by child development researchers is shown in the figure. This is a combination of very high love with a balance between restrictiveness and permissiveness, leaning somewhat toward the side of permissiveness. The general logic here is that love and acceptance are almost totally good for the child, although most writers concede that at some point love could shade into seductiveness or other undesirable forms of highly affectionate behavior, and that extreme acceptance, if carried too far, might "spoil" children or tend to cause them to develop unrealistically high self-esteem or undesirable egotism. Except for such unusual extremes, however, most writers believe that developing children are better off more or less in direct proportion to the degree of love and acceptance they get from their parents (Ausubel and Sullivan, 1970).

The situation is different for the permissiveness-restrictiveness dimension, where there is more disagreement and where most writers counsel a moderate course, although most would prefer erring on the side of permissiveness rather than on the side of restrictiveness. This is because permissiveness tends to foster the development of attributes like initiative, autonomy, independence, and creativity, all of which are ordinarily considered "good." This is especially likely if permissiveness is combined with love and acceptance. Most writers agree on the points made in the previous chapter concerning the problems which can result when children are "granted permissiveness" in decision making or behavior when what they really need is guidance and help (Ausubel and Sullivan, 1970; Baumrind, 1971).

Writers who place the "optimal" point of intersection between these two basic parental dimensions at the place shown in the figure tend to see extreme permissiveness as an abandonment of parental responsibility and as a potentially dangerous practice which can cause children to suffer undesirable consequences from having to cope with situations on their own before they are ready. In some cases, these consequences could be inhibition and a desire for structure and dependency (if the children have had traumatic experiences and become afraid to act on their own). In other cases, the consequences might be egotistical, immature personalities and contemptuous attitudes toward authority figures and rules (in children who became accustomed to doing whatever they pleased whenever they pleased, and could not adjust to societal demands or even to the rights and privileges of other people).

If you agree with the general line of reasoning outlined above, you probably will agree that the optimal mix of parental characteristics is the one indicated in the figure. However, if you are more concerned about developing creativity and independence, less worried about adjustment to societal pressures, and willing to take the risks that come with non-conformity, you probably will see optimal parental behavior as combining love with a higher degree of permissiveness. Conversely, if you are concerned primarily about producing a "normal" and well-adjusted child, and especially if you are more worried about the possible negative consequences of nonconformity than you are excited about its positive possibilities, you probably will see optimal parental behavior as combining love with a greater degree of restrictiveness than that shown on the figure. Obviously, this is a value judgment that individuals and parents acting jointly must make for themselves. Those who choose to combine high love with a fairly high degree of restrictiveness are very likely to produce conforming and well-adjusted children who will be unlikely to rebel against parental demands or against the demands of authority figures generally. However, they will be unlikely to be social leaders or to be particularly creative or dynamic. Conversely, those who choose to combine love with a high degree of permissiveness are likely to produce children who are independent thinking and creative, and likely to be social leaders. Such children begin to think for themselves and become independent of their parents earlier and more totally than other children. Because of their independence, they are less likely to share as many parental values and behavior patterns as other children do, and they are likely to get into "trouble" more often, because they are willing to challenge authority figures and established customs. This can mean anything from minor hassles over rights and privileges to school suspension or arrest for drug use or drag racing.

On the one hand, things that can be done only with a certain degree of creativity and willingness to act independently cannot be done at all if a child does not have the psychological freedom to accommodate this kind of thinking and behavior. On the other hand, not all independence and creativity is used for constructive purposes, so that not all children who have these traits are better off because of them. Such considerations show why decisions about optimal child-rearing methods are and always will be partially value judgments. *Research can help you* by providing information concerning the relationships between adult characteristics and child outcomes, *but it cannot make decisions for you.*

INFLUENCE OF COMPETENCE AND EDUCATION I consider the circumplex model described previously to be valid and useful as far as it goes. However, it is a two-dimensional model limited to love-hostility and restrictiveness-

A three-dimensional model of parenting, indicating the interaction of general parental competence with the love-hostility and restrictiveness-permissiveness dimensions.

permissiveness. I believe that a three-dimensional model like that depicted in the next figure is required to round out a schematic depiction of the relationships between parent and child characteristics.

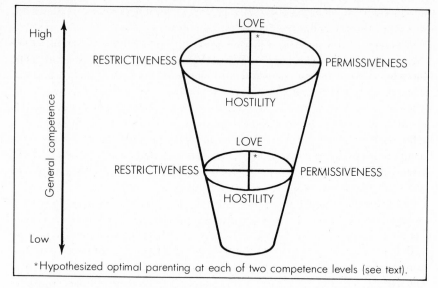

*Hypothesized optimal parenting at each of two competence levels (see text).

The major difficulty with the two-dimensional circumplex model is that it leaves out the important parental differences in general degree of competence discussed in Chapters Five and Six. The three-dimensional model shown in the figure incorporates the two dimensions of the circumplex model, but it adds the third dimension of parental competence in its vertical or depth dimension and its tapered shape. The model tapers inward from top to bottom, rather than remaining cylindrical, in order to represent two ways that more competent parents differ from less competent ones.

First, highly competent parents have *more* schemas, including more schemas that they use in interacting with and raising their children, than less competent parents do; hence the tapered shape. As you move up on the dimension of competence, the model gets wider, representing the idea that newer schemas begin to appear at higher levels of competence. Many schemas which are used by highly competent parents are not used by less competent parents because the latter parents do not possess the schemas, at least not at a level of development sufficient to enable the parents to use them effectively. For particular socialization situations, more competent parents frequently will have more options open to them than less competent parents.

In addition to this difference in sheer *number of schemas* available to parents differing in general competence, there also are correlated differences in *levels of development of those schemas which are held in common.* These differences are represented by the vertical dimension of the model. Higher levels on the model represent more advanced levels of competence. Lower levels represent the ability to use the same schemas, but at less advanced levels.

Two examples will be given to illustrate these points. First, consider the knowledge, equipment, and time involved in teaching a young child to read at home. If we think of this complex of behaviors as a single schema, we can state that some individuals possess it and some do not. Certain parents realize that it is a good idea to teach their children to read and know how to go about doing so. Other parents do not realize this, or do not know how to go about doing so. This particular schema, then, would be one of those that begins to appear at a certain point on the vertical dimension of the model. Below this starting point, the schema does not exist as a viable option to the parent. In contrast, consider schemas such as toilet training or teaching children how to eat independently. These can be considered universal schemas, in that all parents know that they need to accomplish these goals, and all try to do so, in some fashion. Such schemas exist at every level of the model, but people differing in levels of competence differ in the efficiency with which they are able to use them. Highly competent parents will be much more proactive and systematic in the ways they approach these tasks.

Differences in general competence levels even affect the major dimensions of love-hostility and restrictiveness-permissiveness. More educated and competent individuals are more likely to be effective communicators and to use verbal schemas to get across cognitive information to their children. Two parents who are equally loving toward their children still will differ, because one parent could be more verbally articulate and thus more able to express the precise and detailed nature of feelings *about* the child *to* the child. Similarly, two parents may be equal in restrictiveness, but the more articulate parent could communicate the reasons for rules and expectations more completely and understandably than the less articulate parent.

This means that socialization interactions which are equivalent from the standpoint of love-hostility or restrictiveness-permissiveness will differ in their cognitive impact upon the child. They also may differ in their effects upon the child's social and personal development because of this difference in impact upon cognitive development. As a result, differences in competence levels will cause differences in child outcomes, even though the general relationships between parental love-hostility and restrictiveness-permissiveness and child outcomes are the same.

A combination of optimal warmth and moderately high permissiveness is likely to produce a creative, independent, social leader. If the parents are highly competent and the child ends up this way, too, the result is likely to be a successful politician, business manager or owner, or professional. Such persons will be successful not only in terms of occupational title and income, but also in terms of peer status. In politics, they would be likely to be elected to high office and party leadership. In business, they would be likely to rise to the top of the company, to be elected to head the chamber of commerce, and to sit on the boards of trustees of various companies and banks. In the professional world, such persons would be likely to be leaders, creative contributors, and persons who are elected to office or selected for awards and honors.

Children raised in similar fashion but by parents of lesser competence, if they ended up at similar competence levels themselves, probably would not become professionals and would not be likely to get far in politics or business (although, among persons who did succeed in these areas without the benefits of education and connections, this type of person would be especially frequent). Their creativity and leadership qualities would show up at whatever levels of occupation and social status they occupied. If they went into business, they would be likely to form their own business and be their own bosses, rather than work for someone else. If they worked in blue collar occupations, they would be very likely to be made supervisors or elected union shop stewards. They would be the ones that others would look to for leadership. In social life, they would be likely to be elected heads of organizations such as the P.T.A., sports leagues and teams, and religious and fraternal groups.

In contrast to these kinds of children raised with love and fairly high permissiveness, children raised with love and fairly high restrictiveness are likely to turn out differently. They probably will be happy and well adjusted, and will attain occupational success commensurate with their educational levels, but their conformity and dependency needs make them unlikely to become dynamic and independent leaders. Among highly educated children in this group, those who enter politics at all would be unlikely to run for office and more likely to work in bureaucratic roles. Those who enter business would be more likely to work for large corporations offering secure jobs than to go into business for themselves, and more likely to prefer jobs that call for dependability and responsibility than jobs that call for decision making and leadership. They would be more likely to be civil lawyers than criminal lawyers, account executives than sales executives, or administrative staff rather than administrative leaders. They would be less spectacular, both in their successes *and* in their failures, than more dynamic and independent types (Ausubel and Sullivan, 1970).

Those who grew up without benefit of higher education would have blue collar or lower-middle class white collar jobs, but again, they would show a preference for jobs calling for responsibility and dependability and offering security over jobs calling for dynamic leadership and offering greater opportunities at the cost of greater risks. In the white collar area, they would be found in most civil service jobs (but not those that are politically sensitive) and in business and industrial jobs that require a minimum of decision making or policy setting. In blue collar jobs, they would be dependable, steady workers with good reputations, and would be likely to be well-accepted by coworkers and neighbors, but unlikely to be looked to for leadership. They would lead quite conventional and for the most part satisfying lives.

Children raised by highly educated parents who nevertheless treated them with hostility and restrictiveness would be likely to become highly educated neurotics. They might be gross underachievers, because their personality problems would interfere with education and/or ability to perform on the job. If they managed to find and hold a job that they could handle satisfactorily, they would be more or less continually unhappy people with disturbed personal and social adjustments. Many of them would seek psychotherapeutic help, while many others would be forced to rely heavily on defense mechanisms to help them maintain their shaky adjustments.

Children raised by parents with similar traits, but without benefit of higher education, would have similar difficulties, but they probably would be more serious, because fewer resources would be available to them. First, they would not have as much education or general competence, so that they would not have the occupational and social advantages that usually accompany these qualities, and they would not have these qualities available as resources to draw upon in trying to cope with their personal problems. As a result, they probably would have to depend even more heavily upon defense mechanisms and to use more regressive and distortive defense mechanisms than individuals with similar problems but more resources. They would be relatively unlikely to seek psychotherapeutic help voluntarily (although psychotherapy has become more socially acceptable and better known than it used to be), and more likely to end up being forced to get psychotherapeutic help because they experienced a schizophrenic break or some other serious collapse of their defense mechanisms (see Chapter Eleven).

Finally, children raised by parents who combined hostility with an apathetic and rejecting form of permissiveness would be likely to develop antisocial tendencies, but again, the form that these took would depend upon education and general competence. Those with relatively little education and competence would tend to be juvenile delinquents as children and criminals as adults. Furthermore, they would be likely to become acting out, aggressive criminals, convicted of such offenses as assault, mugging, or robbery. If they did not get involved in such serious crimes, they still would have trouble in interpersonal relationships, because of their hostility. This would show up in such problems as feuds with fellow workers or neighbors, continuous fighting with spouses, broken marriages, and general problems with authority figures.

In contrast, children raised by parents who were similarly rejecting and apathetically permissive but much more educated and competent would be unlikely to be arrested for criminal or antisocial behavior, especially if they managed to attain as much education and general competence as their parents. People like this usually channel their antisocial tendencies into more socially acceptable forms of behavior, or use their intellectual resources to figure out ways to "get even" without being discovered. If they did become full-time criminals, they probably would choose forms of crime that require high competence and involve maximal rewards and minimal likelihood of punishment (sophisticated organized crime activities, forgery, carefully planned robberies involving vast sums of money or valuables, or sophisticated swindles or frauds). More than likely, they would not become full-time criminals, but instead would become individuals who practiced criminal activities in the process of working at a legitimate occupation (doctors and dentists who deliberately pad their bills and cheat the government and insurance companies; lawyers who charge exorbitant fees or work for organized crime; high level professionals and businessmen who are much more interested in figuring out ways to gain power and/or make money, even if they have to use immoral or illegal means, than they are in providing services to their profession or to the public at large). These individuals are what have been called "white collar criminals."

This has been an oversimplified schematic model that attempts to integrate many complex factors and assumes many things that may not hold true in a particular case. Nevertheless, it is useful in integrating the material to be presented on the relationships between parent and child characteristics. It provides a basic overview for this broad topic, indicating some of the major relationships that have been discovered and some of the hypothesized cause and effect mechanisms that presumably explain them. It will be used as a general basis for discussion of the relationships between parent and child characteristics throughout the rest of the book.

Remember, however, that statements are *probabilistic,* and that there always are many exceptions. Some well-educated people become murderers or down-and-out winos, and some people manage to overcome miserable backgrounds to become happy and successful. Good starts do not guarantee continued success, and poor starts do not create insurmountable obstacles.

SELF-DEVELOPMENT

Parents and other adults can do many things to promote optimal self-concept and general personality development. Perhaps the most important one is accepting children for what they are as individuals and valuing them positively. Children should be secure in the knowledge that they are loved implicitly, that love is not contingent upon their being successful in mastering goals or meeting expectations (Rogers, 1961).

This is what is meant when it is said that adults should reject unacceptable child behavior but not reject the children themselves. Like most of the important expectations that develop in young children, a sense of being loved and accepted is developed not so much through hearing parents verbalize these feelings directly as through interpreting the attitudes and expectations that parents communicate in their more general behavior. This includes not only what is said to or done to children directly, but the general context in which things are said and done. This also includes the things that are said about children to other people in addition to the things said directly to them. Often, unverbalized assumptions and expectations concerning children are more important in the long run than the direct messages they receive.

For example, consider the following two hypothetical reactions to a child who has taken some cookies without permission and denied it to the parent.

1. "I know you took the cookies, so don't tell me that you didn't. Taking the cookies without permission was bad enough, and you only make it worse by not telling the truth. When I ask you about something, I want you to tell me the truth, even when you do something wrong. You see, if someone doesn't tell the truth all the time, you can't believe him, and you don't like it, either. Would you like it if I promised you something and then didn't give it to you, or if I told you that I didn't have any cookies when I really did have some but hid them? . . . Well, I don't like it when you or anybody doesn't tell me the truth, either."

2. "What do you think you are doing telling me that you didn't take any cookies? Do you think I am stupid? Do you think you can fool me? You're a liar, and I know it, so you are not going to get away with it! Go to your room, and if I catch you lying to me again, I'll really give it to you!"

In both examples, the parent is trying to get the child to understand that it is wrong not to tell the truth. However, there are vast differences in the overt verbal messages and even greater differences in the covert communication of assumptions and expectations. In the first example, the parent reacts primarily with an attitude of concern, and concentrates on trying to get the child to understand the seriousness of the problem and the importance of telling the truth. In the second example, the parent responds with an attitude of anger and rejection, and punishes the child as well. The overt content of the first parent's message is much more likely to teach the child the intended concept and to be successful in getting the child to adopt the desired behavior.

The assumption implied in the first parent's response is that the child did not realize the seriousness of this behavior, and the expectation implied is that the behavior will change once the child realizes its implications, particularly its effect upon the parent. In contrast, the response of the second parent contains the implicit assumption that the child knew these implications but went ahead deliberately, trying to get away with it, as well as the implied expectation that such behavior automatically calls for punishment. Another implied expectation is that punishment will not succeed in changing the behavior. Even as the parent is banishing the child, he or she also is threatening the child with additional punishment the next time (if caught). This shows the child that the parent expects the behavior to be repeated, and that the parent and the child are embroiled in a game of "cops and robbers." The parent presumably must remain constantly vigilant in order to "catch" the child the next time, too.

All of these ramifications are not likely to result from single incidents like those in the two examples above, but if parental behavior of a certain type is repeated daily, the implicit assumptions and expectations begin to sink in. Adults who wish to foster a positive self-image in children should treat them as basically good and well-meaning persons who can and will do the right thing as long as they understand the situation (although they may need guidance occasionally). If consistently treated this way, children are likely to become this way, through self-fulfilling prophecy effects. Conversely, children who are treated consistently as persons who will deliberately misbehave at every opportunity (and lie about it if they get caught) very likely will turn out that way, for the same basic reasons.

Children who are treated as good persons are likely to develop self-concepts of being good persons; children who are treated with implicit love and acceptance consistently are unlikely to develop feelings of self-doubt or feelings that they need to prove themselves or their personal worth; children who feel accepted for what they are are not likely to develop inferiority feelings because of physical features, real or imagined deficiencies, or relative status with respect to other children, including siblings; children whose strivings for independence and mastery are encouraged or at least tolerated are not likely to develop inhibitions; children whose emotions are accepted are unlikely to develop guilt feelings about "unacceptable" emotions; children who are expected to listen probably will listen; and so forth.

These and a long list of other relationships which could have been cited all are part of the self-fulfilling prophecy principle: if you expect children to be or to become certain kinds of persons, and if you treat them in ways consistent with these expectations, they are very likely to fulfill your expectations. In addition to this general principle, there are several more specific behaviors that are relevant to specific aspects of self and personal development.

MASTERY AND ACHIEVEMENT MOTIVATION   In the area of mastery and achievement motivation, a combination of modeling, guidance, and encouragement is helpful. Modeling comes in the form of the parent's own achievement striving and verbalizations about it. This is one of the major ways of communicating concepts like trying to do one's best and trying to improve are important, and that comparisons with others are relatively unimportant. If children see parents concentrating on the task at hand and not worrying about how they are doing compared to other people, they are likely to pick up similar orientations in achievement situations themselves.

Guidance can be important in situations where children are clearly striving to master some task or goal, but need help. Sometimes, they are not ready and need more practice at previous steps, but sometimes a child will be able to master the next step if given a demonstration or some suggestions. This is one place that a parent can directly influence a child's achievement (which also tends to build achievement motivation because, in general, success breeds a desire for additional success). Encouragement is important in situations where the child has been frustrated repeatedly or has reached a plateau in the development of a particular schema. Children who do not overcome the problem with persistent practice or by implementing a suggestion that the parent makes will be very much encouraged by hearing the parent provide the information that they are striving for a goal presently beyond their reach, and especially by hearing the parent give encouragement by reassuring them that they will succeed ultimately. If children appear to have reached a plateau such that they are unlikely to make advances for a time because they need practice to the point of overlearning, or because they need to develop certain readiness skills or even maturation, encouragement in the form of reassurance that they ultimately will solve the problem can be very important. This is especially so for developmental tasks that are important to a child who knows that similar children are able to perform them, and fears that failure will lead to teasing or rejection.

It also is important for parents to make sure that their mastery and achievement expectations for children are appropriate not only to their ages but to their individual characteristics. It can be a very satisfying experience for children to have a parent challenge them with some task that they have not yet mastered and to experience the success and related exhilaration that comes with mastering it. It can be equally disappointing if parents make it clear that they would like the child to be able to master a particular goal, but the child is unable to do so. It is even worse if the parent makes a major issue of the matter by persistently reminding the child of the problem or by making invidious comparisons between the child and others who *are* able to solve it. While parents can be helpful to children in aiding them to learn to define goals, discover the limits of their abilities, pursue their interests, and master new schemas, it is vital that parents do so by suggesting tasks that are within the child's reach. Urging children to do something that they are not yet ready to do will not be helpful and may be harmful.

In giving feedback to children, parents can be most helpful by being simple, straightforward, and honest. As noted earlier, children are quite accustomed to minor successes and failures, and thus are unlikely to become upset upon hearing that they did something wrong. Corrective feedback will be perceived and used as such if it is given directly and matter-of-factly. On the other hand, a parent who is upset about the fact that a child has failed to master a goal and who feels it necessary to cushion the child's presumed disappointment by doing things to make the child feel better might overdo it. As a result, the child will not be cheered up and instead will get the idea that the parent is disappointed or upset. Occasionally, children will become upset or fearful because they hurt themselves or experience some kind of trauma in the process of striving toward a goal. Here again, reassurance and a matter-of-fact response are important, not only for showing that everything is presently all right, but also for showing that there is nothing to be afraid of. Once reassured, the child should be encouraged to return to the task if willing to do so. The parent should stand by with an attitude of positive expectancy, to help reassure the child that whatever happened before is unlikely to happen again, and that, in general, there is nothing to fear. Fears of this kind are most easily overcome if the child returns to the source of the trauma at the earliest opportunity (Bandura, 1969).

If a combination of modeling and encouragement are not enough to overcome the child's fear, it is not a good idea to force the child to return to the fear-provoking situation. This can produce terror or inhibition. Instead, a combination of continual modeling and reassurance with occasional suggestions should do the job, and the child should be allowed to move at his or her own pace. The child will return to the situation when ready, but attempts to speed up the process probably will backfire.

AUTONOMY AND INDEPENDENCE   The main task for the parent in fostering the development of autonomy and independence is to learn to set limits on the child's freedom of choice and behavior in such a way that the child can accept the limits as understandable and legitimate. Children should not become angry or resentful, or start to doubt their judgments about their own capabilities. This is accomplished primarily through what Baumrind has called "authoritative" child rearing: whatever limits are placed upon children are placed for their own good, and the reasons for them are explained. To the extent that parents tend to exercise authority in this way and succeed in making children realize this, the children are likely to accept limits as legitimate and understandable and unlikely to become either fearful and inhibited or hostile and resentful toward authority figures.

"Setting limits" is a somewhat negative term which should be avoided when possible. The term "socializing" the child is preferable, because in most areas socialization requires, or at least is accomplished most effectively through, positive instruction and modeling rather than more negative methods. Especially in regard to curiosity and exploration, placing limits upon the child's behavior is a necessary and important part of socialization. There are some things that young children cannot be allowed to touch or do under any circumstances, and others that can be allowed only under proper adult supervision. These limits must be made clear to children to the point that they will accept them, even when no adult is around to enforce them.

Since limits are necessarily negative and restricting, it is important for adults to be very clear about the limits that they intend to impose. Once the "list" is determined, the adults should be clear in presenting it and firm and consistent in enforcing it. Children should *know* that there are certain things that they cannot touch and do at all, and certain other things that they cannot touch or do unless they have permission or supervision. Clear-cut limits of this kind should be presented in a way that communicates not only firmness but positive expectations and assumptions about the child. Although it might be relevant and important to point out to the child the consequences of violating them in situations where danger is involved, presentation of limits should be done in a way that does not imply or directly express a threat of punishment if the child should not obey. Instead, the assumption that the child will obey should be made throughout, with attention being limited to the dos and don'ts involved in the limit setting without being extended to questions about what will happen if there is disobedience. Children should be told to stay out of the street because cars can hurt them, or to always tell a parent where they are going if they leave the yard so that the parent will know where they are. Limit setting should stop here, though. Parents should not go on to state that children will be punished if they are found in the street or if they should run off without telling the parent where they are going.

Another important consideration in setting limits is the question of whether the prohibition on the child is a permanent and total one, or, more typically, a temporary one. Unless parents quite seriously mean that the child should *never* touch or do something under any circumstances, they should avoid limit setting behavior that would imply this ("You are never to go near the fireplace—do you understand?"). Instead, limit setting should be accomplished in a way that implies that the rule might or will be changed at a later time when the child no longer needs to be prohibited in this way. In discussing a fireplace, the parent should point out to the child that fire burns, that even when there is no fire, the coals sometimes are hot enough to burn, and that, in general, it is dangerous to inspect or explore the fireplace except when supervised. The prohibition is not "Stay away from the fireplace," but "Stay away from the fireplace unless I am around to see that you don't get hurt." The latter is much more understandable and acceptable to the child, and it is flexible so that it can be changed later without making the parent seem inconsistent.

The matter of consistency is especially important in regard to communication of expectations. Children will pick up any discrepancy between what the adult tells them vs. what the adult really expects them to do, and they generally will come to conform to what the adult *expects* rather than to what the adult *says*. Thus, "You can ride your bike on the sidewalk but not in the street," is a clear-cut prohibition likely to be obeyed by the child if the adult is serious and consistent in verbalizing and enforcing it. The statement "Be careful when you ride your bike in the street," is an instruction about how to ride the bike in the street which implicitly includes permission to do so. In contrast to both of the above examples, which are clear-cut, a statement like, "I don't like it when you ride your bike in the street," is ambiguous. In part, it is a criticism of the child, but it is not a clear-cut prohibition against riding in the street. It implicitly communicates the expectation that the child will continue to ride in the street.

Learning to count. The teacher concentrates on teaching the meanings of, and differences between, six and seven. Her verbal presentation is bolstered with concrete manipulable objects which include large, clear representations of the two numerals and counting sticks that can be used to provide physical and visual meaning to the "number words" that the teacher and child use. (NFB Photothèque/Photo by Sue Fitwilson)

By itself, such a statement will not reduce the child's tendency to ride in the street. Nor will it make the child more careful when doing so, because it does not contain any useful information about what the child *should* do.

A certain amount of adult-child conflict is bound to occur in regard to prohibitions of the flexible sort that are changed as the child develops. Conflicts can be avoided by parents who realize that a child is ready to assume new privileges and responsibilities. However, there are bound to be times when children decide that they are ready to do something that they are not allowed to do presently (stay up later, walk or ride in the street, cross the street, use sharp tools, handle certain self-care activities on their own, and so on). The child may be just testing reality, asking the question partly because an older sibling or a neighbor's child is allowed the privilege, and partly just to hear the parent explain the situation. At other times, however, the child's request will go beyond this, and will constitute a serious request for a change in the rules based upon a serious belief that the child is now ready for new privileges and responsibilities.

Such situations are handled best if parents respond in a problem centered way, taking the child's request seriously and thinking about it seriously. Instant refusals made without giving any thought to the matter, criticisms of a child for "pestering," and similar authoritarian responses to such requests are inappropriate. They will depress and anger the child, and they will create or reinforce an adversary relationship between the child and the parent, in which the child attempts to "get away with" as much as possible. If parents think about the matter and decide for good reasons that no change in the situation is warranted at this time, they should explain these reasons. If they really are good reasons, children will understand, although they still may grumble. If parents should decide to grant the child's request, they should clearly spell out the new set of expectations, outlining both what the child can and cannot do and why. If the parents are unsure about whether or not the child is ready to handle the new responsibility, they can allow it on a trial basis, spelling out clearly the criteria to be used in deciding whether or not continued permission will be granted (that the child will ride the bike only on certain prescribed streets, will look both ways before starting, and so forth).

Although there is no need or good reason to become overly formalistic about such "contractual agreements," this is essentially what they are. The parent outlines the conditions under which the child will have to operate in order to be granted the privilege. This clarifies for both parent and child the explicit nature of the agreement. Of course, children should be allowed (and in fact encouraged) to participate actively in working out such agreements, to the extent that they are inclined and able to do so. Like anyone else, young children are more disposed to keep an agreement that they participated in making than to follow a rule imposed strictly from the outside (Gordon, 1970).

DEPENDENCY   Because young children are especially susceptible to traumatic experiences and to undergoing regressions to less mature forms of coping, it is especially important that adults have accurate knowledge and expectations in the area of dependency behavior. Many parents unwittingly cause their children great fear and anxiety by being insensitive to their needs for reassurance and understanding. A child who has become upset over a frightening or humiliating experience and comes to the adult seeking solace and reassurance should receive it. This includes boys as well as girls and children who are "too old to cry" as well as younger children. Children who get the solace and reassurance they need are likely to get over their distress quickly and return to their normal states.

In contrast, children are likely to suffer ill effects if they are teased, rebuffed, or otherwise rejected in an expressive dependency situation. They may succeed in suppressing crying or other signs of distress, particularly if they are threatened with punishment for crying or if they are told that they are acting like a baby, but this does not mean that the problem is solved. In fact, it is likely to linger longer and become more serious under the circumstances. In situations where children are genuinely scared and confused, whether for "good reasons" or not, being rebuffed by an adult to whom they come for solace and reassurance can be seriously upsetting. The result might be the development of general inhibition, the lowering of self-esteem, and/or the development of symptoms such as nightmares or a general increase in expressive dependency needs. With older children who are clearly grumbling or pouting in order to try to avoid something rather than being genuinely distressed, it sometimes is effective to *gently* chide or tease them for acting like a baby. However, preoperational children usually have not yet developed either the ego strength or the cognitive sophistication to pretend to be upset when they are not, so that when they appear to be upset and in need of solace and reassurance, these needs should be met.

An important aspect of expressive dependency that parents frequently mishandle is what Freud would call "Oedipal behavior." Sometime during childhood, typically around ages four through six, the child emotionally works through the transition from close and dependent relationships with adults to a vast reduction in this dependency and a greater orientation toward peers. One manifestation of this is a temporary increase in expressive dependency needs, manifested by such behavior as a frequent desire to sit on the parent's lap, hug or kiss the parent, or be held and cuddled. Such behavior usually is directed toward both parents, but typically primarily toward the mother. Problems sometimes occur if parents do not provide enough affection at these times, or if the parent of the opposite sex becomes irritated and jealous. The latter is most likely to occur in connection with a young boy who persistently seeks physical affection from his mother, including during times when the father is interacting with her and becomes irritated both at being interrupted in general and at the specific nature of the boy's behavior in particular.

There is more than a grain of truth in Freud's discussion of the Oedipal situation. Fathers sometimes do become jealous and irritated with their young sons' attempts to share physical affection with the mother. However, as noted previously, the child does not have lust for the mother or jealousy of the father because of his relationship with the mother, as Freud hypothesized. Instead, such behavior is a developmental phase that helps the child get through the transition from being home bound and dependent upon the parents to being peer oriented. The fact that fathers typically get more irritated with such behavior in their sons than in their daughters suggests that "jealousy" is an appropriate term for describing the fathers' reactions. Many fathers *are* jealous, at least in the sense that they resent the child's continuous attempts to interrupt or disrupt the father's own interactions with his wife.

Other factors are involved too, of course. First, daughters often show more of this kind of affection toward fathers than sons do, so that fathers are less likely to be annoyed or feel "left out" when daughters show the same kinds of behavior toward mothers. Also, fathers tend to become more upset with expressive dependency needs shown by sons than by daughters, because of sex role considerations. In our culture, it is considered appropriate or at least acceptable for females and for infants of both sexes to express emotions such as fear, anxiety, and desire for physical affection and reassurance. As boys get older and begin to be perceived more clearly as boys rather than as infants, this behavior becomes much less acceptable. Consequently, many fathers perceive such behavior on the part of their sons as evidence of immaturity or girlishness, and become upset and angry about it.

This does not mean that parents of either sex should drop everything in order to accommodate the expressive dependency needs of children of either sex whenever they appear. However, expressive dependency needs should be recognized for what they are and met in appropriate ways. As part of building frustration tolerance and independence, and because parents have their own rights and needs, parents will have to delay or refuse certain child requests at certain times. But in general, particularly with expressive dependency needs, children will be best off in the long run if these needs are met as fully and quickly as possible. In any case, it is important for parents to avoid the tendency to do the exact opposite of what children need by snapping at them, telling them to go away, or otherwise denying them the solace and reassurance that they require. Needless to say, it is doubly unfortunate if such adult behavior springs from jealousy.

FEARS   Young children often have fears that appear to be irrational from the adult point of view because children are so vulnerable to trauma. The most important thing for adults to bear in mind is that children's fears are quite real, even when there is no basis for them in reality. Children will quickly come to see this and get over their fears if they are given the proper information and reassurance, but they will not profit from being berated for being afraid.

Some fears will disappear quicker and easier if adults provide not only reassurance, but a degree of assistance or accommodation. Leaving the bedroom door slightly open or installing a night light helps children conquer fear of the dark, especially if it is provided "so you can see if you need to get up" rather than "so you won't be afraid." It provides a little light, so that children can get used to darkness gradually without having to adjust to *total* darkness.

Fears of animals, strangers, and amusement park rides, among others, will disappear faster if adults accompany children, holding their hands and modeling comfort and enjoyment, than if adults limit themselves to verbal reassurances. Young children still are comforted by physical contact, and verbal reassurances are much more convincing when accompanied by modeling (such as feeding and/or petting feared animals).

INSTRUMENTAL DEPENDENCY   Instrumental dependency, in which children seek adult help when they cannot handle something themselves, usually involves fewer problems than expressive dependency, because the child behavior involved is less upsetting to the parents. As with expressive dependency, it is important that parents recognize instrumental dependency for what it is, a developmental phase marking the transition to independence, and not simply a series of irritating requests. The best way to deal with instrumental dependency is to *minimize the need for it* by arranging toy storage and other considerations so that children can do things for themselves and seldom need adult help. Even where this is done, requests for help will be frequent. Where adults handle such requests appropriately, they will tend to be made only when children really do need help and after they have tried to solve the problem themselves. The appropriate adult response is to provide the help asked (or, in some cases, to suggest that the children shift to another activity if they are trying to do something that is beyond their present capabilities).

In this connection it is important to repeat that parents should not couch their expectancies for one child with reference to general norms or to the behavior of an older sibling or another child. Johnny should not be expected to know how to tie his shoes by himself by a certain age just because Jimmy learned at that age or because that is the mean age at which children learn this skill. Johnny's readiness to learn to tie his shoes by himself will depend upon his individual maturation rate and experience with shoe tying, and these must be used as the basis for formulating expectations and giving feedback.

Reasonable requests for help which represent instrumental dependency should be honored, both because this is what children want and because it is the quickest way to help them move toward independence. Although it sometimes may seem otherwise, young children do ask adults to get them four or five separate things in the space of half an hour because they really do want those things, and not because they enjoy bothering adults.

Arbitrary limits on such help, such as "I'll get you one more thing and that's all," should be avoided when possible, because young children do not have the same attention span that adults do. If the adult is tempted to berate the children by suggesting that they ought to be able to do for themselves what they want the adult to do for them, this calls for some thought. Perhaps the adult is right, in which case the children should get instructions they need in order to know how to handle the matter themselves in the future. If the children cannot accomplish the task themselves, they will continue to need help.

How much help they get, and how often, will depend upon the situation.

Again, parents also have rights and needs, so that children will have to learn that they cannot expect help immediately all of the time. If the parent is busy with something that cannot be interrupted, they will have to wait for help or shift activities. If the parent is too tired or preoccupied to be able to do something like read to them, they will have to learn to accept parental needs for rest or relief from interruption. Children will understand, provided that parents delay or refuse them pleasantly and with explanations rather than drive them off angrily.

SOCIAL DEVELOPMENT

Most social development occurs in interactions with peers. Adults can facilitate such development primarily by arranging for children to have satisfying interactions with peers and to be available to help the children work out conflicts or problems that may arise during play. Most of these are resolved by the children themselves, but occasionally something will come up that calls for adult intervention.

Probably the most important thing for parents to keep in mind in these situations is to fight the temptation to take over and do more than they need to do. This will satisfactorily solve the immediate problem, but it will not give the children an opportunity to work out things on their own. This is something that they must learn to do eventually, and adults can help them learn by allowing them to work out some things on their own and by encouraging them to offer suggestions or at least to take an active part in deciding how to resolve problems even in situations where the adult does have to intervene. A major consideration when an adult does intervene in a peer conflict is the importance of obtaining accurate information about what happened. Given the preoperational child's extreme egocentricity and desire to please adults, it is common for young children to attempt to lay the entire blame for any problem on one or more peers and deny all blame or responsibility of their own. Adults need to learn to accept this and take it in stride, delaying responses or actions until they get a clear idea of what has happened, and resisting the children's attempts to get them to take sides. This is important for all adults, but it is especially important when parents deal with conflicts involving their own children. In these situations, most parents have a predisposition to believe their own children, because they do not like to think that their children might be at fault. Obviously, they are going to be at fault sometimes, however.

Much of the help that adults need to give preschool children comes in the form of helping them settle disputes and learn to share toys and generally play together cooperatively. This is done most easily and efficiently by avoiding blame and punishment and instead giving the children instructions, information, and explanations. Helping the children to develop empathy and the ability to see things from others' perspectives by articulating Golden Rule morality is especially helpful ("How would you feel if Johnny did that to you?"). When a dispute over the use of a toy occurs, it usually is both sufficient and optimal to confine the response to a brief mention of the importance of sharing and a specific suggestion that children take turns. Where possible, the suggestions should be made so specific that the children can keep track themselves, such as by suggesting that one child build a block tower as high as possible, until it falls, and then let the other child try. Where the children cannot keep track of these things themselves, it may be necessary to help temporarily by agreeing that each will get so much time per turn and letting them know when their time is up. Children need to gradually learn to work out methods of taking turns and deciding when a turn is up on their own, without adult help.

The same general approach (instilling Golden Rule morality) also applies to conflicts with peers other than those involved in squabbles over toys. Aggression, teasing, name-calling, telling a peer to go home, and the like, all should be gently but firmly criticized on the ground that they are unkind behaviors that children would not like if someone did it to them.

CONFLICTING VALUES AND BEHAVIOR PATTERNS   Assuming that the parents are consistent, young children will be exposed to a consistent and mutually supportive set of socialization pressures. As they play out of the home more and become more peer-oriented, children increasingly will encounter values and behavior patterns that conflict with or simply are different from those to which they have been exposed. This will present the parent with at least two new sets of problems.

The first set of problems concerns unacceptable behavior on the part of peers. When peers say or do things that parents consider unacceptable, parents will have to confront the playmate with the conflict and set firm limits. Usually it is best to simply inform the child that the behavior in question is not allowed in *this* house, and assume that this prohibition will be accepted. It may be necessary to send some children home, if they persist with prohibited behavior despite continued warnings. This usually is not a major problem with young children, because they are still adult-oriented and inclined to do as they are told.

A more complex set of problems arising from peer relationships involves children's exposure to different or even conflicting values or behaviors. This will lead them to come home with thorny questions about differences in religious affiliation and church attendance, parental occupations, and general differences in life styles and value systems. Unless they have been exposed to something that the parent feels is clearly wrong or immoral, children should be informed that the habits of other families are merely different, not better or worse, than those of their own family. Differences of opinion related to value systems, political philosophies, and the like, should be presented as these and nothing more. There should be no implication that there is something wrong or evil about a peer's family because they differ in these areas.

Finally, it is important for parents to assume the proper perspective concerning their child's developing peer-orientation. Once adult-orientation peaks, it will begin to decrease, and peer-orientation will show a corresponding increase. As a result, the same child who used to want to cuddle up or to spend a lot of time with the parents may lose interest in the parents and even rebuff parental physical affection. Ordinarily, this is not rejection of the parents in any true sense of the word; the child simply wants to go out and play with friends.

Parents must learn to psychologically "let go" of their children at the same time that they are helping them to develop. If children are to develop their own unique personalities to their full potentials, free of unnecessary parental restraints and of guilt caused by unnecessary parental overprotection or interference, parents must be prepared to "let go" when the children are ready. This process begins initially when the parents are confronted with the necessity of releasing their "baby" to the world of children and peers.

BROKEN FAMILIES   A particular familial difference which will affect almost all children some way and will require explanation is the broken family. Unprecedented divorce rates make it likely that a third or more of all children (the rate varies with geographical locale and other factors) will come from single parent families or families in which one or both parents have been married previously. These children will need honest but positively oriented explanations of what happened and what it does and does not mean for the family in general and for them in particular. This is a specialized topic and several complete books are available on it. The main thing, as usual, is to see that children in such families realize that they are different from the majority but understand that this difference should not cause shame, inhibition, resentment, or other negative emotions that would affect their happiness or ability to get along with peers.

Socialization also is required for children in intact families who ask questions about playmates from broken families. They need honest and informative answers, but the answers must be phrased in ways that will not upset them or damage their relationships with their less fortunate peers. Many such children get upset when contacts with peers from broken families make them realize for the first time that the break up of their own family through parental separation or death is a possibility. They may even show temporary regression and a resurgence of expressive dependency while they work this through. Their questions usually will be answered best if answered matter-of-factly. Separation and divorce can be explained by noting simply that sometimes parents do not get along well and find it best for everyone concerned to separate. This will satisfy most preoperational children, provided that the message is delivered convincingly without any suggestion that separation or divorce is immoral or that there is something wrong with playmates' parents who have chosen these options. Parents who are happily married might wish to reassure their own children that usually it is best if couples enjoy each other and stay together, and that they are glad that they are happily married, but they should not go beyond this by painting separated or divorced parents as "bad people."

A similar combination of nonchalance and reassurance is needed when children ask about parental death. They need to be told that most people do not die until they get old but that sometimes people die younger, and that this is what happened to the deceased parent about whom they are asking. This can be followed with reassurance that such events are unusual and infrequent enough that there is no need to worry about them (assuming that there is not, in the case of the family involved). Children also may need corrective information concerning playmates who do not have a parent in the home, because contact with such families may confuse their knowledge about the biology of parenthood. They may wonder, for example, how playmates who do not have fathers were born. Usually, children who ask such questions ask them because they think that playmates who do not have fathers in the home *now* never had fathers at any time. A brief explanation that they did (or do) have a father who was together with the mother when they were born will clear up the mystery.

Another major topic in this general area is the series of problems facing parents in the single-parent families. Again, it is beyond the scope of this book to try to treat this in any detail, and several useful books written for single parents are available. It is worth noting, here, though, that such parents must cope with heavy burdens, and that neighbors can help immeasurably by treating them with friendliness and compassion and by making children feel welcome in their own homes. In addition, parents who are of the same sex as the missing parent in a neighboring family can serve as role models and surrogate parents to these children, to the extent that they have time and willingness to do so.

AGE ROLES   Generally, children are happiest and play best with children close in age to themselves, so that parents should make an effort to provide play experiences for their children with age peers. Usually, appropriate friends will be available in the neighborhood. If not, parents can provide such experiences by sending the child to a preschool or by contacting other parents with children of similar age and arranging for the children to visit each other's homes and play together occasionally.

Given the contrasting experiences that result from being the oldest or the youngest in a play group, it is probably most beneficial to children if they get both kinds of experiences. Playing with older children will expose them to new ideas and activities and will be generally stimulating, while play with younger children will allow them to assume leadership roles. As noted previously, most problems or squabbles which develop in play groups among young children are solved quickly by the children themselves, but adults should be prepared to help if necessary. In particular, older children should be encouraged to take the role of a friendly "big brother" or "big sister" to a younger child, as opposed to bossing around the younger child in a more negative sense. Younger children who may become upset because they cannot do what older children can do may need some reassurance that they will be able to succeed later when they are as old as the playmate. Younger children who are repeatedly frustrated in their attempts to play with older children probably should be encouraged to play with younger ones instead, until they become able to play with the older children more successfully.

SEX ROLES   It is difficult to give confident suggestions concerning sex role socialization, not only because different individuals and groups differ in their values and beliefs about optimal sex roles, but also because these differences are very intense and presently are undergoing changes due to the women's liberation movement and other social forces. Many people are now striving for *androgeny*. This is a term which has been coined by those who believe that it is optimal to socialize children of both sexes to have the good qualities typically associated with either of the two sexes, but not to have the bad qualities associated with either sex role. The concept is not quite the same as "unisex," which refers more to an attempt to obliterate sex roles altogether. The concept of an androgenous person does imply that such a person would be superior to both the traditional male and the traditional female, because this person would have the positive qualities but not the negative qualities of the traditional persons. The androgenous person would have such traditional masculine qualities as autonomy, independence, mechanical and spatial abilities, inventiveness, and social leadership, but would not feel restricted or ashamed about showing negative or tender emotions, and would not tend to be overly or inappropriately competitive or aggressive. Similarly, the androgenous person would have such socially valued female traits as good verbal abilities and school achievement, social sensitivity and tactfulness, and comfort in being suitably emotionally expressive across a wide range of situations. At the same time, such negatively valued feminine traits as dependency, passivity, and a restriction of interests to home and family matters would be lacking.

Many psychologists now believe that socializing children to develop into androgenous persons is a desirable and quite feasible child-rearing goal. As with most other things, it requires primarily modeling, communication of expectations, and reinforcement of the desirable traits and behaviors. With boys, it would mean avoidance of some of the traditional sanctions against emotional expressiveness and feminine interests, as well as encouragement, positive expectations, and positive sanctions for developing desirable traits typically associated with females. For girls, the same parental socialization factors would be involved, except that it would mean avoiding disapproval or punishment for "tomboyishness" or other traditionally masculine interests and behaviors, as well as encouragement for the development of such traits as independence, leadership, creativity, and athletic skills. This is all relatively easy to accomplish, at least in theory, because characteristics and behaviors are "masculine" or "feminine" only to the extent that people think that they are. Sex typed characteristics are socially defined rather than rooted in biological sex differences, for the most part. The cross-sex traits involved in the concept of androgeny are socially desirable ones, so that there is every reason to believe that truly androgenous persons of either sex would be admired by peers of both sexes (Spence and Helmreich, 1972).

Cross-sex socialization must not be carried too far, however, because there are social sanctions against it. It probably would be a mistake for parents to pressure children to become involved in cross-sex activities against their wills, particularly if such activities were to cause them to experience peer rejection or ridicule. In the first place, such pressure is likely to be unsuccessful, and perhaps harmful in the long run. A child might go along with the pressure as long as it is maintained, but might resent it and avoid conforming to it whenever the parents were not present to enforce it. If parental pressure ran strongly counter to the rest of the child's experience (input from peers, the media, and general observations), it would almost certainly be rejected.

Most adults have a few "pet peeves" that are leftovers from childhood memories of being forced to do something that they hated. Usually they remember these experiences and vow they will never cause any child of their own to undergo comparable distress. Given the pervasiveness and strong sanctions in the area of sex roles, even during the presently changing social scene, it is likely that strong parental pressure to become involved in cross-sex activities, no matter how well meant, would be resented and would backfire for similar reasons.

A second argument against attempting to socialize a child toward unisex is that it is a hopeless cause. Biological sex differences are real, and they presumably will continue to be in effect and considered important. To act as if they do not exist is to deny reality. Simply because biological sex differences exist, and also because sexual activity is such an important part of life, it seems likely that sex role differences will persist in areas such as clothing styles and personal grooming and adornment, even if sex role differentiation becomes vastly reduced and persons of both sexes become androgenous. In any case, whatever may happen in the long run future, short run sanctions against strong deviations from sex role norms continue, and parents who push their children toward unisex will subject them to ridicule and harassment, if not worse.

Parents concerned about the behavior of preoperational children, whether connected with sex role or not, should bear in mind that few specific behaviors have any special long run importance or significance. The fact that children generally conform to whatever is considered appropriate behavior for a child of their sex in the neighborhood in which they live during these years is not necessarily going to end up traditionally sex typed. For proof of this, one need only look at the present generation of researchers and writers advocating changes in traditional sex roles. Most were raised more or less traditionally, and some were very traditionally sex typed and unconcerned about sex roles until well into their adult lives. Personal traits can and do change much more quickly and easily than we sometimes realize, and because much of our behavior is situation-specific role playing which we learn how to do originally without much difficulty or conscious awareness. We persist in behaviors out of sheer habit more than proactive, deliberate choice. The meanings that a particular behavior has to a person, and the importance of that behavior in the person's general scheme of things, are more important than the mere existence of the behavior itself. Parents should not become upset if their daughter is more interested in football than dancing lessons (or vice-versa). Play interests and activities are important, but they do not become the foci of children's lives unless the children lack healthy relationships with the *people* in their lives. Even here, solving the problem requires repair of distorted human relationships, not mere diversion from the play activity.

Parents should not worry if social pressures cause them to allow their children to do things that they prefer them not to do, or if the children do a few things that cause problems or embarrassment. Most child behavior during the preoperational period results either from egocentric exploration or from modeling, and has only short-run significance. The way that a child perceives a particular behavior usually is more important than the behavior itself, and parents can influence perceptions of behavior even when they cannot influence behavior itself.

Even though the behavior itself usually comes from exploration or from modeling someone other than the parents, children's perceptions of its meaning (if they think about its meaning at all) usually come from the parents, either in the form of answers to questions that they ask, or in the form of

Socialization Attaches Meaning to Experiences

I would like to present a personal example of socialization. If it were up to me, the right to own or carry a hand gun would be limited to law enforcement officers, and there would be specific regulations concerning their use (as in Great Britain). The basic reason for my belief is my experience working in an urban ghetto, where I encountered more muggers and dead and wounded teenagers than I care to remember. As a result, I see hand guns as a menace to society.

Nevertheless, our children own toy guns, and they "play guns" regularly. This is because my wife and I realize that it would be utterly futile to try to prevent them from having contact with guns by refusing to purchase guns for them, attempting to prevent them from watching television shows involving the use of guns, or keeping them away from playmates who have and use guns.

The net effect of such actions would have been to cut them off from playmates and drastically restrict their television viewing opportunities. Also, the heavy focus on guns probably would have produced a fascination with them, and it is likely that they would have used sticks or other substitutes to "play guns" anyway. In short, present society being what it is, it is not possible for children to live in the real world without encountering guns.

Consequently, parents must socialize by helping children learn to place guns in perspective, drawing distinctions between "playing guns" and the real thing. This is not especially difficult, because "playing guns" does not necessarily carry over into adulthood. I am a good example here. I had many different guns and often "played guns" in childhood, and yet I ended up with the attitudes described above. This is because my parents and other significant socializing agents in my life modeled and preached such concepts as Golden Rule morality, prosocial behavior, and respect for the rights and privileges of others, and did not go about settling arguments or problems by shooting people. Thus, I learned that guns and shooting were enjoyable so long as they were confined to fantasy play, but that real guns were lethal weapons not to be played or trifled with.

Modeling and the media. This boy is "playing dead" during a mock gun battle. He is helped along by a very realistic-looking toy gun. Chances are that he learned this form of play from modeling peers and television characters. Is all of this good, bad, or what? (Jean-Claude Lejeune / Stock, Boston)

comments about their behavior. Almost regardless of what specific behavior children might engage in, parents can expect things to work out well in the long run if they: (a) avoid negative over-reactions which may leave the children guilty and inhibited or may cause them to become fascinated and obsessed with this particular behavior that stirred up such an unexpectedly strong parental reaction; and (b) consistently preach, practice, and reinforce ideal values and personal characteristics.

FAMILY CONSTELLATION VARIABLES   Regardless of the number of children in the family, their sexes, or their spacing, the most important thing for parents to do when they have more than one child is to recognize and accept (in the positive sense of the word) each child's individuality. This will minimize sibling rivalry and will help each child develop a sense of positive identity and self-esteem. This is accomplished through positive behavior such as communicating acceptance and affection toward each child, as well as through avoiding such behaviors as expressing disappointment that a child was not of the opposite sex or did not measure up to a standard set by an older sibling, or, more generally, avoiding drawing invidious comparisons between siblings.

Parents can help build self-esteem in older children and also help them to accept younger siblings by developing "big brother" or "big sister" images. This is done by helping the older sibling see that he or she plays an important role in setting an example for the younger sibling and in helping the parents by sharing child-rearing tasks. These tasks should be presented as privileges ("Would you like to feed the baby?"), and not as chores. If an older sibling is asked to teach something to a younger one, parents should compliment the older sibling on his or her teaching job in addition to praising the younger one for learning the new skill.

Beyond creating this kind of self-image, it is important to maintain a good balance between common and separate activities by siblings. Siblings should be encouraged to play together frequently, and older siblings should be both allowed and encouraged to take responsibility for teaching things to younger ones and for helping them with such tasks as getting their clothes on or their shoes tied, learning how to use toys or play games, learning reading or arithmetic, taking a bath, or other skill learning. Such shared activities allow the siblings to enjoy each other's company during pleasant interactions, and they provide the older one with opportunities to exercise responsibility and accomplish goals. This should not be carried to the point that the siblings are "pushed together" all of the time; each should have his or her own set of friends, unless they are so close together in age that it makes sense for them to be part of the same peer group. Similarly, while it is beneficial for an older sibling to take some responsibility for a younger one, this should not be overdone to the point where the older sibling feels put upon or where the parents are evading their own child-rearing responsibilities.

With younger siblings, one important goal is to develop a positive orientation toward the older sibling as a friendly and helpful big brother or big sister to whom they can turn for assistance or information. It also is important to "create reality" for the younger siblings if they become upset because they are not allowed to do something that the older one is allowed to do or are unable to accomplish something that the older one can do. Parents can help here by reassuring the younger ones that they will be able to do what the older sibling can do when they get older, and by giving the reasons behind any differences in treatment or privileges accorded the siblings based upon their ages or levels of development. The main goal here is to see that the younger sibling understands that parental policies are based upon good reasons and not upon favoritism of the sibling.

In addition to modeling appropriate attention and reinforcement themselves, parents can promote good interaction among siblings by encouraging them to take an interest in and to express appreciation for one another's accomplishments. If this is done right, there will be little sibling rivalry. Instead, siblings will learn to take a measure of familial pride and to express genuine appreciation for one another's accomplishments. A certain amount of teasing among siblings is not only normal but probably healthy. This is because children generally are more comfortable with and accustomed to both giving and receiving the unvarnished truth than adults are. Assuming that teasing remains within acceptable limits and does not become vicious or destructive, it can be quite constructive in puncturing egocentric notions and helping children develop accurate concepts about themselves and their accomplishments. Much valuable socialization is accomplished in precisely this way. Parents should not be too quick to put a stop to arguments or teasing among siblings, particularly if it remains realistic and centered on questions of fact and does not become more personal and emotional. Productive disputes with siblings (or peers) can increase children's understanding of the rules of games and/or their willingness to follow them; cause them to receive realistic and helpful feedback about skills they are trying to master; learn that attempts to throw their weight around or "act big" are considered more funny than impressive; and so forth. If interchanges should become nasty, parents always can intervene by labeling certain behavior as inappropriate and by reasserting the expectation that siblings will get along and help one another rather than fight. If children become upset as a result of something they have been told, it may be necessary to reassure them, although this should be done in a way that stresses factual realism. Any part of what the children were told which is true should not be denied, although it might be reinterpreted in a way more acceptable to the child than the way it was told originally (children who get glasses and are called "four eyes" can be reassured that they are normal, and instructed to inform siblings and peers that they now can see better).

MORAL DEVELOPMENT

Most comments concerning optimal parental fostering of moral development in preoperational children either have been made already or should be obvious from what has been said. Briefly, parents should do the following (Hoffman, 1970; Martin, 1975).

1. Provide an atmosphere of acceptance and warmth to foster a positive self-concept and a prosocial attitude toward others.
2. Practice what you preach.
3. Communicate positive expectations by treating children as if they are (or are on their way toward becoming) the kinds of person you want them to become.
4. Present socialization demands in positive ways, as expectations and ideals, rather than in negative ways through threats, criticisms, or punishments.
5. Make sure that there is a good reason for each socialization demand made upon children, and explain this reason to them at a level they can understand.
6. Take into account children's unique individuality by accepting them for what they are and by adjusting expectations as they change.
7. Stress general principles rather than situation-specific rules and stress the intention behind a behavior rather than only the behavior itself. In general, approach the task of socialization as primarily one of providing information and guidance rather than setting limits and punishing.

Parents who consistently practice this kind of child rearing are very likely to succeed in producing children who become genuinely moral persons. Such persons will take into account the potential effects of their behavior on other people and themselves in making decisions about what they will and will not do. Such children also are likely to be reflective, in the sense that they proactively think about their behavior before and during action, anticipating consequences and adjusting accordingly rather than behaving impulsively. Note that these are *process goals*, stressing the "how" rather than the "what" of behavior. Process goals stand somewhat in contrast to *content goals*. Socialization based on content goals would involve telling the child that certain behaviors are good and that others are bad. At first this seems attractive, because generally it is easier to understand and communicate than the process goal approach. However, the content approach has a very serious drawback: very few behaviors are either always good or always bad. Most behaviors, and especially most behaviors performed by ordinary people considered normal and well adjusted, are "good" under certain circumstances and "bad" under other circumstances. An oversimplified content approach is likely to lead to incorrect moral judgments much more often than the more flexible process approach. Also, it is much more likely to produce unnecessary and unfortunate feelings of guilt and shame.

Feelings of shame or guilt are not effective for making people avoid immoral behavior. There is no point in deliberately increasing children's sense of shame or guilt following some transgression, on the mistaken assumption that this will "teach them a lesson." A parent who wants to get children to voluntarily change some behavior pattern should concentrate on showing them why their present behavior is inappropriate, showing them how to act instead, and projecting the expectation that they will change in the desired direction. If the parent should fail to do these things, and instead should only berate the children, efforts to change behavior are likely to fail. The children are likely to persist in the undesirable behavior pattern, at least when they think they can get away with it, except that they will begin to feel ashamed or guilty afterward. Successful behavior change is accomplished through the positive and prescriptive methods outlined above, and not through punitiveness or guilt induction.

Punitiveness and guilt induction are not merely ineffective; they are harmful. Consistent punitive treatment of a child will reduce self-esteem and build up undesirable characteristics such as mistrust, hostility, and aggression. Punitive child rearing backfires completely. It not only fails to accomplish its goals; it leads to the opposite results. Consistent guilt induction without punitiveness has a somewhat different outcome: it is *undesirable* because it tends to be *successful*.

Guilt induction may or may not succeed in producing the desired behavioral outcomes, depending upon other factors (primarily love-hostility). It usually will succeed in producing an individual who is guilt-prone and burdened with a rigid, inhibiting conscience. Such a person will be prone to internal conflicts and the anxiety that they produce, and thus will have to rely heavily upon defense mechanisms (Chapter Thirteen). Even if socialization should be "successful," in the sense that people avoid behaviors that their parents taught them to avoid, they are likely to lead conflicted and unhappy lives. Consistent guilt induction involves placing a heavy and unpleasant burden upon the child without need or reason.

Preoperational children and children in the earlier stages of middle childhood are especially susceptible to developing feelings of shame and guilt. Piaget, Kohlberg, and others have shown that they have not yet developed the cognitive schemas needed to be able to gain a broad, objective perspective upon themselves and their behavior, being instead egocentric, action-oriented, and non-reflective. As a result, they acquire moral codes through a process that Freud called *introjection*. This was Freud's term for the process by which children internalize moral codes verbalized by their parents or other socializing agents. The moral codes are acquired directly from these external sources, but over time, children begin to internalize them and repeat them as if they were their own ideas and had been there all along. Through introjection, moral codes acquired at a young age are maintained throughout childhood and into adolescence. At adolescence, many of the moral codes are questioned by the adolescent undergoing an identity crisis (Chapter Fifteen), so that the moral codes become modified or at least reevaluated. Many are never reevaluated and stay with the person throughout life, knocking around somewhere in the brain more or less in the same primitive and rigid form that they had when acquired originally.

Because moral restrictions originally introjected in situations involving intense shame or guilt are least likely to be reevaluated at adolescence and most likely to produce internal conflict and cause a person to resort to defense mechanisms, parents should avoid unnecessary induction of guilt and shame. This is true in general, but it is especially important during the preoperational stage when children begin to become oriented toward morality but are still extremely adult oriented, concerned about pleasing adults, and likely to take literally whatever they are told. At these ages, children often introject what adults tell them, including overly generalized and rigid prohibitions which can cause them inhibition or conflict for the rest of their lives if they are not reevaluated and adjusted at adolescence. Creating this kind of crippling shame and guilt is not too difficult, if you work at it consistently. The following behaviors are probably most important in establishing shame and guilt within the child.

1. Develop a lengthy and rigid set of prohibitions, and tell the child that everything on the list is wrong at all times and under any circumstances.
2. Introduce shame and guilt at every opportunity by reacting with blame and rejection, telling children that they are terrible or worthless if they do any of the things on the list.
3. If rejection and verbal criticisms do not succeed in reducing children to pitiful anguish, reinforce by telling them to get out of your sight, refusing to speak to them, telling them to go away and not talk to you, suggesting

that they are ruining your life, or staging a tirade or crying jag to show them that whatever they have done is so horrible that it has left you badly shaken.

4. If you are religious, tell them that God is keeping track of their every thought and action and will see that they are punished for every transgression, after death if not before. If you are not religious, produce the same effect by appealing to a force powerful beyond the child's comprehension, such as by suggesting that any wrongdoing will come back to haunt them sooner or later, that everyone must pay the piper.

5. In general, stress the negative. Call attention in particular to the idea that any specific misbehavior on the part of the child is an indication of a general deficiency or evil nature.

6. Let children know, both implicitly and explicitly, that they are not good, that they never were any good, and that they never will be any good.

If you want to induce shame and guilt in a child, it is not difficult to do. Hopefully, the considerations raised so far in the book, combined with those discussed in Chapter Thirteen, will convince you that this is not a good idea. The above should not be taken to mean that children should never experience shame or guilt; only that adults should never deliberately increase their sense of shame or guilt beyond that which is *naturally experienced.* Children who are reared according to the positive principles discussed earlier will experience shame or guilt if they should do something that they know is wrong. This will be true whether or not the parent spells it out for them, and whether or not they are caught. When it is obvious that children know that they have done something wrong and are already sorry for having done so, there is little point in doing much other than expressing the expectation that they have learned their lesson and will not repeat the misconduct.

Occasionally, adults will necessarily induce some shame or guilt by showing children that they have done something wrong when they did not realize it. This is likely to occur, for example, after one child mistreats another and then has this uncharitable behavior pointed out effectively by an adult. In the process of questioning and talking to children to show them that they would not like to be treated that way, the adult probably will make them feel somewhat ashamed or guilty. This is perfectly normal and natural. However, the adult should not unnecessarily deepen the guilt or harp on the problem. Instead, children should be given instructions about how to behave in the future, along with the expectation that they will do so.

This section on moral development will be concluded with two brief observations and a general comment. First, the socialization methods advocated in this chapter are based on the *long run* goals of producing an individual whose behavior is under self-control and who acts in moral and prosocial ways toward fellow human beings. In giving long run goals priority over short run goals, sometimes methods are advocated that are less efficient and somewhat more difficult and time consuming than certain other methods which are more effective in the short run. However, achievement of short run obedience or conformity at the cost of long run immorality or guilt-ridden inhibition is no achievement at all. Furthermore, developmental considerations dictate that parents must think in long run terms in selecting child-rearing strategies. Parents have their greatest effects in the early years, when children are likely to internalize what adults tell them and less likely to encounter contradictory influences from peers or other sources. If parents want their children to respect and listen to them, and if they want their children to be individuals who think before they act and who take the consequences of their actions into account in judging what to do and what not to do, they will have to lay the foundation for this by establishing a solid relationship of mutual love and respect when the child is young. If they do, the strategy probably will pay off. This does not mean that the child ultimately will do everything that the parents would like, because the child probably will develop value systems that differ somewhat from those of the parents. However, if children regulate their behavior and make decisions according to the processes outlined above, they are unlikely to go far wrong.

In contrast, parents who sacrifice long run success by using short run methods, raising children in an authoritarian or *laissez-faire* manner rather than an authoritative manner, are likely to find that: (a) the older the children get, the less they are like what the parents want them to be like; and (b) the older the children get, the less respect they have for their parents' opinions or demands.

A second observation worth noting explicitly is that child-rearing methods have been advocated that would produce an individual who is extremely moral in interactions with other people but who at the same time is virtually free of shame and guilt. At first this may sound a little strange to readers who were under the impression that prosocial moral behavior resulted primarily from shame, guilt, or fear of punishment. Since this is not the case, there are no reasons for, and several reasons against, creating any more shame, guilt, or fear in a child than is necessary. If you understand that these unpleasant feelings do not increase a person's morality, but nevertheless feel somehow that they are helpful or necessary, ask yourself why you think this way, and take the time to find the answer.

Finally, as a general comment, neither this chapter nor the book as a whole provides "cookbook recipes" for dealing with specific situations. It is not possible to write such a book because each individual parent and child, as well as each individual problem situation that arises in child rearing, is unique. In order to give prescriptive advice with any legitimacy or confidence, one must know a fair amount about the individuals involved, the previous family history, the particular events that led up to the problem, and the problem itself. This can be done by a counselor or therapist working on a specific problem with a specific family, but it cannot be done in a book. Hence this book stresses the development of an optimal relationship with a child and on the use of optimal child-rearing processes.

The relationship and the processes mentioned above are important, however. In fact, they are far more important than particular actions taken in response to particular situations. If parents have established relationships of mutual love and respect with their children, and if they consistently describe, model, expect, and reinforce proactive, rational, and humanistic behavior, they are likely to be successful both in the short run and in the long run. Their children are likely to grow up moral in their behavior toward others and loving and respectful toward their parents, although they will not necessarily always agree with their parents on matters involving personal preferences or value judgments. They will be independent and psychologically free of their parents in their thinking and morality (and other matters as well), and yet they will be likely to remain emotionally and socially close to their parents and to have relationships with them which are much more mutually satisfying than the kinds of relationships that children who remain overly dependent upon their parents have.

Establishment of an ideal relationship and approach to child rearing leaves the parents much more margin for error in specific situations. A solid relationship of mutual love and respect is not going to be ruined by a few mistakes in judgment, over-reactions due to stress or frustration, or other relatively minor and isolated incidents. Where the basic relationship and important problem solving abilities are present, difficulties such as these can be ironed out through rational discussion. Both the parents and the children will have the ability to do so and also the motivation, because they will value the relationship and wish to maintain or reestablish it. The methods advocated in this book sometimes are more difficult or time consuming in the short run, but this is a minor price to pay for the very great advantages that they bring in the long run.

SUMMARY The findings of a great many studies relating parent behavior to child characteristics can be simplified with models that reduce a variety of parental traits to the central dimensions of love-hostility and restrictiveness-permissiveness. Advice about ideal child rearing always must be qualified, because it always involves value judgments about what constitutes an ideal person. The most commonly agreed upon statement is that ideal child rearing involves very high parental love combined with medium parental permissiveness. Loving parents usually have children who are secure, confident, outgoing, optimistic, and sociable. Parents who are moderately permissive, granting their children autonomy as much as possible but enforcing the limits that they do impose, tend to have children who are curious, creative, and initiatory. In combination, these parental traits are associated with child outcomes valued by most (but not all) people.

These socialization approaches are affected by parental education and competence, and these variables need to be taken into account in predicting what is likely to happen in particular situations. Two sets of parents who are similar in love-hostility and restrictiveness-permissiveness but different on the education and competence dimension are likely to have children who are similar in their general personal traits but different in their educational attainment and general competence. The result will be similar traits manifested in different ways and in different societal strata.

The chapter extrapolated from primarily correlational studies to provide prescriptive suggestions for child rearing. These necessarily were probabilistic statements rather than indications of universal cause and effect linkages, but if instituted consistently, they are likely to produce children who think before they act and act according to the ideals to which they have been exposed. Specific suggestions were made concerning self-development, mastery and achievement motivation, autonomy and independence, fears, social development, accommodating to conflicting values and behaviors, broken families, age roles, sex roles, sibling relationships, and general moral development. Moral behavior is instilled primarily by modeling and positive socialization techniques, rather than by threats and punishments. A related point is that guilt and shame are not effective deterrents to misbehavior, and that optimal socialization proceeds by building positive behaviors rather than by trying to eliminate undesirable ones. These points will be expanded in Chapter Thirteen.

DALE, PHILIP. *Language development: Structure and function,* second edition. New York: Holt, Rinehart and Winston, 1976.

This is a good general introduction to the topic of language development for beginners. It covers theory and research about the natural development of language as well as the theoretical controversies between linguists and others and among linguists themselves, but without drifting to jargon or difficult presentations. It also is unusually rich in examples, and, in addition to the presentation by the author, there are brief excerpts from the writings of prominent linguists.

DODSON, FITZHUGH. *How to parent.* New York: Signet, 1970 (paperback).

This is what I consider to be the best available popular book for parents seeking help and advice for dealing with preschool children across a broad range of topics. The Spock book is useful primarily for infancy, and the Gordon book referenced at the end of Part III is useful primarily for older children. Dodson has done an excellent job of bringing together a combination of psychological knowledge, common sense, and personal and parental wisdom to create an unusually well-written and valuable popular book on child rearing. Especially helpful are the lengthy appendices which provide suggestions for play equipment for children of different ages, free and inexpensive children's toys, children's books of interest to preschoolers, children's records, and other books for parents. All in all, this is an extremely valuable reference. More recently, Dodson has come out with a companion volume meant explicitly for fathers, entitled *How to father.*

GOSLIN, DAVID (ED.). *Handbook of socialization theory and research.* Chicago: Rand McNally, 1969.

Along with the Mussen handbook listed below, this handbook provides one of the two handiest single sources of information about child development and socialization. As the title implies, the present handbook emphasizes socialization, although much purely developmental material is included in it. The chapters, written by top authorities in the field, cover a broad range of topics and attempt to integrate theory with research.

JONES, MOLLY. *Guiding your child from two to five.* New York: Harcourt, Brace and World, 1967.

This book is a comprehensive guide to socialization of preoperational children, stressing the child guidance techniques favored in traditional nursery schools. Some may find the degree of programming and structuring advocated here to be more than is necessary or desirable, but the book has good practical advice on ways to arrange the environment and to motivate children to comply with parental socialization demands with minimal resistance. Practical tips on a great variety of topics are offered.

KRUMBOLTZ, JOHN, AND KRUMBOLTZ, HELEN. *Changing children's behavior.* Englewood Cliffs, New Jersey: Prentice-Hall, 1972 (paperback).

This is one of the best of a great many books about how parents can apply the principles and methods of behavior modification to child rearing. The authors are committed to the behavior modification approach, but they avoid the extremism and artificiality that marks some other books by behavior modifiers, recognizing that behavior modification techniques need to be blended into a broad pattern of child rearing and not relied upon completely. This book is a good place to begin for those interested in the behavior modification approach to child rearing.

LICKONA, THOMAS (ED.). *Moral development and behavior: Theory, research, and social issues.* New York: Holt, Rinehart and Winston, 1976.

This volume presents 20 essays on moral development and related issues by some of the leaders in the field. It is the most important single source of theory and data in this area for those interested in pursuing issues in moral development in depth.

MUSSEN, PAUL (ED.). *Carmichael's manual of child psychology,* third edition, two volumes. New York: Wiley, 1970.

This two-volume set constitutes the most important single source of information about child development and related topics existing today. It is meant primarily as a handbook for the specialist conducting research and teaching courses in child development, but readers interested in particular topics may find it a valuable source of information and references. Used along with the Goslin handbook referenced above, it will present and/or lead you to the best available scientific information on a topic relating to child development or socialization, something which clearly cannot be said for the majority of popular books on child rearing and related topics.

SMETHURST, WOOD. *Teaching young children to read at home.* New York: McGraw-Hill, 1975.

This is a handy how-to-do-it book for parents who want to teach their preschool children reading. In contrast to certain other books on the same topic, it neither promises dramatic results if some presumably "crucial" method is used nor assumes that teaching preschoolers is of paramount importance. The author believes that it is good for children to learn to read, providing that parents teach them sensibly and that the children themselves respond favorably. Where this is the case, this is a handy and useful manual containing specific and sequenced instructions and numerous references to other materials and sources.

WHITE, ROBERT. *The enterprise of living: A view of personal growth,* second edition. New York: Holt, Rinehart and Winston, 1976.

One of the more readable and at the same time more scholarly books available on the development of personal adjustment and personality generally. Traditional theory and research discussions are supplemented with life history data, clinical studies, and even examples from literature. The book is unusually electic and integrated in its presentation. It combines many of the central concepts stressed in the present book, including the organization of cognitive structure, the importance of developing a sense of competence, and the development of coping and defense mechanisms to rely upon in dealing with stressful situations.

PART FOUR

THE CONCRETE OPERATIONAL YEARS

Physical and Cognitive Development in Middle Childhood

The next six chapters will deal with middle childhood, or, to use Piaget's term, the period of concrete operational thought. This period extends from when the child makes the transition from preoperational thinking to the achievement of concrete operations (anywhere from as early as age five or six to as late as age eight or nine, depending on the child), and continues until the physiological changes marking transition into adolescence begin. The latter typically happen between about ages 10 and 13 in girls, and anywhere between 12 and 16 in boys.

This division into general stages of development is only one of many possible such divisions. In dividing development from birth through adolescence, different writers use age norms, stage theories, school grade levels, and various combinations of these. Sometimes their differences are merely semantic differences or differences in individual preference, but sometimes they are more substantial. Many writers would

323

not divide development into stages at all, because they reject stage theories and the stage concept.

The divisions used in this book are based on Piaget's four major stages: infancy (the sensorimotor period); the preoperational period; the period of concrete operations; and the period of formal operations. I think that Piaget is right in claiming that there are numerous *qualitative* differences between individuals in these different stages, enough to justify the use of the term "stage" to describe them and to provide a rationale for organizing the book around them. However, I find the substages discussed by Piaget to be more quantitative than qualitative, and therefore they are not given much attention. Although the Piagetian stages form the basis for the organization of the major parts of the book, readers should keep in mind the following three important points.

1. Transitions between stages are uneven and lengthy rather than sharp and clear. Children do not become operational over night, and it is typical for them to be operational in their thinking on some topics (those with which they have had the greatest input and experience), but still to be at the preoperational stage in their thinking about other topics (those with which they are less familiar).

2. The existence of stages and the transitions between stages are seen as almost completely dependent upon the child's cognitive development, and little if at all upon the child's age. Quantity and quality of experiences that children have had are basic to their development. Age is related to these, of course, because children have more experiences as they get older. However, independent of these experiences, age by itself is not particularly important and is not a very reliable norm for use in categorizing children.

3. Throughout the book, there is a systematic difference from Piaget: much greater stress is placed upon environmental stimulation and much less stress upon internal maturation as causal mechanisms underlying development. Although the major stages, and consequently the commonalities among children at these stages, are accepted, I am more concerned about the development of individual differences in children than about the universals shared by all children within a stage. The organization of the book follows Piaget to a degree, but the content has been influenced heavily by Gestalt-field theory and by behavioristic theory.

GENERAL CHARACTERISTICS OF CONCRETE OPERATIONAL CHILDREN

Many of the characteristics of concrete operational children already have been discussed at the end of Chapter Six in the section on the changes that occur as children make the transition from preoperational to concrete operational thinking. Briefly, children's cognitive structures become well enough developed and assimilated to one another to form an organized, integrated Gestalt. Their concepts are largely correct (insofar as they go) and are much more stable and much less susceptible to being strongly influenced by apparently contradictory information. Children with concrete operations clearly grasp the concept of object permanence, the distinction between internal and external events, the distinction between the stable and invariant aspects of the environment and those aspects that are random or accidental and could be changed, and they grasp basic thinking and reasoning operations. In short, they now think logically and in general operate much more like adults, although there still are many gaps in their knowledge and experience, and they will not be able to deal with purely abstract content until they achieve formal operations several years later.

It is during the concrete operational years that societies generally socialize children by teaching them the knowledge considered to be important for everyone in the culture to possess. This is done both formally, through schools, religious education, and other explicitly educational institutions, and informally, through such socialization forces as parent and peer modeling, toys and games, and, in technically advanced cultures, children's books and television programs. Cognitive development during these years will be discussed at length in the following section.

Virtually every writer who has approached middle childhood from a stage theory perspective has noted that this is a time of relative stability and tranquility. Piaget notes that the important qualitative changes that mark development in the earlier years fade out, and that the period of concrete operations is marked primarily by the quantitative expansion of knowledge and skills. Freud noted that, once the turbulence of the earlier stages subsides, the child settles down into a period of several years of relatively stable and tranquil development, which he termed the "latency" stage. Even researchers interested in individual differences and personality characteristics note that characteristics salient at ages five or six tend to persist until adolescence, when the child undergoes a restructuring of personality.

Part of this stability and tranquility exists because the child, although no longer as egocentric as before, still is not very self-reflective, either. Children in the concrete operational stage tend to be wrapped up in the play and work activities of childhood. They spend much of the day developing their knowledge and skills at school, and most of the rest of their time playing and acquiring new skills in interactions with their peers. Earlier preoccupations with parents and other adults and with meals and individually-used toys are replaced by a new preoccupation with peers and play. Children literally will play from morning to night, often will have to be called in to eat even if they have not eaten in hours, and almost certainly will have to be reminded often about such matters as personal hygiene and responsibility for clothes and possessions. These children will be too wrapped up with calling friends and going out to play to leave much time or interest for these other "unimportant" matters.

Noting these themes in children's interests and activities, Erikson (1963) has called middle childhood the stage of *industry vs. inferiority*. Children not only are eager to interact with peers and succeed at the developmental tasks expected of them, they are emotionally involved in these activities. Their self-concepts are likely to be influenced strongly by their relative success in meeting expectations and in achieving peer acceptance.

Success (as perceived, at least) tends to breed more success, as well as self-confidence and achievement motivation. The result is what Erikson calls a sense of "industry," an orientation toward and enjoyment of new challenges and of polishing existing skills to perfection through practice. Too much failure (or even perceived failure) will have the opposite effects. Failure will breed more failure, because children will become anxious, self-conscious, and inhibited. They may come to fear and try to avoid situations that children with a sense of industry look forward to and enjoy. In some children, the ultimate result may be a pervasive sense of inferiority. They feel personally inadequate themselves, and they are certain that they are rejected and considered inferior by peers.

Like other self-perceptions, those connected with the stage of industry vs. inferiority depend even more upon subjective perceptions shaped by feedback from others than they do upon objective performance. Children who are relatively successful in absolute achievement and acceptance may come to feel inferior if they *believe* (correctly or not) that they are seen as inferior or that they are rejected by others. The reactions of everyone in their environments are important to children, but they become less adult-oriented and more peer-oriented as they progress through these years. Gradually, the peer group becomes the most important single influence upon many children, and it is a potent force for most of the others.

When given instructions by adults, most children of this stage still comply without serious opposition or rebelliousness. Directions from adults concerning what they should or must do tend to be accepted and introjected without much thought. These include both specific instructions (brush teeth after every meal, no balls in the house, and so forth) and more general moral principles (such as, the Golden Rule and the Ten Commandments). Children acquire and "file" these items of information with the same casual acceptance that marks their learning about facts. However, as we shall see in Chapter Thirteen, the moral concepts that they learn at the knowledge level are not always acted out consistently in their behavior.

Although children in the concrete operational stage share many commonalities in their thought processes, they also show great individual differences. These individual differences increase with age as their unique genetic makeups and unique environments combine to reinforce the development of some attributes and to minimize the development of others. Those attributes that are reinforced heavily become increasingly obvious and stable, so that eventually they form the central traits that define children's "personalities."

PHYSICAL DEVELOPMENT DURING THE PREOPERATIONAL YEARS

Assuming adequate nutrition and normal childhood play activities, physical development in middle childhood could be expected to take care of itself. However, a majority of the children growing up in the world today, including millions in the United States, do not have adequate nutrition. Partially because of this, their physical development, cognitive development, and general energy and stamina levels often are impaired.

Inadequate nutrition is unavoidable in some countries at present, but it is avoidable in the United States. Perhaps a more enlightened population, or, more likely, a population that begins to understand the implications of our drastically reduced birth rate, will change this unnecessary and unfortunate situation (when we come to the realization that the country simply cannot afford the tremendous human waste, let alone the human misery, that we tolerate at present). The combined implications of the world energy situation and our own rapidly changing population statistics make our children vital national resources requiring protection and nurturance, in the same sense that our air, water, forests, and energy sources are. Insurance that all children receive adequate nutrition not only is necessary to insure the individual welfare of such children, but it is becoming increasingly important to insure the welfare of the nation at large.

Not all child malnutrition is related to poverty. Pediatricians and others concerned with child health have been reporting an alarmingly high and increasing proportion of nutritional problems among middle and upper class children. These are caused by unbalanced diets, in which the child gets too much food or the wrong kinds of foods. Such children eat mostly carbohydrates (soda pop or other sugared drinks instead of milk, heavily sugared cereal with little or no nutritional value, snack foods, and desserts) and not enough foods that provide protein and vitamins (meat, fish, dairy products, grains, nuts, and fruits and vegetables). Parents who allow their children to form such eating habits are not doing them any favors, even though insistence upon balanced diets may mean depriving the children of "goodies" that they want. This matter is important enough that it should be insisted upon forcefully and consistently. Desserts and snacks are fine as supplementary treats, but *not* as substitutes for balanced diets.

Where children are getting adequate nutrition, they probably should be allowed to eat whatever they want (within the family budget), *up to a point*. This point is the intake level at which the child begins to accumulate fat due to overeating. Children should not be allowed or encouraged to stuff themselves with so much food (*including* nutritious food) that they begin to get fat. Excess weight is one of the major threats to general health and even life in adulthood, and studies show that the majority of obese adults got in the habit of overeating when they were children. Often, this was because their parents insisted that they finish everything on their plates, or eat a certain portion of food whether they wanted to or not. It is important that children get a nutritious and balanced diet, but at the same time, it also is important that their food intake be matched to their body sizes and physical activity levels, so that they do not accumulate excess weight.

As mentioned previously, physical growth patterns are very uneven and are dependent upon internal maturation which is not under the control of the parents, the child, or anyone else. Because of the variety of growth patterns, children show much greater individual differences at a given age than do

Individual differences in physical development. These two boys are the same age and in the same classroom, but they are very different in physical size and body shape. In this case, their differences obviously are not preventing them from having a good time together, but physical size could be important in other respects. For example, consider the card chair and work table behind the boys. If the smaller boy sat there, might the table be too high for him to work efficiently? If the larger boy sat there, would there be enough room between the chair and the table to allow him to sit comfortably? (Elizabeth Crews/Jeroboam)

adults. People who are unfamiliar with this can see it for themselves by visiting an elementary school classroom, where they will see children in the same classroom who differ so markedly in height and general size that it is hard to believe that they are the same age. The striking differences are due to differences in growth patterns. It is not at all uncommon for a fourth grade classroom to contain a few children who are five feet or more tall and/or of muscular build, and a few other children who are barely three feet tall and/or immature in appearance. All of this is perfectly normal and not particularly important, unless it becomes important to the children themselves because of what they hear from adults or other children. This is why it is important for adults to accept and respond appropriately to whatever physical appearance and stature a child may have at a given time, and to avoid assuming or making predictions about the future based upon what they see at the moment. Differences in the amount and kinds of development that will occur later during the adolescent growth spurt will cause many relatively small children to become larger than average adults, and vice-versa. Since these maturational phenomena are not controllable or very predictable, the adult role here is primarily one of responding appropriately to a child rather than one of systematically shaping the child in certain directions.

Essentially, the goal is to see that the children's self-concepts, including their concepts of their bodies and physical abilities, are both accurate and satisfactory. Accuracy is important so that children will know what they can and cannot do, and thus will not be frustrated trying to do things that are beyond their present abilities. Satisfaction is important if children are to be comfortable and secure, and to avoid feeling shame or inadequacy because they are not big enough, fast enough, skilled enough, attractive enough, and so forth.

Problems sometimes arise because children want to do new things that their friends do, but physical limitations prevent success. For example, the first child in a play group of six- to eight-year-olds who gets a two-wheeled bicycle probably will set off a wave of desire among playmates to get two-wheelers of their own. However, some of the playmates will not be large enough and/or well-coordinated enough to ride bicycles yet, and this may cause frustrations and feelings of inadequacy. Parents may be able to overcome the problem through careful instructions and/or additional equipment such as training wheels. Such children will need assurance that they will be able to ride bikes as well as their friends eventually. Usually, such reassurance is sufficient to satisfy the child. Most frustration is temporary, and so are the self-doubt and feelings of inadequacy that come with it. Children who are almost but not quite able to ride a bike probably will practice until they are able to ride successfully, while children who simply are not ready probably will temporarily drop the idea of learning to ride and instead return to their previously preferred activities. This may lead to a temporary change in choice of playmates, because children who learn to ride bikes and enjoy doing so may begin to seek one another out, while children who do not have bikes or are not yet able to ride them successfully may come together to do other things. All of this is perfectly natural. It represents an intuitive recognition by the children that they need to play with other children of similar abilities and interests.

The bicycle example is only one of a large number of examples of physical skills that children will want to try because other children are doing them and/or because they look interesting. Other common interests include swimming, tree climbing, gymnastics, horseback riding, dancing, playing musical instruments, and sports. When a child expresses interest in taking lessons in one of these activities or in including them in informal play with friends, adults first must "create reality" by providing realistic feedback concerning the appropriateness of the activity given the child's present level of development, the time constraints, the family budget, and safety considerations. Adults should be encouraging and interested in the children's experiences and progress, if they do try out new activities. However, children should know that the activity can be abandoned, temporarily or permanently, if it proves to be too difficult or becomes boring. Parents understandably are frustrated when their child pleads for an opportunity to be allowed to do something that requires them to invest time or money, and then drops the activity after deciding that it was not such a good idea after all. It is much better for the child if the parents grin and bear it when these things happen than if they insist that the child continue with the activity because they have invested in lessons or equipment. It may help to convince the child to stick with it for at least an agreed upon time, but if this does not work out, additional pressure will only mean continued frustration of the child and continued bad investment by the parents.

One final point worth noting about physical growth in childhood is that girls generally mature earlier than boys and maintain this advantage throughout childhood. This means that, contrary to the situation with adults, the average girl of a given age is as large or larger than the average boy. This sex difference is true not only in sheer physical size, but also in motor coordination, athletic ability, and other factors related to physical development. Parents should be aware of this sex difference, so that they do not develop inappropriate expectations or become upset because they think that there is something wrong with their child. Ideal parental behavior related to physical growth in middle childhood will be discussed in greater detail in Chapter Ten.

COGNITIVE DEVELOPMENT IN THE CONCRETE OPERATIONAL YEARS

Much of what Piaget has had to say about cognitive development in the concrete operational years already has been discussed, so it will be treated only briefly here. Most of the discussion in the present chapter will concern cognitive development as viewed from the perspective of learning theory and psychometric theory. First, however, let us characterize children at the concrete operational stage as seen by Piaget, considering both what they *are* and what they *are not*.

Even though considerable development has taken place, children in the concrete operational stage still are heavily action-oriented in their learning. They are capable of dealing with concepts and of learning through instruction in ways that they were not capable of previously. Still, most of their learning occurs, both in school and out, through direct, concrete experiences involving observing and manipulating objects. Although they have become operational, many of the characteristics of preoperational thought remain, particularly in areas in which they have had little or no experience or instruction. In some ways, children at the concrete operational stage still are egocentric, still have difficulty taking the role of another person and seeing things from that person's perspective, still can be fooled by certain kinds of conservation tasks or other confusing tasks which make it difficult to remain clear about what is necessary and unchangeable vs. what is accidental and changeable, and still show the kind of illogical thinking that was typical earlier.

On the other hand, these problems now are more the exception than the rule. Children have developed a stable and integrated set of schemas that they can use to analyze objects, contemplate possibilities, and solve problems. They usually think logically in the adult sense of the term, proceeding without contradiction from original premises and arriving at correct conclusions if the original premises were correct. Because of the combination of the build-up of concepts and experiences and the development of logical reasoning abilities, children now can correctly solve problems that left them completely puzzled earlier. For example, the development of numerical concepts and of the understanding of object constancy enables them to solve conservation tasks by reasoning that nothing has changed unless something is added or taken away. Once children understand this fundamental concept, they tend to be right *every time* in answering questions about whether one container has more, the same, or less of something than another container, after some manipulation has been performed. If the experimenter should do something like pinch off a piece of clay in a conservation of mass experiment or palm a few objects in a conservation of number experiment, operational children will realize that some kind of trick has been played on them. They will not give up their concepts or back down from their reasoning if they are certain that they are correct, as they would have done earlier. Instead, they will stick with their responses and state that the experimenter has tricked them or that something unusual has happened.

A major development that aids children in thinking logically is acquisition of *reversibility*. This is Piaget's term for the ability to reason both forward and backward in a chain of logic. One example already has been mentioned: the concept that a substance remains the same if nothing is added or taken away. Children also come to understand the reverse of this concept: if you add something or take something away, you change the original amount. Children can solve problems which involve manipulating an object and asking whether or not it has changed, and they also can explain how an object has changed, if a change is observable. Similarly, they can make predictions about what will happen in an experiment if they have had sufficient experience with the materials and operations involved to enable them to reason backward from what they have seen before in order to predict what will happen if the procedure is reversed. For example, if two full glasses of water are poured into a pitcher that was empty, they will understand intuitively that, if the water is poured back into the glasses, the result will be that both glasses again will be full and the pitcher will be empty.

These concepts do not all appear immediately when the child becomes operational, nor do they all appear at the same time. These are just a few of many examples of the more general phenomenon that characterizes concrete operational thought: *the ability to reason logically from causes to effects and vice-versa.* In this sense, the thought processes of the concrete operational child are precisely the same as those of the logical adult using formal operational processes. There are several differences, however.

First, until they reach the stage of formal operations, children can use logical reasoning abilities only when concrete objects are available for manipulation and/or when they can visualize an operation which they have seen performed in the past. They cannot deal with purely abstract material, except to memorize certain things without really understanding them. This is why abstract subjects such as theology or philosophy, and the more abstract aspects of the sciences, are not taught until high school and later. Young children might be able to memorize a verbal definition of an infinity, an amino acid, or Einstein's relativity theory equation, but they would not have the slightest idea of the meaning of what they were saying. Consider the pledge of allegiance to the flag. Although virtually every child knows it by heart, few young children understand much of what it means. Part of this is simply vocabulary. If you don't know what words like "pledge," "allegiance," or "indivisible" mean, obviously you do not know what the words of the pledge mean when you recite them. An even more difficult problem is comprehension of the concepts involved. Young children recite the pledge to the flag in a very concrete way—they think of the pledge as something that one says in the presence of the flag in order to honor it (that is, to honor the flag as such, rather than the nation for which it stands). Only much later does a child come to understand that "I pledge allegiance to the flag . . ." is an oath of loyalty to the nation. Similarly, the word "indivisible" will be repeated many thousands of times before the child comes to understand its full meaning. This happens only after the child learns about the history of the country, the Civil War, and all of the other knowledge that one must possess in order to understand why the word appears in the pledge and what it means.

In addition to highly *complex and abstract concepts,* children have difficulty with *figures of speech,* especially those which use vivid imagery but refer to something entirely different from what the words usually mean. While children might understand the phrase "too many cooks spoil the broth," they usually understand it only in direct relationship to soup cooking. Ordinarily, they do not generalize the phrase. Other phrases are so confusing that the child will not understand them at all, or will develop a concept which is quite different from what they really mean ("He saw the handwriting on the wall"; "They pulled themselves up by their own bootstraps"; "It's time to fish or cut bait"; and so forth). Understanding the general meaning of these language idioms requires sophisticated development not only of language but also of a large number of concepts that must be understood and assimilated to one another before the abstract meaning can come through. This process takes several years. Most children do not develop this kind of understanding until the stage of formal operations, and many never develop it at all.

CONTENT OF LEARNING   Piaget approaches children's thought from a primary interest in *process.* He is concerned mainly with discovering the processes that the child develops in coming to understand the world and in thinking and problem solving. He has studied the acquisition of fundamental concepts of logical reasoning and mathematics, and has described the stages involved in the acquisition of such concepts and the ways that they become assimilated to form a logical system. Except for those few concepts he considers to be fundamental and universal to cognitive development, Piaget does not pay too much attention to the *content* of learning.

Throughout childhood, the fund of available schemas becomes vastly multiplied as the child acquires new knowledge and skills. In Piagetian terms, these include sensorimotor schemas, cognitive schemas, and verbal schemas. This expansion of the intellect is primarily *quantitative* (adding more schemas) rather than qualitative (developing higher level schemas), but it is quite important. In our culture, it is accomplished primarily through the school, although children acquire many schemas in their out-of-school activities also.

Just as the development of object constancy and of certain logical and mathematical concepts are seen as fundamental by Piaget, the acquisition of the tool skills of reading, writing, and arithmetic are seen as fundamental from the perspective of school learning. These are the major tasks of the first few grades of elementary school. During these years, both because of the development levels of the children and because of the nature of the teaching-learning situation, schooling concentrates on concrete, specific knowledge and skills, many of which have a heavy motor component that requires continuous practice to reach perfection. In the early grades, we see that children master fundamental tool skills by insuring that they: memorize letter names, letter-sound combinations, the meanings of punctuation marks, and other important skills related to the development of early reading; practice making line segments and gradually learning to make letters and then words, adding new tasks as they gradually learn to write and print; memorize mathematical tables dealing with the four basic operations of addition, subtraction, multiplication, and division, and practice using these skills by working computation problems.

Educational critics have objected to this approach to curriculum in the early grades, arguing that too much emphasis is placed on teaching isolated facts and basic skills and not enough on concepts and thought processes and that this will stifle curiosity and creativity (Silberman, 1970). However, both developmental considerations and educational research indicate the contrary (Brophy and Evertson, 1976). First, the heavily motoric-orientation of young children, even after they have achieved concrete operations, means that they can and do profit from skill instruction involving repeated practice and from activities which involve an opportunity to directly observe or manipulate some object, but they do not profit much from purely verbal interchanges of the kind that older children and adults can learn from. To the extent that children *can* deal with purely verbal learning, they will get the most out of this kind of learning if it deals with objects and events with which they are familiar, and if it stresses concrete facts and observable relationships but does not get into overly complex or abstract material. Developmental considerations suggest that traditional schooling in the early elementary grades is appropriate to the needs and abilities of the children (Brophy and Evertson, 1976).

Learning theory approaches to intelligence and concept development yield similar conclusions. For example, Gagné (1970) has a hierarchical model of learning and instruction which is based on analysis of the tasks that the child must perform, in contrast to Piaget's model, which is based upon analysis of the abilities possessed by the child. Gagné's eight levels of tasks are shown in the

A Hierarchical learning model. (From *Educational Psychology Instruction and Behavioral Change*, 1970, published by Meredith Corporation. Reprinted by permission of the authors, Francis J. DiVesta and George B. Thompson.)

DESCRIPTION OF TYPES OF LEARNING

A LEARNING STRUCTURE FOR BASIC SKILLS OF READING

Type 8   *Problem solving*
Involves thinking skills; combinations of two or more principles to arrive at a unique solution

Type 7   *Principle learning*
Acquisition of a clear understanding (not rote learning) of statements relating two or more concepts in the manner of "If A, then B"

Principles:
  Organization of paragraphs and larger units
  Order of English expression

Type 6   *Concept learning*
A common classifying response is made to groups of objects, events, or ideas, the individual members of which appear to be dissimilar

Concepts:
  Printed nouns, verbs, prepositions, connectives

Type 5   *Multiple discriminations*
Learning to discriminate among many similar-appearing stimuli and to respond to them in as many different ways

Multiple discriminations:
  Distinguishing similar words

Concepts:
  Stimuli of oral speech

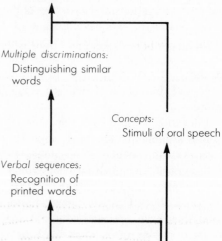

Type 4   *Verbal association*
Learning to link combinations of words as stimuli with words as responses. Language also provides the basis for implicit 1 links called mediators

Verbal sequences:
  Recognition of printed words

Type 3   *Chaining*
Learning to link a chain of two or more stimulus-response connections

Chaining:
  Recognition of printed letters by sound

Chaining:
  Oral production of words

Type 2   *Stimulus-response learning*
The acquisition of precise connections between a given response and a discriminated stimulus

$Ss \rightarrow R$ *learning:*
  Language sounds

$Ss \rightarrow R$ *learning:*
  Simple words

Type 1   *Signal learning*
The learning of a general, diffuse response to a signal as in classical conditioning. It is not clear that Type 1 is a prerequisite for Type 2

334

figure opposite. He has presented both logical arguments and experimental data to support the idea that children will learn a task most easily when it is analyzed and presented according to this scheme. First, the task must be broken sequentially into separate components, and these components must be taught in the proper order. Second, some components may be divided into subtasks according to the scheme shown in the figure, so that each subtask can be taught in a way that starts with the simplest and most fundamental knowledge and proceeds to the highest level or terminal knowledge.

In summary, the basic idea is that each subtask involved in a larger task should be taught in its proper sequence and in a way that begins with the simplest aspects and proceeds gradually and systematically to the most complex aspects. Numerous other learning theorists and developmental psychologists have stated variations of this fundamental idea. Gagné's scheme is presented here primarily because it is one of the most complete and useful ones for planning instructional sequences. In combination with Piagetian developmental psychology, it provides a powerful method of determining what kinds of content and instruction are appropriate for children at particular levels of development.

Another learning theory approach to intellectual development which fits with that of both Piaget and Gagné is that of Ferguson (1954; 1956). Ferguson places great stress on the concept of *overlearning*. Overlearning refers to the development of a skill or knowledge area to the point where additional practice does not lead to any additional development or new learning. Before a child reaches the point of overlearning, increased practice leads to increased ability on the task. Once the point of overlearning is reached, increased practice no longer leads to improvement and the child has reached a peak of performance. Overlearning has proved to be an important and fundamental concept. We now know that abilities learned to the point of overlearning tend to stick with us throughout life and to be available for use whenever we need them, while abilities learned only partially and not to the point of overlearning tend to be lost over time through forgetting.

Ferguson thinks of what we call "intelligence" as the total number of schemas which have been developed to the point of overlearning and thus are available for thinking and problem solving in new situations (what Piaget would call accommodation). In Ferguson's terms, a more intelligent person has more schemas developed to the point of overlearning than a less intelligent person. As a result, more intelligent persons will have more associations to a given stimulus, and more schemas available for immediate use in a situation requiring thinking or problem solving. These persons will be able to solve more problems, partly because they possess schemas that less intelligent persons do not possess, and partly because the schemas that they share in common are developed more highly. This makes them less susceptible to production deficiency problems (inability to use or coordinate efficiently schemas which one possesses and which are relevant to the present situation).

INDIVIDUAL DIFFERENCES   Ferguson's perspective helps bridge the gap between Piagetian theory, which concentrates on studying universals in child development, and social learning and socialization approaches, which concentrate on shaping the child's development through systematic intervention efforts and trying to understand individual differences. A group of fourth graders all might be at the level of concrete operations from a Piagetian perspective, and in this sense, their mental development would be identical. However, it is obvious that they differ considerably from one another (in their daily classwork and on IQ tests or other measuring devices).

According to Ferguson, these individual differences (and differences in groups, for that matter) result from a combination of differences in genetic potential and differences in environmental factors which increase or decrease the likelihood that a given skill or concept will be developed to the point of overlearning. Children who grow up in an environment that virtually insures that they develop a particular skill to the point of overlearning are very likely to acquire this skill to the maximum levels that their genetic potentials allow. Children who grow up in an environment that places less stress on the development of this skill (or no stress at all) are much less likely to develop the skill, let alone to develop it to the point of overlearning. For example, an adult who never has seen a typewriter will not even know what it is, let alone how to use it efficiently. Adults who know what a typewriter is and have fooled around with one a few times but never have learned to type will be unskilled, but at least they will know what the typewriter is for and will have a general idea of how to get started. Adults who took typing many years previously but never learned to type efficiently will have a greater advantage, but they probably will have forgotten most of what they learned in the typing course, and their advantage will be slight. Finally, adults who had learned to type to the point of overlearning but had not typed in several years could sit down at a typewriter and begin typing. Very quickly, probably in an hour or two, they could type with a high degree of efficiency. Similarly, someone who learned roller skating, water skiing, or bicycle riding to the point of overlearning as a child could quickly recapture these skills as an adult, even though many years without practice may have intervened. The same thing occurs with cognitive abilities, but it is less easy to see.

Ferguson's theory also helps explain *individual differences in the development of new skills*. Here, Ferguson combines the idea of *transfer* of schemas already available because they are developed to the point of overlearning with the idea of the *emergence* of specific aptitudes for a specific task (the child's genetic potential). Again, although the general principles hold up for cognitive as well as sensorimotor tasks, they are easier to visualize and understand with sensorimotor tasks. Consider piano playing, for example. If a group of children (or adults, for that matter) all began piano lessons at the same time, the brightest ones would make the most progress in the first few weeks. In Ferguson's terms, the brightest ones would be those who had the greatest number of schemas developed to the point of overlearning and thus available for use in accommodating to the task of learning to play the piano. Many of the schemas most important for progress in the early weeks would be verbal and cognitive ones rather than sensorimotor ones. These would be relevant to understanding instructions, learning to read music, learning the names for the parts of the piano and the types of notes and finger movements involved, and so forth. Thus, an IQ score or some other measure of brightness probably would be a good predictor of progress in learning to play the piano during the early weeks of instruction. However, once past the basics, learning to play the piano with a high degree of skill involves orchestration of great number and variety of schemas, many of which are sensorimotor schemas involving finger dexterity, eye-hand coordination, and the like. Thus, the farther along one gets into piano playing, the more important specific aptitude becomes, and the less important general intelligence becomes. Consequently, after a year or two of piano lessons. IQ would be virtually useless as a predictor of piano playing skill. Tests of psychomotor coordination and finger dexterity would be much more useful at this point.

General intellectual abilities determine the degree to which a person is prepared to cope with a particular kind of task when mastering the basics, but as the person goes to higher levels, general abilities become less important and specific aptitudes for specific tasks become more important. These ideas go a long way toward explaining the emergence of individual differences in ability patterns. In combination with the ideas discussed previously concerning the cognitive environment of developing children, they help explain individual and group differences in measured intelligence and other performance indicators.

PSYCHOMETRIC THEORY   This brings us to the psychometric approach to intelligence and to the controversies concerning IQ tests and interpretations of the meanings of group differences in IQ (intelligence quotient). Some writers, notably Jensen (1969), assign great importance to IQ scores and to the group differences that show up in them. Others see IQ as useful for limited purposes but minimize the importance of the group difference data. Still others claim that IQ tests are useless and misleading and thus should be abolished altogether.

The present controversy would be painful and ironic to Alfred Binet, the man who invented what we now call intelligence tests. Binet was one of a group of French psychologists who began to develop psychology as a separate discipline late in the 19th century. Binet took on the task of developing a method to identify children who were likely to do poorly in school while they were still young, so that they could be singled out for special and more intensive treatment. The motivation for the development of the first IQ tests was a prescriptive and humanitarian one. Ironically, one of the major objections to intelligence tests these days is that they simply label or stereotype children without providing any useful information about how to deal with them, so that the children get worse treatment than they might have gotten if the tests had not been given in the first place.

Binet went about the job in a common sense, practical way. First, he analyzed the school curriculum to determine the kinds of abilities that students needed in order to succeed in school. Then he devised tasks and tests to measure these abilities (vocabulary, direction comprehension and direction following, persistence, working quickly and efficiently, identifying similarities and differences, and so forth). Once he had identified important abilities and developed ways to measure them, he only needed to make sure that the tasks would *discriminate* (tests that are too easy or too hard are not good because everybody passes or fails: they must be mostly of medium difficulty to insure that children of different ability levels get different scores). Because of age differences in general abilities, this meant that different forms of the test had to be made for different ages. Tests that predicted school performance nicely for seven-year-olds were useless for twelve-year-olds, because most twelve-year-olds could pass all the items. Similarly, tests that predicted nicely for twelve-year-olds were useless for seven-year-olds, because they were much too hard for the younger children.

Once problems such as these were worked out, Binet had a collection of tests suitable for children at each age. The tests successfully discriminated the children and correlated strongly with present and future school performance. Binet himself did not introduce the term "IQ." He thought of his tests as a battery of useful tools for making predictions about future school performance, and not as a measure of a single ability or attribute called "intelligence."

Binet's tests were translated into English and revised by Terman and Merrill (1960) early in the twentieth century at Stanford University, and eventually were published as the "Stanford-Binet Intelligence Scales." More than just a translation and revision were involved here. By the time the first version of the Stanford-Binet Scales was published, several ideas basic to the psychometric point of view had become attached to this test battery in particular and to intelligence testing in general. These ideas have been influential ever since, coming under widespread attack only very recently.

One fundamental change was the reification of the concept of intelligence (reification refers to the tendency to treat an abstract concept that does not actually exist in reality as if it did exist). The fact that the Stanford-Binet Scales were referred to as an intelligence test, coupled with the fact that both the concept and the phrase "intelligence test" became popular, eventually resulted in the following.

1. The seemingly obvious point that there is a great variety of human abilities important in thinking and problem solving was lost. In its place was substituted the term "intelligence," coupled with the idea that the term referred to an underlying single ability.

2. Common use of the term "intelligence test" eventually led to the idea that the test battery was really a single test that measured a single entity called "intelligence."

3. Based on the same general kinds of evidence that Jensen uses today, it became common to say that "intelligence" was fixed at conception and constant throughout life. Each person presumably was genetically endowed with a certain amount of this fundamental ability called "intelligence." This remained constant throughout life and could be measured with intelligence tests.

Lost in the shuffle were the facts that intelligence tests were composed of collections of tasks chosen solely because they predicted school achievement; that different tasks which had no relationships to one another (although scores on them usually correlated) all were considered to be measures of a single underlying entity called "intelligence"; that there is no genetic basis for postulating "intelligence" as a phenotype with a single underlying genotype (and in fact, genetic data suggest the opposite); and that many human abilities known to be very important in adult life are not measured on "intelligence tests," because they do not predict performance in school.

All of this was aggravated by the immense popularity that intelligence testing achieved, particularly after introduction of the concept of IQ. The IQ concept caught on immediately, apparently because of its deceptive simplicity and presumed usefulness. The concept *is* simple, at first glance. The original formula was IQ = mental age over chronological age times 100. Chronological age is simply the child's age since birth, and multiplying by 100 is just a mechanism to get rid of the decimal point in the intelligence quotient. Thus, the meaning of IQ boils down to mental age (adjusted for chronological age).

What is mental age? Mental age was a concept developed by reasoning backward from the scores of children of different chronological ages. For example, suppose that a perfect score on the test was 117 points, and that the average child aged eight years, six months scored 47 points. Working backward from data like these, testmakers arbitrarily defined mental age as equivalent to the score made by "average" children of a particular chronological age. If the average child aged eight years, six months scored 47 on the test, anyone, regardless of their actual age, who scored 47 on the test would be said to have a mental age of eight years, six months. Similarly, if children aged exactly ten years averaged 58 points on the test, anyone who scored 58 on the test would be said to have a mental age of ten years, 0 months. This definition of mental age rests purely upon convention; *there is no logical basis for it.*

Returning to the formula, we now can see that IQ is nothing more than a measure of the child's *relative* standing *on the test*, compared to other children the same age. A child who is exactly ten years old and scores 58 points on the test will be assigned a mental age of ten years. This will be the same as the child's chronological age, so that the formula will work out to an IQ = 100. This will make him or her the "average" child. Children who score more than 58 on the test will have mental ages higher than their chronological ages, and the formula will yield IQs higher than 100. These children will be "above average." Similarly, children who score less than 58 will be assigned mental ages less than ten years, and the formula will produce IQs less than 100, making them "below average." Modern-day IQ tests do not use this exact procedure for statistical reasons, but the basic underlying logic is precisely the same. IQ is now, just as it was then, merely a measure of a child's standing on the test relative to other children the same age.

The tests are understood somewhat better and have been improved in certain respects. Nevertheless, no existing IQ test even vaguely approaches measuring every important human ability, and no test measures any single ability that merits the label of "intelligence" or the assumption that the test score is a direct measure of specific brain function. Quite the contrary. The Stanford-Binet, although revised several times, still is essentially a collection of tasks that differ by age level and have no obvious relationship to one another. They are included on the test for the same reason that items were included originally: they are good predictors of school success.

Other tests are somewhat more specific and/or organized. Certain tests labeled as IQ tests are essentially vocabulary tests, particularly the group administered tests. Other IQ tests are divided into subtests which are internally consistent and distinct from one another (such as vocabulary, memory, knowledge of factual information, ability to put together a puzzle quickly). In all cases, however, the specific items and subtests making up what are called IQ tests are included because they predict school performance and/or correlate highly with the Stanford-Binet, and not because they have any direct or known relationship with the size, developmental level, or functioning efficiency of a particular part of the brain. It is a fair statement to say that IQ is a reflection of a child's ability to cope with a mixed assortment of tasks which, for reasons that are not entirely clear, predict school performance.

IQ tests *are* successful in performing their original purpose: predicting school success. IQ tests in general, and the Stanford-Binet in particular, are the best available predictors of future school success, as well as the best available estimates of general ability to cope with present school demands (usually, even better than achievement tests). Such testing is both useful and effective for these purposes (Jensen, 1969). Perhaps the strongest argument in their favor is that they sometimes uncover previously unrecognized abilities in children who have been underestimated. The other major use argued for IQ tests is use in research. Both of these uses are questionable, as will be discussed later.

Having discussed what IQ tests *can* do, let us summarize and reflect upon what they *cannot* do.

1. They cannot measure children's *potential*, either in general or in specific areas.
2. They cannot indicate the degree to which children are achieving their potential; they can only place them relative to other children their age.
3. They give no information about how or why children have come to be the way they are.
4. They give *no* information about what teachers or others should do in order to maximize children's cognitive development in the future.
5. They cannot predict success at things other than schoolwork, not even things that seem related, such as occupational success, creativity, or general accomplishments. IQ scores are correlated with these criteria, but not strongly enough to make them very useful as predictors. The average person could predict just as well on the basis of a few minutes of conversation with someone as with IQ scores.
6. They do not predict such socially important variables as morality, mental health, maturity, emotional stability, motivation, persistence, and other important qualities that make a difference in the degree of success a person achieves in coping with life generally.

On balance, I would like to recommend that we drop the terms "intelligence" and "IQ," as well as the use of IQ testing, on the grounds that they are useless and often misleading. This is easier said than done. The IQ concept and the notion of intelligence as a unitary entity reflecting some underlying structure in the brain are so deeply embedded in our culture that they will be with us for many years to come, unfortunately. Thus, I find it necessary to discuss at length the nature-nurture controversy as it relates to IQ tests, even though I would prefer not to. The whole business is an artificial problem created by people who take seriously test data which are inherently ambiguous and should be ignored.

THE NATURE-NURTURE CONTROVERSY   Arguments about the degree to which a given trait (phenotype) is controlled by the genotype established at the moment of conception (nature) vs. controlled by the environment which shapes the person after conception (nurture) have been carried on in almost every area of psychology. One of the reasons that people get excited about this particular issue is its social implications. If it can be established that an observed group difference exists because of differences in the genes, and if this group difference is socially important, it follows that the group with the more favorable traits has more favorable genes. Furthermore, because the trait is controlled by genes, it usually cannot be affected significantly by environmental intervention. (However, the diet treatment for PKU disease and certain other exceptions to the general rule show that environmental interventions can make a difference in genetically controlled traits. Theoretically, one could argue that this might be possible for *any* such trait.)

Considerations of genetic determinism soon lead to the suggestion that people with the "wrong" genes be sterilized, so that they do not pass them on to another generation. As prenatal medical procedures become more sophisticated, the same kinds of people who favor such sterilization will be pressing for mandatory genetic checks on fetuses, and mandatory abortions in cases where the fetus turns out to have "objectionable" genes. This kind of thinking has been around ever since human genetics began to be understood, and it probably will be around indefinitely. Alarmists concerned about intelligence frequently advocate, or at least imply, the desirability of sterilizing persons who are abnormal due to genetic defects and/or persons whose IQs fall below a certain level. Ethical considerations aside, both of these suggestions make sense from a eugenics point of view (improve the human race through selective breeding), at least in theory. However, available data provide little support for them in practice. First, a large proportion of individuals born with genetic defects already are sterile and/or do not live long enough to have children. Second, the majority of such individuals are cared for in special institutions where they are segregated and supervised closely, and where the likelihood that they would have children is minute.

The concern about individuals with low IQs but no known genetic deficit appears to be misplaced. For one thing, the children of these individuals tend to show regression toward the mean in their IQ scores. If a man and woman who both have IQs of about 80 should marry, their children will average notably higher than 80 in IQ. This also works the same way at the upper end: children of parents with extremely high IQs tend to have IQs that are relatively high but not as high as their parents'. In short, raising the IQ in the population through selective breeding is not a viable option at the moment. The reason seems to be that, as noted above, IQ is a single index estimating a very large number and variety of mental abilities, and these mental abilities are affected by a large number of genes, possibly virtually every gene that we have. Selective breeding to improve general intelligence in the population *might* become feasible *if* our knowledge of human genetics and neurophysiology become immeasurably greater than it is at the moment, but until such time, eugenics is a pipe dream.

An historical analysis reveals that the dire predictions of eugenicists simply have not come true. The United States is an excellent example. Given that it was populated largely by immigrant peasants, and given that the IQs of rural peasants typically are the lowest in a country, the average IQ in the United States should be low and getting lower all the time. This clearly is not the case. Comparisons across decades are difficult to make because of differences in the tests used at different points in time, but if anything, it is likely that the general intelligence of the population has gone up, not down, and that the general intelligence of the population of the United States compares favorably with that of virtually any other country.

Faced with these data, eugenicists sometimes respond by noting that immigration may have been selective, that the people who made the decision to pack up and move to the United States might have been brighter than average. There are no data to substantiate this claim, and we already know that traits like motivation and persistence are not measured by IQ tests. Thus, the ideas of eugenicists in the area of human abilities appear to be just another example of how misleading it can be to use the term "intelligence" and to act as if IQ tests were measuring some single entity that existed in the brain and was controlled by a single gene or a small number of genes. This simply is not the case.

GROUP DIFFERENCES IN IQ   Over the years, the nature-nurture controversy with regard to IQ scores and group differences has gone from one extreme to the other and back again. Early users of IQ tests conceived of intelligence as a single ability which was fixed at conception and would not change throughout life (except for damage to the nervous system). Despite occasional criticism, this view was predominant until the 1950s. Psychologists and educators believed it despite overwhelming contradictory evidence. Either they did not see the evidence or they interpreted it in ways consistent with their own theories. Although it was known that repeated testing of the same child yielded different IQ scores, the differences were chalked up to situational measurement errors. The idea that the differences might have been real and reflective of changes in the child's general intellectual functioning was seldom given serious consideration. The fact that certain individuals show predictable gains and other individuals show predictable losses over time in measured IQ was largely ignored (Hunt, 1969).

Beginning in the 1950s, and continuing through most of the 1960s, this attitude was almost completely reversed. Data showing systematic changes in IQ were highlighted, and some of the weaknesses in the views accepted earlier were critiqued scathingly. In a landmark publication, Hunt (1961) brought together evidence from a large variety of sources to support the proposition that intelligence is affected significantly by the quality of the environment, particularly early experience during the first few years of life. At around the same time, the fact that IQ tests had little or no diagnostic usefulness for teachers or psychologists interested in working with children became more clear, and emphasis began to shift from prediction to intervention. Psychologists interested in group differences criticized IQ tests on the grounds that they were biased toward the experiences of the typical middle class and urban family and thus were somewhat unfair to other families, particularly families who came from a different kind of culture. This led to charges that IQ tests were biased in such a way that favored groups got artificially high scores and unfavored groups got artificially low scores (Hess, 1970).

These and other forces led to an almost complete reversal in thinking about the meaning of IQ scores in the late 1950s and 1960s. It suddenly became fashionable, if not nearly mandatory, for psychologists and educators to view an IQ score merely as an index of the child's *present* intellectual *functioning*, and certainly *not* as an index of any inherent and unchangeable *capacity*. Optimism ran high that early intervention programs such as Project Headstart would raise the IQs of the economically disadvantaged children enrolled in the programs. For a few years, there was a great wave of enthusiasm, which for a time was so strong that no amount of contradictory data could shake it. Positive results were received with an attitude of "See, we told you so." Negative results were ignored or explained away. This brings us to Arthur Jensen, who dropped a bomb on all of this enthusiasm with his highly publicized critique, which began with the flat statement that compensatory education for the purpose of increasing intelligence had failed (Jensen, 1969).

JENSEN AND GROUP DIFFERENCES IN MEASURED IQ   Before attempting to discuss some of these complex issues, groundwork will be laid by clarifying a few points that have become confused in the uproar over the article by Jensen and its aftermath.

First, Jensen's article is a scholarly paper which reviews a large body of evidence relevant to the points he raises and which draws logical (although not necessarily correct) conclusions from them. Second, the great bulk of the paper is devoted to discussion of data, and most of the conclusions drawn are put forward very tentatively and carefully. Third, despite the accusations of some critics, and despite the fact that racists and others have made use of Jensen's paper to support questionable or even clearly immoral purposes, Jensen himself only is trying to clarify the roles of genetic and environmental influences upon the development of intellectual abilities. If everyone else who has jumped into this controversy had been as scientifically responsible as Jensen has been, perhaps the controversy would have generated much more light and much less heat than it has so far.

Jensen's implications can be faulted on several scientific grounds. Depending upon one's value system, Jensen also can be faulted for drawing scientific attention and resources to relatively unimportant and unproductive questions when they might have borne more fruit if directed to more productive questions. Briefly, his article has increased the tendency (not caused it; it already was there) to focus on the negative by asking what is wrong with groups that score poorly on tests rather than focus on the positive by asking how groups that score well on tests develop their cognitive abilities. He also has focused attention on arguments over the relative contributions of nature vs. nurture to ultimate cognitive development, instead of on how the environment can be optimized to insure that genetic potential, whatever it may be, is developed fully. Many have called him a racist or a Nazi for his views. I consider Jensen's emphases to be misplaced, and I disagree with many of his conclusions.

In his 1969 article, and in subsequent publications, Jensen has brought together data and arguments supporting a nativist interpretation of IQ and of group differences in measured intelligence, and has argued effectively against the environmentalist position. In the process, he has sharpened the argument considerably, although in my opinion he also has shown that it cannot be settled definitively on the basis of available data. To illustrate this, I will briefly discuss the major points made by writers on both sides of the argument, showing how *all* of them can be either disproven or interpreted in such a way as to make them consistent with the other side's position.

First, Jensen and others have produced much data concerning the *heritability* of IQ, or the degree to which it is inherited through the genes. These data show beyond serious doubt that whatever abilities IQ tests measure have strong genetic components. Jensen argues that the genetic components are extremely strong, and that most of the rest of the variance in IQs is due to prenatal factors. He concludes that the environment affecting the child after birth has little or no important effects upon IQ except among those growing up in extremely deprived environments (such as understaffed and poorly equipped orphanages). However, Jensen's heritability estimates are inflated. People who are related to one another genetically show similarities in IQ not only because they share similar genes, but also because they share similar environments. This environmental factor inflates the correlations of IQs of people who are related to one another, but to an unknown degree (Scarr-Salapatek, 1975).

Jensen's heritability data implicitly assume that there will be no important or systematic environmental differences from one generation to the next. However, if systematic environmental interventions were instituted that made a difference in IQ, heritability estimates would *change*. Heritability estimates are of little value in any case. If the environment were maximized so that everyone reached his or her full potential, the heritability of IQ would be 100%

(because all environmental variance had been removed). Obviously, though, this would *not* mean that IQs were determined solely by the genes.

This brings us to Jensen's famous statement that compensatory education had failed. While it is true that most attempts to alter the measured IQ or achievement of disadvantaged children have failed to produce sustained positive results, it is *not* true that *all* such attempts have failed. In fact, certain well-designed and well-funded programs have produced modest but significant long-term results. In IQ terms, such programs have taken children who scored between 90 and 100 or so at around 4 years of age and caused them to gain 5 to 10 points, on the average, and to retain these gains over several years of follow up. Meanwhile, comparable children with similar IQs at preschool were dropping 15 to 20 points with age (the familiar "cumulative disadvantage" phenomenon).

Such results may not seem spectacular, but they are both statistically and practically significant. Their significance is perhaps best appreciated by moving away from IQ scores and projecting probable life circumstances. Individuals who reach age 18 or so with measured IQs of about 105 would be quite capable of finishing high school, mastering basic tool skills well enough to be able to use them in everyday living and working, and acquiring sufficient knowledge and skills to be able to get good jobs and participate as full-fledged, functioning members of society. In contrast, individuals who reach 18 with IQs of 75 or 80 are almost certain to be high school dropouts, barely literate, and marginally employable or unemployable due to lack of relevant knowledge and skills.

Another set of data central to Jensen's argument comes from studies of twins. First, the IQs of identical twins separated at infancy and placed in different adoptive homes tend to be correlated highly, much more so than those of ordinary brothers and sisters (not twins). Also, the IQs of adoptive children, including those placed early in infancy, tend to correlate more closely with those of their natural mothers than they do with those of their adoptive mothers. Again, Jensen interprets these data as evidence that intelligence is almost totally controlled by the genes.

These data do provide more evidence of strong genetic components in measured IQ, but they are not as convincing as Jensen would have us believe. First, the studies are correlational rather than experimental, and most of them do not contain enough information about the families involved to allow confident interpretation of what the data might mean. Given that most adoption agencies try to find the best possible homes in which to place children, it seems likely that the variation in the environments in which adopted children were placed was probably much less than the variation in the kinds of homes from which they came. If so, the genetic component of IQ would be overestimated and the environmental component would be under-estimated (Gottesman, 1968).

Somewhat more convincing are data showing that the IQs of identical twins are very closely intercorrelated, while those of fraternal twins are not correlated much more closely than those of ordinary brothers and sisters. At first, these data seem to strongly support Jensen's contention that measured intelligence is almost completely inherited. However, the data still are correlational rather than experimental, and many are of questionable validity (Kamin, 1974). Even if twin study data are taken at face value, it can be argued that the very high correlations of IQs of identical twins are due to identical environments at least as much as to identical genes.

Jensen's other arguments and data also can be interpreted from an environmentalistic perspective. Although they are consistent with Jensen's genetic emphasis, they do not convincingly demonstrate it. The same problem exists with the arguments and data presented by environmentalists, which are open to opposite interpretations by Jensen and other nativists.

One of the major arguments used to counter Jensen has been the "cumulative deficit" or "cumulative disadvantage" argument. This argument is based upon the fact that observed differences in the measured IQs of urban vs. rural people, high vs. low SES people, or blacks vs. whites increase throughout the developmental years. For example, a group of upper middle class children tested at age four will average about 110 on an IQ test, while a group of lower class children will average about 95. Even at age four, there is about a 15-point difference between low and high SES groups. This difference increases (cumulates) as the children get older. Tested as adults, middle class children who had IQs of 110 when they were four years old will average 110 to 115. In contrast, lower class children who averaged 95 when they were four years old will average 75 to 80 as adults. In short, middle and upper class children maintain or gain in average IQ (remember that these are group data, not individual data), while lower class children drop 15 or 20 points in average IQ.

The drop in the lower class group usually is interpreted as a result of the cumulating effects of growing up in a disadvantaged environment which does not stimulate cognitive development very effectively. As a result, disadvantaged individuals do not show the same rates of cognitive development as do more advantaged individuals, so that the disadvantaged individuals fall increasingly behind with age. Because IQ is a relative measure indicating where an individual stands with respect to other people, a decreased rate of intellectual development will mean a lower IQ. The lower IQ does not mean that the person has become "dumber" in any absolute sense. He or she has not lost brain cells or brain functioning. It does mean that ability to handle the kinds of intellectual tasks included in IQ tests is relatively lower, compared to other people's, than it was previously. Knowledge and skills have been gained since the last testing, but not as many or as rapidly as with most other people. As a result, relative standing, and consequently IQ, is lowered.

This argument seems persuasive at first, but Jensen and others have interpreted it from the nativist position. Drawing analogies to genetically based physical growth curves, they suggest that systematic changes in IQ merely are correlated with environmental differences rather than caused by them. Instead, they claim, intellectual development rates are genetically programmed the same way that physical development rates are. Some people are genetically destined to develop at faster rates and for longer times than other people, so that they end up with considerably higher IQs.

This same reasoning is applied to observed increases over time in urban vs. rural and black vs. white IQ differences, and also to data showing that children with certain traits (achievement motivation, independence, striving for mastery) tend to maintain or gain in IQ over time, while children with other traits (passivity, anxiety, fear of failure) tend to drop in IQ over time. Environmentalists would say that these personal traits are caused by child-rearing and other socializing influences, and that they in turn influence intellectual development. Jensen and other nativists would say that they merely are other manifestations of genetically programmed differences. Neither argument is convincing in its own right, and neither can refute the other. Jensen also has pointed out that a person's environment is not necessarily completely a function of outside influences. Individuals literally create their own environments through their own initiatives. To the extent that this happens (and it undoubtedly does, to some degree), it reinforces Jensen's argument that personal traits associated with intellectual differences do not cause these differences but merely are parts of a larger pattern of development controlled by the genes. Just as genetic influences on intelligence cannot be denied altogether, neither can environmental influences. Jensen accepts the importance of a good prenatal environment (maternal health, diet, and medical care; favorable placement in the womb; normal birth; and so forth) with little or no quibbling, so that the argument is mostly about postnatal effects.

Perhaps the most gripping example of environmental effects is the famous study done by Skeels (1966). The major part of the study was completed over 40 years ago in rural Iowa. Skeels studied 25 infants who were being cared for in a minimal way at a poorly funded and staffed state institution for orphans and children who had been removed from their natural parents for one reason or another. After pretesting them and matching groups as well as he could under the circumstances, he arranged for about half of the infants to be removed from the institution and placed into an institution for feeble-minded women. One of these experimental infants was given to each unit in the women's institution, and the infants immediately became the centers of attention and interest. Even though the women were feeble-minded, the infants got a very rich environment because they were stimulated, cuddled, and played with almost continuously. Gradually, friendly rivalries developed, in which different groups of women would attempt to teach "their" infant a particular word or skill so that they could claim that theirs was the first to learn it. While these experimental infants were getting an unusually rich and varied early experience, the infants left in the previous institution spent most of their days lying on cots. Staffing was such that the adults usually had time to do little other than feed and change them. Cuddling and stimulation were minimal.

After about a year of this treatment, the infants were retested. The experimental group showed dramatic gains in their scores on infant intelligence tests. The control group showed modest deterioration, even though they were quite low to begin with. In reporting these results, Skeels attacked the idea that intelligence was fixed at conception, and argued that the data indicated the importance of the environment for stimulating intellectual development. His results were not accepted by very many professionals. In fact, he was criticized severely because the sample was too small, because his tests were unreliable, because his groups were not perfectly matched, and because of numerous other real or imagined methodological deficiencies. The consensus of the profession opinion makers of the time was that the study was so bad that its results should be disregarded. Skeels never lost faith in his findings and ultimately completed a follow up study which produced results so awesome that even Jensen has had to accept them. Skeels returned about 30 years later, when the infants were adults, and managed to find or at least find out about every single one of the 25 original infants. He found that the IQ test results held up, but other data were even more striking.

As it turned out, the control infants who had been left in the state orphanage remained there or in similar institutions throughout childhood, but the experimental infants who spent a year in the institution for feeble-minded women then were placed in adoptive homes and raised in family environments. The two groups of infants had very different life histories *after* the experimental year, as well as very different environments *during* it. The follow up revealed that only one person in the control group ever became self-sufficient and "normal" in any sense of the word. A few had died, and the rest still were institutionalized or were being cared for by relatives. All were completely dependent, unable to hold jobs, unmarried, and generally not functioning in society.

The situation was completely reversed with the experimental group. All of these people were alive, and only one was institutionalized. Furthermore, those living outside of institutions not only were alive, they were married, employed, and generally living productive and "normal" lives. As a group, they were quite ordinary on several indexes of marital adjustment, personal adjustment, and general mental health, and their children were quite average in measured IQ and school achievement.

Data like these do not require statistics in order to demonstrate that they are "significant," and they demonstrate convincingly that the environment does indeed affect intellectual development, at least under some circumstances. Jensen accepts this much, but he claims that significant environmental effects upon intellectual development occur only under very unusual and special circumstances. He argues that improvements in the environment will have significant effects only when the environment is extremely poor to begin with. Where this is the case, he concedes that improving the environment will improve intellectual development. However, he argues that there is a certain level of environmental quality, which he refers to as the environmental threshold, beyond which further improvements no longer will make any difference.

Jensen accommodates the data of Skeels by claiming that they apply only to children being raised in extremely poor environmental circumstances. At the same time, he maintains his claim that environmental changes will make little difference in the intellectual development of the great majority of children. Jensen never has stated exactly where the "environmental threshold" lies. He never has described just how bad he believes an environment must be in order to expect environmental improvements to affect IQ. However, his writings seem to imply that the environmental threshold lies somewhere below the quality of environment typically found in the worst slums. Jensen accepts Skeels' data, but he does not accept the idea that their implications generalize to children growing up in families, no matter how disadvantaged.

Jensen also counters data showing that some compensatory programs have succeeded in raising IQs, even those showing a significant difference over time between a treated experimental group and an untreated controlled group. Here Jensen does not dispute the IQ scores as such, but does dispute their meaning. He notes that IQ gains of 5 or 10 points can be achieved through repeated testing or through giving the child a few tips about test taking skills, and consequently he attributes much of the difference to this. Also, he distinguishes between what he calls Level I skills (basically rote memory and association learning) and what he calls Level II skills (thinking and problem solving skills that we usually mean when we use terms like "intelligence" or "IQ"). Following up on this point, he states that, even where IQ gains might represent real gains rather than improved rapport or test taking skills, the gains are on test items involving Level I skills which are not really the essence of intelligence (such as, Level II skills).

It should be noted that Jensen is largely correct in this assessment. Studies of compensatory programs have shown that it is much easier to produce significant gains on achievement tests and tests of skills that Jensen would classify as Level I skills than it is to achieve significant gains on intelligence tests or tests of skills that Jensen would classify as Level II skills. Some of the tasks that are included on IQ tests are more amenable to environmental influence than others. However, at the same time it should be noted that Jensen is elusive and inconsistent in his discussion of IQ. When it is convenient to his argument, he talks as if IQ tests were measuring a single intellectual ability. At other times, when it is more convenient for formulating an argument about some other point, Jensen speaks of Level I versus Level II skills and of IQ tests as gross estimates of a person's general standing on a variety of intellectual abilities rather than as an index of a single ability called "intelligence." Jensen is hardly alone in his attempt to have his cake and eat it too, but these shifts back and forth between different conceptualizations of the meaning of IQ tend to weaken the force of his arguments. If we were to stick with one interpretation of IQ and apply it to all of his writings, certain of his arguments would be strengthened, but others would be demolished. His presentation would be somewhat more consistent if he came straight out and said that "intelligence" was equated with Level II abilities. He often implies this, but he avoids stating it directly because of the difficulties it will cause him.

There are other arguments for environmental effects upon intellectual development, but, like Jensen's nativist arguments, they are not convincing because they can be countered with alternative interpretations. To my knowledge, there do *not* exist *any* data that convincingly establish the relative effects of nature and nurture on intellectual development, and I suspect that there will not be any such data for a very long time, *if ever*. I will explain why I believe this shortly. First, however, to illustrate the utter futility of trying to answer this question with available data and methods, I will discuss an important study that was designed explicitly to address these issues in a sophisticated way that took into account most of the relevant criticisms of earlier work.

Lesser, Fifer, and Clark (1965) designed and carried out a study which approached the problem by controlling for both genetics and environment. Children were selected from each of four racial/ethnic groups living in ethnic neighborhoods in New York City: blacks, Italians, Jews, and Puerto Ricans. Efforts were made to insure that subjects in each ethnic group were as genetically "pure" as possible. All Italian subjects were individuals whose parents or grandparents all had come from Italy and whose genealogies showed no evidence of non-Italian ancestors. Each of the four groups was well-controlled genetically in this fashion.

Within each of the four groups, two levels of social class were established, using multiple criteria of education, occupation, and income. Middle class subjects came from families in which the father was well-educated and held a high paying professional or managerial job. Lower class subjects came from families in which the father was relatively poorly educated and held a relatively low paying and unskilled or semiskilled job. The four groups were genetically distinct from one another, but two distinct social class groups were identified within each of the four genetic groups.

Equal numbers of children in each of these eight groups then were tested with an IQ test that yields not only a total score but subscores for verbal, perceptual speed, spatial, and mathematical ability. Testing was done under conditions carefully planned to make the test data as perfect as possible. This included care taken to put the children at ease, using testers of the same racial or ethnic group as they themselves (including bilingual testers where necessary), and the like. Test scores then were analyzed by group and by subtest.

The results were striking and dramatic. First, within all four racial/ethnic groups, there were large and significant SES differences, both in general IQ and in scores on each of the four subtests. The typical finding that middle class subjects score above average and lower class subjects score below average was replicated for all groups. However, the really fascinating data concern the subtest profiles. Each of the four racial/ethnic groups had a *unique* subtest *profile* which appeared in *both* the low and the high SES subgroups. For example, Jewish subjects scored relatively higher on verbal abilities than they did on the other three tests. High SES Jewish subjects scored generally high on the test as a whole, but particularly high on verbal ability. Low SES Jewish subjects scored generally low on the test as a whole but notably higher in verbal ability. The same kinds of data were observed for each of the other three groups: despite the social class difference in general level of performance on the test as a whole and on each of the subtests, a distinctive group pattern emerged for each of the four groups which was unique to that group but observable in both the high SES and the low SES subgroups.

At first, these data seemed to settle the issue once and for all. Environmentally-oriented observers noted that the social class differences appeared despite the care taken to insure genetically pure samples, and they inferred that the evidence strongly supported the idea that the environment has important effects upon intellectual development. Furthermore, even most of the pattern differences observed could be interpreted from an environmentalist perspective. The elevated verbal scores in the Jewish samples surprised no one. Jewish culture always has placed strong stress on the development of verbal abilities (based originally on a stress on learning to read the Scriptures), so that it was not at all surprising to find verbal abilities particularly well-developed among Jews. These data fit very nicely with Ferguson's theory of intellectual development mentioned previously. Jewish culture presumably causes a greater number and variety of verbal schemas to be developed to the point of overlearning, so that Jewish individuals score particularly highly on verbal tests relative to perceptual speed, mathematics, or spatial tests.

Instability of IQ

The stability of measured IQ and its relationship to other variables was investigated in depth by McCall, Appelbaum, and Hogarty (1973). The findings from this particular study, along with the multitude of findings from other studies reviewed in connection with it, powerfully underscore the major points made about IQ in this book. This was a longitudinal study, involving repeated administrations of IQ tests to *the same individuals* between ages 2 1/2 and 17. As others had found previously, these investigators found that prediction of later IQs from tests given prior to age three is difficult, and prediction from test data prior to age two is impossible (at least with IQ test data; more recent work using Piagetian measures and other approaches to early intellectual abilities have been more promising). After about age three, IQ correlations became significant and began to rise, but even so, change rather than stability was the rule. Changes across the age range studied *averaged* 28.5 IQ points.

Furthermore, changes were not random. Instead, they were correlated consistently with other variables. High SES children tended to maintain or gain in IQ, while low SES children tended to drop. Children who gained in IQ were described as independent and competitive in their preschool years, and as independent, scholastically competitive, self-initiating, and problem solving during elementary school. Additionally, the parents of the children who gained in IQ provided encouragement and stimulation of cognitive activities in the home, and they used rational rather than fear-oriented approaches to child rearing.

As with other data related to the nature-nurture controversy, these data are correlational. Nevertheless, they support the argument that measured IQ can be affected either favorably or unfavorably, depending upon the relative quality of the environment, and in particular the quality of cognitive stimulation provided by parents.

However, the data are not as simple as they seem. Racial and ethnic groups represent *gene pools*, not identical sets of genes. As Jensen and others correctly point out, the SES differences observed in the study could have resulted because the high SES subjects within each of the four racial/ethnic groups had genes more favorable to intellectual development than the low SES subjects. Furthermore, they note, the pattern differences in relative scores on the subtests are, if anything, more amenable to a genetic interpretation than an environmental one. Perhaps the elevated verbal scores among Jewish subjects occur because the gene pool affecting these individuals contains an unusually high concentration of genes favorable to good verbal development, so that Jewish cultural traditions have nothing to do with it or are effects of the genes rather than causes of verbal abilities.

Arguments like these left the findings of this study just as ambiguous as previous findings. The authors did a follow up study which attempted to get around these interpretation differences. Remember that the four groups included in the original study not only were genetically "pure," but also were living in racial/ethnic neighborhoods in which the cultural traditions of each group were maintained. The gene pools and the cultural traditions of each group were confounded together. Consequently, the authors repeated the study, but this time added an Irish group that was genetically pure but was disbursed throughout the metropolitan area rather than living in an Irish neighborhood and practicing traditional Irish customs. Inclusion of the Irish group allowed a somewhat better assessment of genetic influences independent of cultural influences (Stodolsky and Lesser, 1967).

Again, the findings of the follow up study seemed clear-cut at first. The data from the groups living in ethnic neighborhoods generally replicated the original study. The Irish group also showed the same kind of SES difference in relative performance, but the Irish children did *not* show any particular pattern on the subtests. They were neither especially high nor especially low on any of the four subtests. Environmentalists at first took these data to mean that the subtest patterns in the other four groups were due to living in neighborhoods which preserved their cultural traditions, and that the Irish group had become homogenized and assimilated into generalized American culture, so that their originally distinctive Irish pattern had been lost. In short, they took these follow up data as strong confirmation of the environmentalist position.

Nativists again pointed out that the SES difference could reflect differences in genes rather than in environments, and they were unimpressed by the suggestion that an originally existing (but unknown) Irish pattern on the subtests had been lost due to Americanization. They pointed out (correctly) that the absence of any particular pattern in the Irish group can be explained just as well genetically as environmentally. Perhaps the Irish gene pool does not contain a mixture of genes that either favors or disfavors the development of any of the four abilities measured on the test, so that, in effect, the Irish are genetically programmed to have "flat" profiles. Thus, we are back where we started.

INADEQUACY OF AVAILABLE DATA   By now, it should be quite clear that available data on the nature-nurture issue in the area of intellectual development are not sufficiently convincing to allow any firm conclusions. The very same evidence can be argued either for or against both positions. Many findings seem convincing at first, but upon reflection, it becomes clear that they are not. In my opinion, this will continue to be the case until and unless we make gigantic strides in human genetics and in understanding the relationships between specific genes and intellectual functioning.

In order to unambiguously answer questions concerning group differences in intellectual abilities, we would have to have indisputable measures of an individual's genetic make-up, at least on genes related to intellectual abilities. We already know that intellectual abilities are related to a vast number of genes, but we know virtually nothing about which genes are related to which abilities, let alone about the specific mechanisms through which these relationships are mediated. If a person's mathematical abilities are to some degree determined by his or her genes, there is much knowledge that would have to be acquired before we could state the person's potential for mathematical learning. First, we would have to identify all of the genes that were relevant in determining mathematical potential. Second, we would have to acquire knowledge about the neurophysiological processes controlled by these genes which were relevant to mathematical ability. Third, we would have to know the specific relationships between particular mathematical abilities and particular neurophysiological processes. There are other things that we would have to know, too, but this list is already long enough to make the point: our existing knowledge in these areas does not amount to a drop in a bucket. Furthermore, there are no prospects that significant gains will be made in the near future. Development of this kind of knowledge would require a proliferation of knowledge in genetics and neurophysiology so extreme as to boggle the imagination. The task is not impossible, at least in theory, but in practice it is a long, long way off at the very least.

Lacking this kind of knowledge, we are stuck with debating the issue on the basis of essentially irrelevant and inadequate evidence. Although the questions involved are legitimate and important, there is little point in persisting with these efforts when they are doomed to failure from the beginning. Instead, investigators would be better advised to spend their time figuring out ways to optimize the development of individuals as they are at present. At least this would be of some benefit to these individuals and to society at large. In contrast, production of still more data that will not answer the questions in any definitive way does not do anyone any good.

CONCLUSIONS ABOUT THE NATURE-NURTURE CONTROVERSY IN INTELLECTUAL DEVELOPMENT   As mentioned in the beginning of this section, the controversy is not going to go away. This section will be closed by drawing some conclusions based on the available evidence, such as it is. I believe the following.

1. Existing group differences in measured IQs are *real*. They do not

disappear when attempts are made to improve rapport with the examiner, improve comfort in testing situations, or use only "culture fair" tests (Jensen, 1969). The existence of these group differences *at present* says nothing about the degree to which they are genetically influenced, nor about the degree to which they may change in the future. Bear in mind that most of the ethnic groups now looked upon as middle class and generally bright once were looked upon as lower class and generally stupid.

2. It seems quite clear that both the genes and the environment affect intellectual development. The question is not whether or not they affect it, but in what ways and under what circumstances.

3. It appears that genetic influences are strongest, and therefore that the possibility of significant environmental influences are weakest, at the extremes of the distribution of IQ scores. A child with a very high IQ who is growing up under very favorable environmental circumstances is *unlikely* to be affected significantly by attempts to improve the environment even further. Similarly, at the bottom end of the IQ distribution, the majority of individuals scoring very low IQs do so because they have biological defects (mongoloidism, PKU disease, or other genetic defects) or because they were victims of birth accidents that damaged their brains (such as hydrocephalics, children who suffered damaging oxygen deprivation). Persons who have defective nervous systems for reasons such as these are never going to be completely normal, although their functioning levels can be maximized to some point through proper treatment.

4. Genetic influences appear to be least extreme, and therefore environmental influences appear to be most important, toward the middle of the IQ distribution. Among people born without any known biological defects, the quality of the environment will affect intellectual development significantly. I believe that Jensen is incorrect in saying that these effects are restricted to persons being brought up in extremely unfavorable environments. Instead, I believe that environmental effects have a general and cumulative influence upon the person, although I agree that the degree of influence is reduced as IQ increases. The possibilities for having a really important effect upon children who test out at 90 or 95 when they are four years old are much greater than they are for children who test out at 115 or 120.

5. I believe that Jensen is correct in stating that certain intellectual abilities appear to be much more amenable to environmental influence than others. I think he also is correct in stating that what he calls Level I abilities are more amenable to environmental influence than what he calls Level II abilities. The changes that can be achieved are quite significant, however. If we are talking about a preschool child who scores 95 or so on an IQ test, the difference between a favorable and an unfavorable environment can be the difference between an ultimate IQ of somewhere between 100 and 110 vs. somewhere between 70 and 80. This is highly significant, not only in IQ terms, but in life terms, as

mentioned previously. So, while I do not claim that it is possible to turn everyone into a genius by maximizing the environment, I do claim that, with the exception of biologically damaged individuals, maximizing the environment would make it possible for everyone to be functionally literate, capable of performing a variety of jobs skillfully, and generally capable of participating as an active and self-sufficient member of society.

6. Consequently, I think that social scientists interested in child development should leave the nature-nurture controversy to geneticists and neurologists. Instead, they should concentrate on developing a clearer picture of what "maximizing" the environment means and on attempting to disseminate this knowledge to the general public.

PSYCHOMETRIC MODELS OF INTELLIGENCE   Jensen's distinction between Level I and Level II abilities is only one of a large number of classifications of abilities or models of intelligence that have been put forward based upon logical or factor analyses of test data. Several writers tried to distinguish between verbal and non-verbal tasks, but this concept broke down when it became obvious that the "non-verbal" tasks required thinking and reasoning, which involve talking to one's self. The verbal vs. non-verbal distinction was based on the nature of the overt response to the task (saying something vs. doing something), and not on the mental operations involved in solving it.

Many others used factor analysis methods to attempt to develop models of intelligence. Spearman (1904) introduced the concept of g (general intelligence). He noted that different subtests or ability tests tend to intercorrelate with one another to greater or lesser degree, suggesting that they share in common a factor which is responsible for this intercorrelation. This common factor, present to some degree on all IQ tests, was labeled g by Spearman. The factor never has been defined adequately, so that the familiar definition of intelligence as being what intelligence tests measure is pretty much the truth.

Spearman's model of intelligence postulated the g factor as the only important factor, and equated it with "general intelligence." Performance on a particular task would be a function of g and the person's specific aptitude or ability on that task. In this respect, the model is similar to Ferguson's model discussed previously, except that Spearman tended to treat the general ability factor as if it were an index of a single underlying ability, whereas Ferguson clearly treats it as an estimate of the number and variety of schemas developed to the level of overlearning. In contrast, other models built on factor analysis methods tended to minimize the importance of the g factor relative to subfactors such as verbal abilities, mathematical abilities, or spatial abilities. This approach led to a search for a relatively small number of what Thurstone (1938) called "primary mental abilities."

Other writers, notably Cattell (1971) and Guilford (1967), developed much more complex models involving large numbers of separate abilities. Guilford's model is somewhat more useful than most of the others, because it is based in part upon logical analyses of the tasks involved in intelligence tests and not merely upon factor analyses of them.

All of these models share a common weakness: they are based upon intelligence test data. As noted above, intelligence tests are limited to verbal and paper and pencil activities that predict school performance. They do not include numerous other abilities that are socially important or skills that cannot be measured quickly and simply. Consequently, what are called "models of intelligence" can be described more narrowly (and accurately) as "models of the factor structures of intelligence tests." For more basic and useful models of intellectual functioning, we need to look to Piaget, Ferguson, and others who have written in the areas of cognitive development and human learning.

Ironically, of all of the various models proposed by psychometrically-oriented writers, Jensen's Level I vs. Level II distinction may be the most important and useful. However, it must be understood as a dimension upon which different tests can be placed rather than as description of two completely different kinds of tests. All tasks involve some degree of Level I ability and some degree of Level II ability, although Jensen has identified a few tasks which are almost completely one or the other.

It also should be kept in mind that the child, and not just the test, determines the degree to which Level I abilities and Level II abilities are required or used. The very same task (such as a Piagetian conservation task) can be a Level I task for a child who already has overlearned everything about this particular kind of conservation and thus is capable of giving the correct answer with little or no thought, but it will be a Level II task for children who have not yet learned it and must reason it out to the best of their abilities.

With these qualifications in mind, Jensen's distinction is a useful one, both for describing the nature of tasks in terms of the kinds of demands they make upon children's mental abilities, and for describing the ways that children approach tasks. The model is especially useful when combined with Ferguson's ideas about overlearning and the availability of schemas for use in thinking and problem solving. Basically, a Level I task is one which the child already has overlearned or can learn very quickly and easily by using other available skills previously overlearned. The new learning involved is assimilated easily, and the task itself involves minimal accommodation.

In contrast, a Level II task is one that children have not seen before or at least have not overlearned. They must approach it through Level II thinking and reasoning abilities. Consequently, the task will be somewhat difficult, and will present more of a problem of accommodation than of assimilation. Relatively few overlearned schemas will immediately transfer to the new task, so that they will have to generate possible solutions and discover a correct one through trial and error.

Jensen's Level I and Level II distinction helps integrate psychometric data with data from cognitive development and learning, although Jensen himself stays primarily within the psychometric tradition. Combined with Ferguson's ideas, this distinction helps explain both individual and group differences on tests and test items. Furthermore, it allows for both genetic and environmental influences to be included in the explanation. For example, the group differences that have caused so much argument among psychologists and educators tend to exist largely with Level II tasks, and minimally or not at all with Level I tasks. This is explainable on the grounds that our culture apparently causes the abilities that Jensen calls Level I to be developed to the point of overlearning in almost everyone (and the genes apparently equip almost everyone to develop these abilities to the point of overlearning). Conversely, the differences that appear in Level II tasks apparently appear because of a combination of genetic differences in Level II ability potential and environmental differences in the degree to which Level II abilities are stimulated to the point of mastery at the level of overlearning.

Jensen's distinction also can be tied in with the important concept of *production deficiency*. A typical production deficiency task presents children with a number of items to memorize. If they attempt to do it through sheer rote memory, they will take longer than if they use clustering techniques. Children who presumably have the ability to cluster but do not do so are described as having production deficiency. Using Jensen's terms, we also could say that they approach a task that is done most easily using Level II skills in a less efficient manner that relies on Level I skills. Carrying this further and invoking Ferguson's ideas, we might say that the production deficiency occurs because the child has not yet mastered the relevant Level II skills to the point of overlearning, and consequently cannot use them for thinking and problem solving in a task such as this, where they would be helpful.

This has been just one of a great many possible illustrations of how ideas drawn from apparently disparate sources can be brought to bear on the same problem. The result often is recognition that differences are more apparent than real, and that terms used by one group of writers often are essentially equivalent to a different set of terms used by a different group. It also illustrates how ideas from different groups of writers can be used to complement and supplement one another to form a richer and more complete explanation than would be possible using only the ideas of one group. I have found this to be the case almost all of the time, which is why I advocate a reasoned eclecticism, rather than an identification with a more limited theory, as the most sensible approach to psychology as it exists today.

OTHER ASPECTS OF INTELLECTUAL DEVELOPMENT   So far, we have discussed in some detail intellectual development as described by Piaget, by learning psychologists, and by developers of intelligence tests. However, there are certain other aspects of intellectual functioning that generally are considered to be important, but are not discussed to any great degree by any of these major sources of information about intellectual development. These include such traits and abilities as curiosity, social intelligence, divergent thinking, and creativity.

None of these qualities is associated especially closely with IQ test scores. *Curiosity* appears to result from a combination of tolerating and particularly encouraging children's investigations of things of interest and satisfaction of equilibration needs. It is a habit of going beyond the obvious aspects of things (that can be seen through observing them passively) by observing them in a more active way, generating questions and hypotheses about them, and following through by systematically attempting to answer the questions or test the hypotheses through deliberate action.

Although the data are far from clear and simple, they suggest that children who develop curiosity and related questioning and hypothesis generating skills tend to come from homes in which the parents tolerated, or better yet, encouraged and rewarded, the curiosity behavior that virtually all children show in early childhood. In contrast, other parents apparently extinguish this curiosity by ignoring children's discoveries or even by regularly punishing them for exploratory behavior. If kept up long enough, this can inhibit and ultimately even extinguish a child's tendency to generate questions and hypotheses about things and follow through by testing them out (Watson, 1957).

The same general child-rearing behaviors appear to be related to *divergent thinking,* or the tendency to "break set" by generating perceptions, associations, and concepts that differ from commonly accepted and acknowledged facts. Divergent thinkers can generate unusual associations to words, think up unusual uses for common objects, and otherwise inject their own perspective into their outlook on the world rather than simply accommodate to "reality" as it is presented to them. They usually indulge in more free and more "far out" fantasy, and they have the ability to look upon ordinary things from extraordinary perspectives. Divergent thinking abilities of this kind usually are considered central to *creativity,* since by its very nature creativity requires inventiveness and the ability to generate a new idea that contrasts with standard or accepted "reality" (Wallach, 1970).

Creativity, while generally acknowledged to be extremely important, is a slippery and ill-defined concept. Some writers have argued that it is just a part of general intelligence, or at least is not distinguishable from it, but comparisons of the contrasting achievements of people of equal general intelligence would seem to dispute this (MacKinnon, 1962). To date no one has come up with generally accepted definitions or tests of creativity. It remains as one of those personal qualities that we can recognize when we see, but cannot define clearly enough to measure. Several researchers have attempted to measure it through tests of divergent thinking abilities, often calling these tests of creativity (Torrance, 1962). Although the tests do measure divergent thinking abilities, they do not measure creativity as the word is usually understood. They seldom correlate with behavioral measures of creativity or with ratings of creativity based upon general behavior or upon inspection of specific creations.

Part of the problem in coming up with criteria of creativity in general and divergent thinking in particular is finding a way to separate ideas and activities that are both innovative and worthwhile from ideas and activities which are innovative or different but no more insightful or in any way better than existing ideas or activities (in some cases, they clearly are worse). Creativity tests ask children to generate unusual uses for common items or ways to improve common toys. Responses are scored for *originality*. The most original responses show great variability in *quality*. Some reveal a perceptiveness and inventiveness that would be accepted as creativity by almost anyone. Others clearly are original but also are bizarre. If anything, they are likely to be perceived as indications of mental disorder. Until problems such as these are overcome, creativity research with children is unlikely to get very far.

A few studies have been done comparing retrospective reports of early childhood experiences of adults judged to be highly creative compared to those of adults in the same field judged to be low in creativity. The data are unsurprising, but they do help fill in the picture and provide support for other data on socialization methods that foster cognitive development. In general, highly creative individuals report being exposed to a rich variety of experiences as children and being encouraged to ask questions and to test out their ideas through active experimentation. Also, they typically were encouraged to pursue their interests in collections, hobbies, development of knowledge about particular fields, development of particular talents and skills, and the like (Wallach, 1970).

Social intelligence (tact, being able to see others' perspectives, avoiding hurting others unintentionally, making friends easily, and so forth) is extremely important throughout life, but is *not* measured on IQ tests. It is partially related to intelligence, in that people very low in general intelligence usually also are low in social perceptiveness. However, the converse is not true. High intelligence does not guarantee or even necessarily make highly probable social perceptiveness or social intelligence generally. Many very intelligent people are unpopular, unhappy, and generally inept in social situations.

Social intelligence appears to be fostered primarily through social experience. Children who spend much of their time playing with peers tend to learn much more about people and how to deal with them than children who spend most of their time with adults. Adults do play an important role in interpreting confusing or upsetting events to young children and in modeling social behavior and providing general information about social interaction. On the whole, the children who end up most socially intelligent tend to be those who get good modeling and information from adults and a good range of experiences in interacting with other people, especially peers. Children who do not get enough experience with peers frequently end up somewhat withdrawn or even inept in social relationships with peers, while children who spend a lot of time with peers but get little modeling and information from adults (or worse, get the wrong kind of modeling and information) often end up with self-esteem problems or problems of antisocial behavior. For example, parents who encourage their children to settle differences with their fists, rather than by discussing problems and agreeing upon solutions, are encouraging the development of generally hostile and antisocial behavior.

In summary, these specialized aspects of intellectual development, which are not measured by IQ tests, typically are fostered by a combination of allowing or encouraging the child to learn through experience and backing this

Group sand play. This picture shows a truly cooperative activity, in which continuous discussion and planning has resulted in a fairly complex fort. Individual exploration and discovery in the process of play are still important, but the social aspects of play and the desire to produce something that will be realistic or "cool" (or both) are now more important. (Photo by Evan Evans)

Group play in childhood. The girls in this picture are clearly in the stage of concrete operations, and this is reflected in their play. They will still discover things about rollerskating and master the skill to increasingly higher levels, but these aspects of rollerskating are now subordinated to the desire to interact with peers, have fun as a group, and think up interesting ideas that add to the enjoyment of familiar forms of play by providing new twists. The girls have progressed from individual skating to such complex activities as coordinated synchronized skating and playing tag. (Photo by Evan Evans)

direct learning with modeling and provision of information by adults. The experience is important in providing opportunities for stimulation and practice of the behavioral aspects of these qualities, while the socialization by adults is important for developing the intellectual aspects.

COGNITIVE STYLES   Research on cognitive and personality development converge in studies of characteristics known as *cognitive styles*. This term refers to individual differences in the ways that people process information in perceiving and use strategies in responding to tasks. Like curiosity, divergent thinking, and creativity, they are related to IQ, but only weakly, and they show systematic relationships with contrasting patterns of socialization.

One of the first cognitive style distinctions made was between *levelers* and *sharpeners* (Gardner, Jackson, and Messick, 1960). This distinction refers to a polar dimension describing how people perceive and remember stimuli. It builds upon some of the early work of the Gestalt psychologists, illustrating one way that people with different predispositions can look at the same stimuli and see different things. Consider a geometric figure that is almost but not quite square, being slightly rectangular. Levelers will tend to "level" or even out minor differences in order to impose a simple structure. As a result, they are likely to see such geometric figures as squares, or at least to see them as more square than sharpeners see them. If asked to reproduce such figures from memory, levelers are likely to draw perfect squares. In contrast, sharpeners pay attention to minor departures from "good form," so that they are especially likely to notice and remember the fact that the geometric figure was not perfectly square but was in fact a rectangle. Furthermore, if asked to reproduce it from memory, they may exaggerate the rectangular shape a little ("sharpening" it).

Differences between levelers and sharpeners have not been studied as thoroughly as differences in the cognitive styles to be discussed below, but they appear to be related to differences in defense mechanisms as they relate to general education and competence (see Chapter Thirteen). In particular, levelers seem likely to develop into the kinds of people who rely primarily upon repressive defense mechanisms while sharpeners seem likely to develop into those who defend by "sensitizing" their attention to stimulus details (Byrne, 1964). Furthermore, there is good reason to believe that such stylistic differences are learned through socialization, especially parental modeling.

A second cognitive style distinction, introduced by Kagan and his colleagues and since investigated intensively, is *conceptual tempo*, or cognitive reflectivity vs. cognitive impulsivity. Stress is placed on the word "cognitive" here, because this cognitive style refers *only* to individual differences in attending to and responding to information in cognitive situations. It has nothing to do with behavioral impulsivity (Bentler and McClain, 1976; Kagan and Kogan, 1970). Differences in conceptual tempo are perhaps most obvious (and are measured) in matching-to-sample tasks. In these tasks, children are shown a sample drawing of an object or geometric figure, and then are asked to indicate which of a number of other drawings is exactly the same as the sample. All of the other drawings are similar to the sample in varying degrees, but only one is exactly like it, so there is only one correct response. Cognitively impulsive children respond to such tasks by inspecting the response alternatives very briefly and then quickly selecting what they believe to be the correct one. They have short response latencies (they respond quickly), but they make a lot of errors because they do not take enough time to carefully compare each alternative to the sample. Often, they do not even inspect all of the alternatives at all (Kagan and Kogan, 1970). They respond as soon as they come to an alternative that is not obviously wrong. In contrast, cognitively reflective children take their time before responding, carefully considering each of the alternatives and eliminating choices until they arrive at the one they believe to be exactly the same as the sample. Because of this difference in response style, reflective children take much longer to respond, but they make many fewer errors.

This cognitive style is of interest for many reasons, one of which is that it is related to early reading progress (Kagan and Kogan, 1970) and probably is related to general success in completing school tasks. Like most learned behavior, it probably is influenced most strongly by modeling, although other aspects of socialization such as specific instructions and reinforcement probably are important, too. In this case, Kagan and others have shown that cognitive reflectivity can be socialized at school as well as at home. Kagan, Pearson, and Welch (1966) found that cognitively impulsive boys who spent a school year in the classroom of an unusually reflective teacher had become notably more reflective themselves at the end of the school year.

Several investigators tried to develop ways to teach reflectivity by teaching children to delay their responses in matching to sample tasks and similar cognitive tasks. These attempts were successful in getting children to delay their responses, but the children made just as many errors as before. These data, along with many others, illustrate that the key difference between cognitively impulsive and reflective children is not the time they take to respond, but what they do with that time. In particular, it is the systematic search and comparison strategies that reflective children use, and not just more time, that enables them to succeed more often. Following up on this, Meichenbaum and Goodman (1971), using an applied behavior modification technique known as "cognitive modeling," succeeded in making impulsive boys more reflective by teaching them problem solving strategies. Use of the strategies necessarily involved more time in responding, but the data showed clearly that it was the strategies and not the greater time that produced improved performance. Furthermore, the study as a whole showed that reflectivity can be induced relatively quickly and easily with a well-designed treatment.

A third major cognitive style dimension, investigated by Witkin and his associates (Witkin, Dyk, Faterson, Goodenough, and Karp, 1962), is known as *psychological differentiation*, or *field dependence* vs. *field independence*. This dimension also has roots in Gestalt psychology, particularly in the notion that perceptions of stimuli are affected strongly by contextual variables. People who are field dependent or low in psychological differentiation have difficulty differentiating a stimulus from the context in which it is imbedded, so that they are highly susceptible to having their perceptions of the stimulus affected by manipulations of the surrounding context. People who are field independent or high in psychological differentiation have the opposite pattern. They have learned to separate stimuli from background or context, so that they are not very susceptible to changing their perceptions of stimuli when changes in context are introduced.

This cognitive style shows itself in a remarkable variety of situations. One of the most basic is the situation in which the stimulus is the person's own body. This has been shown in experiments in which people are put in specially constructed chairs in specially constructed rooms that make use of optical illusions to confuse them about directionality and the force of gravity. Field dependent individuals are seriously confused by these situations, so that they do not do very well when asked to estimate the degree to which their bodily position differs from vertical upright or when asked to change positions so that they are upright. Some people are off as much as 45 degrees, indicating that they literally do not know which way is up in this situation. In contrast, extremely field independent individuals are impervious to these manipulations and able to indicate the vertical direction accurately despite almost any kind of distractors (Witkin, Dyk, Faterson, Goodenough, and Karp, 1962). These individual differences in susceptibility to perceptual distortions concerning bodily orientation are related to parallel susceptibilities to other kinds of perceptual distortions in spatial relationships and figure ground relationships, especially distortions caused by interference from confusing contextual clues. This cognitive style shows up in cognitive tasks like embedded figure tests, in which familiar stimuli are embedded in larger and more complex configurations that tend to mask them ("Can you find five animals in this picture?"). Individuals high in psychological differentiation are good at these kinds of tasks, but field dependent individuals have difficulty with them.

This same cognitive style shows up in the personality area of dependence upon vs. independence of social influences. The same people who are field dependent in bodily orientation and embedded figures test situations tend to be people who are especially susceptible to socialization pressures. They tend to adjust to others by accommodating to their expectations and to the pressures they exert. In contrast, field independent individuals are much less susceptible to social pressures. Depending upon other factors, this makes them more likely to be independent minded and perceived as creative leaders, or, if they lack positive qualities, to be rejected and seen as nonconforming or stubbornly headstrong. Given these differences, it should not be a surprise to learn that males typically are more psychologically differentiated than females (Maccoby and Jacklin, 1974), although this is another difference that may disappear as the effects of the women's liberation movement set in.

An addition to demonstrating the pervasiveness of psychological differentiation as a cognitive style, Witkin and his colleagues have identified certain socialization practices that relate to it (Dyk and Witkin, 1965). One important correlate (cause?) of psychological differentiation is what has been called independence training (Whiting and Child, 1953), a combination of expectations and reinforcement for independent and autonomous action rather than dependence upon adults. Field dependence (or low psychological differentiation) has been associated with overprotective and/or authoritarian parenting, in which children were discouraged or punished for aggressive or independent behavior and dominated by parents in most aspects of their lives. Their parents were quick to "jump in" to settle arguments or give orders, rather than let children work things out on their own.

The parents of more highly differentiated children tended to be warmer and more close to their children emotionally, and to spend more time with them sharing common experiences. The role of fathers was especially important here, particularly for the development of differentiation in boys. These parents exercised control through what Baumrind calls "authoritative" methods, avoiding unnecessary over-control and authoritarian punitiveness, but maintaining necessary limits. In addition to these more general traits, parents of highly differentiated children socialize this development more specifically through modeling differentiation in their own behavior and encouraging it in their children. They not only allowed but encouraged and approved of children's assertiveness in exploring the environment, acting independently, making decisions, developing self-reliance, and assuming personal responsibility for their own affairs.

Only three of a much larger number of cognitive style dimensions that have been identified or proposed have been discussed (Sigel and Coop, 1974). Various dimensions stressed by different writers tend to overlap, and research on these topics is plagued by conceptual and measurement problems. The area is an important one, and probably will continue to receive much attention. It represents the borderline or area of interface between cognitive development and personal development, and most if not all development of different cognitive styles appears to result from contrasting socialization and formation experiences. Cognitive styles are at the crossroads of several different areas of psychological inquiry.

LINGUISTIC DEVELOPMENT IN THE CONCRETE OPERATIONAL YEARS

Language development during this period generally parallels cognitive development, in that the changes are almost all quantitative (expansion of vocabulary and general verbal abilities) rather than qualitative (development of higher level verbal skills). Production deficiency is a major problem early in this period, and it remains a problem for those children whose verbal schema development does not keep pace with their development of sensorimotor and cognitive schemas. A good part of language development depends directly upon the modeling and general "linguistic environment" provided in the home. Although peers certainly teach children many things, most language development is stimulated through interactions with adults, primarily parents and teachers.

All children at these ages still have the ability to pick up language simply by hearing it, but familial differences in social class begin to make a greater difference now. The conversations heard in most middle and upper class homes contain much more cognitive and linguistic stimulation than the conversations heard in most lower class homes. Middle and upper class children continue to develop their vocabulary and general language skills at high rates, while lower class children develop at much slower rates, because they encounter new words and new concepts less often.

Bernstein (1962) has noted that these differences depend not merely on general intellectual differences, but also on differences in occupations and other out-of-home activities that are associated with social class. Well-educated people who work at professional or other cognitively stimulating jobs are likely to do a lot of reading related to their work, or to spend time discussing it. They also are likely to regularly read newspapers and magazines and to watch the news on television. Furthermore, they tend to belong to more professional and social organizations, to become actively involved in political and religious organizations, and, in general, to have a broad range of experiences and interactions. A child growing up in this kind of home is exposed to all of this stimulation, and will be involved in conversations concerning it. One result will be a much bigger vocabulary. Another will be the development of more linguistic schemas to the point of overlearning, which will occur through sheer repetition of them in many different conversations covering many different topics. Within these social class differences, individual differences in habits such as reading, writing, watching television, carrying on conversations, and hobbies and interests will make a difference in the child's exposure to language and mastery of linguistic schemas. Children who are encouraged or at least allowed to pursue interests in these areas are likely to develop their linguistic abilities faster and farther than children who do not have such experiences.

Ordinarily, the child's language will be affected most strongly by the language spoken in the home, so that accents and dialects existing there will appear in the child's speech also. These are not of any great importance in their own right, although they may become important if the school system or the social system in which the child grows up makes an issue of them. In any case, they are no cause for concern. Anyone who is motivated to do so can learn to eliminate an accent or dialect with little difficulty. The best examples of this are radio and television personnel, all of whom tend to speak in a relatively homogeneous and bland Middle Western accent. Few of these people talked that way originally. Many of them had dialects or accents associated with racial or ethnic groups, and many had thick accents associated with geography (northeastern twang, southern or western drawl, and so forth). They learned to eliminate this with relative ease during their career educations.

In general, cognitive development is much more important than language development, increasingly so throughout development. An intelligent person can change language relatively easily, and even can learn to speak in an entirely new language if necessary. Language instruction will not compensate for all of the important experiences that are needed to stimulate general cognitive development. Radio and television personnel again make good examples here. With their highly developed verbal skills, they are able to read the news with smooth deliveries, even though at times it becomes clear that they do not have much understanding of what they have just read.

The opposite problem (difficulties in communicating knowledge that really is there) exists in people whose development of verbal schemas has not matched their development of sensorimotor and cognitive schemas. In most cases, this will cause no great problem, because most such individuals tend to be in occupations that require them to use the knowledge that they possess but not to communicate it to others (skilled workers). However, individuals who possess a lot of cognitive and sensorimotor knowledge and who are called upon to pass it along to others will have difficulty in doing so unless they develop their communication skills. Fortunately, this is not very difficult for them to do, if they have the motivation to do so.

In general, language development is of some importance but is clearly secondary to cognitive development, and gaps in language development can be filled in later with relative ease by a person who is able and motivated. Adults working with children therefore should do what they can to foster language development (primarily provide a good language model), but they should not make a major issue of particular language usages or problems of pronunciation, since these will tend to disappear of their own accord over time. Language development generally will be associated closely with general cognitive development, and both will depend largely upon the variety and quality of stimulating experiences to which the child is exposed.

SUMMARY   Once they achieve concrete operations, children use the same kinds of logical reasoning that adults do, although they cannot yet handle purely abstract material. Their schemas become assimilated and coordinated into an internally consistent and coherent cognitive structure, which allows them to make connections between events, reason forward from causes to effects and backward from effects to causes, and conserve the universal and invariant aspects of objects even when formerly confusing changes in surface appearances are made. Unstable and spotty knowledge gradually merges into a stable and integrated cognitive structure.

Physical development normally proceeds smoothly if children get adequate nutrition and maintain typical play levels and activities. Play usually is not a problem, but nutrition often is, even in high SES families. Children need nutritious and balanced diets to insure continuous healthy physical growth, and they also need monitoring of their diets to see that they do not become dangerously unbalanced toward carbohydrates and/or do not lead to excess fat accumulation. Growth continues to proceed unevenly, with brief growth spurts alternating with longer periods of minimal growth. Growth spurts often introduce new opportunities to children, as they become big enough to do things that they could not do before. This will affect play preferences and even playmate preferences, at least temporarily.

Children remain in the period of concrete operations throughout middle childhood, so that they do not make major gains in cognitive development from the Piagetian perspective. Within this stage, they make great quantitative strides in the number and variety of schemas they acquire. Much of this occurs as a result of deliberate instruction at school, although children continue to learn through play and other informal activities as well. This kind of learning has been studied in detail by experimental child psychologists and learning psychologists, who have developed a large literature about it. Among the more important contributions are the learning hierarchy of Gagné and Ferguson's theory of the development of human abilities as outcomes of the combination of genetic potential interacting with environmental and cultural factors that cause specific schemas to become overlearned and thus available throughout life for repetition and for transfer to new situations.

Psychometric approaches to the measurement of intellectual abilities in children began with Binet's efforts to develop tests capable of identifying problem low achievers while they were still young, so that the schools could provide them with special help. Very soon the concept of intelligence tests and several related concepts took hold and remained in vogue for about 50 years. Then, in the 1950s and 1960s, the idea of intelligence as a single entity, fixed at conception and measured adequately by so-called intelligence tests, came under attack, and an extreme nativist point of view was supplanted by an extreme environmentalist point of view. For a time, it was believed that the early years were absolutely crucial to cognitive development, and that poor achievement and other problems associated with the disadvantaged could be eliminated through early intervention programs. This enthusiasm later soured, and presently most psychologists hold a more moderate position on the nature-nurture issue. The arguments and data put forth by Arthur Jensen and the responses of his critics were reviewed in some detail to illustrate the nature-nurture controversy as it applies to intellectual development. It was shown that no existing data are definitive, and that no definitive data are likely to be forthcoming in the foreseeable future. One major implication of this is that nature-nurture questions should be left to the biological sciences, and that social scientists should concentrate on questions concerning optimizing child development by optimizing environments.

Many writers have tried to categorize intellectual abilities and/or types of tasks or tests. So far, none of these schemes has proved to have much practical usefulness, although Jensen's distinction between Level I and Level II abilities might have, especially if elaborated to take into account individual differences in children as well as differences in task demands. Curiosity and creativity are two intellectual abilities that provoke continuing interest, but so far without many definitive findings. Another important aspect of intelligence includes the complex of social skills that we could include under the label "social intelligence." This important set of skills is not measured by conventional IQ tests, and has not received attention that it deserves, although this is starting to change.

Cognitive styles have produced considerable research activity in developmental psychology and psychology generally. They are interesting individual difference variables, and they have both theoretical and practical implications because they combine cognitive development with personality development and appear to be shaped through socialization. The cognitive style variables leveling vs. sharpening, conceptual tempo, and psychological differentiation were discussed, although many other such dimensions have been identified or proposed.

Social class differences in the frequency and functional use of language in the home have relatively greater impacts upon children during these years than they did previously. This probably is one reason for the cumulative disadvantage problem discussed throughout the book. Children whose environments are rich in cognitive and linguistic stimulation learn many more words to overlearning and thus have larger vocabularies. They learn to use words for communicating, thinking, and problem solving more effectively. Still, as in other developmental stages, language is important but not nearly as important as general cognitive development.

CHAPTER TEN

Fostering Physical and Cognitive Development in Middle Childhood

In general, the socialization factors that favor development in the preoperational years should continue throughout the concrete operational years, although they need to be adjusted as children get older and become capable of carrying on true dialogues with adults. Many of the primary factors important for fostering optimal physical, cognitive, and linguistic development were mentioned briefly in Chapter Nine. These and other factors will be discussed in more detail now.

PHYSICAL DEVELOPMENT

As noted, physical development proceeds more or less automatically in most children, *if* they get adequate nutrition and exercise. Since most children get adequate exercise on their own, the main job facing parents here is providing adequate nutrition. Assuming adequate income (problems here would require intervention from a social agency), the primary socialization goal is to instill good eating habits in children. Hopefully, this not only will insure good nutrition in childhood, but also will involve placing and keeping food in proper perspective and learning good eating habits that will persist throughout life.

Although children become more and more able to tolerate the three meal a day regimen that most adults follow, they still require a larger number of smaller meals, compared to adults. They still should not be expected to eat as much as adults at regular mealtimes, particularly supper, and they should be given snacks in mid-morning and mid-afternoon if they request them. Ideally, these snacks should be good tasting but also nutritious (such as; fruits, nuts, cheese, peanut butter, milk, fruit juices). Children usually will prefer candy or ice cream treats, of course, and there is no reason why they should not get these occasionally too (assuming that their diets are adequate).

Problems often arise because children demand too many of the preferred but not very nutritious foods, badgering parents for larger or more frequent servings and failing to eat as much as they should at mealtimes because of snacks that were too large or eaten shortly before meals. It is important that both parents and children view snacks as meal supplements, not substitutes, and that children get enough food to satisfy their hunger but not be allowed to stuff themselves needlessly. It is worth repeating: adult obesity begins in childhood with the development of the habit of overeating typically and compulsively.

GENERAL PHYSICAL GROWTH   Children get a lot of good exercise in the normal course of playing with their friends. Furthermore, play takes so many forms that all parts of the body typically get sufficient exercise. Usually there is no need for adults to cause children to get specific kinds of exercise. In particular, unless children want to do so, there is no reason to insist that they perform calisthenics or other exercises that adults use to keep in shape. An active child is always in shape.

Promoting optimal physical development mostly involves providing children with equipment and physical exercise opportunities suited to their developmental levels and their interests. Ordinarily, children will enjoy almost any physical activity or sport, provided that they are physically developed enough to be able to attain a reasonable degree of success. The main problem facing adults when discussion of a new activity comes up is to determine whether or not the child is ready. Where possible, it is a good idea to find out if children really are ready to do something that they want to do (when there is any doubt). The fact that playmates are able to perform a task does not necessarily mean that a particular child will be able to do it or will still want to do it after trying a few times. Assessing readiness is especially important when the activity involves some investment, such as purchase of a good bicycle, a trampoline, or a musical instrument. Usually, it is possible to arrange for children to try out activities provisionally by using borrowed items or arranging for them to take lessons in activities like swimming, gymnastics, or dancing. A few sessions should be enough to allow adults to judge children's readiness for an activity. Children get feedback about their own abilities and about the nature of the activity, so that they can reevaluate their interests after they have had some experience.

Respecting and accepting the child's size and level of skill development is essential. Sometimes it will be necessary to tell children that they are not ready or able to do something that they want to do (or think they want to do). This is accomplished best with feedback which is straightforward and honest, but presented in a positive and accepting way. Children should emerge from such experiences with a genuine understanding and acceptance of why it is not a good idea for them to seriously pursue the new activity at the moment, but without any sense of shame or inadequacy because they cannot do something that their friends can do. It helps, of course, if, in addition to specific feedback, adults give children some general information about individual differences in bodily growth rates and other aspects of maturation.

In addition to helping children recognize and accept maturational advances and limitations, it is important for adults to do so themselves. The same goes for respecting children's interests. It does children no good, and it may do some harm, to insist that they join a ball club, take dancing or music lessons, or receive some other kind of formal instruction in a skill or sport before they are ready to do so or when they do not want to do so. It sometimes is claimed that enforced experiences of this kind will teach the child mental or physical "discipline," but the data suggest otherwise.

Even worse, of course, are adult attempts to live out their own frustrated dreams vicariously by trying to get children to do things that they were unable to do themselves. Most adults are aware of the dangers of these things at some level, but this can be forgotten in the excitement of involvement with an activity, particularly a competitive sport. Probably the best example is Little League, where parents who are otherwise sensible and understanding typically get caught up in the excitement of the game and in their own aspirations for their child, so that they end up doing and saying things which are embarrassing or even destructive. In short, the watch words for physical development are: encouragement and opportunity, yes; badgering and demanding, no.

DEVELOPMENT OF SPECIFIC SKILLS The development of specific skills should be left mostly up to the child. Ideally, children will have had opportunities to sample and participate in a great variety of activities and sports. Typically, they will become highly interested in some of these, hopefully those for which they are well-suited physically. When a good combination of readiness and high interest exists, the time is ripe for enrolling the child in lessons or formal organizations, but not before. Insofar as possible, parents should follow their children's expressed interests in arranging for them to become involved seriously in specific motor skills or sports.

There are two areas where parents should exert some specific pressures. First, both because it is something that can be enjoyed throughout life and because it is a skill that should be learned for safety's sake, I think that it is important that all children learn how to *swim*. They need not learn to become expert swimmers or divers, but they should learn to enjoy the water and be able to swim well enough to insure safety. So-called "swimming lessons" are offered for children as young as a year old, but children do not learn to swim in a real sense until they are at least three or four. Where possible, it is a good idea for parents to have professionals give the children a few lessons to get them off to a good start. After this, parents usually can handle the rest of the job themselves. Most pools offer Red Cross swimming lessons free or at low cost.

It also is a good idea for parents to watch while small children are getting swimming lessons. Professional instructors usually are masters of the arts of communicating positive expectations and encouragement, minimizing fears, and avoiding doing or saying things that make children feel that they are incompetent or in danger. They also know specific and efficient techniques for teaching particular skills. Parents can pick these up through careful observation, and can practice them with the child later.

Once three- or four-year-old children become comfortable in the water and interested in "swimming," they are ready for enjoyable outings with the parents. Swimming practice, not to mention mutual enjoyment and physical contact, can be standard features of family swimming. At pools, parents can wade out several feet and then let children swim back to the side of the pool, increasing the distance gradually as the children gain efficiency and stamina. At beaches, young children can swim back and forth between parents and/or responsible older siblings. When they tire, they can be held (both to provide support needed for resting and to take advantage of natural opportunities for warm and physically close interaction). Older children who have mastered basic swimming and mainly want to practice strokes, try for new "records," and just have fun, do not need continuous interaction. They will need supervision for a few more years, until they are both skilled and responsible enough to practice water safety habits *continuously.*

In addition to a specific effort to insure that children learn how to swim, I think it is a good idea for parents to emphasize the learning of sports and recreational activities that can be enjoyed *throughout life.* This is one area in which the schools and other socialization institutions in our society have been remiss until relatively recently, stressing team sports which place a premium on size, strength, and specialized athletic skills at the expense of such activities as gymnastics, swimming, bowling, tennis, table tennis, handball, squash, golf, skating, and other recreational activities and sports that almost anyone can become involved in and that do not require a large number of players or expensive equipment or facilities.

An additional advantage to these kinds of activities is that both males and females can participate in them meaningfully and enjoyably. This becomes important later for providing couples and families with activities that they can do together. In this connection, it is worth noting again the importance of encouraging girls to get involved in physical activities and sports, and to caution once again about the dangers of pushing boys to try to do things that they do not want to do or that are beyond their present capabilities. This is one area in which our traditional sex role socialization has been very unfortunate, tending to minimize the involvement of girls and women in sports and physical activities and to channel boys only into certain activities, particularly ones at which only a small percentage are likely to succeed and which are not very practical as lifelong interests. Children of both sexes will be much better off to the extent that we rid ourselves of the tendency to look upon sports as primarily masculine activities with implications of competition and proving oneself. Instead, we should begin to look upon them as physical activities that children and adults of both sexes can participate in primarily for fun.

Much of the material on cognition in the previous chapter dealt with the concept of intelligence and the nature-nurture controversy concerning IQ test scores. The present section will concentrate on how parents can help foster cognitive development at home and on how society begins to socialize the cognitive development of the child through formal schooling during the concrete operational years and beyond.

COGNITIVE DEVELOPMENT

FOSTERING COGNITIVE DEVELOPMENT AT HOME   The school is an extremely important institution of the child's life, and its effects should not be minimized. Nevertheless, in most cases, the home and particularly the parents remain the primary influences upon child development throughout childhood. The child attends school for only six or seven hours a day, five days a week, nine months a year. This is a relatively small portion of the total time available for socialization, and the vast majority of the remaining time is spent in and around the home. Furthermore, even though the school is set up explicitly to concentrate on cognitive development and to leave socialization in other areas to the home and other institutions (for the most part), some of the most important cognitive development that goes on in childhood occurs in the home.

The basic mechanisms for stimulating optimal cognitive development in the home are provision of materials and opportunities to satisfy curiosity and learn through exploration; preaching *and* practicing active intellectual involvement with the environment; and maintaining a close and cooperative relationship with the school. Provision of opportunities for intellectual development includes both the purchase or construction of stimulating equipment and materials and the desire to spend time using them with the child. It would be nice if children really were intrinsically motivated to learn everything that they could about the environment, and if they did so on their own initiative, as some writers seem to believe, but this is not the case. A rich physical environment naturally will provide more stimulation and potential activity than a barren one, but instruction, modeling, and interactions with adults will be needed if children are to make optimal use of whatever environments they have.

As mentioned before, the child does not extract *meaning* from the environment through osmosis or some other automatic process. Many things never will be noticed unless attention is called to them, and many questions never will be generated by the children themselves. Knowledge can be stimulated by adults who provide information, demonstrations, and stimulating questions or suggestions. Ideally, most of this should take place during informal interchanges that occur regularly every day because parents and children spend a lot of time together. Learning should not be restricted to times when the child comes to the parent with a request or when the parent decides to teach something to the child. The latter situations are important and should occur regularly, but a great deal of socialization also should occur during casual conversations and interactions at mealtimes, while watching television, and in other informal situations throughout the day.

Effects of Television

There is much interest and controversy about the nature and strength of affects that television watching has upon children. Correlational data overwhelmingly support the conclusion that, to the extent that viewing has any effects at all, it is likely to induce modeling and imitation (Stein and Freidrich, 1975). Children who watch aggressive cartoons tend to be more aggressive in their play than other children, and children exposed to aggressive cartoons in experimental situations tend to be more aggressive immediately afterward than children exposed to neutral cartoons. The likelihood of imitation of characters seen on television or other media varies with many factors, so that effects upon specific children are difficult to predict. Effects are unlikely to be very strong except in unusual cases, but where effects do appear, they are likely to involve imitation rather than catharsis. Children's desires to act out aggressively are likely to increase rather than decrease as a result of watching aggressive television programs, (if these desires are affected at all).

There is little reason for concern that exposure to a single program will have much of an effect, but many observers believe that a constant diet of violence and aggression, cumulated over time, is likely to brutalize children by making them familiar with these negative emotions and behaviors and likely to imitate them in frustrating situations. Research in this area is difficult and no definitive data are available yet, but the great weight of evidence favors the position of those who fear that exposure to undesirable modeling will have undesirable effects over the position of those who believe that such exposure will produce catharsis and will have desirable effects. Such data raise serious questions about censorship and control of television programming, particularly that directed at children.

More recently, studies have shown that television can have positive as well as negative effects. For example, Coates, Pusser, and Goodman (1976) found that viewing "Sesame Street" increased rates of positive reinforcement given to playmates and adults by preschool children. The frequencies of social contacts initiated by these children also increased following viewing of the program. Increases were significant for children with initially low scores in these categories, but there were no significant effects on the behavior of children initially scored high. Even more encouraging effects were found for the viewing of "Mister Roger's Neighborhood." All children significantly increased their rates of positive reinforcement and social contacts with other children and adults after viewing this program. These findings make sense based on the content of the programs themselves, and they illustrate that television models can have positive as well as negative effects. Other studies have shown that viewing such programs can increase self-control, sharing, cooperation, and preferences for children of other racial or ethnic groups (Gorn, Goldberg, and Kanungo, 1976). The potential societal benefits of all of this seem obvious and important.

Parents can both stimulate and model intellectual activity when children are young by purchasing and using books, chalk boards, table games, and card games, *and using them with the children.* As the children get older, parents can expand on this base by getting their children library cards, encyclopedia sets, globes, and other equipment and supplies which will allow the children to follow up on intellectual interests they pick up at school.

Elementary school children become very interested in hobbies and collections. These are valuable, not only as enjoyable activities in their own right, but also as methods of stimulating cognitive development and interests. Stamp and coin collections, rock collections, animals and plants, arts and crafts projects, and other things that children can take a continuing interest in are stimulating and informative as well as enjoyable.

Within space and budget restrictions, it is helpful to provide children with a desk and a bookcase of their own for reading and writing, and to keep them

Science class in elementary school. These students have mastered the basic tool skills and are able to use them for learning about other things—in this case, botany. They not only can understand and profit from, but will enjoy, such activities as planting things and keeping systematic records of the results, based on concrete experimentation such as that shown here. (The student at the left is measuring the height of the plants, and entering it on the record along with similar measurements taken earlier.) All this is very meaningful to the students because they have participated in this experiment themselves and are personally monitoring its results. (Elizabeth Hamlin / Stock, Boston)

378

supplied with paper and writing materials and with arts and crafts materials. Children also can be encouraged to watch the many excellent educational television programs which now are available for them, although this should be confined to positively oriented suggestions rather than to insistent demands (which might make them take a negative attitude toward the shows involved).

As children get older, cognitive development as well as development in other areas can be facilitated by gradually allowing them to assume responsibilities around the house and to observe and help their parents in the process of conducting household chores and repairs. Where possible, it is a good idea to allow children not only to watch but also to participate directly in these activities, such as by using their own tools to tighten loose screws, to assist with painting jobs, to assume certain responsibilities for household chores, and so on.

Intellectual stimulation also is provided from movies, trips to museums and other informative and interesting places, and family vacations. Summer camp programs, programs offered by organizations such as scout troops or the YMCA or YWCA, and enrollment in specialized lessons also are useful. Such experiences allow children to become exposed to a great variety of stimulation, and they lead to the development of more specific interests that the child can follow up more systematically later. Such experiences will be most valuable, of course, if adults ask questions, listen to the child's answers, and make comments of their own about things that the child has not thought about or mentioned. Shared interactions of this kind show children that adults are interested in their activities and experiences, and they stimulate reflection about the meanings of these activities. In Piagetian terms, they stimulate the development of cognitive schemas related to previously developed sensorimotor schemas.

Probably the most important experience for parents to consistently question children about and discuss with them is the school experience. In this way, parents can show that they consider school to be important and that they are interested in their progress at school. Furthermore, by establishing and maintaining a continuing dialogue about what is happening at school, parents can keep abreast of developments, find out about potentially troublesome problems early enough to do something about them before they get worse, and help children interpret and cope with situations which are confusing or frustrating. Additional comments about home-school relationships will be made below.

ELEMENTARY SCHOOL   School typically is the first and most important of society's institutions that children encounter and learn to cope with. Although it is a necessary and vital institution, school presents a somewhat distorted and unnatural environment to children, and both parents and teachers should try to keep this in mind. For economic and other practical reasons, instruction at school is not conducted in the individualized and informal manner that was described as ideal for parent-child interaction in the home. Instead, children are taught in large groups and in a step-by-step fashion which works reasonably well in general but which rarely is ideally suited to the specific needs of any individual child at any given moment.

As a result, although school can and should be thought of in positive terms, it also represents a systematic set of demands and frustrations that children must learn to accept and cope with. It is unnatural and often difficult for young children, especially boys, to sit quietly at a desk or table for a long period of time and work persistently on pencil and paper assignments. It also is difficult for young children to remain quietly attentive and await their turn instead of calling out an answer to a question or making a comment about whatever is being discussed at the moment. The same is true for moving around only in orderly lines, getting drinks and using the washroom only at specific times, trying to cooperate with obnoxious or aggressive classmates, and numerous other aspects of the artificial environment that schools create (usually by necessity) in order to try to accomplish their goals with the available resources.

As noted previously, if the parents are providing a rich cognitive environment in the home, further enrichment through specialized tutoring or enrollment in a school that claims to "accelerate mental development" is pointless. This does not mean that parents should take the attitude that the school knows what it is doing and needs no assistance or investigation. Quite the contrary. Parents should arrange to observe in the schools they intend to send their children to, and should ask questions about anything they find confusing or objectionable. If they believe that there are important and significant differences between teachers working in the grade that their child is about to enter, they should see the principal and request that the child be placed in the classroom of one of the teachers they consider to be acceptable. Most principals will do what they can (so will most teachers, for that matter). If the principal neither complies nor attempts an explanation, parents should give notice that they intend to pursue the matter with the school district administration or the school board, and they should be prepared to do just that, if need be.

If this sounds like an unusual or extreme measure, this is only because most of us have been conditioned to accept the gradual erosion of parental responsibility for the socialization of children and the gradual depersonalization and institutionalization of the school. These historical developments have been very unfortunate, because the family is much better equipped than the school to handle most aspects of child socialization, and parents should neither shirk their responsibilities in this regard nor allow them to be assumed by the school or any other societal institution. Schools were created to serve the needs of the community, and school officials who do not remain aware of this fact will need to be reminded of it, forcefully if necessary.

Before taking any action at all on a problem area, parents must be sure that they have all of the relevant information and are clear about the problem itself, the reasons for it, and the solution options that are realistically feasible. In the first place, there almost always are two sides to a story, and parents need to hear explanations from relevant school officials before making decisions about what (if anything) to do. Parents should make sure that they are not acting on misinformation, thus causing rather than solving problems, and also that they have identified the true source of the problem. There is a tendency to blame teachers for virtually all problems, when very often the teacher is doing something only because the principal or the school district demands that it be done. While parents should be encouraged to take an active role in monitoring what is going on at the school that their children attend, caution should also be used to avoid jumping to conclusions. Information should be gathered before making decisions or taking action, and there should be an attempt to solve problems through *informal personal* contacts conducted in a *positive* and *friendly* manner.

If a child is assigned to an inept teacher and it is clear that nothing can be done to change the assignment, parents still can make the best of a bad situation by helping the child and perhaps also the teacher. The child will need suggestions or instructions about how to cope with the teacher and with specific problems that come up repeatedly at school. If children's complaints about such situations are legitimate, they should be treated as such. Parents should try to avoid making them worse by unnecessarily criticizing or ventilating hostilities against the teacher. Instead, ask questions about what is going on, to get an idea about what things are bothering the child and what the teacher is like. Children probably will respond honestly and at length if parents truly want to know and if children are questioned in low key and informal ways.

Once the information is gathered, try to help the child solve the problem by providing specific suggestions about what to do to cope with it, how to minimize it, or how to escape it. If the teacher is overly reactive and punitive, parents can suggest ways that the children stay out of trouble by avoiding bad habits such as sitting near and fooling around with friends during class. If the teacher's behavior cannot be justified in any way (such as bitter personal criticism directed at the children with minimal provocation), the parent will have to affirm the child's perception that this behavior is wrong, and perhaps agree to try to do something about it, but meanwhile, the child will have to accept the need to find ways to cope with it.

Parents might be able to help teachers, too, by arranging for a conference to discuss the problem and share information and perceptions. If the teacher is at all aware of the problem and willing to try to do something about it, the meeting is almost certain to produce some kind of useful outcome if the parent retains an attitude of concern and a focus on the problem (avoiding blame and criticism). If the teacher is completely uncooperative and does not offer any information to change the parent's perception that the teacher is at fault, it is time to consider transferring the child or going to the principal.

If it looks like the child is going to be stuck with the situation for the rest of the year, realistic information should be given, but in as positive a light as possible. The child can be reminded that the situation is temporary and that the parent understands, so that there is no need to worry. Reassurance may be needed to the effect that the teacher probably will not follow through on threats that have upset the child or that the teacher did not really mean some

This picture illustrates the kind of home-school cooperation that parents and teachers should try to establish. Note the friendliness, informality, and generally positive atmosphere that pervades the whole scene. Sitting together on the floor and some of the other specifics shown in this picture would not be feasible at higher grade levels, but the same kind of warm and personal relationships can be established. (Elizabeth Hamlin/Stock, Boston)

unjustified criticism or was simply wrong in making it. Even here, unless it is hopelessly unrealistic to do so, parents have nothing to lose and may gain a little by trying to remain positive and holding out the hope that the situation will improve once the teacher has the chance to think things over.

What was said about teachers holds for principals, too. Often, they enforce policies only because they are handed down from above. It is not always possible for them to accommodate parental requests concerning assignments of children to teachers, because too many may desire to be assigned to and/or to avoid certain teachers. Principals usually are in no position to transfer teachers during the school year, and they must keep classroom rosters reasonably balanced. Not all requests can be honored, and not all problems are under the principal's control. As a final caution, parents should have convincing reasons for any demands they may make. Education has been plagued with fads, usually introduced with much ballyhoo but little supporting data (Dunkin and Biddle, 1974). Popularity or currency does not make an idea or teaching method good.

At the moment, there are *no* clear-cut criteria for judging teacher effectiveness (Good, Biddle, and Brophy, 1975). The methods used by the teacher or the school usually are not very informative. Fads come and go. For a few years, a fad may be hailed as the answer to all problems, but eventually it fades away and becomes replaced by something else, often something contradictory. For example, present fads in early elementary school include the discovery learning approach and the open classroom. These are being pushed enthusiastically in all parts of the country, even though there is no evidence to support them, and in fact, logical analyses suggest that they are more likely to be harmful than helpful (Strike, 1975). In any case, they probably are of no great importance, because they are not closely related to the most important aspect of schooling, *the quality of teacher-student interaction.* As with child rearing by parents, the quality of the teacher-student relationship is far more important and influential than the presence or absence of particular curricula, methods, or school organization forms.

Probably the most reliable indicators of the effectiveness of schooling are the degree to which children *like school* and the degree to which they are *learning.* In the early grades, this means in particular the degree to which they are mastering basic reading, writing, and arithmetic. The nature of the student population at the school needs to be taken into account here, too. Even the best teacher is going to have difficulty in a school that is overcrowded, underfunded, and burdened with an unusually large number of children with adjustment problems.

This cautionary note is one element of the larger, two-sided question involved here. I already have stated that I think parents should be much more assertive and active in getting involved with the school and with their children's teachers than most parents have been in the past. However, it is essential that parents treat teachers in ways that show appreciation of them and perception of them as professionals trying to do their best for all of the children in their classes (until and unless the facts suggest otherwise). You should treat the teacher the same way that you would treat a close and respected friend. Problems should be investigated and solved through personal visits and phone calls rather than through more formal mechanisms such as letters or unnecessary and irritating behavior such as going over the teacher's head to talk to the principal or someone else. Also, when parents go to discuss a situation with a teacher, they should be prepared to hear a side of the story that may shock them. Many children do almost everything that their parents want them to do in and around the home, but are very different in other environments, especially the school. Occasionally, parents respond to teachers' descriptions of their children with disbelief and anger, because "their child never does" the things that the teacher is describing. However, in many cases, the teacher is completely correct.

Even where what a teacher is doing *is* objectionable to the parents, it is important for them to get the facts down rather than simply march in and blame the teacher. The behavior may be objectionable to the teacher, too, but it may be required by the school administration. Or, even where something is not specifically mandated or forbidden, teachers may be unable to do something that is a good idea and that they want to do, because of too many other and more important commitments and responsibilities. The "look before you leap" rule is a good one to follow in any situation, but especially so in situations where a teacher is *apparently* incompetent or unprofessional.

In addition to meeting and establishing a close working relationship with their children's teachers, parents can help the school to foster cognitive development in areas directly related to the school curriculum by reinforcing it at home. Usually this will not mean or require extra work, unless a child is seriously behind and needs tutoring. The school curriculum as it is set up in the elementary schools in our country is really not highly demanding for most children, and much time is left for overlearning of the basic skills of reading, writing, and arithmetic. This is as it should be, because children will be relying on these skills for the rest of their lives. They will be better off to the extent that they have overlearned them and can produce and use them as needed, automatically and without difficulty. The importance of this has not always been appreciated by critics of the schools. In particular, those who favor learning through discovery and/or teaching through methods which minimize teacher talk and maximize student talk and interaction often take a dim view of teaching the fundamentals to the point of overlearning. They take an even dimmer view of teaching these fundamentals through teacher structured lessons which require the children to practice skills, get feedback, and continue practicing to the point of overlearning. However, both theory and available data suggest that this is not only beneficial but probably necessary and ideal for children in the early grades (Brophy and Evertson, 1976).

Using one's "learning to learn" skills in order to satisfy curiosity and generally manage one's own learning in an independent fashion is wonderful, but it cannot be done until one has mastered the rudimentary tool skills involved. Furthermore, children who get past the third or fourth grade without being at least functionally able to read, write, and do basic mathematical calculations may have great difficulty catching up later. The school curriculum, starting at about fourth grade and continuing thereafter, relies primarily on methods involving having the students read and then follow up by working on assignments or projects or having discussions. All of this works fine with children who can read and write and do fundamental arithmetic, but it is confusing and discouraging for children who cannot.

From a developmental perspective, all of this is painfully obvious. You have to stand before you can walk, and so forth. Nevertheless, the vast majority of children who get beyond the early elementary grades without mastering the fundamentals are *not* given tutorial or other high-powered instruction in these fundamentals designed to help them catch up. Instead, they are taught *as if* they had mastered the fundamentals. The result is that they fall further and further behind as the material becomes more complex and more removed from their ability to even understand the instructions.

Correcting this is primarily a matter of school reform which needs to be carried out on a societal scale, but it affects families directly when one or more of their children is involved in one of these kinds of failure cycles. Where this is the case, parents should not hesitate to discuss the matter at length with teachers and other relevant persons and insure that proper steps are taken to see that the children get the kinds of instruction that they need. They also should be prepared to invest time and energy of their own to help.

Regardless of how well their children are doing in school, parents can be of great help to teachers by establishing partnership relationships and by reinforcing the importance of school and the progress of the children. The most obvious way to do this, of course, is to take time to inspect and comment upon the worksheets or products that children bring home from school and to review report cards with children in a way that communicates that they are considered important. Parents should show that they appreciate the progress that the children are making, and at the same time express hopes for improvement (where this is appropriate).

Less obvious, but perhaps more important, is indicating the value placed upon school and upon careful work at school. This is done by asking questions about the teacher and about school assignments, by showing an interest in children's school work (not just the work that the children have been instructed to show the parents), and by "testing" the child in informal ways at mealtimes and other discussion times through verbal games, knowledge games, riddles, mathematical challenges, and the like. It is crucial that these activities be conducted in an atmosphere of challenge and enjoyment ("I'll bet you can't get this one!"), not an atmosphere of force or punitiveness ("You'll stay here until you get them all right!"). The first approach helps the children to develop the idea that learning is fun, while the second approach is almost certain to cause children to develop the idea that learning is an unwelcome chore forced upon them from the outside and done only to please adults and avoid punishment.

Self-Fulfilling Prophecies

The notion that many characteristics of children are acquired as a result of self-fulfilling prophecies of their parents is accepted widely, although there is little direct research on the matter. However, the topic of self-fulfilling prophecies in teacher expectations has been researched thoroughly in the last few years.

Interest in the topic was generated by the highly publicized study *Pygmalion in the Classroom* by Rosenthal and Jacobson (1968). In this study, teachers were led to believe that certain of their students were "late bloomers" who would show a surge in achievement during the coming academic year. Although these students were selected randomly, testing indicated that those identified as "late bloomers" did in fact achieve at unexpectedly high levels, at least in the first two grades. The initial enthusiasm and subsequent controversy created by this study led to a large and continually growing body of research on the origins and effects of teacher attitudes and expectations concerning students.

Brophy and Good (1974) reviewed several hundred of these studies and concluded that, although self-fulfilling prophecy effects are not automatic or even particularly widespread, teacher attitudes and expectations can affect students' achievement and/or attitudes. For example, various studies have revealed that teachers who do not expect particular students to understand or learn particular content are likely to treat these students by waiting less time for them to respond if they do not answer immediately, moving on to other students more quickly rather than staying with these students and giving them a chance to experience success, praising them less often when they do well and criticizing them more often when they fail, rewarding them inappropriately when they do reward them, failing to give them feedback more frequently, giving them less attention and calling on them less often, seating them physically farther away, and, in general, demanding less from them. Obviously, such treatment, if extended across a school year, would minimize the learning progress of the students involved.

Other studies have shown that teacher attitudes also can have self-fulfilling prophecy effects. Sometimes teachers treat students that they like in favorable ways, and students that they dislike in unfavorable ways. If this is kept up consistently, it will not be surprising if the liked students respond positively to the teachers and the disliked students respond negatively, even though the nature of the teacher-student interaction might have been different if teachers started with different attitudes.

In general, most of the data on teacher attitudes and expectations confirm the self-fulfilling prophecy hypothesis: to the extent that teachers (and presumably parents) consistently treat children as if they are, or are in the process of becoming, a certain type of individual, to that extent the children are more likely to become the kinds of individuals they are expected to become.

Behavior of this sort sets up a series of related self-fulfilling prophecy effects. Children learn to anticipate learning situations favorably, which increases the likelihood that they will enjoy them. Such anticipation, coupled with the development of positive expectations about their own competence and skill, makes it likely that they will develop expectations of success, which in turn will make it easier for them to actually achieve success later. Furthermore, children with these qualities tend to engender positive attitudes and expectations in their teachers, who then are likely to treat them with positive attitudes concerning their personal qualities and positive expectations concerning their abilities and interests in learning. All of these things together are likely to result in both better teaching and better learning (Brophy and Good, 1974).

Unfortunately, the reverse can also happen. Parents can minimize the likelihood of this problem by doing all of the things described above. However, sometimes teachers do develop inappropriate negative attitudes and expectations toward some of the children in their classes, and end up treating them inappropriately. This can be seen in such behaviors as underestimating children's learning abilities and placing them in reading groups or other learning groups which are below the level at which they should be placed; failing to even attempt to teach them certain things because of the mistaken impression that they cannot learn them; interacting with them less often and less positively; failing to give them feedback about the quality of their work often enough to minimize mistakes, or to spend enough time giving feedback to insure that the children really understand the concept being taught; and the like (Good and Brophy, 1973). Parents who suspect that something like this is going on should attempt to do something about it, although, again, they should be prepared to hear the teacher out and perhaps find out some new and unpleasant things about their child. While it is true that teachers sometimes develop completely inappropriate and unfortunate attitudes or expectations about children, it also is true that most of the attitudes and expectations that teachers develop are accurate. They are understandable and normal reactions based upon the children's qualities, rather than unfounded and inappropriate prejudices. Even where children are limited in ability and/or likeability, there still are certain teacher behaviors that are optimal for them, and other ones that are harmful. Parents and teachers, working together, should plan to see that each child's school experience is as optimal as possible.

CURIOSITY, CREATIVITY, AND SOCIAL INTELLIGENCE

Although all children apparently are born with curiosity, the degree to which they form the habit of following up curiosity through exploratory behavior is dependent upon the kinds of socialization they get. Like any other habit, exploration to satisfy curiosity can be strengthened or weakened by encouragement and reward (vs. discouragement and punishment). Parents can encourage primarily by inviting children to observe and ask questions about things that interest them and to take part in activities. As the children get older, encouragement also will mean providing materials and experiences relevant to the development of interests, insofar as this is feasible.

Of course, some limits will have to be placed on curiosity and exploration. Children cannot be allowed to destroy valuable household appliances simply to satisfy their curiosity about what is inside them, for example. However, they can be given old appliances to play with and take apart, can be allowed to watch and participate in household repairs, can be provided with information sources and materials and opportunities for exploration, and so on. More generally, they can and should be provided with the knowledge that their parents approve of their curiosity and exploratory behavior and not only are willing to tolerate it but are positively interested in fostering it. This means, among other things, taking time to observe and listen, making meaningful comments and asking serious questions, and following through by arranging for appropriate experiences and by obtaining needed materials.

Creativity, in the sense of producing new and worthwhile insights or inventions, usually comes only after children have mastered the basics of an area to the point of overlearning. Children may have creative ideas at any time, of course, but many of them will be unfeasible because they lack the necessary skills to put them into practice. Children's involvement in arts and crafts often is equated with creativity, although when used in this context, the term probably is inappropriate and misleading. Usually, until the fundamental skills involved in a talent area are mastered, such activities are more appropriately described as exploratory behavior than as creativity.

It probably is true that children who are both encouraged and allowed to develop skills and to use them in an exploratory way are more likely to develop true creativity in an area than are children who are not afforded these

opportunities or who are repeatedly told to do things "the right way" instead of allowed to explore alternatives. If socialization is sufficiently restrictive, the likelihood that creativity will emerge is minimized. While it is an overstatement to claim that children all possess creativity naturally and will show it unless it is somehow stamped out through rigid socialization, it probably is true that rigid socialization will reduce the tendency to think creatively. This factor, combined with the absence of factors that would foster the development of creativity, will minimize the degree of creativity that ultimately appears.

It should be kept in mind that the word "creativity" has been used here, for purposes of communication, as if it referred to a single ability, but this is no more true than it is of the term "intelligence." Creativity is mostly specific to areas in which individuals develop a deep and continuing knowledge and interest. It is not a generalized characteristic which appears in every facet of the person's activity. There are exceptions, of course, such as Leonardo da Vinci, who was creative in an astounding number of different fields. Individuals who are recognized as creative in one field usually are not particularly creative in other fields. They probably are more divergent thinkers, however, because

Group activities are increasingly important in middle childhood and pre-adolescence, but individual practice of skills continues as well. Although she is part of a larger musical group, this girl is concentrating intensely on playing the recorder. This probably indicates a special interest and pride in this skill, although she may be responding to more general motives such as the desire to please others or to master a challenging task. (NFB Photothèque/Photo by Michael Semak)

387

they were raised with socialization techniques which fostered this line of development. People who are truly creative in one or more areas are not likely to be creative in all areas. They are likely to score higher on tests of divergent thinking, because they share in common a background of socialization factors which fostered divergent thinking in general as well as creativity in certain areas in which they were particularly interested.

What we call social intelligence usually is fostered by allowing children to have experiences with a variety of different kinds of people and by continually engaging them in dialogue about these experiences. Experiences alone are not enough; dialogue which involves feedback and explanations is required in order to lend meaning to the experiences and to stimulate the development of cognitive and verbal schemas which apply to them. Over time, such schemas become organized into larger schemas such as tactfulness, sensitivity, sociability, leadership skills, and other traits that we normally consider to be part of what is called "social intelligence."

A few people develop these skills to a high degree intuitively. These are people who develop certain good habits and observational skills largely without awareness. Like other people who have sensorimotor and cognitive schemas without corresponding verbal schemas, however, they will find it difficult to analyze or explain their social sensitivity and intelligence to other people. Even though these skillful people might be unusually accurate in judging other people and unusually successful in responding to them, they will neither understand nor be able to explain the processes they use in performing such activities.

In summary, the implications for parents in relation to the development of these specialized intellectual skills are very similar to those related to the development of the kinds of skills measured by IQ tests. Such skills are not learned through formal instruction, but they are stimulated through socialization which favors development and inhibited through socialization which restricts it. Furthermore, the socialization involves much stimulation and provision of information, not just affective acceptance and encouragement, contrary to the impression often given by writers interested in these areas. Parents who want to actually foster such development, rather than merely allow it, need to go beyond acceptance and reinforcement by providing stimulation, information, feedback, modeling, and other input that stimulates development in a more positive and direct way.

COGNITIVE STYLES Parents also need to foster the development of cognitive styles. Children probably are more likely to become sharpeners than levelers if exposed to a variety of situations requiring them to notice fine details, describe them, and remember them. Children probably are more likely to become cognitively reflective rather than cognitively impulsive if adults stress the processes involved in responding correctly over the speed with which answers are given, and if adults model and reinforce rational problem solving strategies rather than random or impulsive guessing. Finally, children are more likely to become psychologically differentiated (field independent) if allowed to assume as much independence as they can handle responsibly and if encouraged to contribute their opinions to discussions and to become increasingly self-reliant.

All of these cognitive style differences are easier to develop if children are generally bright and competent, but each involves a personality component as well as a cognitive one. Regardless of their levels of cognitive development as manifested by IQ test scores or rate of development through Piagetian stages, children's development in desirable directions on cognitive style variables can be increased or decreased depending upon environmental influences, especially home influences.

As noted earlier, language development tends to take care of itself if the child is spoken to frequently enough and in a variety of meaningful contexts. There is no need for adults to be concerned about normal childhood difficulties in pronouncing certain sounds and words or about the development of accents or dialects. These linguistic attributes will change in time if general cognitive development proceeds well and if there is any need or reason to change them.

LANGUAGE DEVELOPMENT IN THE CONCRETE OPERATIONAL YEARS

The main work of parents in stimulating language development is to include the child as a continuing participant in family discussions. This means interactions initiated by the parents as well as by the child, and it means including the child in discussions about matters of general concern rather than only matters relating directly to the child. Children should not only be allowed but encouraged to participate in discussions at mealtimes, discussions involving decision making about purchases, household repairs, vacations, or other topics of interest to everyone in the family, and discussions about neighbors, politics, current events, and other topics that are normally discussed in the home.

As a general rule of thumb, there are only two types of discussions from which the child should be excluded, and where steps should be taken to insure that the child does not hear (as opposed to carrying on the discussion in hushed tones or whispers which the child can and probably will want to overhear). The first type of discussion concerns delicate matters which the adults simply do not want children to know about or hear about. The second involves discussions about the children themselves, such as trying to make decisions about how to handle a behavior problem which has come up. Discussions like these should be conducted when children are out of the house or asleep. Also, they should include agreement about what *will* be told to the child in situations where the problem involves something that requires some sort of explanation or feedback.

Other than these two exceptions, stimulation of language development and communication skills is mostly a matter of conversing with children regularly about a variety of topics. This requires a genuine interest in children and their activities, as well as a general interest in hearing their opinions about matters of concern to everyone in the family.

PREPARING CHILDREN FOR ADOLESCENCE

The physical changes that occur at adolescence are of extreme importance to children. Even the brightest and best adjusted children are likely to have some problems comprehending and adjusting to the physical and emotional changes that occur in themselves and their friends during the preadolescent years. Parents can help minimize such problems by preparing the children ahead of time. This must be done when girls are about nine or ten years old and when boys are about eleven or twelve, at the *latest.*

First, it is important to provide children with basic factual information. This can be done in part by purchasing for the children any of a number of well written books addressed to this purpose. Even with the aid of such books, a certain amount of direct discussion with parents will be needed, because the books will raise as many questions as they answer. This whole process is much easier, of course, if the parents have been open and honest with children all along, keeping sex and sex differences in proper perspective, speaking about them naturally and honestly, using appropriate terms for bodily parts, and the like. Even where all this has been done, though, some additional, more specific preparation for adolescence will be needed when the time comes.

Boys, and especially girls, need information about menstruation, so that they will know what to expect and will not become upset when the process begins. Ideally, they should have been allowed to observe and ask questions as young children when their mothers had menstrual periods. Now, they need information about how often they come, how long they last, what they feel like, what sanitary pads are, why and how they are used, and so forth. Girls also will need to know what to expect concerning the adolescent spurt in physical growth, breast development and the wearing of bras, the use of makeup, and other things related to the transition from being a young girl to being a young woman.

Boys also need specific instruction about coping with bodily changes as they enter adolescence. This includes purchase and instruction in the use of athletic supporters and shaving equipment, along with information about such matters as erections, wet dreams, and masturbation.

Children of both sexes should be encouraged to talk about dating and relationships with the opposite sex. This will encourage them to share such information with parents, and it will help make sure that they feel comfortable in seeking information or guidance when they need it. Where children do not feel comfortable in asking their parents questions, they will tend to ask their friends. They will pick up much useful information this way, but mixed in with it will be a certain amount of misinformation that get passed along from youth to youth in a particular area.

Children of both sexes also need information about the great range of individual differences in onset of maturation. Late maturers in particular will need firm reassurance, backed by a wealth of factual information, to insure that they do not feel ashamed or that there is something wrong with them.

Other information will be required in greater or lesser degree by other children, depending upon whether they are early, average, or late in maturing and upon the quantity and quality of information that they get from sources other than their parents. It is important for parents to do as much as they can to help their children to prepare for and comprehend the changes that occur at adolescence, and to maintain a continuing, open, and honest dialogue about these as well as other matters, so that the children will feel comfortable in coming to them for information or advice.

SUMMARY

During the preoperational years, children must gradually accommodate to the eating customs in their societies, which in our society means learning to become hungry at mealtimes three times a day. Most children learn this without great difficulty, although it takes time.

Adults can stimulate the development of sensorimotor schemas by matching opportunities provided to children to the children's own readiness and interests. Children will develop interests in a great variety of physical activities, all of which will be good for their general development if they are ready for them and thus able to attain reasonable success. There do not seem to be any "crucial" activities or experiences, although there are many good reasons why children should learn to swim and should learn lifetime sports in addition to the more traditionally taught team sports and childhood pastimes.

Cognitive development is relatively easy to stimulate in the home if parents take the time to do so by reading to children, listening to them read, playing games with them, carrying on extended discussions with them, including them in planning and decision making which involves the whole family, and providing specific educational experiences when opportunities arise.

More formalized cognitive development occurs at school, where the children learn the fundamentals of the three R's in the first few grades and then begin accumulating much information about a great variety of topics. All of this goes on at the level of concrete operations and thus does not involve fundamental qualitative changes in the cognitive structure, but a great number and variety of quantitative additions are made. Parents can reinforce this by emphasizing the value of schooling in their words and actions and by developing close home-school relationships. It is important for parents to get to know their children's teachers, ideally early in the year and under purely social circumstances, rather than only after some problem arises. Parents and teachers will be much more effective working together and sharing information than they will be working in isolation from each other or at cross purposes from each other. Parents should not hesitate to initiate corrective action when school problems come up, although such problems are most likely to be solved if good relationships have been established previously and if interactions involve information sharing and mutual problem solving rather than blame and mistrust.

There are many aspects of cognitive development that are not measured well or even at all by intelligence tests or Piagetian tasks. These include curiosity, creativity, social intelligence, and a variety of what have been called "cognitive styles." Most of these characteristics involve personal orientations as well as cognitive elements. In many cases, data are available to indicate that certain kinds of socialization are associated with one kind of development, and other kinds of socialization are associated with a different kind of development. Even where data are sparse, there are strong reasons to believe that cognitive styles are affected strongly by parental modeling and other socialization influences. Among the more important parental characteristics that seem to foster optimal cognitive development on these dimensions are expectations and reinforcement for independent and self-reliant behavior by children, and stress on rational and reflective rather than impulsive decision making and problem solving.

During these years, children complete their acquisition of the basic grammatical structures of the language spoken in their environment, but their vocabularies and their abilities to use language expressively to communicate or to think and solve problems are affected strongly by the nature of language that they hear used in the home. These abilities are likely to be fostered most strongly in homes which provide rich linguistic stimulation and modeling. This involves talking to children often, and in particular, talking to them in purely social interactions rather than only household management and disciplinary situations, encouraging the children to talk and listening to them rather than only talking to them, and including the children in the family conversations about a great variety of topics.

Finally, parents will need to prepare their preadolescent children for the physical and social changes that occur during these years. We tend to think of "adolescence" as starting about age 13 or 14, but children need information much earlier than that, girls no later than age 9 or 10 and boys no later than 11 or 12. This will be discussed in more detail in Chapters Fifteen and Sixteen.

CHAPTER ELEVEN

Personal Adjustment and Moral Development

The achievement of concrete operations and the other intellectual changes that mark the transition into middle childhood also affect children's personal adjustment and moral development. The development and expansion of their fund of schemas include schemas relating to self-concept and to interactions with others. Compared to adults, school age children still are quite egocentric. As this childish egocentrism gradually breaks down, children become increasingly able to see themselves as others see them. Also, an increasing proportion of their behavior becomes consciously planned and monitored. Conversely, the tendency to behave without much conscious awareness of what they are doing (while doing it) or much memory for what they did (after they have finished) gradually is reduced.

Schemas about self-concept and about interactions with others include schemas relevant to moral development. Children now have reached the "age of reason," so that they can begin to distinguish right from wrong. They develop what we call a *conscience*, or the awareness that certain behavior has moral implications.

Freud divided conscience into a positive part and a negative part. He called the positive part the "ego ideal," and included within it all of the child's schemas which, taken together, described the idealized person that he or she was striving to be like. He called the negative part the "superego," which included all of the negative moral scruples and proscriptions defining certain thoughts and actions as immoral and evil.

Other writers have made similar distinctions. They seem useful for some purposes, but generally unnecessary. First, the distinction between failure to meet moral standards because one has fallen short of an ideal vs. failure to meet moral standards because one has done something considered evil seems to be more of a semantic distinction than a real one. Either way, the effects upon the person are likely to be similar. Second, there is no more reason to use the term "conscience" than there is to use a term like "intelligence." Although we often reify conscience with images such as a voice telling us what to do, there is no physical part of the brain, corresponding to conscience, which is "reserved" for schemas relating to morality.

Instead, studies of learning and memory organization have shown that schemas retained in long-term memory are "filed" in such a way that related schemas (those which are closely associated with a particular schema) tend to be activated at the same time that some particular schema is activated (Craik and Lockhart, 1972). For most people, schemas activated in response to the stimulus word "murder" include not only definitions and synonyms, but visual images of murders and emotions like anxiety and revulsion. The latter feelings would be especially likely if for some reason we were thinking about committing murder ourselves. What we call "conscience" does not exist in reality as an organized entity. Instead, we have a vast variety of schemas and associated emotional reactions concerning ideas or behaviors that we see as good or bad.

MORAL DEVELOPMENT

Traditionally, moral development research has been divided into three main topics: moral judgment, moral affect or feelings, and moral behavior (Hoffman, 1970). This division has been based in part on differences in focus among these three areas, but it also has persisted because measures of development in these three areas are not correlated very highly with one another. Common sense says that they should be, but they are not (Hoffman, 1970).

As noted previously, neither the ability to make intellectualized moral judgments nor the degree to which a person feels guilty about having done something wrong is related to moral behavior very strongly. As a result, I believe that undue emphasis has been given to moral judgment and guilt feelings, and not enough to the socialization practices involved in producing successful coping strategies and prosocial moral behavior. The topic coverage in this and the next chapter will reflect this.

MORAL JUDGMENT   Moral judgment research has been carried on primarily by Piaget, Kohlberg, and other investigators working from a cognitive developmental perspective. This is because moral judgment is basically a cognitive ability. It is a specialized aspect of generalized cognitive development, and consequently it is much more related to other indexes of cognitive development than it is to moral behavior. In a very real sense, moral judgment tasks are closer to conservation tasks and other Piagetian-oriented measures of cognitive development than they are to indexes of morality based upon observations of behavior.

The *cognitive consistency* that comes with the achievement of concrete operations allows the emergence of systematic and *stable moral judgments*. Previously, children's moral ideas were just as unstable and susceptible to change based on new experiences as their schemas in other areas were. The stability and internal consistency of schemas that is part of the transition to the stage of concrete operations includes those schemas which relate to morality.

Although they still are somewhat egocentric, children now are more aware of their behavior and of its consequences for themselves and others. They also are more knowledgeable about and interested in the goodness or badness of various behaviors, although their conceptions of morality remain quite naive. They still react primarily to observable behavior and only minimally to personal intentions and situational circumstances. They know that doing something wrong on purpose is worse than doing it without thinking about it or by accident, but some of the finer points involved in distinguishing between immoral behavior and justified or understandable behavior still are beyond their grasp.

Children have trouble distinguishing true moral situations from situations involving rules that are nothing more than social conventions. They may be just as concerned about such matters as whether the rules of a game are being followed properly (insofar as they understand them) or whether others have said "please" or "thank you" when they were supposed to, as they are about matters that adults see as more important, such as lying or stealing (Piaget, 1932).

To the extent that children *are* capable of making true moral judgments, they are made only about very concrete situations with which they have had personal experience. Most of their "moral judgments" are not judgments at all in any real sense; they are verbalizations of moral schemas introjected from parents and other authority figures. Children will repeat these things when they are asked what is the right thing to do in certain situations, even though they may have little or no understanding of what they are saying. This is what Piaget often refers to as "merely verbal" knowledge—verbal schemas without corresponding cognitive schemas implying true understanding. This also is why Kohlberg characterized children of this age as having a "good boy" or "good girl" orientation toward morality. Most children want to be thought of as "good" by adults who are important to them, and so they learn to say all of the "right" things and, to some degree, to conform to the ideal standards of behavior which they have been taught. However, their verbalizations are much more consistent and predictable than their behavior is.

An important key to the development of moral judgment appears to be experience and socialization that help the child to develop the ability to take the role of another person. Until children can learn to put themselves in another's place, and thus to understand how their own behavior affects others, moral teachings remain just words to be memorized and repeated upon demand rather than ideals to be taken seriously and used for guiding behavior. This is why socialization practices that stress explanations which help children see how their behavior affects others and ultimately themselves are effective, not only for promoting moral judgment but also for motivating the children to seriously pursue the espoused ideals (Hoffman, 1970).

This simplistic type of moral judgment gradually develops into what Kohlberg calls an authority maintaining moral orientation as children approach adolescence. They learn to generalize from individual and concrete situations in order to develop broader moral rules. Gradually, these rules become assimilated to one another and form an increasingly stable and internally consistent *system*. In the process, the focus of concern gradually changes from pleasing the parents and other specific adults important to the child to a broader and less personal orientation toward morality. Children come to understand that individuals must act responsibly and morally, not just to please others and to avoid punishment, but to insure the smooth functioning of society.

Gradually, ideas about morality, particularly about antisocial crime, become connected with ideas about the laws of God and/or man, and with ideas about the need to insist upon certain behaviors and to forbid others for the sake of the common good. This still is basically concrete operational thinking. It does not involve the abstract moral judgments which appear at higher stages, but it is much more generalized and systematized than the "good boy" or "good girl" morality seen earlier.

Children usually are extremely naive concerning authority figures. For a number of years they tend to think that their parents are much smarter and more important than they really are. Partially for this reason, they tend to accept what their parents tell them with little or no questioning (assuming that the parents are reasonably consistent in what they say). They also tend to believe that anybody with prestige or authority necessarily is a good person interested in helping the child personally and society in general. This includes politicians, policemen, firemen, postal workers, doctors, and teachers, among others. Much of this is "programmed" by society, through control of what is taught to children at school and shown to them on television. For a time, most children simply cannot comprehend the idea that the president or a police officer might be immoral. This comes later, when the child is able to separate the person from the office and from the uniforms and other trappings associated with the office (Hess and Torney, 1967).

Although much of what we teach children in this regard is unrealistic, it is not necessarily bad. Given children's apparent need for heroes to provide ideals and for authority figures whom they can depend upon for guidance, and given the cognitive development that must occur before children can make some of the distinctions discussed above, presenting them with simplistic ideals and a generally sugar-coated picture of the world when they are young might not be such a bad idea. While I do not want to overstress this point and end up supporting the romanticized "pristine sanctity of childhood" idea, I do think that there is much to be said for trying to see that children are as happy as possible and for withholding information about some of the uglier and more distressing aspects of reality, where possible. Unnecessarily forcing children to confront unpleasant or threatening realities before they are ready to take them in stride can be traumatic for them, perhaps so much so that their ability to deal with the real world effectively as adults will be harmed rather than helped. In general, then, preserving "childhood innocence" probably is desirable, at least up to a point.

MORAL AFFECT   Moral affect includes feelings of pride and self-satisfaction that occur because one has avoided temptation or lived up to one's ideals, and feelings of guilt and shame that occur when one does something believed to be wrong. People show great individual differences in the nature and intensity of the moral affect that they develop. Most of these emotional reactions are established in early and middle childhood, in connection with the establishment of coping and defense mechanisms (to be described below).

Moral affect will arise spontaneously when children discover that they have done something particularly praiseworthy or blameworthy. Typically, there is nothing in particular that adults need to do here, although it sometimes may be appropriate to reinforce positive affect when congratulating the child for having done something particularly good. As mentioned previously, there is no point in deliberately increasing negative affect in cases where the child has done something bad. If the adult does an effective job of communicating the reasons why the misbehavior is wrong and should not be repeated again, the child will spontaneously feel a degree of shame or guilt when this is appropriate. There is no reason for the adult to deliberately increase these negative feelings, since this will not make the child any less likely to repeat the misbehavior but it may undermine self-concept or have other undesirable effects on personal adjustment. The key to promoting good moral development lies in promoting a good personal adjustment and an understanding of and consideration for the rights and feelings of others, not in engendering guilt or shame.

MORAL BEHAVIOR   Moral behavior is equated here with treating others as one would like to be treated (the Golden Rule). By far, the most important factor affecting the behavioral aspect of moral development is parental example, or *modeling*. In judging the morality of an act, it is customary to take into account the person's *intentions* and degree of *awareness* in addition to the behavior itself.

The development of moral intentions and of awareness of the moral implications of behavior is closely related to the development of *coping and defense mechanisms*. The latter topics usually are discussed in reference to

Temptation. These boys know they should not be doing this, but they have been unable to resist the temptation. Yet, they do not do this often, so why are they doing it now? One probable reason is that parents and other authority figures are not around to inhibit them. Another is the presence of peers who may taunt them if they ''chicken out.'' Can you think of some other reasons that influence resistance to temptation, either in this situation or in others? (Anna Kaufman Moon/Stock, Boston)

personal adjustment rather than moral development. However, I consider these two areas to be so closely related as to be inseparable, and they will be discussed jointly. If the development and operation of coping and defense mechanisms are understood, so are the weak relationships among moral judgment, moral affect, and moral behavior.

Earlier, we spoke of the need for children to develop tolerance for frustration and the habit of coping with problems by persistently seeking ways to overcome them rather than by giving up or by exploding in rage. Coping now will be discussed as it relates to dealing with *internal conflicts*. These conflicts arise for the first time because of the cognitive consistency needs that appear and become increasingly stronger as the child moves into and through the stage of concrete operations. The point has already been made that moral schemas are among the many schemas which form the child's cognitive structure. Just as inconsistencies among cognitive schemas tend to produce a sense of discomfort and motivate the child to take action to eliminate them, inconsistencies among moral schemas have similar effects.

COPING AND DEFENSE MECHANISMS

Inconsistencies can exist between two or more different behaviors, between two or more different cognitions, or between conflicting cognitions and behaviors. When children are not aware of such inconsistencies, they present no problems. Awareness of inconsistencies can lead to feelings of guilt or anxiety, especially where the cognitions or behaviors involved have implications regarding morality and general self-worth. For example, most of us, children included, have a strong need to think of ourselves as good, praiseworthy people. This is basic to a healthy self-concept. It is so important that anything that conflicts with it is very threatening. Conflicts might include, for example, becoming aware that we held racial, sexist, religious, or ethnic prejudices; that we had acted selfishly in situations where we should have shared or been more cooperative; or that we had done something that we considered wrong. Recognition of such discrepancy (often called "cognitive dissonance") probably would produce feelings of guilt or anxiety and motivate us to do something about the situation.

If we were capable of *coping*, we would take appropriate action to *resolve the problem* as well as we could and to see that it did not occur again. Coping requires what Piaget calls equilibration. If the conflict is between two contradictory behaviors, resolution involves thinking about the behaviors in relationship to our ideals and general moral codes, and then changing one or both of them. If the conflict is between two cognitions, coping involves seeking information (if necessary) and then changing one or both of the cognitions. If the conflict is between cognition and behavior, it involves changing either or both to make them conform with one another rather than conflict. In any case, coping involves a true resolution of the conflict achieved by changing one or both of the conflicting elements (Murphy, 1962).

Typically, coping involves changing the undesirable aspect to make it conform to the more general and more desirable aspect. Coping with a conflict

402

involving the cognition that one is a generally good and prosocial person and the cognition that one has certain irrational and antisocial prejudices ordinarily would involve eliminating the prejudices. The conflict also could be resolved by changing the more socially desirable cognition to make it conform to the conflicting one. The prejudices could be maintained and the idea that one is a generally good and praiseworthy person could be abandoned or else redefined in such a way that such prejudices no longer would be considered imperfections. The latter kind of conflict resolution (or resolution of cognitive dissonance) does solve the internal conflict, but not in a socially desirable way. It involves the use of *defense mechanisms* rather than coping mechanisms.

This distinction between coping mechanisms as actions which not only resolve conflicts but do so in socially desirable and effective ways vs. defense mechanisms which resolve conflicts but not in desirable ways is a somewhat arbitrary one. So far, no one has composed a commonly accepted "standard" list of coping mechanisms, or a clear separation of coping mechanisms from defense mechanisms. As will be discussed in some detail below, defense mechanisms sometimes are appropriate or at least preferable to the available alternatives. Nevertheless, to facilitate communication, the word "coping" and the term "coping mechanisms" will be used to refer to conflict resolutions which not only resolve the conflict but also change the person in a *socially desirable* manner, while the word "defending" and the term "defense mechanisms" will be used to refer to responses which resolve the conflict (at least temporarily), but do *not* change the person in a socially desirable direction.

Coping mechanisms include: confronting a problem directly and continuing to generate possible solutions to it until an effective one is discovered; gathering needed information; getting help from someone else because you are presently unable to handle the problem yourself (instrumental dependency); and consciously dropping certain habits or forming new ones. They involve gathering information and/or taking action to eliminate the undesirable cognition or behavior which is causing the conflict. In contrast, defense mechanisms remove the conflict from conscious awareness, but they do *not* involve genuinely coping with it because they allow the conflicting elements to continue, including the socially undesirable ones. Defense mechanisms allow people to live with these discrepancies by keeping them out of their minds, while at the same time continuing with the discrepancies. Obviously, coping mechanisms are preferable to defense mechanisms because they involve genuine solutions to the problem. Defense mechanisms provide only the illusion of solution, while the problem continues. Furthermore, time spent defending is time lost from possible coping and time gained for the problem to get worse.

Defense mechanisms take up a certain amount of energy. Although it certainly is possible to fool oneself, it is not easy or cost free. People who keep conflicts under control through the use of defense mechanisms are at a double disadvantage compared to people who truly cope with their problems. The problem itself remains with them, and in addition, energy is expended in maintaining the defense mechanisms which keep it out of conscious awareness.

People who rely heavily on defense mechanisms have diminished reality contact (the degree to which their perceptions of themselves and others are accurate and complete). Defense mechanisms allow us to fool ourselves at the expense of avoiding or distorting certain aspects of reality that we are not willing or able to perceive accurately. This takes up energy and causes other difficulties as well. The result is less energy available for coping and the problem of trying to cope when we have incomplete or inaccurate information without realizing it.

Nevertheless, *if a person is not able to cope,* defending, even at the expense of reality contact, usually is preferable to a total absence of defense mechanisms. This is especially so if the person is highly vulnerable to anxiety and guilt because of deep-seated conflicts, or is defending against serious antisocial or destructive impulses which could lead to disaster if they got out of control.

VULNERABILITY   The term "vulnerability" refers to the degree to which people are susceptible to intolerable anxiety, guilt, or fear of loss of control because of conflicts that they cannot cope with successfully. As a general rule of thumb, *the more vulnerable people are, the less they will be able to solve problems through coping mechanisms and the more they will be forced to try to deal with them through defense mechanisms.* The more vulnerable people are, the more likely they are to have problems with reality contact. In extreme cases, they may be out of contact with reality altogether (psychotic) or able to deal only with certain aspects of reality, and even here, only within certain "safe" limits (seriously neurotic).

Despite these disadvantages of defense mechanisms, they often are beneficial. This is especially so when they involve no distortion of reality, but merely the avoidance of unpleasant thoughts or memories. The simplest example is *repression,* which involves systematically keeping painful thoughts or memories out of conscious awareness without realizing that one is doing so (more about how this works later). Almost all of us have had certain unfortunate experiences that are best forgotten, because nothing positive will result from thinking about them further, and such thinking will be painful. Some people, such as survivors of horrifying war experiences or natural disasters, have a large number of very vivid memories that they are best off repressing for their own good. Non-distortive defense mechanisms can promote health and happiness and, in effect, function as coping mechanisms (especially when they keep our minds off of painful experiences which we cannot change or cope with in a more active way).

Another situation where defense mechanisms are preferable to the available alternatives occurs with people who are extremely vulnerable to very threatening internal conflicts. If coping is not a viable option for them (for the present, at least), defending usually is much preferable to the collapse of all defenses. People using defense mechanisms under conditions of such heavy pressure usually have seriously impaired reality contact and coping resources, because of the time and energy invested in defending. Even so, they are better off than they would be if their defenses collapsed. In the latter event, they would suffer severely traumatic emotional disturbances, and would develop symptoms such as anxiety and depression, or they would lose control and act out antisocial impulses.

Consider children who are small, ill-coordinated, unattractive, dumb, friendless, unloved, and lacking the slightest idea of how to go about coping with any of these problems. Given their extremely high vulnerability and the extremely unfortunate realities that they would have to face, good reality contact without any defense or coping mechanisms could be so painful and damaging to self-esteem that they might give up all hope of ever coping successfully. They might instead become withdrawn and depressed, perhaps ultimately suicidal. Individuals like this would be better off in the long run if they avoided some of these pressures, at least temporarily, through a variety of defense mechanisms, even at a considerable cost of reality contact. This could "buy time" in which they might learn to cope in more effective ways.

I have made a point of stressing that clear reality contact (accurate perception) is not always good, and that the use of defense mechanisms is not always bad, because many writers have equated good reality contact with mental health. These writers are essentially correct in cases where the person's conflicts are purely internal. Here, achievement of good reality contact *would* eliminate the need for defense mechanisms and lead to successful coping. However, this is not the case where external reality is painful or traumatic for the person. Here, people do not so much need to learn how to recognize reality as they need to learn to cope with it. This may take a long time and require a very slow, gradual shift from defending to coping.

Heavy reliance on defense mechanisms, even to the point of temporary psychosis, usually is preferable to collapse of defense mechanisms and the development of morbid depression or homicidal or suicidal tendencies. People tend to think of psychosis as the most extreme form of mental disorder. This can be argued reasonably for certain forms of schizophrenia and other psychoses which appear to be primarily genetically based and which have no known cure. The prognosis (likelihood of a successful future adjustment) for people who are driven to temporary psychosis because they are vulnerable to extreme threat is relatively favorable, certainly much more so than the prognosis for individuals whose defense mechanisms collapsed or never developed and who therefore have become morbidly depressed or antisocial and dangerous. In short, coping with problems clearly is the best solution, but, where this is not possible, defending against them usually is better than being overwhelmed by them.

Vulnerability depends partly upon the degree to which the conflict involves things seen as central to people's self-concepts and general adjustment, and partly on the degree to which they possess coping mechanisms they can use to deal with the problem effectively. *The more crucial and important the conflict, and the fewer coping mechanisms available, the greater the vulnerability.*

Where vulnerability is low, awareness of the conflict will produce very mild and only slightly negative reactions, such as confusion or puzzlement. Where vulnerability is high, awareness of the conflict will produce debilitating shame or guilt or fear of loss of control. Where vulnerability is low, the problem usually can be coped with rather easily or kept out of awareness using defense mechanisms involving little or no distortion of reality. Where vulnerability is high, the problem cannot be coped with at all, and it will be so threatening as to cause the person to defend against it desperately, using a variety of defense mechanisms including many that involve distortion of reality.

In general, five separate kinds of responses to threats and conflicts can be identified, ordered as follows: (a) from those most likely to be used in low vulnerability situations to those most likely to be used in high vulnerability situations; (b) from those which solve the problem, through those which do not solve it but also do not distort reality, to those which distort reality; (c) from active coping, through passive non-response, to active defense mechanisms.

1. *Coping.* Here, the person is least vulnerable. The conflict is not threatening and can be perceived without difficulty. The person copes with it by taking action to eliminate it for good.

2. *Inaction.* Here, the person may be at any degree of vulnerability, although in most cases, vulnerability will be low. The person will perceive the discrepancy, but will neither take action to solve the conflict through coping mechanisms nor take action to remove it from conscious awareness through defense mechanisms. The conflict will remain open to conscious awareness. If vulnerability is low, emotional response will be minimal. An example might be a discrepancy which is recognized but not considered particularly important, as when one reads that a mile is 5260 feet instead of 5280 feet. Most people would react to this by chalking it up as a typographical error or simply a mistake, and would not bother to check it out. Vulnerability would be low here, because the discrepancy involves cognitions that are not central to the self-concept and do not have important moral implications. Also, the discrepant information is almost certainly wrong. There will be little pressure to take it seriously, so that the person can ignore it with little effort. In contrast, if the conflict involved discrepancies that had serious personal implications (such as the thought that the person might be a homosexual), vulnerability might be very high. In the absence of coping or defense mechanisms that would remove the conflict or at least get it out of conscious awareness, the person might become obsessed with it and experience deep shame, guilt, or anxiety (especially if homosexuality were considered awful or evil). In high vulnerability situations people usually respond by defending against such perceptions rather than by accepting them passively and experiencing painful emotions.

3. *Repression.* The first level of defense mechanisms involves simple *repression*, often backed by other mechanisms, but *no memory distortion*. Levels 1 and 2 involve no repression, although they might involve *suppression*. Suppression refers to recognizing conflicts but deliberately putting them out of one's mind by thinking about something else or otherwise distracting oneself. It is a form of escape from the conflict, but

it is done consciously and deliberately. In contrast, repression occurs more automatically and without conscious awareness (this will be discussed in detail below). However, even repressive mechanisms simply keep the threatening material out of conscious awareness; they do not involve distortion of reality perception or of memory.

4. *Memory distortion*. The next level of severity of defense mechanisms involves both repression *and* memory distortion. Original perception is accurate, but repression and other mechanisms produce incomplete or inaccurate memories. The threatening content not only is kept out of conscious awareness through repression, but the memory is distorted. Events are remembered in a way that is more acceptable to the person's self-concept and moral ideas than they would be if remembered more objectively. Unacceptable elements are lost and/or transformed and remembered as different from what actually occurred.

5. *Perceptual failure*. The most severe forms of defense mechanisms, which involve loss of contact with reality, cause threatening events to fail to register in consciousness in the first place. Previously listed defense mechanisms allowed for *accurate initial perception* of what happened, with some perceptions being later repressed out of conscious awareness and/or distorted to make them conform to the person's self-concept. At the highest vulnerability levels, certain events are so threatening that they cannot even be perceived. They are kept out of consciousness altogether through the use of rather extreme defense mechanisms. These and other defense mechanisms will be discussed in more detail in connection with the figure. First, the relationships between defense mechanisms and general competence will be discussed.

COPING AND DEFENSE MECHANISMS RELATED TO GENERAL COMPE-TENCE   Although intellectual abilities do not relate very strongly to morality as measured by behavior toward other people, they do relate to aspects of personal adjustment (coping and defense mechanisms) and to the nature of mental and behavioral disorders that are likely to appear if an individual should develop such problems. Criminologists long have noticed systematic differences in the kinds of crimes committed by poorly vs. highly educated criminals. These differences in antisocial behavior are precisely what would be predicted based on general knowledge about differences in intellectual abilities.

Briefly, less intelligent and educated individuals tend to act out in more direct and behavioral ways, and in less sophisticated ways, than more intelligent and educated individuals. Where the crime involves money, the first type of person is more likely to become involved in armed robbery or mugging, while the second type is more likely to become involved in forgery or embezzlement. Where violence is involved, the first type of person is more likely to become involved in barroom brawls, domestic fights, and unpremeditated manslaughter that occurred because they were in the right place at the wrong time and lost their temper. In contrast, the second type of person is unlikely to get involved in violence. If they do, they are likely to do so in sophisticated and premeditated ways, such as murdering someone for profit while making it look like an accident.

What has been called "white collar crime" is committed almost exclusively by well-educated and intelligent individuals. This is because crimes such as sophisticated frauds, tax cheating, swindles, or stock manipulation conspiracies are essentially intellectual activities that involve highly developed skills and careful planning. These crimes are not viable options to less competent individuals, because they lack the skills necessary to pull them off successfully.

Differences in intellectual competence show up in coping and defense mechanisms as well as in "styles" of morality. In general, an equally stressful stimulus is going to be more threatening to less competent people than to more competent people. *More competent people will be less vulnerable* to it because they have a greater number and variety of coping and defense mechanisms available for use in responding to it.

Even where vulnerability is equal, the particular forms of defense mechanisms that appear will differ with individuals' intellectual competencies. In general, proceeding from lower to higher levels of general competence, coping and defense mechanisms will differ as follows.

1. Direct, primarily action-oriented approaches vs. symbolic, primarily fantasy-oriented approaches.

2. Naive and rather obvious (to others) defense mechanisms vs. more sophisticated and credible defense mechanisms which tend to be successful in covering the person's poor reality contact.

3. Rigid and brittle defense mechanisms vs. more flexible and adaptable ones.

4. Limited and specific defenses vs. a more general pattern of interrelated defenses that forms a sort of "character armor" which is much less vulnerable to collapse but also much more difficult to change.

5. Likelihood of psychotic reactions in high vulnerability situations vs. likelihood of neurotic reactions in high vulnerability situations.

In summary, more competent and better educated individuals can deal with an equivalent threat with a greater number and variety of coping and defense mechanisms, and they can weave these mechanisms into a systematic pattern more effectively (Haan, 1963). As a result, they can respond to stress with less effort and less likelihood of a collapse of their defenses. Nevertheless, even the most competent and highly educated individuals can be driven to loss of control, psychosis, or suicidal depression if their defenses should collapse completely.

These observations about how general competence and degree of vulnerability interact to affect behavior in conflict situations are summarized in the following figure. The figure is ordered vertically from low (top) to high (bottom) *vulnerability,* and from low (left) to high (right) *competence.*

At the first level (Level 0), there is no vulnerability at all, because there is no conflict. Here, people's thoughts and actions correspond with their ideals and

General competence and education, vulnerability to stress, and coping and defense mechanisms.

Degree of vulnerability	Degree of general competence and education*
	Low ———————————————————————→ High
0	*No vulnerability.* There is no conflict between conscience and desires, which are acted out directly. Person is well adjusted (if desires are prosocial) or sociopathic (if desires are antisocial).
1	*Low vulnerability with coping.* Conflicts are minor and are solved through coping mechanisms — no need to rely on defense mechanisms. As above, general adjustment and morality depend upon desires (prosocial vs. antisocial).
2	*Low vulnerability without coping or defending.* Conflicts are not solved through coping mechanisms, but vulnerability is low enough that the resultant stress can be tolerated without resorting to defense mechanisms. The person occasionally experiences shame, guilt, anxiety or other stressful emotions when conscience is violated. Adjustment is generally good (but not as good as that of persons at the above levels), while morality again depends upon desires (prosocial vs. antisocial). The person may use suppression but not repression.
3	*Medium vulnerability, repression.* Mild to major maladjustment due to continual reliance on defense mechanisms. These are repressive rather than projective; threatening material is excluded from awareness but there is no other, more direct, distortion of reality. Unacceptable desires are repressed, but they have indirect effects on behavior through defense mechanisms. Nervous tension Repression Direct escape, avoidance Indirect escapism (sports, entertainment, hobbies, fantasy) Rationalization Compartmentalization, intellectualization Compulsions, phobias, obsessions Conversion reactions, somatization Fugue states, fainting, multiple personalities
4	*High vulnerability.* Conflicts are intense enough to force reliance on projective mechanisms in addition to repressive mechanisms. Initial perception is not distorted, although events perceived accurately may be interpreted in terms of projected motives or meanings. Memory is distorted, through a combination of repression and projection. General adjustment is poor, as is reality contact, but unacceptable desires are repressed and held in check as long as defenses continue to work. Displacement of emotional responses, projection to substitute outlets Projection of interpretations which distort the meanings of events Reversal: projection of own desires and emotions onto others
5	*Extreme vulnerability.* Conflicts are so intense that the person is driven to defense mechanisms which distort basic perception and produce loss of reality contact. The person's whole defense system is in danger of collapse, leading to acting out of the unacceptable desire and/or extreme anxiety and depression. Denial Hallucinations

*In general, among persons similar in type of conflict, degree of vulnerability, and type of defense system, those who are more competent and educated are likely to use defense mechanisms that are intellectual (vs. behavioral), sophisticated (vs. psychologically naive), ambiguous (vs. obviously interpretable), symbolic (vs. direct), flexible (vs. rigid), systematized (vs. limited and specific), and neurotic (vs. psychotic).

moral codes. In most cases, this means good personal adjustment as well as good moral development, although individuals still will differ in their general competence and life circumstances, along the lines described in Chapter Seven. However, a few such individuals would be sociopathic criminals. These would be people whose behavior never conflicted with their ideals or moral codes for the simple reason that their ideals were themselves immoral, and their moral codes non-existent. Occasionally, people will choose a specific criminal or a generalized criminal mode of behavior and pursue this as an *ideal*. This is mentioned briefly in passing just to point out that absence of conflict or of the need for coping and defense mechanisms to deal with conflict does not necessarily mean that the person is well-adjusted or prosocially moral.

Level 1 on the figure refers to low level vulnerability situations in which the person possesses coping mechanisms capable of solving the problem. The development of general intellectual competence involves something of a trade off here. On the one hand, more intelligent and perceptive people are going to become aware of more conflicts than less intelligent and perceptive people. On the other hand, they are going to have both more and more effective coping mechanisms available for resolving conflicts, so that they will be better equipped to deal with such low vulnerability situations. Individuals at this level of adjustment all will have good reality contact, in the sense that their perceptions will be accurate, but the more competent ones will have many more such perceptions. As a result, their "reality" will be richer and more complex than the "reality" of less perceptive individuals. They will be more cognitively developed, but *not* better adjusted or more moral.

Level 2 on the figure refers to low vulnerability situations in which the person responds by doing nothing at all rather than by either coping or defending. As mentioned above, the vast majority of such situations involve discrepancies not considered important enough to merit follow up. However, this level also can include situations where the emotional response to a conflict is minor but irritating enough to cause people to resort to suppression, deliberately putting problems out of their minds when the problems become irritating. This method of dealing with conflict can persist indefinitely, as long as vulnerability does not increase.

Defense mechanisms at Levels 3, 4, and 5 of the figure all involve repression. Because this basic concept is extremely complex and somewhat controversial, it will be explained in some detail before the discussion of the figure is continued.

CONCEPT OF REPRESSION   Most people with knowledge or experience relating to psychology use the concept of repression freely, although they are not always clear about what it means. A few diehards still refuse to accept it, primarily on the grounds that it cannot be produced automatically in the laboratory by using well-established and replicated procedures. This criticism is correct: repression cannot be produced "on demand." Furthermore, the chances of someone discovering a method to produce it experimentally are minimal, partly because of the many ethical problems involved in such research.

Even most experimentally oriented psychologists accept the concept of repression, because they have seen it in action in treatment facilities or in themselves or in their friends. These days, there is little serious opposition to the concept. Just to be sure that we understand what we mean when we use this term, let us analyze it in some detail.

Recall that the term "suppression" refers to deliberately and consciously putting something out of the mind because it is irritating or mildly anxiety arousing. This is not technically a defense mechanism; no unconscious avoidance or distortion of reality is involved. The conflict is not systematically excluded from conscious awareness. Instead, it merely is suppressed when it becomes irritating. Vulnerability is low, so that the person can think about and even discuss the situation, although it will be somewhat unpleasant to do so.

Repression is very different. It is *systematic, automatic, and unconscious.* To accept the concept of repression, we have to accept *all* the following: (1) an experience or thought occurs which is registered in short-term memory and filed in long-term memory; (2) the person is sufficiently vulnerable to this experience or thought that he or she cannot tolerate remembering it or thinking about it; (3) consequently, whenever the threatening experience or thought starts to enter conscious awareness, it is systematically blocked; (4) as a result, it is as if the person has simply forgotten the experience or thought (repressive mechanisms work so efficiently and automatically that the person either is totally unaware of them or is temporarily disoriented for a moment or two without knowing why); (5) this systematic vigilance against unacceptable material persists indefinitely and works automatically; but (6) the person remains completely unconscious of the whole affair (Maddi, 1976).

Repression is the *simplest* of the various defense mechanisms, and yet it involves all of this. When first confronted with this analysis, many people respond by concluding that all of the things involved in repression simply could not happen so systematically and automatically, or at least that they could not happen without conscious awareness. However, this is not the case. Relatively little is known about the brain and nervous system, but what is known suggests that all of this is not only possible but probable.

The key to repression apparently lies in what has been called the "gating function" of the midbrain. This refers to the fact that only a small portion of incoming stimulation which potentially could reach conscious awareness ever does so. For example, consider yourself reading this material. Ever since you began, you have been getting visual input from your eyes, auditory input from your ears, scents from your nose, taste sensations from your mouth, kinesthetic sensations from the nerve endings just under your skin, other kinesthetic sensations from nerves inside of your body, and stimulation from your own brain (tendencies to let your mind wander off into daydreaming or into worry about things that concern you at the moment). All of this input has been coming in continuously and simultaneously, and any of it could become conscious at any time. Now consider your left foot. Since you are paying attention to it, you can feel numerous kinesthetic sensations. These sensations did not begin just now. They have been coming in to your brain *all along*, but you have been systematically gating them out in order to pay attention to this book and to other things that were more important to you than the feelings in your left foot.

If you think about it a moment, you can see easily that life would be completely impossible if we had to pay attention and respond to every possible stimulus reaching us at every moment. The reason that we do not have to do so is that our brains are equipped to "gate out" stimulation that is of little or no importance and to "let through" stimulation that is important at the moment. This enables us to concentrate on and react to important input without being distracted by unimportant input.

In brief, this works as follows. Stimulation from all of the afferent (incoming) nerves in our body, including stimulation from memories "filed" in our cortex, flows continuously through the nervous system and into the brain. When it gets to the midbrain area, the gating function operates so that most of it terminates there. A small portion is fired past the midbrain and into the cortex, where connections are made with efferent (outgoing) nerve systems that begin a return flow back through the midbrain and out to the appropriate nerve endings or organs. This cycle must be completed *before* anything can enter our conscious awareness, be registered in short-term memory, or be filed in long-term memory. Only those experiences which get past the "gate" and make this round trip ever get registered in consciousness. Furthermore, memory impulses flowing into the midbrain must make another "round trip" in order to become conscious again (Maddi, 1976).

This gating function is an important *adaptation mechanism* that enables us to cope with everyday life. It makes it possible for most adaptation needs to be handled automatically (particularly basic skills that have been overlearned, such as walking and talking), so that we can concentrate on the things that we are deliberately trying to do at the moment. More and more functions get subsumed under this automatic mechanism with age, as more and more skills are developed to the point of overlearning. When we first learned to walk, we had to walk very slowly and deliberately, consciously moving each foot and devoting our full attention to the process. Once we learned walking to the point of overlearning, we began to walk automatically and unconsciously. Now we pay attention to our walking only when there is a special reason to do so (such as, walking across a field full of rocks or holes, walking up a ramp, avoiding obstacles). Most of our walking is done effortlessly and with minimal conscious awareness. The same is true for eating, talking, writing, driving, and numerous other important but overlearned skills.

In effect, our brains have been programmed to take care of these functions automatically and without "bothering" us by making us aware of them, unless special circumstances require that we pay attention (reaching a curb, realizing that a fork is too full, seeing someone driving on the wrong side of the street and heading toward us, and so forth). Under these circumstances, functions that usually are unconscious and automatic suddenly become very conscious. This happens because the "program" controlling brain functions related to these activities has gotten a "special alert" message. This causes incoming stimulation that usually is gated out at the midbrain to be shot into the cortex, so that we become conscious of it and able to react to it. For a detailed discussion of the brain mechanisms and functions involved in this, see Pribham (1971).

In summary, our brains are set up to gate out certain stimuli so that we can concentrate on others. This includes gating out *stimulation already stored in memory* in the brain. When such stimulation is gated out simply because we are concentrating on other things, the gating function is operating in its usual adaptive way. The only difference is that the gated out stimuli are coming from the inside rather than the outside. This is not repression; the stimuli are gated out simply because we are more interested in other matters, not because they are threatening to us. When the stimuli are not gated out, we daydream or drift into reverie. We remember and think about things that have happened to us in the past. Obviously, this is not repression, either. Sometimes *memories are gated out because they are unacceptable to us,* and this *is* repression.

Somehow, in a way that is not completely understood, the gating mechanism that continually screens out unimportant stimuli so that we can focus on important ones sometimes also systematically functions to screen out stimuli that are too threatening. Apparently, the process involves sending "special alert" messages of the kind that open the gate for stimuli that usually are gated out, except that in the case of repression, the special alert causes the gate to close rather than open. Although all of this happens without awareness and in a fraction of a second, the neurophysiological mechanisms are there.

Incoming nerve impulses are processed in two stages. The first is an *arousal stage,* in which the impulse is sent to the midbrain and scanned for passage through the gate (vs. termination). If the impulse is passed through to the cortex to complete a full cycle, the arousal stage is followed by a recognition or *registration stage* involving perception of the stimulus and registration of it in short-term memory. If you are walking along talking to a friend, paying little or no attention to your walking, impulses from your feet and legs will be gated out automatically if no problems come up. This will change if you should step in a hole or onto an object. You will experience a quick arousal message telling you to change your focus of attention, followed by perception and other relevant responses to the interruption of smooth walking. You may have to take steps to make sure that you do not trip or that you go around the object in your way.

Repression involves a similar two-stage process, except that the result is gating out of the perception rather than intensification of it. The initial arousal alerts the gating mechanism to the presence of an unacceptable stimulus, and there is enough time for gating to occur so that the stimulus will not pass through the gate, reach the cortex, and enter conscious awareness. Known neurophysiological mechanisms are capable of mediating repression, despite its complexity and seeming impossibility.

At this point, the most meaningful questions concern not the existence of repression, but the mechanisms involved in developing and using it. In any case, all of the defense mechanisms listed at Levels 3, 4, and 5 of the figure involve repression. They also involve additional defense mechanisms (also carried out unconsciously, or at least without awareness of their real meaning), presumably because repression alone is not enough to screen out the intolerable stimulation and must be "reinforced" through additional mechanisms.

OTHER DEFENSE MECHANISMS   Level 3 of the figure includes repression and a variety of defense mechanisms that often are used in connection with basic repression. All of these other defense mechanisms usually are described as reinforcing or assisting repression by providing distractions from threatening stimuli or by providing other outlets for desires and impulses that the person is not able to express directly. These mechanisms, even when used frequently and predictably, usually are considered evidence of neurosis rather than psychosis, and are considered normal in the sense that we all tend to use some or most of them at various times. They allow us to "fool ourselves," in the sense that we keep certain unacceptable material repressed and do not have full insight into the real reasons for our behavior. Our reality contact is not affected to the extent of distorting memory or perception. Instead, unacceptable memories and perceptions are kept out of conscious awareness. This is the basic difference between the mechanisms listed at this Level 3 and those listed at Levels 4 and 5, which *do* involve some distortion of reality in addition to repression.

The simplest repressive defense mechanism is repression itself, without the "assistance" of other mechanisms. It can be effective, provided that vulnerability is not too high and the likelihood of encountering the threatening stimulus is low. Repressed desires and fears related to homosexuality usually can be kept out of awareness without difficulty. However, repressive mechanisms would tend to cause the individual to avoid areas frequented by homosexuals, avoid reading about homosexuals, and to change the subject when discussions of homosexuality came up. If the repressed desire is something that cannot be avoided so easily (for example, a sexual desire for a neighbor or fellow worker that one sees every day), repression almost certainly will not be sufficient by itself. In situations like these, both vulnerability and the frequency and intensity of threatening situations are high, so that other defense mechanisms may be required.

One rather direct mechanism is *escape*—the person changes habits to avoid the threatening situation. This could mean moving away from the tempting friend or fellow worker, or driving the person away through rude treatment. Some people try to escape their problems through alcoholism, drug addiction, and other behavior disorders. These usually do not function very effectively as defense mechanisms, however. Often they are signs that defenses are failing and stress is becoming overwhelming.

Where direct escape of this sort is not possible, *escapism* through *obsessions*, *compulsions*, *phobias*, and *fantasy* can be relied upon instead. The person can become compulsively involved in work (or in other compulsions such as cleanliness, neatness, sports or hobbies) to preoccupy attention so completely that intrusion by the threatening or tempting stimulus is unlikely. Such

414

compulsions work in two ways. First, as mentioned, they compel attention. They require concentration in order to be carried out. Second, they provide people with something to do most of the time, and thus minimize the times the mind wanders and is more open to intrusion by threatening or tempting stimuli.

Obsessions are similar in function, differing from compulsions only in that they involve concentration on thoughts rather than on physical activity. Obsessions can include such simple things as continuous preoccupation with tunes, rhythms, words, or other ideas that keep running through the mind; continuous thought and worry about real or imagined problems, either personal or impersonal (political problems, the state of the economy, and so forth); or *phobias*, which are continuing and irrational fears concerning unlikely or impossible dangers. Like compulsions, obsessions and phobias minimize the likelihood of intrusion of unacceptable material by keeping the mind occupied on other things. *Fantasy* works the same way.

Compartmentalization refers to situations where the person is aware of the presence of two contradictory ideas or behaviors, but does not recognize the contradiction. Compartmentalization often is assisted through the use of separate labels for essentially the same thing. Certain forms of behavior in someone we dislike are labeled as cowardice, while the same behaviors in ourselves or others that we like are labeled "prudence" or "recognition of reality." The same is true of such distinctions as "prejudice" vs. "facing the facts," "power grabbing" vs. "taking bold and exciting new initiatives," and "caving in to pressure" vs. "achieving a reasonable compromise."

Another form of compartmentalization is to preserve a general rule but allow for a few specific exceptions to it. The best example of this used to be "some of my best friends are black," although this now has become such a joke that it doesn't function as a compartmentalization mechanism anymore except for people who are extremely naive. Many of the "games people play" described by Berne (1964) and others are ways to maintain compartmentalization. All of these mechanisms have in common the fact that they allow people to perceive contradictory ideas or behavior accurately while at the same time failing to perceive the contradiction itself. The ideas or behaviors are perceived and discussed in such a way as to make them seem unrelated, and thus not contradictory. Many people who oppose racism ideologically send their children to segregated private schools "to get quality educations" or may lament the fact that "outdated policies" keep their private club segregated, while doing nothing to try to change these policies or change clubs.

Another mechanism, used primarily by highly competent and educated people, is *intellectualization*. Like compartmentalization, it allows for accurate perception of potentially conflicting thoughts or behaviors, but not of the conflict itself. The person becomes obsessively involved with the purely intellectual aspects of the situation, so much so that little or no time is left for recognition of the conflicting and potentially emotionally upsetting aspects. A violence prone person might keep this potential repressed through intellectualization mechanisms such as developing detailed knowledge and library resources about the history of weapons or war, by acquiring an elaborate weapons collection, or even by striving to become a criminal lawyer or judge.

An especially effective method of intellectualization is to "ignore the forest" and instead "analyze a single tree" in great detail. The most obvious examples of this occur in the writings and speeches of politicians and journalists who want to deal with complex and conflicting situations in oversimplified ways. The writings of extreme "hawks" or "doves" about the war in Southeast Asia provide good examples of this. Extreme hawks bent over backward to interpret everything in a way favorable to their position, even such embarrassments as the My Lai massacre or the corruption of many of the individuals and governments that we were supporting. Extreme doves did the same thing, attempting to justify atrocities and blood baths and to portray as heroes political and military leaders who had blatantly negative qualities in addition to their positive ones. It has been said that if you look at a situation in a purely intellectual and analytic way long enough, eventually it will disappear altogether. This is how intellectualization works.

Another defense mechanism of sorts is the development of symptoms of *nervous tension*. Such symptoms are defense mechanisms, at least in part, because they apparently help maintain repression. On the other hand, they are signs that maintaining the repression is causing the person to undergo considerable strain, and that collapse of all defenses is a possibility. The most simple and direct types of nervous tension include the kinds of symptoms that we usually refer to when we use the term: general anxiety, jumpiness, fitful sleep or insomnia, irritability, fatigue, distractibility, difficulty in concentrating, and the like. All of these are symptoms suggesting that some sort of conflict is threatening the person's peace of mind and well-being. If the problem remains repressed, the person will not become upset about it, because he or she will not be aware of it. However, the strain of keeping it repressed may result in nervous tension symptoms.

A more extreme defense mechanism involving nervous tension, once common but now seen only in naive individuals, is the *conversion reaction* (formerly called hysteria). Such reactions usually develop when a person has a strong vulnerability to a conflict and is in a position where the threatening stimuli are constantly at hand. Another common form appears when people who are highly vulnerable but quite well-defended through escape mechanisms suddenly and unexpectedly receive a jolt for which they were not prepared (for example, a person with repressed fears of homosexuality who is approached by a homosexual looking for action).

Conversion reactions are so called because the anxiety and tension caused by the conflict presumably become "converted" into an hysterical symptom. One form is simple fainting, in which the person awakes anywhere from a few seconds to several hours later, with only a vague memory for what happened and no memory at all for the specific triggering event. A more extreme (and rare) reaction of this type is the *fugue* state, in which people lose awareness of who they are and what is happening, so that they wander around for a time in a state of total confusion, and then emerge from this confusion with little or no memory of their past life. The rarest and most extreme reaction of this kind is the multiple personality, in which the person's conscious awareness and memory become compartmentalized in such a way that selective parts are organized into two or more different personalities, one or more of which is completely unaware of the existence of the other(s). The most famous case of this sort has been publicized in the book and movie *The Three Faces of Eve* (Thigpen and Cleckley, 1974).

These forms of conversion reactions which involve the total personality are fascinating, but they are rare and getting rarer as people become more sophisticated about psychology. The more common conversion reactions are much more limited. They typically involve impairment of sensory or motor functions in people who have nothing wrong with their nervous systems. People with sensory conversion reactions temporarily lose vision, hearing, touch, or other sensory functions, even though they have suffered no neural damage. Other conversion reactions involve loss of motor functions, so that the person is partially paralyzed in some part of the body even though the nervous system is functioning properly. Often conversion reactions of these kinds are related in some way to the internal conflict. For example, a person with an urge to masturbate or to use the hands to attack someone else might develop a conversion reaction involving inability to move the hands or arms. Such a reaction not only reinforces repression by providing the person with a symptom to focus attention on, it also physically prevents the possibility of acting out the forbidden behavior.

Conversion reactions involve loss of sensory or motor functions even though there is nothing wrong with the person. It also is possible to develop a different type of bodily symptom in response to conflict: *somatization*. Somatization symptoms are caused by nervous tension and anxiety, just like conversion reactions, but they involve actual damage to the body. Some such reactions are temporary, such as fatigue, elevated blood pressure, and other bodily changes that can occur when a person is temporarily under heavy stress. In some individuals, where stress is continual or where vulnerability is high, permanent damage to bodily organs can occur. Examples include such disorders as ulcers, colitis, asthma, tics, and various aches and pains in all parts of the body. This is *not* to say that *all* such conditions necessarily are psychologically caused (that is, caused by nervous tension resulting from some kind of internal conflict). All of these conditions can be purely physiological, resulting from a combination of bodily predisposition and unfavorable environment (poor diet, air pollution, and so forth). However, it also seems clear that many of these kinds of bodily ailments are caused primarily if not solely by psychological factors.

Nervous tension that is frequent and strong enough can begin to adversely affect some part of the body, and in some cases the effects are permanent. Stomach ulcers occur because the stomach overproduces acids needed for digestion. In certain individuals, nervous tension can cause over-production of these stomach acids, and eventually they may wear a hole in the wall of the stomach, producing an ulcer. The ulcer itself is physiologically equivalent to an ulcer that developed for purely biological reasons. It will require medical treatment, even if the psychological problem that caused it originally is solved.

All of these various defense mechanisms discussed in connection with Level 3 of the figure are used in support of basic repression. All are carried on in the same way that basic repression is carried on. The person is completely unaware of the underlying conflict producing the symptoms, and also is unaware that the symptoms are psychologically caused. Reactions are not necessarily confined to repression in combination with *one* other symptom. In fact, five or six separate defense mechanisms can be observed in the same individual over a short period of time. The frequency and variety of defense mechanisms observed, and the general tendency to rely on such mechanisms, depend upon the person's vulnerability to the conflicting material. The specific nature of the defense mechanisms also depends upon the person's general intellectual development. All of these factors develop over time in response to socialization influences, especially parental modeling.

Persons of limited competence and education are more likely to develop conversion reactions than more educated people. The latter are not able to "fool themselves" through such mechanisms, so that the mechanisms will not work for them. Instead, if they develop bodily symptoms in reaction to psychological stress, they will develop somatization problems. Highly educated individuals, especially if they have had psychology courses, are unlikely to develop extremely obvious obsessions or compulsions. Instead, they are more likely to develop defense mechanisms involving sophisticated compartmentalization and intellectualization, or perhaps escapist fantasy which they indulge in regularly but keep to themselves. In short, their defense mechanisms are more sophisticated and less obvious to other people. Such defense mechanisms generally are more effective, but they also are more difficult to eliminate through intervention. In fact, despite higher competence and better education, a person with extremely well-functioning and sophisticated defense mechanisms is much more difficult to change than a person with a similar conflict but less successful defenses.

Persons using defense mechanisms listed at Level 4 of the figure not only "fool themselves" by keeping certain unpleasant aspects of reality out of their conscious awareness; they go beyond this by transforming and distorting original events so that the events are remembered as different than they really were. The basic mechanism here is *projection*, although repression still is important as an even more basic mechanism. Projection involves perceiving or remembering situations in an egocentric and personally unique way which differs from the perceptions of others who were present. Just as repression is a basic adaptation mechanism that becomes a defense mechanism only when used systematically and for the purpose of closing out unacceptable realities, projection also is a basic perceptual mechanism that ordinarily is adaptive but can be used for defensive purposes under stress.

Actually, *all of our perceptions involve projection.* When we observe the environment around us, we do not observe some kind of immutable and objective reality. Instead, we observe certain aspects of the environment that are important to us, and we observe them from a very personal perspective. Another person observing in precisely the same situation would not have precisely the same experience. That person would pay attention to some things that we ignore, would ignore some things that we pay attention to, and generally would have a different point of view and a different memory of the situation. Projection is simply a word that indicates that perception and memory are subjective. Information is perceived and filed in memory not in an objective way, but in a highly subjective way which involves interpretation of the meaning of an experience in addition to simple registration of its objective aspects. Projection is a continuous process. When used in certain systematic and distorting ways for the purpose of avoiding conflicts, it becomes a defense mechanism.

Displacement involves perceiving an original experience accurately but quickly repressing it because it causes strong emotional stress, especially anger or frustration. The reason for the repression usually is that the person cannot express the anger or frustration directly. As a result, these negative feelings emerge later at the expense of someone or something else. The negative feelings are "displaced" onto a safer or more convenient object. A person may get mad at the boss but repress this anger for fear of being fired, and then later "take it out on" someone else by picking a fight or overreacting to a minor incident and using it as an excuse for exploding in rage at someone else who poses no threat. In cases like these, the anger is displaced from the original frustrating but powerful or dangerous person to a less powerful or dangerous person or object. The result presumably is a catharsis: by taking out anger against a substitute person or object, we get rid of the anger. Displacement is helpful to an extent, although it is not very effective because it causes new problems of its own and its effectiveness is temporary at best. It does nothing to solve the real problem, and it creates difficulties with the victim of the displaced hostility and aggression.

A somewhat more distortive defense mechanism in this category is *projection*. Where immediate perception of external events is involved, the perception of observables is accurate. However, the person using the defense mechanism projects motives or other non-observables which give the situation a twisted meaning. For example, people with delusions of persecution who observe others talking and looking in their direction may infer that they are talking about them or plotting against them. Or, they may believe that someone is trying to poison them because they made them a drink that involved an ingredient which was not put into anyone else's drink. Such paranoid delusions can become extremely complex and can involve severe distortions of reality, although the person still perceives external events accurately to a degree. That is, the distortion is in the *meaning* assigned to these events, not in the *perception* of the events themselves.

Another kind of projection involves projection of internal desires and emotions onto other people, so that feelings that really are coming from the inside are perceived as coming from someone else. A person with repressed homosexual tendencies might avoid a person of the same sex because of a belief that this other person is homosexual, and a person with repressed anger against someone else may be unaware of that anger but perceive that the other person seems to be angry with them. A common form of this type of projection has been called *reversal* or *reaction formation*. Both terms refer to a direct reversal of the real but repressed feelings ("I hate him" becomes "he hates me").

These examples of projective defense mechanisms all have been fairly primitive ones involving fairly obvious and distorted paranoia. Some defense mechanisms based on projection are quite sophisticated and difficult to detect. Consider people who feel jealousy and hostility toward a fellow worker but have repressed these feelings and are sophisticated enough to conceal them from others as well. Such people are not likely to verbalize grossly distortive paranoid ideas, such as that the other person is trying to kill them or is plotting against them. However, by selectively interpreting what the other person does, they might succeed in damaging the person's reputation and perhaps even in creating the false impression (at least initially) that the other person dislikes them and has a tendency to treat them unfairly.

Sophisticated projective mechanisms of this kind can be quite effective, partly because they are not obvious and thus can be maintained indefinitely without being punctured, and partly because they are likely to result in self-fulfilling prophecy effects. If you treat other people consistently in a way that suggests that they do not like you, chances are that eventually they will come to dislike you, even though they may have been neutral or even positive at first. Individuals with self-concept problems ("I am worthless" becomes "he doesn't think much of me") and people with hostility problems ("I hate him" becomes "he hates me") are especially likely to develop these kinds of projective defense mechanisms if vulnerability is high enough.

People with defense mechanisms like these often have badly distorted memories, even when their original perceptions were reasonably accurate. If they started a fight with another person, they may remember the incident later as a fight that the other person started, without any provocation on their part. If they lied to the other person, they may remember the incident as having told the whole truth, or even that the other person lied to them. If they attempted to seduce the other person, they may remember the incident as a seduction directed at them. Because of distortions like these, it is commonly said that people who rely on projective defense mechanisms have "poor reality contact." *This is not the same as immorality,* because immorality implies deliberate, intentional misbehavior. People with very well-functioning defensive systems honestly believe their own delusions. When they say something that is factually untrue, they are not lying; they are telling the truth as they see it. Their vulnerability is so high that they must defend themselves from the real truth, and, as long as their defense system works successfully, the real truth will remain hidden and they will continue to honestly believe their own version.

It is because of this capacity for certain defense mechanisms to distort a person's perception or memory that defense mechanisms and moral development are being discussed together in the present chapter. Because of the operation of certain kinds of defense mechanisms, many actions which are immoral from the standpoint of the victim are not immoral from the standpoint of the perpetrator, because defense mechanisms prevent the perpetrator from perceiving his or her own behavior accurately and realizing its moral implications. Not everyone who fails to practice what he or she preaches is a hypocrite. Defense mechanisms allow some people to consistently violate their expressed moral principles without realizing that they are doing so, even when this is obvious to everyone else. Such people are most commonly at Level 3 and especially Level 4 of the figure.

Level 5 of the figure represents the most serious, widespread, and extreme form of defense mechanism, in which contact with reality is completely lost, at least for a time. Even in the more extreme forms of defensiveness at Level 4, original perceptions are accurate, at least in part. Distortion occurs because original perceptions are embellished with non-existent motives or emotions, and/or because memories are distorted. At Level 5, distortion extends to the original perception itself.

One mechanism is *denial*, or perceptual constriction, as it is called by those who do not accept the existence of a true denial mechanism. Denial refers to the failure to see something that is literally right in front of your eyes, the failure to hear something that you could have and should have heard, or, more generally, avoiding the perception of a threatening situation by blocking it out of awareness. Whereas repression refers to the process of keeping something out of conscious awareness after it has been experienced at least once, denial refers to avoiding a threatening experience in the first place.

Denial is such a gross distortion of reality that it cannot be maintained for long. This defense mechanism can be successful only with isolated incidents. Something that keeps happening repeatedly cannot be handled with denial, because the defense mechanism will break down in the face of consistent pressure. Such a breakdown could lead to a reaction of depression and anxiety or possibly to psychosis.

The most serious defense mechanism is *hallucinatory projection*. Here, external reality (or internal reality, in the case of unacceptable thoughts or impulses) is shut out entirely. It is replaced by projected internal reality that is experienced as if it were coming in from the outside. These are hallucinations, seeing and hearing things which simply are not there. People who are actively hallucinating literally are not in contact with reality. They are temporarily psychotic. The nature of hallucinations depends upon the underlying conflict and upon the background of the individual. Hallucinations induced by drugs (including alcohol) usually are not organized into any particular system or theme. They may be pleasant, as when the person sees flashes of color or non-existent animals, or they may be frightening, as when the person sees giant insects ready to attack or feels a sense of falling through space and believes that he or she is about to crash and die.

Where hallucinations result from extreme vulnerability to internal conflict rather than temporary reaction to a drug, they are more likely to be repetitive, systematic, and related in some way to the conflict. Their specific content will depend to a degree on the competence and education of the person. In cases where people have extremely high vulnerability to masturbatory desires, it is possible that repeated and escalating desires to masturbate might drive them to the point of psychosis. One common form that hallucinations take in these situations is the belief that some external person or source of power is influencing them, so that their actions are involuntary and they are not responsible for their behavior. Unsophisticated people would be rather vague in explaining this, perhaps suggesting that some unknown and undescribed force was operating or that the devil was controlling them through remote control electrical waves.

In contrast, more sophisticated people with the same basic defense mechanism probably would not tell a story so grossly unbelievable, because they would not be able to believe it themselves. Even in a state of psychosis, they would come up with a story more credible than the examples given above. Both delusions and hallucinations might be interwoven into the belief that their sexual organs were abnormally active because of a neurological or hormonal disturbance that the doctors were not able to understand or do anything about yet, and in the meantime masturbation was necessary for relief of the discomfort caused by this unfortunate condition. Although equally psychotic, this systematic explanation is much more detailed and difficult to disprove than some of the more simplistic ones described above, and it reveals a degree of knowledge about neuroanatomy and physiology. Even people whose vulnerability is such that they must resort to the most extreme forms of defense still reflect their general social class and educational backgrounds in the kinds of symptoms they develop.

In this book, moral development is grouped with self-concept and personal adjustment. This arrangement is somewhat unusual. More typically, the cognitive aspects of moral development (moral judgment) are treated in conjunction with Piaget, and the behavioral aspects of moral development are discussed along with aspects of social development and personality. However, I believe that the present organization is more appropriate, for two major reasons. The first has already been mentioned: decisions about the morality or immorality of an act usually involve some discussion of the person's conscious awareness and intent, and coping and defense mechanisms are directly involved in this. Secondly, what is conventionally looked upon as morality from the theological or philosophical point of view usually is looked upon as mental health or good mental adjustment from the psychological point of view. Conversely, behavior looked upon as immoral from the philosophical or theological point of view tends to be looked upon as symptomatic of psychological disorder, from the psychological point of view. The points of view are quite different, but the personal qualities of interest and the predisposing socialization factors are essentially the same.

The link between these two perspectives has been recognized by several writers. Perhaps the most prominent and obvious was Freud himself. He saw the development of sociopathic and other antisocial behavior disorders as reducing essentially to an overly weak conscience or superego, and saw neuroses as reducing essentially to the development of an overly strong conscience. A notable recent example has been the writings of Mowrer (1964),

PROMOTING GOOD PERSONAL ADJUSTMENT AND PROSOCIAL BEHAVIOR

who describes neuroses as essentially a struggle with tendencies toward immorality. Although it is not typical to treat moral development and personal adjustment together, there certainly is a basis for it in psychological writings, particularly in the writings of clinical psychologists and psychiatrists interested in psychological disorders.

The differences in point of view were discussed in Chapter Two. From the theological or philosophical perspective, behavior thought of as immoral involves breaking the laws of God or man. From the psychological perspective, behavior thought of as disordered involves insufficient development of prosocial motives and habits and/or poor reality contact and the development of symptoms of psychological disorder. These problems have been discussed at length already. From a moralistic point of view, individuals who have developed a "normal" conscience and a prosocial orientation but who nevertheless fail to live up to their ideals are hypocritical and immoral. From a psychological point of view, these same individuals are immersed in conflict between their ideals and their impulses and desires, and those who cannot cope with their conflicts end up relying on defense mechanisms which allow them to violate their ideals without being aware of what they are doing. The combination of continual turmoil due to stress, and continual reliance on defense mechanisms which take up energy and impair reality contact, results in behavior which might be looked upon as hypocritical or evil from a moralistic standpoint.

It can be argued that both positions are equally valid, with the differences being simply differences and nothing more. I believe that the psychological perspective is more useful, because it goes beyond simply labeling the person and provides some explanation and understanding which lead to suggestions about intervention. As most of us know, behavior that is "over-determined" because the person is under heavy stress and tends to rely on it is not changed through sermons, logical appeals, or other moralistic approaches. This is most obvious with regard to behavioral deviations such as alcoholism, but it is true for any kind of behavior that is part of a pattern of defense mechanisms protecting the person from powerful conflicts. Psychological approaches to such problems are by no means universally effective or even well-articulated. Nevertheless, they do provide deeper insights into the nature of the problem, and successful treatment approaches have been developed for at least some behavioral disorders.

Consideration of the developmental and socialization factors involved suggests another reason for considering morality and personal adjustment together. Whether one views socially unacceptable behavior from the point of view of mental health vs. psychological disorder or from the point of view of prosocial behavior and morality vs. immorality, the same kinds of socialization factors are involved. Optimal socialization that produces happy, well-adjusted, and generally mentally healthy individuals also produces individuals who are moral in their attitudes and behavior, at least by the standards of Golden Rule morality. Conversely, undesirable socialization practices which produce individuals who develop mental or behavioral disorders have negative moral implications, because these same individuals behave in ways that are generally considered to be immoral. In summary, then, the mental health perspective and the moralistic perspective are closely intertwined, both in regard to the kinds of behavior on which they focus and in regard to the kinds of socialization practices which lead to these behaviors.

SUMMARY

Typically, moral development is divided into moral judgment, moral affect, and moral behavior. Moral judgment is a primarily cognitive ability that relates more closely to cognitive development than it does to moral behavior. Moral affect refers to feelings of personal satisfaction in connection with having done something good, or, more typically, feelings of guilt or shame related to violations of conscience. Moral behavior refers to the degree to which people follow the Golden Rule in being prosocial vs. antisocial in their interactions with other people.

A consistent finding of studies of moral development, and one which frustrates those who want to believe that personality is highly integrated, stable, and consistent, is that measures of the three major areas of moral development do not correlate very highly if at all. Individuals who score highly on moral judgment tests are not necessarily more moral in their behavior than individuals who score lower, and not necessarily more likely to feel ashamed or guilty if they violate their consciences. Similarly, guilt and shame, even when quite extreme, frequently do not prevent people from engaging in the kinds of behaviors that produce these negative emotions. As discussed in Chapter Seven, "morality" does not appear to exist as a stable personal trait. Instead, moral behavior tends to vary with situational differences.

The primary reason for the low relationships among moral judgment, moral affect, and moral behavior appears to be the development and use of coping and defense mechanisms. This is especially true of defense mechanisms, because they allow individuals to retain conflicting or unacceptable ideas or behaviors (that normally would be eliminated) by keeping them out of conscious awareness. There are a great variety of defense mechanisms, varying in sophistication and general effectiveness. Many of them are used only by poorly educated and generally unsophisticated people, while others are so complex that high levels of intellectual competence are needed to sustain them. Like many other things, the kinds of defense mechanisms that people use result from the interaction of their genetic potentials, the cognitive stimulation they receive, and the nature of the socialization to which they are exposed.

Independent of these factors which determine the kinds of defense mechanisms that people use *if* they use defense mechanisms, the degree to which people are pressured to rely on defense mechanisms depends upon their vulnerability to anxiety and stress. Socialization factors relevant to general intellectual development already have been discussed in some detail. Socialization factors relevant to vulnerability and use of coping and defense mechanisms (and thus relevant to moral development as well) will be discussed in the following chapter.

CHAPTER TWELVE

Fostering Personal Adjustment and Moral Development

What factors are likely to produce an individual who is both *prosocial* in moral orientation and *well-adjusted* personally? Good prosocial orientation is accomplished primarily by helping children incorporate prosocial ideals and a predisposition to take into account the rights and privileges of others in planning and monitoring their own behavior. Good personal adjustment is accomplished by seeing that the moral ideals transmitted to children are realistic and flexible enough to adapt to changing realities, as opposed to being overly rigid and in conflict with normal behavioral dispositions. It also is important that the child receive sufficient modeling and instruction to know how to operationalize moral ideals in interpersonal behavior. Children not only need to be told what to do, but need to be shown how to do it *and* told why they should do it.

PRACTICES AND TECHNIQUES

Much of the material in the present chapter assumes that the kinds of socialization practices discussed previously have been practiced all along. In fact, most of what is said in the present chapter about fostering moral development and personal adjustment boils down to continuations and elaborations of the main themes discussed in Chapter Eight. The problems are more complex, and children now are more reflective about themselves and other people, but the kinds of treatment and information that they need remain basically the same. These include the following.

1. Basic acceptance and love, to provide a positive self-concept and a prosocial orientation toward others.
2. Exposure to Golden Rule morality, presented consistently in adult verbalizations and modeled consistently in adult behavior.
3. Insistence upon minimal standards of behavior, although these standards are adjusted from time to time to take into account changes in the child, and are presented to the child positively rather than punitively.
4. Explanations of the reasons behind demands whenever the child does not appear to understand them fully, stressing in particular the consequences of behavior and the reasons why these consequences are desirable or undesirable.
5. Positive attitudes and expectations which continually reassure children that they are both expected to be and considered to be well meaning and prosocial in their orientation, even though at times they will need to be given some realistic feedback about undesirable behavior.
6. Continuous dialogue with adults who are interested in the children's concerns, personal and social problems, and other matters, and who are prepared to provide both support and information.

Children consistently exposed to this kind of socialization are likely to become *both* prosocial in their moral orientation and conflict-free in their personal adjustment. This means *minimal vulnerability* to conflict, for the simple reason that conflict itself is minimal. The child will have solid resources available to resolve conflicts through appropriate *coping* mechanisms, and thus will not have to depend upon defense mechanisms. Furthermore, such a child likely will develop moral judgment and role taking skills rapidly, so that, among other things, the proportion of moral ideals adopted in a genuine and personal sense will be maximized. Conversely, the proportion retained at the level of introjection and thus verbalized but not necessarily implemented in behavior will be minimized. The result will be a child who has maximal cognitive development and a prosocial orientation in both attitudes and behavior, and yet is relatively free of conflicts and the shame, guilt, and anxiety that conflicts entail.

Children who do not develop this kind of optimal morality and personal adjustment usually show one or both of two problems in their socialization history. Children who are relatively free of conflict but who are *antisocial* in their behavior usually were raised by parents who rejected them, treated them brutally or otherwise undesirably, and provided inappropriate modeling in their own behavior. Children growing up in circumstances like these understandably develop antisocial attitudes in response to the mistreatment that they receive. This predisposes them to distrust others and to want to get even or to protect themselves by adopting a "you have to get them before they get you" attitude. Predispositions to behave along these lines then are reinforced by the kinds of modeling that the children receive. They may suppress or displace their resentments while they are still young and small enough to be vulnerable to punishment, but once they become big and brave enough to act out, they are likely to become as bad as or worse than their parents. In extreme cases, the result is assaultiveness and general criminality.

The other major path to distorted development involves rigid and unrealistic expectations which are forced upon children continually and backed by powerful sanctions for failure to comply. This sort of socialization will have undesirable effects even if the parents are mostly warm and accepting, although problems will be much greater if they are not. The basic difficulty here is that rigid but unrealistic expectations cannot be lived up to and thus will cause conflicts. The more rigid and unrealistic the expectations, the more frequent and intense the conflicts. Also, the more intense the sanctions, the greater the vulnerability. Both pressure from conflicts and vulnerability to such pressure will be greatest when rigid and unrealistic expectations are backed by strong and threatening sanctions, particularly threat of total withdrawal of parental acceptance and/or threat of punishment by God. For children raised in religious environments, the latter threat can be an extremely powerful one for insuring conformity, but if the demands to which they are expected to conform are unrealistic, the result can be an individual who is extremely guilt-ridden and forced to rely continually on *defense mechanisms* in order to keep out of conscious awareness ideas or desires which are too threatening to contemplate (Peck and Havighurst, 1960).

It is for this reason that socialization methods based on developing a *positive commitment to ideals* are recommended over methods based upon inducing guilt or fear of punishment. Where the latter approaches do work, they do so at a price; conformity is achieved, but only in the context of guilt, anxiety, and a need to depend upon defense mechanisms because of high vulnerability to conflict. Furthermore, when fear and punishment-oriented methods do *not* work, the result is a cynical and resentful person or a person who hypocritically verbalizes certain ideals because they are socially acceptable but does not live up to them in behavior when opportunities arise to get away with something without being punished. This approach to socialization frequently backfires, and even when it "works," it produces conformity at the cost of serious personal adjustment problems.

These contrasts are extremes, of course. Few parents fit the stereotypes described, and few children show such extreme contrasts in development. The relationships are probabilistic and cumulative: to the *extent* that socialization approaches one extreme, the probabilities of extreme outcomes increase. The basic aspects of a positive approach to socialization listed above are discussed in detail below, particularly as they apply to the socialization of children during the concrete operational years.

This picture illustrates many of the aspects of parent-child relationships described as ideal in this book. Can you see what some of these are? Do you tend to like and identify immediately with the man in the picture? Why or why not? (James Motlow / Jeroboam)

LOVE AND ACCEPTANCE   It is worth noting once again that love and acceptance from parents and important others form the basis for both positive self-concept and a prosocial orientation toward people. Furthermore, establishing and maintaining a close, warm relationship with children provide a solid basis for the more specific aspects of socialization which occur over the years. Occasional mishandling of these individual interactions will *not* do much harm if a good basic relationship is present, because the individuals involved will value and like each other enough to overcome undesirable effects of isolated incidents. Parents who handle a particular situation poorly have little to fear if their general relationship with the child is marked by mutual love and respect.

The situation with parents and children in this regard is much like that with married couples. Couples who are deeply in love and who place their relationship above all other considerations find it relatively easy to work out disagreements, and they rarely stay angry for long or hold grudges. However, marriages lacking this kind of commitment to the relationship are very fragile. The partners do not feel a strong commitment to each other and to the relationship, so that they are more likely to say or do something that they know the other person will not like, or even to deliberately insult or hurt them. Children are much the same way with respect to their parents.

As the child becomes more clearly defined as a unique individual, acceptance becomes important not only in the general sense but in the specific sense. This already has been discussed in Chapter Ten in regard to the necessity of accepting the child's physical appearance and degree of school success, and the same is true with regard for all of the other unique qualities that the child possesses. Ideally, these should be carefree years. The children are not yet mature enough to assume responsibility for themselves or others, and they usually are not affected seriously by burdens that are assumed by adults. Most children will be carefree and happy during the concrete operational years if they are cared for in a way that provides basic security and a positive self-concept. These in turn tend to be coupled with a prosocial moral orientation.

Parents who are child-oriented in the first place will find it easy to provide this kind of love and acceptance if they maintain an orientation toward enjoying the children for what they are, both generally and at specific ages. This means accepting philosophically and with a minimum of frustration the inevitable irritations and regressions that appear, and focusing instead on the charming and delightful aspects of each child's emerging personality. With the proper psychological set (be alert to observe and enjoy the positives), and by taking time to observe and interact with children, it is not difficult to see and appreciate their charms. These observations should be communicated directly to the children, both to provide information which will help them develop an accurate and positive self-concept and to help cement the parent-child relationship.

Acceptance of this kind also will have the effect of freeing children from unnecessary pressures and making it easier for them to feel secure and comfortable with themselves. This kind of security provides a buffer to help the child over the rough spots that occur in everyday interaction with peers. Basically secure children emerge from squabbles with peers quickly and without scars or grudges. In contrast, children without this kind of security have difficulty in peer relations and tend to become bullies (if they are strong and aggressive enough to get away with it) or to become rejected or victimized by their peers (if they are not). Parents who share a good relationship with their children can help them cope successfully with peer difficulties by "creating reality" for them, explaining the situation in a way that will make it understandable and acceptable to the child and providing guidelines for dealing with the problem constructively in the future. Some children become hurt and upset when peers rebuff them or threaten not to play with them anymore. They will be relieved by reassurance that the peers did not really mean what they said and were acting out of anger or jealousy (if this is the case). Where problems are more serious and persistent, adults can suggest ways to cope prosocially and probably effectively (verbalize feelings to the peer; assert self without resorting to violence), thus reducing the chance that inferiority feelings and/or hostility will develop.

Sometimes parents can best reassure children that they are loved and accepted simply by leaving them alone for awhile. As children become increasingly self-reflective, they begin to think about problems, particularly interpersonal conflicts in which they were at least partially at fault. When something like this happens and a child shows no desire for information but does want to be left alone, this wish usually should be honored. Parents can be most helpful here by being willing to let the child have time to think things through, by remaining willing to listen and provide information upon request but avoiding intruding themselves, and by providing the child with reassurance that he or she retains parental acceptance and confidence. This can be very helpful to a child who has made a mistake, faced up to it, experienced a certain amount of guilt or shame, and now needs to resume "normality."

Such reassurance also is important immediately after a child has tried and failed to do something that he or she considers to be extremely important. If one is deeply ego-involved in a game, a contest, or some other test of personal or team ability, losing can produce depression and loss of self-esteem. Understanding and sympathy from parents can help a child get over this quickly. If children are insecure because their parents tend to make love and acceptance conditional upon their behavior, they will feel a more deep and lasting self-devaluation following failure. This will be even worse, of course, if the parents respond with rejection.

Reassurance of continued love and acceptance also is important in helping the child make the transition between a moral orientation based on pleasing adults and an orientation toward discovering and coming to terms with reality. For most children, concern with pleasing adults is so strong that they frequently will lie in order to tell adults what they think they want to hear, especially if the truth seems threatening or unacceptable. Adults can help here by making it clear that they want and expect the truth and that mistakes are understood to be normal parts of growing up.

In summary, love and acceptance of the child are the most basic and pervasive parental qualities important for fostering good personal adjustment and a prosocial moral orientation. They make up for many deficiencies elsewhere, but nothing really makes up for their absence.

PREACHING AND PRACTICING PROSOCIAL MORALITY   Parental love and acceptance will produce self-acceptance and a sense of security in children, and this will pave the way for the development of a general prosocial orientation and a Golden Rule morality in interpersonal relationships. These do not appear automatically. They are shaped by the socialization forces to which children are exposed, and they are produced most surely and efficiently when the parents consistently and clearly articulate Golden Rule morality in the ideals that they verbalize and in the example they set by their own behavior. As noted previously, when there is a discrepancy between what children see and what they hear, they tend to imitate what they see and ignore what they hear. This becomes more and more evident as they develop greater awareness of and sensitivity to hypocrisy and inconsistencies.

If parents articulate laudable ideals but do not live up to them themselves, their children are likely to become equally hypocritical. If parents exhibit Golden Rule morality in their interpersonal behavior but give the children little or no systematic instructions or feedback, the children are likely to end up imitating their parents' behavior for the most part, but learning to do so will involve a lot of unnecessary trial and error, frustration, and confusion. Children do not automatically imitate everything that they see. The importance of certain behaviors may escape them unless it is called to their attention explicitly. Although practice is much more important than preaching, providing children with clear and understandable expectations for behavior helps eliminate confusion and the need for learning through trial and error.

It is important for parents to remain aware of the specific language that they use in giving their children instruction and feedback. Overly specific *or* overly generalized statements can come back to haunt you as children become able to observe discrepancies between parental preaching and practice. Generally, it is advisable to discuss specific situations in some detail, explicitly recognizing and taking into account the situational factors involved in determining what is considered to be appropriate and inappropriate behavior. Overly broad generalizations ("you must *always* tell the *complete* truth") should be avoided, because the parents do not really mean this. When they violate it themselves, they will appear hypocritical to the children.

Perhaps the most important parent modeling occurs in parents' relationship to each other. If they consistently treat each other with kindness and respect, and if they resolve conflicts in problem-centered and non-destructive ways, children probably will begin to do the same things themselves. Many studies have revealed that a harmonious relationship between the mother and father is associated strongly with positive indicators of personal adjustment in children, and that parents' feelings for each other and treatment of each other can be as important as their interactions with children. As noted previously, children pick up many things from observing and imitating their parents' behavior, but in particular, they pick up behavior associated with their later roles as adults (Maccoby, 1961).

Another important but negative kind of parent modeling occurs in relationship to *defense mechanisms*. In general, if one or both parents tend to rely consistently on a particular kind of defense mechanism, the children will be disposed to do the same. Parents who tend to repress consistently are likely to have children who also repress consistently; parents who often develop headaches or other particular bodily disturbances in relation to stress are likely to have children with the same reactions; and so on. This is unlikely to create problems *between* parents and children, because parents with particular kinds of defense mechanisms are likely to accept the same kinds of behavior in their children. Such defensive behavior may irritate *other people*, particularly if distortion of reality and/or socially unacceptable behavior is involved. This is yet another way that parents "create reality" for children by inducing generalized expectations concerning what is "normal." Children growing up in homes where even minor tension leads to splitting headaches come to see this as both normal and expected. It even may be commented upon or joked about, although the defensive function of the headaches will not be recognized. Instead, frequent headaches (and frequent taking of pills to alleviate them) will be accepted as normal parts of life.

FLEXIBLE RULES AND STANDARDS   As noted earlier, children need guidance in the forms of rules and standards of conduct, and parents will need to enforce these rules as necessary. If parents have done a good job of establishing the kind of loving and respectful relationship described previously, rule enforcement will not be a serious problem. In fact, in the ideal situation, physical punishment and even threats of physical punishment should be unnecessary, at least after the first few years of life. If the children understand that parental guidance is intended for their own good, they are likely to comply without serious resistance. Parents who have established this ideal kind of relationship need only to continue it in order to continue being able to get their children to comply with expectations without serious hassles. Parents who have not established this kind of relationship need to do their best to establish it, and this may involve "unlearning" some bad habits as well as establishing some new ones.

These comments do *not* mean that adults who have established good relationships with their children will not have disagreements with them or problems in seeing that all rules are followed. First, it will be necessary to adjust expectations and rules continually. Children get older and are increasingly capable of taking care of themselves and making their own decisions. Because of individual differences in parental values and in children's rates of development, it is impossible to give any simple set of guidelines or timetables. Both adults and children have to adjust as they go along, and this process necessarily involves a certain amount of disagreement and conflict. Solutions can be reached with a minimum of ill feeling where a good relationship exists, but even so, a certain amount of temporary frustration and aggravation is to be expected.

Children will continue to test limits by agitating for changes in rules or even by deliberately going beyond agreed upon limits in order to see what will happen. This kind of testing can be minimized if adults remain consistent (and in agreement with each other) in articulating and enforcing guidelines. Inconsistency encourages testing, while consistency encourages children to seek changes by initiating discussions rather than by deliberately disobeying in order to see what will happen. In addition to being consistent, adults can minimize conflicts over rules by being open-minded when children do seek a change in a rule. Serious inquiries initiated by children should be considered seriously by adults. Ideally, there should be a discussion of the situation, involving presentation of arguments by the children and provision of feedback by the adults. Dialogue should continue until some agreement or mutual understanding is reached. If the rule is changed, the degree to which it has been changed should be spelled out clearly, unless the rule has been abandoned altogether (Gordon, 1970). If the discussion concerns a change in bedtime, the old rule should be replaced with a very clear new one which reflects the new agreements and which provides very specific guidelines to both parents and children concerning what is and is not expected in the future. If the parents find the children's arguments unconvincing and are not willing to change the rule, they should explain their reasons as fully as possible and provide some guidelines that would help the children understand what will be required before they *would* be willing to change the rule. If the parents are unclear as to whether or not they are ready to do what the child requests, they can agree to give it a try, but be very explicit about the agreement being temporary and subject to review at a specific time in the future. In any case, agitation for change by children should result in a *reasoned discussion* of the pros and cons of the situation, followed by an *agreement* which is unmistakably clear in its specifics and which is agreeable to all parties, insofar as possible.

One place where punishment or threats of punishment may be required with children of these ages is the general area of responsibility for personal hygiene and care of possessions. This should not be allowed to become a major source of conflict, because children's failure to do what is expected of them in these areas almost always is a matter of forgetfulness due to preoccupation with other things rather than deliberate defiance of the parents. Nevertheless, very few children voluntarily initiate such activities with any regularity between the ages of six or seven and adolescence and beyond. Frequently, it is necessary to remind them or even order them to take baths, brush their teeth, pick up their clothes or toys, and the like. Few children of these ages reach the point where all of these things are done automatically, without any parental reminding. It is reasonable and appropriate to make it clear to children that such responsibilities and duties are not discussible or negotiable, and that there is no point in attempting to argue about them or avoid them. Where forgetfulness has been unusually extreme and irritating, it might be appropriate to punish the children or to threaten to do so if they do not shape up.

Any punishments used should be *minimal* ones designed to get children to become more thoughtful and reflective about their responsibilities, as opposed to more extreme punishments that involve more revenge than socialization. It might be appropriate to require such children to give their rooms a thorough cleaning and straightening instead of going out to play with their friends, or to require them to miss a television show and instead spend their time doing chores that should have been done earlier. On the other hand, it would be inappropriate to go to the extent of physical punishment, to cause the child to miss a special event like a birthday party or field trip, or to impose a punishment involving pointless overkill, such as not being allowed to play with anyone for a week. Resorting to even the mildest of punishments is, or should be, the *final step* in a sequence of behaviors used in dealing with such problems. Parents first should simply remind children about their responsibilities and assume that this is all that will be required. If it turns out that the children do not respond, the parents then should remind the children in a more extended and forceful way, pointing out that failure to do things that should have been done automatically and without reminders was bad enough, but failure to respond to reminders is frustrating and aggravating. If the children still do not respond, punishment then would be appropriate, although, even here, parents should go out of their way to make it clear to the children that they are being punished only because they left the parents with no other alternative.

In summary, parental guidance necessarily must involve a certain amount of insistence upon conformity to expectations, backed by a willingness to enforce these expectations if necessary. However, the whole enterprise goes most successfully when a positive approach is used. This means presenting expectations in a positive way, stressing that they are being imposed for the child's own good and that the child will be expected to understand this and respond appropriately. From the child's point of view, doing what one is supposed to do then becomes a matter of doing something for a good reason, not simply to avoid punishment. When punishment is required, the children should see that they brought it on themselves. When these kinds of perceptions and attitudes are achieved through effective socialization practices, things are likely to go most smoothly and effectively, and the necessarily authoritative role of the parents is least likely to interfere with the establishment of a mutually loving and rewarding relationship with the children.

PROVIDING EXPLANATIONS AND RATIONALES   This important feature of good socialization is closely related to the point discussed immediately above. When parents provide children with explanations and rationales underlying their expectations for behavior, they accomplish two things. First, they stimulate children's cognitive development, particularly in regard to the behavior being discussed. Second, they help children to understand that parental expectations and demands flow from a concern for the children's health and safety, as opposed to authoritarianism or an enjoyment of "bossing them around."

Explanations and rationales which help children see the effects of their behavior on themselves and other people are especially helpful, because they help break down egocentrism and help the children to develop ability to take the role of another person. This ability is fundamental to the development of prosocial attitudes and behavior. It also is basic to moral development at the cognitive level, particularly to true understanding of the Golden Rule. Even children who are relatively immature and extremely concrete in their thinking can understand that someone else probably would not like certain behavior if they themselves would be angry when someone else did the same thing to them. Asking questions such as "How would you feel if someone did that to you?" or "How do you think other people feel when they are treated that way?" can help children to make the connections between their behavior and its implications. Such perceptions and cognitions help the children to understand the rationales underlying socialization demands, and at the same time help them to accept such demands emotionally.

PROJECTING POSITIVE EXPECTATIONS, PROVIDING REALISTIC FEED-BACK   Positive expectations and self-fulfilling prophecy effects remain important throughout childhood. In general, children are likely to become the kinds of people that their parents expected them to become, and likely to act pretty much the way their parents expect them to act. *Regardless* of the way that a particular child may be acting at the moment, it is important for parents to project generally positive expectations concerning personal adjustment and moral development. Children should be treated as basically likeable and praiseworthy, and their lapses should be treated as oversights which are uncharacteristic of them and unlikely to be repeated. Children exposed to a steady diet of expectations like these probably will fulfill them. Conversely, children treated as if they constantly must be guarded and threatened in order to insure that they do not misbehave are likely to fulfill these prophecies by eventually becoming sneaky and disobedient.

Along with positive expectations, children need straightforward feedback when they act inappropriately. Such feedback can actually reinforce positive expectations if it is given with an attitude of surprise and disappointment at the child's misbehavior, and if discussions conclude with a statement of the expectation that the child will not repeat such behavior in the future. This is to be distinguished from a threat or warning that the misbehavior will be punished if it is repeated. The latter can have the effect of telling the child that the adult expects similar misbehavior again, or at least, that the child's tendencies to misbehave are so strong that threats of punishment are required to curb them. Again, if expectations like these are communicated to children, they are likely to be accepted and eventually fulfilled.

MAINTAINING AN OPEN RELATIONSHIP   Socialization problems can be minimized, and the joys of parenthood can be maximized, if a good relationship is established and maintained. It is important to stress *maintaining* such relationships as well as establishing them. Like a marriage that goes sour because the partners begin to take each other for granted and do not work at maintaining their relationship, close parent-child relationships can deteriorate over time if taken for granted or neglected. Although parents probably should not attempt to become "buddies" to their children, they should become genuine friends who share mutual love and respect. Parents and children should share interest in one another's activities and a desire to talk about them, in the same sense that any good friends share these qualities. This means, among other things, a continuing two-way dialogue, in which both parties share information and experiences.

This is in contrast to parent-child relationships in which parents initiate interactions only when they wish to give their children directions or corrections, and children initiate relationships only when they want to ask a question or to fulfill a specific need. Relationships like these evolve in families where the parents gradually but consistently condition the children to talk to them only when there is a specific reason to do so (because the parents are uninterested in interacting with them otherwise). Obviously, such relationships do not encourage children to form the habit of telling their parents what is going on in their lives and seeking advice and guidance with their problems. Nor do they motivate children to look up to and respect their parents.

COPING, DEFENSE MECHANISMS, AND MORAL DEVELOPMENT

In this section, the material discussed in Chapters Eleven and Twelve will be summarized and integrated, stressing in particular the implications for socializing children. The main point is that *children who develop high moral ideals in combination with low vulnerability to conflict and stress are most likely to develop both good personal adjustment and prosocial morality.* Furthermore, they are likely to practice the Golden Rule in their interactions with others habitually and effortlessly, even though fear of shame, guilt, or punishment is not an important motivating factor. Conversely, children raised more punitively may develop a strong set of these kinds of fears and a high vulnerability to conflict and stress, but they are more likely to have impaired personal adjustments, to rely heavily on defense mechanisms, and to be less moral in their interpersonal behavior despite this higher vulnerability.

Ideals usually are acquired in a straightforward manner through parental preaching and practice. If parental preaching and practice are consistent and realistic, children are likely to adopt them. If they are consistent but unrealistic (overly rigid morality which involves forbidding or seriously restricting things which are natural and harmless), children are likely to adopt the ideals but not necessarily to act them out in behavior. In these cases, there will be some vulnerability to anxiety because of continuing conflicts between desires and conscience. The children probably will eventually develop defense mechanisms that allow them to act out some of their desires while simultaneously avoiding the feelings of guilt that are unconsciously attached to this process. Alternatively, if parental socialization is not only consistent but extreme enough, the children may defend against the desires themselves and become rigidly moralistic like their parents.

Parents who want to avoid these problems and produce children who are highly moral but not highly vulnerable to guilt and anxiety can do so. There are two main goals: maximizing the degree to which children come to see socialization demands as reasonable and appropriate, and minimizing the degree to which they become vulnerable to guilt and anxiety.

The first goal, *maximizing the degree to which children see socialization demands as reasonable and appropriate*, is accomplished primarily by the following.

1. Make sure that socialization demands *are* reasonable and appropriate in the first place.
2. Keep them flexible and open to discussion and change as the children change.
3. Take care to provide explanations and rationales, so that the children see the reasons for the demands.
4. Consistently treat children with positive expectations communicating the idea that they are or are trying to be good persons doing what is right.

The second goal, *minimizing vulnerability to anxiety and guilt*, is accomplished primarily by the following.

1. Treat lapses as stemming from ignorance, carelessness, or forgetfulness, but *not* from evil intentions, deliberate defiance, or other underlying qualities that would imply that the child is an evil person.
2. Discuss the details and situational factors which qualify the morality of specific situations, as opposed to ticking off lists of overly generalized and unrealistically labelled "sins," thus helping the child learn other perspectives and develop a moral sense based upon the Golden Rule rather than upon inappropriately rigid ideas about good vs. evil.
3. Minimize the use of punishment by using it as a last resort when explanation and persuasion have not worked, and make it clear that it is being used only to underscore the seriousness of parental intent to enforce rules, not as parental indulgence in sadism, revenge, ego trips, and so forth.
4. Stress commitment to positive ideals, showing determination to live up to them, and reaffirm the implications of behavior (including requiring children to make restitution in situations where this is appropriate), but avoid inducing unnecessary shame or guilt or causing children to feel that they are filled with powerful impulses and negative emotions that could go out of control at any moment.

In general, children become highly vulnerable when they develop ideas or desires that they believe to be evil. Sometimes the conflict is purely internal, in that the ideas or desires would not be considered evil by most other people. This is especially true of ideas. Fantasy, including sexual fantasy, is perfectly

This is the view from below when adults "talk at" children in authoritarian tones. If you were in this boy's place, would you be listening intently to the cognitive content of the message? If not, what might be going through your mind? (David Powers/Jeroboam)

normal, in childhood as well as throughout life. Unfortunately, some children are taught that certain ideas are wrong in themselves. They come to believe that they are evil if they even have such ideas, let alone act upon them. Unrealistic socialization of this kind causes much needless guilt and reliance on defense mechanisms.

The same is true for many desires and impulses. Many children have been taught that normal desires and impulses (such as masturbation) are evil, so they fight to suppress or even repress them because they cannot tolerate the guilt that would result if they should act them out. Again, socialization of this type is unreasonable and usually unfortunate in its consequences, especially when children develop fears of loss of control. They not only believe that their desires and impulses are evil; they also believe that those desires are extremely strong and likely to be acted upon (because people are basically weak or fundamentally immoral, because the devil or some other strong evil force is tempting them persistently, and so forth). Ideas like this maximize vulnerability, often to

438

the point of panic, so that the person becomes heavily reliant upon defense mechanisms. Bear in mind that this vulnerability does not necessarily increase morality, and in fact is likely to decrease it.

Sometimes, however, children will develop genuinely dangerous or antisocial desires. In these cases defending *is* necessary, both from the view of personal adjustment and from the view of morality. Conflicts like these usually reflect conflicts in the real world rather than purely internal conflicts caused by inappropriate socialization *content*. One route is through exposure to conflicting ideals and models. The child picks up conventional morality in some degree from certain models and socialization sources, but picks up antisocial modeling and socialization from other sources. Probably the worst combination is when one or both parents model immorality and inappropriate behavior in general and, more particularly, mistreat the child and consequently increase the likelihood that he or she will develop resentment and antisocial tendencies. The antisocial modeling burdens the child with unacceptable desires and impulses that must be kept in check continually, while the conventional morality provides a degree of conscience and general moral orientation that will motivate the child to try to keep them in check.

The situation becomes more serious when the balance of socialization forces is tipped more heavily toward inappropriate socialization and modeling. This minimizes prosocial tendencies and maximizes antisocial tendencies. Children raised under these circumstances, where parents and important others in their environment are providing primarily immoral modeling and where they are being mistreated continually in ways that build up resentment and antisocial tendencies, are going to develop widespread and strong antisocial tendencies themselves. Usually, there will be at least some positive forces that develop conscience and prosocial tendencies, and there will be realistic fear of punishment or retribution for unacceptable behavior. These influences will provide some motivation for such children to attempt to hold their antisocial tendencies in check. However, their resources for doing so will be limited, as will their chances for complete success. The end result will be sporadic acting out in the form of antisocial behavior, or, in extreme cases, the development of a basically antisocial, criminal mentality. With these children, punishment and threats of punishment are virtually useless, except for inhibiting acting out in the short run. These children perceive punishment (usually correctly) as revenge or as attacks upon them, and not as justified responses to their own antisocial behavior. This is why parents who use grossly inappropriate socialization techniques for a number of years rarely are successful in reversing the situation once they realize that a child has become a serious problem. This also is why threat and punishment-oriented methods of dealing with juvenile delinquents and criminals do not work. In fact, children of this kind provide just one of many different examples of the more general fact that punishment does not work if relied upon as the basic mechanism for socialization. It may be necessary as a stop gap measure to enforce limits, but it does nothing to change underlying desires or impulses. In short, it attempts to treat symptoms without treating causes. More often than not, it is not even effective for treating symptoms, because it increases resentment and desires to get even.

In summary, the "bottom line" here is that the best solution to problems is to prevent them altogether rather than to take remedial actions after they have been allowed to develop. Going back a step further, I would add that the idea of preventing problems should be kept in proper perspective. It should be seen as an outcome of good positive socialization, and not as a primary goal. Parents who are concerned mostly with preventing problems are likely to use essentially negative approaches involving communication of negative expectations about the child and reliance upon threat and fear. In contrast, parents who develop a good relationship with a child, communicate positive expectations, and rely on basically rational and positive socialization methods will not have to worry much about problems. The few that they do have are unlikely to be persistent or serious.

SUMMARY   Following up on the points made in earlier chapters, it was suggested that ideal moral development and general personal adjustment are accomplished by socializing children to develop high moral ideals in combination with low vulnerability to conflict and stress. Genuine commitment to moral ideals (as opposed to introjection and verbalization of moral norms without commitment to using them as guides to behavior) is most likely to result in genuinely internalized self-control and prosocial morality. Such children learn to act morally because of a sense of fairness and justice, and not because of conscience pangs or fear of punishment. Minimizing vulnerability to conflict and stress helps promote general happiness and mental health. This is recommended both because it has benefits in its own right, and because burdening children with unnecessary guilt or anxiety does not increase their levels of morality.

Throughout the concrete operational years, the same general kinds of parental traits and socialization methods which were important earlier continue to be important. Love and acceptance of children is fundamental, and preaching and practicing prosocial morality, enforcing rules and standards while keeping them flexible, providing explanations and rationales, projecting positive expectations while still providing realistic feedback, and maintaining open relationships also are important.

Children acquire prosocial ideals most easily if their parents articulate them and model them in their own behavior. This includes behavior toward each other and other people as well as behavior toward their children. As always, if there is conflict between what parents say and what they do, children will tend to imitate what parents do and ignore what they say (or learn to repeat it but not pay any attention to it).

Vulnerability to conflict and anxiety is minimized through positive approaches to socialization. This means keeping socialization demands reasonable and appropriate, keeping them flexible and open to change as needed, providing explanations and rationales, and treating children with positive expectations, even when they slip up. Children treated this way consistently are likely to respond positively, thus minimizing the need for parents to resort to authoritarian or punitive methods. Eventually, they will develop truly internalized and sophisticated levels of moral development and moral understanding, and these moral concepts will be used in guiding their interpersonal behavior.

CHAPTER THIRTEEN

Social and Personality Development

The general themes of development of personality and social behavior during the concrete operational years are similar to those related to development in other areas during these years. Most children reach relative stability in personal and social traits, tending to be leaders vs. followers or happy vs. unhappy throughout the concrete operational years. However, these general traits are affected by a continually broadening set of experiences with the environment. These include new knowledge and experiences, new interests and skills, and the transition from home to school and peer group.

Parental influences continue to be strong, usually the strongest influences affecting children. At this time new influences begin to appear and take on a growing importance. Perhaps the peer group is the most important of these. Most children are extremely peer-oriented during these ages, strongly desiring to play with peers most of the time and frequently choos-

The young boys obviously idolize these tennis stars, chasing after them, trying to be helpful, imitating their clothing and manners, and generally modeling them. Children will tend to do this with adults whom they regard as heroes. During childhood such adults are likely to be those who do things with which children can identify, such as excelling at sports or singing or acting. Scientists, philosophers, and individuals who make important but nonglamorous humanitarian contributions to the betterment of the world might not be recognized until much later, if at all. Is this just the way things are, or does it reflect our socialization methods? (Tim Carlson/Stock, Boston)

ing the opportunity to play with peers over opportunities to go to a movie or on a family outing. Motivation to play with peers tends to persist even among children who have unfortunate peer group experiences. Much socialization occurs in contacts with peers, who provide both models and direct socialization concerning values and attitudes.

These days, such socialization influences also are provided through the media, especially television programs. Interest switches from children's programs to situation comedies featuring families and then to action dramas. Early preferences are for programs and cartoons with simple plots in which super heroes overcome the forces of evil. Initially, such super heroes provide food for imagination and fantasy play, and later they become sources for thoughtful consideration of questions about what is or is not possible for humans and what is good vs. evil. In a very real sense, Superman, Superwoman, and the rest provide stimulation and socialization, not just entertainment.

Beginning around age eight or so, interests shift from these simplistic, "larger than life" characters to shows featuring familiar family situations or heroes in roles familiar enough to allow realistic identification (police officers, medical personnel, rescue-workers, and other familiar community figures). Shows which feature children prominently are especially popular. Child viewers often concentrate their attention on child characters, especially ones their own age and somewhat older. Such characters provide models for behavior and help build expectations about what life will be like in a year or two.

Similar stimulation and information can be gotten from books, which were the main sources of such information prior to television. Books still are important sources for children who have learned to read for pleasure and who do so regularly. For other children, and even for avid readers, television generally is a much more powerful influence because of its absorbing realism and capacity for immediate impact. The child is drawn into the experience as a participant observer, as it were. This kind of impact is much more difficult for books to achieve, and it is possible only for children who possess at least minimal reading skills and interests.

The major societal institution affecting social and personal development during these years is the school. Here, children come into contact with large numbers of age mates, in contrast to the small play groups typical of early childhood. They also encounter teachers with whom they often spend several hours a day. Typically, this is their first continuing and close association with an adult outside of the family. In addition to stimulating cognitive development, these experiences expand children's knowledge about other people and provide challenging situations which have not been encountered before. These stimulate the development of new coping strategies. Stimulation from other adults and organized experiences also affect some children (those in church or Sunday school activities, camps, scouts and similar groups, and the like). Like school, these experiences broaden horizons and provide new challenges.

In general, key personal and social traits deepen and become more stable and characteristic of individual children, although temporary regressions to earlier forms of behavior and/or departures from normal activities are frequent. Sometimes these occur when a child has become upset over some traumatic experience, but this is not necessarily or even usually the case. Often, they occur because the child decides to try out something new, is temporarily influenced by the suggestions or behavior of a friend, is going through a developmental transition (which often involves a temporary breakup of previous stability as a new and higher level of stability is developed), or for other basically positive reasons. Although children in these age ranges tend to be stable relative to younger children, many changes and considerable development are taking place.

A major difference is that development is a little harder to see, because now it mostly involves relatively minor cycles of instability, followed by development, followed by the achievement of a new stability, but all *within the general outlines established previously*. Although a child who is a social leader at age six will tend to be a social leader at age 12, there will be a great expansion in quantity and development in quality of social skills and knowledge related to social leadership during these years.

What goes on here is parallel to what goes on in intellectual development. Most 12-year-olds have IQs similar to those they had when they were six, indicating relative stability in intellectual development (compared to age mates). If attention is shifted from *relative* abilities to a comparison of *absolute* abilities at the two ages, a striking broadening and deepening of abilities is evident. The same kinds of changes go on in the social and personality areas, but they are less easy to see.

PERSONALITY
DEVELOPMENT

Mischel (1971) and other behaviorists have argued that the term "personality" has little meaning because behavior varies drastically across situations, primarily in response to situational reinforcement contingencies. This argument has considerable merit. As we have noted, "traits" often considered to be characteristic of individuals, such as honesty or willingness to help others, usually are unstable across situations. At the very least, "personality" is much less stable and generalized than traditional personality theorists would have us believe.

On the other hand, whether or not you use the term "personality," people do develop certain central traits which are characteristic of them. Such traits are recognized by virtually everyone who knows them, and usually by themselves as well. While it is probably correct to say that no trait is evident in *all* situations, many are sufficiently characteristic of a person and sufficiently evident in enough situations that they become recognized as central to the person's "personality." Some of the more noticeable traits of this sort include introversion vs. extroversion, outgoing friendliness vs. social withdrawal, confidence vs. inhibition, leader vs. follower, preference for group vs. individual activities, competitiveness, cooperativeness, and happiness. Other traits are generalized in some children but more typically are situational. These include self-confidence and level of aspiration, independence, dependency, and behavioral morality.

Typically, the most salient and stable aspects of personality result from systematic socialization. The child is expected to show certain behavior and then is rewarded for doing so. Such socialization may or may not be deliberate or conscious, but it tends to be systematic. Where it is less systematic, because children get minimal attention to certain behaviors or conflicting expectations and reinforcements, the behaviors involved are much less likely to become stable and central aspects of personality. Where clear-cut role expectations exist, these help determine which behaviors will be retained and stabilized and which will be dropped or will become more situation specific. For example, as children develop traits which become noticeable and therefore open to differential attention and reinforcement by others, traits which are considered appropriate for their sex are likely to be reinforced and maintained, while traits considered more appropriate for the opposite sex are likely to be neglected or punished and dropped (Kagan and Moss, 1962).

Children's personalities also will be molded by the numbers and kinds of experiences that they have. Part of the reason for the stability seen in these years is that the major forces which have been acting upon children to cause them to develop certain characteristics by age six continue to operate on them in much the same way. This means continuation of pressures to develop in the same general directions. The influence of these socialization forces will be reduced somewhat as children encounter new stimulation from peers, media, and the school. They will continue to operate and usually will continue to have the same general kinds of effects on the children. Also, motivational factors relevant to Erikson's (1963) industry vs. inferiority stage continue in effect throughout these years, providing more pressures for stability.

Aspects of personality, particularly self-concept, also are influenced by children's *reference groups*. Reference groups are groups that children know and identify with to the point that they use them as bases for judging themselves. They judge themselves "with reference" to the group. Children who are intelligent or strong relative to other children in their reference group think of themselves as intelligent or strong. Compared to others in the reference group, they are. However, compared to children in the nation or the world at large, they might be only average or even below average. This is a key point about self-concept and other aspects of personality that Coopersmith (1967) and others have discovered. Children (and adults, for that matter) judge themselves by *relative standards* involving comparisons with reference groups, not by absolute standards. Sometimes the pool of potential reference groups is extremely limited because of limited experiences, so that the reference groups children use will correspond closely to the groups with which they are familiar. If children become exposed to a variety of possible reference groups with contrasting characteristics, they will identify with a subset of these groups that they consider to be similar or relevant to themselves, and will use only these groups as bases for judging themselves.

In the past, before the rapid development of inexpensive mass transportation, and especially before television, most individuals were limited in their exposure to possible reference groups. Many spent most or even all of their lives within very small geographical areas and within homogeneous cultural and socio-economic groups. Mass transportation and television have removed these limits. Most children now growing up in urban ghettos or rural poverty who rarely get very far from home still learn much about other children and adults from watching television.

In some cases, these changes may have profound influences on self-concepts. Children growing up in disadvantaged circumstances usually do not feel particularly disadvantaged when they know little or nothing about dramatically different and more attractive environments. Most children now are aware of such environments. In the past, such children would have to be content with fantasizing themselves as royalty or movie stars, thus substituting romantic dreams for the real thing, at least for a time. Now, television provides much more realistic models which can provide both motivation and information important for raising aspirations realistically. On balance, this probably is good, because it broadens their vistas and provides a much greater range of models and potential reference groups. This assumes, of course, that genuine opportunity will be there for those eager to take advantage of it. If those who raise aspirations or expectations after exposure to vicarious models are denied the opportunity to realize them, the result will be frustration, self-devaluation, and, perhaps, resentment.

SELF-CONCEPT   Self-concept continues to depend primarily upon the degree to which the child is accepted and encouraged by significant others, particularly parents. Changes occur with age as new significant others such as peers and teachers enter the picture, and as new interests and activities are

These boys are well into middle childhood and able to combine individual skills in the use of tools learned earlier with increasing sophistication in group planning and cooperation, in order to work together to build impressive go-carts. Although the atmosphere of the activity is essentially playful, the construction involved is genuine and not mere play, and the boys are working without adult supervision. Early childish observation and immature modeling of adult construction skills have evolved to genuine construction skills as good as or better than those possessed by many adults. (Photo by Evan Evans)

taken up. The self-concept of the preoperational child was based almost entirely on physical activities which could be observed directly by both the children themselves and by significant others, and which tended to provide immediate feedback concerning degree of success. Much of this continues throughout childhood, as children take up new physical activities such as sports and games. School skills provide another major set of activities that bring both immediate feedback about success and responses from significant others, now including teachers and classmates in addition to parents and others in the home. In general, success breeds positive motivation and failure breeds avoidance, so that most children come to prefer activities at which they excel and to dislike or even fear or hate activities that bring failure and a sense of inferiority.

The same tends to be true with other kinds of skills and interests. In middle childhood children begin to develop interests and hobbies engaged in just for enjoyment, which do not have connotations of success or failure. These include such diverse activities as reading, collections, games and pastimes, and arts and crafts. In most of these activities, success and failure is less relevant than in more clearly physical activities such as sports, and is more difficult to judge. Adults can encourage such activities by making suggestions and providing materials, and can add to the child's sense of enjoyment by showing genuine and continuing interest in them. Usually this is most satisfactory to the child if done through questioning and listening rather than through praise. Questioning and listening imply that adults consider the activity worthwhile and accept the child's involvement, while evaluational remarks go beyond showing interest by introducing success and failure criteria. This can change an enjoyable hobby into an achievement task.

The core of self-concept in middle childhood still is made up of physical and easily observable attributes rather than more subtle personal traits. When asked to describe themselves, children typically will give their age and sex, school and grade, home address and description of the rest of the family, and a brief list of favorite skills and hobbies. Usually, they do not go on to give personal or interpersonal traits, as adults do. These traits exist, of course, but children still are oriented toward the concrete and observable. The same is true when they describe friends and acquaintances to someone else. If questioned, though, they can make such discriminations as whether or not another child is fun to be with, is fair in treating others, and so on (Schmuck and Schmuck, 1975).

Parents can help foster self-concept development by continually projecting acceptance of the child as he or she is, positive expectations and attitudes, and genuine interest. As far as possible, the child should be free to explore in order to satisfy curiosity, and encouraged to follow interests and develop hobbies. These and other aspects of parental role in fostering personal and social development will be discussed at the end of this chapter and in the next chapter.

INTERPERSONAL TRAITS   Most interpersonal traits are modeled or shaped in the home, at least at first. A child whose parents are introverted and whose attempts to initiate interactions meet with little response is likely to become introverted also. Conversely, another child with extroverted parents who interact frequently and who express emotion spontaneously is likely to follow their example and to be rewarded for doing so. Children who are encouraged to play with peers and to bring peers into the home regularly are likely to become very peer-oriented, but not children whose parents foster and reward adult dependency, are overly concerned and controlling with regard to peer interactions, and do not want active children messing up their orderly home. Likely results include greater dependency upon the parents and greater preference for solitary activities and adult-like activities involving the parents as opposed to group activities with age mates.

As children get older and more experienced, their interpersonal relationships become more differentiated. Preschoolers usually are limited, both by developmental factors and by geography, to a few friends on the block and perhaps a few relatives that they see often. Once children enter school and become able to meet and visit with new friends farther away, they begin to form friendship groups based upon *similarity of preferences and interests* and upon complementary personalities which enable them to play well together and enjoy one another. Children who enjoy similar activities will tend to seek one another out, so that common interests and compatibility eventually become more important than geographical convenience in determining who plays with whom (Byrne, 1969).

Of course, sex also takes on primary importance, even though sex typing pressures are reducing. Between age five or so and age 10 or 11, cross-sex play is reduced drastically, and that which does occur goes on mostly at school or among relatives. Cross-sex age mates who live next door will drift apart, the boy seeking other boys and the girl seeking other girls. They may be willing and able to play well together if alone, but usually they will avoid each other if peers are around, because they want to avoid being teased.

The more popular and adaptable children will develop "categories" of friends, differentiated on the basis of context. They may call certain friends if they want to swim or ride bikes, but will avoid friends who cannot or do not want to swim or ride bikes. At other times, they may call other friends for quieter or more intellectual activities, if these friends are good at and enjoy such activities, but will not call their swimming and bike riding friends if these friends do not enjoy such activities. Most children have certain friends at school that they enjoy socializing and working cooperatively with, and certain other friends that they play with after school because of shared interests in play activities in this context. Sometimes the friends are the same, but often school friends are not easily accessible after school or do not share the same kinds of after school interests. After school friends sometimes are not accessible in school, because they are in different rooms or grades.

Cultural Differences in Cooperation and Competition

Spencer Kagan and Millard Madsen (1972) and their colleagues have conducted a series of studies indicating that, compared to Mexican and Mexican-American children, Anglo-American and Afro-American children are less cooperative and more competitive. Their studies are very interesting and very convincing, partly because they use realistic game situations in which children participate with gusto, and partly because their results have been unusually clear-cut.

In games where children can play either competitively (trying to get the rewards for oneself only) or cooperatively (working together with others in the game to maximize everyone's rewards), Mexican children are more likely to be cooperative and American children more likely to be competitive. Mexican-American children are in between. These results have been obtained in several studies, and they indicate rather clearly that these differences are real and that they are related to cultural socialization of the values placed on cooperation and, especially, competition.

In what is perhaps their most striking study, Kagan and Madsen (1972), studied the behavior of American vs. Mexican children aged seven through nine in situations in which they were playing a game much like

Chinese checkers. The idea was to start at your own goal and move toward the opposing goal, with the winner being the first to reach the opposing goal. Each move made by each child could be classified as an attempt to move toward the other goal and thus win the game, a sideways move that was not helpful in moving toward the other goal, or a backward move that not only was not helpful in winning the game but helped the other child to win. There were two conditions, a competition condition, in which the winner got a prize, and a "rivalry" condition, in which the children of interest were told that no one would get a prize if they won the game, but that their opponents would get a prize if they lost the game.

The competition condition was a one-against-one game of the kind that children typically play, and competition (meaning an attempt to win the game and thus win the prize) was appropriate for both players. In this condition, 92% of the moves of the Anglo-American children were forward moves made in an attempt to win, but only 77% of the moves that the Mexican children made were forward moves. In a straightforward competitive situation where competition was appropriate, both cultural groups were primarily competitive, but the Americans were more competitive. In this case, it should be pointed out that the behavior of the Mexican-American children who were not competitive was somewhat inappropriate, at least by American standards.

The most interesting, instructive, and in some ways frightening results were obtained in the "rivalry" condition. Here, forward moves intended to win the game represented some combination of motives to win and motives to deprive the opponent of an opportunity to win and to get the prize. This condition yielded differences which are not merely significant but strikingly large. In this condition, 78% of the moves of the American children were forward moves geared to win the game, while only 8% were neutral moves and 14% were backward moves. In sharp contrast, the percentages for Mexican children in the same condition were 36% forward moves, 22% neutral moves, and 42% backward moves. When placed in a condition where winning would bring personal satisfaction but losing would allow the opponent to get a prize, the Mexican children tended to allow the opponent to win and get the prize, but the American children were extremely competitive.

Taken together, the data from this and several other experiments conducted by these authors and their colleagues indicate that Mexican children sometimes avoid competition when it is appropriate, but that American children have a much stronger tendency to be competitive and rivalrous even when it is inappropriate by our own standards. Among other things, this indicates that our socialization in the area of achievement motivation has failed to make clear enough distinctions between achievement and competition, so that the majority of our children appear to be motivated to compete for the sake of winning even at someone else's expense and at no particular gain to themselves.

Many of the games and pastimes we associate with childhood in our culture are found in identical or similar form in many other cultures. These boys are playing a French version of what we call "hopscotch." Note that although the game appears to be basically the same and played under similar circumstances, the players are boys, not girls, and they are all wearing shorts. What does this suggest about childhood sex roles? (IPA/Jeroboam)

In general, it probably is to a child's advantage to have many friends and a large variety of kinds of friends (except for extremely antisocial types). This exposes the child to more types of individuals and situations, and thus encourages the development of more coping mechanisms. This in turn makes for greater ease and skill in making new friends and in coping with new situations. Such breadth of experience and flexibility and adaptability are important for popularity and leadership, both in the present and in the future.

Such experiences also lead to greater self-insight, since the child will be exposed to more reference groups and more dimensions on which to make comparisons. Exposure to different kinds of families, different value systems, different foods, different cultural traditions and practices, and the like, tends to be both educational and enjoyable. As children reflect upon such experiences, they gain insights about the range of human differences and some of the reasons for the differences, and they begin to pose questions about matters that interest and puzzle them. If their parents are open to such questions and disposed to take the time to provide useful answers, the result will be optimal development of social knowledge and skills. These include such important ones as the ability to empathize with different kinds of individuals and the ability to take a tolerant or even positive attitude toward human differences (as opposed to the chauvinistic attitude that you and your group are right and anyone else is wrong).

SOCIAL DEVELOPMENT

Age roles, sex roles, family constellation factors, and other factors previously important for development continue to be important now. Like home influences, these other continuing influences remain in effect, but their relative importance diminishes as the child moves out of the home and into the school and the peer culture.

AGE ROLES   Age remains important throughout childhood, although its importance diminishes gradually. One support for it is the lock step curriculum typical of most schools, which automatically means that older children have been exposed to more schooling than younger ones. This, coupled with the fact that older children usually are larger and more mature than younger ones, gives the older children an advantage in play groups which are mixed in age composition. The age difference factors discussed in Chapter Seven continue throughout childhood, although with less importance with each passing year.

Age gradually recedes in importance compared to maturity, physical size and coordination, and similarity of interests and temperament. Except for things related directly to school knowledge, small differences in age, such as six months or even a year, are relatively trivial in middle childhood, whereas they were of great importance in early childhood. Even so, age still is psychologically important to most children. Older ones often will try to pull rank on younger ones, and will do so regularly if they can get away with it. Most children much prefer being thought of as older than they are, and they usually will revise their age upward when asked how old they are (most seven-year-olds are "seven-and-a-half" or "almost eight"). The same is true with regard to school grade: as of the last day of the school year, children consider themselves to be in the following grade, even though they will not actually begin until the fall.

Children tend to use age and school grade as norms in judging themselves and others. A child who excels in a sport or other activity often will brag that he or she can do just as well as the others even though the others are older, or will express surprise that an older friend cannot do as well as a younger friend. Older children who find that younger children can equal or surpass them at activities they consider important rarely mention this, although they notice it and may be affected negatively by it. In fact, if the disparity is extreme enough, and especially if other children or adults should comment upon it, such children are likely to withdraw from the activity rather than face continued embarrassment.

Age roles have considerable psychological importance even though they have relatively little physical importance. Children usually develop the expectation that those who are the same age should be able to do a given task with roughly equal skill, and they comment upon noticeable differences from this expectation. Those who exceed expectations feel pride, while those who fall short feel shame. Such experience with age norms usually provides children with their first encounters with something they will have to cope with the rest of their lives: individuals who differ noticeably from what is statistically normal and expected are considered deviant, and deviancy usually has positive or negative connotations attached to it.

Age differences begin to become more important again as children approach adolescence. Typically, children who have not yet entered adolescence receive a good portion of their information about it from older children. Although throughout childhood children tend to look up to and imitate those who are slightly older than themselves, this tendency is exaggerated as they begin to approach adolescence and come to understand that they will be moving into a

454

new state in life. Except for entry into junior high and high schools, we do not have clear-cut "rites of passage" from childhood into adolescence (or adulthood) as some societies do. Nevertheless, we make many informal distinctions between children and adolescents, and these are communicated in various ways to children. As they approach adolescence physically, and as they begin to develop formal operations and other cognitive structures signifying the transition to a more mature intellectual perspective, children in the 10 through 12 age range tend to pay careful attention to real and vicarious adolescent models and to seek out information from adolescent acquaintances (where possible).

SEX ROLES   Separation of the sexes increases to peak at around age eight or nine, and then decreases gradually until adolescence. In general, children play primarily with others of their own sex, and conform to culturally prescribed sex role differences in home responsibilities and behavior and in dress and appearance. Sex roles have loosened up recently, but they still are powerful influences and there still are powerful sanctions against notable deviance, particularly for boys (Maccoby and Jacklin, 1974).

Children gradually learn about bodily differences between the sexes and come to understand that these are the real differences. Ordinarily, they learn this while they are still young, and under circumstances such that they do not attach any great importance to the information. Only later, as they approach adolescence, do children begin to understand that sex differences are far more important than they had realized (some children find this out much earlier, of course, especially if they live in crowded conditions or for whatever reason have acquired knowledge about sexual intercourse).

Camping out in a group is an experience that most pre-adolescents anticipate, relish, and remember fondly, even if everything went wrong from an adult perspective. This particular experience gives these boys a "legitimate" opportunity to learn and practice cooking, general kitchen work, bed maintenance, and other tasks normally associated with females and housework in traditional sex typing. Chances are that some of these boys would feel conflict about participating in these tasks at home because of sex-role socialization, but in this setting they do so with obvious interest and enjoyment. (George Bellerose/Stock, Boston)

Among most preadolescent children, sex is important because of the role behaviors attached to it, not because of sexual intercourse or related matters. Boys learn that they are supposed to play with other boys, and girls with other girls. Children of both sexes learn that certain kinds of behavior are expected of boys but not of girls, and vice-versa. Most conform to these expectations to some degree, especially when they have been socialized strongly and explicitly. Sex role prescriptions tend to be tighter for boys than for girls, and penalties for violating them are both more likely and more intense. Sex role differences tend to be more extreme among children in lower class environments than among children in middle class environments. This derives both from socialization in the home and from socialization by peers. The greatest pressure to conform to rigid sex role expectations is exerted on lower class boys, and the least on middle class girls.

Segregation by sex leads to different playmates, different kinds of play, and the development of different social and personal characteristics. Girls tend to play in pairs or small groups, and much of their play involves activities such as fantasy play with dolls and related equipment, table games, playing school or other play involving imitation of adults, arts and crafts, and reading and other school related activities. Girls also participate in certain kinds of feminine sex-typed physical activities (jumping rope, dancing) and in physical activities that are considered appropriate for both sexes (bike riding, swimming, bowling, games of tag, and the like). Most girls also can partake in "boy" activities if they want to, although they may have to overcome some resistance and/or put up with some teasing.

Boys tend to play in larger groups, partly because of the nature of the play considered appropriate for them. The fantasy play of younger boys involves pretending to be super heroes, cowboys, and the like, or imitating more familiar adult models by playing with automotive garage sets, trains and trucks, and so on. Boys usually play outdoors more than girls, and their play tends to be more active and boisterous. Younger boys will play a lot of chase games and spend a lot of time riding tricycles or bicycles, while older boys will begin to play group sports (Hartup, 1970).

As they move toward adolescence, boys tend to spend a great part of their free time outside of the home, engaging in team sports and "hanging around." Girls also spend a lot of time socializing and exchanging information, but usually in the home and usually in pairs or small groups. They begin to make a transition from what we usually think of as childhood play into more typically adolescent activities such as listening to records, practicing dances, planning slumber parties and other social activities, babysitting, working on arts and crafts and various hobbies, and perhaps taking lessons such as dancing or gymnastics. They also begin to do more things with and for their mothers, assuming responsibility for household duties and learning how to cook, sew, and perform other domestic skills.

Boys also do the above things to some extent, but not as much and not as soon. They do tend to do things with their fathers and to learn male sex-typed skills such as the use of tools for household repairs and do-it-yourself

456

construction jobs. They also assume responsibility for household tasks, usually masculine sex-typed ones such as cutting grass, shoveling snow, performing repairs, and painting the exterior of the house. These statements about sex-typed activities are group generalizations, of course. The degree to which they are sex typed in a given family depends upon the attitudes of the parents and children, the number and sexes of children, and numerous other factors. Sex typing of this kind is breaking down, and probably will continue to do so. It is neither particularly unusual or unnatural for boys to be doing some of the things listed above as typical of girls, or vice-versa.

FAMILY CONSTELLATION FACTORS   Investigations of family constellation factors have yielded many findings, but most are weak or ambiguous. The only one that continues to hold up as a solid generalization is that firstborns tend to be more thoroughly socialized than later borns. Other studies suggest influences such as a tendency for parents to baby the youngest child and a tendency for children with cross-sex siblings to be less extreme in their sex typing than children from all-boy or all-girl families. Such findings have face validity and probably are true to some extent, but they are weak general tendencies rather than strong probabilities. Sex typing probably depends more on expectations and reinforcement from family and friends than upon family constellation factors. Many last born children are not babied but are relatively ignored or prematurely pushed by parents eager to get rid of the work involved in raising young children.

The tendency of firstborns to be more heavily socialized to parental expectations is a fairly strong one. Firstborns usually are given some responsibility for caring for and babysitting their younger siblings (especially firstborn girls), as well as chores to perform around the house (especially firstborn boys). In general, the work involved in such duties usually is more than compensated by other considerations. First, such children usually get allowances or some kind of direct compensation for the work that they do, and they have a special place in the pecking order within the home. Even if the parents do not call any special attention to the fact that they are the oldest, they usually will impress this upon their younger siblings and use it, with varying degrees of success, as a way to get what they want. This can make a difference in decisions about what television show will be watched, who will get to use something first, and the like. Also, firstborns are older and have had more experience in dealing with the parents, and thus they are likely to be more successful than their younger siblings in getting the parents to follow their wishes.

These advantages are compensated by certain disadvantages. The main one is that the firstborn must "break in" the parents. Every change involving the firstborn is a new event for the family, and often change is agreed to only after much discussion and argument. Most parents tend to be relatively over-protective towards their firstborn, primarily because they are unsure of themselves when faced with requests for permission to do something new or to change rules concerning bedtime or other limits. Not wanting to make mistakes, parents tend to be conservative in these situations, agreeing to changes only when they are reasonably sure that there is no danger involved. Once they have been through this with their firstborn, they tend to be more sure of themselves and quicker to agree to changes with later borns. The firstborn must constantly exert pressure against parental over-protectiveness, setting precedents and paving the way for later born siblings to get the same privileges with little or no hassle. This may be an additional reason why firstborns tend to be particularly responsible, dependable, and achievement-oriented. Even when they do succeed in getting parental agreement to go along with something new, there usually is the stipulation that it will be a try-out to be evaluated later. Consequently, firstborns tend to be socialized to look upon permission to do things as a privilege and to expect to be held accountable for their behavior and to have to prove themselves worthy of parental trust.

In contrast, because of the difference in parental behavior in parallel situations, later borns are more likely to look upon such permission granting as a right rather than a privilege, and are less likely to feel the need to prove themselves worthy to the parents or to anyone else. Over time, differences like these will tend to make firstborns both more traditional and more sensitive to the reactions of others (even the *possible* reactions of others). Later borns are more likely to confine their planning considerations to the probable consequences of behavior for themselves, with less concern about what others may think.

SOCIAL RELATIONSHIPS   As mentioned previously, social relationships become much more complex and differentiated as children meet large numbers of peers at school and become increasingly able to travel in order to spend time with friends of choice. Children become increasingly peer-oriented throughout these years, so that they are strongly motivated to do the things that peers value. Much of this is done out of positive interests, because peers have told them about a television show, game, food, or other enjoyable experience. Often, not only the child but the family as a whole will be enriched by new ideas and experiences introduced through friends.

The negative side here is that most children feel strong pressure to conform to whatever peers say and do. This will lead to incidents such as refusals to wear certain kinds of clothing or to play with certain toys, as well as imitation of words and fads presently current at school or in after school play groups. This can be exasperating (deliberate use of obscenities or seemingly endless raucous laughter anytime someone passes gas), but most of it is potentially enjoyable if adults recognize it for what it is and take a positive attitude where possible (knock-knock jokes, gymnastic tricks, riddles, clothing fads, and so forth).

Within relevant constraints such as the family budget and school dress codes, it probably is best for the family to go along with a child's wishes on matters of clothing and appearance. Mothers may think that their daughters look better in dresses and curls, but daughters may disagree and wish to conform to peer norms that girls should have short (or long) hair and dress in sweatshirts, blue jeans, and tennis shoes. This kind of clothing probably is more functional and practical than dresses, and the matter really resolves to a disagreement over taste, not substance. If forced to go to school in a dress, a girl may suffer teasing from peers, and even if she does not get teased, she may feel that they look upon her as square.

Similarly, consider the plight of a boy forced to confront his fashionably long-haired friends sporting a short hair cut. The importance attached to these things may seem funny to adults, but they are not at all funny to children. In fact, they can be of primary importance, so much so that they might make the difference between a feeling of security and acceptance vs. a feeling of shame and unworthiness. Adults should avoid doing anything which will unnecessarily embarrass or humiliate children in relationships with peers.

Parents can help here all along, of course, by *minimizing vulnerability*. Vulnerability to self-devaluation can be minimized by developing a strong sense of security and self-esteem in the first place, and then maintaining it consistently. In addition, parents can help their children cope with peer rejection by staying conspicuously open to discussion of problems that might come up, listening carefully to the child's story and providing realistic feedback and suggestions for coping with similar situations in the future. Except under special circumstances (such as when a child has been beaten up by an older bully), it usually is best if parents discuss the situation with the child but then let the child handle it, rather than trying to intervene and handle it themselves. By intervening unnecessarily or too often, parents can make the child dependent upon them for help whenever difficulties arise, and can cause the child to be seen this way by peers and teased because of it ("Why don't you go tell your mommy?").

Children who are upset by conflicts with peers should be given help in comprehending the situation and deciding what if anything to do about it. They should not simply be ordered to handle it themselves without any guidance at all. If they knew what to do, they probably would have done it already, or at least would not be so upset. The fact that they *are* upset indicates that they need guidance, and ordering them to solve the problem without providing any guidance is, to repeat an earlier example, similar to tossing infants into water and ordering them to swim. By questioning the children and providing useful feedback, parents can minimize both vulnerability and the damage that the incident causes, and can build coping strategies by making specific suggestions about what to do. Much of this is accomplished by "creating reality." Although they are much more sophisticated than preoperational children, children in the concrete operational stage still are rather naive when it comes to deciding whether to take a threat or remark seriously. They also are largely ignorant of motives for behavior, and often an unpleasant situation is much easier to take in stride if recognized for what it is (such as an attempt to save face) than if taken seriously at face value (such as a serious intention never to play with the child again).

Another important place that parents can help children cope in optimal ways is by helping them recognize and accept their physical attractiveness, social desirability, and other aspects of self-image and peer popularity. There is little to be gained by "protecting" a child from the truth about physical ugliness or deformities or about membership in a low status social group, since this only increases the potential impact of these problems, which are going to assert themselves anyway. Children who have unchangeable physical characteristics which may bring them rejection need sympathetic but honest information about their problem. They need to be reassured that they are as good as anyone else, despite what others may say, but also to be prepared for possible rejection with information about how to respond to it if it occurs.

Conversely, although it is not often recognized as a problem, children who are unusually attractive, athletic, or otherwise endowed with characteristics likely to make them popular with peers also need realistic information about their good fortune. They should understand that they were lucky to be born with these valued qualities, and should be taught courtesy and compassion toward those who were not. Adults who deal with such children regularly should try to be sure that these qualities do not become dominant parts of their self-concepts, because such qualities will be less valued later. Many individuals who are very attractive physically as children or preadolescents are less so as adults, and, except for the handful of professional athletes, athletic ability is not as valued among adults as it is earlier. Children who become accustomed to and expect special treatment because of such physical characteristics are in for some bitter letdowns later.

THE SCHOOL

The importance of school as a factor in child development probably has been overrated relative to the family and peer group. Nevertheless, school is an extremely important institution affecting children. It typically is the first institution that a child learns to deal with *as an institution*, coping with it *as an individual* rather than as a member of the family (in contrast to early experiences with churches or other institutions). Also, schools are institutions set up explicitly *for* children, and this gives schools a special interest value and importance in their eyes. Children spend about half of their waking hours at school on school days, and typically they are under the care of a single teacher who gets to know them quite well. The potential for general socialization and for impact upon personality development is high. The actual impact varies with children's ego involvement in teachers and schools vs. peers and other influences, with the kinds of teachers that they have, with the degree of importance attached to school success by the family, and with the nature of their experiences at school.

Starting school speeds up the tendency to move away from the family and toward peer groups and other societal influences. Not only are children systematically removed from the home for six to seven hours, five days a week, but they come into contact with a great number and variety of *new peers*. As mentioned earlier, this multiplies their experiences and opportunities for forming friendships based on common interests. Children typically become deeply invested in their new friends, wanting to visit back and forth at one

460

another's houses, invite one another to birthday parties and other social events, and the like. For at least the first few grades of school, children will turn down an opportunity to do almost anything else in favor of an opportunity to go and visit a friend at the friend's house.

School also is important as a series of challenges and a source of relative *status*. Children are expected to master the skills taught in the curriculum, and their relative success in doing so tells them and others something about their general brightness vs. dullness (and perhaps also their maturity, persistence, work habits, or general adjustment). Children typically start school eager (except for a few, usually temporary, cases of "school phobia" experienced by children who are upset at the prospect of being left alone in a strange environment without their parents). Initial enthusiasm subsides, and children's positive attitudes toward school gradually deteriorate as they get older. Relatively few come to detest school, but few remain enthusiastic about it, either. Most settle into the idea that school is where they will spend much of their time for the next several years and that it is "okay," neither particularly good nor bad (Jackson, 1968).

Status differentiation appears in differential teacher-student interaction and other aspects of schooling practically from the first day. Teachers develop beliefs, attitudes, and expectations about children very quickly (Brophy and Good, 1974). Some of these are based upon purely physical attributes such as size and appearance, while others are based on observations of the quality and cleanliness of clothing, speech and mannerisms that provide clues to the nature of the home background, general responsiveness, happiness vs. unhappiness, presence or absence of school readiness skills that may indicate intelligence and/or home preparation factors, and the like. Teacher perceptions tend to concentrate on children's attributes most relevant to their roles as students, although teachers notice and react to more personal characteristics, also (Brophy and Good, 1974).

Just as in the home, there is a great potential for self-fulfilling prophecy effects when teachers react to children on the basis of early contacts with them. Most erroneous impressions are corrected quickly, because teachers get to observe children repeatedly. However, self-fulfilling prophecy effects can occur when teachers make up their minds that children have certain qualities and then treat them as if they do. Since children develop reputations in schools, both in their cumulative record folders and in the teacher grapevine, such effects can continue as they pass from one teacher to another. The fact that children get a new teacher each year (typically) does minimize the danger here, although it also minimizes the degree to which any one teacher gets to know a child very closely.

Independent of self-fulfilling prophecy effects and other personal and social outcomes that can result when a unique teacher encounters a unique student, certain structural factors built into the nature of the schooling as we know it today have effects upon all children. First, the lock step curriculum provides elaborate norms about the kinds of knowledge and skills children "should" possess at given chronological ages. This can cause problems, for a number of reasons. People tend to over-react to such norms, forgetting that 50% of us are "below average" on anything, that children in the same grade differ considerably in maturity and even chronological age, and that children having difficulties in one area do not necessarily have difficulties in others. There is a tendency to treat children as *generally* "bright," "average," or "dull." These generalizations fit certain children accurately, but not others (Hopkins and Bracht, 1975). Furthermore, even where they do fit, there is a tendency to forget that mastery of the school curriculum is not the essence of life. It clearly is very important, both in childhood and in later life. However, academic achievement is only one of a large number of skills important for adults. Mastery of the curriculum does *not* guarantee the ability to apply what one knows in an occupation, the social intelligence necessary to insure effective interpersonal relationships, creativity or originality, motivational structures that help people get the most from their abilities, or even "common sense."

I am not arguing here for elimination of competition, grades, or other aspects of schooling that tell children their relative status compared to their peers. Attempts to eliminate these things inevitably fail. Children develop consensual agreement among themselves about the academic "pecking order" in a classroom or school, no matter what teachers may do to try to disguise it (Nash, 1973). There is no point in trying to camouflage distinctions based upon obvious achievement. However, I think that we should deemphasize the importance attached to these distinctions, particularly small distinctions among the great mass of individuals who do not differ in any really significant way. In other words, I am arguing that our concept of "average" should be very broad, taking into account everyone but the most extremely bright and extremely dull children.

Extremely bright children who have the potential to move into the most demanding and learned occupations probably should be encouraged to do so, and all along the way they should be given whatever educational opportunities they are ready to profit from. It does *not* appear to be a good idea to refer to them as "gifted" or to segregate them from their age mates in elementary school, although it probably is helpful to provide them with enrichment activities and special projects which challenge their abilities and allow them to develop their interests and skills. It is possible for elementary schools to provide such children with extremely rich and high quality educational experiences, while at the same time minimizing the degree to which they develop elitist attitudes toward peers, suffer peer rejection and become bookworms, or otherwise develop undesirable peer relationships or social characteristics because of their status as "different."

Children who are extremely dull or who are brain damaged provide an even greater challenge to the schools, since they usually will have difficulty in mastering the curriculum at even a minimal level and often are rejected by peers. Here again, except for those whose handicaps require special tutorial instruction (the blind or the deaf, for example), it probably is best for dull children to remain in heterogeneous classrooms with other children rather than to be segregated into "special education" classes. Teachers can help such children by creating an atmosphere of cooperation in the classroom which, among other things, will enable these children to be tutored or otherwise helped by their brighter classmates rather than ignored or rejected by them. More importantly, teachers and other school officials can make sure that such children are diagnosed properly and given whatever educational experiences will be optimal for them. It should be self-evident that attempting to teach a child using materials and methods that assume functional reading ability will not work if the child cannot read, but this is precisely what is done in an amazing percentage of cases. Furthermore, many of these children could achieve reasonably well in school if taught to read functionally, although they will remain hopelessly unable to cope as long as they are unable to read. Except for individuals with extensive brain damage, it is reasonable to expect every child to become functionally literate and to master the basics of reading, writing, and arithmetic in school, regardless of whatever else may or may not occur. This not only is important to cognitive development, but it has ramifications for self-concept, employability, the chances for a "normal" adjustment in later years, and quality of life generally. Even where they are grossly behind "grade level," dull children benefit from "social promotion." Their peer adjustments are much better than if they are held back and required to go to school with younger children, and their achievement also is improved. Although such children typically remain *relatively* behind their age mates, they ultimately reach *absolute* levels of achievement higher than those reached by children required to repeat grades (Kraus, 1973).

In addition to all of the other reasons for its importance, school represents the first systematic societal "assessment" of children, and, by implication, of their families. It has enormous potential for preventive mental health through early identification and treatment of children headed toward distorted personal adjustments, although this potential has not been capitalized upon as yet. Even taking into account the dangers of self-fulfilling prophecies and misperceptions, information from kindergarten or first grade teachers about children is generally accurate and useful for identifying children likely to become maladjusted later. Poor social or personal adjustment usually results from a poor home environment, and these forces have had five or six years to influence children by the time kindergarten or first grade teachers encounter them. Most such children already show signs of distorted development, and teachers usually spot them. Our society has not yet developed mechanisms to capitalize upon this knowledge. Teachers themselves usually have neither the time nor the expertise necessary to intervene successfully. Furthermore, successful intervention usually will require working with the entire family, and teachers have little realistic opportunity to do this in most cases. All we do at the moment is watch and talk about such children as they grow up to become increasingly withdrawn, antisocial, or otherwise disturbed. Typically, we do not do anything to insure that they get treatment until their problems become so severe and compounded that the chances for successful treatment are minimized.

This is understandable, but not excusable. Part of it stems from traditional American opposition to unnecessary government interference in individual or family lives. The attitude is that socialization is the primary duty and responsibility of the family, and that it should not be "usurped" by other institutions. This is fine in theory, but it ignores the facts that many parents are inept or ignorant, unable to raise children successfully without some kind of help, and that others do not care about or even want their children, and thus lack even the motivation to try to raise them properly. Another aspect involved here is distrust of mental health professionals. Much of this is based upon the bad image that "child psychology" has had, most of it deserved, until recently. Much of the rest has been based upon the notoriously poor records that intervention "experts" have compiled in trying to deal with adults who are severely disordered. Between the explosion of knowledge about child development that has occurred in the past 15 years or so, and the fact that a disordered individual can be changed much more easily if helped while younger than if allowed to develop into a much more seriously disturbed adult, genuinely effective preventive health measures now are realistic options.

These considerations lead to the strong recommendation that such measures be instituted, for humanitarian reasons alone. There also are other reasons. Not the least among them is that women's liberation, access to inexpensive and effective birth control, and other factors have produced an unprecedented but probably permanent change in attitudes about children. Among other things, birth rates have plunged to the point that we are now below zero population growth, and there is no prospect that they will increase significantly in the future. This means that our society is headed for an unprecedented change in age structure, with many more individuals being middle aged and older, and many fewer being younger, compared to what we have been used to in the past.

Among other things, one implication of this is that we no longer can afford to remain unconcerned about child development and familial effectiveness, as we do now. Instead of looking upon children as national resources existing in perpetual overabundant supply, we are going to begin to look upon them as limited and increasingly precious national resources to be cherished and carefully nurtured. We must abandon the "method" of benign neglect, allowing a certain percentage of our children to develop into antisocial criminals, illiterate unemployables, or others unable to cope with society and thus supported by it in one way or another. Instead, we will have to concentrate on more positive and preventive measures designed to insure that each individual child develops in an environment that is as optimal as possible, thus minimizing both human waste and societal strain.

Whether we want to do it out of the goodness of our hearts or whether we want to look to more materialistic motives such as staggering taxes and the collapse of social security, we are going to have to institute preventive mental health measures, and soon. Although a great variety of measures are needed (such as, parent education for individuals who have not yet had children as well

464

as those who have, adequate nutrition and medical care for pregnant mothers of all social class backgrounds), one of the most obvious needs is a system to identify high risk children when they enter school and see that they get assessment and, if necessary, systematic intervention.

OTHER SOCIETAL INSTITUTIONS

Children's social and personal development also can be affected by experiences with church or Sunday school, camping, scouting, YMCAs and YWCAs, and other societal institutions. Such institutions are similar to the school in the kinds of opportunities (and dangers) they provide, although typically they do not have as strong an influence as the school. They can be especially important for children who are having difficulties in school, if they provide such children with opportunities to pursue interests that give them satisfaction and a sense of self-esteem. Also, counselors, coaches, and other adults in such institutions often are objects of hero worship by children, and thus are in positions to influence them.

In general, such activities are almost always good for children. This assumes, of course, that children are voluntarily attending activities they want to attend, not being forced to attend them because parents think they need such activities or want to get rid of them for a time. This assumes that parents respect children's rights to change their minds, and avoid brow-beating them into continuing with something because they liked it when they started or because time and money invested in the activity will be "wasted" unless the child continues. This changes a potentially happy and broadening set of experiences into a source of continual distress, usually eliminating any positive benefits that might result and maximizing negative outcomes. We all know adults who were forced to continue to do something that they did not want to do as children (such as take piano lessons). They typically resent their parents for making them do it and loathe the activity they were forced to do.

It is helpful, of course, if parents build positive expectations and enthusiasm for such activities when first presenting them to children, encouraging whatever accomplishments may be involved. However, parents must be prepared emotionally for the possibility that children's initial enthusiasm will disappear, and thus be prepared to allow children to discontinue activities without making them feel guilty or ashamed.

THE FAMILY

Despite all the other institutions and experiences that children encounter during the concrete operational years, the family typically continues to be the most important influence. This is maximized, of course, if parents are generally effective and continue to maintain open communication with their children. The family usually will be the major source of values and morality, defense mechanisms, general happiness, and insight into self and others.

Responsibility typically develops primarily in the home as the child encounters allowances, chores, and opportunities to exercise choice. The combination of modeling and reinforcement coming from parents is likely to determine such general personal characteristics as happiness vs. unhappiness, aggression vs. affiliation and cooperation, extroversion vs. introversion, and degree of competitiveness.

Parental modeling also provides information about adult sex and spouse roles and about parent roles. Adult males usually act as their fathers did in the ways that they interact with their wives and children, and adult females tend to act as their mothers did.

Another major set of social and personal qualities which is influenced heavily by modeling from parents concerns *locus of control*. Depending upon parental modeling, children are likely to develop systematically toward the idea that they can control their environments and are personally responsible for what happens to them vs. being unable to control their environments and not responsible for what happens to them. This has implications for coping and defense mechanisms, for frustration tolerance and responses to problems, for political participation and interaction with formal and informal groups, and for other aspects of the general dimension of attempting to change vs. passively accepting the environment. For example, during these years, the growing child becomes increasingly aware of politics. Children who frequently hear their parents discussing elections and other political matters, who see their parents vote and work in political campaigns, and who otherwise are exposed to politically involved and active parents are likely to become politically involved and active themselves as adults. In contrast, children whose parents show little or no interest in politics are not likely to develop such interests themselves. Regardless of degree of political activism, political party membership and general political leanings tend to be affected strongly by the parents. Conservative parents tend to raise conservative children, and liberal parents tend to raise liberal children (Hess and Torney, 1967).

Changes sometimes occur if the child experiences upward mobility later. It is more than a comic line or stereotype to talk about a person switching political parties, church affiliations, and general attitudes if a transition is made between a primarily lower class mode of living and a primarily middle or upper-middle class mode of living. People of all ages tend to use reference groups in forming their own attitudes and beliefs. If they are trying to become accepted by their reference group (rather than being in it securely already), they may go out of their way to try to be like the reference group in an attempt to gain such acceptance.

As a result, *specific* parental church affiliation and attendance, political affiliation and activity, social attitudes and practices, and the like often are changed if a person moves into a new social class or subculture. More generalized personal characteristics formed in the home tend to persist throughout life. Adult behavior as a spouse relating to a spouse and as a parent relating to a child already has been mentioned. Some of the other things that typically are learned in the home and then retained throughout life include the following.

1. Familial closeness and emotional expressiveness toward relatives and friends.

2. Work attitudes and habits (work as enjoyable and fulfilling vs. necessary but unrewarding).
3. Recreational attitudes and habits (types of recreation and general activity level; individual vs. group activities).
4. Reading habits (subscriptions to newspapers and magazines; book reading; use of libraries).
5. Donating and other examples of altruistic behavior toward the needy.
6. Neighbor roles (meeting and sociability vs. withdrawal and avoidance; interest in interacting and cooperating vs. a "My home is my castle" attitude).
7. Television and movie habits (time spent in these activities; types of programs preferred).
8. Leisure time activities generally.
9. Virtues and "vices" (politeness and good manners with family and friends; politeness and good manners with strangers; drinking; smoking; use of obscene language; and so forth).
10. Salient traits (independence vs. conformity; introversion vs. extroversion; and so forth).
11. Noise and activity levels tolerated and expected.
12. Expectations concerning cleanliness and orderliness in the home and general environment.
13. Expectations concerning clothing and personal appearance.
14. Preferences in eating (types of food eaten; recipes used to prepare such food).
15. Religious, racial, ethnic attitudes and prejudices.
16. Expressive mannerisms (gait, use of hands, general posture, non-verbal communication behavior, accent).

The above list could be greatly expanded, but it is long enough to make the point that, regardless of what may happen outside of the home, parents have broad effects upon children through modeling and selective reinforcement. They are the overwhelmingly predominant influences upon children for the first five years or so of life, and they remain the major influences for the next seven or eight at least. Regardless of what may happen to children later, the early expectations, habits, and general characteristics formed in these years tend to persist. They may be changed or adapted to new situations in varying degrees, but they usually remain in some recognizable form.

The qualities that a child picks up at home are a base from which adaptation to out-of-home situations occurs. Except in unusual situations, this base remains, rather than becoming supplanted by a new base developed through peer experiences or other out-of-home experiences. Single events usually do not have any great important or permanent effects upon children, but things which are repeated day after day over a number of years tend to become deeply ingrained and resistant to change. It is common, for example, for adolescents and young adults to drop out for a while to "do *their* thing," only to end up much like their parents a few years later.

Many of the things most resistant to change, and consequently many of the areas where children most resemble their parents, involve *conditioning*, somtimes without awareness by either the children or the parents. Most expressive mannerisms are learned this way. Few parents systematically teach their children to communicate non-verbally in certain ways, to talk with a certain kind of accent, or to walk a certain way, and few children consciously imitate their parents in these areas. Nevertheless, comparisons of parents and children usually reveal numerous examples of learning expressive mannerisms through modeling.

The same tends to be true with other things that are modeled consistently. Independent of conservative vs. political ideology, and independent of prejudices or other antisocial attitudes that may have been picked up from parents, children of polite and altruistic parents will tend to be polite and altruistic themselves, and children of selfish or paranoid parents may become selfish or paranoid themselves. These are just more examples of the general point made several times previously that children tend to imitate what they see and not what they hear, if there is a difference.

The home has been described as a base for personality development. It also is a base in another sense: a source of love, information, treats, reassurance, and other supports that the child needs for smooth and optimal development. Another important thing that the home provides is a place for solitude and quiet reflection. Most observers talk of the concrete operational years as years of relative quiet and stability, both in cognitive and personal development. However, many things are going on, even though dramatic changes may not be evident. In the social and personal area, children are assimilating schemas to one another, trying to make sense out of themselves, their families, their friends, and the world generally.

This is the same kind of process that occurs in the more strictly cognitive areas of learning, and the same kind of assimilation of knowledge and experience from different areas into a coherent system which goes on there also goes on in the area of social and personal development. Although children do not show the rapid and obvious changes that they showed earlier in the preschool years and will show later during adolescence, many important changes take place during the concrete operational years. These involve such things as filling in gaps in knowledge about themselves and others (through a combination of getting information from parents or others and firsthand experience); finding out about the diversity that exists in the people of the world, the nation, the neighborhood, and the immediate peer group, and forming opinions and reactions to this diversity; broadening and deepening understanding of where one's self and one's family fit in the greater scheme of things; gradually losing childish romanticism and coming to see the world as it really is (often painfully); coming to terms with the fact that certain frustrations are unavoidable; working through the emotional trauma that result from unpleasant experiences; learning to accept responsibility for one's behavior, including behavior that implies mistakes in judgment or even unacceptable morality; learning that you cannot please everyone yourself or even keep

ASSIMILATION OF SOCIAL AND PERSONAL SCHEMAS

people that you like from hurting one another; learning that there is always someone who can do something better than you can; and a great many other things.

A preadolescent who has had favorable development will work through all or most of these things and emerge with healthy and realistic concepts of self and of others. Such a child is very different from the preoperational child who knows little if any of this, and is also different from the preadolescent who has had an unfortunate childhood and has been unable to develop in these areas for lack of knowledge and information, emotional freedom to grapple with moral issues, overwhelming stress, or other debilitating problems.

In addition to being the kinds of ideal parents outlined all along, parents can help this assimilation process that goes on in middle childhood by giving children time to be alone and *think* when they seem to need it. Often, quiet periods are times when major advances in social and personal development are taking place, even though it may appear to a parent who jumps to a false conclusion that the child has merely gone to his or her room to pout. In fact, successful parents may encounter times like these more often than less successful parents, because they are raising their children to be responsible and reflective. This means that, at times when the children *do* do something inappropriate, they may become upset and need to think about it at some length. They may need quiet and privacy, partly because of a sense of shame which makes them want to get away from the people they feel they have let down, and partly just so that they can think. Once they have had time to think things over and reach conclusions, they will be emotionally ready to rejoin the family and resume their "normal" activities, although they genuinely will have "learned a lesson."

SUMMARY   During the concrete operational years, children move out from "home base" and begin to cope with the demands and challenges of peer groups and the school. Home influences remain in effect and remain important, but now proportionately more stimulation and socialization comes from peers, teachers, books, television, and other media influences. Combined with children's increasing knowledge and sophistication, these influences broaden their vistas concerning themselves, their families, and the world generally. Depending upon the children's relative preparation and on their relative success in coping with these new experiences, they may find them challenging and enjoyable or frightening and painful. Again, the dominant theme of these years is the struggle to achieve general success and a sense of industry and to avoid becoming discouraged by failure to the point of developing a widespread and deep sense of inferiority.

As part of the general stability acquired during these years, children begin to become more stable in their social and personal traits, although specific behavior still is highly situational. In particular, preexisting traits which are valued and reinforced are especially likely to become more stable and obvious with age. If the same general kinds of socialization forces that have been affecting the child in the first six years or so of life continue to have the same effects, the child will be similar six years later on such variables as general happiness, introversion vs. extroversion, self-confidence, leadership tendencies, competitiveness, and ability to get along with others. The same will be true for gestures, mannerisms, and expressive movements.

Systematic change may result if children identify with a model or a reference group that differs considerably from their parents. In extreme cases, they may consciously pattern their behavior after that of the model or reference group, because they want to be that way themselves and/or because they want to be accepted by the individuals they are imitating.

Children's relative satisfaction with themselves depends less upon objective achievement or status than it does upon where they stand relative to their reference groups. A bright but not unusually gifted child who nevertheless is notably brighter than other children at school is likely to develop tremendous self-confidence and self-esteem, and a child who would be well-adjusted under other circumstances but is rejected by the immediate peer group for some reason is likely to be miserable and perhaps become withdrawn and inhibited. These perceptions can change later when adolescents and adults develop a broader perspective about the range of human differences, but in early and middle childhood, the reactions of immediate reference groups "create reality" for children because they provide the primary if not the only source of information by which they can define and evaluate themselves.

Such feedback is quite potent because, in contrast to the largely physical activities of earlier years that gave objective feedback about success and failure, information about one's social attractiveness and general acceptability comes from the subjective reactions and judgments of others. Until they get old enough to gain some perspective and to begin to develop friendships along common interests, children will be forced to adjust to peers with whom they are thrown together for geographical or other reasons having little or nothing to do with their own preferences. Sometimes, the result is isolation and rejection of children who would do all right under other circumstances. Parents and teachers can mitigate this if they keep informed about children's relationships with peers and help them over rough spots.

Age and sex roles and family constellation variables still have effects in middle childhood, although they gradually dwindle in importance, and children become more differentiated as individuals and develop friendships with children that they like and get along with well. Norms and fads generated by peer group and media influences begin to become more important, showing themselves in games and pastimes, clothing preferences, local slang, and, in general, desires to be or possess whatever is "in" at the moment.

Children learn an amazing amount at school, but most of their school related interests and perceptions concern the personal characteristics of teachers and events going on in the peer group rather than the content of the curriculum. Even so, they are aware of their relative status at school, both academically and socially. Teachers (especially in the academic sphere) and peers (especially in the social sphere) sometimes have self-fulfilling prophecy effects upon developing children, treating them in stereotypic ways long and consistently enough to make them begin to fulfill these expectations. This is not an important problem for most children, but it does happen. In general, it is better for children in the long run if they are passed along to the next grade even if they do not master the content of the present grade. This is less disruptive and damaging to their social relationships, and in the long run, it produces somewhat better achievement compared to the achievement of children who are retained in a grade one or more years.

The startling devaluation of children which has developed over the last few years, coupled with the apparently permanent adoption of birth control and family planning by the vast majority of parents, means that the country is in for an unprecedented change in the age structure of the society over the next generation. We no longer can "waste" children the way we have been doing, and we are fast reaching the point where it will become essential that each child's potential be maximized through optimizing the environment. A great many things are involved in this, including many mentioned in various places throughout the book, but perhaps the most important is the development of effective methods to identify high risk children early enough to institute effective treatment before problems become deeply ingrained and difficult to reverse.

The stress on movement out of the family and into the peer group and the stress on the socialization roles played by the school, the media, and other influences, sometimes make us forget that the family remains by far the strongest socialization influence upon most children. A brief list of personal traits that typically are learned in the home during childhood and retained throughout life was given near the end of the chapter. It serves as a reminder that, although children can and do change in many ways as they develop, parental and home influences in the early years are strong and for the most part permanent. No matter how much we may change in lifestyles, reference groups, and surface traits, few of us ever really get very far from our roots, if those roots took firm hold.

CHAPTER FOURTEEN

Fostering Social and Personality Development

The most important general themes relevant for fostering optimal social and personality development during the concrete operational years should be familiar by now, because they are the same ones that are important in other areas. These include, most fundamentally, acceptance, love, and encouragement of children, combined with flexible and reasonable limits. Parents also need to provide positive guidance and information and to avoid negative attitudes and expectations or stereotyping in ways that produce undesirable self-fulfilling prophecy effects.

Parents also must be consistent with their choices concerning the degree of independence and latitude they allow. Wide tolerance means allowing children freedom to experiment and sometimes fail, maintaining confidence that things will work out for the best in the long run. A contrasting pattern of vigilant protectiveness and control of the child and the environment will minimize problems ad failures, but this form of child rearing becomes more difficult as children get older. Furthermore, it can backfire by glamorizing forbidden activities in the eyes of the children.

Whatever general lines of approach are taken, it is important that parents remain open to change, both in children and in their own attitudes. Failure to do this will impair communication as children learn that it is easier to omit certain information or even lie to parents than to endure what they perceive as pointless hassles. When possible problems appear, it is important for parents to take the time to gather information and think things over before making decisions.

If proper relationships and lines of communication have been established and maintained, adjustments in rules and limits should be relatively minor and easy to make. Where parents have not formed and maintained these kinds of relationships, clashes with children become increasingly serious as the children get older. Even those who were adult-oriented and easily cowed by a show of authority when they were younger can be peer-oriented and hostile toward authority as they grow older. As always, such problems are handled best by preventing them in the first place. Secondarily, problems which were not prevented should be minimized and dealt with in ways that involve true solutions satisfactory to all concerned, not merely authoritarian exercises of parental power.

A major difficulty for parents during these years is the need to adapt as their children become increasingly peer-oriented. Children pick up numerous ideas and desires from peers, including many that parents reject or feel unsure about. On one hand, it is important for parents to establish unequivocally with their children that "my friends do it" or "my friends' parents say it's okay" never are sufficient reasons for anything. Given the extreme pressures for peer conformity that children feel, and given that many children see arguments like these as reasonable, parents can expect to be badgered with them virtually continuously unless parents make it clear that they consider them irrelevant or at least incomplete. The pros and cons of a contemplated activity must be discussed on the basis of more rational considerations such as the probable effects of the activity on the children and others in their lives.

Information about the activities of friends or the attitudes of friends' parents can be useful in finding out about the contemplated activity and in making decisions about it, so that it *is* relevant to a degree. Parents should acknowledge this, but at the same time make it clear that the mere fact that a friend is allowed to do something is not a valid reason for approving the activity themselves. Having established this much, it also is important for parents to show that they are open to new ideas and to changes in existing rules or agreements. Sometimes children will be persuasive in arguing that existing limits are overly restrictive or that they now are responsible enough to merit new independence or privileges. On the other hand, some suggestions may strike the parents as immoral, unacceptably dangerous or expensive, or otherwise unfeasible. Here, parents should explain their reasoning to the children rather than simply refuse their requests without proper explanation.

New arrangements can be tried out provisionally, subject to review at a later time. Very often, this is the best short-term solution to new demands, because many involve activities with which parents are unfamiliar. This happens for many things that firstborn children request, and it also happens frequently when children encounter age mates from a different ethnic or cultural background. Such interactions may involve requests for new foods, opportunities to do things that parents know little or nothing about, and the like. Initially, parents may react to such requests with confusion and puzzlement rather than clear rejection. Getting information and giving new ideas a try is much more sensible than refusing them without good reason. Many times, these interactions can lead to experiences which are enriching not only for the children but for the whole family, as when peer contacts result in new favorite recipes, recreational activities, and the like.

When confronted with a brand-new idea which leaves parents confused, it usually is best if they familiarize themselves with the idea. Often this will involve getting to know their children's friends and families better, since the simplest way to acquire the information usually is to observe or talk with the friend or parents involved. By "trading notes" this way, parents can enrich their own lives and expand their social experiences in addition to obtaining the information necessary to deal with the request. If an investigation convinces the parents that the idea is a bad one, they should explain this to their children in ways that make their reasons clear while at the same time avoiding any unnecessary criticism of friends or parents of friends. This is important for several reasons. First, as always, parents will be most successful in establishing limits when they give rational reasons that their children can understand. Second, criticism of friends or parents of friends is likely to be resented, and it may cause the children embarrassment or rejection if the friends find out. Finally, if parents regularly refuse their children's requests and at the same time criticize the individuals responsible for implanting the ideas, their children may come to look upon the parents as hopelessly square. Ultimately, this can cause them to stop asking for permission and to begin to become sneaky.

PERSONALITY DEVELOPMENT

By the time children start school, some of their more salient characteristics have become obvious. If these characteristics are ones that the parents desire and have been trying to foster, it is highly likely that parental behavior has been generally appropriate and that favorable development along the same lines will continue (assuming, of course, that parents make the necessary adjustments to emerging developments in their children). Conversely, if children aged five or six have developed salient and apparently stable characteristics which conflict with parental socialization goals, it is very likely that the parents have been behaving inappropriately. Where the discrepancy between what the parents wanted and what they have is clear enough to be noticeable and troublesome, and where parents are confused as to the reasons, they should seek professional help. It may be that they have been over-reacting to essentially minor and normal problems, or that they have unrealistic expectations. If the problem is real (that is, if the child already shows noticeable adjustment problems and is judged likely to get worse unless intervention is undertaken), the time to act is *now*.

As noted in the previous chapter, salient characteristics that are obvious by age five or six are likely to become more deeply ingrained over the next several years, because the same kinds of environmental factors (primarily parental factors) which have produced them continue to operate. This is likely to be the case unless parents make fundamental changes in their attitudes and interactions with the child. Unfortunately, the parents most likely to be able to do this without outside help are the parents least likely to need to do it. In contrast, parents who are doing a poor job because they are grossly ignorant or because they are poorly adjusted themselves are unlikely to seek help on their own. They may do so, however, if motivated by a friend or relative, a neighbor, or a teacher. Pediatricians, social workers, and others who come into contact with families also can fill this role.

This is much easier said than done, of course. Presently, our society has no systematic mechanisms for early identification of high risk children, and a critical shortage of individuals with the characteristics and training necessary to intervene successfully when such children and families are identified. This problem is likely to be remedied gradually, as the nation begins to come to grips with the fact that children are precious national resources (see previous chapter). Even if appropriate personnel were available, there still would be the problem of unwillingness to "get involved." Unless we want to continue to passively watch children predictably grow up to be antisocial or otherwise seriously disturbed, some people are going to have to get involved. Those people are *us*. For starters, police or child welfare officials should be alerted whenever child abuse is observed or even strongly suspected. This particular problem is so serious that action should be taken *immediately*, preferably by total cooperation with the authorities. Those who cannot bring themselves to do this much should at least attempt to get someone else to do so, or, if absolutely necessary, should request an investigation anonymously.

I also strongly recommend getting involved with families of children who show signs of disturbed development but not of severe child abuse, even though many would call this recommending that people involve themselves in other people's business. I maintain that the quality of child rearing which parents provide *is* other people's business. The problem is that we tend to look upon it as everyone's business, and consequently as no one's. For reasons mentioned earlier, it is more important than ever that we all begin to look upon it as *our* business when we see a child clearly headed toward distorted development, and that we attempt to do something about it. Where the parents are friends, a direct approach underscoring the potential seriousness of the problem and need for intervention would be ideal. Where this is not a viable possibility, try something that has a good chance to achieve the same results, such as approaching a mutual friend, a clergyman, a teacher, or someone else who knows the child and family and might be in a better position to speak to the parents. If necessary, take a chance and call up the parents to assess their willingness to discuss the child. If they are aware of the problem, they may be more than willing to discuss it with someone else who is willing to speak frankly with them. If they are not aware of the problem, they may be responsive if they are basically well meaning and can be made to see that their child is headed for serious trouble unless some changes are made. Frequently, parents know little or nothing about their children's activities outside the home.

In contrast to the above, it is *not* a good idea to call the police in situations like this. There is little that the police can do other than try to reason with the parents, and they are unlikely to be able to do this successfully except where the child has done something serious enough to require police intervention. Furthermore, the police cannot provide treatment; they can only arrest the child, which is unlikely to lead to positive outcomes. Disturbed children and their parents need treatment-oriented help, and this is not likely to result from conviction for juvenile delinquency.

The remainder of the chapter will concentrate primarily on optimizing the development of children already off to a good start. However, the present point is worth stressing again: adults who observe serious adjustment problems in their own or other people's children should do something about them, and do so immediately. This does not mean that children who reach adolescence in a disturbed state cannot be helped; they can. However, helping these individuals is much more difficult than it is when they are still young. Where action clearly is needed, action should be taken. Do not wait for things to get worse or for someone else to "get involved."

SELF-CONCEPT   As noted in the previous chapter, parents can optimize self-concept development by continually projecting acceptance, positive expectations and attitudes, and genuine interest. In addition, as time and budgets allow, they can provide freedom and opportunities for children to satisfy curiosity and develop interests and hobbies, and, in general, to "find themselves." We often think of this as happening during the adolescent identity crisis, but much of it happens earlier.

Assuming basic acceptance, the primary method of encouraging children to pursue their interests is to continually show interest in what they are thinking about and doing and to encourage their efforts at creativity and hobbies. Genuine accomplishments should be praised, and frustrations and difficulties should be eased through provision of realistic feedback about the difficulties involved in the task and about the limits of the child's present abilities. Parents can show interest by asking questions and asking to see demonstrations of abilities or examples of creations. Often, they can share interests and hobbies with their children, ideally where both parent and child are genuinely interested in the activity (as opposed to the parent becoming involved only to try to please the child).

Parents must learn to tread the fine line between encouraging activities and praising accomplishments on the one hand, but still allowing children freedom to change their minds about what they are interested in and to experience failure without deep or lasting disappointment, on the other. If parents give an activity too much build-up or go too far in making it clear that they badly want to see success, a child may feel compelled to continue with it and succeed at it. Failure then may lead to a deep sense of unworthiness. Taken together, these considerations add up to being ready and willing to allow children to pursue a broad variety of interests, but knowing that they will drop most of them once they become familiar enough with the project to realize they do not want to continue. Nevertheless, encouragement of each new venture is provided. This is tricky, but it can be done. A good initial response is "I'm glad and interested to hear that you are doing————; tell me about it or show me." If initial interest fades, parents can make it clear to children that this is "okay" through remarks such as "Well, you've learned a lot about————, maybe now it is time to move on to something else." Parents also can reinforce their willingness to allow children the freedom to change their minds by bringing the subject up when it is appropriate. For example, if children are taking lessons, they will have to re-register for these lessons periodically. At registration times, parents can check to make sure that children want to continue with the lessons rather than simply assuming that they do and signing them up for more.

The reason that parents can afford to be much more open and less directive about hobbies and interests (as compared to behavioral limits and moral values) is that these are matters of individual preference. Children are mature enough to know what they like once they have had concrete experiences. Since interests and hobbies presumably are opportunities for them to do what they want to do (in addition to opportunities to develop cognitively), it makes little difference what specific activities they come to prefer. It usually is best for parents to follow children's wishes rather than to try to force or badger them into continuing with activities that they do not enjoy. This is especially important when a child wants to do something different from what peers are doing. Unless the desired activity is immoral or unfeasible for some reason, why not? Again, what is typical is not necessarily ideal, and a child who does something different may be better off than other children, regardless of what other children or adults might think about it.

In addition to allowing children to find themselves through interests and hobbies, parents help develop self-concept by gradually increasing responsibilities and opportunities to exercise choice, commensurate with age and level of maturity. In general, children should get increased privileges (allowances, later and more flexible bedtimes, opportunities to do new things) and increased responsibilities (specifically assigned jobs such as making their beds, taking out garbage, and helping with other household activities) as they get older.

It probably is *not* a good idea to tie allowances directly to their duties, although it might be a good idea to pay the child extra money for performing special jobs. Where continuing responsibilities are going to be considered *duties* (that is, jobs that the children will be expected to perform all of the time), these expectations should be made very clear. The rationale should be

This Mexican girl is assuming a task typically associated with females: serving a meal. Differences in customs between Mexico and the United States are obvious in the types of food and drink being served. However, a difference related to sex roles is evident also: Note that the girl's father not only is assuming responsibility for supervision of the younger child, but is holding the child warmly on his lap without any evidence of self-consciousness or intention to get rid of the child at the first opportunity. This is no accident. Mexican males are socialized to show affection, including physical affection, toward the members of their family, whereas many American males are socialized quite differently. (Andy Mercado/ Jeroboam)

As children get older they become more capable of assuming responsibilities, and usually more interested in doing so, at least up to a point. This girl may have been just playing several years ago when she modeled her mother, but now she is doing the family wash. In many ways, this picture illustrates traditional sex-role socialization: Girls typically assume responsibility earlier and more heavily than boys, and a certain degree of sex typing exists in the tasks assigned to and/or assumed by boys vs. girls. This girl is relatively young for independently handling the task of doing the wash in a laundromat, but the task itself is associated with the female sex role. (Owen Franken/Stock, Boston)

that the children now are able to assume responsibility for some of the jobs that must be done around the house, and that it is appropriate for them to do so because they are members of the family who are expected to share the work as well as the benefits. This should be discussed as long as is necessary to get the children to understand, but it should not be tied up with the matter of allowance, at least not in a direct "this much money for this particular work" sort of way.

Instead, allowances should be given to children freely, primarily because they begin to need money of their own and become increasingly capable of exercising choices about how to spend this money. It might help to note that the allowance is given partly in recognition of and appreciation for the help that the child provides around the house, but it should not be tied to household duties in such a direct way that failure to perform them leads to deductions in allowance. Failure to perform duties should be dealt with directly, without mention of allowance. Otherwise, the allowance becomes a club used to control children rather than an enabling privilege.

Allowances should be given to children as theirs to spend as they wish, even though this will mean a lot of teeth-gritting and tongue-biting. Six- and seven-year-olds will spend most of it on candy or cheap toys, and even ten- and eleven-year-olds frequently will abandon grandiose plans to save up for something big in favor of "blowing it" on movies, records, or other less expensive items that they want immediately. If the money really is theirs, its use is up to them (within limits discussed and agreed upon). Furthermore, it is through experiences like these that children learn to make sensible decisions and to balance short-range desires against long-range goals. This requires firsthand personal experience, which means making mistakes.

If children are not allowed to make these kinds of mistakes, they are unlikely to learn much, and they may end up having to make them on a much greater scale later. This does not mean that children who are not given freedom to learn through exercising choice in matters like how to spend their allowance will become individuals who buy impulsively, but it does mean that children who have this kind of freedom and experience are likely to develop a sense of responsibility and hierarchical priority of goals and values as they learn from their experiences, good and bad.

These comments concerning privileges, responsibilities, and allowances are part of a broader point: as children emerge from infancy and differentiate into increasingly unique and sophisticated individuals, they should be treated as members of the family, not as second-class citizens who are controlled but who do not have input into decision making or opportunities to participate as a full-fledged group member. Parents and children are not equals, and parents should not attempt to be "buddies" to their children. On the other hand, children are entitled to their rights and to respect, like other individuals. This includes such matters as opening their own mail, privacy in general, use of the telephone (limits may have to be set here, but children should be allowed to use the phone in circumstances parallel to those in which adults typically use it), input into decision making about television programs or weekly menus, freedom to get certain kinds of snacks at will (commensurate with responsibility), access to newspapers and magazines, and the like. As children develop, adults and other family members will have to adjust to their emerging needs. For example, if there are only two chairs in the family room that are located near lamps and thus appropriate for reading, some additions or new arrangements will be required when children begin to read themselves. While an adult may be justified in staking first claim to a particular chair, there is no need to forbid children from sitting in this chair at times when the adult is not using it. Children will need places of their own that are suitable to their sizes and needs.

All of these may seem like little things, and in isolation, they are. Taken together, they make a difference in the degree to which children see themselves as developing to higher levels of responsibility and status. Those who are allowed few privileges and opportunities to exercise choice, and who are treated as if they are still infants, are likely to act like infants. Conversely, those who are given continual acceptance and respect and are treated as responsible individuals are likely to become worthy of this treatment. They are likely to become more differentiated and sophisticated in their knowledge about themselves and others, more realistic but at the same time more satisfied with themselves as individuals, more capable of thinking before taking action and of exercising choices rationally, and more likely to see themselves as able to attain their goals by taking realistic and effective action (vs. seeing themselves as unable to have much effect on the environment because of forces beyond their control).

INTERPERSONAL TRAITS   Interpersonal traits picked up as a result of modeling parents usually please parents, because the children are behaving as they do. Most of the interpersonal traits that parents become concerned about are developed in reaction to influences from outside the home. If objectionable child behavior results from parental modeling, parents will need to change their own behavior if they expect the child to change. Again, parents cannot reasonably hope to succeed with a "do as I say, not as I do" approach to child rearing (consider smoking, drinking, and obscenity).

If something like this happens, it is a good idea to discuss the situation with the child, perhaps developing a mutually agreed upon contract concerning future behavior. In calling attention to the child's objectionable behavior, the parents should make it clear that they realize that they do the same thing themselves. In calling for changes on the part of the child, they also should make it clear that they intend to make changes themselves. This, of course, must be followed by appropriate behavior consistent with what was said.

If parents are concerned about their child being overly adult-oriented and dependent and/or insufficiently experienced with peers, they can take steps to correct this. First, some soul searching is in order. Is the problem largely accidental (there are not many age mates in the area for the child to play with), or have the parents contributed to it heavily by being overly protective or restrictive? If the latter, change in parental behavior is needed. If the former, steps such as relocating or enrolling the child in activity groups that will involve peer interaction can help.

In any case, it usually is best *not* to discuss problems like this with the child. Telling dependent children that they are dependent probably will only depress them and make them even more dependent. Similarly, making an issue of forcing chidren to make their own decisions rather than depend on adult authority is likely to worsen matters by increasing both the children's awareness of their dependency and the likelihood that they will see it as a problem. In attempting to reduce dependency, anxiety, fears, and the like, it is best to proceed slowly and covertly, moving the children along in small steps without calling attention to the fact that systematic manipulation is taking place. To the extent that this is accomplished, the children are likely to make slow but sure progress without even realizing it, so that inhibitions, anxiety, dependency, and similar problems gradually become replaced by initiative and self-confidence.

Such children become accustomed to acting independently and making decisions on their own, without being particularly conscious or concerned about the process. Meanwhile, parents convey acceptance and approval in covert ways, largely by simply letting the children do these things without interference. Unnecessary criticism of bad decisions should be avoided, of course, but so should praise of good decisions (since this will focus attention on the decision-making process, something that should be avoided with children who are anxious about it).

Characteristics picked up from interactions with peers are more likely to cause problems for parents than characteristics picked up from the parents themselves. Attempting to keep children away from these peers usually is neither feasible nor wise. Instead, successful parents counter such problems primarily through good socialization practices with their own children, and to a lesser degree by socializing other people's children.

There are four main considerations. The first is establishment and maintenance of a good general relationship and good communication, the same fundamental points stressed several times previously. This makes possible the second aspect: detailed discussion of the problem, in which parents and children share perceptions and in which the parents clarify the problem and take the lead in working out possible solutions. In this way, parents can make clear to their children that they do not approve of and will not tolerate (beyond explicit limits) aggression, property damage, name calling and pointless arguing, petty but malicious teasing, and similar problems that can result when two peers have difficulty getting along or when several gang up on or exclude an unpopular scapegoat. By stressing Golden Rule morality, parents can help make their children see why such behavior is wrong, and by providing information and suggestions, they can help them learn to behave more acceptably in such situations in the future.

A third consideration is that children treated this way at home tend to be the more popular ones who become social leaders. As a general rule, children who are secure and happy tend to be prosocial in their relationships with peers. This leads to peer popularity, the ability to play well with others, and the ability to work out solutions which are mutually acceptable to all without having to appeal to an adult to settle it. Furthermore, such children are unburdened by needs to compensate for difficulties at home through defense mechanisms in play, thus freeing them to concentrate on having fun. Children like these tend to be more fun to be with, both because they have a good time themselves and because other children have a good time when they are with them. As a result, other children will tend to value their friendship and look to them for leadership. A bonus for parents of such children is that the children not only are well-adjusted in their interpersonal behavior, but they also are the group leaders that establish the norms and generally set the tone for what is expected and acceptable in the peer group. In short, if you are generally successful in getting your children to do what you want and in helping them to become the kinds of individuals who become social leaders, you will minimize conflicts between your values and those of the peer group.

Finally, parents can and should do a certain amount of socialization of other people's children when problems occur in and around their own homes. They can make it clear to peers that certain behavior is not allowed in their home, even though other parents might allow it, and they can enforce this by sending home children who fail to heed their warnings. Occasionally, this will lead to an embarrassing encounter with other parents. Usually it will not, because few children voluntarily tell their own parents that a peer's parents have sent them home for misbehaving, and most parents agree that action should be taken to correct misbehavior. Such actions by parents may or may not succeed in inducing generalized change in the peers, but they probably will succeed in changing the behavior of peers when they are playing with the parents' children. Sometimes this is the most that can be accomplished, at least in the short run, especially if parents do not agree on what is acceptable behavior by their children.

More seriously embarrassing problems for adults often occur in conjunction with undesirable social relationships in the peer group. Ill will sometimes results when children have been fighting or when name calling or scapegoating has occurred. Such incidents usually are not serious except when adults over-react to them; it is common for children to argue or even fight one minute and return to happy cooperative play the next. Isolated incidents usually are best minimized, although it is a good idea to remind the children involved that they are expected to play together well and enjoy one another rather than get into fights.

Problems that are repeated continually will require more intensive intervention, preferably after the parents involved have traded notes in order to get the full facts (as opposed to trading accusations or insults without facts). If it is clear that one child has been acting as a bully, that child's parents should immediately take steps to change this behavior. If several children have been picking on or excluding one child, the parents of the latter child should try to identify the source of the problem. Children who are unpopular with their peers usually are unhappy in more pervasive and fundamental ways. This shows up in peer relationships in such traits as jealousy, hostility, attempts to "buy" friendship, argumentativeness, and a general tendency to take the fun out of play by complaining or bickering. Typically, such children are trying to make up for deficiencies in acceptance, love, or other fundamental aspects of support at home. Other parents can help by urging their children to be more patient and understanding with such a child, and by strongly forbidding any malicious teasing or scapegoating. The problem is likely to persist unless the more fundamental reasons for the rejected child's unhappiness are remedied. This is another situation where intervention by professionals may be needed to achieve a true solution. Although their problems are not as serious, at least to others, as those of malicious or sadistic children likely to become antisocial criminals, children who are unpopular to the point of consistent rejection by peers also need help. If they continue in the same vein, they are likely to end up as socially inept adults with tendencies toward very poor self-concepts, withdrawal from other people, and depression or paranoia.

It should be reemphasized that this is a discussion of children who show *persistent and generalized difficulties* in getting along with peers, not problems involving isolated personality conflicts or temporary jealousies or arguments. Probably the most characteristic aspects of such children are generalized unhappiness and an air of resentment that is expressed in passive ways rather than in more clearly antisocial or aggressive ways. Sometimes the reasons for the child's difficulties are understandable, as when a child has lost a parent, is growing up in a neighborhood where everyone else has much more money and possessions, or is otherwise suffering the stigma of being different in an undesirable way. The causes for such problems usually are less obvious, but the ultimate cause is rejection in one form or another.

SOCIAL DEVELOPMENT

Many of the implications of data on social development already have been discussed in connection with personality development. The following material deals with several special topics, elaborating upon previous discussions. Topics include age and sex roles and family constellation factors.

AGE ROLES

Like sex roles and most other roles, age roles are more constricting than facilitative. There are certain positives regarding age roles that adults can emphasize with children, and they also can help minimize the negative effects that age roles can have. Without overdoing it, adults can accentuate the positive by reinforcing children's sense of pride on birthdays and other occasions marking achievements of new status levels related to age. Discussions of age in relationship to parental ages and to the ages of siblings and friends help deepen children's understanding of themselves and others. Until they are nine or ten, children look forward to birthdays with great anticipation. Parents can add to this by helping them count the days until the birthday arrives, discussing birthday parties and presents, talking about how they have changed since they were babies (in positive ways likely to maximize interest and self-esteem), and the like.

Birthdays are less central in the lives of older children, but they still enjoy and benefit from experiencing a special day on which they receive presents, special attention, their favorite meal and dessert, and so on. Around age nine or ten, children lose interest in the large group type of party that they enjoyed earlier. They will enjoy large group parties again as adolescents. In the meantime, they usually prefer an opportunity to have a friend or two stay overnight or accompany them to a movie or a special treat rather than to have a large group party like they had in the past.

The fact that similarity of interests rather than geography and age begins to predominate in choice of friends and play activities will require some readjustment by parents. Usually, it is wise for parents to *encourage* their children to play with other children, but *not* to *demand* that they play with specific children (or siblings) or make them feel guilty if they do not. As children become more differentiated in their personalities and interests, it is typical for them to become close to new friends and to gradually reduce or even lose contact with earlier friends. For the parents, this means getting to know new sets of parents of new friends, as well as some potentially embarrassing interactions with parents of old friends that their children do not wish to play with anymore. This problem will be minimized, of course, if parents have taken care to teach their children Golden Rule morality in general, and methods of disengaging with former friends in ways that do not involve rejection or hostility, in particular. Changing friend patterns also will require parents to adjust to increased use of the telephone by their own children and by other children who call their children, organizing in cooperation with other parents for parties and other group activities, making arrangements for overnight sleeping by or with friends, and so forth.

Unless siblings are very close in age, parents will have to adjust to the fact that age role considerations will cause older siblings to want to spend time with age mates rather than younger siblings. Insisting that older siblings let younger siblings tag along usually is unwise, since it is likely to produce resentment in the older siblings and to cause the younger siblings to have to try to play with older children almost all of the time. Instead, it is wiser for parents to emotionally "let go" of their children as they become increasingly peer-oriented, adjusting to and trying to optimize these developments rather than trying to delay the inevitable. Inclusion of younger siblings can be suggested, but parents should be prepared to back off if they run into strong resistance or if the younger siblings cannot participate in an activity meaningfully.

To the extent that age roles become an issue in peer groups, parents can minimize potential negative effects by providing realistic information. Older children who try to get their way just because they are older can be told that they will need better arguments than this if they expect to be listened to. Younger children subjected to such manipulation attempts can be reassured that there is no need for them to defer simply because another child is older. Where arguments about age cause peer conflicts, parents can help by minimizing the importance of age differences and perhaps by suggesting other, more fruitful and enjoyable activities. The importance attached to age differences can be minimized most successfully through expressions of utter disinterest rather than through extended lectures or explanations. Children who attempt to capitalize on the fact that they are older than others get the message in a hurry when the adults casually respond with total ignoring or with a quizzical expression, a slight shrug, and the question "So?"

SEX ROLES Adjusting to the effects of sex roles on children's social behavior also involves accepting the inevitable, so parents might as well enjoy it. Despite much talk and some action concerning adult sex roles, children's sex roles remain deeply entrenched. Since childhood sex roles are passed along from one child to another and learned primarily from peers rather than adults, sex role pressures on children have not changed much despite changes at the adult level. Greater flexibility and movements toward androgeny can be expected in the future, but these probably will take a long time. In the meantime, we can expect to continue to see boys and girls who got along fine begin to "hate" each other in middle childhood, despite both parental embarrassment and elegant rational appeals and explanations. Parents who have children the same age but of opposite sex and who enjoy getting together socially can expect to have to endure a few years during which their children go to elaborate lengths to make it clear that they do not like or want to associate with each other.

This is largely posturing and empty talk, of course, and frequently the children will play well together after going through the expected rituals of mutual distaste. When peer pressure in the sex role area is especially strong, or when other peers are present who might tease or tell tales, children may flatly refuse to associate with the opposite sex. Adults should make it clear that they consider this to be silly, but should stop short of demanding or forcing the children to play together when they do not want to. This will only worsen matters, partly because it increases the attention and therefore perceived importance of the "problem," and partly because it is difficult to play with *anyone* when an adult is standing over you ordering you to "play." If the adults simply drop a casual remark or a humorous put down to the effect that the children are being silly and are missing a chance to have fun together and then leave the children alone, the children probably will work things out.

A special problem exists where the children involved are all male except for one female, or vice-versa. Unless the isolated child is both willing to play with children of the opposite sex and able to cope with ritual opposition, it is likely that he or she will be excluded from the group. Furthermore, it is likely that he or she will be *happy* to be excluded from the group and will prefer solitary activity to enforced group play. Ordinarily, parents should respect this preference. Even though such sex role behavior is incomprehensible from the adult perspective, the forces acting upon children are very real and very strong. Forcing the issue probably will produce only embarrassment or resentment, although discussing the situation later with the children individually can help them to see that their behavior is both silly and uncharitable. Parents can minimize the force of sex role pressures upon their own children by "creating reality" for them, and they may even succeed in spreading this attitude throughout a peer group if their children are among the leaders. Even so, few parents or children will be able to avoid embarrassing or annoying experiences related to sex roles. Parents should be prepared to respond to them in good humor, and also be prepared to reassure their children if an upsetting experience should occur.

In general, cross-sex play is good. That is, children who play well with other children of *both* sexes tend to be better off in several ways than children who are strictly sex-typed, even when social class differences are taken into account. Such children usually are more independent minded and creative, less susceptible to peer pressures, and more likely to have a greater number and variety of friends and experiences (Maccoby and Jacklin, 1974).

Occasionally, boys who grow up in a family with no brothers and several sisters, especially if no father is present in the home, will show some effects. The effects are neither simple or entirely predictable. Many such boys develop feminine sex role behaviors in varying degrees. These usually include interest in and knowledge about activities typically considered feminine. They sometimes also include the development of expressive mannerisms considered feminine, an event likely to cause the boys to be seen as "sissies" or "swishes" (Maccoby and Jacklin, 1974). These aspects of feminine sex role behaviors have nothing directly to do with sexual adjustment. The vast majority of males who have these characteristics for these reasons have normal masculine sexual adjustments (that is, they are heterosexual and comparable in sexual adjustments to other men who are more clearly masculine in their sex role characteristics).

A different reaction to this same situation is what has been called "over-compensatory masculinity." This is sometimes seen in boys whose masculine sex role adjustments are threatened by their status as the only male in the family. Some such boys respond by becoming stereotypes or caricatures of "macho" masculinity by joining teenage or motorcycle gangs, developing swaggering and aggressive mannerisms, and the like (Lynn, 1974). This is a special case of the use of the defense mechanism reaction formation. Such boys repress the idea that they might be "unmasculine" (whatever that means), and instead develop the conscious idea that they are models of "masculinity" (as they interpret it).

Similar, but usually less extreme, effects can occur in situations where a girl is the only girl in a family with a number of brothers. One reason that extreme effects are less frequent is that there usually is a mother present in such families, whereas father absence is a much more typical pattern in single parent families. Girls developing in such families often become tomboys, picking up masculine interests and developing abilities in masculine-oriented skill areas. Here again, this has nothing directly to do with eventual sexual adjustment; most such girls develop into normally adjusted heterosexual women.

Concerning sexual adjustment, as noted previously, children explore and experiment with sexual activities in early and middle childhood. For most children, such sexual activity is confined to exploration and masturbation until adolescence. Sexual adjustment as such usually is not established until then. This will be discussed in more detail in the next chapter.

During middle childhood, the main task for parents in the area of socialization of sexual adjustment is to continue to let children guide them in making decisions about how much attention to devote to the topic of sex. This whole area would be a "non-problem" if parents could be as casual and open about it as children are. Most adults have an aversion to discussions about sexual matters. Often they clam up altogether, give only minimal and unsatisfactory answers, or, when they do provide information, do so in obviously agitated ways. Where this happens, the chances are good that the children never will ask them questions about these matters again, with the unfortunate result that they will get most of their sexual information from peers, and thus get a mixture of fact and fiction.

The main problem here is that some of the fiction that children pick up from others scares them into believing that there is something wrong with them. To avoid the needless pain that accompanies such experiences, parents should see that children are informed about sex when they need the information (parenthetically, let me stress that we are talking about *sex* here, not just reproduction, menstruation, adolescent development of secondary sex characteristics, and other matters not directly related to sex).

Virtually everyone in our society pays lip service to the idea that parents should educate their children about sex (as opposed to schools or other organizations), but very few parents do so. Surveys show that few children received much information about sex from their parents, and that most of those who did received much more information from peers or other sources. The problem seems to be parental anxiety. Parents need to think about and try to emotionally work through the facts that sex is a normal and important part of life, our tendency to become anxious about it is a leftover from earlier days with no good reasons to support it, there is no reason why parents should feel anxious or ashamed about their own sexual activities or about discussing them with their children, and that children are going to need and get sexual information somewhere. They are better off getting factual information from their parents than a mixture of fact and fiction from peers.

Some children will ask directly, but most will show their desire for information through indirect means. Parents should be alert for these clues and prepared to follow up on them when a child shows interest in the information. It is important to be prepared to respond in a hurry when the child does develop this desire. Parents who feel anxious or inadequate to handle the entire task in a verbal discussion can at least purchase for their children any of several well-written sex education booklets prepared for precisely this purpose, and then can follow up the reading with a discussion in which they encourage the children to ask whatever questions they desire and in which they attempt to answer these questions in a complete and straightforward manner.

Finally, concerning information about sex, it is important to point out that the same principles apply here as to any other aspect of information seeking by children. That is, children do not move from a state of no knowledge or interest whatsoever to a readiness to learn everything that there is to learn. Instead, they proceed in stages, taking in limited amounts of information at a time, according to their levels of cognitive development and kinds of personal experiences. A child who presently is interested in the specifics of sexual intercourse probably should be given this information, but unless there is evidence of interest in less directly related areas such as sexual deviations or parental opinions about what constitutes normal and appropriate vs. abnormal and inappropriate sex, these matters might best be left unmentioned until some future time when there is more evidence that the child wants information of this sort.

FAMILY CONSTELLATION FACTORS   Socialization implications related to birth order and family constellation factors mostly involve considerations of what *not* to do. Basically, all children need the same kinds of fundamental support from their parents. In order to minimize some of the common dangers associated with birth order differences, parents should be especially alert to avoid "dumping on" the oldest child, "losing" middle children, or "babying" the baby. Each child needs to be treated individually according to unique needs and interests, without being either overprotected and restricted or pressured and pushed. Parents should be enablers, encouraging and helping children to get experiences and try out things as much as possible, but within clearly defined limits.

Like age roles, birth order should be minimized as a relevant variable in family discussions and arguments. Firstborns should not be allowed to have their way just because they are the oldest; nor should last borns be given special consideration that their siblings did not get just because they are the youngest. Any special treatment given to children should be based upon good reasons having to do with the children's needs and the specifics of the situation, but not with sex, age, or birth order as such.

BROKEN FAMILIES   A special kind of family constellation problem that must be faced by some families is the absence of one of the parents due to death or divorce. In the case of death, a certain amount of trauma and depression is unavoidable, although it tends to dissipate gradually with time. There often is an initial period in which individuals react with rage and resentment. Typically, this is followed by acceptance coupled with depression. After some time, the depression lifts and the person is capable of resuming previously "normal" behavior. In the meantime, about all that can be done in such unfortunate situations is to keep open communication and discuss the situation continuously for as long as family members see the need to do so. This probably will help them work through their grief, to accept the situation, and begin to develop an orientation toward building a new future life.

In the case of separation or divorce, it is important for the good of the children, no matter how much genuine cause for resentment might be present, that the parents minimize the degree to which they show animosity toward each other in front of the children or run down each other in conversations with the children. Such behavior will produce resentment or at the very least depression in the children, even where the complaining parent is completely justified. This is because children in middle childhood still are closely identified with both parents. They are not yet able to emotionally disengage to the point of being able to look upon them somewhat objectively, the way that individuals who have passed through an adolescent identity crisis are able to do. Consequently, no matter how bad parents may be, children still will try to see them in positive ways and identify with them. The alternative, breaking off identification and seeing themselves as essentially on their own, usually is much too threatening for children to accept yet. When families are broken due to the loss of one of the parents, it is important that the traumatic effects be minimized and the quality and strength of emotional bonds among family members be solidified. This means minimizing blame and complaints, providing realistic information, and taking steps to develop a new adjustment that is as good as is possible under the circumstances.

Where a single parent is left to raise a family without a spouse, certain problems are inevitable. In the first place, this parent will have much more work to do, and consequently much less time to devote to leisure and to the children, and more demands probably will have to be made upon the children to perform household duties. Furthermore, the children of the same sex as the absent parent will not have an adult role model of the same sex present in the home. These are problems which can be handled successfully, not sources of inevitable damage. The term "broken home" has been used so much that we have become conditioned to thinking that all children from such homes are necessarily going to be scarred in important ways, but this is not the case. A broken home obviously is less ideal than a happy, unbroken home, but parents and children who work at it can minimize or even eliminate negative effects. Responsibility for "working at it" extends to include the parent who is absent from families broken by separation or divorce.

A single parent cannot and should not attempt to provide a role model for children of the opposite sex by trying to do everything that the missing parent did or would have done. A woman raising boys without a husband in the home should not go to the extent of becoming proficient in sports and participating with her sons in them, unless she is genuinely interested in doing so. It is important that single parents develop (if they have not already) an understanding and appreciation for sex-typed activities engaged in by their children of the opposite sex. While there is no need for them to participate in these activities themselves, it is important for them to appreciate and encourage their children's participating. Much of this can be accomplished through discussions in the home, although it helps to come out to watch children participate in plays, contests, or athletic events.

A form of irrational behavior seen frequently in parents who have suffered a painful separation or divorce is failure to distinguish between the specific objectionable characteristics of their former spouse and general sex-typed characteristics which have nothing to do with them. Occasionally, such individuals will decide that men in general or women in general are bad, and even will go to the extent of teaching and reinforcing this idea with their children. Needless to say, this is likely to harm both the general self-concept and the sexual adjustment of opposite sexed children who are subjected to a continuing diet of rejection of anything associated with masculinity or femininity (whichever applies). Parents should avoid running down each other in front of their children, and also should avoid comments like "just like a man," or "just like a woman."

In summary, in addition to handling immediate crises with minimal emotional damage to all concerned, the major task facing single parents is *not* to develop a bisexual orientation and attempt to be a role model for their opposite sex children. Instead, it is to continue to minimize the after-effects of the trauma, to avoid taking out anger against the spouse on children of the same sex, and to develop genuine interest in and appreciation for the sex-typed activities of children of the opposite sex (if they have not done so already).

SOCIAL RELATIONSHIPS   As pointed out in the previous chapter, the major task facing adults who must respond to peer conformity pressures on children is to learn to enforce limits in ways that make them acceptable and understandable to the children involved and do not place the parents in direct conflict with the peer group. Conflicts over matters of personal taste should be avoided by letting children do what they want to do, as long as this is feasible.

The pressures on children to conform to peer norms should be recognized and accommodated to some degree, although parents can help reduce these pressures by making their own children less susceptible to them. This is done primarily by getting across the fundamental point that an idea is not necessarily good just because someone else favors it. The familiar "if Johnny jumps off a cliff, are you going to do it, too?" has become a cliche, but similar comments help make this point. Such comments must be followed, of course, by discussion and explanation sufficient to enable children to see that limits are being enforced for good reasons and out of concern for their welfare. If peers are allowed to do things the parents consider dangerous or unwise, parents can express concern for the peers' welfare and surprise at the behavior of the peers' parents. Where questions of value systems or morality are involved, parents will have to express their disapproval, but ideally in ways that do not imply total rejection of the peers or their parents.

Much has been made of the fact that schools have become increasingly impersonal organizations remote from the needs of individual students and from personal contacts with parents in the community. This has happened essentially because parents have let it happen. Individual parents can take action to see that it does not happen in their case, even if it is generally true of the schools their children attend. Steps can be taken to initiate close,   **THE SCHOOL**

492

continuing, and mutually helpful home-school relationships. These include meeting and talking at some length with the principal and with each teacher who teaches a child. There is no need to wait for the school to initiate such contacts or to confine them to PTA meetings. Where schools encourage visits, parents should respond. Where schools do not take the initiative, parents should do so themselves, visiting the school to establish initial contact and calling or visiting again in the future if the need should arise.

When parents make it clear to the school that they are concerned about their children's school experiences and have every intention of monitoring them closely through continual discussions with the children and through frequent visits to the school, they are likely to get a positive response. Ideally, of course, this should be done in a friendly and mutually cooperative way, so that productive relationships develop spontaneously and parents feel free to call the school, and vice-versa, whenever there is any reason to do so. Active and continual initiation of contacts with the school are a good idea for parents even where school officials do not reciprocate positively. At minimum, such activity will put the school officials on notice that *this* particular family cannot be taken for granted, and it will increase the likelihood that children in the family will be assigned to the more capable teachers.

In dealing with their own children, parents should underscore the importance of schooling by showing continuing interest in what is going on at school, inspecting and commenting upon work brought home, and generally indicating that they consider school to be important and want their children to do their best. Where children are doing well, parents will not need to give them much help, but they can reinforce effort and success by showing appreciation for accomplishments and by challenging them to tackle new projects or inviting them to show off their skills. Where children are having difficulty, parents should take the time to give them necessary help. In some cases, this may mean time spent virtually every day tutoring children in fundamental skills (in the early grades) or helping them with their homework (in later grades).

Where parents are puzzled or upset about what is happening to their children at school, they should not hesitate to talk to teachers or other school officials. They should demand an immediate stop, for example, to such things as public ridiculing of children for failure to understand something or punitive treatment which serves no purpose and clearly is unwarranted. This assumes, of course, that parents have taken the time to get the facts, rather than jumping the gun by acting on information from the children which may be incomplete or distorted.

Parents also should go out of their way to make it clear to teachers that they welcome information about their child, good or bad. Teachers see children in an organizational setting interacting with one another while their parents are not around, and consequently they see many things that parents do not get a chance to see themselves. Also, teachers have more experience with observing children in the grade levels that they teach, and often are better able to judge the degree to which a child is well-adjusted and the nature of the problem if the child is poorly adjusted. Information of this kind from teachers can be invaluable in alerting parents to a growing problem early enough for them to take action to correct it with relative ease compared to what will be necessary if the problem continues without intervention for several more years.

Where children report serious social problems at school, such as beatings or extortion by older students, parents should take immediate action to see that the situation is corrected before it gets worse (which it will unless stopped quickly). Ordinarily, contacting the school and providing all the known facts along with the expectation that the school will take the steps necessary to correct the situation will be sufficient. If the school is unwilling or unable to stop serious problems like these, parents should not hesitate to threaten or follow through with actions such as contacting the central school administration or the police. Contacting the parents of the students responsible for such problems also is effective in most cases, since the parents usually are not aware of their children's behavior and usually will disapprove of it and try to stop it.

In general, it is a good idea to let children work out disagreements among themselves on their own (although with discussion and suggestions from parents), but parents will have to get involved in situations like these that the children cannot reasonably be expected to solve. Juvenile delinquents must learn that they cannot get away with unacceptable behavior, and their victims must know that they can rely on their parents and on school officials to help in situations that they cannot handle themselves, if they are expected to help solve such problems rather than reinforce them through passive submission.

OTHER SOCIETAL INSTITUTIONS

Parents have access to a great variety of societal institutions (formal and informal organizations) that can be sources of enjoyment and useful experiences for their children. They can take advantage of these resources by arranging for their children to participate in the activities of these organizations, along the lines of their interests. Such organizations need to be *supported*, not simply used. Parents must be prepared to do their part by volunteering as group leaders, drivers for trips, coaches, Sunday school teachers, or other adult roles.

A special source of mutual satisfaction is doing things together, such as playing some sport or activity. As children reach ages eight or nine, they begin to be able to participate meaningfully with adults in common activities, and this ability increases from then on. Where parents and children share interests, participating together in activities related to these interests is one good way for them to spend time together and solidify their relationships.

Like teachers, adults who work with children in various institutional settings can be important sources of information and assistance to parents. Group leaders, coaches, and other adults may be able to provide parents with important information. Furthermore, where they have become objects of hero worship or identification, they can do much to encourage desirable development in the children. Much of this will go on anyway, but good relationships between such individuals and the children's parents can result in sharing of

494

information that will help the adults to make the best use of their opportunities to have positive influences on the children.

The potential importance of such adults in a child's life is magnified when one of the parents is absent from the home and the child develops a close relationship with some other adult who is of the same sex as the missing parent. While such adults cannot and should not try to be parent substitutes in a total sense, they can provide important experiences for children who are not getting similar experiences at home because one of their parents is missing. Where situations like this exist, the parent should make sure to see that the adult is informed, both to insure that the adult knows the situation and is aware of the special place that he or she has in the child's scheme of things, and so that friendly communication with the parent is established in case opportunities to share important information should come up.

THE FAMILY Despite all the development that takes place in childhood, and despite the increasing importance of peers and other influences outside of the home, the primary and overwhelming importance of the family is the "bottom line" to the story of personality and social development, at least in childhood. A partial listing of some of the personal characteristics that typically are initiated and maintained through familial experiences was given in the previous chapter. This list, along with the information present so far in the book as a whole, indicates the depth and breadth of familial influences on the developing child. Most fundamentally, the family is the basis for the child's identity and security, even in homes where the child is neglected or rejected. Except in unusual situations, children need to identify with their parents as a way to provide identity and self-definition and to provide the security necessary to deal with strangers and cope with the world generally. Rejected children usually end up rejecting their parents later when they become mature enough to strike out on their own, but during the concrete operational years, most of them remain dependent upon their parents.

Parents also are the main sources of the child's values. If they present values in authoritarian ways, the values will tend to be rigidly and perhaps permanently introjected at an unconscious level rather than carefully considered at a conscious level. The ultimate result may be defensive or immoral behavior, because values which remain at the level of unconscious introjection usually are expressed purely verbally and do not actually govern behavior. They may produce guilt if not repressed, but they are not the same as consciously adopted values which are used as moral codes which guide one's life. In middle childhood it still is possible for parents to "succeed" with authoritarian methods. This "success" is short lived and illusory, however, because the children are almost certain to react negatively later.

Because children still are adult dependent and parents still are the primary authority figures in their lives, parents remain the most important influences on the child and continue to be the individuals with the best chances of changing the child for good or ill. Parents who establish and maintain optimal relationships with their children can expect their children to continue to develop along positive lines and to work out lives that are appropriate and satisfactory for them, although they may not necessarily be what the parents would have preferred. On the other hand, parents who neglect their children or treat them in arbitrary and authoritarian ways can expect to see them become unhappy and resentful, and ultimately blame them (largely correctly). It never is too late to change, however, so that parents who do become aware of unfortunate behavior on their part probably can repair most if not all of the damage done if they make an honest effort to do so and get whatever help may be necessary.

As the child nears adolescence and begins to assimilate schemas into increasingly stable and interrelated patterns, dependence upon the parents for identification and security becomes greatly diminished. Since the children are moving from repetition of introjected values to serious thought about moral issues and about themselves and others, the opportunities for parents to have important and permanent effects upon children remain high during these years. This assumes, though, that parents have established and maintained good relationships and continuing communication with the children. If they have, they can help children fill some of the gaps in their general knowledge about themselves and other people, and they can help smooth the adjustment problems that come with the transition from childhood innocence to adolescent turmoil and confusion.

ASSIMILATION OF SOCIAL AND PERSONAL SCHEMAS

In fact, despite common assumptions about generation gaps and adolescent rejection of parents, parents who have established good relationships with their children are likely to continue them permanently, and to remain important figures in their children's lives throughout adolescence and beyond. Their role gradually shifts from one of being a largely unquestioned authority figure to one of being a sounding board and friend. Parents no longer will be treated as if they possessed special knowledge or wisdom, like they were treated when the children were younger, so that their opinions will be treated as opinions rather than taken as facts. However, where good relationships have been established, children will be predisposed to give careful consideration to what their parents think, for the very good reason that their parents have shown themselves to be reasonable, thoughtful, and helpful in the past. On the other hand, if parents have not shown these qualities, children who begin to think for themselves will be unlikely to seek parental opinions about *anything*, and likely to reject the opinions that they get without asking.

In this section, and in the book as a whole, I have stressed strongly the important and primary roles that parents typically play in shaping the development of their children in almost every aspect of life. However, I want to make it clear that I am *not* suggesting any automatic determinism here. The nature and strengths of socialization effects that parents have on a given child *cannot* be predicted in advance.

DISCLAIMERS

They could be predicted to a large degree if the fact that a child would be biologically normal, the fact that the parents both would live long enough to see the child through at least early adulthood, and the precise nature of parental attitudes, values, beliefs, and child-rearing practices could be known *in advance*. Even here, however, there would be numerous exceptions to the general rule of accurate prediction.

First, there always is the possibility of accidents or tragedies befalling the child which have permanent effects upon subsequent development. Second, peer influences and other influences outside the home are only partially controllable by parents, and it is possible for children to go wrong in one way or another even when parents did everything that could reasonably be expected of them. Another difficulty with making predictions is that conditions change. Things that were effective or appropriate at one time become out-dated and even dysfunctional later. In an age in which time has speeded up in breath-taking fashion, parents routinely are confronted with problems that no one *ever* was confronted with before. Other complicating factors could be discussed, too, but the point here already should be clear: no one can guarantee to parents that their children will turn out in certain ways if the parents behave in certain ways.

A related point is that, while it may be true in most cases that the parents are more responsible than anyone else for the ways that their children turn out, there is no point in *blaming* parents for past problems. Blaming parents, whether they deserve it or not, is as pointless as trying to socialize children by merely punishing them rather than showing them how to act. It will produce hostility, resentment, or guilt, but it will not do anything to change behavior in desirable directions. In short, parents who are not doing a good job need *help*, not criticism. Furthermore, unless there is direct evidence to the contrary, it should be assumed that parents are trying their best, and that whatever errors that they make are due to ignorance or poor judgment rather than apathy or evil intentions.

Part of the reason for adopting this attitude is the same self-fulfilling prophecy effect mentioned in connection with children: if you treat parents as if they are well-intentioned people trying to do their best, you maximize the probability that they will fulfill this expectation. Investigations of unsuccessful parents, including even most parents guilty of child abuse, have shown such parents to be overwhelmed by a combination of ignorance and frustrations, rather than to be malicious or sadistic individuals who behaved as they did because they wanted to. Most realized that they were not doing what they should have been doing, but they did not know how to break the cycle of unfortunate behavior in which they had become entangled. This should be kept in mind by anyone who becomes involved with parents of disturbed children. Unfortunately, it is far too common for people to limit their involvement to blame and castigation, rather than providing more positive and useful help.

SUMMARY

For the most part, adult behavior important for fostering social and personal development during the concrete operational years is similar to that important for fostering moral development in general personal adjustment, as discussed in Chapter Twelve. In addition, the present chapter focused on how the widening social sphere of children will bring parents into contact with peers, parents of peers, the school, and other people and institutions that their children deal with, and these contacts will involve both opportunities and frustrations for the parents. It was stressed that conflicts arising from these situations are likely to be resolved most successfully if the parents enforce and explain limits where they feel the need to do so, but avoid unnecessary criticism of peers or the parents of peers in the process. It also was noted that problems within peer groups are most likely to be solved easily if the parents involved are in close and continuing communication with one another, sharing information and acting cooperatively for the common good.

Parents can promote the development of independence and responsibility by allowing children as much autonomy as they can handle successfully and by allowing them to make decisions and have input about such matters as money and how it is spent, clothing styles, and leisure time activities. As children become more mature and responsible and begin to act more like adults, they should be treated correspondingly. This includes such matters as respecting privacy and showing respect as well as expecting them to assume heavier responsibilities for household management and other family tasks.

The payoff to the kinds of child-rearing strategies discussed throughout the book becomes more obvious as children near adolescence, when they begin to test limits more often and more intensively and when obedience based upon fear or threat of punishment gives way to sneakiness or defiance. Parents who have maintained close and open relationships with their children can continue to maintain such relationships, and their children are more likely to listen to and respect their opinions about acceptable and unacceptable behavior. Furthermore, their children are more likely to become the popular and leadership-oriented children in the neighborhood, meaning that they are more likely to be the opinion setters and leaders rather than the followers in the peer group. This also will minimize the frequency of conflict between parental values and ideas picked up from peers, compared to families where the children are actively rebelling against their parents.

Age roles, sex roles, and birth order continue to have effects throughout childhood, mostly irritating effects caused by ritualistic behavior connected with sex roles or squabbling connected with age roles. Unless it is really serious, this kind of posturing is usually best treated by ignoring it. If comments are made, they should imply that these topics are unimportant or even silly, so that children's tendencies to see them as important will not be reinforced.

497

Throughout these years, children will need information and guidance about aspects of social and personal development. In addition to value conflicts resulting from exposure to peers and other influences outside of the family, this includes information about sex differences and sexual behavior, about the reasons for and implications of broken homes, and about how to deal with disturbed individuals encountered in the neighborhood or at school.

Parents should make a point of getting to know the parents of the friends of their children, exchanging information and cooperating in solving problems. The same is true with regard to getting to know the children's teachers and any adults in organizations that children belong to. Parents should get to know these individuals and pass along any information that is important for them to know, and they should be prepared to help out by volunteering to help the teacher or school or the child organization to the extent that they are able to do so.

The chapter closed with several disclaimers. Special efforts were made to call attention to these in order to repeat once again that the suggestions given in this book, although based on data, are probabilistic ones. Most parents who follow them will get good results, but humans are too complex for anything to happen automatically or with certainty, especially anything as complex as human development over a large number of years. This is why the quality of the parent-child relationship has been stressed consistently as more important than the use of any particular technique or method, and why it has been stated repeatedly that it is never too late to change the course of development, even though it may get more difficult with age. It is important for all of us to resist the desire for quick and easy solutions and to persist with difficult and time consuming, but ultimately more effective, attempts to optimize the environment of every developing child.

ANNOTATED BIBLIOGRAPHY, PART FOUR

Freud, Anna. *The ego and the mechanisms of defense.* New York: International Universities Press, 1946.

This volume, written by Sigmund Freud's daughter Anna, was the first comprehensive treatment of defense mechanisms in a single volume, and it stands today as a classic in the field. Although it contains numerous references to aspects of psychoanalytic theory which have been long since discarded, it still is worth reading for its historical value in helping give perspective on how knowledge about defense mechanisms developed and what kinds of cases were used as examples.

Havighurst, Robert. *Developmental tasks and education.* New York: Longmans Green, 1952.

This volume presents Havighurst's concept of developmental tasks in detail, and discusses their implications for education. The latter makes the volume particularly interesting for teachers, although it is of value for anyone interested in a stage approach to child development. A weakness of the concept is that the stages often are limited in generalization to western industrial cultures within the Judeo-Christian tradition, but this provides strength at the same time, because the stages are defined externally according to cultural demands as they relate to age, and not internally according to poorly understood genetic or maturational mechanisms.

Lickona, Thomas (Ed.). *Morality: A handbook of moral behavior.* New York: Holt, Rinehart and Winston, 1975.

This handbook brings together in one volume contributions from some of the major writers on topics relating to moral development and moral behavior. The value of each individual piece is enhanced by the opportunity to compare and contrast it with contributions by others who write from different points of view.

Redl, Fritz, and Wineman, David. *Children who hate: The disorganization and breakdown of behavior controls.* New York: Free Press, 1951 (paperback).

This book is based on the authors' experience with a group of extremely disturbed and mostly delinquent boys. It outlines in detail and gives good examples of a variety of defense mechanisms used by such individuals in order to rationalize away or otherwise avoid taking responsibility for their own behavior or for changing it. It is an excellent portrayal of the thinking and behavior of individuals who grow up in the kinds of environments least favorable to the development of moral judgment and moral behavior, and provides a nice contrast to writings on the defense mechanisms used by more conventional but neurotic people who suffer internal conflicts but usually keep their interpersonal behavior under control.

TERKEL, STUDS. *Working.* New York: Pantheon, 1973 (paperback).

This volume should be mandatory reading for anyone who has grown up in a segregated suburban middle class environment and knows little or nothing about lower class life, especially as it exists in the slums and ghettos of our large cities. It also is important reading for anyone who doubts the validity of the concepts of socio-economic status or social class. This is so even though the book is not a sociological text or even a formal treatment of the subject. Instead, it is a series of interviews conducted by Terkel with a variety of people, a format that he has used successfully with a number of popular books. In this book the focus is on working, so that in each case people talk about their jobs, what the jobs mean to them, and how the jobs affect their lives and life styles. These interviews are fascinating to read in any case, which is why the book is so popular. For present purposes they also provide unusually clear insights into social structure, social class, occupations and education, and related topics.

PART FIVE

ADOLESCENCE

CHAPTER FIFTEEN

Adolescent Development

Development continues throughout life. However, this book will end with a consideration of development during the adolescent years, primarily because the socialization roles of parents are reduced drastically once their children emerge from adolescence as young adults. Readers interested in pursuing the topic can do so as several excellent books on adult development and aging already are available, and the topic of life span developmental psychology presently is very active. Several stage theorists, notably Erikson (1963) and Havighurst (1953), have discussed developmental stages or tasks important to adjustment in adult life, and much information is available about the influences of such factors as higher education, social class and reference groups, marriage and parenthood, occupational status and success, physical health, and numerous other factors that affect adjustment in the adult years (Bischof, 1976).

OVERVIEW AND GENERAL CONSIDERATIONS

Defining the adolescent years is not easy, particularly in our society. Smaller and simpler societies often have informal but widely recognized or even formal ceremonies or "rites of passage" to mark the transition from childhood to adolescence or from adolescence to adulthood. Some even make a direct transition from childhood to adulthood, not recognizing adolescence as an intervening stage. Many of these rites of passage are far from appealing. They may involve proving oneself by living alone in the wilderness for a long period of time, or by submitting to painful ordeals, sometimes exotic ones such as scarification of the sex organs (Young, 1965). However, societies with these formalized or at least generally recognized rites of passage into adulthood do save their youths from most of the confusion and frustration of attempting to "find themselves."

In contrast, complex industrial societies, especially the United States, have no formal rites of passage, either from childhood to adolescence or from adolescence to adulthood. Furthermore, we do not even have generally recognized informal ones. Instead, we have a large number of different and often conflicting criteria. States differ in their laws concerning the age at which one can quit school, drive a car, vote, buy liquor, get married without parental permission, work full time, and so forth.

In addition to these legal considerations, there are numerous informal methods of determining whether or not an individual is considered an adolescent vs. a child or an adult vs. an adolescent. These include such things as graduation from school, being finished with school and fully employed vs. still in school and partially employed, being independent of one's parents, being married, having children, and being financially independent. Expectations and norms in different geographical areas and social class levels vary drastically. In some segments of society, youths of 15 or 16 are expected to get married and to become self-sufficient, and they are treated as adults if they meet these expectations.

In other segments of society, youths who did this would be considered irresponsible or at least abnormal, even if they succeeded in becoming self-sufficient. Here, youths are expected to attend and graduate from college (at the very minimum) before entering a full-time occupation, and are not expected to marry or have children until this time (unless they are among the relatively few who can afford it). These individuals, although highly intelligent and educated, may be treated as adolescents by their parents and other adults until they are 24 or 25 years old.

The key concept here probably is *role*. Societies which are relatively static and closed have a limited number of rather specific and binding roles, and children are socialized toward fulfillment of one of these roles practically from birth. This eliminates much of the searching for identity and creation of an acceptable role in society that goes on in our country and in similar ones, but at the same time it tends to "lock in" youths to the roles carved out for them by their societies and forced upon them whether they want them or not. In contrast, the United States, with its cultural diversity and geographical size and mobility, offers most youths a staggering array of choices and possibilities concerning occupational and other adult roles. Certain families and certain segments of society channel their children toward specific roles and away from other ones, but the degree of pressure and specificity is nowhere near that found in simpler and more static societies.

In many other cases, perhaps a majority, children and youths get relatively little specific socialization regarding adult roles, although they may get socialization concerning the general kinds of expectations that their parents hold for them (attend school and graduate with at least a minimum degree or certificate; take a certain kind of job paying a certain amount of money at minimum; marry and have children; and so forth). The process of sorting through all of the possibilities open to an individual and arriving at a feasible and satisfying set of roles is time consuming and difficult. The industrialization and complexity of our society, and the higher education that comes with it, have acted to prolong adolescence as well as to blur the distinctions between childhood and adolescence and between adolescence and adulthood.

This probably is good to some degree, because it allows adolescents more of the time they need for exploration and self-discovery. On the other hand, these years involve much confusion and frustration, as adolescents try out (and frequently fail at or have unfortunate experiences in) various roles and activities.

It is difficult to generalize about adolescents, because children become more and more differentiated and unique with age. By adolescence, and especially after the major part of the adolescent growth spurt and the adolescent search for identity have passed, individuals have fewer and fewer common traits which allow discussion of them as a group. In many ways, it makes more sense to discuss them as individuals and as young adults. Because of these complexities, the following section on adolescence will *assume* that the kinds of child rearing discussed in previous sections of the book have been followed reasonably well. The adolescent chapters will focus on psychologically *normal* individuals. Those who are seriously disturbed, such as psychotics or criminals, will not be discussed in any detail. Readers interested in these abnormal populations should consult sources devoted to them specifically.

Adolescence typically is thought of as a time of turmoil in our society, and it usually is, to some degree (however, this is not true in all societies). Much of the reason for this is the fluidity and openness of society, which presents adolescents with opportunities but also choices, usually too many choices for them to make smoothly or easily. Adolescence is a time of change in many areas of life, and these changes come in rapid succession. The result is that the period of relatively carefree stability that most children develop during middle childhood breaks down, and the adolescent enters a period of intense self-preoccupation and search for identity. Physical, cognitive, and social milieu changes occur all at once. Individually, and especially in combination, these changes allow adolescents to see and do things that they could not see and do before, but they also force them to come to grips with new challenges and problems.

Physical changes in the body which occur at maturation introduce sexuality as a new and important aspect of living. The development of secondary sexual characteristics and the growth spurt that occurs at adolescence introduce many new physical features which act both as sources of pride and satisfaction and as problems requiring adjustment. Cognitive development, particularly the attainment of what Piaget calls formal operations, allows adolescents to deal with abstract concepts in areas like mathematics, logic, and moral and political philosophy. These new abilities also allow adolescents to see some of the contradictions and falsehoods embedded in their previously accepted beliefs and attitudes. Consequently, they are forced to reassess these beliefs and attitudes.

The combination of cognitive development and increased and continued development of independence from the parents eventually enables adolescents to begin to question the values and attitudes that previously were introjected through parental socialization. Sometimes, this causes adolescents to consciously adopt the same beliefs and attitudes that previously were introjected and verbalized but without genuine understanding. It often results in a rejection of these beliefs and attitudes and in a search for a different set that is more acceptable. This produces a degree of conflict with parents and other authority figures, as well as a period of confusion and searching for guidance.

The combination of new intellectual abilities with continued movement toward independence from the parents also means that adolescents are exposed to more and more individuals and reference groups who provide different and often conflicting items of information and directions of influence. Much time is spent trying to sort through personal beliefs, parental beliefs, religious teachings, social mores and ideals, and the specific opinions and influences of peers and individuals influential in the youth culture. Ultimately, adolescents must resolve these conflicts and arrive at an internally consistent and satisfying set of beliefs, attitudes, expectations, and behaviors. This multi-faceted process usually is referred to as the "adolescent identity crisis," a term popularized by the writings of Erikson (1968).

Adolescence also is a time when parents "lose" their children. This happens in a physical way as children develop into adolescence and beyond. During adolescence it also happens in a psychological way. Due to the factors of development and new input mentioned previously, adolescents become more and more independent of parental control and direct influence. In fact, unless they are willing to resort to extreme and unfortunate measures, parents no longer can *control* adolescents in any real sense. At best, they have a "jawboning" influence based upon respect and accumulated good will.

This influence can be quite strong where a good relationship exists and communication lines are open, although there still will be a subtle difference between parents as respected sources of information and guidance vs. parents as authority figures with final say and control. Parents who have not developed this kind of relationship will "lose" their adolescents quite literally. That is, once the adolescents are old enough to defy the parents and get away with it, the parents no longer will be able to exercise much control over them, other than to throw them out of the house.

In addition to losing control, parents also lose the ability to "do for" their children. When young children have problems with peers, parents often can solve the problem for them by taking some action such as removing their children from the distressing situation or dealing with the peers and/or the peers' parents in order to solve the problem. Usually, of course, it is best if the children are allowed to solve such problems themselves to the extent that they are able, but sometimes they do require adult help. In many cases, the adults can solve the problem completely on their own if they are disposed to do so. This ability is diminished and eventually lost as children move into adolescence.

Parental attempts to solve adolescent problems with peers (other than discussion of the problem with their offspring at home when the peers are not present) usually will only compound the problems. Independence of parental dominance also means loss of parental protection and leadership; for the most part, adolescents must solve their own problems on their own. They will be better equipped and generally more successful at doing so, of course, if parents have helped them all along to develop qualities such as independence and leadership, self-esteem and self-confidence, and the habit of carefully considering the consequences of actions before undertaking them.

Although it seems paradoxical at first, parents whose children psychologically "leave them" the earliest will be the most successful in coping with adolescent problems (assuming, of course, the adolescents have the qualities just mentioned and are not "leaving" the parents because of rejection and hostility). In contrast, parents who have maximized their children's dependency upon them for guidance will "hold onto" their children longer, but their children probably will have more difficulties and will take more time in working through the adjustment problems that come with adolescence.

PHYSICAL DEVELOPMENT

Physically, adolescence begins when the primary sex organs mature. Associated with this event are the development of the secondary sexual characteristics and the sudden increase in rate of growth known as the adolescent growth spurt. Measures of height, weight, bone growth, and other aspects of physical development show a decrease in relative gain per year throughout childhood, but growth accelerates for several years during the adolescent growth spurt. Once the adolescent growth terminates, the individual is a physically mature adult who will not experience additional physical growth of any consequence. This physical maturity may be achieved at ages as young as 15 or 16 in some individuals, but in others it may continue until the mid or even late 20s.

All of this is totally under genetic control, for all practical purposes. Diet, exercise, and other factors will affect general appearance, particularly muscle development and degree of excess fat. Diet, exercise, or body building attempts will not significantly affect the rates or ultimate forms of development. At present, there is no known way to slow down or speed up development, or to minimize or maximize it. Individual adolescents will have to adjust to changes in their bodies *as they emerge*. Parents and socialization sources can help, of course, by providing information and reassurance where necessary.

Much of the growth during adolescence is in the long bones of the arms and legs. This means that the individual becomes taller and thinner (and usually somewhat gawky and ill-coordinated) for a time. Problems are exaggerated

Nature and Nurture in Physical Growth

Nature and nurture interact to produce phenotypes in any human characteristic, but they seem to be easier to see and discuss in areas relating to physical development and physical growth. In a review of these topics, Tanner (1970) identifies several ways in which the environment can interact with genes to influence the course and ultimate forms of growth. This review and others like it make it very clear that even something seemingly simple like physical growth is extremely complex genetically, and much more complex still when the interaction of genetics with environment is considered.

Genetic control of the growth rate is largely independent of genetic controls relating to the ultimate size that individuals attain, and also largely independent of the genetic mechanisms involved in producing the ultimate physical shape of the body. Furthermore, each of these lines of genetic determination is affected by environmental influences. Environmental influences are often temporary and very specific to a particular aspect of growth. For example, changes in the rate of growth produced by environmental stimulation will not necessarily affect the general bodily shape or physique at physical maturity. Growth and maturation rates are known to be affected by such environmental conditions as climate and temperature, nutrition, disease, and even psychological disturbances.

Over the last hundred years or so, geneticists have observed what they call the "secular trend." This has been a worldwide tendency for children to develop into taller individual adults than their parents. It appears to be related primarily to nutrition and health factors, because it has been observed in close relationships with the modernization of countries and cultures, and in particular the establishment of good nutrition and medical care throughout a community or nation. In general, people are taller and heavier today than they used to be in the past, and there are cross-national differences in height and general bodily build related to better nutrition and medicine.

A similar secular trend, believed due to similar reasons, has been noted for females' age at menarche. Menarche refers to the onset of menstruation, and thus the start of physical maturation in girls. A century ago, girls began menstruating at about age 16. This average age has dropped steadily through the present time, so that modern girls reach menarche at about age 12 on the average, and a great many begin three or four years earlier.

when the growth spurt is rapid (some individuals grow six inches in a few months), but adjustment problems occur to some degree for almost all adolescents. Much of the apparent gawkiness and lack of coordination of adolescents is due to continued reliance on overlearned sensorimotor schemas which now need to accommodate to new situations. A popular cigarette commercial for a company that produces an extra long cigarette shows funny situations that result in the cigarette being broken at the end because the smoker is used to a shorter cigarette. This is analogous to what happens to adolescents who experience rapid growth. It is not so much that they lack coordination, as that they have not yet adjusted to their new heights, new arm lengths, new leg lengths, and so forth.

Usually, these adjustments are made without any great physical or emotional difficulty, although a few adolescents who become self-conscious about their bodies because of this factor may need some reassurance. Girls in particular are more likely to become concerned about growing too tall. Parents of girls who are headed for taller than average status should help prepare them through a combination of realistic information and the building of positive expectations and self-concepts, rather than allow the girls to develop the idea that being tall is an unfortunate handicap.

The reverse is usually required with boys, who typically are happy to find themselves growing taller but upset to find that they are not developing as early or as much as their friends are. Adjusting is not a problem for boys with good self-esteem and realistic information and expectations. Boys who are heavily invested in athletics, particularly in sports which place a premium on size and strength, may need some realistic guidance in readjusting their expectations if it becomes clear that they are not going to attain stature that stardom in the sport requires.

Related to the question of rate and ultimate form of development is the question of onset of the adolescent growth spurt. Again, the consequences differ by sex. Social adjustment problems usually are greatest for girls who mature very young and for boys who are very late. Such girls will need guidance concerning adjustment to their new status and to the problem of being among the first to mature, while such boys will need continued reassurance that there is nothing wrong with them because they mature later than other boys. The boys might find it reassuring to know that, on the average, very early maturers have a shorter growth spurt and tend to end up somewhat shorter and smaller than later maturers do. The later maturers not only start later, but they tend to continue to grow for a longer time, eventually surpassing the early maturers who towered over them when they were 13 or 14 (Tanner, 1970).

The onset of adolescent maturation is controlled genetically, and the ultimate form of development for any individual is not open to much change. Consequently, it is important for all individuals, regardless of sex, size, early vs. later maturation, or anything else, to develop both realistic and positive self-concepts concerning their bodies and physical capabilities. Those blessed with desirable features should learn to make the best use of them (but not to become too heavily invested in them, because physical factors are far more important at adolescence than later on), while those who are less blessed should be helped to accept the realities of the situation and to adjust by scaling their expectations for physical activities to realistic proportions based upon their physical development. They also should be reassured that everyone has a unique pattern of strengths and weaknesses, so that the fact that they were not blessed physically does not mean that they are inferior to others.

The area of physical development provides many examples of the point made earlier that parents can only help their adolescents respond to adjustment problems; they cannot solve the problems for them. Adolescents who develop prominent physical features are likely to be called nicknames based on those features, mostly ones that they dislike (such as "Shorty," or "Jughead"). Parental attempts to keep their adolescents away from peers who use these nicknames, or to try to get the peers to stop using them, are virtually certain to result in increased use of the nicknames. These things cannot be escaped; adolescents must learn to accept and adjust to them with as much good humor as they can muster.

Another important area of physical changes that requires knowledge and adjustment by adolescents is the development of secondary sexual characteristics. In addition to the development of the sex organs, boys develop bodily hair on most parts of the body and must begin shaving, and adolescent maturation brings about the development of strength and muscular patterns associated with adult males. With girls, the development of secondary sexual characteristics is even more obvious than the development of primary sexual characteristics, since the development of the ovaries and related structures occurs inside the body. Along with this primary sex organ development comes the development of the breasts and of the general bodily form associated with adult females, as well as menstrual periods and the hormonal (and sometimes physical and emotional) reactions which accompany them.

Adolescents of both sexes need information about the development of primary and secondary sexual characteristics in both sexes. In particular, they need realistic expectations about what will happen to them, so that they can look forward to these changes positively and adapt to them smoothly. If this is handled properly, boys will look forward to the day that they purchase a jock strap or begin shaving, and girls will look forward to wearing bras and other undergarments associated with adult females. When properly informed, girls also will accept and perhaps even look forward to menstrual periods, because of the role that menstruation and the related hormonal changes within their bodies play in initiating and maintaining the development of feminine physical and physiological characteristics.

Both sexes undergo voice changes, although these usually are more pronounced for boys than girls. Most adolescents know about this and take it in stride, although a few who are ignorant about what is happening will need information, and a few who have been involved in singing activities may have to be prepared for the possibility that they no longer may have good singing voices. Adults can expect notable changes in the eating habits of adolescents of both sexes, particularly during growth spurts and among adolescents who are physically active. The combination of rapid growth and heavy physical activity that frequently exists among adolescents produces a huge increase in appetite, which in turn is based upon a genuine increase in nutritional needs. An adolescent who formerly would not finish a single hamburger at supper might want to eat two or even three or four, and many adolescents switch from drinking milk by the glass to drinking it by the quart. Although there obviously is a borderline between heavy nutritional needs and stuffing oneself, many adolescents will want to, and should, eat perhaps twice as much as adults do. This may be appropriate for a time (assuming a balanced diet, of course).

The aspect of adolescent development which probably is the most important but least talked about is the development of primary sexual characteristics or sex organs. In boys, this includes the regular production of sperm by the testes (which are present but usually not active in producing sperm earlier), the development of the penis, and the appearance of pubic hair in the genital area. In girls, this means development of active ovaries which begin to produce eggs, resulting in a mature reproductive system enabling the girl to become pregnant and bear children, as well as a changed hormonal balance, making her more interested in and receptive to sexual experiences.

Adolescents of both sexes will find themselves becoming sexually aroused in the same sense that adults do (as opposed to the more general bodily arousal associated with childhood sexuality), and many will follow up on such arousal with masturbation or other sexual activity, including copulation. Needless to say, the bodily changes involved are inevitable realities which require knowledge and adjustment, and parents and other socialization sources must provide solid knowledge if smooth adjustment is to be expected.

COGNITIVE DEVELOPMENT

As far as is known, the important cognitive developments that occur during adolescence have nothing to do with the physical developments that occur at about the same time. The cognitive developments apparently result from the attainment of at least a minimal degree of schemas which have been developed to the point of overlearning at the concrete operational level and have been assimilated to one another to form a higher, hierarchically organized and internally consistent, cognitive structure. Like other stage phenomena, this transition does not occur overnight, nor does it occur concurrently in different knowledge and skill areas. It will occur earlier for areas which the individual is most familiar with and skilled in, and later or not at all for areas with which the individual is less familiar or is unfamiliar.

Different writers use different terms when discussing adolescent changes in intellectual abilities, but they tend to reduce to essentially the same thing. Piaget (Flavell, 1963) speaks of the transition from concrete operations to formal operations. Although much is involved in this transformation, the hallmark is the development of the ability to think in symbolic terms and comprehend content meaningfully without the benefit of concrete objects or even visual or other imagery which would enable the individual to deal with the material in a concrete way. Formal operations refer to the logical and mathematical concepts and rules of inference that mature individuals use to conceptualize and discuss abstract content which is difficult or impossible to represent concretely. Included here are the content and mental operations involved in comprehending abstract philosophy and logic, abstract mathematics, and other principles and concepts which are mostly or entirely abstract and which can be addressed only through verbal and conceptual means.

In Piagetian terms, the development of formal operational thought means that the individual understands for the first time the meanings of many words (verbal schemas) that were used but not understood previously. Many of these are introduced for the first time at adolescence, particularly concepts associated with philosophy and mathematics. Many are familiar words that simply were not understood before. Consider the National Anthem, the Pledge of Allegiance, or the Ten Commandments. Most children learn these by heart, or at least know something about them, but they do not truly understand what the words mean until they attain formal operational thought.

Piagetian theory implies that once formal operations are acquired as generalized schemas, it is possible, at least theoretically, for an individual to master all existing knowledge. In practice, of course, this is not possible. For example, a developmental psychologist would do well to master all of the important knowledge in this relatively specialized field. Psychology has become so diversified that no single individual could master all of the important knowledge in all of its branches today, and certainly no one could master all of the important knowledge in all of the various sciences. In practice, even highly educated individuals with well-developed formal operations tend to use them only in certain areas (those with which they are most familiar due to occupational necessity or individual interest).

Like any other schemas, formal operations follow the general laws of learning as described by Ferguson (1954; 1956). If not mastered to the point of overlearning, they are likely to be forgotten. If mastered to the point of overlearning, they not only are likely to be retained, but they are likely to be generalized to new situations and used when relevant for solving new problems. For individuals who master them and use them regularly, they can become generalized information processing devices much like the "learning to learn" schemas used by younger children. Such individuals can and do use symbolic abstractions and inferential deduction and induction in approaching problems, both new and old. Whereas children formerly might have solved difficult arithmetic word problems successfully but laboriously through a variety of concrete operational schemas, they can translate these word problems into simple algebraic problems and solve them in a few seconds if they have mastered algebraic symbols and rules. The problem and the ultimate answer arrived at are the same, but the developmental level and degree of efficiency with which the problem is approached and solved are different.

Piaget would speak of such individuals as using formal operations, and people using less technical terms would say that these individuals were very abstract in their thinking processes and able to deal with abstract information successfully. Jensen (1970) would say that they had attained and developed highly their Level II information processing skills, so that they could solve problems with peak efficiency (and also solve a greater number of problems), compared to individuals limited to Level I skills. Regardless of the language used, the key difference is the ability to conceptualize complex and abstract material without having to rely on concrete props.

This is the difference between a person who can follow a trouble shooting guide in repairing a television set or automobile, but is stumped by a problem not included in the guide, vs. a person who can conceptualize the workings of a television set or automobile in abstract terms, identify the point in the sequential chain of events at which the problem occurs, and generate hypotheses as to the nature of the problem and its solution. Certain formal operational schemas, particularly the fundamentals of logic and mathematics, appear to be especially significant because they are universal (they are true whenever they apply to a situation) and because they generalize to many situations.

Mastery of these schemas to the point of overlearning and functional ability to use them in situations where they would be maximizing the efficiency of information processing and problem solving corresponds roughly to the development of highly advanced intellectual abilities as discussed and measured by writers rooted in the psychometric tradition. Individuals who get extremely high scores on intelligence tests, particularly the kinds of abstract tests that Jensen refers to as "Level II" tests, tend to have these kinds of schemas developed to this level of functional usefulness. Such people usually have highly developed behavioral (sensorimotor), cognitive (perceptual, logical, mathematical), and verbal schemas as well. In addition, they have assimilated their schemas into unusually consistent and well-organized systems which function very efficiently. The major exception to this assimilation, and the major reason why high intelligence does not necessarily guarantee high morality or good mental adjustment, is the blocking of assimilation by defense mechanisms, particularly repression. The adult's cognitive structure can be represented by the following figure. Assuming that the individual is reasonably well-adjusted, most material retained in long-term memory will be accessible to conscious awareness. In addition to this immediately accessible and usable material, there will be a smaller amount stored in short-term memory which may or may not "stay with" the person. That which stays will be retained in long-term memory; the rest will be forgotten.

Another area includes material which exists in memory but is not open to conscious awareness because it is systematically and continuously excluded through repression and other defense mechanisms. Because much assimilation of different schemas occurs during the process of actively thinking about things, repressed material not only remains out of conscious awareness, but usually also remains relatively isolated, not assimilated to the rest of the individual's cognitive structure. This is only one of many ways in which the cognitive developments that occur at adolescence interact with social and personal developments.

Schematic cognitive structures of adults with good and poor reality contact.

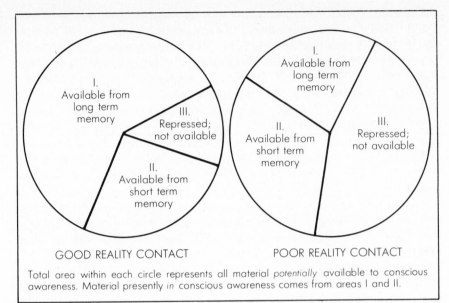

I.
Available from
long term
memory

III.
Repressed;
not available

II.
Available from
short term
memory

I.
Available from
long term
memory

II.
Available from
short term
memory

III.
Repressed;
not available

GOOD REALITY CONTACT

POOR REALITY CONTACT

Total area within each circle represents all material *potentially* available to conscious awareness. Material presently *in* conscious awareness comes from areas I and II.

COGNITION AND PERSONALITY   As mentioned earlier, to the degree that individuals develop formal operations, they develop the ability to comprehend the more abstract aspects of material. This means that certain familiar material learned only at a verbal level will be understood conceptually for the first time. These cognitive developments provide the basis for the questioning and testing of authority figures and traditions that is so typical of adolescents. Throughout childhood, children learn and repeat the value systems they are taught by their parents, their teachers, their religious instructors, or other socialization agents. Because moral and political philosophical principles tend to be abstract, much of this learning is confined to what Piaget likes to call the "merely verbal" level. Often, there is little or no genuine understanding of the fundamental issues involved.

In Freudian terms, values are *introjected* in childhood. That is, they are learned without much conscious awareness but are repeated regularly in certain contexts. Often the fact that they were learned originally from another source is forgotten, and individuals come to believe that the ideas are their own, if in fact they think about them at all. Such verbal schemas are just that: *verbal.* Unless assimilated to corresponding behavioral schemas, they will not act as guiding principles of morality or politics. This lack of assimilation, along with the operation of defense mechanisms in some cases, is the reason why moral judgment as measured by verbal means does not correlate well with moral behavior as measured by the nature of interpersonal interactions.

The development of formal operations in adolescents enables them to understand certain moral, political, and philosophical ideas and values for the first time. Where this occurs, the result will be serious consideration of the ideas, not just repeated introjection, as in the past. Sometimes, the individuals will conclude that the idea or value is *correct.* This will not change their verbalizations much, but it will lead to assimilation of related verbal, cognitive, and behavioral schemas. Instead of repeating in parrot-like fashion an idea or value introjected long ago, the individual now will be verbalizing an idea or value which has been consciously considered and *adopted.* This is a very important *qualitative difference.* Among other things, values which are consciously adopted are likely to be implemented in behavior and used as general guides for behavior, in contrast to values which never are consciously considered and thus remain at the level of introjection and "merely verbal" learning.

However, conscious consideration of an idea or value by an individual who has developed formal operations also opens up the possibility of recognizing contradictions or other objectionable aspects of the idea or value, with the ultimate result that the individual will *reject* it. When this happens, the previously introjected value will be replaced by a new one. This process could happen in the space of a few seconds or could take years, depending upon the scope of the problem and its importance to the individual. In any case, whether conscious consideration leads to adoption or rejection of previously introjected values, the qualitative aspects of the situation change considerably once such conscious deliberation has taken place. If introjection is replaced by conscious adoption, the result is likely to be a much closer correspondence between preaching and practice. If the result is rejection of the old value and replacement by a new one, the result is likely to be a different kind of preaching, as well as practice that corresponds with this new preaching. If conscious deliberation and value adoption never take place, introjection is likely to continue, but so is the poor correspondence between preaching and practice.

Cognitive development also can lead to rejection of authorities or traditions for a different reason: adolescents consciously consider a value and determine that it is a good one, but at the same time become capable of seeing that the people who preach this value do not practice it themselves. This leads to the development of resentment, the perception of authority figures as hypocritical, and so on. Thus, paradoxically, the development of cognitive abilities that lead to true understanding of value statements for the first time can lead to rejection of authority figures, not only when it leads adolescents to reject previously introjected values, but sometimes also when it leads them to consciously adopt and commit themselves to previously introjected values. Adolescent rejection of authority figures will be discussed in more detail in the later section on personality development.

LANGUAGE DEVELOPMENT   As in middle childhood, language development in adolescence consists mostly of added vocabulary, and it is both stimulated and limited by more fundamental factors of cognitive development, for the most part. Much new vocabulary is learned as individuals are exposed to new concepts and subject matter areas. Many verbal schemas that previously were learned in isolation become assimilated with cognitive and sensorimotor schemas for the first time (the person comes to understand what certain words and phrases *mean* for the first time).

A common misconception about language learning in adolescence and beyond is that it is more difficult at these ages than it is for young children. This idea is widely believed, although there are no data to support it and and some to contradict it. Apparently, it developed because children of immigrants tend to pick up a new language quicker and more completely than their parents. Some took this to mean that children could learn language, and particularly a second language, more easily than adults. The reasons for this commonly observed phenomenon appear to lie in motivation and practice factors rather than ability factors.

Investigations of language learning reveal that, as with learning in other areas, ability is the most important single variable. When motivation and opportunity to learn are equalized, adults generally learn quicker than children. To the extent that it is true that adults who move to a new country do not pick up the language as easily or quickly as their children do, the reasons lie in lack of desire and/or in the fact that they continue to converse with each other in the old language and thus get less practice in using the new one, compared with the children, and not in any age-related reduction in language learning ability (Cazden, 1972).

PERSONALITY DEVELOPMENT

Whereas middle childhood is a time of relative stability in personality development, adolescence is a time of upheaval and change. Much of this is in response to and/or because of the physical and cognitive changes already discussed, although there also are changes in peers, reference groups, and other social and personal influences. The previously notable stability in personality and self-concept gives way as reflection and new experiences lead to the questioning of previously accepted roles and values and the exploration of new ones. A process analogous to the transformation from introjection without much thought or awareness to conscious deliberation and decision making, which occurs in the area of moral development, goes on in personality and self-concept development in general. Several stage theorists have identified developmental tasks or crises which contribute to these changes, along with the physical and cognitive changes described previously.

STAGE THEORIES   A stage theorist who is especially notable in this regard is Sullivan (1953). Sullivan outlined six stages from birth through late adolescence, writing from a psychoanalytic perspective similar to Freud in some respects and to Erikson in other respects. Unique among stage theorists, Sullivan spoke of pre-adolescence as a separate developmental stage, marked in particular by a change in orientation from a desire to spend time with large groups of friends to a desire to spend much time with one special friend or buddy, typically a child of the same sex and about the same age. According to Sullivan, children who pair off in such "buddy" relationships develop interest in and insight into themselves and others by discussing each other at great length and providing each other with honest feedback about their strengths and weaknesses, their impressions upon others, and their general reputations.

Differences in maturity can be social and personal as well as physical. In Switzerland, as in the United States, most adolescents seek to expand their freedoms and "flaunt it if they have it." These two girls appear similar in age and physical maturity, but the one at the right clearly is "into" makeup, hair and clothing styles, smoking, and other symbols of what she regards as "in." The other girl is more mysterious. She may be wishing she had the qualities that her friend has, or she may be wondering what her friend is trying to prove and why she needs to "play the role" so obviously. Is this girl socially inhibited and constricted, or is she coolly sophisticated? (Cary Wolinsky/Stock, Boston)

This insight never has been researched thoroughly, but it fits my own experiences and observations. While such relationships are not universal, they do seem to be rather common among pre-adolescents, and they do seem to facilitate the development of insight and psychological sophistication. I believe that the key here is the loss of interest in childhood games and the development of interest in oneself and in how one is perceived by others. The aspect of having one special "buddy" is somewhat secondary; continuing dialogues which involve frank exchanges of information and opinions that produce new insights and psychological sophistication can be carried on with several friends, not just one. I believe that Sullivan was right in stressing the importance of these kinds of discussions for producing such development, and also was correct in noting that interest in such discussions peaks in the pre-adolescent years. Actually, the phenomenon probably is more related to intellectual development than to physical or sexual development. It probably is yet another aspect of the transition from concrete to formal operational thinking.

Freud (1938) stressed the appearance of the *genital stage* in adolescence. He saw this stage as marked by and based upon the physical maturation of the primary sex organs, which, among other things, flooded the individual with new libido coming from a new source. This new libido presumably was

519

channeled into "normal" sexual activities by "normal" people, although it could be diverted into defense mechanisms by disturbed individuals.

Psychoanalytic writers less biologically oriented and more socially oriented than Freud speak of "regression in the service of the ego" (Kris, 1952). This is a psychoanalytic term for the *break-up of previously established stability* (which often is accompanied by rebellion against authority, posturizing, and other "adolescent" behavior that is considered regression to earlier developmental levels). Eventually, it is *supplanted by a reorganization into a new and more sophisticated level of functioning.* The "regression" involved is said to be "in the service of the ego" (as opposed to being a manifestation of defense or of collapse of defense mechanisms) in the sense that it is considered necessary to insure that the previously established stability will be broken up sufficiently and permanently, allowing the rebuilding of a new and more sophisticated kind of stability.

The idea here is a simple one: people cannot shift quickly and easily from one well-organized structure to another. Instead, they must have the time and the experiences necessary to break down the first structure enough so that they can develop a new structure. This same basic idea is implied in concepts from many other sources, such as unlearning before relearning, sowing wild oats before settling down, "getting it out of your system" before being emotionally able to accept and move on to something else, and the like.

Erikson (1968) has written the most widely publicized and accepted psychoanalytic version of stage phenomena in adolescence. He refers to the same general kinds of things mentioned above, but he speaks of the search for identity (self-definition, a sense of direction and inner harmony, "finding oneself"). Individuals who have been successful in this quest have consciously considered the beliefs, attitudes, and value systems which had been introjected previously, worked through any inconsistencies or confusions, and developed an internally consistent, realistic, and satisfactory new system. This includes not only morality in the narrow sense, but also self-concept, ideals, self-definitions, and other related concepts having to do with how individuals describe themselves, both as they are now and as they want to be.

Erikson has stressed the concept of "role" in discussing the adolescent identity crisis, using the term "role diffusion" to refer to situations in which individuals are confused and searching with regard to self-definition and values. He speaks of them as trying out one role after another, sometimes directly by acting out in behavior, and sometimes vicariously through fantasy. This aspect of Erikson's stage theory strikes a responsive chord in most people, since most of us can remember this kind of confusion and search for identity, including both direct and vicarious attempts to "try out" various roles, during adolescence. A few examples are as follows.

1. Spending a lot of time in front of the mirror, experimenting with hair styles, cosmetics, and clothing.
2. Deliberately trying to create a certain kind of impression or reputation, either in general or in certain specific situations (such as at high school dances or in the classroom).

3. Developing hero worship for prominent figures in sports, politics, or entertainment, carefully studying them and trying to imitate them.

4. Attending unfamiliar church ceremonies, seeking opportunities to have contact with unfamiliar racial or ethnic groups, developing interests in unfamiliar philosophies, or otherwise exploring the possibilities involved in cultural groups or life styles different from your own.

5. Fantasizing yourself having qualities or playing roles which were grossly unrealistic and which you would be embarrassed to admit to someone else even now.

These are some of the activities typically engaged in by virtually every adolescent, including those that *seem* to be supremely self-confident and "together." There is more than a grain of truth in the concept of "regression in the service of the ego." It *does* seem to be necessary to tear down a stable structure, at least to some degree, before it can be rebuilt into a different kind of structure. This seems to be as true for personality as for physical structures. Much of the "adolescent" behavior that vexes adults, particularly authority figures, is regressive in one sense but progressive in another. It is a way station in the development from childhood to adulthood, helpful and perhaps even necessary as part of the process of identity formation.

Erikson's next stage, which he locates in early adulthood, but which, especially lately, occurs in many individuals in adolescence and in concurrence with the search for identity, is the crisis of intimacy vs. isolation. This is similar to Freud's genital stage, except that there is less emphasis on sex and more on emotional intimacy, self-disclosure, and, sometimes, love. The idea here is that there is a social expectation, as well as an internally felt desire, for the initiation and maintenance of a close, intimate, loving relationship with another individual. In the past, and to some extent in the present, this has been considered as universal. Lately many have argued that too much intimacy, or the wrong kind, is more an undesirable binding commitment than a natural and rewarding relationship indicative of normality and mental health. Those who reject intimacy as inherently natural or desirable can be persuasive, as can those who value intimacy but reject the idea that it must be limited to heterosexual and/or monogamous relationships. Traditionalists usually reject these views, looking upon them as rationalizations for difficulties in establishing intimacy and/or stable heterosexual relationships. Many differences here are purely semantic, but the question of whether genuine intimacy can be attained outside of monogamous heterosexual relationships is a real one.

My own view is that intimacy is extremely important and rewarding, especially but not necessarily if combined with a stable heterosexual relationship. Other forms of intimacy also can be very rewarding, but they bring problems, at least at present, because of social opposition to homosexual relationships and to "illicit" heterosexual relationships. It should be clear that the problems here lie primarily if not solely in societal opposition to alternative life styles, and not in anything inherent in these kinds of relationships themselves.

Just as identity vs. role diffusion seems to be the most crucial developmental crisis for the generation of individuals who became adolescents in the 25 years or so following World War II, the intimacy vs. isolation crisis seems to be more of a problem for present-day adolescents and young adults. The symptoms are many. The topic of self-disclosure is very popular in psychology, apparently because many individuals have difficulty in being open and honest with others about their inner ideas and feelings (Jourard, 1968). There has been a retreat from commitments to other individuals, as seen in the questioning of the institution of marriage, discussion of trial marriages, and generalized discussion of commitment as a problem. The popular encounter groups and other group experiences designed to teach people to break through their rigid inhibitions stress becoming open and spontaneous in interactions with others. The widespread interest in such groups indicates a felt need for learning how to feel and express intimacy (it is difficult to say whether this is a real difference in needs from previous generations or simply a difference in *consciousness* of needs).

Many young people argue that there is only a difference in consciousness, claiming that they are no different as a group than previous generations except that they are more conscious of desires to be open and uninhibited in interactions with others. However, most state that the problem really is more important than previously. Some commonly offered explanations include a lack of close emotional relationships with parents who were preoccupied with jobs and other aspects of their own lives, the high rates of societal change and personal mobility ("How can I make a commitment when I don't know where I'm going to be tomorrow?"), and The Bomb ("How can I make a commitment when I don't know if *anybody* is going to be here tomorrow?"). Assuming that the problem is real, all of these factors probably are involved to some degree. I would add a fourth candidate: the breakdown of traditional men's and women's roles as spouses and parents. When well-established roles like these dissipate, a period of confusion sets in, because people must find their own way without having the role to "tell them what to do." If and when a new consensus develops about these roles, there should be less of this kind of confusion. The process probably will take a long time, and it may result in a proliferation of acceptable roles rather than merely a change from one set to another. When this occurs, there should be less trouble with the crisis of intimacy vs. isolation.

So far, isolation has been mentioned but not discussed. Individuals who do not develop intimacy with others *are* isolated, even though they may have many acquaintances and superficial social relationships. Unwilling or unable to discuss fundamental and important things with others, they are left to their own devices (or perhaps to a professional therapist) to work out their problems and concerns. Many do so successfully, but many suffer needless anxiety or embarrassment because of misinformation or groundless fears that would have been cleared up if they had had opportunities to get good feedback about themselves. This could occur in the kinds of "buddy" relationships discussed by Sullivan, and/or in the kinds of intimate relationships that Erikson stresses in adolescence and in adulthood.

SELF-CONCEPT   Like most things in adolescence, self-concept undergoes questioning and change, eventually emerging in a much sharper and more clearly delineated form. As with the change from introjection to consideration and conscious adoption in the moral area, personal qualities previously taken for granted or not given much consideration tend to be considered and evaluated, and individuals undertake systematic changes in areas where they are dissatisfied. Where development has been generally successful, such stock taking usually produces self-satisfaction for the most part. Even so, it is typical to discover at least some qualities that lead to embarrassment and shame, followed by attempts to change to more socially desirable patterns.

Individuals with good reality contact (that is, those who can perceive reality accurately because they are not heavily defended against it) usually make these adjustments smoothly. Those with many personal difficulties may become seriously distressed or even depressed. Such concern, combined with the heightened self-consciousness typical of adolescents, makes them vulnerable to over-reactions such as "I'm no good; nobody likes me; I want to kill myself." Usually, these fears are worked through emotionally through fantasy and support from others (assuming that the person is not isolated in the sense discussed above), but sometimes they have tragic consequences, and most of the time they impair social relationships. Youths who think that they are unworthy and socially rejected will act in ways that "turn off" their peers, setting off a vicious circle of self-fulfilling prophecy effects.

One of the more famous anecdotes in the self-fulfilling prophecy literature occurred in this connection. Both as a potential good deed and as something of a cross between a joke and an experiment, several college men agreed to flirt with and generally pay a lot of social attention to a young woman who was socially inexperienced and who obviously had difficulties with self-esteem. She was shy and withdrawn, usually staying on the fringes of groups without participating in interactions. Consequently, she usually was overlooked when the young men were considering potential dates. The young men, without the young woman's knowledge, systematically greeted her, initiated conversations with her, asked for dates, and so on, but remaining careful all the while to avoid becoming obvious about it. This effort apparently was successful, because neither the young woman herself nor anyone not in on the "game" realized what was happening. As a result, the young woman changed systematically over the school year from a withdrawn wallflower into a social butterfly. She eventually became much more active, sociable, self-confident, and attractive, both in general and as a date. Interestingly, all of this happened with respect not only to the young men involved in the original scheme, but also to other school mates. She became popular among the women, and many young men having nothing to do with the original scheme began asking her out.

This anecdote is a good one for illustrating how expectations can operate as self-fulfilling prophecies. It also is instructive to consider what might have happened to the young woman if she had not been selected for this unofficial "experiment." Chances are that she would have continued to be socially inept and withdrawn, unless she managed to form an intimate relationship with at least one other person, got involved in some group or activity that provided her with opportunities for social learning and reinforcement, or initiated self-change efforts with the support of a therapist.

Although data are not available on the point, it is very likely that this young woman's self-concept changed in the course of the year from something like "I am dull and uninteresting; nobody would want to talk with me or ask me out," to something like "I am popular and socially attractive; these are among my better qualities." This story also illustrates the point that *self-concept is influenced heavily by one's immediate peers and reference groups* (Coopersmith, 1967).

Somewhat independently of their status in the absolute sense, people in general and adolescents in particular use immediate peers and reference groups as guidelines in judging themselves. Those who are successful in meeting peer and/or reference group norms or expectations usually feel satisfied and successful. Conversely, those who do not meet such norms or expectations usually feel failure, even though they may be doing quite well compared with people in general. In fact, investigations of self-concepts of adolescents in different social class groups usually show no group difference, even though the middle class adolescents tend to have higher IQs, more advantageous home backgrounds and life circumstances, and generally better prospects for future success. Apparently the reason that social class differences typically are not found is that lower class youths usually have adopted lower class attitudes and value systems, and tend to use lower class norms as criteria for self-evaluation. Because of this, and because they often are ignorant of the life circumstances and prospects open to more advantaged youths, lower class youths tend to be happy and self-satisfied if they are succeeding in meeting the expectations and aspirations to which *they* have been socialized. Success and self-satisfaction, then, are determined primarily by the attitudes of family and friends (assuming that these are the primary reference groups), and not by the norms of the middle class, of society in general, or of other *potential* reference groups that are too far removed from the immediate present to function as *actual* reference groups.

Such reference group phenomena make life easier for some adolescents, but complicate it for others. For lower class adolescents, they reduce or even eliminate much of the self-devaluation that would result if more general societal norms or specifically middle class norms were used for forming self-judgments. For adolescents growing up in middle and upper class families and general environments, reference group phenomena lead to individuals feeling needs to meet very high standards for success. As a result, many individuals who are quite well-adjusted and successful by absolute standards nevertheless consider themselves to be failures or to be inadequate because they do not meet the norms for *their* reference groups.

Independent of particular reference groups, adolescents are notably self-centered and self-conscious. They are so preoccupied with themselves and their images that essentially trivial things such as pimples, square haircuts, clothing, mannerisms, or blushing and other signs of embarrassment can become extremely important sources of concern. This all is part of making the transition from childish egocentrism in which there is relatively little knowledge of or concern for the perceptions of others, to self-confidence and related traits which come with successful resolution of the adolescent identity crisis.

MORAL DEVELOPMENT   Much of what happens in the area of moral development in adolescence already has been discussed, particularly the questions of whether or not previously introjected norms are called into question and evaluated actively, and, if they are, whether or not they are accepted. Norms and values which are accepted in an active way are more likely to be used in guiding behavior than introjected norms that are verbalized without much serious thought and without much assimilation to their cognitive and behavioral implications. This lack of assimilation is a major reason for a lack of correspondence between preaching and practice.

Individuals who develop formal operations usually also move into the last two of Kohlberg's (1969) six stages of moral judgment development. Individuals who attain stage five develop a kind of legalistic and philosophical morality, based upon the ideas of individual rights and privileges, contractual obligations, and the obligations to follow civil or religious laws. This is a cognitive advance over the previous level of authority maintaining morality, primarily because it involves conscious deliberation and personal commitment to values. This increases the likelihood that these values will be implemented in behavior and will be held for their own sake, as opposed to the earlier introjection of rules which were not always implemented in behavior (and even when they were, tended to be implemented mostly for the sake of pleasing authority figures).

Kohlberg's sixth stage involves moving beyond external legalistic notions of morality to the development of an internally consistent and philosophically sophisticated conscience comprised of an integrated set of general moral principles which are used to guide behavior. An important difference between the fifth and the sixth stage is the acquisition of the ability to distinguish between what is legal vs. what is moral, as well as the attainment of the related concept that legal activities sometimes can be immoral and vice-versa.

Individuals who have reached this stage of moral judgment development have reached a point where they can judge the morality of situations by assimilating them to their elaborate system of moral judgment schemas, without having to depend upon external sources such as civil or religious bodies of law. They have developed and internalized a generalized system of humanistic morality which transcends specific civil and religious codes by taking into account situational and motivational factors in addition to actual behavior. As a result, such individuals may see a given act as moral or justified in one situation but immoral or unjustified in another. Their morality is quite consistent, although this consistency may not be apparent unless they are questioned or otherwise given opportunities to explain the general, abstract moral principles which guide them in forming moral judgments.

SOCIAL RELATIONSHIPS   As adolescents pass through crises and become more mature and socially skilled, friendships and activities become more focused upon common interests and personal characteristics. Although there usually is some experimentation with the unfamiliar, most adolescents (and adults) associate primarily with friends from similar home backgrounds who have similar value systems and interests. Social class differentiation sets in at adolescence and becomes stronger thereafter, with children from lower class homes gravitating toward one another as the class groups become more and more different. Except for small schools where everyone knows everyone, adolescents from strikingly different social class backgrounds usually avoid one another, except for participation in team sports or other organized activities which cut across social class lines (Coleman, 1961).

Within social classes, friendship groups tend to differentiate according to common interests and personal characteristics. Many groups form because of common interests in, for example, motorcycles, specific sports or recreational activities, or more intellectual pursuits such as debating or working on the school paper.

Social group differentiation along SES and personal similarity lines is accentuated by school. Elementary school children typically are grouped heterogeneously. De facto housing segregation often produces some homogeneity in the school as a whole, but, within these limits, heterogeneous grouping and changes in class rosters from year to year expose children to most of their age mates who attend the school. In contrast, junior high and high schools usually track students according to ability groups, so that those in tracks designed to prepare them for college tend to interact only with one another, rarely or even never attending classes with students in vocational tracks or other tracks.

Much of this is unavoidable, because students in these different tracks *require* different courses, to a considerable degree. Schools could group heterogeneously in humanities, social science, and personal interest courses, if grades and competition were deemphasized in favor of general participation and interaction. Arrangements like these probably would be helpful, especially in large schools, because in many areas de facto housing segregation is such that adolescents have little or no direct knowledge of how individuals of different social classes, ethnic groups, and/or races think, feel, and live. Many of the group animosities that exist in our society might be broken down if such individuals had enough contact with one another to allow them to see that most group stereotypes are wrong. This assumes, of course, that such contact is conducted under voluntary or at least acceptable circumstances; throwing groups together against their will when they view each other with animosity is likely to increase the animosity.

Such heterogeneity widens the pool of potential reference groups for individual adolescents. This could have long-range positive consequences, even if short-range social relationships continue to be limited primarily to friends of similar background. Adolescents exposed to individuals and groups with unfamiliar value systems and life styles can take it upon themselves to learn more about these life styles if the life styles are appealing to them. In contrast, they will not learn much about different life styles if they never are exposed to them. There can be some vicarious learning through reading and media influences, of course, but direct experiences are much more powerful and meaningful.

THE YOUTH CULTURE   The desire of most adolescents to rebel against or at least differentiate themselves from adult life styles, combined with the prolongation of adolescence in our society and others like it, has resulted in the emergence of a "youth culture." This term refers to the music, clothing, lingo, new forms of entertainment and recreation, drinking and dope fads, and other things which are associated with adolescence, both by adolescents themselves and by society in general. The specific content of the youth culture changes with time (very rapidly lately because of the pervasiveness of the media), partly because of normal changes in tastes and preferences, and partly because aspects of the youth culture which become assimilated into society in general lose some of their appeal to certain adolescents.

Here is a scene from one of the more recent additions to the youth culture—the outdoor rock concert. Notice the intense emotional involvement: everyone seems mesmerized, and a few are even shrieking hysterically. Did you do this a few years ago? Why? More generally, why should an adolescent girl begin to shriek as soon as a rock star starts to sing, especially if the star and the song are familiar, and she may even have the same performance on a record or tape at home? (Jeff Albertson/Stock, Boston)

Each generation of adolescents seems to produce several "trademarks" which are valued as signs of being current and socially acceptable to peers. They also differentiate adolescents from children and, especially, adults. This aspect is a source of pride as well as identification, because it helps give adolescents a sense of uniqueness, togetherness, and accomplishment. Most of what is involved in the youth culture at any given time is relatively trivial in an absolute sense, but usually it is a source of much interest and discussion both within the youth culture and within society at large, and usually it involves at least some elements of rebellion against or change in traditional practices.

Most fads soon become boring, even to the adolescents who popularize them, while those things that have genuine value or appeal tend to be co-opted by society at large—hence the necessity for continued innovation. Even so, most people retain a special fondness for and identification with things that made up the youth culture when they were adolescents, even though this dates them. For example, I feel a certain pride in being part of the generation tha. popularized rock and roll music, but I find that younger friends and acquaintances frequently never have heard of some of my favorite artists, that they learned about many of them from 1950s nostalgia activities, and that I engender amazement when I proclaim acid rock to be nothing but electronically produced noise.

In general, given that most of the youth culture is related to fun and recreation, society should enjoy it rather than worry about it. However, this probably would only motivate adolescents to become more inventive until they hit on something that succeeded in worrying their elders. A few things have been genuinely dangerous (playing "chicken" with cars or motorcycles, gang initiation rites involving violence or destruction, experimentation with truly dangerous drugs), but most things involved in the youth culture are matters of taste and personal preference. The attention given to them by adults and by the media usually is all out of proportion to their importance, and the worry and criticism they engender usually is groundless.

SEXUAL RELATIONSHIPS   Masturbation is common throughout childhood, but it usually is an almost purely physical activity not accompanied by elaborate sexual fantasies. This changes in adolescence, as fantasies of sexual activities, based initially on ideas picked up from the media, from erotic literature, or from friends, and based later on actual experiences, become the focal points of masturbatory activity. Although masturbation has been a cause for much moralizing and worrying, studies of it have revealed that it causes no harm and tends to be associated with good sexual adjustment later. This association does not necessarily imply causality; it probably only means that adolescents who masturbate for sexual pleasure also tend to become heterosexually active earlier and somewhat more successfully than adolescents who do not. The primary causal variable probably is the degree to which sex is viewed as enjoyable and positive vs. forbidden and sinful, not masturbation per se (Kinsey, Pomeroy, and Martin, 1948).

Early heterosexual activities are, both figuratively and literally, groping explorations. When carried on by young adolescents who have not yet developed the motivation or intellectual capacities to sustain intimate personal relationships, such sexual exploration usually is done for its own sake without much if any connotation of intimacy. Having heard much about sex, adolescents quite naturally want to find out about it, in the same sense that they want to find out about driving cars. Unfortunately, learning about sex usually turns out to be more difficult than learning to drive a car, although driving a car is probably more complex and difficult (from a purely mechanical standpoint).

The problem is that sexual taboos so far have succeeded in excluding systematic and sanctioned sexual socialization from our society (systems for such socialization do exist in other societies). As a result, adolescents usually learn by trial and error, and under the worst of conditions. Learning usually takes place in clandestine circumstances, often in hurried or physically difficult situations, and usually with guilt or inhibition on the part of one or both parties. Contrast this with the usually more satisfactory and successful conditions under which adolescents learn to drive cars. Fortunately, most sexual adjustment problems are overcome by most people, although not without much needless frustration and self-doubt, and not without a certain percentage of failures (individuals whose sexual experiences are so frustrating and unsatisfactory that they avoid sex in the future or confine themselves to autoeroticism).

Parents can help here by providing educational materials and information, and by remaining conspicuously interested in and available for advice about sex and sexual activities. Because of the taboos surrounding the subject, many adolescents will not feel comfortable in discussing sex with their parents, even if the parents remain open and interested. Parents simply may have to accept this, although they still can prevent many potential problems by insuring that their children get good information about sex and thus are not misled by erroneous beliefs. When adolescents *are* willing to talk about sex, a combination of information and reassurance can be very helpful. It is common for adolescents to believe that there is something wrong with them if they have any difficulty at all in their sexual activities, to believe that they are homosexual if they masturbate or find themselves attracted to members of the same sex, to believe that sex is more satisfying or appropriate for males than females, or to believe that sex is most satisfying when orgasms are simultaneous. These and other myths, half truths, and misconceptions about sex can be cleared up by parents who find out about them, much to the relief of their son or daughter.

Other socialization about sex will have to depend upon parental values. Parents who believe that there is only one correct or acceptable set of values and ideas about sex should be particularly careful in trying to socialize their children, because there is a danger that they will end up preaching rather than socializing, and that their efforts may backfire if they spend so much time denouncing certain activities that these activities become glamorous in the eyes of the children. Again, beginning in adolescence, parents have only a "jawboning" influence over their offspring; they cannot control their activities directly. Consequently, parents will be most successful in getting their message across if they present their point of view calmly and reasonably, in a way that recognizes that value judgments are involved and that honest disagreement is possible. This may not succeed in convincing the offspring to follow parental values entirely, but it probably will motivate the offspring to seriously consider them. At the same time, it will minimize the likelihood that the offspring will want to challenge values for the sake of discovery or rebellion.

PREPARING FOR ADULTHOOD

There are great individual differences in the amounts of time and the degrees of difficulty involved in making the transition from childhood through adolescence into adulthood. In general, of course, adolescents who have the emotional freedom to explore and discover, who have the security and socialization base provided by a good home, who have highly developed coping skills and minimal vulnerability to threat, and who have highly developed social skills, are likely to encounter the least difficulty. Even for them, some problems will be involved, and the time taken to reach maturity might be considerable. In fact, the time for full transition into adulthood sometimes is longer for the brightest children from the highest social class backgrounds, because they stay in school longer, get married later, become financially independent later, and delay clear transition to adult status in many other ways.

Adolescence probably always will be a difficult period in a complex society, but it is inordinately and unnecessarily difficult in these times. We can and should set up mechanisms to make it easier for adolescents to "find themselves," by increasing the variety and availability of information sources and by developing new and more meaningful *adolescent roles*. At the moment, adolescents have no real role at all, except to go to school, try to stay out of trouble with their parents or other authority figures, and participate in the youth culture. This is unfortunate and wasteful, because it means several years of "hanging around," participating in sports or recreational activities that have begun to lose their glamour but are continued for lack of meaningful alternatives. In particular, only a small percentage of our adolescents ever get an opportunity to do meaningful and satisfying *work*. There has been much talk of changing this by setting up more combination school and work programs, and by creating more employment opportunities that adolescents could participate in on a part-time basis.

I think that it would be to everyone's advantage if such plans were implemented. I think it is a good thing, up to a point, that we tend to look upon adolescence as a time for young people to socialize, sow wild oats, and generally find themselves and mature before being expected to fulfill adult roles. However, I think that it would make more sense to phase them into adult roles gradually, or at least to make this kind of phasing in a viable alternative for those who choose it, than to do as we do now, expecting adolescents to mature into full-fledged adults virtually overnight when they get married and/ or begin full-time work. In the first place, this expectation is wildly unrealistic.

No one can make an immediate transition from a life involving minimal responsibilities and stress on entertainment and pleasure to a life laden with several important new responsibilities all coming at the same time, without experiencing difficulties. Second, we are wasting valuable resources. There are many service jobs and part-time jobs of all kinds that adolescents can and would want to perform, but mechanisms to bring this about do not exist for the majority. Third, as a result, a great many adolescents are bored stiff. Many get in trouble because they are looking for excitement. Many jobs have the potential for acting as maturing influences on adolescents; they are more than just mechanisms for allowing them to earn money and keeping them off the streets. Societal investment in the creation of more such jobs would more than pay for itself in the work productivity of the adolescents involved, the reduction in crime and other problems that result from sheer boredom, the maturing influences that job responsibilities and earning an income provide, and the increase in cooperative contacts between adolescents and adults, which would promote mutual understanding and tolerance.

We also need to develop mechanisms to provide adolescents with solid information about marriage and parenthood. We often tend to assume that they already know about these things, because they have grown up in a family. Some families are far from ideal as models. In the process of growing up, few children pay much attention to behavior related to spouse and parent roles.

"Hanging out." Although it looks almost like a parody, this picture illustrates the youth culture as it exists in our country, in this case for adolescent males. Is this a good idea (or even necessary), or is it a reflection of the absence of anything better to do? (Elizabeth Hamlin/Stock, Boston)

Consequently, although most adolescents have picked up a lot from their parents through modeling, they seldom have given much *systematic thought* to the subject or gotten much systematic information about it. In fact, to the extent that they have thought about marriage and parenthood at all, they probably have romanticized and idealized views ("they got married and lived happily ever after"). Even many of those who should know better have such views, because most people tend to think that problems happen only to others, not themselves. At minimum, adolescents should get enough information to insure that they enter marriage and parenthood (if they do) with their eyes open. Much information exists about the factors that make for stable and satisfying marriages, and about the behaviors that make for success as a parent. Relatively little of this ever reaches adolescents or young adults, and that which does usually arrives too late to do much good. It will be obvious by now, if you have read the rest of the book, that marriage and parenthood are heavy responsibilities involving commitment of time, energy, money, and virtually everything that one has to offer.

Furthermore, ideally in the case of marriage, and clearly in the case of parenthood, this commitment is a *permanent* one, and it should not be entered into lightly or halfheartedly. At minimum, we as a society should set up mechanisms to insure that all who are contemplating such a commitment receive enough information to insure that they realize what they are getting into and are prepared to go through with it. While it would be too much to expect this to completely eliminate unhappy marriages, divorces, and inept parents, it would go a long way toward minimizing these problems. Here again, the benefits to society would be multiple, and worth the costs many times over.

SUMMARY   The adolescent years involve qualitative changes in physical and cognitive development, and these changes bring about new changes and problems in social and personal development. The most important cognitive changes are those related to the development of what Piaget calls formal operations. Within the purely cognitive sphere, these developments allow adolescents to understand highly abstract materials for the first time, and to begin to use formal operations to think symbolically and solve problems more efficiently. Another effect of these cognitive developments is to enable (and motivate) adolescents to begin to seriously think about and question abstract moral values that they introjected in childhood without really understanding them.

If such reflection causes adolescents to determine that they agree with the values, they are likely to adopt them consciously and deliberately, so that they begin to use them to guide behavior. If reflection leads them to reject these values, they will begin a search for newer and more acceptable ones. Meanwhile, some values are likely to be retained at the level of introjection because they are never considered seriously or systematically, either because the adolescent has not had occasion to do so, or because these values have been socialized in ways that make even thinking about or questioning them too threatening.

Adolescents also reflect about other things, especially their changing bodies and the implications that these changes have for sexual and social relationships, and their personal characteristics and interactions with others. This process seems to be facilitated by the formation of close personal relationships with one or more friends who provide honest feedback about how adolescents are perceived by their peers. This information usually has strong influences upon self-concept and general personal satisfaction, because these self-perceptions tend to be influenced most strongly by immediate reference groups.

Two of the important themes of development in the adolescent years are the search for identity (finding one's self) and the attempt to develop intimacy (developing relationships in which even the most private thoughts and concerns are shared). Those who solve the quest for identity without undue difficulty emerge with a sense of who they are and what they want out of life, while those who do not may spend years trying out different roles and generally attempting to work out some kind of satisfactory adjustment. Similarly, those who achieve intimacy without undue difficulty become capable of initiating and maintaining intimate relationships which involve personal commitment and self-disclosure, while those who do not solve this crisis are inept, inhibited, and/or fearful about close relationships with others, and may avoid them or withdraw from them if they should develop.

The importance of socialization methods that place a premium on thoughtfulness and rational decision making is most clear when children reach adolescence and become less and less subject to parental control. Parents who have maintained an optimal relationship with their children will maintain a strong personal influence based upon a history of respect and affection as the children move through adolescence, but parents who have relied upon fear-oriented methods will find that they have little if any influence at all once their adolescents no longer are subject to threat. Adolescence probably always will involve a certain amount of generational conflict, but there is much more of this at present than there need be, because adults often over-react to aspects of the youth culture which really are matters of taste rather than values, and which have no genuine importance. Perhaps the major problem facing present-day adolescents is not what adults do, but what they do *not* do. Specifically, they do not provide meaningful adolescent roles likely to stimulate or assist development. This is true in general, but it is most obvious in the world of work, where we could be but are not providing adolescents with opportunities to become involved in meaningful jobs that would provide a sense of accomplishment and responsibility and would help ease the transition from present adolescent roles involving stress on recreation and minimal responsibilities to adult roles with heavy responsibilities coming all at once.

CHAPTER SIXTEEN

Fostering Adolescent Development

Parenthood becomes especially frustrating when children enter the adolescent years. For one thing, the rewards that come with close relationships tend to be reduced, because adolescents develop lives of their own outside of the home and spend less time with their parents, even where good relationships exist. Also, this is a time of sporadic conflict and frustration, as adolescents test limits, criticize or get into conflicts with parents, or do things that upset or outrage them. Adolescents tend to stop expressing affection and gratitude directly the way that younger children do, and it may be several years before they begin to express positive feelings for their parents in more mature ways. In the meantime, parents may feel frustrated and unappreciated.

Where a good relationship exists, this need not be the case. The changes in adolescents reflect their preoccupations with self, peer group, and the youth culture, but not rejection of or hostility toward the parents. This is difficult for some parents to accept, particularly when their adolescents use the home primarily as a place to sleep, eat, and get clothes cleaned, seldom participating in family activities and seldom saying much when they do. If given sufficient time, understanding, and emotional freedom to work things through, these same adolescents will develop into young adults who show love and respect for their parents. In the meantime, parents will have to grit their teeth and bear it when their adolescents do such things as pretend that they do not see them on the street when they are with their friends.

Adolescents are not the only ones that have to adjust during these years; parents must change, too. Although they still retain ultimate responsibility for legal minors, parents no longer can (or at least, they should not) act as authority figures in the same way that they did when the children were younger and more clearly dependent upon them. Commensurate with their adolescent's maturity, responsibility, and other aspects of readiness to function independently, parents must begin to allow this independence and to interact with the adolescent more as a young adult than as a child. This is a difficult transition for parents to make, and of course it is compounded by the resistance to parental authority that most adolescents show.

Parents who are most successful at this transition tend to have the same kinds of qualities that have been stressed as important for parent-child relationships. During adolescence, certain particulars are especially important.

1. Maintain continuous dialogue with adolescents about their activities. The burden on the parents is greater here. They will have to initiate more interactions than they did in the past, because most adolescents volunteer less information. Parents should remain continuously informed about their adolescent's friends and activities.

2. Although the need for clarity about what rules are "non-negotiable" and what rules can be changed is ever present, it becomes paramount during adolescence. Pressure for new freedoms and responsibilities increases in rate and intensity, and it is important for parents to be clear and consistent about their position on an issue so that they can respond rationally when pressured to change rules or agreements.

3. It is important for parents to make efforts to get to know their adolescent's friends and their families, both to establish positive relationships and lines of communication, and to avoid allowing themselves to end up in direct conflict with peers.

4. Where parents still do exercise authority, it is helpful if they minimize the degree to which they flaunt or show it. Adolescents should be socialized to expect to ask for and get approval for something new or out of the ordinary, but parents should be prepared to give approval unless they have good reasons for refusing. This way, parents retain their status as authority figures, but at the same time, their adolescents get to do most of what they want to do, and conflicts are minimized.

5. When adolescents reach the point where parents no longer can exercise

537

control in certain areas, this fact of life should be recognized and discussed explicitly. Parents probably will be most successful if they explicitly state that they no longer expect to (or even want to) exercise control, but, at the same time, that they do expect to maintain continuous communication and to be truthfully and completely informed about what their adolescents are doing. If they disapprove, they can express their disapproval and give their reasons for it, but they should stop short of futile gestures such as empty threats or ultimatums which cannot be enforced. Such behavior only will cause adolescents to minimize communication with parents, or even to tell them what they want to hear (if this differs from the truth).

6. Parents can minimize the generation gap by avoiding needless criticism of youth culture activities which involve personal taste but not morality or legality. Better yet, they can express interest in the youth culture by asking their adolescents questions about the latest music, clothing, fads, dances, or entertainment forms. This need not (and should not, unless genuine interest is involved) extend to the point of parental attempts to participate in these youth culture activities, but it will provide much common ground for discussion and will help keep adolescents aware that their parents maintain an open mind toward new or different ideas.

As the roles and influence of parents decrease, the roles and influence of peers and societal institutions increase in adolescence. Consequently, many of the suggestions offered here concerning optimizing adolescent development have to do with activities by adults and by institutions outside of the home. As adolescents begin to develop interests in out-of-home activities, adults sponsoring or conducting these activities can serve as models and general socialization influences upon them. This occurs partly because they see the adolescents on a regular basis and thus get to know them, and partly because the adolescents often admire them and thus are especially likely to be influenced by them. Parents build the foundation for general development and remain as strong influences, sometimes stronger than they realize, but teachers, coaches, church personnel, camp counselors, work supervisors, and others who come into contact with adolescents on a regular basis can have significant effects upon them.

Given the genetic basis for physical development, the primary facilitative roles for adults here are as sources of information and reassurance, in particular to adolescents who have unusual difficulties because of early or late onset of maturation or because of physical features, awkwardness, or other problems that embarrass them. Being prepared to deal with increases in food intake during growth spurts also is important, not only in providing for the necessary food, but also in avoiding making adolescents feel guilty or abnormal because of their appetites.

PHYSICAL DEVELOPMENT

The development of primary and secondary sex characteristics provides

That burger looks big, but for an adolescent, especially one in the midst of a growth spurt, it may be little more than an appetizer. Adolescents undergoing growth spurts develop sharply increased appetites, including desires for snacks and meals in addition to regular meals, as well as more food at ordinary mealtimes. (Frederik D. Bodin / Stock, Boston)

another opportunity for parents to solidify their relationships with adolescent sons and daughters. Mothers often can become very close to adolescent daughters by providing information about, and acting as sounding boards concerning, undergarments, feminine hygiene products, and cosmetics and grooming products. Fathers can help build self-esteem and confidence in daughters by commenting, sometimes seriously and sometimes jokingly, upon emerging milestones in physical and sex role development.

Similarly, fathers can solidify relationships with sons by providing information and acting as sounding boards concerning athletic equipment and activities, tips on shaving and masculine grooming, and the relative merits of masculine cosmetic and hygiene products. Also, mothers can help build self-esteem and confidence in sons by commenting, again sometimes seriously and sometimes jokingly, upon increased physical strength or muscular development, mature looks or attractive features, and the like.

In situations where adolescents' aspirations in physical areas exceed realistic possibilities, parents, coaches, and other adults will need to provide realistic information in ways that the youths can accept without serious loss of self-esteem. Athletes who have little chance to make a team (or to participate much if they do make the team) should not be misled into unrealistically high expectations. Where size or body type precludes success at a particular sport or physical activity, this information should be passed on honestly and clearly. At the same time, efforts should be made to suggest alternative activities capable of providing similar satisfactions (such as other sports, intramural participation rather than participation on the school team, participation as a student manager or other assistant to the coaches). Those who wish to persist in an activity even after receiving this kind of information probably should be allowed to do so, however. Adolescents who want to stay on a team even though they know that they are unlikely to see much action probably are getting important benefits from such participation. There is always the possibility that a growth spurt or other physical change will enable them to achieve more success.

Those who become stars at sports and physical activities will need to keep such success in perspective. They are likely to be lionized by the peer group, at least during junior high and high school years, and they may develop unrealistically high aspirations and expectations if they do not realize that this status is short lived. Parents and coaches should help these individuals to realize the importance of education and career planning. Even for outstanding all-star types, the chances of becoming a professional or Olympic athlete are very slim, and even if they make it, careers are short. In some ways, adolescents who are outstanding at sports or other physical activities are more in need of adult guidance than those who are disappointed because they cannot achieve the levels of success to which they aspire.

If adolescents have been introduced to physical activities that can be continued throughout life, these activities provide another natural basis for solidification of relationships with parents. Although adolescents usually like to avoid family outings and activities that they enjoyed as children, they often respond positively to invitations to swim, bowl, play golf, bicycle, play tennis, or engage in other sports and recreation activities with their parents. These occasions not only allow parents and adolescents to spend time together; they also make it likely that they will enjoy the activities and one another's company.

COGNITIVE DEVELOPMENT

The cognitive development that occurs in adolescents involves fundamental changes that force parents to begin to interact with them in new and different ways. They must gradually make the transition from being "all knowing" authority figures who provide information and guidance, to being fallible individuals with uneven patterns of knowledge (less knowledge than their offspring in many areas) and with unique attitudes and value systems which are open to question (and probably will be questioned). This transition is difficult, as is any transition from being an authority figure to being a friend without special authority or even expertise. It is made more difficult, of course, by the close emotional relationships between the individuals involved, and by adolescent idealism and intolerance of hypocrisy (which often results in sarcasm and accusations directed against parents). These reactions are understandably irritating, but the worst part of it is that a certain portion of them will be true. Whenever adolescents do succeed in finding disparities between parental preaching and practice, the only sensible course for parents (painful, though it is) is to admit the disparity and take steps to eliminate it. Denials, refusals to listen, or attempts to dismiss the adolescents as "too young to understand" will only undermine credibility. On the other hand, this is a two-way street. Assuming that information is conveyed in an atmosphere of caring and concern (as opposed to getting even), parents can and should show adolescents where their behavior does not follow *their* preaching. In particular, adolescents who are concerned about matters of justice, charity, and humanism, but mostly in the abstract or as they apply to oppressed peoples elsewhere, may need to be reminded that these concepts also apply to such mundane matters as fulfilling home responsibilities, demonstrating civility and good manners in interactions with parents and siblings, and the like.

In the areas of social and political philosophies and value systems, dialogues with parents, including arguments, probably are good for all concerned (assuming that at least a minimal level of mutual respect is maintained). Usually, there will be some truth to both points of view, so that both the parents and the adolescent stand to gain from such discussions and arguments. In general, parents can provide adolescents with realistic information about areas in which adolescent idealism is unrealistic or has not taken into account factors which reveal a simple situation to be much more complex than it seems at first. Conversely, stimulation from idealistic adolescents can help force parents to reassess their own value systems, and perhaps also to recognize areas in which they have become complacent or hypocritical.

Much more of the latter kind of influence goes on than most adolescents or even adults realize. In the early 1970s, there were wholesale changes in the attitudes of most American adults concerning such topics as the war in

Southeast Asia, the military draft, premarital and extramarital sex, and the esthetic attractiveness of long hair, mustaches, and/or beards on males. While there were many different reasons for these changes, discussions and arguments with adolescents and young adults probably were the most important influences. Similar changes are occurring for similar reasons in attitudes and beliefs about sex roles, drugs, conservation, and quality of life. What starts out as a dialetic ends up as synthesis acceptable and beneficial to all. The generation gap is usually a good thing (again, assuming that arguments do not degenerate below an irreducible minimum of civility and mutual respect).

Adults not only change their opinions, they develop new interests, just as adolescents do. Here again, much is to be gained by all through the sharing of information about newspaper and magazine articles, books, and movies, new foods and recreational activities, hobbies, or specific areas of knowledge. Adolescents may be taking school courses in fields that their parents are unfamiliar with, and parents might be interested in hearing about these topics or even reading about them. Conversely, parents can help adolescents acquire new information and assimilate specific facts to abstract principles by providing information that they are in a unique position to give (personal experiences and observations related to historical events that adolescents have read about but do not remember; information about what life was like before certain inventions or social conventions became widespread, and how these innovations changed their lives; or information about what goes on at work or activities conducted outside of the home). In addition to providing adolescents with food for thought, such interactions can increase their understanding of and respect for their parents.

PERSONALITY DEVELOPMENT

Adolescents must solve the crises of identity and intimacy on their own for the most part, but parents and other adults can help by providing information and reassurance. Regarding identity, adolescents will benefit from hearing parental perceptions about their qualities and parental opinions about activities or occupations that they might enjoy and be successful at. Of course, these will be more valuable if they are based upon objective assessment of the adolescents as they are, as opposed to unrealistic parental dreams or aspirations. If parents have suggestions to offer concerning fields of specialization or occupational roles, they should explain the reasons for these suggestions in addition to simply making them. Presumably, they will be based upon realistic interests and/or talents that the adolescents possess.

It also seems to foster progress toward a sense of identity if parents provide adolescents with information about the family tree. At least, most adolescents are strongly interested in hearing this information. Pictures, scrapbooks, and anecdotes related by parents and other relatives help adolescents develop a sense of familial definition and identification, help provide an historical perspective upon their own lives, and help foster the development of a mature and satisfying sense of identity. In addition, they are intrinsically interesting in their own right. Even though such information has little or no direct bearing on

The family in this picture is reliving cherished moments together as they go through family photo albums. This is one of many ways that all members of a family can participate in an enjoyable common activity that tends to cement family bonds, the sense of identity, and the sense of belongingness. (Cary Wolinsky/Stock, Boston)

the adolescents' immediate or future lives, it seems to be very satisfying and to fill a deep need. Adopted children who are unable to obtain information about their natural parents often report a sense of void and dissatisfaction, and sometimes undertake efforts to obtain such information, even though in other respects they are quite well-adjusted and are close to their adoptive parents. Apparently, most of us have been socialized to want to learn about our genetic and historical backgrounds. In any case, this is one area where parents and other relatives are uniquely able to help adolescents achieve a sense of identity.

In cases where notable problems of role diffusion are combined with obvious low self-esteem, adults other than the parents might be in a better position to help than the parents are. Often, low self-esteem is the primary cause of the other problems. In turn, it is caused primarily by parental rejection. More positive input from other adults, particularly information about intellectual and personal strong points, vocational and avocational possibilities, and other guidance that might provide some confidence and some sense of direction to such adolescents, is extremely valuable. Many individuals who were depressed and lonely throughout most of childhood and adolescence literally have had their lives changed when some adult who noticed one more of their positive qualities took an interest in them and gave them some guidance. Guidance counselors in high schools probably have the most obvious opportunities to do this, but any adult that adolescents know and respect is a potential source of both self-esteem and self-definition for those who are confused and in need of guidance. Programs which provide adolescents with more information than they usually get about occupational possibilities would be valuable here, particularly ones that go beyond simply collecting files of brochures by bringing in adults to discuss their work with students on a face to face basis.

Adult opportunities to help adolescents and young adults with the problem of intimacy vs. isolation are much more limited. Adults help primarily by *modeling* intimate relationships. If this has not occurred, adults are unlikely to be able to do much, even if they want to, by the time children reach adolescence. Vicarious modeling through movies, books, television, and other media presenting intimacy models and stories provide the primary socialization about the value of intimacy and about specific behaviors associated with it. Ultimately, however, the achievement of intimacy usually depends upon whether or not the person meets someone sufficiently attracted to him or her that the formation of an intimate relationship is possible, and upon whether or not the person is prepared to respond. Contrary to the romantic notion that only one specific person in the whole world is "waiting" for another person, anyone can become involved intimately with a large number of other individuals. When he or she settles on one particular individual, it usually is due to a combination of intimacy interests or inclinations signaled by the other individual with situational factors that favor the development of an intimate relationship.

Unfortunately, some individuals are not prepared to respond with intimacy and self-disclosure, even when conditions are optimal. These individuals are the ones that Erikson calls "isolated." Due to a combination of low self-esteem, inexperience, confusion about their own identities, mistrust of their feelings and reactions, and general inhibition, they cannot bring themselves to allow intimate feelings to develop (or, if they have developed, to express them). Sometimes, persistence on the part of a patient and loving partner can overcome these inhibitions. In fact, this probably is the single most effective "treatment" that such individuals could experience. Even so, in some cases personal adjustment problems are so deep and widespread that even persistent advances from an idealized lover are not reciprocated.

SELF-CONCEPT   Adults help adolescents build and maintain positive self-concepts by projecting positive attitudes and expectations toward them. However, these must be kept realistic. Well-meant reassurance which involves denying obvious reality will only depress the adolescent. Realities must be recognized and accepted, both by the adolescents themselves and by parents and other adults who deal with them. It is helpful if the adults not only provide realistic information about undesirable attributes but also guidance about how to adjust to them or make the best of bad situations.

Adults also can help adolescents to weather the emotional strains of broken friendships and romances, or experiences involving failure or rejection, by maintaining a secure home base. Adolescents who know that they are accepted and valued at home are likely to have or develop the ego strength required both to face up to their problems (vs. attempting to deny them) and to adjust to them without serious loss of self-esteem (vs. recognizing them but becoming depressed or upset as a result).

In general, the importance of parental focus upon the good points of their offspring and minimizing attention to weaknesses remains important in adolescence (as it is at any point in the life cycle). Everyone has strengths and weaknesses, and happiness pretty much boils down to capitalizing upon strengths and learning to live with weaknesses without feeling shame or guilt. Anything that adults can do to promote this coping pattern will be in the general best interests of their adolescents, in addition to specifically fostering self-esteem and positive self-concepts.

MORAL DEVELOPMENT Adults can help adolescent moral development primarily by being open to and prepared for challenges to their authority and, more specifically, to their beliefs and value systems. Although arguments and conflicts are virtually inevitable, adults have nothing to fear here if their beliefs and value systems are internally consistent and based upon sound assumptions and logic. In short, if adults really are correct, they should be able to convince their adolescent (or anyone else) of this. If they cannot, they should reassess their position and perhaps change it, or at least recognize that the position involves value judgments and not clear-cut right vs. wrong.

Problems with fear-oriented approaches to socialization become very clear at adolescence, because offspring now are physically and mentally developed enough to recognize that they have little to fear because threats will not be enforced. Where this happens, the result is loss of parental control, and often the emergence of antisocial behavior as well. This is especially likely where there has been a heavy emphasis on fear as the basis for socialization, so that parents have not built a positive and prosocial moral orientation which acts as an *internal* guide to behavior in their offspring. Sometimes, behavioral inhibition through fear can be continued by religious socialization stressing eventual punishment for sins by an all-knowing God. Behavior inhibition achieved this way comes at the expense of the development of more sophisticated and internalized moral judgments. A large percentage of moral ideas and values will be retained at the level of introjection, because the adolescent will believe that it is wrong even to think about or question them. Unless such ideas and values *are* consciously questioned, they cannot be consciously adopted. If not consciously adopted, they are likely to remain as verbalized values but not to become assimilated to behavior or to act as guides to behavior. The result is likely to be a person who never gets beyond Kohlberg's fourth stage of authority maintaining morality.

Although it is successful and in many cases appropriate to deal with *young children* by protecting them from certain realities that may be too threatening for them to handle at the moment, it is neither practical nor wise to try to do this with *adolescents* who develop genuine moral curiosity as part of their broader cognitive development. First, most adolescents will be exposed to values and ideas conflicting with those espoused by the parents anyway, so that attempts to protect them from contact with such ideas are likely to fail. Second, and more important, true internalization of moral value systems can occur only when adolescents have had a chance to deliberate on the matter and make a conscious decision and commitment to a value system. This, in turn, can occur only when they have the emotional freedom to undertake this kind of analysis (and, ideally, the opportunity to exchange ideas with parents).

Moral reasoning directed at adolescents during arguments is more likely to be effective if it stresses Golden Rule morality ("How would you feel if someone did that to you?") and/or impersonal, objective logic ("All right, suppose you did do it. What would happen then?"). This helps focus the adolescents' attention on their own behavior and its consequences, minimizes the likelihood that the adults will be perceived as authority figures trying to force their values on the adolescents, and promotes the assimilation of separate moral ideas into larger clusters and eventually into a single integrated system (Kohlberg's sixth stage). It also minimizes arguments, since the adults take the role of reality therapists pointing out alternatives rather than the role of authority figures granting or refusing permission. It helps, of course, if adults refrain from saying "I told you so" when an adolescent goes ahead and does something that the adult had predicted would be a mistake. If it indeed was a mistake, the adolescent will be more than sufficiently aware of it, and will need guidance rather than further embarrassment.

SOCIAL DEVELOPMENT

As their children move into adolescence, parents must accept and adjust to the fact that they increasingly will lead lives of their own and reduce their participation and emotional involvement in family activities. The desire to spend time with peers is both very strong and quite normal, so that parents who try to prevent or delay it are fighting a hopeless battle. Adolescents should continue to be invited to participate in family outings and activities, but they should not be made to feel guilty if they turn down these invitations to participate in a peer group activity. Forcing them to go only will produce arguments and unpleasantness before and during the family activity, not to mention embarrassment afterwards ("Why weren't you at the dance Saturday night?" "Uh, I had to go out with my family."). Sometimes, parental needs to be flexible here may even extend to hallowed family traditions such as holiday gatherings involving all of the relatives. It is reasonable to exert pressure on an adolescent to attend such gatherings when the alternative is, for example, going to a movie with a friend. If the alternative is accepting an invitation for a holiday dinner at the home of a steady date, a more genuine dilemma is involved. It will be necessary to work out an arrangement enabling the young couple to divide their time between the two families. Often, this will require the parents to explain things to disappointed relatives, but this is unavoidable and should not be allowed to become a bone of contention between them and their adolescent.

SEX ROLE   Sex role pressures from outside the home are bad enough without parents adding to them. Instead, parents should act as resources to provide information and support to adolescents who have difficulties in this area. One fundamental point that all adolescents should be aware of, regardless of their degree of success in meeting expectations or gaining approval from peers of either sex, is that sex-typed activities are stressed much more strongly during adolescence than they will be later in life. Boys who are popular primarily because of athletic achievement and girls who are popular primarily because of physical attractiveness should understand that these assets will recede in importance later, and that they will need to develop fully rounded personalities.

Similarly, boys who are frustrated or ashamed because they are poor athletes, and girls who are ignored or rejected because they are physically unattractive, can be reassured that the heavy stress placed on these sex-typed attributes during adolescence is temporary, and that these problems need not prevent them from leading happy and well-adjusted lives. In general, with all kinds of adolescents, stress should be placed on the development of personality traits which will be important to popularity and general happiness throughout life: prosocial moral orientation; personal integrity and credibility; liking for oneself and for others; social conversational skills (including listening and responding as well as talking and initiating); and a reputation for fairness, common sense, and good judgment.

Parents should keep tabs on their adolescents' friends. The best way to do this usually is to encourage them to bring their friends home, and to make the friends welcome if they do come. Parents with a large enough house, a well-stocked refrigerator, and the patience of Job may wish to consider offering the use of their house for pajama parties, card games, or other social occasions. Where this is done, it will be important to leave the adolescents in privacy after visiting with them a while. They are likely to feel inhibited (and unlikely to want to return) if parents insist on staying around or even staying within earshot, even though what they are discussing may be entirely innocent. This is yet another of the many adjustments that parents have to make: when children are young, they often are shuffled outside of the house or into another part of the house so that the adults can have privacy; in adolescence, it is the offspring who want privacy, and the adults who must accommodate to this desire.

Where late or all night gatherings go on in someone else's home, parents should satisfy themselves that the planned activities are appropriate and that one or more responsible adults will be present in the home. Occasionally, this may mean calling up a complete stranger to ask questions. If so, parents should not hesitate to do so. The vast majority of parents will take this for what it is—a sign of parental concern and responsibility. They are not likely to regard such calls as insults or criticisms of their own parental competence, because they would do the same thing in the same circumstances.

Eventually, parents have to "let go" in the total sense, recognizing that their adolescent or young adult has become old enough and responsible enough to come and go freely without seeking permission or being supervised by *anyone*.

Here again, this is an inexorable reality that parents cannot prevent, so that they have nothing to gain and much to lose by trying to do so. Furthermore, it is too little and too late to try to control the behavior of adolescents and young adults through close supervision or chaperoning. At this point, individuals are controlled (or not controlled) by *internal* moral standards and value systems developed over a long period of time. If parents have done a good job of helping their offspring develop such standards, they can have reasonable confidence that the adolescents will follow them. In contrast, if behavior has been suppressed through punitive methods and internal control mechanisms have not been developed, controls are unlikely to appear at adolescence, certainly not overnight. Internal standards still can be developed, but this process will take the kinds of dialogues discussed previously, not more control or punitive treatment.

The effect upon parents of the differentiation of adolescent society along social class and personal characteristic lines depends on parental aspirations and reference groups. Parents prejudiced in favor of people similar to themselves and against those different from themselves are likely to be satisfied with the emergence of a similar pattern of friendships in the adolescent group. Many higher social class parents will be disturbed to discover that their sons or daughters (especially daughters) are associating with lower class friends, in particular where marriage is a possibility. Although people of higher social status are not always aware of this, lower class parents may be equally disturbed to discover that their sons or daughters are associating with people that they look upon as snobs or "blue bloods." The same is true for adolescent friendships which cross racial or ethnic lines.

If parental reactions in this area involve nothing but blind prejudice, this will be evident and adolescents will ignore them. If parents have a genuine basis for worrying about certain friends of their adolescents, they should be able to explain the basis for their fears in ways that the adolescents can understand. It probably is unrealistic to expect the adolescents to respond by *immediately* agreeing to drop the friendship, but such a talk is likely to prevent the adolescents from being influenced in unfortunate ways by their friends, because forewarned is forearmed. Here, as in any situation, it is vital that parents stress logical reasons and avoid giving the appearance that they dislike the friend because of prejudice, lack of understanding, or other irrational reasons.

THE YOUTH CULTURE   Much can be said to parents about the reactions of fear and loathing that aspects of the youth culture in vogue at the moment may engender in them, but all of it can probably be summed up in the cliche "Don't knock it unless you've tried it." Youth culture activities frequently engender utter hysteria in adults, especially in self-appointed guardians of the public morals and mores. Witness the ludicrous statements made over the years about the presumed awful effects of masturbation, unisex clothing styles, or marijuana, for example. Although almost everyone now can look back and laugh at the ideas that masturbation will lead to blindness, that unisex clothing was part of a communist plot to undermine the moral fiber of America, or that marijuana produces brain damage and all manner of physical and personal deterioration, the fact remains that numerous adults believed these and other equally ludicrous fears about the youth culture.

The problem, of course, is that anyone who believes and makes such statements to an adolescent (or to anyone else who has tried the custom or substance and knows what the effects and meanings are) will lose *credibility*, probably not only on that particular subject, but on things *in general*. The typical reaction is "If they believe *that*, how can I take them seriously when they talk about *anything?*" Unfortunately, this is quite understandable, even though the reasons that lead frightened parents into believing such nonsense also are understandable.

People look to their reference groups for information, attitudes, and values. If parental reference groups do not include scientific sources of information or representatives of the youth culture, and especially if they are concentrated heavily upon personal acquaintances similar to themselves in age and belief systems, it is not hard to understand how parents can develop strong reactions of disgust or hysterical fear about aspects of the youth culture commonly believed to be dangerous or destructive. Lacking firsthand experience, they go by what they hear. What they hear from adults whom they know and respect is all negative, and this will outweigh what they hear from their adolescent offspring (who, after all, have not yet developed the track records for credibility that their friends have). If everyone they know says that pot is an extremely dangerous substance likely to turn a perfectly normal adolescent into a vegetable, they are likely to believe it, no matter what their son or daughter tells them.

The moral here for young people is to try to understand why parents react as they do, and to bear in mind that they usually act out of concern for their offspring rather than a desire to flaunt authority (or some other negative motive). The solution is provision of firsthand information from highly credible sources, not shouting arguments. For adults, the moral here *is* to try it before you knock it, or at least to make sure that you get reliable information rather than merely repeat what your friends say.

Given that most youth culture activities involve matters of taste (music, clothing styles, slang phrases, and so forth), there is no point in putting them down or becoming irritated by them. For the open minded (and occasionally, the adventurous), there usually is much to be gained by giving some of these new things a try. My own life has been enriched in many ways by suggestions from the young people that I come in contact with at the university and/or by opportunities to share in their activities. In short, openness to the youth culture has kept me younger (or, at least, has given me the illusion of being younger).

Another good reason for adults to remain open to the youth culture is that it is oriented toward fun and recreation. Too many adults get so bound up in their own personal problems and in the problems of the nation and the world that they forget how to relax and enjoy themselves. Frequent contact with young people and involvement in youth culture activities is a good antidote to this, and one of several ways that adolescents and young adults can benefit middle-aged and older adults. Throughout most of the book, the stress has been on the role of adults in socializing the young. However, it is worth pointing out that, when two individuals interact, they influence each other; the influence is not only from the older one to the younger one. Adolescents and young people generally can and will enrich the lives of adults if the adults allow them to, just as adults can and should socialize young people.

SEXUAL RELATIONSHIPS   Socialization in this area really does not differ in any important way from socialization in any other area; it is treated separately here simply because so many people make such a big issue out of it. Basically, the problems facing adults here are the same problems faced in any other aspect of emerging independence and new activities on the part of adolescents.

1. Adjusting to emerging developments and realities, rather than attempting to deny them or to "protect" adolescents from sexual involvement.
2. Provision of information and maintenance of conspicuous availability as a resource person.
3. Articulation of a value system concerning sexual relationships, stressing the reasons underlying attitudes at least as much as the attitudes themselves.
4. Recognition that, at some point, the adolescent will be old and mature enough to act independently, and that attempts to block this will only fail and lead to conflicts.
5. Provision of honest feedback concerning reactions to dates and potential marital partners, but stopping short of attempting to pressure the adolescent into either staying or breaking up with a present romantic interest.
6. Provision of information about birth control, and willingness to assist in obtaining birth control devices if this is requested (adults with qualms about this should bear in mind that, given the situation, the probable alternatives are either that the adolescent will get the materials elsewhere or that an unwanted pregnancy will result).
7. Where relevant, there should be frank discussion and eventual agreement on an explicit set of rules concerning sexual behavior conducted in the home by an adolescent who is living in the home. Parents who want to reject this outright can do so successfully, although they should not be surprised to see their adolescent move out of the home at the first opportunity if this becomes a major issue. At the other extreme, parents who have no qualms or concerns about it should take into account the possibility that other parents might. They should come to some kind of agreement with their own adolescent about how this problem will be handled.

Ultimately, the bottom line regarding socialization in the area of sexual mores is the same as elsewhere: if parents have reasonable values and attitudes, if they have taken the time to articulate and explain these, and if the general nature of

These adolescents and young men are doing their part in a neighborhood cleanup project. This is but one way that adolescents can be given meaningful roles to play in society. An additional benefit of activities such as this is that they allow adolescents to work together in cooperation with adults under generally positive circumstances, helping minimize generation-gap problems. What other kinds of adolescent roles could we create that would have these advantages? (Harry Wilks / Stock, Boston)

their relationships with their adolescents is characterized by warmth and mutual respect, the adolescents probably will accept parental values. Where they do not, they will have good reasons for choosing to act as they do. In contrast, if parents do not know what they are talking about or try to control their adolescents through threats and overprotective supervision, they can expect to be rudely disappointed.

TRANSITION TO ADULTHOOD

It is worth stressing again the importance of *time* and *emotional freedom* in determining whether or not problems are worked out successfully. These are among the more important things that parents can provide, by making the home a secure "home base" for their adolescents.

Time is important because, as noted frequently, even where a problem is identified and the ultimate solution is known, people cannot change overnight from one clear-cut structure and set of habits to another. Just as time is needed to recover from a divorce or the death of a spouse, time is needed to change central aspects of self-concept, to recover from severe social rejection or a broken romance, or to work through the problems that come with school failure or trouble with the law. Parents will be most effective if they grit their teeth and try to be patient when adolescents go through difficult periods which involve brooding, displaced hostility, and general uncivil and irritating behavior.

Although certain things cannot be tolerated, it is helpful if parents are understanding when their adolescents go through these emotional crises, learning to take them in stride and to avoid taking personally remarks or behavior which are symptomatic of an underlying problem and not really directed at the parent. Very often, adolescents need not only time but *time alone,* walking around "aimlessly" or lying on their beds thinking about their problems. Much of this time is spent fantasizing, daydreaming grandiose scenes in which the adolescents are happy and all-powerful rather than unhappy and frustrated, or perhaps thinking about how miserable everyone would be if they committed suicide or ran away and never came back. These and other typical adolescent fantasies, while childish from an adult perspective, are important in helping adolescents to emotionally work through disappointments and frustrations, enabling them to "return to their old selves" again. Both the time itself and the activities conducted during it are important, sometimes more important than doing a particular chore that can wait until tomorrow or eating a meal that might be missed or eaten cold later.

Parents should try to remain alert to recognize times when their adolescent offspring are preoccupied with these kinds of problems and need time to be left alone to work them out, and they should respect this need insofar as they can. It is a good idea to ask what is wrong and offer to talk about it, but if this offer does not bring a positive response, it usually is best to leave the adolescent alone. When he or she finally emerges, it is helpful to indicate that there is *no* need to discuss the problem. This can be done indirectly through a remark like "We saved you some dinner—it's in the oven." The adolescent will talk about the problem if and when he or she is ready.

Emotional freedom is related to the ratio of continued introjection vs. deliberation of values. If parents succeed in implanting the idea that it is wrong even to think about something, such thoughts will flood the adolescent with guilt. He or she will not be emotionally free to deliberate the matter, and thus the value will be retained but at the level of introjection rather than conscious adoption. Where emotional freedom has been blocked in several different areas, the adolescent might be quite inhibited and guilt-ridden, leading eventually to neurotic symptoms if the forbidden thoughts cannot be repressed. To prevent problems of this kind, it is important for parents to express disapproval calmly and with emphasis on their reasons for it, rather than to over-react and make the adolescent feel unnecessarily ashamed or guilty.

The problems of prolonged adolescence and conflicting criteria of developmental status are as confusing to parents as they are to adolescents. Despite continued interest, we know much more about what *not* to do than about what *to do* here. For example, it is clear that attempts to differentiate by chronological age (you can date when you are 14; you can drink liquor in the house when you are 18) do not work because of individual differences in interests and maturity levels. For similar reasons, distinctions based on legal age or on considerations such as whether or not the adolescent is living at home or is being supported by the parents also do not work. They are correctly viewed by adolescents as arbitrary and authoritarian exercises of parental power, and they are likely to be resented and violated.

The degree of parental influence depends upon the degree of "jawboning" influence that they have, and this in turn depends upon their own credibility and the nature of their relationships with their adolescent. Usually, things work out best if agreements are made about general principles of behavior. Overly specific rules and regulations are likely to be broken sooner or later by even the most conscientious adolescents, because they do not take into account unforeseen events. This makes the rules themselves a farce, unless the parents want to take the drastic step of throwing the adolescent out of the house, which hardly is a solution. Ultimately the answer is prevention and positive socialization, not control and "discipline."

Where adolescents develop realistic career or life plans, these should be respected, even though they may not match what the parents had in mind. If an adolescent wants to be something other than a doctor, parental pressure to become a doctor will only be irritating and pointless. The same is true for pressure to get married or to have children. In general, parents will be most helpful if they are supportive of their adolescents' occupational aspirations, although they should not be so enthusiastic as to interfere with emotional freedom if the adolescents should change their minds. Where adolescents have unrealistic ideas, parents should not hesitate to straighten them out by providing realistic information that they are not taking into account. Parents also need to be prepared for the possibility that career or marital plans may call for the young adult to move away from the home, possibly several thousand miles. This is commonplace in our highly mobile society, but it does not sink in on most parents until it hits them directly. Formerly, it was quite reasonable for parents to expect that their children would live nearby when they grew up, but not anymore.

A FINAL NOTE It should be very clear by now that parenting is a serious responsibility involving total commitment, much hard work, many frustrations, and no guarantees. It also has many rewards. The roles and responsibilities of parents are sources of identity and satisfaction, because they are so important. Doing a job well is something most of us value and enjoy, and parenting is a very special job. Despite the work and frustrations, children are more or less continuous sources of joy, amusement, and personal satisfaction. Watching them grow up, and being a vital part of the process, is fun and exciting. Close parent-child bonds provide the satisfactions that come with rewarding intimate relationships. All these rewards make it worth the trouble and effort for those who enter parenthood properly prepared and with their eyes open. However, this is saying a lot.

The present book has barely scratched the surface of things that parents need to know. If you find the prospect of doing these things challenging and worthwhile, fine; if you do not, this is fine, too, provided that you react logically and avoid having children. Remember, once a child is born, it will be too late to change your mind. Therefore, if you do not want children or are not sure, *do not have a child*. If you think you might want children but not right now, *wait*.

If you think you can minimize parental responsibilities by hiring help, talk to psychiatrists and psychologists, most of whose clientele had every material advantage, but nevertheless ended up seeking psychological help.

Basically, it comes down to this. If you are male, would you want yourself for a father? If you are female, would you want yourself for a mother? If your answer is "no," this may be an indication of a need for some personal reassessment (but not necessarily). If your answer is "yes," and if you feel that you do want children and are ready to assume the responsibilities of parenthood, try it, you'll like it!

SUMMARY

This chapter presented suggestions about how parents and other adults can help adolescents through the adjustments that come with changes in physical, cognitive, personality, self-concept, moral, and social development. Most of these suggestions involve the same general kinds of parental behavior stressed throughout the book, although these general approaches need to be adjusted to take into account the increasing sophistication and independence of adolescents. If done successfully, the result should be a gradual and relatively easy transition from childish dependency upon adult authority figures to friendship with and respect for loved adults by independent and competent adolescents and young adults.

As a final note, the question of whether or not you should have children was raised. It is one that you must answer for yourself, although you should be in a much better position to answer it now than you were when you started this book, and you can get additional information by talking to parents and by consulting some of the follow-up references listed in the annotated bibliographies. Do not worry if you cannot answer the question right now; eventually you will, and the decision you make probably will be the correct one. Finally, do not expect to answer the question with complete and total certainty. There almost always is at least a little fear of the unknown when we undertake some new venture, and this can be expected in prospective parents. Minor fears of this kind do not mean that you are "not ready," and they should not deter you from having children if you want them.

ANNOTATED BIBLIOGRAPHY, PART FIVE

BERNE, ERIC. *Games people play: The psychology of human relationships.* New York: Grove Press, 1964.

This brief book provides an easy introduction to Berne's transactional analysis approach to behavioral dynamics. It is especially useful for developing insights into the dynamics of adolescent-adult conflict, because Berne's theorizing lends itself to this kind of conflict most particularly. It also is an enjoyable book to read. Many of the "games" discussed in it will be recognizable as basically the defense mechanisms discussed in the present book.

COLEMAN, JAMES. *The adolescent society.* New York: Free Press, 1961.

A classic reference on the youth culture and on the world of the adolescent, particularly as it revolves around school activities. Some of the specific topics are a little dated, but the general principles are still valid today. For example, at the time, conflict between adolescents and school authorities centered around such issues as smoking tobacco and dress codes, whereas today these issues have receded and issues such as drugs have become more prominent. However, the basic dynamics underlying the nature of adolescent conflict with authority figures in the schools remain essentially the same.

ERIKSON, ERIK. *Identity: Youth and crisis.* New York: Norton, 1968 (paperback).

In this volume, Erikson outlines in detail his theory about the adolescent identity crisis, the reasons behind it, and the probable outcomes of different kinds of adjustment to it. This is an important basic source for anyone interested in adolescence and/or in Erikson's theories.

JOURARD, SIDNEY. *Disclosing man to himself.* Princeton: Van Nostrand, 1968.

This book discusses the problem of self-disclosure in detail, presenting some of Jourard's theorizing and research on the topic, which has assumed increasing importance in recent years. In many ways, this and related books probably will be to the 1970s and 1980s what Erikson's works were to the 1960s and early 1970s. The book is especially relevant to adolescents and young adults coping with the crisis of intimacy and having difficulties with self-disclosure and commitment, but it is an important reference for anyone interested in these topics.

LEMASTERS, E. *Parents in modern America: A sociological analysis.* Homewood, Illinois: Dorsey Press, 1974.

This is an excellent source book for young people interested in learning more about what is involved in being and becoming a parent. It will be useful for creating realistic expectations and exploding myths, and providing the kind of information needed in order to make intelligent decisions about whether or not one really wants to be or should be a parent. It explodes some of the more romantic myths about childbirth and parenting, without taking the completely negative tone that has cropped up recently.

McCANDLESS, BOYD. *Adolescents: Behavior and development.* Hinsdale, Illinois: Dryden, 1970.

This is a basic text on the psychology of adolescents, covering in great detail the theories and data relevant to this part of the life cycle.

MANASTER, GUY. *Adolescent development and the life tasks.* Boston: Allyn and Bacon, 1977.

This is a basic text on adolescent development that is similar to the present one in its attempt to present general principles and integrate materials usually covered separately. It is written from a humanistic viewpoint but gives detailed attention to cognitive development in adolescence. It builds on Havighurst's concept of developmental tasks, delving in greater detail into the developmental tasks facing adolescents today and their implications for individuals.

REFERENCES

ADAMS, B. Birth order: A critical review. *Sociometry*, 1972, 35, 411–439.

AINSWORTH, M. Object relations, dependency, and attachment: A theoretical review of the infant-mother relationship. *Child Development*, 1969, *40*, 969–1025.

ALLPORT, G. *Becoming: Basic considerations for a psychology of personality*. New Haven: Yale University Press, 1955.

ALLPORT, G. *The individual and his religion*. New York: Macmillan, 1950.

AUSUBEL, D. AND SULLIVAN, E. *Theory and problems of child development*, second edition. New York: Grune and Stratton, 1970.

BALDWIN, A. *Theories of child development*. New York: Wiley, 1967.

BANDURA, A. *Principles of behavior modification*. New York: Holt, Rinehart and Winston, 1969.

BAUMRIND, D. Current patterns of parental authority. *Developmental Psychology Monograph*, 1971, *4* (No. 1, Part 2).

BAYLEY, N. Behavioral correlates of mental growth: Birth to thirty-six years. *American Psychologist*, 1968, 23, 1–17.

BECKER, W. Consequences of different kinds of parental discipline. In M. Hoffman and L. Hoffman (Eds.). *Review of child development research*, Volume one. New York: Russell Sage Foundation. 1964.

BELL, R. Stimulus control of parent or caretaker behavior by offspring. *Developmental Psychology*, 1971, *4*, 61–72.

BENTLER, P. AND McCLAIN, J. A multitrait-multimethod analysis of reflection-impulsivity. *Child Development*, 1976, *47*, 218–226.

BERNE, E. *Games people play: The psychology of human relationships*. New York: Grove Press, 1964.

BERNSTEIN, B. Social class, linguistic codes, and grammatical elements. *Language and Speech*, 1962, *5*, 221–240.

BIJOU, S. AND BAER, D. *Child Development: Readings in experimental analysis*. New York: Appleton-Century-Crofts, 1967.

BISCHOF, L. *Adult psychology*, second edition. New York: Harper and Row, 1976.

BLOOM, B. *Stability and change in human characteristics*. New York: Wiley, 1964.

BOWLBY, J. *Attachment and loss. Volume 1. Attachment*. New York: Basic Books, 1969.

BRAINE, M. Children's first word combinations. *Monographs of the Society for Research in Child Development*, 1976, *41*, No. 1 (Serial No. 164).

BRONFENBRENNER, U. Developmental research, public policy, and the ecology of childhood. *Child Development*, 1974, *45*, 1–5.

BRONSON, G. Infants' reactions to unfamiliar persons and novel objects. *Monographs of the Society for Research in Child Development*, 1972, *37*, No. 3 (Serial No. 148).

BROPHY, J. Mothers as teachers of their own preschool children: The influence of socioeconomic status and task structure on teaching specificity. *Child Development*, 1970, *41*, 79–94.

BROPHY, J. AND EVERTSON, C. *Learning from teaching: A developmental perspective*. Boston: Allyn and Bacon, 1976.

BROPHY, J. AND GOOD, T. *Teacher-student relationships: Causes and consequences*. New York: Holt, Rinehart and Winston, 1974.

BROWN, R., CAZDEN, C., AND BELLUGI, U. The child's grammar from I to III. In J. Hill (Ed.). *1967 Minnesota Symposium on Child Psychology*. Minneapolis: University of Minnesota Press, 1969.

BRUNER, J. *Toward a theory of instruction.* Cambridge, Massachusetts: Belknap, 1966.

BRYAN, J. Children's cooperation and helping behaviors. In E. Heatherington (Ed.). *Review of Child Development Research,* Volume 5. Chicago: University of Chicago Press, 1975.

BYRNE, D. Attitudes and attraction. In Berkowitz, L. (Ed.) *Advances in experimental social psychology,* Volume 4. New York: Academic Press, 1969.

BYRNE, D. Repression-sensitization as a dimension of personality. In Maher, B. (Ed.). *Progress in experimental personality research,* Volume 1. New York: Academic Press, 1964.

CAMPBELL, D. On the conflicts between biological and social evolution and between psychology and moral tradition. *American Psychologist,* 1975, *30,* 1103–1126.

CATTELL, R. *Abilities: Their structure, growth, and action.* Boston: Houghton-Mifflin, 1971.

CAZDEN, C. *Child language and education.* New York: Holt, Rinehart and Winston, 1972.

CHOMSKY, N. *Language and mind,* second edition, New York: Harcourt, 1972.

CLARKE-STEWART, K. Interactions between mothers and their young children: Characteristics and consequences. *Monographs of the Society for Research in Child Development,* 1973, *38,* Nos. 6–7 (Serial No. 153).

COATES, B., PUSSER, H., AND GOODMAN, I. The influence of "Sesame Street" and "Mister Rogers' Neighborhood" on children's social behavior in the preschool. *Child Development,* 1976, *47,* 138–144.

COLEMAN, J. *The adolescent society,* New York: Free Press, 1961.

COOPERSMITH, S. *The antecedents of self-esteem.* San Francisco: Freeman, 1967.

COOPERSMITH, S. AND FELDMAN, R. Fostering a positive self concept and high self-esteem in the classroom. In R. Coop and K. White (Eds.). *Psychological concepts in the classroom.* New York: Harper and Row, 1974.

CRAIK, F. AND LOCKHART, R. Levels of processing: A framework for memory research. *Journal of Verbal Learning and Verbal Behavior,* 1972, *II,* 671–684.

DALE, P. *Language development: Structure and function,* second edition. New York: Holt, Rinehart and Winston, 1976.

D'ANDRADE, R. Sex differences and cultural institutions. In E. Maccoby (Ed.). *The development of sex differences.* Stanford: Stanford University Press, 1966.

DAVIS, C. Results of the self-selection of diets by young children. *Canadian Medical Association Journal,* 1939, *41,* 257–261.

DELACATO, C. *The diagnosis and treatment of speech and reading problems.* Springfield, Illinois: Thomas, 1963.

DENNIS, W. Infant development under conditions of restricted practice and minimum social stimulation. *Genetic Psychology Monographs,* 1941, *23,* 143–189.

DEUTSCH, M. The role of social class in language development and cognition. *American Journal of Orthopsychiatry,* 1965, *35,* 78–88.

DICK-READ, G. *Childbirth without fear: The principles and practice of natural childbirth,* second revised edition. New York: Harper and Row, 1959.

DODSON, F. *How to parent.* New York: Signet, 1970.

DUNKIN, M. AND BIDDLE, B. *The study of teaching.* New York: Holt, Rinehart and Winston, 1974.

DWECK, C. AND BUSH, E. Sex differences in learned helplessness: I. Differential debilitation with peer and adult evaluators. *Developmental Psychology,* 1976, *12,* 147–156.

DYK, R. AND WITKIN, H. Family experiences related to the development of differentiation in children. *Child Development,* 1965, *36,* 21–55.

EBBINGHAUS, G. *Memory,* 1885. (Translated by H. Ruger and C. Bussenius.) New York: Teachers College Press, 1913.

ELKIND, D. The child's conception of his religious identity. *Lumen Vitae,* 1964, *19,* 635–646.

ERIKSON, E. *Childhood and society,* second edition. New York: Norton, 1963.

ERIKSON, E. *Identity: Youth and crisis.* New York: Norton, 1968.

FERGUSON, G. On learning and human ability. *Canadian Journal of Psychology,* 1954, *8,* 95–112.

558

FERGUSON, G. On transfer and the abilities of man. *Canadian Journal of Psychology*, 1956, *10*, 121–131.

FERSTER, C. AND SKINNER, B. *Schedules of reinforcement*. New York: Appleton-Century-Crofts, 1957.

FESHBACH, S. Aggression. In P. Mussen (Ed.). *Carmichael's manual of child psychology*, third edition, Volume 2. New York: Wiley, 1970.

FESTINGER, L. *A theory of cognitive dissonance*. Stanford: Stanford University Press, 1957.

FLAVELL, J. *The developmental psychology of Jean Piaget*. New York: Van Nostrand, 1963.

FLAVELL, J., BEACH, D., AND CHINSKY, J. Spontaneous verbal rehearsal in a memory task as a function of age. *Child Development*, 1966, *37*, 283–299.

FLAVELL, J., BOTKIN, P., FRY, C., WRIGHT, J., AND JARVIS, P. *The development of role-taking and communication skills in children*. New York: Wiley, 1968.

FREUD, A. *The ego and the mechanisms of defense*. New York: International Universities Press, 1946.

FREUD, S. *The basic writings of Sigmund Freud*. Translated by A. Brill. New York: Modern Library, 1938.

GAGNÉ, R. *The conditions of learning*, second edition. New York: Holt, Rinehart and Winston, 1970.

GARDNER, R., JACKSON, D., AND MESSICK, S. Personality organization in cognitive controls and intellectual abilities. *Psychological Issues*, 1960, *2*, Monograph 8.

GESELL, A. The ontogenesis of infant behavior. In L. Carmichael (Ed.). *Manual of child psychology*, second edition. New York: Wiley, 1954.

GESELL, A. AND THOMPSON, H. Learning and growth in identical infant twins. *Genetic Psychology Monographs*, 1929, *6*, 1–24.

GLASS, G. AND ROBBINS, M. A critique of experiments on the role of neurological organization in reading performance. *Reading Research Quarterly*, 1967, *3*, 5–51.

GLUCKSBERG, S., KRAUSS, R., AND HIGGINS, E. The development of referential communication skills. In F. Horowitz (Ed.). *Review of Child Development Research*, Volume 4. Chicago: University of Chicago Press, 1975.

GOOD, T., BIDDLE, B., AND BROPHY, J. *Teachers make a difference*. New York: Holt, Rinehart and Winston, 1975.

GOOD, T. AND BROPHY, J. *Looking in classrooms*. New York: Harper and Row, 1973.

GORDON, T. *P.E.T.: Parent effectiveness training*. New York: Wyden, 1970.

GORN, G., GOLDBERG, M., AND KANUNGO, R. The role of educational television in changing the intergroup attitudes of children. *Child Development*, 1976, *47*, 277–280.

GOTTESMAN, I. Biogenetics of race and class. In Deutsch, M., Katz, I., and Jensen, A. (Eds.). *Social class, race, and psychological development*. New York: Holt, Rinehart and Winston, 1968.

GUILFORD, J. *The nature of human intelligence*. New York: McGraw-Hill, 1967.

GUTTMACHER, A. *Pregnancy, birth, and family planning: A guide for expectant parents in the 1970s*. New York: Viking, 1973.

HAAN, N. Proposed model of ego functioning: Coping and defense mechanism in relationship to I.Q. change. *Psychological Monographs*, 1963, *77*, No. 8.

HALL, C. AND LINDZEY, G. *Theories of personality*, second edition. New York: Wiley, 1970.

HAMBLIN, R., BUCKHOLDT, D., FERRITOR, D., KOZLOFF, M., AND BLACKWELL, L. *The humanization processes: A social, behavioral analysis of children's problems*. New York: Wiley-Interscience, 1971.

HARLOW, H. AND HARLOW, M. Learning to love. *American Scientist*, 1966, *54*(3), 244–272.

HARTSHORNE, H. AND MAY, M. *Studies in deceit*. New York: Macmillan, 1930.

HARTUP, W. Peer interaction and social organization. In P. Mussen (Ed.). *Carmichael's manual of child psychology*, third edition, Volume 2. New York: Wiley, 1970.

HAVIGHURST, R. *Human development and education*. New York: Longmans, 1953.

HEATHERINGTON, E. AND PARKE, R. *Child psychology: A contemporary viewpoint*. New York: McGraw-Hill, 1975.

HERRON, R. AND SUTTON-SMITH, B. (Eds.). *Child's play*. New York: Wiley, 1971.

HESS, R. Social class and ethnic influences upon socialization. In P. Mussen (Ed.). *Carmichael's manual of child psychology*, third edition, Volume 2. New York: Wiley, 1970.

HESS, R., SHIPMAN, V., BROPHY, J., AND BEAR, R. *The cognitive environments of urban preschool children*. Chicago: School of Education, University of Chicago, 1968.

HESS, R. AND TORNEY, J. *The development of political attitudes in children*. Chicago: Aldine, 1967.

HOFFMAN, M. Moral development. In P. Mussen (Ed.). *Carmichael's manual of child psychology*, third edition, Volume 2. New York: Wiley, 1970.

HOPKINS, K. AND BRACHT, G. Ten-year stability of verbal and nonverbal IQ scores. *American Educational Research Journal*, 1975, *12*, 469–477.

HUNT, J. *Intelligence and experience*. New York: Ronald, 1961.

HUNT, J. *The challenge of incompetence and poverty: Papers on the role of early education*. Chicago: University of Illinois Press, 1969.

JACKSON, P. *Life in classrooms*. New York: Holt, Rinehart and Winston, 1968.

JARVIK, L., KLODIN, V., AND MATSUYAMA, S. Human aggression and the extra Y chromosome. *American Psychologist*, 1973, *28*, 674–682.

JENSEN, A. Hierarchical theories of mental ability. In Dockrell, B. (Ed.). *On intelligence*. Toronto: Ontario Institute for Studies in Education, 1970.

JENSEN, A. How much can we boost I.Q. and scholastic achievement? *Harvard Educational Review*, 1969, *39*, 1–123.

JOURARD, S. *Disclosing man to himself*. Princeton, New Jersey: Van Nostrand, 1968.

KAGAN, J. AND KOGAN, N. Individual variation in cognitive processes. In P. Mussen (Ed.). *Carmichael's manual of child psychology*, third edition, Volume 1. New York: Wiley, 1970.

KAGAN, J. AND MOSS, H. *Birth to maturity: A study in psychological development*. New York: Wiley, 1962.

KAGAN, J., PEARSON, J., AND WELCH, L. Modifiability of an impulsive tempo. *Journal of Educational Psychology*, 1966, *57*, 357–365.

KAGAN, S. AND MADSEN, M. Experimental analysis of cooperation and competition of Anglo-American and Mexican children. *Developmental Psychology*, 1972, *6*, 49–59.

KAMIN, L. *The science and politics of I.Q.* Potomac, Maryland: Erlbaum, 1974.

KESSEN, W., HAITH, M., AND SALAPATEK, P. Human infancy: A bibliography and guide. In P. Mussen (Ed.). *Carmichael's manual of child psychology*, third edition, Volume 1. New York: Wiley, 1970.

KINSEY, A., POMEROY, W., AND MARTIN, C. *Sexual behavior in the human male*. Philadelphia: Saunders, 1948.

KLINGER, E. AND MCNELLY, F. Self states and performances of preadolescent boys carrying out leadership roles inconsistent with their social status. *Child Development*, 1976, *47*, 126–137.

KOCH, H. The relation of certain formal attributes of siblings to attitudes held toward each other and toward their parents. *Monographs of the Society for Research in Child Development*, 1960, *25*, No. 4 (Serial No. 78).

KOHLBERG, L. A cognitive-developmental analysis of children's sex-role concepts and attitudes. In E. Maccoby (Ed.). *The development of sex differences*. Stanford: Stanford University Press, 1966.

KOHLBERG, L. Stage and sequence: The cognitive-developmental approach to socialization. In D. Goslin (Ed.). *Handbook of socialization theory and research*. Chicago: Rand McNally, 1969.

KOHLBERG, L., YEAGER, J., AND HJERTHOLM, E. Private speech: Four studies and a review of theories. *Child Development*, 1968, *39*, 691–736.

KOHLBERG, L. AND ZIGLER, E. The impact of cognitive maturity upon the development of sex-role attitudes in the years 4 to 8. *Genetic Psychology Monographs*, 1967, *75*, 84–165.

KRAUS, P. *Yesterday's children: A longitudinal study of children from kindergarten into the adult years*. New York: Wiley-Interscience, 1973.

KREITLER, H. AND KREITLER, S. Children's

560

concepts of sexuality and birth. *Child Development*, 1966, *37*, 363–378.

Kris, E. *Psychoanalytic explorations in art.* New York: International Universities Press, 1952.

Kroeber, A. *Anthropology today: An encyclopedic inventory.* Chicago: University of Chicago Press, 1953.

Kuhn, D. Short-term longitudinal evidence for the sequentiality of Kohlberg's early stages of moral judgment. *Developmental Psychology*, 1976, *12*, 162–166.

Kuhn, T. *The structure of scientific revolutions.* Chicago: University of Chicago Press, 1962.

Lecky, P. *Self-consistency.* New York: Island Press, 1945.

Lesser, G., Fifer, G., and Clark, D. Mental abilities of children from different social-class and cultural groups. *Monographs of the Society for Research in Child Development*, 1965, *30* (Serial No. 102).

Lewis, M. and Rosenbloom, L. (Eds.) *The effect of the infant on its caregiver.* New York: Wiley, 1974.

Lynn, D. *The father: His role in child development.* Monterey, California: Brooks/Cole, 1974.

Maccoby, E. The taking of adult roles in middle childhood. *Journal of Abnormal and Social Psychology*, 1961, *63*, 493–503.

Maccoby, E. and Jacklin, C. *The psychology of sex differences.* Stanford: Stanford University Press, 1974.

Maccoby, E. and Masters, J. Attachment and dependency. In P. Mussen (Ed.). *Carmichael's manual of child psychology*, third edition, Volume 2. New York: Wiley, 1970.

MacKinnon, D. The nature and nurture of creative talent. *American Psychologist*, 1962, *17*, 484–495.

Maddi, S. *Personality theories: A comparative analysis*, third edition. Homewood, Illinois: Dorsey, 1976.

Martin, B. Parent-child relations. In F. Horowitz (Ed.). *Review of child development research*,

Volume 4. Chicago: University of Chicago Press, 1975.

Maslow, A. *Motivation and personality*, second edition. New York: Harper and Row, 1970.

May, R. (Ed.). *Existential psychology*, second edition. New York: Random House, 1969.

McCall, R., Appelbaum, M., and Hogarty, P. Developmental changes in mental performance. *Monographs of the Society for Research in Child Development*, 1973, *38* (3, Serial No. 150).

McClelland, D. Risk-taking in children with high and low need for achievement. In J. Atkinson (Ed.). *Motives in fantasy, action, and society.* Princeton, New Jersey: Van Nostrand, 1958.

McDavid, J. and Harari, H. Stereotyping of names and popularity in grade school children. *Child Development*, 1966, *37*, 453–459.

Meichenbaum, D. and Goodman, J. Training impulsive children to talk to themselves: A means of developing self-control. *Journal of Abnormal Psychology*, 1971, *77*, 115–126.

Merton, R. The self-fulfilling prophecy. *Antioch Review*, 1948, *8*, 193–210.

Miller, L. and Dyer, J. Four preschool programs: Their dimensions and effects. *Monographs of the Society for Research in Child Development*, 1975, *40*, Nos. 5–6 (Serial No. 162).

Mischel, W. A social-learning view of sex differences in behavior. In E. Maccoby (Ed.). *The development of sex differences.* Stanford: Stanford University Press, 1966.

Mischel, W. *Introduction to personality.* New York: Holt, Rinehart and Winston, 1971.

Moore, N., Evertson, C., and Brophy, J. Solitary play: Some functional reconsiderations. *Developmental Psychology*, 1974, *10*, 830–834.

Mowrer, O. *The new group therapy.* Princeton, New Jersey: Van Nostrand, 1964.

Murphy, G. *Human potentialities.* New York: Basic Books, 1958.

Murphy, J. Psychiatric labeling in cross-cultural perspective. *Science*, 1976, *191*, 1019–1028.

Murphy, L. *The widening world of childhood.* New York: Basic Books, 1962.

NASH, J. *Developmental psychology: A psychobiological approach.* Englewood Cliffs, New Jersey: Prentice-Hall, 1970.

NASH, R. *Classrooms observed: A teacher's perception and the pupil's performance.* London: Routledge and Kegan Paul, 1973.

NEIMARK, E. AND SANTA, J. Thinking and concept attainment. In M. Rosenzweig and L. Porter (Eds.). *Annual review of psychology,* Volume 26. Palo Alto, California: Annual Reviews, 1975.

O'BRYANT, S. The effects of success and failure and cooperation and competition on children's altruism. Unpublished doctoral dissertation, The University of Texas at Austin, 1975.

ORTONY, A. Language isn't for people: On applying theoretical linguistics to practical problems. *Review of Educational Research,* 1975, *45,* 485–504.

PARTEN, M. Social participation among pre-school children. *Journal of Abnormal and Social Psychology,* 1932, 27, 243–269.

PAVLOV, I. *Conditioned reflexes.* Oxford: Clarendon Press, 1927.

PECK, R. AND HAVIGHURST, R. *The psychology of character development.* New York: Wiley, 1960.

PIAGET, J. Piaget's theory. In P. Mussen (Ed.). *Carmichael's manual of child psychology,* third edition, Volume one. New York: Wiley, 1970.

PIAGET, J. *The construction of reality in the child.* New York: Basic Books, 1954.

PIAGET J. *The moral judgment of the child.* (Translated by M. Worden.) New York: Harcourt, Brace and World, 1932.

PIAGET, J. AND INHELDER, B. *The psychology of the child.* (Translated by H. Weaver.) New York: Basic Books, 1969.

POLLACK, R. Some implications of ontogenetic changes in perception. In D. Elkind and J. Flavell (Eds.). *Studies in cognitive development.* New York: Oxford University Press, 1969.

PREMACK, D. Reinforcement theory. In D. Levine (Ed.). *Nebraska symposium on motivation.* Lincoln, Nebraska: University of Nebraska Press, 1965.

PRIBHAM, K. *Languages of the brain: Experimental paradoxes and principles in neuropsychology.* Englewood Cliffs, New Jersey: Prentice-Hall, 1971.

REST, J. Developmental psychology as a guide to value education: A review of "Kohlbergian" programs. *Review of Educational Research,* 1974, *44,* 241–259.

ROBBINS, M. A study of the validity of Delacato's theory of neurological organization. *Exceptional Children,* 1966, *32,* 517–523.

ROBINSON, M. Parent-child development centers: An experiment in parent intervention and R and D strategies. Paper presented at the biennial meeting of the Society for Research in Child Development, 1975.

ROGERS, C. *On becoming a person.* Boston: Houghton-Mifflin, 1961.

ROHWER, W., AMMON, P., AND CRAMER, P. *Understanding intellectual development: Three approaches to theory and practice:* Hinsdale, Illinois: Dryden, 1974.

ROSENTHAL, R. AND JACOBSON, L. *Pygmalion in the classroom: Teacher expectation and pupils' intellectual development.* New York: Holt, Rinehart and Winston, 1968.

RUBIN, K., MAIONI, T., AND HORNUNG, M. Free play behaviors in middle- and lower-class preschoolers: Parten and Piaget revisited. *Child Development,* 1976, *47,* 414–419.

SCARR-SALAPATEK, S. Genetics and the development of intelligence. In F. Horowitz (Ed.). *Review of Research in Child Development,* Volume 4. Chicago: University of Chicago Press, 1975.

SCHACHTER, F., KIRSHNER, K., KLIPS, B., FRIEDRICKS, M., AND SANDERS, K. Everyday preschool interpersonal speech usage: Methodological, developmental, and sociolinguistic studies. *Monographs of the Society for Research on Child Development,* 1974, *39,* No. 3 (Serial No. 156).

SCHACHTER, S. The interaction of cognitive and physiological determinants of emotional state. In P. Leiderman and D. Shapiro (Eds.). *Psychobiological approaches to social behavior.* Stanford: Stanford University Press, 1964.

562

SCHAEFER, E. A circumplex model for maternal behavior. *Journal of Abnormal and Social Psychology*, 1959, 59, 226–235.

SCHMUCK, R. AND SCHMUCK, P. *Group processes in the classroom*. Dubuque: William C. Brown, 1975.

SEGALL, M., CAMPBELL, D., AND HERSKOVITS, M. *The influence of culture on visual perception*. New York: Bobbs-Merrill, 1966.

SERBIN, L. AND O'LEARY, K. How nursery schools teach girls to shut up. *Psychology Today*, 1975, 9 (No. 7), December, 56–58, 102–103.

SIGEL, I. The development of classificatory skills in young children: A training program. *Young Children*, 1971, 26, 170–184.

SIGEL, I. AND COOP, R. Cognitive style and classroom practice. In R. Coop and K. White (Eds.). *Psychological concepts in the classroom*. New York: Harper and Row, 1974.

SILBERMAN, C. *Crisis in the classroom*. New York: Random House, 1970.

SKEELS, H. Adult status of children with contrasting early life experiences. *Monographs of the Society for Research in Child Development*, 1966, 31, No. 3 (Serial No. 105).

SKINNER, B. *Science and human behavior*. New York: Macmillan, 1953.

SMILANSKY, S. *The effects of sociodramatic play on disadvantaged children: Preschool children*. New York: Wiley, 1968.

SPEARMAN, C. "General intelligence" objectively determined and measured. *American Journal of Psychology*, 1904, 15, 201–292.

SPENCE, J. AND HELMREICH, R. Who likes competent women? Competence, sex role congruence of interests, and subjects' attitudes toward women as determinants of interpersonal attraction. *Journal of Applied Social Psychology*, 1972, 2, 197–213.

SPIVACK, G. AND SHURE, M. Childrearing and the development of interpersonal cognitive problem-solving ability. Research and Evaluation Report No. 33, Hahnemann Medical College and Hospital, 1975.

SROUFE, L. A methodological and philosophical critique of intervention oriented research. *Developmental Psychology*, 1970, 2, 140–145.

STEIN, A. AND FREIDRICH, L. The impact of television on children and youth. In E. Heatherington (Ed.). *Review of child development research*, Volume 5. Chicago: University of Chicago Press, 1975.

STEVENSON, H. *Children's learning*. New York: Appleton-Century-Crofts, 1972.

STODOLSKY, S. AND LESSER, G. Learning patterns in the disadvantaged. *Harvard Educational Review*, 1967, 37, 546–593.

STONE, L. AND CHURCH, J. *Childhood and adolescence: A psychology of the growing person*, third edition. New York: Random House, 1973.

STRIKE, K. The logic of learning by discovery. *Review of Educational Research*, 1975, 45, 461–483.

SUCHMAN, R. AND TRABASSO, T. Stimulus preference and cue function in young children's concept attainment. *Journal of Experimental Child Psychology*, 1966, 3, 188–198.

SULLIVAN, H. *The interpersonal theory of psychiatry*. New York: Norton, 1953.

SUTTON-SMITH, B. AND ROSENBERG, B. *The sibling*. New York: Holt, Rinehart and Winston, 1970.

TANNER, J. Physical growth. In P. Mussen (Ed.). *Carmichael's manual of child psychology*, third edition, Volume 1. New York: Wiley, 1970.

TERMAN, L. AND MERRILL, M. *Stanford-Binet Intelligence Scale. Manual for the third revision: Form L-M*. Boston: Houghton Mifflin, 1960.

THIGPEN, C. AND CLECKLEY, H. *The three faces of Eve*. New York: Popular Library, 1974.

THOMAS, A., CHESS, S., AND BIRCH, H. The origin of personality. *Scientific American*, 1970, 223, 102–109.

THURSTONE, L. *Primary mental abilities*. Chicago: University of Chicago Press, 1938.

TORRANCE, E. *Guiding creative talent*. Englewood Cliffs, New Jersey: Prentice-Hall, 1962.

TYLER, L. *The psychology of human differences*, third edition. New York: Appleton-Century-Crofts, 1965.

VELLAY, P., ET AL. *Childbirth without pain*. New York: Dutton, 1960.

VYGOTSKY, L. *Thought and language.* Cambridge, Massachusetts: M.I.T. Press, 1962.

WACHS, T. Relation of infants' performance on Piaget scales between twelve and twenty-four months and their Stanford-Binet performance at thirty-one months. *Child Development,* 1975, *46,* 929–935.

WALLACH, M. Creativity. In P. Mussen (Ed.). *Carmichael's manual of child psychology,* third edition, Volume 1. New York: Wiley, 1970.

WATSON, G. Some personality differences in children related to strict or permissive parental discipline. *Journal of Psychology,* 1957, *44,* 227–249.

WATSON, J. *Psychological care of infant and child.* New York: Norton, 1928.

WATSON, J. AND RAYNOR, R. Conditioned emotional reactions. *Journal of Experimental Psychology,* 1920, *3,* 1–14.

WEIKART, D. A comparative study of three preschool curricula. Paper presented at the biennial meeting of the Society for Research in Child Development, 1969.

WERNER, H. *The comparative psychology of mental development.* New York: International Universities Press, 1957.

WHITE, B. *The first three years of life.* Englewood Cliffs, New Jersey: Prentice-Hall, 1975.

WHITE, R. *The abnormal personality,* second edition. New York: Ronald, 1956.

WHITE, R. Motivation reconsidered: The concept of competence. *Psychological Review,* 1959, *66,* 297–323.

WHITING, J. AND CHILD, I. *Child training and personality: A cross-cultural study.* New Haven: Yale University Press, 1953.

WHORF, B. *Language, thought, and reality: Selected writings.* Cambridge, Massachusetts: Technology Press, 1956.

WITKIN, H., DYK, R., FATERSON, H., GOODENOUGH, D., AND KARP, S. *Psychological differentiation.* New York: Wiley, 1962.

YARROW, M. AND WAXLER, C. WITH BARRETT, D., DARBY, J., KING, R., PICKETT, M., AND SMITH, J. Dimensions and correlates of prosocial behavior in young children. *Child Development,* 1976, *47,* 118–125.

YOUNG, F. *Initiation ceremonies.* Indianapolis: Bobbs-Merrill, 1965.

ZAJONC, R. Family configuration and intelligence. *Science,* 1976, *192,* 227–236.

GLOSSARY

ACCOMMODATION Piaget's term for the process of adapting to stimulus situations by changing existing schemas or developing new ones. Accommodation corresponds roughly to the development of new learning. *See* assimilation.

ACHIEVEMENT MOTIVATION General term referring to the motivation to succeed by meeting or surpassing some objective or internally set standard.

ADOLESCENCE That part of the life cycle which begins with sexual maturation (ordinarily around ages 10–13 in girls and 12–15 in boys).

ADULTOMORPHIZE Attribution to young children of adult concepts, motives, or other mature experiences or characteristics which they have not yet developed.

AFTERBIRTH The placenta, umbilical cord, and other temporary biological structures that were needed in the womb between conception and birth but which no longer are necessary and must be expelled from the mother's body following the birth of the baby.

ANAL EXPULSIVE PERSONALITY Freudian term for a particular kind of adult personality marked by sloppiness, messiness, and vulgarity, especially concerning the use of terms relating to urination and defecation. Hypothesized to result from unfortunate toilet training experiences during the anal stage. *See* adultomorphize.

ANAL RETENTIVE PERSONALITY Freudian term for an adult personality type marked by neatness, orderliness, obsessive concern with cleanliness, and penuriousness regarding money or other valuable possessions. Believed to result from unfortunate experiences during toilet training during the anal stage. *See* adultomorphize.

ANAL STAGE The second of Freud's developmental stages, so-called because he believed that the most important event occurring during this stage was toilet training and the experiences and socialization connected with it. *See* adultomorphize.

ANDROGENY A form of sexual adjustment which combines the better features of the two traditional sex roles but eliminates the less desirable ones.

ANIMISM Piaget's term for a particular type of egocentric thinking by preoperational children. Animism refers to the tendency of such children to believe that everything is alive (at first), and later, that everything that moves is alive.

ARTIFICIAL INSEMINATION Impregnation of a fertile egg cell (insemination) through artificial means rather than through normal sexual intercourse. Typically accomplished using a hypodermic needle to infuse sperm cells collected previously from a male donor.

ASSIMILATION Piaget's term for the process of adapting to stimulus situations using previously existing knowledge and abilities. Aspects of situations that can be assimilated are aspects that require no change or new learning. *See* accommodation.

ASSOCIATIVE PLAY One of a series of stages in the development of social play as outlined by Parten. At this stage, children who previously engaged in parallel play which involved playing in close physical proximity but without any true interaction or cooperation begin to interact and cooperate. There is more verbal interaction than actual cooperation in associative play, with the children exchanging comments about their own and each other's activity.

AUTHORITARIAN A general personality type, and, more specifically, an approach to child rearing. Authoritarian individuals respond primarily to their own and other people's relative positions of power and authority, rather than to considerations of logic or the common good. *See* authoritative, and *laissez-faire*.

AUTHORITATIVE A term introduced by Baumrind to describe an approach to socialization that strikes a happy medium between authoritarian and *laissez-faire* methods. Authoritative parents are affectionate and child-oriented, and they present rules and limits with explanations and concern for children's feelings, but they also make sure that these rules and limits are enforced.

AUTOEROTICISM Self-stimulation for sexual pleasure, usually involving both masturbation in some form and sexual fantasies to initiate and sustain sexual arousal.

AUTONOMIC NERVOUS SYSTEM That part of the nervous system controlled mostly by the lower regions of the brain and thus operating automatically and without conscious effort. Includes the neural mechanisms regulating heartbeat, changes in internal physiology in response to different physiological needs (fight or flight reactions to stress, digestion processes following intake of food, and so on), and mobilization of the energy and physiological supports needed for vigorous work or exercise. Autonomic processes ordinarily cannot be affected systematically through conscious willful action, but they do react to conscious experiences. *See* homeostasis.

AUTONOMY A term that refers both to the state of, and the awareness of, need for, or achievement of, independence in making decisions and guiding one's actions.

BABY TALK The traditional term for well-meant but unnecessary and sometimes condescending attempts to accommodate to the speech of babies by imitating or by using terms that adults think babies will understand or prefer in contrast to more normal speech ("din-din" for dinner). *See* simplified speech.

BEHAVIOR MODIFICATION The systematic application of Skinnerian principles of behavior analysis in order to modify behavior in particular ways. It is the applied aspect of the Skinnerian approach to learning and the general analysis of behavior.

BEHAVIOR MODIFIERS Those who develop and implement procedures for applying Skinnerian principles for the purpose of modifying the behavior of individuals who are judged to need such modification for some reason.

BEHAVIORAL SHAPING The procedures used by behavior modifiers in order to change behavior systematically (also refers to the results of such activity). Behavioral shaping involves systematic application of applied behavioral analysis procedures in order to move people systematically through successive approximations from where they started toward a desired end state.

BEHAVIORISM One of the major approaches to the study of psychology in general and child development in particular, and perhaps the most influential. Modern behaviorists concentrate on overt behavior instead of unmeasurable subjective experience, show concern with methodology, and have a tradition of care in conducting and reporting experiments, a tendency to view organisms as relatively passive and under the control of stimuli and reinforcements, a preference for experimental over correlational observational study, and an aversion to hypothesized internal constructs like "stage," which they look upon as unnecessary and as merely descriptive but not explanatory.

BELIEF A relationship or item of information that a person thinks to be factual, whether it is or not. Along with attitudes and expectations, beliefs both result from prior experience and shape future experience (in part through self-fulfilling prophecy effects).

BILATERAL PRINCIPLE One of the basic general principles of physical development. Human bodies are generally bilateral, with most organs and bodily parts on the left side of the body having counterparts on the right side. During development, corresponding organs or bodily parts typically begin development at about the same time and progress at about the same rate, although it is typical for one member of each pair to be dominant over the other to some degree.

BLANK STATE A term (taken from the Latin *tabula rasa*) describing the theory that infants are born with little or no genetic programming of their later intellectual or personal attributes.

BREECH BIRTH Births in which the newborn does not emerge in the typical head down and head first fashion.

CAESARIAN SECTION Term for the removal of an infant from the womb through an operation involving an incision in the abdominal wall and removal of the infant from the incision rather than through the birth canal.

CANALIZATION A basic developmental process. Initially, behavior is relatively undifferentiated and the probabilities of alternate potentials are similar. As a result of repeated experiences in doing one of a number of possible alternatives, options which were more equally likely earlier become differentiated. Established paths are taken more and more frequently until they become overlearned and retained as characteristic features, while other alternatives which might have been equally likely are unexplored or gradually dropped in favor of the preferred behavior. *See* differentiation.

CATHARSIS Release of pent-up emotional tension and/or the gratification of needs that occurs when people break through barriers to expression of the desired behavior and act it out. Theoretically, the catharsis that occurs at this time involves both an immediate sense of relief and gratification and a release of the pent-up needs to perform the behavior. Some believe that this will reduce the likelihood that it will be performed again in the future (at least the near future).

CENTRAL-DISTAL PRINCIPLE A basic principle of physical development. In general, internal (central) organs and bodily systems develop earlier and to a greater degree of completion than more external (distal) parts.

CEPHALO-CAUDAL PRINCIPLE A basic principle of physical development. In general, development occurs earlier and proceeds to a greater degree of completion for parts of the body at or near the head area than it does for parts of the body at or near the tail area.

CERVIX The outer end of the uterus which normally is quite narrow but which dilates considerably during the birth process in order to accommodate the passage of the infant through and out of the birth canal.

CHROMOSOMES Microscopic but extremely vital collections of genes, the biological entities responsible for transmission of heredity. Humans have 23 pairs of chromosomes, each containing many genes.

CIRCUMPLEX MODEL A model depicting the relationships among variables, showing them arranged in a circle in which variables adjacent to one another are closely and positively related, variables 90 degrees apart from one another are unrelated, and those 180 degrees apart from one another (across the circle) are negatively related.

CLASSICAL CONDITIONING Conditioning paradigms, based originally on Pavlov's dog salivation studies, in which existing (unconditioned) responses are conditioned to appear in reaction to the presence of a conditioned stimulus which did not have the power to evoke them before. This is accomplished by presenting the conditioned stimulus immediately prior to the unconditioned stimulus which already has the power to evoke response, and repeating this until the organism associates the two stimuli and begins to react to the conditioned stimulus the same way it reacts to the unconditioned stimulus. *See* instrumental conditioning.

CLONING A biological procedure whereby exact genetic duplicates of individuals are created.

COGNITION A general term referring to intellectual activity such as thinking and problem solving. It usually is distinguished from affect, which refers to the emotional aspects of experience.

COGNITIVE CONSISTENCY A term popularized by Festinger and hypothesized as a general principle of human psychology. It is stated that humans spontaneously seek cognitive consistency and will take action to remove any inconsistencies among their beliefs, attitudes, or behaviors. In this book, it is claimed that cognitive consistency motives do not take effect until the child becomes operational and achieves a stable cognitive structure.

COGNITIVE DEVELOPMENT General term referring to the development of the intellectual processes involved in thinking and problem solving. Piaget and others have shown that a sequence of qualitatively distinct stages is identifiable in cognitive development. As individuals achieve a higher stage, they are capable of doing things that they were not capable of doing previously.

COGNITIVE ENVIRONMENT A term used by Hess and his colleagues to refer to the quality of intellectual stimulation, parental competence, and general aspects of the environment in which children grow up that affect children's cognitive development.

COGNITIVE SCHEMA A concept, intuitive understanding of a relationship, or some other aspect of intellectual knowledge or skill that is developed through experience and available for inclusion in the person's cognitive structure. The structure includes verbal schemas and sensorimotor or behavioral schemas in addition to cognitive schemas.

COGNITIVE STIMULATION Experiences of novelty, incongruity, exposure to models or instruction, or other experiences that are believed to stimulate the development of new cognitive schemas.

COLIC General term for variety of digestive difficulties which can cause infants to experience severe pain and consequently cry intensively and at length, without responding to attempts by parents or others to calm them down.

COMPARATIVE PSYCHOLOGY A branch of psychology concerned with comparing the behavior of different species in smaller situations.

COMPARTMENTALIZATION A fairly sophisticated defense mechanism. Inconsistent and/or threatening material is recognized and retained in memory, but the individual manages to avoid seeing the implications of, or connections between, compartmentalized items, so that inconsistency or inappropriateness does not become apparent. *See* defense mechanism.

COMPULSION A defense mechanism which diverts attention from threatening material by preoccupying the mind and body with physical "duties." The compulsive behavior may or may not be symbolically related to the dynamic cause of the conflict. *See* obsession, defense mechanism.

CONCRETE IMAGERY A kind of imagery that children at the stage of concrete operations need in order to think and solve problems in the absence of physical objects that they can inspect and manipulate. These include the visual images and memories of previously seen and manipulated objects, along with other kinds of imagery relating to concrete experience, such as memories of sounds or smells.

CONCRETE OPERATIONS Piaget's term for the logical operations that children attain in middle childhood, such as the ability to reason backward as well as forward in a chain of causal reasoning, or the ability to conserve invariant properties despite changes in overtly observable but variable ones. They depend on the presence of concrete objects and direct experience and/or the imagery and memory of such objects or experience. Concrete operations cannot be applied successfully to purely abstract content.

CONCRETE PROPS Physical objects available for observation or manipulation by children who have not attained the stage of formal operations and children whose development of concrete operations has not advanced far enough to allow them to think and reason continuously without such props.

CONSCIENCE Popularly, "conscience" refers to self-generated thoughts about the morality of actions which are based upon previous learning. Within psychoanalytic theory, the moral aspects of personality are split into the ego ideal, which embodies the values and positive ideals toward which the person strives, and the conscience, which embodies the negative restrictions on freedom of thought and action that the person has

learned from socialization or general experience. Violation of conscience produces conflict, which in turn produces shame or guilt if recognized or the development of defense mechanisms to prevent such recognition if it would be too threatening to accept. *See* ego ideal.

CONSERVATION LEARNING The learning of what Piaget calls conservation—the ability to retain continuing recognition of the status of invariant properties of objects, even if other properties should be varied.

CONTIGUITY A basic principle of learning, referring to a closeness in time between the occurrence of two events. If different stimuli occur contiguously (close together in time), they are more likely to be associated together. Furthermore, if they occur repeatedly in the same order, the first one is likely to become seen as the cause or at least the signal for the appearance of the second one.

CONVENTIONAL MORALITY Kohlberg's term for individuals who are at the third and fourth of his six stages. In contrast to individuals at the first two stages, these individuals are truly moral, in the sense that their behavior is governed by considerations about its consequences for and effects on others, and not just by a desire to escape punishment or gain material rewards. Morality at this level is rather absolute and authoritarian, leaving little room for exceptions to general rules based on situational factors.

CONVERSION REACTION A defense mechanism, formerly called hysteria, involving the loss of functional use of sensory or motor abilities even though there is nothing wrong with the person biologically. The problem created by this kind of reaction helps distract the person from the threat that causes it, and sometimes it also results in restrictions or discomfort that provide some of the punishment the person may feel is necessary at some unconscious level. *See* defense mechanism.

COOPERATIVE PLAY The highest of the social play categories articulated by Parten. Children who attain this level play in a truly cooperative fashion, interacting socially and working cooperatively on tasks that require their joint participation and cooperation.

COPING Responding to challenges and threats with adaptive behavior intended to meet the challenge and/or overcome threat. *See* defense mechanism.

568

CORRELATION The degree to which two variables share an association (correlation) with each other. Correlations vary from 0.0 to ± 1.0, depending upon the strength and direction of relationship. Variables which are unrelated, such as height and day of week upon which one was born, correlate about 0.0. Variables with strong positive relationships, such as IQ and scores on standardized achievement tests, show high correlations like 0.75. Variables with mild negative relationships, such as number of children in the family and standardized achievement test scores, show weak negative correlations, such as —0.30.

CORTICAL CONTROL Psychological processes under the control of the cortex, or the higher brain functions. Cortical control is involved in deliberate and systematic perceiving and searching, information processing, thinking and reasoning, deliberately undertaken adaptive behavior, and other things which involve conscious awareness and especially deliberate systematic activity. *See* autonomic nervous system.

CREATING REALITY Actions taken in ambiguous situations which move people from a state of confusion toward the development of clear-cut expectations or beliefs. This can be done directly through instruction or explanation, or indirectly through modeling or other kinds of communication that lead onlookers to develop their own expectations as to what is going to happen or interpretations about the meanings of what is happening.

CREDIBILITY The degree to which a source is considered generally believable and reliable, or the degree to which a particular idea is considered believable or probable.

CRITICAL PERIOD A relatively short period of time (usually a few moments to a few weeks) during which some developmental event of interest occurs. Most typically, it is the onset of some new biological structure or psychological phenomenon. The critical period usually extends from the beginning of the new phenomenon until some point is reached after which anything which has happened is irreversible. *See* irreversibility.

CROSS-CULTURAL Research that involves comparing different cultures.

CULTURE The aggregate of physical artifacts, history, beliefs, attitudes, traditions, and behaviors which are shared by all the people that a given culture embraces, in greater or lesser degree.

CULTURE FAIR TESTS This term came into popularity in the late 1950s and early 1960s, when it was recognized that standard IQ and achievement tests were biased in favor of members of certain subcultural groups and against members of others. "Culture fair" tests are tests which have been examined and revised in order to eliminate biased items by sticking with items that refer to universal human experiences, items that are equally "fair" to all who take the test because no one is likely to have had specific experience with them, and/or items that have the latter properties and also avoid the need for language by presenting examples non-verbally and calling for non-verbal responses.

CUMULATIVE DEFICIT This term drew attention to the fact that the differences between groups increased with age, presumably because of the cumulation of the effects of different environments. Lower class children compared to middle and upper class children, blacks compared to whites, rural children compared to urban children, and so on, not only scored less well on standardized tests, but gradually fell farther and farther behind as they got older.

CUMULATIVE DISADVANTAGE This term refers to the fact that group differences which are relatively small when children are young gradually get larger and larger until they reach some maximum point and stay there. The term "disadvantage" is preferred over the term "deficit" by most writers, because it does not contain the negative connotations of "deficit," and because it helps draw attention to the fact that poor environments put children who are raised in them at a disadvantage when they are compared with or forced to compete with other children raised under more advantageous circumstances. The term "cumulative" is retained as a reminder that the group difference increases with age, at least until a maximum point.

DEFENSE MECHANISM A general term that refers to the many ways people can respond to conflicts in ways that keep the conflict itself or at least the unpleasant emotions associated with it out of conscious awareness, even though the conflict remains unresolved. *See* coping.

DEFERRED IMITATION A particular type of imitation that is considered to reflect important cognitive advances in infants when it begins to appear for the first time. The infant imitates actions seen hours or days earlier. This indicates that schemas which include memories of these actions have developed and are retained, because such deferred imitation would not be possible without the development of these abilities.

DELUSION A special type of false belief which is maintained for defensive purposes. The delusion helps the individual who maintains it avoid recognizing conflicting material and/or having to experience the painful emotions that would ensue if such recognition occurred.

DEMOCRATIC Within the realm of developmental psychology, this term is often used to describe a particular kind of child rearing—socialization characterized by concern about the child's wishes, willingness to grant wide latitude and autonomy in letting the child follow those wishes, and willingness to take the time to carefully explain and justify any limitations that are placed upon the child. *See* authoritarian and *laissez-faire*.

DENIAL An extremely distortive defense mechanism involving failure to notice or at least register things that are going on literally before one's face. *See* defense mechanism.

DEVELOPMENT Progression toward higher and more differentiated stages in a sequence from smaller and undifferentiated through larger and more differentiated structures. *See* growth.

DEVELOPMENTAL PSYCHOLOGY An approach to psychology which views the subject matter from the perspective of concentration on its developmental aspects. Developmental psychology is more a point of view or approach than a substantive area. Developmental psychologists are relatively more interested in such matters as the identification of universal sequences and stages of development, describing and explaining the nature and timing of each stage and the way it contrasts with other stages, predicting future development on the basis of what is known about past development, and reconstructing the course of previous development of symptoms or other behavior patterns of interest in individuals being examined at the moment.

DEVELOPMENTAL SPURT Development usually proceeds unevenly, with relatively short periods of very rapid development separated by longer periods of reduced growth and slow consolidation of the development that took place during the last rapid growth period.

DEVELOPMENTAL TASKS Havighurst uses the concept of developmental tasks to describe normal human development from a developmental perspective. Developmental tasks are challenges facing each developing child within a culture or subculture. Until they are mastered, such tasks typically form the core of motivation and interests in children, and after they are mastered, they serve as bench marks for describing children and comparing them to one another. Developmental tasks are sequenced and keyed to age for the most part, although they differ considerably across cultures.

DIFFERENTIATION A term referring to the general level of development attained by an organism at any given point in time. Differentiation implies a combination of growth from small to large, increase in level of complexity or specificity from low to high, and development from global mass movements toward highly circumscribed and specific responses involving only those aspects of the organism most relevant to the task at hand. *See* canalization.

DISEQUILIBRIUM One of Piaget's major motivational constructs. People are said to be in disequilibrium with regard to a stimulus situation if one or more stimuli in the situation are partially (but not fully) assimilable into existing schemas, and thus capable of eliciting curiosity and exploratory behavior designed to reduce the disequilibrium. If this happens, the person will accommodate to these stimuli by developing new schemas and exercise these new schemas with the new stimuli until a point of equilibrium is reached. At this point, the disequilibrium from that particular stimulus will have been eliminated, and the motivation for continued exercise of the new schemas will disappear. Attention now will turn to some other aspect of the situation which is in disequilibrium and thus is capable of motivating attention and action. *See* equilibration.

DISPLACEMENT A defense mechanism in which anger or other unpleasant emotions are displaced from their real source and vented against a substitute, usually a substitute that is safer than the cause of the anger. *See* catharsis, defense mechanism.

DIVERGENT THINKING The ability to generate original, unusual, inventive, non-conforming, or otherwise "creative" ideas. Originality (uniqueness) probably is its most distinctive feature.

DOMINANT GENE Genes are arranged on chromosomes in pairs. One of each pair of genes came from the person's father and one from the mother. It is common for individuals to resemble either their father or their mother almost completely, rather than looking like a cross between the two. This is because many genes are dominant or recessive with respect to each other. If a gene is dominant, the phenotype associated with it will show up not only when the person has two dominant genes, but also when the person has one dominant gene and one recessive gene. In contrast, phenotypes associated with recessive genes appear only where people have two recessive genes. *See* recessive genes.

ECLECTICISM An attempt to take the best of various theories, even theories which might disagree with one another in part, and weave them into an integrated approach to the field that hopefully contains all of the advantages of the best parts of the individual theories which were retained, but none of the disadvantages of the parts which were discarded.

EGO Freud's term for the part of the personality concerned with "executive functions" such as conscious monitoring of experience, making decisions, and maintaining satisfactory adjustment by balancing conflicting impulses and desires. Since Freud first used it, the term has been used in many different ways by many different writers. Often, it is used more or less synonymously with the term "self-concept."

EGO IDEAL A Freudian concept referring to the positive part of the superego, which contained all of the ideals and values to which the person aspired. The negative part of the superego, the conscience, contained the moral proscriptions against activity defined as immoral. *See* conscience.

EGOCENTRIC SPEECH A particular kin of speech noted in preoperational children who are thinking out loud or acting out fantasies when playing alone, or who are speaking to another child during ostensibly social play but without truly carrying on a conversation. Piaget considers it to be little other than further evidence of childish egocentrism, but other writers believe that it has a functional value in helping children to learn to use speech for thinking and problem solving.

EGOCENTRISM Piaget's term for the general nature of the mind of the child during the sensorimotor period and most of the preoperational period. Children this young have not yet learned to view things from the perspectives of other people, so that they necessarily see situations from their unique and self-centered perspectives.

ELABORATED CODE LANGUAGE Bernstein's term for the kind of language used in formal and scientific communication and in some of the everyday interpersonal communication of individuals high in educational and occupational status. The full message is conveyed by the words themselves, without any supplementing with gestures, implicit references to the immediate context, or other embellishments. *See* restricted code language.

EMBRYO An organism in the early stages of prenatal development. In humans, the embryonic stage lasts roughly the first two months of pregnancy.

EMBRYOLOGY The science dealing with the development of organisms from conception to birth, but particularly the differentiation of these organisms from initially global masses of protoplasm to increasingly differentiated bodies with recognizable parts and subparts.

EMPIRICAL Referring to the scientific collection of objective factual data. The term is often contrasted with "theoretical."

ENVIRONMENT At the broadest level, the environment is anything external to the organism. Thus, the prenatal environment includes the womb and anything that affects the womb via the mother's bloodstream or as a result of the mother's physical activities. The postnatal environment theoretically includes the whole world, animate and inanimate, immediate and remote. The effective environment for any particular organism is the immediate environment that affects the organism in some way, or at least could affect it. It is this effective environment that is referred to in nature-nurture debates.

ENVIRONMENTALIST A general term for a psychologist or other theorist about humans who postulates that humans are mostly or entirely "blank slates" at birth and thus are mostly or entirely open to shaping through the environment. *See* nativist.

EQUILIBRATION Piaget's primary motivational concept. Although he recognizes the roles of the genes and maturation, the physical environment, and direct and indirect socialization, Piaget also believes that people are motivated by unique personal equilibration needs. Equilibration is his term for the individual's postulated need to remain in a continuous but dynamic state of equilibrium with the environment, ignoring or paying minimal attention to stimuli that are of minimal interest but exploring and manipulating stimuli that are partially assimilable to existing schemas but which force some accommodation and thus elicit motivation. *See* disequilibrium.

ETHOLOGY A branch of comparative psychology that has examined the interactions between genetic programming and the specifics of the immediate environment, and also the question of what happens when naturalistic environments are artificially manipulated. Ethological studies of birds, fish, and other species led to important discoveries about imprinting, critical periods, and irreversibility in development. *See* comparative psychology.

EUGENICS This term refers to both the science and the social movement connected with the science of improving races or species through selective breeding.

EVOLUTIONARY PERSPECTIVE The approach of those who seek to understand how or why existing human traits are adaptive and hope to predict how changes in the environment might ultimately lead to changes in human biology, physiology, or psychology.

EXPECTATIONS Beliefs about what will happen in a particular situation, how it will affect oneself, and how one should respond to it. Expectations are generally accurate and based upon past experience, and if situations should change, expectations usually change, too.

EXPERIMENT The classical scientific method for determining cause and effect relationships. Ideally, an experiment involves controlling all possible factors that might influence the outcome, except for the factor to be manipulated, so that manipulations of this factor can be monitored for their effects. If they have effects, a causal linkage will have been established. If no effects are observed, the experiment will have failed to support the causal hypothesis.

EXPRESSIVE DEPENDENCY The kind of emotional dependency in which young children look to parents or others for comfort and support when they become frightened or upset. *See* instrumental dependency.

EXPRESSIVE LANGUAGE The language that a child can and does use in conversation or composition. *See* receptive language.

EXTERNAL STIMULI Stimuli which impinge upon people from the external environment. They include sights, sounds, smells, tastes, and a vari-

ety of physical stimuli that induce sensations of touch or pain, along with social stimulation (the words and actions of other people, the media, and so on). *See* internal stimuli.

EXTRINSIC MOTIVATION Motivation to pursue some goal or engage in some activity for reasons other than enjoyment of the activity itself. This includes monetary or concrete rewards, social rewards such as approval or adulation, the desire to win a competitive event, and so on. *See* Premack principle, intrinsic motivation.

EXTROVERT A personality type originally described by Jung and since verified by many others. Extroverts are marked by gregariousness and enjoyment of the company of others, friendliness and sociability, relative absence of inhibitions about revealing themselves to others or about "performing" in front of a crowd, talkativeness, and so on. *See* introvert.

FACTOR ANALYSIS A statistical technique to analyze patterns of intercorrelation in order to determine what variables correlate highly with one another and form clusters (factors). The variables that load together on a common factor are all correlated with one another in a common pattern, and they are not highly correlated with other variables on other factors.

FAMILY CONSTELLATION FACTORS Factors such as birth order, number of children in the family, father presence or absence, mother presence or absence, spacing between siblings, and other aspects of family composition or constellation that might affect child development.

FEEDBACK The information that one gets about the consequences of one's actions. Typically, this feedback acts to shape actions in the future, in that actions which lead to desirable outcomes tend to be repeated, and actions that lead to undesirable outcomes tend to be dropped. *See* reinforcement.

FETUS The developing prenatal infant between about the beginning of the third month and the termination of pregnancy.

FERTILIZATION The union of a male sperm cell with a female egg cell to produce a zygote and thus initiate the development that will eventuate in the birth of an infant.

FORM OF DEVELOPMENT Along with rate and sequence, form is one of the three basic aspects of development. Form refers to the observable na-

572

ture of the phenotype, both during development and once development has reached maturity. In physical development, form refers to the person's height, general shape and body build, and so on. In intellectual development, form refers to the general level of development (corresponding to IQ or some similar index) and also to the profile pattern of abilities in different areas (such as strong in verbal abilities compared to spatial abilities, or vice-versa). In the area of sensorimotor or behavioral schemas, form refers to the particular behavior that is characteristic of the person (general skill at a particular task; method used to pursue the goals; general smoothness vs. disorganization; and so on). In expressive language, form refers to the speaking vocabulary and communication skills used by the person. In general, the form of a particular sequence of development is the ultimate result of that sequence. It is a joint product of nature and nurture, and is unique with each individual.

FORMAL OPERATIONS Piaget's term for the highest level of cognitive development in his sequential scheme. It is achieved at about age 12 or so (if it is achieved at all), although it has nothing to do with physical maturation. Formal operations are achieved when the individual can understand abstract concepts and use them to think and solve problems, without requiring the support of concrete objects or imagery.

FREE ASSOCIATION The attempt of an individual to verbalize as many associations as possible to a stimulus word. Many of the so-called "creativity" tests rely on free association in one form or another, as when people are asked to name as many unusual uses as they can think of for common objects such as a brick.

FRUSTRATION TOLERANCE The ability to endure frustration without a collapse of defense mechanisms resulting in uncontrolled anger, depression, or other severe emotional over-reactions. Frustration tolerance is closely related to ego strength and vulnerability. Individuals high in ego strength and low in vulnerability are likely to be high in frustration tolerance, while those low in ego strength and high in vulnerability are likely to break down easily under even mild stress. *See* ego and vulnerability.

FUNCTIONAL STAGE The term "stage" sometimes is used loosely to refer to any kind of observable marker in a sequence of development, but sometimes it is used in a much more specific way which implies functional importance and

even causality. When used in this way, the term "stage" or the activities that go on within a stage considered to be functional are thought to be not merely descriptive of development but actively causal.

GENE Any of several hundred microscopic particles which contain and are responsible for the transmission of heredity from parents to offspring and for the establishment and development of inherited characteristics in the offspring.

GENE POOL Each particular gene exists in two or more different forms (technically called alleles). The distribution of the two or more alleles for a particular gene ordinarily would not be the same for a subpopulation of people as it would be for all of the individuals in the world taken together as a single group. The term "gene pool" refers to the variety and distribution of gene types available within a particular subpopulation (the term refers to populations and not to individual people). Gene pools differ from one another in varying degrees, although it is generally stated that the differences are relative rather than absolute. *See* chromosome, eugenics.

GENETICS The study of factors involved in inheritance, especially the attempt to identify the genes which exist in particular species, understand how they are transmitted from one generation to the next, and identify the relationships between genes and the observable characteristics (phenotypes) that the genes influence.

GENITAL STAGE The highest stage in Freud's developmental theory, marked by the physical maturation that occurs at adolescence and the psychological changes including the capacity to sustain adult sexual and personal relationships.

GENOTYPE The particular pattern of genes inherited by an individual. The genotype sets limits on, and in some cases controls much more specifically, many of the ultimate observable characteristics (phenotypes) observed in mature individuals. *See* phenotype.

GESTALT Generically, this term is a German word that refers to a pattern or elaborated structure. Within psychology, it refers to a particular approach (gestalt psychology) that stresses subjective experience over objective external reality, the tendency to perceive and remember isolated stimulus events in meaningful organized structures or wholes, and the idea that all experience is mapped into memory in such a way that individual items remain in dynamic interrelationship with one another as part of an organized structure, making it possible for events occurring in one area to influence events in other areas. These ideas contrast sharply with those of behaviorists.

GROWTH Increase in the physical size or mass of an organism. Growth refers to increase in size only, in contrast to development, which refers to an increase in level of complexity or differentiation. *See* development.

HALLUCINATION The subjective experience of seeing, hearing, or otherwise sensing events which are not actually happening. Hallucinations are perceived as occurring or caused by events external to the individual, but they actually are projected from within. *See* defense mechanism, hallucinatory projection.

HALLUCINATORY PROJECTION All perception involves some projection of internal meaning upon external stimulation. This is normal and adaptive. However, under certain conditions, primarily either altered states of consciousness induced by drugs or alcohol or acute panic due to the impending collapse of defense mechanisms, projective activity may intensify to the point that it distorts perception or even dominates it. At this point, individuals are said to be psychotic or out of contact with reality, perceiving and responding to their own hallucinations rather than to what is happening in their environment. *See* defense mechanism, hallucination.

HEDONISM The pursuit of pleasure and the avoidance of pain.

HERITABILITY The degree to which an observable and measurable characteristic of individuals (a phenotype) is affected or controlled by the genes (genotype). *See* gene pool.

HOMEOSTASIS A basic principle of physiology referring to the fact that our autonomic nervous systems regulate bodily functions to keep them within tolerance limits that define the "normal" range. *See* autonomic nervous system.

HOMOSEXUALITY A general term that refers to activities conducted in cooperation with other individuals of the same sex for the purpose of sexual gratification. *See* autoeroticism.

HORMONAL DISTURBANCE Generally, any hormonal disfunction that causes problems or has observable effects upon general health and well-being. This could result from either an underproduction or an overproduction of a particular hormone, leading to a general imbalance in the body and to specific effects related to the specific hormonal disturbance.

HYDROCEPHALIC An adjective or noun used to describe an individual suffering from a birth defect involving an abnormal increase in fluid inside the cavity that contains and protects the brain. This increase in fluid puts pressure on the brain itself, usually leading to some degree of mental retardation or other brain damage, and causes an expansion of the upper part of the head, causing the person to have large and unusual looking head. Damage can vary from minimal to extreme, so that some individuals with extremely distorted heads might have normal or almost normal functioning.

ID Freud's term for the part of the personality that included the instincts and emotions. He saw the id as exerting continual pressure upon the ego to arrange for gratification of impulses and desires. Meanwhile, the superego exerted restraint upon the ego by introducing guilt as a consequence and punishment for indulging impulses believed to be immoral. *See* ego, superego.

IDENTITY CRISIS A term popularized by Erikson but now in general use, referring to the gradual collapse of childish belief systems involving parroting of early socialization, along with the resulting need for adoption of new belief systems, adopted this time in a more adult fashion.

ILLUSION Anything that appears to be something different from what it really is. Illusions represent distortions of objective perceptions due to socialized tendencies to project particular kinds of meaning onto particular kinds of stimuli.

IMAGERY The mental representation of concrete objects or experienced events. Imagery is important in facilitating thinking and understanding in people of all ages, and Piaget has shown that it appears to be essential for individuals who have not attained the level of formal operations.

INSTINCT A pattern of behavior that is universal to all members of a species, genetically programmed to appear in particular kinds of situations, either in general or after certain necessary previous maturation has taken place.

INSTINCT THEORIES Psychological theories that were popular for a brief time around the turn of the 20th century. They postulated a variety of instincts as basic to human psychology, and explained personality and individual differences on the basis of hypothesized differences in the relative strength of these different instincts in different individuals.

INSTRUMENTAL CONDITIONING General term for the kind of conditioning stressed by Skinner and most other modern behaviorists. This involves conditioning of new behaviors by making rewards contingent upon the performance of those behaviors. If the new behavior of interest cannot be conditioned immediately because it does not appear spontaneously, instrumental conditioning procedures are used in order to condition the ultimate behavior gradually in successive approximations, rewarding each new behavior that approximates the ultimate end point more closely than previous behaviors have. *See* classical conditioning.

INSTRUMENTAL DEPENDENCY Children's needs for adult advice or assistance in solving problems that are too difficult for them to solve on their own because of physical or mental limitations. *See* expressive dependency.

INTELLECTUALIZATION One of the more sophisticated defense mechanisms. People using intellectualization respond to threatening material by analyzing it scientifically in great and complex detail. *See* defense mechanism.

INTERNAL CONFLICTS Once the need for cognitive consistency develops, inconsistencies among beliefs, attitudes, behaviors, or other aspects of experience can be stressful and threatening. Internal conflicts refer to inconsistencies or conflicts between different internal events, such as conflicts between a desire to get something accomplished and a desire to relax, or conflicts between impulses to gratify some pleasure need and conscience pangs indicating that such behavior would be immoral. Such conflicts produce stress, and, if they are threatening enough, may be suppressed and lead to the use of defense mechanisms.

INTERNAL STIMULI Stimuli usually are thought of as impinging upon the individual from the outside. However, some stimulation comes from inside the body. One type is internal stimulation coming from organs or other internal bodily parts (hunger pangs, pain sensations). Another kind is the cognitive stimulation (thought, impulses, desires, imagery, memories) which occurs during directed thinking, daydreaming, night dreaming or, in fact, at any time that we pay attention to

the messages that our brains are sending us. When directed and organized, such internal stimulation is important for thinking and problem solving. When it occurs spontaneously, it can be a source of pleasure (pleasant daydreams), a source of pain (nightmares, unpleasant memories), or even a threatening experience which elicits defense mechanisms (the tendency to think about memories, desires, or impulses which are too threatening to be faced). *See* external stimuli.

INTRINSIC MOTIVATION The pleasure or other positive motivation that is derived simply from doing something or participating in an activity, independently of the outcome and of any social rewards that might be associated with the activity. The term "intrinsic" means that the pleasure or motivation is intrinsic to the activity, not to the person. This point has been much misunderstood, because some theorists have postulated that humans are born with an "intrinsic" desire to explore and manipulate their environment. *See* extrinsic motivation.

INTROJECTION Freud's term for the process by which values, ideals, and other behavioral norms picked up originally through exposure to socialization agents eventually become internalized.

INTROVERT An individual who is asocial (but not necessarily antisocial), concerned more with internal events such as thoughts and feelings than with social interaction with others. Introverts often are thought of as shy and inhibited. *See* extrovert.

IQ (INTELLIGENCE QUOTIENT) A numerical index yielded by any of a large number of tests or test batteries purporting to measure "general intelligence." They do not measure "general intelligence," because there is no such thing.

IQ TESTS Any test that purports to measure "general intelligence" and yields IQ scores. *See* IQ (intelligence quotient).

IRREVERSIBILITY This term, along with the term "critical period," is associated with the notion of stages in development. When individuals have advanced from one developmental stage to the next, and when the stage is a truly qualitative one, the advance is considered to be irreversible, meaning that there will be no regression to earlier stages, and the individual will remain at the new stage or at higher stages from then on.

LABILE SCHEMA Piaget's term, meaning changeable or unstable. Piaget points out that schemas developed in particular situations and in the process of manipulating particular objects are labile in the sense that they can be transferred to new situations and/or objects. *See* mobile.

LAD (LANGUAGE ACQUISITION DEVICE) Chomsky's term for an hypothesized innate mechanism, universal to all humans, which enables us to learn language simply by being exposed to it, without any systematic instruction or reinforcement (necessarily).

LAISSEZ-FAIRE A French term that translates roughly "let them do as they wish." In psychology, the term has been applied to the leadership styles of group leaders and to the parenting behaviors of parents. Parents who raise their children with a *laissez-faire* style impose minimal demands upon the children and tend to be lax about forcing the demands that they do articulate. They are permissive to a fault, failing to provide even minimal guidance or restrictions, even where children may need or want them. *See* authoritarian, democratic.

LAMARCKIAN HYPOTHESIS The hypothesis, propounded long ago by Lamarck, that acquired characteristics could be transmitted through the genes. If this were true, the offspring of individuals who had developed specialized skills would have special aptitudes for those same skills.

LATENCY STAGE Freud's developmental stage that corresponds roughly to middle childhood. Sexuality presumably remained "latent" throughout the middle childhood years.

LAW OF EFFECT One of the first and most important of the laws of learning articulated by early learning researchers, and the precursor of modern reinforcement theory. In its most popular form, the law of effect stated that rewarded actions would be repeated and punished actions would be extinguished.

LEVEL I, LEVEL II Jensen's terms for two major clusters of mental abilities required in varying degrees by different kinds of problem solving tasks. Level I abilities are roughly equivalent with associative learning. They include short-term association and memory, rote memorizing, and the learning of isolated facts and skills. Level II tasks are more demanding and require higher level intellectual abilities. In particular, they require well-developed information processing skills including the ability to generate hypotheses about the possible meanings of ambiguous information and the ability to formulate questions and figure out problems, in addition to being able to answer those questions or solve those problems.

LEVEL OF ASPIRATION The level of performance to which an individual aspires when beginning a task.

LINEAR MODEL A statistical model or assumption about the relationships between variables. Many theorists and researchers assume that different variables are related linearly, meaning that an increase in one variable will be associated with an increase in the other variable, throughout the entire range of possible scores on both variables.

LINGUISTICS A branch of science concerned with the study of languages. It is argued in this book that linguists have overstressed the structural aspects of language and failed to give sufficient attention to the functional aspects involved in communication and problem solving.

LOCUS OF CONTROL A name for the internality vs. externality dimension, probably one of the more important individual difference variables yet discovered. Individuals with an internal locus of control believe that they are capable of controlling their environments and their fates through their own actions.

LOGICAL OPERATIONS A general term for the kinds of physical or mental transformations of stimuli that we perform in thinking and problem solving.

MALLEABILITY The degree to which a structure is open to change (vs. being stable or unchangeable). It is generally believed that in most sequences of development, malleability is higher in the earlier stages than it is in later stages when canalization has taken place and clear-cut directions have not only been established but practiced and reinforced for some time. *See* canalization.

MASTERY MOTIVATION A term popularized by Robert White, referring to the idea that humans may not only have motivational systems that make them curious about the environment and likely to explore and manipulate it, but also that they enjoy and are generally motivated by the sense of mastery that comes from perfecting one's skills at particular tasks.

MATURATION The development and emerging of structures and functions according to pre-programmed genetic timetables. Maturation is the internal or "nature" aspect of development, and learning is the external or "nurture" aspect.

MEMORY DISTORTION The result of repression and related defense mechanisms which cause traumatic events originally perceived accurately to be repressed (completely forgotten) or remembered in some distorted fashion, as when an argument started by oneself is remembered later as having been started by someone else.

MENTAL AGE This term was coined and used by those who develop and conduct research with IQ tests. IQ was defined as the quotient of mental age divided by chronological age multiplied by 100 (to eliminate the decimal point). Mental age, in turn, was defined by the test scores obtained from children tested to develop norms for the test. If the average total score on a particular test for children aged eight years, six months were 75, 75 would be equated with a "mental age" of eight years, six months. Then, anyone who took the test and obtained a score of 75 would be declared to have a "mental age" of eight years, six months, regardless of how old they were chronologically. Mental age is a hypothetical construct which has little or no meaning or usefulness in reality. *See* IQ tests.

MENTALISTIC A general term for theories which postulate internal events (motives, goals, values, conscience) which can neither be observed nor measured.

MOBILE A term used by Piaget to describe schemas and by several other theorists to describe affect and energy. Schemas are said to be mobile to the extent that they can be transferred from their original objects or situations to new ones. In the case of schemas, mobility allows for transfer and cumulation of knowledge. In the case of energy and affect, mobility allows for substitute gratification, displacement, and transfer of focus from one object to another. *See* labile.

MODEL A person, fictional character, or even animal that behaves in distinctive ways that observers can notice and imitate. The influence of behavior models can be seen in direct imitation, deferred imitation, or modeling. *See* modeling.

MODELING A special kind of learning that occurs as a result of exposure to a model. Used loosely, the term may take into account imitation as well as modeling, although technically the two concepts differ. Imitation refers to explicit and exact duplication of the model's words and/or actions, whereas modeling refers to a much less specific and precise imitation. When modeling occurs, the observer notices the model's behavior in the original situation, and this behavior later influences the observer's behavior in a generic sense in similar situations. The original situation and the later situations might be anywhere from a few seconds to many years apart.

MONGOLOID An adjective or noun used to refer to victims of Down's syndrome, a chromosomal abnormality which produces varying degrees of distortion of physical features and mental retardation.

NATIVISTS A general term referring to theorists who use and/or prefer known or hypothesized internal events as explanations for behavior (as opposed to environmental events). Nativists typically stress genetic influences, maturation, and sometimes hormones and other biological factors or concepts such as instincts. *See* environmentalists.

NATURE-NURTURE CONTROVERSY A long standing and continuing controversy in psychology over the degree to which human behavior is determined by the genes (nature) or the environment (nurture).

NATURAL CHILDBIRTH A generic term covering several different approaches to childbirth having in common emphasis on childbirth as a biologically normal and ideally enjoyable experience, avoidance or at least minimal use of anesthetics, and reliance upon a combination of provision of information, preparatory practice and exercises, active maternal participation in the birth process and, sometimes, paternal participation as well.

NEO-FREUDIANS Writers who are generally psychoanalytic in orientation but who have rejected the least defensible aspects of Freudian theory, placing less stress on biology and sex and more stress on socialization and learning.

NEONATE Newborn infant for the first month of so after birth; a newborn.

NEUROSIS Any of a great number of different kinds of psychological disorders involving regular reliance upon repression and other defense mechanisms including memory distortion, but not including the kinds of basic perceptual distortion seen in psychosis. Neurotics differ from normals not so much qualitatively as quantitatively, in the degree to which they rely upon defense mechanisms rather than coping and the degree to which this interferes with work efficiency, well-being, and general adjustment. *See* psychosis.

NORMAL CURVE A theoretical statistical concept used in drawing inferences about general populations based upon data from smaller samples. Also used for estimating the "statistical significance" of relationships among variables or differences among groups obtained in research. It is a bell-shaped curve that represents the frequency distribution of scores for the population as a whole on some variables on which scores cluster around a mean and scores different from the mean differ from it randomly rather than systematically.

NORMS Norms are scores on some measure obtained from a sample large enough and presumably representative enough of the population at large to enable the score distributions from this sample to be used as bench marks against which to judge the scores of others who are measured the same way in the future.

OBSESSIONS Recurring thoughts or images that will not go away even if people attempt to get rid of them. They range from repeated musical tunes and visual images to irrational or even frightening thoughts or premonitions. *See* defense mechanism.

OEDIPAL STAGE The stage in Freud's developmental theory between the phallic stage and the latency stage, occurring around ages four through six. At this time, the young child presumably becomes aware of lustful desires for the parent of the opposite sex; fears that the parent of the same sex will recognize this and respond with extreme punitiveness; and consequently identifies with the parent of the same sex, thus submerging childhood sexuality, developing conscience, and developing sex role identification. *See* adultomorphism.

OPERANT CONDITIONING Skinner's term for the approach to analysis and modification of behavior through manipulation of stimuli and reinforcements favored by himself and his followers. *See* instrumental conditioning.

ORAL STAGE The first of Freud's developmental stages, corresponding roughly to the first year of life and also to Erikson's stage of trust vs. mistrust. During this year, the infant is completely dependent upon adult caretakers, and many of the most basic interactions with the environment occur through the mouth (crying, other communication, feeding, spitting, tasting, belching, teething, biting).

ORGANISM A general term used by psychologists, especially behaviorists, to refer to any living thing.

OSMOSIS A basic physiological process by which nutrients, oxygen, waste products, and other basic materials pass through the walls of membranes. In this way, separate organs or even organisms that share a common membrane can exchange materials, even though their systems are not directly connected. This is how biological exchanges between mothers and prenatal offspring take place through the placenta.

OSSIFICATION The gradual accumulation of calcium deposits in soft bony tissue. This process makes the bones progressively harder and stronger, but it also slows down and ultimately stops bone growth.

OVA The Latin term meaning "eggs." In human development, it refers to the egg cells released by the female ovaries. If these cells are fertilized by a sperm cell from a male, the result will be a zygote and the beginning of development of a new human being.

OVARIES The primary female reproductive organs, responsible for producing ova and female sex hormones.

OVERLEARNING A stage in the learning process which is reached when the individual has practiced a particular skill to the limit of ability, so that further practice will not lead to any increase in performance efficiency.

PARADIGM A standard procedure or model followed in developing theories, designing experiments or other research, or conducting other scientific work. Until recently, many scientists thought of "scientific method" as completely objective, universal, and ageless. However, Kuhn has shown that what is considered "scientific" differs across cultures and even within cultures over time. Paradigms which are popular or accepted at the moment are considered to be reputable and "scientific," while those which do not conform are rejected, even though they may be valued at some other time or some other place.

PARALLEL PLAY An early stage in the classification system of Parten, during which young children seem to be aware of and to enjoy the company of other children, but not to communicate much if at all with them. During this stage, the children may play next to each other and do similar things, but without paying much attention to each other even though they are aware of each other's presence. If they do "communicate," their messages are likely to be egocentric statements of concern only to themselves, and unlikely to involve true exchange of relevant information and comments such as occurs in genuine conversations.

PERCEPTUAL DISCRIMINATION   One of the earliest forms of cognitive activity to develop and differentiate, and one of the basic "building blocks" for later cognitive development. The term refers to the gradually increasing ability, based upon observation of repeated patterns of stimulation and sequences of action and reaction, to separate figure from ground and begin to perceive the environment in meaningful and differentiated ways rather than as a global and undifferentiated mass of stimulation. *See* cognitive schema.

PERCEPTUAL FAILURE   This is what happens when individuals in an acute panic state rely upon extremely distortive defense mechanisms and begin to deny or hallucinate. They literally do not perceive what is going on around them, perceiving and experiencing instead either nothing at all or hallucinatory experiences projected from the inside. People undergoing true perceptual failure are in a psychotic state because they are out of contact with reality. *See* defense mechanism, psychosis.

PERIPHERAL PARTS   Parts of organisms that are located away from the central structures and organs and towards the extremities. Peripheral parts are less vital to the life of the organism, although they may be extremely important for everyday adaptation, and they typically develop later than more central parts. *See* central-distal principle.

PHALLIC STAGE   The Freudian developmental stage between the anal stage and the Oedipal stage. During this stage children presumably become preoccupied with their own bodies and the bodies of others, and they develop exhibitionism involving enjoyment of displaying their bodies and their bodily skills. *See* adultomorphize.

PHENOTYPE   The form that development has taken at a particular point in the life of the organism. Phenotypes include any kind of observable or measurable characteristic, such as height, body build, IQ, blood type and composition, eye color, and so on. The term is used most meaningfully in combination with the term "genotype" in discussions of human characteristics known or believed to be at least partially determined by the genes. *See* genotype.

PHOBIA   A defense mechanism involving the development of and obsession with irrational fears. Phobias differ from ordinary fears because the person becomes obsessed with them, because the feared event is extremely unlikely or impossible, and/or because the fear is greatly in excess of any real danger that might be involved. *See* defense mechanism.

PHYLOGENETIC ORDER   The ordering of known biological species from the simplest and earliest developing through the more complex and later developing.

PHYSIOGNOMY   The shape and contours of the body as a whole or any of its subparts, either as measured or as they appear to others. The term is used most frequently with reference to facial appearance and general body build, although it can refer to any aspect of bodily appearance.

PLACENTA   A temporary but vital biological structure which protects and sustains the prenatal development between conception and birth. The placenta includes a membrane through which nutrients, oxygen, and other needed substances are ingested from the mother's body, and through which waste materials are eliminated into the mother's body and ultimately out of it through the mother's own elimination systems. The placenta also includes a protective sac that completely surrounds the offspring and protects it from shock, threatening changes in temperature, and other dangers.

POLYGENETIC   A term used to describe any phenotype that is determined or partly determined by more than one gene. Most aspects of human psychology that are determined genetically at all are polygenetic. *See* phenotype.

PREMACK PRINCIPLE   A basic principle of behavioral analysis which constitutes an operational definition of reinforcement. According to the principle, any behavior engaged in spontaneously at a particular frequency can be used as a reinforcer to increase the frequency of behavior engaged in less often spontaneously. *See* extrinsic, intrinsic, reinforcement.

PREOPERATIONAL   Piaget's term for children who

are past the sensorimotor stage but have not yet become operational and entered the stage of concrete operations (the period corresponding roughly from age two to about age six). *See* egocentric, logical operations.

PROACTIVE   A term used to describe parenting, teaching, or any kind of adaptive behavior characterized by systematic planning, preparation, and follow-through which takes advantage of whatever information or tools are at hand and involves conscious awareness and deliberate decision making all along the way. *See* reactive.

PROJECTION   The process of imposing subjective meaning on objective external reality. In its most general sense, projection is a fundamental human process, one of the basic characteristics of human perception. The term has a more specific meaning as a defense mechanism. In defensive projection, people do not merely project meaning based on previous experiences in the process of perceiving external reality according to purely logical considerations. Instead, they project internal experiences in order to obliterate external reality completely (hallucinations), or they perceive external reality accurately to some degree but project meanings which are inaccurate and unsupported by the facts (delusions). *See* delusion, hallucination, hallucinatory projection.

PROXIMAL-DISTAL   *See* central-distal principle.

PSYCHOSIS   A severe psychological disorder involving temporary loss or at least severe impairment of contact with reality due to reliance on distortive defense mechanisms such as hallucinations and delusions. *See* neurosis.

RATE   Along with form and sequence, rate is one of the three major aspects of development studied by psychologists. Rate of development refers to the speed of progression from the beginning through to the end of a sequence of development. Faster rates mean earlier and quicker development. *See* form, sequence.

REACTION FORMATION   A defense mechanism in which threatening personal thoughts or impulses are repressed and reversed. Reaction formation involves not merely repression of the threatening material, but development of the opposite idea. *See* reversal.

REACTIVE   Term used to describe adaptive behavior in general and parenting in particular. This refers to behavior characterized by absence of forethought and planning and/or present infor-

mation processing and decision making. Instead of controlling the environment and proceeding in an orderly fashion, people who operate reactively allow events to control them and respond impulsively to whatever situations they encounter. As a result, they are less effective and more likely to make mistakes. *See* proactive.

REALITY CONTACT   The degree to which people perceive what is happening to and around them accurately and objectively. Reality contact can be reduced or even temporarily lost altogether through reliance upon distortive defense mechanisms. *See* psychosis.

RECEPTIVE LANGUAGE   The language that we can perceive and understand correctly when we are listening or reading, as opposed to the language that we actually use ourselves when we are speaking or writing. *See* expressive language.

RECESSIVE GENES   One of a set of alleles (different forms of the same gene) which does not express itself in the phenotype to the degree that a dominant gene does, even though it exists equally with the dominant gene in the genotype. *See* dominant gene.

REDUCTION DIVISION   A term for the process involved in the formation of germ cells (sperm and ova); the lining up of paired genes on each of the chromosomes, followed by separation of the genes in such a way that the resulting germ cells contain one member of each original pair.

REFERENCE GROUP   A group (real or imagined, immediate or remote) with whom an individual identifies and tries to imitate and/or please. Our beliefs, attitudes, and behaviors are affected strongly by the reference group or groups with which we identify, and tend to change accordingly if reference groups change.

REINFORCEMENT   One of the most basic processes and principles of psychology. Reinforcement refers to the positive or desirable outcomes that result when particular behaviors are performed. Behaviorists generally and Skinnerians in particular place great stress on reinforcement, believing it to be the key to the establishment and maintenance of behavior. *See* feedback, law of effect, Premack principle.

REPETITIVE SCHEMA   Piaget's term for emerging schemas which are repeated over and over again without external reinforcement and apparently for reasons having to do with equilibration (curiosity, desire for mastery, sheer enjoyment of practicing and improving particular skills).

REPRESSION The most basic and general of the true defense mechanisms. Traumatic events, perceptions or desires are said to be repressed when they are systematically kept out of conscious awareness. True repression is systematic but not conscious or deliberate. *See* defense mechanism, suppression.

RESTRICTED CODE LANGUAGE Bernstein's term for everyday informal language used in primarily social situations. Restricted code language often is grammatically incomplete or even incorrect, and it depends upon shared past experiences and perceptions of the immediate situation, in addition to the actual words used, to help convey the intended meanings. *See* elaborated code language.

REVERSAL An alternate name for the defense mechanism usually called reaction formation. *See* defense mechanism, reaction formation.

REVERSIBILITY This term has two meanings: the degree to which existing development can be changed (reversed); one of the characteristics of the logical operations that children develop when they enter the stage of concrete operational thinking (term popularized by Piaget). Once children attain reversibility in their logical operations, they can reason backward from effects to causes as well as forward from causes to effects. *See* logical operations.

ROLE DIFFUSION Erikson's term for the condition of individuals who have not yet resolved the identity crisis successfully. They continue to search for roles with which they feel comfortable, trying out different roles for a time but discarding most of them because they are not appropriate or satisfying. *See* identity.

SALIENCE Noticeability, or the degree to which a stimulus stands out from the background as a figure which commands attention and interest. The salience of stimuli is enhanced by such characteristics as bright colors, movement, or novelty.

SCHEMA Piaget's term for the basic unit of learning, corresponding roughly to the behavioristic term "habit." Schemas include knowledge and skills involved in adapting to the environment by manipulating it in some way. Sensorimotor or behavioral schemas involve physical manipulation of objects; verbal schemas involve understanding and use of language; and cognitive schemas involve the images and memories associated with past experiences and the logical and other cognitive abilities involved in manipulating these experiences for purposes of thinking and problem solving.

SECONDARY SEX CHARACTERISTICS Bodily changes associated with one sex or the other that accompany changes in the primary sexual organs that occur at adolescence. These include such things as the development of facial and general bodily hair in males, the deepening of the voice, and the gradual delineation of a generally masculine body build. In females, secondary sex characteristics include the development of the breasts and other general bodily changes involved in the gradual delineation of an adult female bodily form.

SELF-FULFILLING PROPHECY A basic principle of human development which refers to the fact that individuals tend to perceive and attempt to conform to the expectations that significant others hold for them. More specifically, a self-fulfilling prophecy is an expectation (prophecy) which is initially false or at least not necessarily true, but which becomes true because people act upon it and thus set in motion a series of events that eventually make it come true.

SENSORIMOTOR SCHEMA A linkage that a child develops between particular stimulus situations or objects and particular adaptive behavior. Sensorimotor schemas involve knowledge about what can or should be done with things in the environment through direct physical manipulation of these things.

SENSORIMOTOR STAGE The first of Piaget's four general stages of development, encompassing roughly the first two years of life. During this time the development of sensorimotor or behavioral schemas is more rapid and systematic than the development of verbal and especially cognitive schemas, which enter the picture more systematically later. Most of the knowledge and skills of children in the sensorimotor stage concern concrete objects in their environment and what the children can do with these objects. By comparison, they have relatively little social or intellectual knowledge, and they do not yet possess logical operations. *See* logical operations.

SEQUENCE Along with form and rate, sequence is one of the three aspects of development concentrated upon by psychologists. Sequence refers to the order in which developmental events occur. True developmental stages occur in universal sequences, meaning that stage one always occurs before stage two, which always occurs before stage three, and so on. *See* form, rate.

SEX ROLE   A term that refers to the complex of personal characteristics and behavior that are expected of males and females, respectively, within a culture or subculture. Also called "gender role," because most of what is involved in sex roles has little or nothing to do with sexual activity. *See* androgeny.

SIMPLIFIED SPEECH   Speech used by adults when talking to infants and very young children, characterized by shorter sentences, emphasis on key terms, and restriction of content to mostly familiar and observable objects and events. *See* baby talk.

SITUATION BOUND LEARNING   Learning which is restricted in application to one or a very small number of similar situations, and which therefore does not generalize to a wider variety of situations to which it might be applicable. Most learning is situation bound at first, and the learning of infants and very young children tends to be situation bound in general. *See* stimulus bound.

SOCIALIZATION   A general term referring to the gradual molding of infants (with initial potential to develop along any or all of a great number of paths) into individuals whose development has become concentrated (canalized) along certain emphasized dimensions at the expense of others which could have been emphasized but which were not. When used more restrictively, the term "socialization" is roughly equivalent to "child rearing." *See* development.

SOMATIZATION   A very complex defense mechanism in which stress producing material is repressed and the stress is channeled into physical symptoms. The result can be the development of genuine physical ailments such as ulcers. These physical problems can occur for purely physical reasons, but when the cause is psychological rather than physical, they function as defense mechanisms and feature somatization. *See* defense mechanism.

STAGE   Loosely, the term "stage" refers to any identifiable marker in a sequence of development. The behavior or other distinguishing characteristics of the stage are mostly or entirely absent until the stage is reached, at which point they become prominent or at least noticeable for the first time. The stage is completed when a new stage is entered. *See* functional stage.

STIMULUS BOUND   The focusing of attention and/or the appearance of a schema are said to be stimulus bound when they are elicited by only a single stimulus or a small class of very similar stimuli. *See* situation bound.

STIMULUS DISCRIMINATION   In the early stages of learning, stimuli tend to be perceived globally. As development progresses, individuals learn to make finer and finer discriminations between similar stimuli, especially if making such discriminations has important adaptational value. As discriminations among stimuli accumulate, differential adaptive behavior to discriminably different stimuli begins to appear. *See* stimulus generalization.

STIMULUS GENERALIZATION   The gradual widening and sharpening of knowledge about the essential common features shared by equivalent stimuli that might differ in gross general appearances but nevertheless might be functionally equivalent and call for similar adaptive response. Stimulus generalization is important in assimilating new situations and new stimuli into existing schemas, because if a strange new stimulus can be recognized as functionally equivalent to more familiar stimuli, existing schemas can be activated to allow more efficient and adaptive responding. *See* stimulus discrimination.

SUBCORTICAL   A general term referring to neurological activity in the spinal cord or the lower parts of the brain below the cortex. Subcortical activity includes the autonomic nervous system, which controls bodily reflexes and the homeostatic activities involved in everyday adaptation. *See* autonomic nervous system, homeostasis.

SUPEREGO   Freud's term for the part of the personality that included the ideals and values toward which the individual aspired (the ego ideal) and the moral proscriptions and inhibitions against unacceptable impulsive behavior or selfish gratification (the conscience). *See* conscience, ego, ego ideal, id.

SUPERSTITIOUS LEARNING   A term to describe what happens when causal inferences are drawn on the basis of contiguity of observed events. Such inferences are quite understandable, especially if the observed contiguities are repeated, although they may be incorrect.

SUPPRESSION   The conscious and deliberate attempt to get one's mind off of unpleasant thoughts by deliberately thinking about something else or getting involved in some kind of activity that will call for concentration and make it easier to forget about the material to be suppressed. In contrast to the defense mechanism repression, suppression is a conscious and deliberate activity and is not actually a defense mechanism. *See* defense mechanism, repression.

TELEGRAPHIC PHRASES   A term for the brief phrases used by infants and young children who are old enough to communicate their thoughts or desires, but who have not yet mastered all of the grammatical rules involved in forming complete sentences.

TESTES   The basic male reproductive organs, which produce sperm cells. *See* ovaries.

TRANSPOSITION PROBLEMS   A class of problems used in research on animals and humans, involving identification of which of two or more alternatives is the "correct" alternative (as defined by reinforcement). Subjects first learn that a particular stimulus is "correct." After this is learned, they then move to a new problem in which the choices are transposed, so that the previously correct stimulus is incorrect, but another stimulus that follows the same rule used in the first experiment is designated as correct.

TRAUMA   A general term for any kind of unpleasant or painful experience, physical, emotional, or mental. Severe trauma can have lasting effects in the form of nervous symptoms, nightmares, inhibitions, or the development of defense mechanisms used in an attempt to repress them. *See* repression.

UNIVERSAL HUMAN EXPERIENCES   Experiences that every human in every culture must necessarily undergo (birth, surviving the first year or so of life in a state of complete dependency upon caretakers, adjusting to socialization demands imposed by parents and by society at large, sex role socialization, and so on).

UTERUS   The technical name for the womb, the organ located in the midsection of the female body which is designed to develop the placenta and other protective structures and generally accommodate and protect prenatal offspring in women who become pregnant.

VULNERABILITY   Openness or defenselessness against unpleasant or undesirable experiences. As used in this book, it refers to the degree to which people have been socialized in ways that make them likely to develop strong feelings of anxiety or guilt, and are thus less likely to cope with threat and more likely to invoke defense mechanisms in an attempt to avoid threat. *See* ego, frustration tolerance.

WHORFIAN HYPOTHESIS   The hypothesis that language structures thought, rather than vice-versa, named after the linguist Benjamin Whorf.

YOUTH CULTURE   A general term referring to the clothing, life styles, leisure-time activities, jargon, and other characteristics associated with adolescence.

ZYGOTE   A cell which is formed when an egg is fertilized by a sperm, thus paving the way for the development of a new human being. The zygote stage is the first stage of prenatal human development.

Index